Principles of
Computer Design

PRINCIPLES OF COMPUTER SCIENCE SERIES

ISSN 0888-2096

Series Editors

Alfred V. Aho, *Bell Telephone Laboratories, Murray Hill, New Jersey*

Jeffrey D. Ullman, *Stanford University, Stanford, California*

1. *Algorithms for Graphics and Image Processing**
   Theo Pavlidis
2. *Algorithmic Studies in Mass Storage Systems**
   C. K. Wong
3. *Theory of Relational Databases**
   Jeffrey D. Ullman
4. *Computational Aspects of VLSI**
   Jeffrey D. Ullman
5. *Advanced C: Food for the Educated Palate**
   Narain Gehani
6. *C: An Advanced Introduction**
   Narain Gehani
7. *C for Personal Computers: IBM PC, AT&T PC 6300, and compatibles**
   Narain Gehani
8. *Principles of Computer Design*
   Leonard R. Marino
9. *The Theory of Database Concurrency Control**
   Christos Papadimitriou
10. *Computer Organization**
    Michael Andrews
11. *Elements of Artificial Intelligence Using LISP*
    Steven Tanimoto

*These previously-published books are in the *Principles of Computer Science Series* but they are not numbered within the volume itself. All future volumes in the *Principles of Computer Science Series* will be numbered.

OTHER BOOKS OF INTEREST

Jewels of Formal Language Theory
Arto Salomaa

Principles of Database Systems
Jeffrey D. Ullman

Fuzzy Sets, Natural Language Computations, and Risk Analysis
Kurt J. Schmucker

LISP: An Interactive Approach
Stuart C. Shapiro

Principles of Computer Design

Leonard R. Marino

San Diego State University

COMPUTER SCIENCE PRESS

Computer Science Press
1803 Research Blvd.
Rockville, Maryland 20850

2 3 4 5 6   Printing   Year   91 90 89 88 87

Library of Congress Cataloging in Publication Data

Marino, Leonard R.
  Principles of computer design.

  Bibliography: p.
  1. Electronic digital computers—Design and
construction.   2. Computer architecture.   I. Title.
TK7888.3.M3524   1985   621.3819′582   84-23812
ISBN 0-88175-064-6

Contents

Preface ix

CHAPTER 1 AN OVERVIEW.................................. 1
  1.1 Computer Organization 1
    1.1.1 Fundamental Characteristics 2
    1.1.2 Structure and Operation 7
    1.1.3 Instruction Set 23
    1.1.4 Programming 42
    1.1.5 Input-Output Operation 55
    1.1.6 Exercises 62
  1.2 Computer Design 63
    1.2.1 Models 63
    1.2.2 Modular Design Procedures 66
    1.2.3 The Levels of Computer Design............ 68
    1.2.4 Exercises 76
  1.3 Computer Packaging and Production 76
    1.3.1 Microcircuits 77
    1.3.2 Macrocircuits 83
    1.3.3 Independence of Design Levels............. 86

CHAPTER 2 DIGITAL ELECTRONICS 90
  2.1 Electric Circuit Review 90
    2.1.1 Resistor Circuits 91
    2.1.2 Capacitance 92
    2.1.3 Inductance 97
    2.1.4 Power Supplies 97
    2.1.5 Informal Circuit Analysis.................. 100
    2.1.6 Power and Energy 102
    2.1.7 Exercises 103
  2.2 Digital Circuits 104
    2.2.1 Diodes and Transistors 104
    2.2.2 Logic Gates 113
    2.2.3 Gate Interconnections..................... 123
    2.2.4 CMOS Logic 126
    2.2.5 Exercises 129
  2.3 Integrated Circuits 123
    2.3.1 Materials Review......................... 133
    2.3.2 nMOS Transistors........................ 134
    2.3.3 Parameter Values 138
    2.3.4 Exercises 143

CHAPTER 3 LOGIC DESIGN:
            COMBINATIONAL NETWORKS 145
      3.1 Switching Functions 146
            3.1.1 Specifications of Switching Functions 146
            3.1.2 Properties of Logic Operations 149
            3.1.3 Exercises 151
      3.2 Gate Networks.................................152
            3.2.1 Logic Gates 153
            3.2.2 Gate Interconnections....................154
            3.2.3 Optimal Design 157
            3.2.4 Exercises 174
      3.3 Switch Networks...............................176
            3.3.1 Formulas for Switch Networks.............176
            3.3.2 Transistors Switches 178
            3.3.3 Tree Networks 178
            3.3.4 Pull-Down Networks 181
            3.3.5 Electrical Considerations 182
            3.3.6 Exercises 186
      3.4 Elementary Word Operations 188
            3.4.1 Logic Operations on Words 188
            3.4.2 Other Operations........................192
            3.4.3 Exercises 193

CHAPTER 4 DIGITAL ARITHMETIC 197
      4.1 Integer Codes..................................198
            4.1.1 Definitions: B2 and 2C Codes 198
            4.1.2 Fundamental Properties 199
            4.1.3 Other Codes 202
            4.1.4 Exercises 203
      4.2 Addition 204
            4.2.1 B2 Addition 205
            4.2.2 Overflow 209
            4.2.3 2C Addition 210
            4.2.4 Addition Instructions 216
            4.2.5 Exercises 218
      4.3 Subtraction....................................219
            4.3.1 The 2C Negate Operation 220
            4.3.2 2C Subtraction 221
            4.3.3 B2 Subtraction..........................223
            4.3.4 Subtraction Instructions...................225
            4.3.5 Ordering Relations and Branch Instructions ..225
            4.3.6 Exercises 229
      4.4 Multiplication 231
            4.4.1 Unsigned 231
            4.4.2 Signed 233
            4.4.3 Programs 234
            4.4.4 Exercises 238
      4.5 Division 239

4.5.1 Unsigned 240
4.5.2 Signed 243
4.5.3 Programs 243
4.5.4 Exercises 245
4.6 Real Arthimetic.............................246
4.6.1 Fixed-Point Representation 246
4.6.2 Floating-Point Representation 249
4.6.3 Fixed- versus Floating-Point Arithmetic......260
4.6.4 Exercises 261

CHAPTER 5 REGISTER TRANSFER LEVEL COMPONENTS ... 263
5.1 Digital Signals 263
5.1.1 Logic Levels and Noise Margins 264
5.1.2 Modelling Digital Signals 267
5.1.3 Signal Paths.............................273
5.1.4 Exercises 281
5.2 Combinational Networks.......................281
5.2.1 Decoders...............................282
5.2.2 Multiplexers 290
5.2.3 Read Only Memory (ROM) 294
5.2.4 Programmable Logic Array (PLA) 305
5.2.5 Arithmetic Logic Unit (ALU)..............310
5.2.6 Exercises 311
5.3 Pulse Generators 312
5.3.1 Clocks 312
5.3.2 One-Shots..............................316
5.3.3 Switches and Reset Circuits 319
5.3.4 Exercises 322
5.4 Memory Components..........................323
5.4.1 Immediate Access Registers 324
5.4.2 Random Access Memory (RAM)...........343
5.4.3 Sequential Access Memory (SAM) 358
5.4.4 Exercises 366
5.5 Sequential Networks..........................368
5.5.1 The Sequential Machine 368
5.5.2 The Synchronous Sequential
      Network (SSN) 370
5.5.3 Sequential Machine Construction...........377
5.5.4 Input Synchronization 382
5.5.5 Exercises 390

CHAPTER 6 REGISTER TRANSFER DESIGN 392
6.1 Fundamentals 392
6.1.1 RT System Structure 392
6.1.2 The Design Process......................394
6.2 A Synchronous One-Shot 394
6.2.1 System Specification and Data Unit 395

6.2.2 CU Structure 396
6.2.3 Sequential Operation 401
6.2.4 CU Combinational Network 404
6.2.5 Timing..................................409
6.2.6 Decomposition..........................416
6.2.7 Exercises 417
6.3 IO Controllers..............................419
6.3.1 The System Bus.........................420
6.3.2 A Programmable One-Shot................428
6.3.3 Parallel-Port IOCs 436
6.3.4 Serial-Port IOCs 444
6.3.5 Exercises 449
6.4 DMA Controllers 451
6.4.1 Specifications 451
6.4.2 Minimizing Chip Area 454
6.4.3 Data Unit 458
6.4.4 Control Unit 468
6.4.5 Chip Layout............................479
6.4.6 Exercises 483
6.5 Processors 484
6.5.1 Fetch-Execute-Interrupt Operation..........485
6.5.2 Data Unit and Chip Layout 488
6.5.3 CU Structure 490
6.5.4 Sequential Operation 494
6.5.5 Exercises 511
6.6 Control Unit Variations......................512
6.6.1 State Registers and Codes 512
6.6.2 Microprogramming 515
6.6.3 Exercises 528

CHAPTER 7 MACROCIRCUIT DESIGN .....,........529
7.1 IC Interconnections 529
7.1.1 Linear Models 530
7.1.2 Device Specifications 533
7.1.3 Non-Linear Models......................537
7.1.4 Exercises 540
7.2 Transmission Lines 540
7.2.1 The Digital Model 541
7.2.2 Computing Solutions 550
7.2.3 Line Termination........................553
7.2.4 Exercises 557
7.3 Noise 558
7.3.1 Electromagnetic Radiation................559
7.3.2 Crosstalk...............................559
7.3.3 Common Impedance Noise 564

REFERENCES...565
INDEX..568
SPECIAL NOTATIONS 578

PREFACE

Computers are multilevel systems. At the processor level a computer is constructed from processors, memories, input-output controllers, and other sophisticated devices. Each of these devices is itself a complex system, constructed at the register transfer level from simpler components (e.g., registers, combinational networks, sequential networks). These register transfer components are constructed at the logic level from yet simpler components (e.g., gates and flipflops), which in turn are constructed from electronic components (e.g., resistors and transistors), which (at last!) are constructed from materials found in nature (conductors, semiconductors, and insulators). In addition, above the hardware levels just mentioned there are software levels that implement programs to control the operation of the computer, using machine instructions as primitive components.

This book has been written with the conviction that every student majoring in computer engineering or computer science should have a fundamental understanding of computers at every level: physics, electronics, logic, register, processor, and programming. Most university programs offer one or more courses at each of these levels, but courses that present the fundamentals of the entire structure compactly and coherently are rare. There are two undesirable consequences of this situation:

1. There is not room in the curriculum to require courses at every level, thus many students graduate with significant gaps in their education.

2. It is left to the student to integrate individual courses into a coherent whole. Some students are eventually successful in this effort while others are not, but all students suffer to some degree from a lack of perspective and motivation while studying the individual levels.

This situation is not necessary. A student is equipped to understand the fundamental principles of every level of computer structure after completing the standard lower-division physics and calculus sequences. As soon as possible after that point in his education, a student should be provided with a coherent view of the whole hierarchy of computer structure. Subsequent courses at any level will then be more meaningful and more effectively integrated into his developing perception of computing machines. This book is the result of my efforts during the past several years to develop a course that would address this need.

Throughout the text, computers are discussed from the viewpoint of the designer, even though the primary objective is to provide an understanding of computer structure, and not necessarily to train designers. The design viewpoint is adopted because it offers the truest insights into the current structure of computers, and provides the best basis for understanding future developments. Also, the inclusion of practical design techniques facilitates the construction of meaningful exercises.

Microcircuit design (i.e., the design of a circuit to be implemented on the surface of an IC chip) and macrocircuit design (i.e., the design of systems using ICs as components) are given equal emphasis in the text. Microcircuit design has become increasingly important to computer system designers in recent years, as the size of the system that can be implemented on a single IC chip has increased. At the same time, macrocircuit design has remained important, both because high-performance computers are constructed from smaller-scale (and faster) chips, and because no matter how large the system on a single chip may be, there will always be the need for systems that are much larger.

The emphasis throughout this text is on the principles of the design process rather than on the details of currently available devices or current practice. This does not imply, however, that the text is oriented toward theory rather than practice. In fact, the reverse is true. Practical systematic design techniques are presented, and difficult issues such as loading, transmission line effects, and noise are considered. Specific devices are used for illustration, but the emphasis is on design principles that are independent of device details. After finishing the text, the student should be equipped to undertake design projects of considerable complexity, using any sort of digital components.

Chapter Summaries

Chapter 1 provides an overview of computer organization, design, and production. In Section 1.1 a particular computer architecture is described which is used in examples and exercises throughout the text. The 6800 microprocessor system architecture was selected for this purpose because it illustrates all of the important aspects of traditional (von Neumann) computer architecture, yet it is simple and uncluttered. It is also an architecture of continuing commercial importance, since all 68xx family processors are compatible with the 6800. Assembler language programming is introduced in this section, and is used throughout the text.

In Section 1.2 an important principle of computer science is introduced, that complexity in a digital computer arises not so much from the inherent complexity of the primitive components from which the machine is constructed (e.g., transistors are used simply as switches), but rather from the overwhelming number of details that must be managed when interconnecting many of these simple components. One of the most important skills that a computer engineer must develop is the ability to manage this complexity of many details. The ideas of using multilevel models and modular design techniques to control complexity are introduced in this section, and applied throughout the text.

In Section 1.3 the major packaging levels, macrocircuit and microcircuit, are introduced, and the economics of computer production are discussed.

Chapter 2 provides a brief review of electric circuits, followed by an introduction to the fundamentals of digital electronics. Simple switching models of transistors are presented and used to analyze logic gate structures. The fundamental roles of capacitance and resistance in determining speed and power dissipation in digital circuits are discussed. The elementary physics and mechanics of integrated circuit operation and fabrication are presented.

A compact presentation of combinational network design is provided in Chapter 3. Several traditional topics are omitted, including formal Boolean algebra and tabular minimization of switching functions. These topics are no longer of fundamental importance in computer design, and are better left to an advanced course in logic design.

Digital arithmetic is presented in Chapter 4. Because of its fundamental importance, and because it is frequently a source of confusion for students, this topic is treated with particular care. A clear distinction is maintained between binary words and the numbers that they represent, and special attention is given to dealing with overflow and representing numerical relations.

Chapter 5 begins with a discussion of digital signalling, that is, the use of voltages to transmit information between components. The major classes of register transfer level components are then discussed: combinational networks, pulse generators, memory, and sequential networks. Microcircuit and macrocircuit implementations of each component are presented.

Chapter 6 describes systematic techniques for register transfer level design. Several design examples are presented in detail, including input-output controllers, a DMA controller, and the 6800 processor. Microprogramming is discussed in the last section.

Chapter 7 is devoted to topics associated specifically with macrocircuit design. Macrocircuit models for IC interconnections are described, and standard electrical and timing specifications are discussed. These models apply to all levels of macrocircuit design, including high-speed MSI/LSI-based systems, microprocessor-based systems, and high-performance systems constructed from custom LSI and VLSI components. Transmission line effects, which are crucial in high-speed systems, are considered in detail. Noise is also considered, but because of the limited background assumed, the discussion is necessarily qualitative. The objective is to provide an intuitive understanding of the principles involved.

Note to Instructors

One of the difficult aspects of teaching computer design is determining the proper amount of detail to include in lectures. A lecture with too much detail will be boring, while one with too little detail may be dismissed as superficial. The optimal amount and selection of detail depends upon the background of the students and the objectives of the course.

In order to allow sufficient latitude to accommodate different situations, a considerable amount of detail has been included in this text. In is not intended that all of this detail be laboriously presented in lectures, although at one time or another almost all of it has been included in my own lectures. It is intended, rather, that lectures focus on general principles, illustrated by selected examples, with much of the detail left as assigned or elective reading.

This text is suitable for a first course in computer design for students of computer science or computer engineering. The only prerequisite is completion of the standard lower division university physics and calculus sequences. With this minimal background, it should be possible to complete the text in two semesters.

The text is also suitable for a course that is preceded by one or more courses in electronics, logic design, or computer organization. Selected portions of the text may then be omitted or covered lightly, making a one semester course possible.

Acknowledgements

Many friends and colleagues have helped me in writing this book. I would especially like to thank Bill Brown, Alex Iosupovici, Chuck Seitz, and Jeffrey Ullman for reading parts of the manuscript and making many excellent suggestions. I am grateful to my brothers Al and Tony for frequent helpful discussions and valued advice. I am indebted to Tom Windeknecht and Hank D'Angelo, from whom I have learned a great deal, and who have significantly influenced the paths that I have taken. Thanks also to the hundreds of students who have sustained me with their interest and curiosity while reading draft versions of this text in the EE373, EE573, and EE503 courses at San Diego State University.

My wife suggested the following dedication for this book: "To my beautiful wife, Kay, and wonderful children, Jesse, Daniel, and Katie, in spite of whom this manuscript was completed." However, while it is conceivable that this work might have been completed sooner without the distractions of my family, it is far more likely that without them it would not have been completed at all. It certainly would not have been completed without Kay's generous support and understanding.

Quotations

I always enjoy reading quotations that provide a sense of history or capture the essense of an important idea with a brief statement. Here are several that are relevant to computer design.

Everything should be made as simple as possible, but not simpler.

Albert Einstein

Achilles: There must be some amazingly smart ants in that colony, I'll say that.
Anteater: I think you are still having some difficulty realizing the difference in levels here. Just as you would not confuse an individual tree with a forest, so here you must not take an ant for the colony. You see, all the ants in Aunt Hillary are as dumb as can be. They couldn't converse to save their little thoraxes.

Douglas Hofstadter

I regard programs as specific instances of mechanisms, and I wanted to express, at least once, my strong feeling that many of my considerations concerning software are, mutatis mutandis, just as relevant for hardware design.

The art of programming is the art of organizing complexity, of mastering multitude and avoiding its bastard chaos as effectively as possible.

(We should) restrict ourselves to simple structures whenever possible and avoid in all intellectual modesty "clever constructions" like the plague.

Program testing can be used to show the presence of bugs, but never their absence.

Edsger W. Dijkstra

As the result of the large capacity of computing instruments, we have to deal with computing processes of such complexity that they can hardly be constructed and understood in terms of basic general purpose concepts. The limit is set by the nature of our own intellect: precise thinking is possible only in terms of a small number of elements at a time. The only efficient way to deal with complicated systems is in a hierarchical fashion.

O. J. Dahl and C. A. R. Hoare

*Inasmuch as the completed device will be a general-purpose comput-
ing machine it should contain certain main organs relating to
arithmetic, memory-storage, control and connection with the human
operator.*

*The utility of an automatic computer lies in the possibility of using a
given sequence of instructions repeatedly.*
A. W. Burks, H. H. Goldstine and J. von Neumann (1946)

*The entire UNIVAC system is constructed of circuits which . . . have
been designed as building blocks, and the entire computer is constructed around these blocks.*
J. P. Eckert, et al (1951)

"To be is to do"—Socrates
"To do is to be"—Jean-Paul Sartre
"Do be do be do"—Frank Sinatra

Kurt Vonnegut

*For my wife Kay
and my parents
Jesse and Mary*

Chapter 1

AN OVERVIEW

1.1 Computer Organization
1.2 Computer Design
1.3 Computer Packaging and Production

This chapter introduces the study of digital computers from three perspectives. Section 1.1 describes the general organization and operation of stored program computers. Section 1.2 discusses some of the issues involved in designing complex systems and presents general systematic methods for dealing with complexity. Computer design serves as a vehicle for the discussion, but the principles apply to the design of any complex system. Section 1.3 discusses the technologies involved in implementing and packaging digital computers. It is these matters more than any other that determine the cost of digital computers, and hence their impact on society.

1.1 COMPUTER ORGANIZATION [1–8]

1.1.1 Fundamental Characteristics
1.1.2 Structure and Operation
1.1.3 Instruction Set
1.1.4 Programming
1.1.5 Input-Output Operation
1.1.6 Exercises

In this section, the fundamentals of computer organization and programming are presented, using the 6800 microprocessor as an example. This particular processor was chosen because it is simple and yet it has all the fundamental characteristics of a modern processor. In addition, the 6800

1

architecture is likely to remain popular for many years, since it is used, with various modifications, by all of the 6800 family microprocessors. This family includes processors significantly more powerful than the 6800 (e.g., the 6809), as well as single-chip microcomputers (e.g., the 6805).

1.1.1 Fundamental Characteristics

In this section are described the most fundamental characteristics of computers. These characteristics are shared by essentially all digital computers.

Digital Representation of Information

Computers are machines that store and process information. Within a computer, information is represented by binary words. A *binary word* (or simply a word) is a sequence of bits. A *bit* is a "binary digit," either 0 or 1. For example, 01101011 is an 8-bit binary word.

Registers.   Within a computer, words are stored in devices called *registers*. There are many different ways to implement registers (see Section 5.4). Regardless of the implementation, however, registers always serve the same purpose: to store binary words.

Placing a word into a register for storage is referred to as *loading* the register, or *writing* into the register. Examining a register to determine what word is stored is referred to as *reading* the register. The word in a register is not changed by reading. After loading a register, the word loaded remains in the register until another word is loaded.

A *memory* is a set of registers that share the same hardware for reading and writing. Memories are classified according to the type of read and write access that they provide.

Mathematically, a register is represented by a binary word variable. The value of the variable at any time is the word stored in the register at that time. We will normally use capital letters or strings of capital letters to denote binary word variables.

Individual bits of a binary word variable are binary variables. These are normally referred to by using the word variable name with a subscript to identify the specific bit, as illustrated in Figure 1.1. The subscript range associated with an n-bit word is usually $\langle n - 1:0 \rangle$, as in the figure for the 8-bit register X.

In block diagrams, registers are represented by rectangular boxes. If it is necessary to represent individual bits (or "cells") of the register, this is done by subdividing the box, as in Figure 1.1. Each cell may contain either a 0 or a 1.

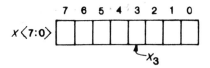

Figure 1.1   An 8-bit register

An 8-bit word is commonly referred to as a *byte*. The byte has become the standard unit for specifying storage capacities. For example, a computer may have 32 kilobytes (32K) of random access memory (RAM); a disk memory may have a capacity of 16 megabytes (16M). The prefixes "kilo" and "mega," when used to specify storage capacities, mean 2^{10} and 2^{20} (rather than 10^3 and 10^6 as in usual scientific notation). Hence, 32K is actually 32,768 bytes and 16M is actually 16,777,216 bytes.

For compactness, binary words are frequently represented by using *hexadecimal* notation. The bits of a word are separated into 4-bit groups, and each group is represented by one hexadecimal digit, as defined in Table 1.1. Hence, for example, the word 01101110 is represented as 6E and 1001010111000111 as 95C7.

Codes.   In order to use binary words to represent information, it is necessary to define a *code* that specifies the particular information value that is represented by each word.

Table 1.1. Hexadecimal notation

4-bit word	Hex digit
0000	0
0001	1
0010	2
0011	3
0100	4
0101	5
0110	6
0111	7
1000	8
1001	9
1010	A
1011	B
1100	C
1101	D
1110	E
1111	F

The three general types of information that are most commonly represented in computers are: text, numbers, and programs.

Text.   The most widely used code for representing text is the American Standard Code for Information Interchange (ASCII, pronounced ass-key), defined in Table 1.2.

Notice that the ASCII character set includes a number of "nonprinting" text and control characters. The SP (space) and CR (carriage return) characters, for example, are part of the text since they separate words and lines. Others such as SYN and ACK are not actually part of the text, but are used to control the transmission of text or the operation of input-output devices.

The ASCII code is a 7-bit code. The registers in most computers, however, are 8 bits or some multiple of 8 bits. For this reason, characters are normally stored as 8-bit words. The eighth bit is either ignored (e.g., made 0 always) or used as a "parity bit" for error detection. The value of the parity bit for a character is chosen so that the total number of 1's among the 8 bits is odd. Any single-bit error that occurs in the transmission of a character can then be detected. No matter which bit changes, the parity of the resulting word is even.

Numbers.   The fundamental code for representing unsigned integers is the *base 2* code (abbreviated B2). If $[X]_2$ denotes the integer represented by the word $X\langle n - 1:0\rangle$ under the B2 code, then

$$[X]_2 = X_0 \cdot 2^0 + X_1 \cdot 2^1 + \cdots + X_{n-1} \cdot 2^{n-1} \qquad (1.1)$$

For example, $[1101]_2 = 1 \cdot 2^0 + 0 \cdot 2^1 + 1 \cdot 2^2 + 1 \cdot 2^3 = 13$.

The most common code for representing signed integers is *two's complement* code (2C code). The 2C code is a variation of the B2 code. Arithmetic under the B2 and 2C codes is discussed in Chapter 4.

Real numbers are represented by fixed-point and floating-point codes. These are also discussed in Chapter 4.

Programs.   Programs are the third type of information commonly stored in computers. Programs are represented by a special code called *machine code*. Programs and machine code are discussed later in this section.

Register Transfer Operations

A computer processes information by doing operations on words. For example, the symbol $+_2$ denotes the operation that takes two words of the same

Table 1.2 ASCII code*

$X\langle 3:0\rangle$ / $X\langle 6:4\rangle$	000	001	010	011	100	101	110	111
0000	NUL	DLE	SP	0	@	P	`	p
0001	SOH	DC1	!	1	A	Q	a	q
0010	STX	DC2	"	2	B	R	b	r
0011	ETX	DC3	#	3	C	S	c	s
0100	EOT	DC4	$	4	D	T	d	t
0101	ENQ	NAK	%	5	E	U	e	u
0110	ACK	SYN.	&	6	F	V	f	v
0111	BEL	ETB	'	7	G	W	g	w
1000	BS←	CAN	(	8	H	X	h	x
1001	SKIP HT	EM	)	9	I	Y	i	y
1010	LF	SUB	*	:	J	Z	j	z
1011	VT·	ESC	+	;	K	[	k	{
1100	FF→	FS	,	<	L	\	l	|
1101	CR	GS	−	=	M	]	m	}
1110	SO	RS	.	>	N	∧	n	~
1111	SI	US	/	?	O	_	o	DEL

*Control character abbreviations:

NUL	null	DC1	device control 1
SOH	start of heading	DC2	device control 2
STX	start of text	DC3	device control 3
ETX	end of text	DC4	device control 4
EOT	end of transmission	NAK	negative acknowledge
ENQ	enquiry	SYN	synchronous idle
ACK	acknowledge	ETB	end of transmission block
BEL	bell	CAN	cancel
BS	backspace	EM	end of medium
HT	horizontal tabulation	SUB	substitute
LF	linefeed	ESC	escape
VT	vertical tabulation	FS	file separator
FF	form feed	GS	group separator
CR	carriage return	RS	record separator
SO	shift out	US	unit separator
SI	shift in	SP	space
DLE	data link escape	DEL	delete

length and produces a third word which represents their sum under the B2 code. The result word is one bit longer than the original words.

The word operation $\hat{+}_2$ is the same as $+_2$ except that the extra bit is dropped, so that the result is the same length as the operands. This is called a *fixed-range* operation. ("Overflow" is possible with fixed-range operations, but this need not be discussed here.)

In similar fashion $+_{2C}$ denotes addition under the 2C code, $-_{2C}$ is subtraction under the 2C code, $+_{FL}$ is addition under our floating-point code, and so on. The definition and implementation of arithmetic word operations are discussed in Chapter 4.

Logic operations on words are simpler (e.g., AND, OR, INVERT, SHIFT). No overflow is possible. These are discussed in Chapter 3.

A *register transfer* (RT) operation is a word operation with the operand words taken from specific registers and the result word loaded into a specific register. For example, $A \hat{+}_2 B \rightarrow C$ denotes the RT operation that takes the words in A and B, performs the fixed-range B2 addition operation, and puts the result into register C. A and B are called the *source* registers for the operation; C is called the *destination* register.

Only the destination register is changed by an RT operation. Source registers are unaffected. A particular occurrence of the operation $A \hat{+}_2 B \rightarrow C$ is illustrated in Figure 1.2. Notice that only register C is changed by the operation. There is no overflow in this example; the fixed-range operation is correct. The integers represented by the operand words are 5 and 7 and the integer represented by the result word is 12.

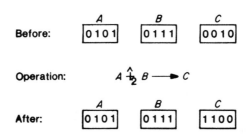

Figure 1.2   An RT operation

Program Controlled Operation

Computers perform complex information processing tasks by doing long sequences of simple RT operations. The RT operations that a computer is capable of performing are determined by the computer's instruction set. Each *instruction* specifies a particular operation, including the source and destination registers for the operation. Instructions are represented by binary words, as defined by the machine code. The instruction set and machine code for a particular processor are presented in Section 1.1.3.

A *program* is a sequence of instructions. The information processing task that is performed by a computer is determined by a program that is stored in the computer's memory. The instructions that constitute the program are "fetched" (i.e., read from memory) and "executed" (i.e., the specified RT operation is performed) one at a time.

The processing task that a computer performs can be changed simply by changing the program that is stored in the computer's memory. This ability to "program" a computer to do different jobs is the most important economic characteristic of computers. The major benefits of this characteristic are two:

1. It allows a single expensive machine to be shared for many small tasks, none of which individually could justify the machine cost.

2. It allows the same machine to be used for many different applications, thus increasing the market size and allowing the machine to be mass-produced. This greatly reduces the cost per machine.

1.1.2 Structure and Operation

The structure of a typical small computer is shown in Figure 1.3. The P, M, IOC, and DMAC blocks communicate with each other via a single communication channel called the *system bus*. More complex communication structures are possible, involving multiple communication paths and switches (see Section 1.2.3). However, the same major components (P, M, IOC, IOD, and DMAC) are used in these more complex structures and the role played by each of these components in the operation of a computer remains essentially the same, regardless of the complexity of the communication structure.

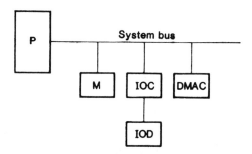

Figure 1.3   Single-bus architecture

In this text we will usually restrict our attention to the single bus structure of Figure 1.3. This is the most commonly used structure for small computers. The more complex structures are used in larger systems. Most of what we say applies to these systems as well (see Section 1.2.3).

Major Components

The major components of the computer, as illustrated in Figure 1.3 are: the processor, P; the primary memory, M; the input-output devices, IOD; the input-output controllers, IOC; and the direct memory access controller, DMAC. We will describe the role played by each of these in the operation of the computer.

Primary Memory.   The primary memory (also called main memory) is a set of registers that are directly accessible to the processor via the system bus. The processor uses the primary memory to provide temporary storage while it is processing information. In addition, the program that controls the operation of the processor is stored in primary memory.

Processor.   The function of the processor is to fetch and execute the instructions that constitute the program, one at a time. These instructions are represented by binary words stored in primary memory. The register transfer operations specified for execution by the instructions may involve source and destination registers in any of the blocks connected to the system bus (i.e., P, M, IOC, or DMAC). Hence, execution of an instruction may involve other blocks besides the processor.

The processor typically contains only a few registers, which provide *immediate access* storage for a limited amount of information. We will look at the processor registers of a particular microprocessor later in this section.

The primary memory contains a much large number of registers. These registers are slightly less accessible to the processor than its own immediate access registers for two reasons:

1. Communication over the system bus is slower than internal processor communication; and

2. Only one register at a time may be accessed via the system bus.

The IOC and DMAC blocks also contain registers that may serve as source or destination registers. These, like the memory registers, are accessible to the processor via the system bus. Instructions that involve these registers are used to control and communicate with the IOC and DMAC blocks.

IO Devices. The IOD block may also contain registers. These registers, however, are not directly accessible to the processor and cannot be specified by instructions as source or destination registers. Only the IOC block has access to IOD registers.

The IOD block includes all of the computer's input-output devices (also called *peripheral devices*). IO devices are used to transfer information into and out of the computer. Usually, information is brought into primary memory via an input device, processed in some fashion by the processor, and then transferred out of the computer via an output device.

Some common output devices are printers, plotters, and displays of all sorts. Common input devices are keyboards, switches, and card readers. A "computer terminal" is a device that combines a keyboard and a display. It is both an input and an output device.

In the near future, verbal input and output may become common. Speakers will serve as output devices and microphones as input devices.

In automatic control applications, various sorts of transducers and actuators are used for input and output. Thermocouples, pressure sensors, phototransistors, and accelerometers are examples of input devices. Motors, solenoids, and valves are examples of output devices. In such applications, analog (continuous) variables rather than digital (binary) variables are involved. Analog-to-digital converters must be used to convert continuous signals into binary words for transfer into the computer, and digital-to-analog converters for output transfer.

The IOD block also includes *secondary memory* devices. These devices are used to provide backup storage when the primary memory is not large enough to hold all of the desired programs and data to be processed.

The processor cannot directly access secondary memory. When it is desired to have a program in secondary memory control the operation of the processor, that program must first be moved into primary memory. Likewise, if it is desired to process some information stored in secondary memory, it must first be transferred into primary memory.

In addition to the functional differences between the primary and secondary memories, there are also important operational differences. The primary memory M is usually a *random access* memory (RAM), while the secondary memories in IODs are usually some type of *sequential access* memory (SAM).

A random access memory is so called because every register in the memory is equally accessible at any time. Registers in a sequential access memory are not equally accessible. At any time only one SAM register is directly accessible. Other registers are accessible only after some "latency time," which is different for different registers.

Examples of sequential access memories are magnetic disk, magnetic drum, magnetic tape, and long shift registers such as charge-coupled device

(CCD) or magnetic bubble shift registers. Consider a single-head magnetic disk. The disk consists of many concentric tracks, with many registers on each track. The disk rotates continuously. At any time, only the register that is currently under the "read/write head" is accessible. To access an arbitrary register it is necessary to move the head to the track containing that register and then wait for the disk to rotate until the desired register is under the head. The time required for these mechanical operations is the latency time. Other sequential access memories have similar latency times.

After the desired register is positioned under the head of a disk, the read or write operation can be quite fast, almost as fast as for a random access memory. If consecutive registers are to be accessed then there is a latency time only for the first register. After that, registers appear under the head one after another in the order required. For this reason, communication with secondary memory is usually done in blocks (e.g., 128 or 256 words in consecutive registers might comprise one block). We shall have more to say about block transfers between M and IOD later in this section.

IO Controllers. Each IO device is connected to the system bus via an IO controller. The IOC plays the role of an intermediary in communication between the IO device and devices connected to the system bus.

For example, when the processor (under program control, of course) wishes to print a character, it will send the character to the printer's IOC via the system bus. The IOC will put this character into a buffer and then transfer the character to the printer. This transfer may involve special control signals and may require a relatively long time. While the IOC is managing the transfer of this character to the printer, the processor continues to fetch and execute other instructions.

DMA Controllers. A DMAC is used to control the transfer of information between an IO device and primary memory. Not all systems have a DMAC. The processor can be used instead of a DMAC to control such transfers. A DMAC is used when either:

1. The processor cannot transfer information as fast as the IO device requires; or

2. The volume of information to be transferred would require too much of the processor's time to allow processor control.

The System Bus [2-4]

The binary signals that comprise the system bus are determined by the processor. The 6800 microprocessor bus is illustrated in Figure 1.4. For simplic-

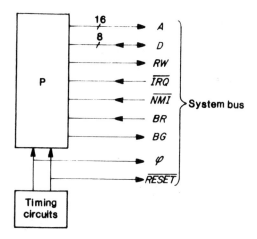

Figure 1.4 The system bus

ity, three 6800 signals of minor importance are omitted in Figure 1.4, and three of the signals shown have different names (see Section 6.3.1). (Essentially the same bus is used by several other processors in the 6800 and 6500 microprocessor families). A brief description of this bus is given here. A more complete description is provided in Section 6.3.1, along with a discussion of other common buses.

The signals $\overline{RESET}$ and ϕ are generated by timing circuits, which are not actually part of the processor. In Figure 1.3 all bus signals are shown as emanating from the P block for simplicity. Some microprocessors actually include these timing circuits on the processor chip (as suggested in Figure 1.3). The 6800 processor, however, does not.

Communication over the system bus consists primarily of *read operations* and *write operations*. The device that initiates a bus operation (either read or write) is called the *bus master*. Either the processor P or the DMAC may be the bus master.

During a read operation, the bus master requests one of the other devices connected to the system bus to send a copy of the word stored in some specified register. The bus master receives the word and stores it in one of its internal registers.

During a write operation, the bus master sends out a word and requests another device to load this word into a specified register.

The device that responds to the bus master's read or write request is called the *bus slave* for that operation. The bus slave may be an IOC, M, or DMAC component. The processor cannot act as a bus slave. The DMAC is the only component that may serve as either master or slave.

Registers in the slave devices are assigned addresses. An address is an integer between 0 and $2^{16} - 1$, represented by a 16-bit word. The bus master specifies the register to be accessed during a read or write operation by putting its address on the address bus A. The RW line is used to indicate whether a read or a write operation is desired: $RW = 1$ for read; $RW = 0$ for write.

The slave devices continuously monitor the A bus. During any bus operation, only that slave device which contains the addressed register responds. Data is transferred, either into or out of that register, via the 8-bit D bus.

Since the D bus is 8 bits, all slave registers must be 8-bit registers. We will use the notation $M[\alpha]$ to denote the 8-bit slave register with address α. Most of the slave registers are in the primary memory M (hence, the M in the notation $M[\alpha]$). However, IOC and DMAC also contain a few slave registers. These registers are assigned addresses, just like memory registers, and we will use the general notation $M[\alpha]$ for these as well as for memory registers. A register in IOC and DMAC usually has another name in addition to its generic name $M[\alpha]$.

The timing for bus read and write operations is illustrated in Figure 1.5. The master timing signal is the periodic "clock" signal ϕ. A bus operation requires one period of the clock. The period begins with a 1-to-0 transition of ϕ, at which time the bus master places the address of the desired register onto the A bus and sets RW to 1 or 0, depending upon whether a read or write is desired. Data is transferred during the second half of the clock period, while $\phi = 1$. If the operation is a read, the slave device puts the word contained in register $M[\alpha]$ onto the D bus while $\phi = 1$, and the bus master copies the word into one of its registers. If the operation is a write, the master puts a word on the D bus while $\phi = 1$ and the slave copies the word into register $M[\alpha]$.

The signals $\overline{IRQ}$ and $\overline{NMI}$ are "interrupt request" inputs. The bar over the signal name indicates that the signal is asserted low, that is, an interrupt is requested when $\overline{IRQ} = 0$ or $\overline{NMI} = 0$. An interrupt request is generated by an IOC when the IO device that it controls needs the attention of the processor for some reason. For example, when a printer is ready to print a character (i.e., the previous character has been printed), the printer IOC may generate an interrupt request. Or, when a key has been pressed on a keyboard, the keyboard IOC may generate an interrupt request.

The processor responds to an interrupt request by branching to a program stored in primary memory called an "interrupt service routine." Under the control of this program, the processor will determine the cause of the interrupt request and respond accordingly. For example, it may transfer the next character to the printer, or take a waiting character from the keyboard.

Interrupt requests at the IRQ input can be "masked" by the execution of the "set interrupt mask" instruction when the currently executing program

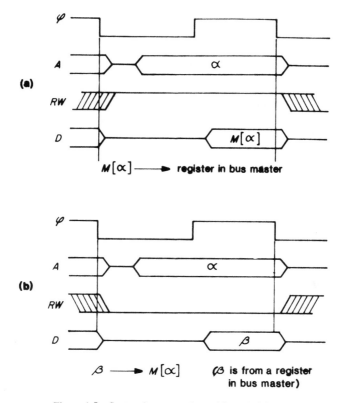

Figure 1.5   System bus operations: (a) read; (b) write

should not be interrupted. The "clear interrupt mask" instruction can be executed to allow $\overline{IRQ}$ interrupts to occur.

Interrupt requests at the $\overline{NMI}$ input cannot be masked, hence the name "nonmaskable interrupt."

The *BR* and *BG* signals (bus request and bus grant) are used to control bus mastership. Only one device can be bus master at any time. When power is first turned on, the processor assumes bus mastership. When the DMAC needs to initiate a bus operation, it must first request control of the bus by asserting *BR*. The processor responds by completing its current bus operation and then asserting *BG*. DMAC then becomes the bus master. The processor will not attempt to initiate another bus operation until *BR* is released. DMAC releases *BR* when it is finished using the bus for the moment, and the processor again becomes the bus master.

The $\overline{RESET}$ signal is used to initialize circuits in the P, IOC, and DMAC blocks. Usually $\overline{RESET}$ is asserted (i.e., $\overline{RESET} = 0$) momentarily after power to the system is first turned on, or after a RESET button is pressed (not shown in Figure 1.3).

Processor Registers

Registers in the processor itself provide the most accessible storage available to the processor. An instruction that specifies a processor register as a source or destination will execute faster than an instruction that specifies a memory register for two reasons:

1. A processor register is immediately accessible, while access to a memory register requires a system bus operation; and

2. Some time may be required for the processor to determine the address of a memory register, but no "address computation time" is required for access to a processor register.

Accumulators.   The registers in the 6800 processor are shown in Figure 1.6. Registers *A* and *B* are 8-bit "accumulators." An accumulator is a register that is used to hold intermediate results during a chain of calculations (e.g., the display register of a calculator is an accumulator). In order to be used in this fashion, a register must appear as a source or destination register in many instructions. This is the case for registers *A* and *B*, as we shall see.

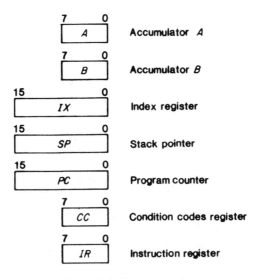

Figure 1.6   Processor registers

The name A is used not only for the accumulator register, but also for the address bus, as we have seen. Usually, it will be clear from the context which is intended. However, when ambiguity must be avoided, an alternative name, $ACCA$, is sometimes used for accumulator A. For symmetry, the name $ACCB$ may be used for accumulator B.

Index Register.   Many instructions specify memory registers as operands (i.e., as source or destination registers). Specification of a memory register requires specification of a 16-bit address. The manner in which an instruction specifies an operand address, or more precisely, the manner in which the processor determines this address from the information supplied by the instruction, is called the *address mode.*

The most straightforward address mode is *extended addressing*: the address of the memory register is simply included as part of the machine code for the instruction. (This address mode is called "direct addressing" in most other processors, but Motorola uses this term for a slightly different mode in the 6800.)

Another address mode used by the 6800 is *indexed addressing*. The processor computes the address of the memory operand by adding 1 byte of machine code to the 16-bit address in the index register, IX.

Indexed addressing is useful for accessing arrays of data stored in memory (e.g., tables, vectors, matrices). Examples of the use of indexed addressing will be provided in Sections 1.1.4 and 1.1.5. A precise description of all the address modes used by the 6800 will be provided in Section 1.1.3.

Long Register Notation.   Three of the processor registers (IX, PC, and SP) are 16 bits long. The letters H and L, used either as subscripts or in-line with the register name, will denote the "high byte" and the "low byte" of these registers. For example, $IXH = IX_H = IX\langle 15:8\rangle$ and $IXL = IX_L = IX\langle 7:0\rangle$.

When 16-bit registers are stored in memory or loaded from memory, two consecutive memory registers are used. In the 6800, the high byte is always at the lower memory address and the low byte at the higher memory address. (Some other processors store 16-bit words in memory in the reverse order.)

The notation $M2[\alpha]$ will denote the 16-bit register formed by "concatenating" (i.e., putting end to end) two consecutive memory registers, lower address on the left. That is,

$$M2[\alpha] = M[\alpha] \circ M[\alpha + 1] \qquad (1.2)$$

The small circle represents concatenation.

Communication over the system bus involves 8-bit operations only. A 16-bit transfer between the processor and memory must be accomplished as two 8-

bit operations. For example, the operation of storing the index register in memory at address α, $IX \rightarrow M2[\alpha]$, must be done as two bus write operations:

$$IXH \rightarrow M[\alpha] \text{ and } IXL \rightarrow M[\alpha + 1]$$

Program Counter. The program counter (PC) is a 16-bit register that contains the address of the next instruction byte to be fetched by the processor. The processor fetches an instruction byte (i.e., a byte of machine code) by putting PC on the A bus and doing a system bus read operation. It then increments PC so that PC "points to" (i.e., contains the address of) the next consecutive instruction byte.

A *branch* (or *jump*) instruction is an instruction that specifies PC as a destination register. The address that is loaded into PC is called the branch address. The processor will fetch and execute instructions from consecutive memory registers until a branch instruction is executed, which may cause it to skip over some instructions or to loop back to a previous instruction sequence.

As with operand addresses, branch addresses may be specified and computed using different address modes. The 6800 branch address modes will be described in Section 1.1.3.

Stack Pointer. A *branch* (or *jump*) *to subroutine* instruction (also called a *subroutine call* instruction) is a special type of branch instruction. In addition to loading a branch address into PC, it saves a "return address" somewhere in memory, from which it may be retrieved later. The return address is the address of the next consecutive instruction after the subroutine call.

A companion instruction to the subroutine call is the *return from subroutine* instruction. When executed, this instruction retrieves the return address that was stored in memory by the previous subroutine call and loads it into PC. Hence, the return from subroutine instruction is a branch instruction for which the branch address is the previously stored return address.

A subroutine is a program that performs a particular task and then terminates with a return from subroutine instruction. When called, a subroutine will perform its task and then branch back to the instruction after the subroutine call. Examples of subroutines will be given in Section 1.1.4.

It is possible for one subroutine to call another, and that subroutine to call yet another, and so on. This is called *nesting* of subroutines. The return addresses from successive calls must be "stacked up" in memory and then retrieved in reverse order when subroutine returns are executed.

The 6800 and most other modern processors store return addresses by using a "stack" structure, which facilitates nesting of subroutines. A stack is a "last in first out" (LIFO) buffer. There are two operations associated with a stack: *push* and *pull*. If R is a register, then the operation "push R" (denoted $R \rightarrow Stack$ in register transfer notation) will store a copy of the word in R on the stack. The operation "pull R" (denoted $Stack \rightarrow R$) will retrieve the word most recently pushed on the stack and load it into R.

In the 6800, the stack is implemented by using the stack pointer register, SP. For an 8-bit register R, the push and pull operations are each implemented as a sequence of two operations, as follows:

$$R \rightarrow Stack \equiv \begin{array}{ll} 1. & R \rightarrow M[SP] \\ 2. & SP - 1 \rightarrow SP \end{array} \qquad (1.3)$$

$$Stack \rightarrow R \equiv \begin{array}{ll} 1. & SP + 1 \rightarrow SP \\ 2. & M[SP] \rightarrow R \end{array} \qquad (1.4)$$

Notice that after any stack operation, SP points to the next available location on the stack. The push operation writes the byte in R into the memory register pointed to by SP, and then decrements SP. The pull operation increments SP, and then reads the word stored in the register pointed to by SP and loads it into R. The word that is "pulled" from the stack is not actually removed from memory by the pull operation; the stack pointer is simply moved past it. The word will be removed when a subsequent push operation writes over it.

A sequence of four stack operations is illustrated in Figure 1.7. Accumulators A and B are pushed onto the stack and then pulled from the stack in reverse order, thus exchanging the contents of A and B. The contents of registers A, B, SP, $M[1232]$, $M[1233]$, and $M[1234]$ are shown before and then after each operation. Memory addresses and register contents are all in hexadecimal notation.

There are instructions in the instruction set for pushing and pulling A and B. A program consisting of these four instructions will perform the sequence of operations in Figure 1.7.

When the stack is used to store a return address, as discussed initially, the 16-bit PC register must be pushed onto the stack. This is actually done as two 8-bit push operations as follows:

$$PC \rightarrow Stack \equiv \begin{array}{ll} 1. & PCL \rightarrow Stack \\ 2. & PCH \rightarrow Stack \end{array} \qquad (1.5)$$

Note that the return address is stored in memory in the standard 6800 order, high byte at the lower address.

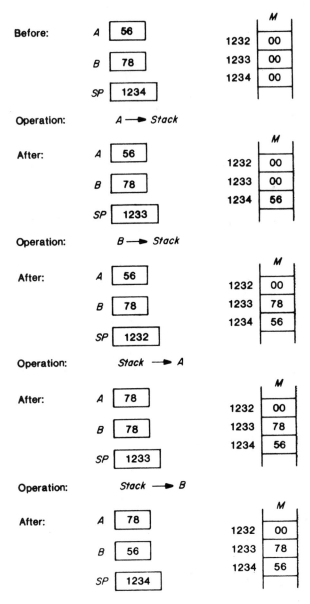

Figure 1.7   Stack operations

The return from subroutine instruction pulls the return address from the stack and puts it into PC. Again, this is implemented as two 8-bit pull operations:

$$Stack \rightarrow PC \equiv 1. \quad Stack \rightarrow PCH$$
$$2. \quad Stack \rightarrow PCL \tag{1.6}$$

Condition Codes Register.   The condition codes (CC) register is actually a collection of six independent single-bit registers, each of which serves a different purpose. Two 1's are concatenated to the left of these 6 bits to form an 8-bit register for system bus operations.

Each bit of the CC register has a name (other than CC_i) that suggests its function. The name of each individual bit is specified in Figure 1.8, together with a brief description of its use.

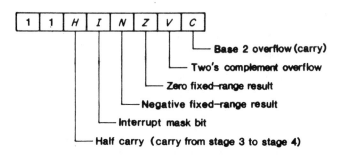

Figure 1.8 CC register

The I bit, CC_4, is used to mask or unmask interrupt requests at IRQ, as described above under "The System Bus." The other bits of CC are used to record certain events that may occur when instructions are executed.

Suppose, for example, that the instruction ADDA is executed. This instruction will add two 8-bit words, one obtained from accumulator A and the other from a memory register, and put the fixed-range result (i.e., the 8-bit result) into A. If all bits of the fixed-range result are 0, then the Z bit is "set" (i.e., $1 \rightarrow Z$); otherwise, Z is "cleared" (i.e., $0 \rightarrow Z$). If the fixed-range result is the correct sum under the base 2 code, then the C bit is cleared; otherwise, base 2 overflow has occurred, and C is set. The V bit is the same as C, except that it is for the two's complement code (i.e., it is the 2C overflow flag). The N bit is set if the fixed-range result under the two's complement code is negative; otherwise, N is cleared. The H bit is set or cleared according to whether or not there was a carry from stage 3 to stage 4 in performing the addition.

A complete understanding of the *CC* bits will be possible only after studying digital arithmetic (Chapter 4). Until then the above explanation will suffice.

Instruction Register.   Register *IR* is used by the processor to hold the first byte of machine code for the instruction currently being executed. This byte specifies the operation to be performed, the processor register(s) involved, if any, and the address mode to be used in computing the address of any memory register involved.

The instruction register is dedicated completely to the above use. It is not available for any other use. Specifically, it does not appear as a source or destination register of any instruction.

Fetch-Execute-Interrupt Operation

Most processors are very similar in their fundamental operation. A basic cycle is repeated endlessly. On each pass through the cycle, the processor fetches and executes one instruction. The address of the instruction is obtained from the *PC* register. Before the end of the cycle, *PC* is updated to point to the next instruction.

Either at the beginning or at the end of the cycle, the processor checks for interrupt requests. If one or more unmasked requests exist, the processor "honors" the highest priority request as follows:

1. Save *PC* and possibly some other processor registers, usually by pushing them on the stack;

2. Put the address of the interrupt service routine (ISR) into *PC*; and

3. Go to the beginning of the instruction cycle (the first instruction of the ISR will be fetched next).

This is known as the processor's *hardware interrupt response*. The essential effect is to save the return address (i.e., the address of the instruction that would have been executed next if no interrupt had occurred) and to transfer control of the processor to an ISR. The ISR is a program that will respond appropriately to the interrupt request (this is the "software interrupt response"). The ISR ends with a "return from interrupt" instruction, which pulls the return address from the stack and puts it in *PC*, thus returning control to the program that was interrupted. It also pulls any other words stored by the hardware interrupt response and restores them to the registers from which they were taken. (Note the similarity between an interrupt and a subroutine call.)

Also, at some point in the cycle the processor checks for bus requests. If there is a bus request, the processor relinquishes control of the bus to another bus master. This is typically accomplished by "floating" the necessary bus drivers (A, D, and RW for the 6800) and asserting the bus grant signal.

The term "floating a bus driver" means effectively disconnecting the internal circuitry from the corresponding bus line, leaving the line free to be used by another bus master. This is normally done by using tri-state drivers (see Section 5.1.3).

After relinquishing control of the bus, the processor waits for the new bus master to finish using the bus. The processor then continues with the cycle.

There is usually a RESET input that overrides all other inputs and internal conditions. Assertion of this input initializes the PC and perhaps some other processor registers, so that the fetch-execute-interrupt operation will begin in an orderly fashion.

This same basic description applies to most modern processors. In the details of operation, however, processors may differ considerably from each other. Some common points of variation are the following:

1. How is the PC initialized by a RESET, and what other registers are initialized?

2. How are the priorities of interrupt requests and the addresses of interrupt service routines determined?

3. What registers are saved besides PC during the hardware interrupt response?

4. When during the cycle are interrupt requests and bus requests checked?

5. What signals are involved in transferring bus control?

The flowchart of Figure 1.9 provides most of these details for the 6800 processor. Following a RESET, the processor initializes PC by doing two bus read operations: $M[\text{FFFE}] \rightarrow PCH$; $M[\text{FFFF}] \rightarrow PCL$. It also disables IRQ interrupt requests by setting the interrupt mask bit.

The processor begins the cycle by checking for bus requests. If $BR = 1$, the processor floats A, D, and RW and sets $BG = 1$ to indicate to the requesting bus master that the bus is free. It then waits for the new bus master to indicate that it is finished using the bus by clearing BR.

If there is no bus request, the processor checks for interrupt requests. INT is an internal variable that is 1 if there is an unmasked interrupt request pending (either at IRQ or NMI). If so, it honors the request by saving the processor state PS on the stack. This requires seven bus write operations.

The address of the interrupt service routine, $a(\text{ISR})$, is obtained by doing two bus read operations, at either address FFF8 or FFFC, depending upon

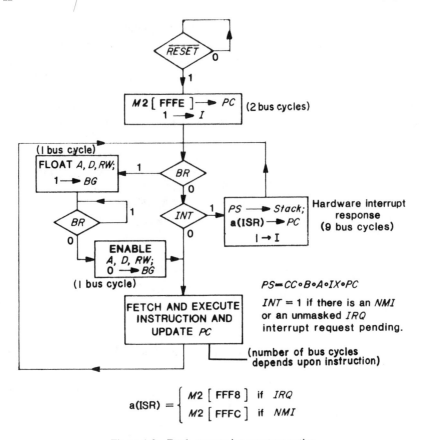

Figure 1.9   Fetch-execute-interrupt operation

whether the interrupt is at IRQ or NMI. If both requests are active, NMI has priority (not indicated in the flowchart).

After loading $a(\text{ISR})$ into PC, the processor returns to the beginning of the cycle and checks again for bus requests. This is better than going directly on to fetch and execute an instruction, because it reduces the maximum response time to a bus request.

If the processor finds $INT = 0$, it goes on to fetch and execute the next instruction. Two of the instructions that it might fetch actually involve the hardware interrupt response, although this is not shown in Figure 1.9. The software interrupt instruction, SWI, is executed by going to the hardware interrupt response box; $a(\text{ISR})$ in this case is $M2[\text{FFFA}]$. The wait instruction, WAI, is executed by pushing PS onto the stack and then going to a "wait state," where it waits for an IRQ or an NMI interrupt. When one of these occurs, it completes the interrupt response by loading a(ISR) into *PC* and then continues.

1.1.3 Instruction Set

Associated with any processor there is a particular set of instructions and a machine code for representing these instructions. The instruction set and machine code for the 6800 processor are described in this section. Extended versions of this same instruction set are used by other 6800 family processors as well.

The complete instruction set is presented here for convenient reference, including a precise description of all address modes. Some of the instructions and address modes will not be fully understood, however, until the background material of Chapters 3 and 4 has been developed.

General Characteristics

Before discussing specific instructions, we will point out some general characteristics of the instruction set.

Instruction Types. Except for a few special instructions, each 6800 instruction is one of the following types:

1. $R1 * R2 \rightarrow R1$ (two-operand register transfer);
2. $f(R1) \rightarrow R2$ (single-operand register transfer);
3. If $BC = 1$ then $BA \rightarrow PC$ (branch/jump).

R1 and *R2* are registers, *at most one of which is external to the processor. R1* may be the same as *R2* for type 2 instructions. *BA* is a branch address. *BC* is a branch condition, involving one or more bits of the *CC* register. * is a double operand word operation. *f* is a single operand word operation, which may be the identity function.

The restriction that at most one of the operand registers specified by an instruction is external to the processor is an important characteristic of the instruction set. It means that no instruction must specify more than one address. This limits the complexity of the instructions and the number of bytes required to represent instructions.

Most of the register transfer instructions are 8-bit instructions. For these, the operand registers *R1* and *R2* are 8 bits each.

A few of the instructions involve 16-bit registers. There are no instructions that mix 8- and 16-bit operands, although such instructions would be useful (e.g., $B \circ A \rightarrow IX$).

The type 3 instruction class includes unconditional as well as conditional branch instructions. An unconditional branch may be thought of as a conditional branch with branch condition 1 (i.e., $BC = 1$ is always true).

Machine Code.   Each 6800 instruction is represented by 1, 2, or 3 bytes. We will refer to these as *BYTE1*, *BYTE2*, and *BYTE3*. Instructions are stored in memory at consecutive addresses, with *BYTE1* at the lowest address, *BYTE2* next, and then *BYTE3*.

For type 1 and type 2 instructions (single and double operand register transfers) *BYTE1* specifies the following:

1. The operation (* or f);

2. Any registers in P (*R1* and/or *R2*);

3. The address mode to be used in computing the address of an external operand register, if any; and

4. The number of bytes used to represent the instruction (1, 2, or 3).

For type 3 instructions (branch/jump), *BYTE1* specifies the branch condition *BC* and the address mode to be used in computing the branch address. Subroutine call instructions may also be included in this class, in which case *BYTE1* also specifies the type of branch (i.e., branch to subroutine or ordinary branch).

Bytes 2 and 3 of the instruction, if present, are used in computing the address of an external operand register. The only exception to this is for an address mode known as "immediate addressing." For this mode, bytes 2 and 3 are the operand itself. With immediate addressing, if an 8-bit operand is needed, *BYTE2* is the operand; if a 16-bit operand is needed *BYTE2* ∘ *BYTE3* is the operand.

Instruction Tables

The entire 6800 instruction set is described in Table 1.3. The leftmost column of each part of the table, Operations, lists the name of each instruction. The next column, Mnemonic, specifies a three- or four-letter symbolic name that will be used to represent the instruction when writing programs. The word "mnemonic" means "an aid to the memory." It derives from the same root as the word "amnesia," which means "loss of memory."

The next major column, Addressing modes, is composed of several subcolumns, one for each address mode that may be used with instructions in that table. Each subcolumn is headed by the name of an address mode and is further divided into three sub-subcolumns headed OP, ~, and #. OP stands

TABLE 1.3. 6800 Instruction Set*

(a) Accumulator and memory instructions

Operations	Mnemonic	Immed OP	~	#	Direct OP	~	#	Index OP	~	#	Extnd OP	~	#	Implied OP	~	#	Boolean/arithmetic operation (all register labels refer to contents)	H (5)	I (4)	N (3)	Z (2)	V (1)	C (0)
Add	ADDA	8B	2	2	9B	3	2	AB	5	2	BB	4	3				$A + M \to A$	↕	•	↕	↕	↕	↕
	ADDB	CB	2	2	DB	3	2	EB	5	2	FB	4	3				$B + M \to B$	↕	•	↕	↕	↕	↕
Add acmltrs	ABA													1B	2	1	$A + B \to A$	↕	•	↕	↕	↕	↕
Add with carry	ADCA	89	2	2	99	3	2	A9	5	2	B9	4	3				$A + M + C \to A$	↕	•	↕	↕	↕	↕
	ADCB	C9	2	2	D9	3	2	E9	5	2	F9	4	3				$B + M + C \to B$	↕	•	↕	↕	↕	↕
And	ANDA	84	2	2	94	3	2	A4	5	2	B4	4	3				$A \cdot M \to A$	•	•	↕	↕	R	•
	ANDB	C4	2	2	D4	3	2	E4	5	2	F4	4	3				$B \cdot M \to B$	•	•	↕	↕	R	•
Bit test	BITA	85	2	2	95	3	2	A5	5	2	B5	4	3				$A \cdot M$	•	•	↕	↕	R	•
	BITB	C5	2	2	D5	3	2	E5	5	2	F5	4	3				$B \cdot M$	•	•	↕	↕	R	•
Clear	CLR							6F	7	2	7F	6	3				$00 \to M$	•	•	R	S	R	R
	CLRA													4F	2	1	$00 \to A$	•	•	R	S	R	R
	CLRB													5F	2	1	$00 \to B$	•	•	R	S	R	R
Compare	CMPA	81	2	2	91	3	2	A1	5	2	B1	4	3				$A - M$	•	•	↕	↕	↕	↕
	CMPB	C1	2	2	D1	3	2	E1	5	2	F1	4	3				$B - M$	•	•	↕	↕	↕	↕
Compare acmltrs	CBA													11	2	1	$A - B$	•	•	↕	↕	↕	↕
Complement, 1's	COM							63	7	2	73	6	3				$\overline{M} \to M$	•	•	↕	↕	R	S
	COMA													43	2	1	$\overline{A} \to A$	•	•	↕	↕	R	S
	COMB													53	2	1	$\overline{B} \to B$	•	•	↕	↕	R	S
Complement, 2's (Negate)	NEG							60	7	2	70	6	3				$00 - M \to M$	•	•	↕	↕	①	②
	NEGA													40	2	1	$00 - A \to A$	•	•	↕	↕	①	②
	NEGB													50	2	1	$00 - B \to B$	•	•	↕	↕	①	②
Decimal adjust, A	DAA													19	2	1	Converts Binary Add. of BCD Characters into BCD Format	•	•	↕	↕	①	③

Cond. code reg.†

25

TABLE 1.3. *(continued)*

(a) Accumulator and memory instructions

Operations	Mnemonic	Immed OP	~	#	Direct OP	~	#	Index OP	~	#	Extnd OP	~	#	Implied OP	~	#	Boolean/arithmetic operation (all register labels refer to contents)	H 5	I 4	N 3	Z 2	V 1	C 0
Decrement	DEC							6A	7	2	7A	6	3				$M - 1 \rightarrow M$	•	•	↕	↕	④	•
	DECA													4A	2	1	$A - 1 \rightarrow A$	•	•	↕	↕	④	•
	DECB													5A	2	1	$B - 1 \rightarrow B$	•	•	↕	↕	④	•
Exclusive Or	EORA	88	2	2	98	3	2	A8	5	2	B8	4	3				$A \oplus M \rightarrow A$	•	•	↕	↕	R	•
	EORB	C8	2	2	D8	3	2	E8	5	2	F8	4	3				$B \oplus M \rightarrow B$	•	•	↕	↕	R	•
Increment	INC							6C	7	2	7C	6	3				$M + 1 \rightarrow M$	•	•	↕	↕	⑤	•
	INCA													4C	2	1	$A + 1 \rightarrow A$	•	•	↕	↕	⑤	•
	INCB													5C	2	1	$B + 1 \rightarrow B$	•	•	↕	↕	⑤	•
Load acmltr	LDAA	86	2	2	96	3	2	A6	5	2	B6	4	3				$M \rightarrow A$	•	•	↕	↕	R	•
	LDAB	C6	2	2	D6	3	2	E6	5	2	F6	4	3				$M \rightarrow B$	•	•	↕	↕	R	•
Or, inclusive	ORAA	8A	2	2	9A	3	2	AA	5	2	BA	4	3				$A + M \rightarrow A$	•	•	↕	↕	R	•
	ORAB	CA	2	2	DA	3	2	EA	5	2	FA	4	3				$B + M \rightarrow B$	•	•	↕	↕	R	•
Push data	PSHA													36	4	1	$A \rightarrow M_{SP}, SP - 1 \rightarrow SP$	•	•	•	•	•	•
	PSHB													37	4	1	$B \rightarrow M_{SP}, SP - 1 \rightarrow SP$	•	•	•	•	•	•
Pull data	PULA													32	4	1	$SP + 1 \rightarrow SP, M_{SP} \rightarrow A$	•	•	•	•	•	•
	PULB													33	4	1	$SP + 1 \rightarrow SP, M_{SP} \rightarrow B$	•	•	•	•	•	•
Rotate left	ROL							69	7	2	79	6	3				M	•	•	↕	↕	⑥	↕
	ROLA													49	2	1	A	•	•	↕	↕	⑥	↕
	ROLB													59	2	1	B	•	•	↕	↕	⑥	↕

Addressing modes

Cond. code reg.†

26

Operation	Mnemonic	IMMED OP	~	#	DIRECT OP	~	#	INDEX OP	~	#	EXTND OP	~	#	INHER OP	~	#	Boolean/Arithmetic Operation	H	I	N	Z	V	C
Rotate right	ROR							66	7	2	76	6	3				M ⎫	•	•	↕	↕	⑥	↕
	RORA													46	2	1	A ⎬ → C → b7…b0 → C	•	•	↕	↕	⑥	↕
	RORB													56	2	1	B ⎭	•	•	↕	↕	⑥	↕
Shift left, arithmetic	ASL							68	7	2	78	6	3				M ⎫	•	•	↕	↕	⑥	↕
	ASLA													48	2	1	A ⎬ C ← b7…b0 ← 0	•	•	↕	↕	⑥	↕
	ASLB													58	2	1	B ⎭	•	•	↕	↕	⑥	↕
Shift right, arithmetic	ASR							67	7	2	77	6	3				M ⎫	•	•	↕	↕	⑥	↕
	ASRA													47	2	1	A ⎬ b7…b0 → C	•	•	↕	↕	⑥	↕
	ASRB													57	2	1	B ⎭	•	•	↕	↕	⑥	↕
Shift right, logic	LSR							64	7	2	74	6	3				M ⎫	•	•	R	↕	⑥	↕
	LSRA													44	2	1	A ⎬ 0 → b7…b0 → C	•	•	R	↕	⑥	↕
	LSRB													54	2	1	B ⎭	•	•	R	↕	⑥	↕
Store acmltr.	STAA				97	4	2	A7	6	2	B7	5	3				A → M	•	•	↕	↕	R	•
	STAB				D7	4	2	E7	6	2	F7	5	3				B → M	•	•	↕	↕	R	•
Subtract	SUBA	80	2	2	90	3	2	A0	5	2	B0	4	3				A − M → A	•	•	↕	↕	↕	↕
	SUBB	C0	2	2	D0	3	2	E0	5	2	F0	4	3				B − M → B	•	•	↕	↕	↕	↕
Subtract acmltrs.	SBA													10	2	1	A − B → A	•	•	↕	↕	↕	↕
Subtr. with carry	SBCA	82	2	2	92	3	2	A2	5	2	B2	4	3				A − M − C → A	•	•	↕	↕	↕	↕
	SBCB	C2	2	2	D2	3	2	E2	5	2	F2	4	3				B − M − C → B	•	•	↕	↕	↕	↕
Transfer acmltrs	TAB													16	2	1	A → B	•	•	↕	↕	R	•
	TBA													17	2	1	B → A	•	•	↕	↕	R	•
Test, zero or minus	TST							6D	7	2	7D	6	3				M − 00	•	•	↕	↕	R	R
	TSTA													4D	2	1	A − 00	•	•	↕	↕	R	R
	TSTB													5D	2	1	B − 00	•	•	↕	↕	R	R

27

TABLE 1.3. (continued)

(b) Index register and stack pointer instructions

Pointer operations	Mnemonic	Immed OP	~	#	Direct OP	~	#	Index OP	~	#	Extnd OP	~	#	Implied OP	~	#	Boolean/arithmetic operation	H 5	I 4	N 3	Z 2	V 1	C 0
Compare index reg	CPX	8C	3	3	9C	4	2	AC	6	2	BC	5	3				$X_H - M, X_L - (M+1)$	•	•	⑦	↕	⑧	•
Decrement index reg	DEX													09	4	1	$X - 1 \rightarrow X$	•	•	•	↕	•	•
Decrement stack pntr	DES													34	4	1	$SP - 1 \rightarrow SP$	•	•	•	•	•	•
Increment index reg	INX													08	4	1	$X + 1 \rightarrow X$	•	•	•	↕	•	•
Increment stack pntr	INS													31	4	1	$SP + 1 \rightarrow SP$	•	•	•	•	•	•
Load index reg	LDX	CE	3	3	DE	4	2	EE	6	2	FE	5	3				$M \rightarrow X_H, (M+1) \rightarrow X_L$	•	•	⑨	↕	R	•
Load stack pntr	LDS	8E	3	3	9E	4	2	AE	6	2	BE	5	3				$M \rightarrow SP_H, (M+1) \rightarrow SP_L$	•	•	⑨	↕	R	•
Store index reg	STX				DF	5	2	EF	7	2	FF	6	3				$X_H \rightarrow M, X_L \rightarrow (M+1)$	•	•	⑨	↕	R	•
Store stack pntr	STS				9F	5	2	AF	7	2	BF	6	3				$SP_H \rightarrow M, SP_L \rightarrow (M+1)$	•	•	⑨	↕	R	•
Indx reg → stack pntr	TXS													35	4	1	$X - 1 \rightarrow SP$	•	•	•	•	•	•
Stack pntr → indx reg	TSX													30	4	1	$SP + 1 \rightarrow X$	•	•	•	•	•	•

28

(c) Branch instructions

Operations	Mnemonic	Relative OP	~	#	Index OP	~	#	Extnd OP	~	#	Implied OP	~	#	Branch test	H (5)	I (4)	N (3)	Z (2)	V (1)	C (0)
Branch always	BRA	20	4	2										None	•	•	•	•	•	•
Branch if carry clear	BCC	24	4	2										$C = 0$	•	•	•	•	•	•
Branch if carry set	BCS	25	4	2										$C = 1$	•	•	•	•	•	•
Branch if = zero	BEQ	27	4	2										$Z = 1$	•	•	•	•	•	•
Branch if ≥ zero	BGE	2C	4	2										$N \oplus V = 0$	•	•	•	•	•	•
Branch if > zero	BGT	2E	4	2										$Z + (N \oplus V) = 0$	•	•	•	•	•	•
Branch if higher	BHI	22	4	2										$C + Z = 0$	•	•	•	•	•	•
Branch if ≤ zero	BLE	2F	4	2										$Z + (N \oplus V) = 1$	•	•	•	•	•	•
Branch if lower or same	BLS	23	4	2										$C + Z = 1$	•	•	•	•	•	•
Branch if < zero	BLT	2D	4	2										$N \oplus V = 1$	•	•	•	•	•	•
Branch if minus	BMI	2B	4	2										$N = 1$	•	•	•	•	•	•
Branch if not equal zero	BNE	26	4	2										$Z = 0$	•	•	•	•	•	•
Branch if overflow clear	BVC	28	4	2										$V = 0$	•	•	•	•	•	•
Branch if overflow set	BVS	29	4	2										$V = 1$	•	•	•	•	•	•
Branch if plus	BPL	2A	4	2										$N = 0$	•	•	•	•	•	•
Branch to subroutine	BSR	8D	8	2											•	•	•	•	•	•
Jump	JMP				6E	4	2	7E	3	3					•	•	•	•	•	•
Jump to subroutine	JSR				AD	8	2	BD	9	3					•	•	•	•	•	•
No operation	NOP										01	2	1	Advances prog. cntr. only	•	•	•	•	•	•
Return from interrupt	RTI										3B	10	1		•	⑩	⑩	⑩	⑩	⑩
Return from subroutine	RTS										39	5	1		•	•	•	•	•	•
Software interrupt	SWI										3F	12	1		•	⑪	•	•	•	•
Wait for interrupt‡	WAI										3E	9	1		•	•	•	•	•	•

29

TABLE 1.3. (continued)

(d) CC register instructions

Operations	Mnemonic	Implied			Boolean operation	Cond. code reg.					
		OP	~	#		5 H	4 I	3 N	2 Z	1 V	0 C
Clear carry	CLC	0C	2	1	0 → C	•	•	•	•	•	R
Clear interrupt mask	CLI	0E	2	1	0 → I	•	R	•	•	•	•
Clear overflow	CLV	0A	2	1	0 → V	•	•	•	•	R	•
Set carry	SEC	0D	2	1	1 → C	•	•	•	•	•	S
Set interrupt mask	SEI	0F	2	1	1 → I	•	S	•	•	•	•
Set overflow	SEV	0B	2	1	1 → V	•	•	•	•	S	•
Acmltr A → CCR	TAP	06	2	1	A → CCR	•	•	⑫	•	•	•
CCR → acmltr A	TPA	07	2	1	CCR → A	•	•	•	•	•	•

* Courtesy of Motorola, Inc.

† Condition code register notes (bit set if test is true and cleared otherwise):

① (Bit V) Test: Result = 10000000?
② (Bit C) Test: Result ≠ 00000000?
③ (Bit C) Test: Decimal value of most significant BCD Character greater than nine? (Not cleared if previously set.)
④ (Bit V) Test: Operand = 10000000 prior to execution?
⑤ (Bit V) Test: Operand = 01111111 prior to execution?
⑥ (Bit V) Test: Set equal to result of N $\oplus$ C after shift has occurred.

⑦ (Bit N) Test: Sign bit of most significant (MS) byte = 1?
⑧ (Bit V) Test: 2's complement overflow from subtraction of MS bytes?
⑨ (Bit N) Test: Result less than zero? (Bit 15 = 1)
⑩ (All) Load condition code register from stack.
⑪ (Bit I) Set when interrupt occurs. If previously set, a nonmaskable interrupt is required to exit the wait state.
⑫ (All) Set according to the contents of accumulator A.

‡ WAI puts address bus, R/W, and data bus in the three-state mode.

for Opcode and refers to the machine code for *BYTE1* of the instruction in hexadecimal notation. Sub-subcolumn ~ specifies the number of clock periods required by the 6800 to fetch and execute the corresponding instruction with this address mode. Sub-subcolumn # specifies the number of bytes of machine code required to represent the instruction with this address mode.

Many instructions may be used with more than one address mode. For example, instruction ADDA may be used with four different address modes. Note that OP is different for each address mode, verifying our previous observations that *BYTE1* specifies the address mode. *BYTE1* of the ADDA instruction with extended addressing, for example, is BB = 10111011; this instruction will be represented by 3 bytes in memory and will be fetched and executed by the 6800 in four clock periods. The 6800 address modes will be defined precisely below.

The next subcolumn, labeled Boolean/arithmetic operation in Table 1.3(a), (b), and (d), specifies the register transfer operation that is performed when the instruction is executed. The register transfer notation used by Motorola is the same as we have been using, with the following variations and additions:

1. All arithmetic word operations are fixed range. Specifically, $+$ denotes $\hat{+}_2$ and $-$ denotes $\hat{-}_2$ (it is shown in Chapter 4 that $X \hat{-}_2 Y = X \hat{+}_2 \bar{Y} \hat{+}_2 1$).

2. $+$ also denotes logic OR.

3. M denotes external register $M[\alpha]$, where α is the operand address as computed by the appropriate address mode.

4. M_{SP} denotes $M[SP]$ (i.e., the external register whose address is in *SP*).

5. If no destination register is specified, then the operation is performed but the result is not loaded into any register. For example, the operation specified for CMPA is $A - M$. Bits of the *CC* register are set as they would be for SUBA, but register A remains unchanged.

In Table 1.3(c) the next to last subcolumn is labeled Branch test. For each conditional branch instruction, this subcolumn states the condition under which a branch *will* be performed. The last several instructions in Table 1.3(c) are not conditional branch instructions. This subcolumn is not used for these instructions.

The last subcolumn of each part of Table 1.3 describes the effect of the instruction execution on each bit of the condition codes register. The following notation is used: "•" means the bit is unaffected; "S" means the bit is set to 1; "R" means the bit is reset to 0 (i.e., cleared); and "↕" means the bit is affected in the "standard fashion," according to the result of the register transfer operation evoked by the instruction.

The $\updownarrow$ notation can be defined more precisely. Let $R < 7:0 >$ denote the fixed-range result of the RT operation [i.e., $R < 7:0 > = R1*R2$ or $f(R1)$]. Then

$N\updownarrow$ means $R_7 \rightarrow N$.

$Z\updownarrow$ means NOR $(R < 7:0 >) \rightarrow Z$ (i.e., $1 \rightarrow Z$ if $R < 7:0 > = 00000000$; $0 \rightarrow$ Z otherwise).

$C\updownarrow$ means $1 \rightarrow C$ if the operation generates B2 overflow; $0 \rightarrow C$ otherwise.

$V\updownarrow$ means $1 \rightarrow V$ if the operation generates a 2C overflow; $0 \rightarrow V$ otherwise.

$H\updownarrow$ means $CARRY_4 \rightarrow H$, where $CARRY_4$ is the carry-in to stage 4 of a $+_2$ operation. (1.7)

There are a few exceptions to these standard interpretations of $\updownarrow$. These are explained in Table 1.3 as footnotes. Several of the "exceptions" are not really exceptions at all, but fall within the standard interpretation. The footnotes in these cases are unnecessary, but correct nevertheless.

Address Modes

The address modes of the 6800 are defined precisely in Table 1.4. The name of the 6800 address mode is listed in the leftmost column, and in the next column a general expression for a 16-bit address is given. This general expression indicates both how the address is represented by the machine code (using bytes 1, 2, and 3) and the computation that the processor must perform to construct the address.

The next three columns provide an example of an instruction using the address mode. The first of these three columns shows how the example instruction would be represented in assembly language. The next two columns give the hexadecimal machine code and the register transfer operation that will be performed upon execution.

The assembly language representation of an instruction consists of two "fields." The first field is the instruction mnemonic. The second field specifies the address mode and any related information.

As mentioned previously, no 6800 instruction may involve more than one operand register external to P, and $BYTE1$ of the machine code specifies any operand registers in P. Hence, we can speak of "the address mode of a 6800 instruction" without ambiguity. It is the address mode used to specify the address of the one and only external operand register, or the branch address if a branch instruction. The second and third bytes of an instruction are used to provide information to be used in the address computation, or to specify the operand itself in the case of immediate addressing.

Direct Mode. A direct address instruction is always two bytes. $BYTE2$ is used to specify the low 8 bits of a 16-bit address. The upper 8 bits are made all 0's by the processor.

TABLE 1.4. Address modes

Address mode	16-bit address	Example		
		Assembly language	Machine code	Execution
Direct	$00 \circ BYTE2$	ADDA $20	9B 20	$A \; \hat{+}_2 \, M[0020] \to A$
Extended	$BYTE2 \circ BYTE3$	JMP $5C20	7E 5C 20	$5C20 \to PC$
Indexed	$00 \circ BYTE2$ $\hat{+}_2 \, IX$	ADDA 5,X	AB 05	$A \; \hat{+}_2 \, M[6025] \to A$ assuming IX = 6020
Immediate	$a(BYTE2)$	ADDA #$20	8B 20	$A \; \hat{+}_2 \, 20 \to A$
		LDX #$4F7	CE 04 F7	$04F7 \to IX$
Relative	$PC \; \hat{+}_{2C} \, BYTE2$	BCS $4C03	4C05 | 25 | FC	$PC \; \hat{+}_2 \, FFFC \to PC$ $4C07 \; \hat{+}_2 \, FFFC = 4C03$
Inherent	None	ABA	1B	$A \; \hat{+}_2 \, B \to A$

To be consistent with other 6800 literature, we will use Motorola's assembly language. This language allows addresses and data to be specified in either decimal or hexadecimal notation. The "$" is used to indicate that the numerals to follow are hexadecimal. If no $ is present, the numerals are decimal. Leading zeroes in either case may be omitted. Hence, in the example "$20" represents hexaddress 0020. The "20" in "ADDA 20," however, would represent hexaddress 0014.

We will use the $ notation only within assembly language statements. Elsewhere, we will always use hexadecimal notation to represent binary words and decimal notation to represent integers, with no special notation to remind the reader of this convention. The intended meaning should be clear from the context. Addresses and machine code, in particular, will always be represented in hexadecimal notation. For example, all of the numerals in the last two columns of Table 1.4 are hexadecimal.

Extended Mode.   An extended address instruction is always three bytes. Bytes 2 and 3 specify a complete 16-bit address.

Both extended and direct modes are characterized by the fact that the address is specified directly as part of the machine code. Extended addressing allows access to the full address range of the processor, while direct addressing allows access only to "page 0" (i.e., addresses 0000 through 00FF; in the 6502 processor this address mode is referred to as "zero page addressing"). The advantage of direct addressing is that the machine code is shorter, so it saves both memory space and execution time. To take maximum advantage of direct addressing, page 0 of memory should be used for frequently accessed information.

In assembly language, both direct and extended addressing are represented in the same way: the address (or some expression representing the address) is simply written in the operand field. The assembler will use direct addressing if the address is on page 0 and extended addressing otherwise.

Indexed Mode.   An instruction using indexed addressing is always 2 bytes. *BYTE2* specifies an "offset" in B2 code to be added to the address in IX to produce the final operand or branch address. Indexed addressing is represented in assembly language by writing the desired offset in the operand field followed by ",X".

Two things should be noted carefully. First, the offset is in B2 code, not 2C code. Hence, the final address is always greater than the address in *IX* (unless the address in *IX* is on the last page of memory, and adding the offset produces a carry-out; the final address is then on page 0 since the carry-out is discarded by the fixed-range operation $\hat{+}_2$). Second, the address in *IX* does not change when indexed addressing is used; the word in *IX* is simply used in the address computation.

Immediate Mode. Ordinarily, we do not think of the immediate address mode as specifying an address. Instead, the immediate mode supplies the operand "immediately" as part of the machine code. Other address modes, by contrast, specify an address, and the processor accesses the operand via a bus operation at that address. If we wish to think of the immediate mode as an actual *address* mode, then the address that is specified is *a(BYTE2)*, the address of *BYTE2* of the instruction.

The immediate address mode is used to specify source operands only, never destination operands. Hence, immediate mode is used to introduce constants into the computation.

Immediate mode instructions may be either 2 or 3 bytes long, depending upon whether the destination register for the instruction is 8 or 16 bits. One example of each is given in Table 1.4.

In assembly language, the immediate mode is identified by the prefix "#" in the operand field. Notice that this is the only distinction between the example for direct addressing in Table 1.4 and the ADDA example for immediate addressing.

Relative Mode. An instruction using the relative address mode is always 2 bytes. Relative addressing is similar to indexed addressing in that *BYTE2* specifies an offset from a 16-bit address in a processor register. There are two differences, however. First, the processor register involved is *PC* rather than *IX*. Second, the offset is represented in two's complement (2C) code rather than base 2 (B2) code.

An 8-bit word in 2C code can represent any integer between -128 and $+127$. Hence, the final address specified by an instruction in relative addressing will be between $PC - 128$ and $PC + 127$. The address in *PC* at this time will be the address of *BYTE1* of the next instruction, since *PC* is incremented after *BYTE2* of the relative address instruction is fetched.

Relative addressing is used only for branch instructions in the 6800. In fact, it is the *only* address mode used for most of the branch instructions. In Table 1.3, notice that relative addressing is the only address mode used for branch instructions whose mnemonic begins with the letter B. Also notice that relative addressing is not used for any other instructions. This means that the instruction mnemonic itself is sufficient to specify relative addressing. No special notation is needed in the operand field, as is the case with other address modes.

In the example, notice that the actual branch address (not the offset) is written in the operand field. This is more convenient for the programmer.

The assembler computes the offset to be used for *BYTE2*. In this example, the branch address is 4C03 and the instruction is stored at 4C05. After the processor fetches *BYTE2* of the instruction, *PC* will contain address 4C07. Hence, the offset should be −4, which is FC in 2C code. The assembler does this computation when it translates BCS $4C03 into machine code.

At execution time, the processor adds *BYTE2* = FC to *PC*, using 2C code for *BYTE2*. As shown in Chapter 4, this is done by extending the leftmost bit of *BYTE2* to the left to form a 16-bit word, and then adding that word to *PC* using B2 addition.

Relative addressing is ideal for branch instructions because most branches in typical programs are to nearby instructions (e.g., loop back a few instructions; skip ahead a few instructions). When it is necessary to branch to an instruction that is farther away, the JMP or JSR instructions may be used.

The advantage of the relative address branch versus the extended address jump instruction is that only 2 rather than 3 bytes of machine code are required.

Inherent Mode. If all operand registers for an instruction are in the processor, then no address need be specified. Such an instruction is said to use the "inherent" address mode.

Since *BYTE1* of an instruction specifies all operand registers in P, all inherent mode instructions are single-byte instructions. In assembly language, inherent mode instructions are characterized by an empty operand field.

Before closing this discussion of address modes, let us review the assembly language representation of the different address modes. Indexed and immediate addressing are distinguished from other address modes by special notations in the operand field: "#" for immediate, and ",X" for indexed. The inherent address mode instructions are distinguished by an empty operand field.

Three address modes share a common representation: direct, extended, and relative. Relative address mode instructions are distinguished from direct and extended by the instruction mnemonic: the relative mode is used if the instruction is a branch with first letter B.

Direct and extended are distinguished from each other by the value of the address that is specified in the operand field. If the address is on page 0, then the direct address mode may be used; otherwise, extended addressing is required.

Specific Instructions

To write programs for a processor, it is necessary to understand exactly what register transfer operation(s) will be performed when the processor executes each instruction. This is specified concisely in the Operation columns of Table 1.3. In many cases, the operation is simple and this specification should be sufficient. In other cases, the operation is more complex and some further explanation or background may be required.

Accumulator and Memory Instructions. The operand registers involved in these instructions are accumulators A and B, and single-byte memory registers. An M in the instruction table denotes memory register $M[\alpha]$, where α is the address computed according to the address mode specified, as defined in Table 1.4. The C bit of the condition code register ($C = CC_0$) is also involved in a few instructions.

The following instructions are straightforward, and should require no explanation beyond the description in Table 1.3(a): the clear instructions (CLR, CLRA, CLRB); the load instructions (LDAA, LDAB); the store instructions (STAA, STAB); and the transfer instructions (TAB, TBA).

The stack instructions (PSHA, PSHB, PULA, and PULB) should be clear from our previous discussion of the stack.

The following instructions perform logic operations: ANDA, ANDB COM, COMA, COMB, EORA, EORB, ORAA, and ORAB. The necessary background to understand these operations is provided in Chapter 3. Also, discussed in Chapter 3 are the shift and rotate instructions: ROL, ROLA, ROLB, ROR, RORA, RORB, ASL, ASLA, ASLB, ASR, ASRA, ASRB, LSR, LSRA, and LSRB. These operations, however, should be clear from the diagrams in the instruction table. Figure 1.10, for example, illustrates the logical shift right operation.

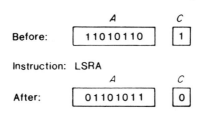

Figure 1.10 Logical Shift Right A execution

Chapter 4 will provide sufficient background to understand the arithmetic instructions: add (ADDA, ADDB, ABA, ADCA, ADCB); negate (NEG, NEGA, NEGB); subtract (SUBA, SUBB, SBA, SBCA, SBCB); increment (INC, INCA, INCB); decrement (DEC, DECA, DECB); and decimal adjust (DAA).

The increment and decrement operations, in fact, can be understood with only the definition of the base 2 code (Section 1.1.1) as background. These are simply the count up and count down operations. If $B = 10111001$ before execution of INCB, then $B = 10111010$ after execution.

The bit test, compare, and test instructions (BITA, BITB, CMPA, CMPB, CBA, TST, TSTA, TSTB) are unusual in that no destination register is specified. These instructions are used to set or clear the bits of the CC register according to the operation specified, but without loading a destination register. The operations are: logic AND for bit test; subtract for compare; and subtract 0 for test.

The test instruction can be understood with no arithmetic background, because subtracting 0 is no operation; the CC bits are simply affected according to the operand specified. The only bits affected are N and Z. Examples are given in Figure 1.11.

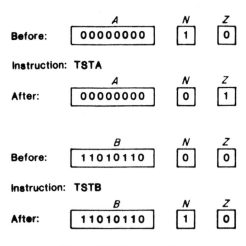

Figure 1.11 Test instruction

IX and SP Instructions.   Table 1.3(b) includes all instructions that specify *IX* and *SP* as operand registers. An X in the Operation column actually denotes *IX*.

The load and store instructions (LDX, LDS, STX, STS) are straightforward, but the notation in the table may be confusing. Using the notation that we have developed, the operation for LDX is $M2[\alpha] \rightarrow IX$ and the operation for STX is $IX \rightarrow M2[\alpha]$, where α in each case is the address computed via the specified address mode. LDS and STS are similar.

The transfer instructions (TSX, TXS) are similar to the transfer accumulator instructions (TAB, TBA), except that $IX-1$ is transferred instead of IX, and $SP + 1$ is transferred instead of SP. The reason for this involves the use of the stack for subroutine communication and will be discussed later.

The increment and decrement instructions are 16-bit base 2 operations.

The CPX instruction is similar to the 8-bit compare instructions (CMPA, CMPB). The CC register bits are affected according to a subtract operation. Unfortunately, only the Z bit is affected according to the 16-bit subtraction $IX - M2[\alpha]$. The N and V bits are affected according to the 8-bit subtraction $IXH - M[\alpha]$. This was probably a matter of design convenience. The N and V bits are usually of no use to the programmer after CPX. CPX is normally used only to check whether $IX = M2[\alpha]$, which is properly indicated by Z.

Branch Instructions.   Table 1.3(c) includes all instructions that may load a branch address into PC.

The first instruction, BRA, is an unconditional branch. The next 14 instructions (BCC through BPL) are conditional branch instructions. The branch address is loaded into PC only if the condition specified in the Branch test column is true.

To understand how the conditional branch instructions are used, consider a simple example. Suppose that we wish to branch to address 1200 if accumulator A contains 65, and to address 1250 otherwise. And suppose that the program that is required to make this decision will be stored at address 1234 (so that both 1200 and 1250 are within relative address range). The following program will work.

```
CMPA  #$65
BEQ   $1200
BRA   $1250
```

The first instruction will set $Z = 1$ if $A = 65$ and $Z = 0$ if $A \neq 65$. The next instruction will branch to 1200 if $Z = 1$, that is, if $A = 65$. If $A \neq 65$, then the BRA instruction will be executed next, which will branch to 1250 as required.

This is a typical, though simple, example of how decisions must be made by a program. First, one or more bits of the CC register must be set up to reflect the decision that must be made. Then conditional branch instructions must be executed to test the appropriate conditions.

When one considers the complexity of the decisions that programs are expected to make, it is surprising that the mechanism for making decisions is so primitive. Every decision, no matter how complex, must be carried out as a sequence of tests on the bits of the CC register.

Most of the branch tests in Table 1.3(c) represent arithmetic relations and conditions. The background necessary to understand these is developed in Chapter 4.

The branch to subroutine instruction (BSR) and the jump to subroutine instruction (JSR) both execute as follows:

$$1.\ PC \rightarrow Stack$$
$$2.\ \alpha \rightarrow PC$$

(1.8)

At the time of execution, PC contains the address of the next consecutive instruction; α denotes the branch address, computed by relative addressing for BSR and either extended or indexed addressing for JSR.

The only difference between BSR and JSR is in the address modes available for each. BSR is used for branching to nearby subroutines, and JSR for more distant subroutines. The same distinction applies to the unconditional branch instructions, BRA and JMP.

The NOP instruction performs no operation. PC is simply incremented to the next consecutive instruction. This is not normally considered a branch instruction. Since NOP does no operation, it cannot be useful in processing information. It is sometimes useful during program development, however, when instructions must be removed from a program without changing the location of other instructions, or when space must be held for instructions to be inserted later.

The return from interrupt instruction (RTI) pulls the processor state from the stack, that is, $Stack \rightarrow PS$. This requires seven bus read operations (see Figure 1.9). An interrupt service routine normally ends with RTI.

Return from subroutine (RTS) pulls a return address from the stack, that is, $Stack \rightarrow PC$. Subroutines normally end with RTS.

The software interrupt instruction (SWI) pushes the processor state PS onto the stack and then branches to the interrupt service routine at the address stored in $M2[\text{FFFA}]$. That is,

$$1.\ PS \rightarrow Stack$$
$$2.\ M2[\text{FFFA}] \rightarrow PC$$

(1.9)

The wait instruction (WAI) pushes PS onto the stack and then suspends processor operation until an IRQ or an NMI interrupt occurs. The processor floats A, D, and RW and holds $BG = 1$ while waiting. This allows other bus masters to use the bus.

CC Register Instructions.   These instructions are used to directly set or clear bits of the CC register. Their operation should be clear from the table.

Instruction Set Variations

The 6800 instruction set is simple, yet typical of modern processors. Variations are primarily in the following areas.

Operations. The 6800 provides a minimal set of arithmetic instructions, just integer addition and subtraction. Larger processors may provide integer multiplication and division as well, and perhaps even floating-point arithmetic instructions.

More complex shift and rotate instructions are also common (e.g., shift n bits rather than just 1 bit).

Operand Size. Except for a few simple 16-bit instructions, the 6800 instructions have 8-bit operands. Larger microprocessors may have a full set of 16-bit instructions in addition to the 8-bit instructions. Minicomputers and larger computers typically have even larger operands (e.g., 32 or 64 bits).

Some microprocessors intended for control applications have instructions with single-bit operands (called bit-manipulation instructions).

Address Modes. Most processors have direct addressing (i.e., the 6800 "extended" mode), immediate addressing, and relative addressing (usually for branch instructions, like the 6800). In addition, most processors have other and more powerful modes of indexed addressing.

Indexed addressing in the 6800 is weak because there is only one index register. Most processors have more than one index register, or "general registers" that can serve either as index registers or accumulators.

The 6800 indexed addressing is also weak because the offset (displacement) is only 8 bits and is part of the instruction (hence cannot be incremented). Other processors provide a full-size offset as part of the machine code, which can be used as a "base address" allowing the index register to step simultaneously through several arrays.

A still more powerful address mode specifies two index registers and a displacement to be added, allowing access to more complex data structures.

Auto-increment addressing is indexed addressing with the index register automatically incremented when it is used. Auto-decrement addressing is similar. These modes are useful for implementing stacks and queues.

Indirect addressing is indexed addressing with no offset. Indirect addressing through a memory register allows memory registers to be used as pointers. Indirect and indexed addressing can be combined by doing first one, then the other (in either order).

Operand Combinations. The 6800 allows only one memory operand per instruction. More powerful processors may allow multiple memory operands. A "symmetrical" processor allows any address mode or processor register to be used for any source or destination register. The 68000 processor, for example, is almost symmetrical.

Branch Instructions. The 6800 provides a good set of conditional branch instructions. Some small processors (e.g., 6502 and 8080) are not as complete. Most large processors provide essentially the same branch tests. Additional branch address modes are usually provided as well.

1.1.4 Programming

In this section the fundamentals of assembly language programming are presented. Program examples are for the 6800 processor, but the emphasis is on fundamental principles (assembly language characteristics, straight-line programs, branches, loops, and subroutines) which apply to any processor.

Assembly Language

Definitions. An *assembly language program* is a sequence of "statements," each of which represents either a processor instruction or an *assembler directive*. Assembler directives are also called *pseudoinstructions*. Directives for 6800 programs are defined below.

A *machine language program* is a sequence of bytes to be stored in specific memory locations. The bytes represent both processor instructions (in machine code) and data. The bytes to be stored in some registers may be unspecified. These are "working registers" for the program, the initial values of which are irrelevant.

An *assembler* is a program that translates an assembly language program (called the *source program*) into a machine language program (called the *object program*). The assembler accepts the source program as input and generates the object program as output.

Directives. Assembler directives for 6800 programs are defined in Table 1.5. The origin (ORG) directive tells the assembler where in memory to place the "object code" generated by the statements to follow. This includes the data bytes and unspecified bytes generated by assembler directives, as well as the machine code for processor instructions.

The form constant byte (FCB) directive is used to place data values into memory. Two forms for the directive are shown. The first form is used to specify numbers (in decimal) or binary words (in hexadecimal). Numbers will be represented in base 2 or two's complement code. Each x_i must be repre-

Table 1.5 Assembler directives

Directive	Interpretation
ORG α	The object code for the statements to follow (until the next ORG) should be placed in consecutive memory locations beginning at address α.
FCB $x_1, x_2, \ldots, x_n$ or FCB '$x_1 x_2 \ldots x_n$'	Put bytes representing the data $x_1, x_2, \ldots, x_n$ into next n consecutive memory locations.
FDB $x_1, x_2, \ldots, x_n$	Put 16-bit words representing the data $x_1, x_2, \ldots, x_n$ into next $2n$ consecutive memory locations.
RMB n	Reserve next n bytes of memory for use as working storage.
y EQU α	Associate address α with label y.

sentable by a single byte (i.e., between -128 and $+255$ for numbers; at most two hexadecimal digits for binary words).

The second form is used to specify ASCII text. Any string of ASCII characters not including " ' " is legitimate. For example,

FCB 'JOHN SMITH'

will put 10 data bytes in memory. Note that the space between N and S is an ASCII character, represented by 20. This will be the fifth data byte.

The form double byte (FDB) directive is similar to FCB, except that each x_i generates a 16-bit word. For example,

FDB $1234,25

will generate 4 bytes of object code: 12, 34, 00, 19.

The reserve memory bytes (RMB) directive generates n bytes of unspecified value (i.e., initial values are irrelevant, but locations are reserved). The corresponding memory registers will be available to the program for use as "working storage."

The equate (EQU) directive informs the assembler that the address α will be represented symbolically in the program by the "label" y. For example,

XYZ EQU $1234

tells the assembler that XYZ will represent address 1234. The instruction INC XYZ will then be interpreted by the assembler as INC $1234.

As an alternative to using the EQU directive, an address value may be assigned to a label by attaching the label to a statement. The address value associated with the label will be the address where the object code for the statement is placed in memory. For example,

```
     ORG $2000
ANN  LDAA #$25
```

will assign the address 2000 to the label ANN.

Syntax. To the assembler, a source program appears as a sequence of ASCII characters. The assembler must separate the program into statements, determine the meaning of each statement, and generate the appropriate object code.

The assembler's job is made easier if the program is required to conform to a rigid syntax that specifies precisely the format for the program. The syntax for 6800 programs is specified in Table 1.6.

The notation used to define the syntax is an informal version of *Backus-Naur form*, which was originally developed to describe the syntax of compiler languages. This notation is used to specify those sequences of characters that constitute "syntactically correct" programs. The notation does not define the "meaning" of a program (i.e., what instructions and directive are represented). This should be clear from our previous discussion.

Names enclosed in angle brackets, "⟨ · · · ⟩", are called *nonterminal symbols*. *Terminal symbols* are the characters that will actually appear in a source

Table 1.6 Assembly language syntax

1. ⟨program⟩ ::= ⟨statement⟩ (CR) $^{\geqslant 1}$⟨statement⟩ (CR) $^{\geqslant 1}$ · · ·

2. ⟨statement⟩ ::= [⟨label⟩]⟨s⟩⟨opcode⟩[⟨s⟩⟨operand⟩][⟨s⟩⟨comment⟩]

3. ⟨s⟩ ::= (SP) $^{\geqslant 1}$

4. ⟨label⟩ ::= ⟨letter⟩ ⟨alphanum⟩$^{0-7}$

5. ⟨letter⟩ ::= A|B| · · · |Z

6. ⟨alphanum⟩ ::= ⟨letter⟩ | ⟨decnum⟩

7. ⟨decnum⟩ ::= 0|1|2| · · · |9

8. ⟨opcode⟩ ::= ⟨mnemonic for processor instruction or assembler directive ⟩

9. ⟨operand⟩ ::= ⟨expression⟩ | #⟨expression⟩ |
   ⟨expression⟩, X |'⟨ascii⟩$^{\geqslant 1}$' |
   ⟨expression⟩ [,⟨expression⟩]$^{\geqslant 1}$

10. ⟨expression⟩ ::= ⟨label⟩ | ⟨constant⟩ |
    ⟨expression⟩ + ⟨expression⟩ |
    ⟨expression⟩ − ⟨expression⟩

11. ⟨ascii⟩ ::= any ASCII character

12. ⟨constant⟩ ::= ⟨decnum⟩$^{1-5}$ | $⟨hexnum⟩$^{1-4}$

13. ⟨hexnum⟩ ::= ⟨decnum⟩ | A|B|C|D|E|F

program. Each rule of syntax specifies how a nonterminal symbol may be replaced by a sequence of nonterminal and terminal symbols. By repeated application of the rules of syntax, all nonterminal symbols can be removed, resulting in a sequence of ASCII characters that represents a syntactically correct source program.

Besides the angle brackets, our informal Backus-Naur notation also involves several other symbols: "::=" means "represents" or "may be replaced by"; the vertical bar "|" means "or"; square brackets "[···]" enclose an optional element; the superscript "i-j" means "repeat i to j times"; the superscript "$\geqslant 1$" means "repeat one or more times." Terminal symbols include all the printing ASCII characters plus a few nonprinting characters. A nonprinting character is represented by a name (see Table 1.2) enclosed in a circle. For example, ⓒⓡ represents the single hex byte 0D (ASCII carriage return).

The first rule of syntax in Table 1.6 states that a program consists of a sequence of "statements," with successive statements separated by one or more carriage returns.

The second rule specifies the format for a statement: an optional label, followed by a mandatory opcode, then an optional operand, and an optional comment. Successive elements of a statement are separated from each other by one or more "space" characters (rule 3).

Rule 4 states that a label consists of a letter followed by zero to seven alphanumeric characters.

Rules 5–7 define a label to be a string of one to eight uppercase letters and numerals, beginning with a letter.

Rule 8 indicates that an opcode is the mnemonic for either a processor instruction (Table 1.3) or an assembler directive (Table 1.5).

Rule 9 specifies all of the possible operand fields for instructions and directives.

Rule 10 is a *recursive* definition; that is, the term that it is defining (⟨operand⟩) appears in the definition. The intended interpretation is as follows. First, an expression may be either a label or a constant. Second, an expression may be formed by writing any two legitimate expressions in sequence, separated by the terminal character +. An example is XYZ+5. (The intended meaning should be clear: XYZ+5 represents the fifth address after the address represented by XYZ.)

The next form introduces expression subtraction. For example, DAN−5−XYZ is an expression, since DAN−5 and XYZ are expressions. When more than one operator appears in an expression, evaluation is left to right. Hence, the last example means (DAN−5)−XYZ, not DAN−(5−XYZ).

Rule 12 defines a constant to be a string of one to five decimal numerals or one to four hex numerals. Longer strings would require more than 16 bits for their representation, hence they can be ruled out syntactically. Note, however, that this syntax limit does not ensure that a constant will not be too large in a particular context. For example, LDAA #$1234 is acceptable syntactically, but it is incorrect since accumulator A is only 1 byte long. The hex constant in this context must be at most two digits. A rule such as this could be represented syntactically, but it is not convenient to do so.

The assembly language described by this syntax is a subset of Motorola's 6800 assembly language. The Motorola language has some additional features that facilitate program development but are not essential. We have omitted them for simplicity.

This assembler is called an *absolute* assembler. It generates object code to be placed in specific locations in memory. A more sophisticated type of assembler, called a *relocating* assembler, produces object code that can be loaded anywhere in memory (with some slight modifications at load time). Relocating assemblers are convenient when developing large programs, or programming in a time-sharing environment, because they allow postponement of the decision of where to place a program in memory. We will not discuss relocating assemblers further.

Straight-Line Programs

The simplest program structure is the straight line, consisting of a sequence of instructions that are to be executed once only, in sequential order. There are no branches.

Example 1. Consider the task of adding decimal 21 to the number stored in memory register 1234. That is,

$$M[1234] \; \stackrel{+}{}_2 \; 15 \; \rightarrow \; M[1234]. \tag{1.10}$$

Immediate addressing can be used to introduce the constant 15. But there is no instruction that allows an immediate constant to be added directly to a memory register. Hence, the memory word must first be moved into an accumulator where the addition may be performed. The program follows, placed in memory at address 2000. The RT operation for each instruction is shown in the comment field.

```
ORG   $2000
LDAA  $1234        M[1234]  →  A
ADDA  #21          A +₂15  →  A
STAA  $1234        A  →  M[1234]
```

The machine code for this program is shown in Table 1.7.

The bus operations that will occur when this program is executed are listed in Table 1.8. Notice that four bus cycles are used for LDAA and two for

Table 1.7 Machine code for Example 1

Address	Contents	Symbolic instruction
2000	B6	
2001	12	LDAA $1234
2002	34	
2003	8B	
2004	15	ADDA #21
2005	B7	
2006	12	STAA $1234
2007	34	

ADDA, both as specified in Table 1.3. STAA, however, uses one less bus cycle than the number of cycles specified. This means that the bus is actually idle for one clock period, because of the inability of the Motorola processor to work fast enough. We will see why this might happen in Chapter 7 when we study processor design.

Table 1.8 Sequence of bus operations for Example 1

A	RW	D	Operation
2000	1	B6	Fetch *BYTE1* of LDAA and put in *IR*
2001	1	12	Fetch *BYTE2* of LDAA
2002	1	34	Fetch *BYTE3* of LDAA
1234	1	M[1234]	Read operand and put in *ACCA*
2003	1	8B	Fetch *BYTE1* of ADDA and put in *IR*
2004	1	15	Fetch *BYTE2* of ADDA and add to *ACCA*
2005	1	B7	Fetch *BYTE1* of STAA and put in *IR*
2006	1	12	Fetch *BYTE2* of STAA
2007	1	34	Fetch *BYTE3* of STAA
1234	0	ACCA	Write *ACCA* to M[1234]

Example 2. Consider the task of exchanging the contents of *IX* and the double accumulator $A \circ B$. For example, if before execution $IX = 1234$, $A = 56$, and $B = 78$, then after execution $IX = 5678$, $A = 12$, and $B = 34$.

In the program to follow, working registers WRX, WRA, and WRB are

assigned to page 0 to allow the use of direct addressing. The program starts at
address 3000, represented by the label XCHG.

```
          ORG   0
    WRX   RMB   2
    WRA   RMB   1
    WRB   RMB   1

          ORG   $3000
    XCHG  STX   WRX
          STAA  WRA
          STAB  WRB
          LDX   WRA
          LDAA  WRX
          LDAB  WRX+1
```

It is left as an exercise to specify the machine code and the sequence of bus
operations for this program.

Branches

A program may be invested with the ability to make decisions through the use
of branch instructions. To be implemented in a program, a decision must be
reduced to a sequence of the available branch tests. The *CC* register must be
set up prior to each branch test so that its value reflects the condition to be
tested.

Example 3. If the byte in accumulator *B* is the ASCII character Ⓒ then
clear *B* and branch to ENDLN; otherwise, branch to NEXT. Suppose that
both ENDLN and NEXT are within relative address range.

```
    ORG   $2000
    CMPB  #$0D          1 → Z if ACCB = Ⓒ
    BNE   NEXT          branch if Z = 0
    CLRB
    BRA   ENDLN
```

The assembler would not be able to translate this program into machine
code, because the address values of the labels NEXT and ENDLN are unknown. These labels are said to be "undefined."

A label is *defined* (i.e., an address value is attached to it) when it appears in
the label field of a statement. In a complete program, NEXT and ENDLN
would both appear as labels of instruction statements somewhere in the
source program.

When writing and testing a program in pieces, however, some of the labels referred to in a program segment may not be defined within that segment. The equate directive may be used to define the labels temporarily so that the segment can be assembled. For example, in our program segment we might include the statements

```
NEXT   EQU  $2030
ENDLN  EQU  $2050
```

Later, when the complete program is to be assembled, these temporary equate statements can be removed.

The programs that we write as examples will often involve undefined labels. We will not bother to insert equate statements, although this would be necessary if the program were to be assembled, or even if the machine code were to be generated by hand.

Also, we will usually omit the origin statements in our examples, unless placement in memory is relevant to the example. These would also have to be inserted before assembly.

Example 4.   If the ASCII code for LDX is stored in $M3[1234]$, then branch to MNELDX; otherwise, continue in a straight line.

```
        LDAA  $1234
        CMPA  #'L'
        BNE   CONT
        LDAA  $1235
        CMPA  #'D'˙
        BNE   CONT
        LDAA  $1236
        CMPA  #'X'
        BEQ   MNELDX
CONT    ...
```

This program represents the required decision as a sequence of three branch tests.

Loops

Much of the power of the digital computer derives from its ability to do the same computation repeatedly. In a program, this is called a *loop*. A loop consists of a program segment (in the simplest case, a straight-line segment; in more complex cases, the segment may involve branches and even other loops) ending in a branch back to the beginning of the segment. Usually, this branch is a conditional branch; at the end of each pass through the loop a decision is made whether to make another pass. This is called the loop *exit test*.

If it were necessary to write programs without loops, even programs for simple computations would be enormously long. The 6800 processor executes over 100,000 instructions every second. A program without loops that is to control the 6800 for 1 minute would be 6 million instructions long. The machine code for the program would be about 12 million bytes. Only a tiny fraction of this program could fit in the primary memory (maximum size, 64K bytes). About 25 floppy disks would be required to store the program.

The idea of a loop is important in hardware as well as in software. The fetch-execute cycle (Figure 1.9), for example, is a loop. The control unit that controls the sequential operation of any nontrivial digital system always involves a loop (Chapter 6).

In fact, loops are important in almost all types of systems (e.g., motors run in cycles; buses repeat the same schedule; the seasons). Loops provide a way to obtain infinite (or at least endless) operation from a system of finite complexity.

In high-level computer languages (compiler languages) loops are implemented by statement types provided for that purpose (e.g., DO statement in Fortran; WHILE, FOR, and REPEAT statements in Pascal; FOR statement in Basic). In assembly language, loops must be constructed using branch instructions.

Example 5. Count the number of 1's in accumulator A. Flowcharts are often used to provide a visual representation of the sequential operation of programs involving loops and other branches. A flowchart for this program is shown in Figure 1.12.

Accumulator B is used as the 1's counter. B is cleared before entering the loop. On each pass through the loop, the LSR instruction shifts A right one bit. The rightmost bit goes to C, where it can be tested, and a 0 is inserted at the left end. B is incremented if $C = 1$. If A is not yet 0, not all 1's have been counted yet, so another pass is made through the loop; exit from the loop occurs when $A = 0$.

```
          CLRB
LOOP      LSRA
          BCC    EXTST
          INCB
EXTST     TSTA
          BNE    LOOP
```

The BCC instruction is used to skip over INCB when the A bit that has been shifted into C is 0. The TSTA instruction sets up the exit test by setting $Z = 1$

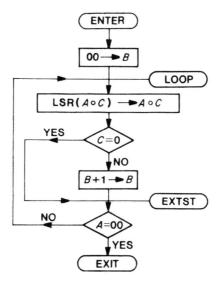

Figure 1.12 Flowchart for Example 5

if $A = 0$. The flowchart is keyed to the program via the labels, which identify corresponding points in the flowchart and program.

Instruction Step Simulation.   Instruction step simulation involves stepping through a program one instruction at a time, and tracing the changes that occur in "program registers" (i.e., processor and memory registers that are involved in the computation). Specific initial values and input data are supplied as required.

An instruction step simulation for the program of Example 5 is illustrated in Table 1.9. The program registers in this case are accumulators A and B and CC bits C and Z. The simulation involves recording the changes in these registers as each instruction is executed. The initial value of A is chosen arbitrarily to be 05. The initial values of B, C, and Z are irrelevant.

Instruction step simulation is a tedious process, which is seldom done by hand in such detail as in Table 1.9. However, when writing a program or reading a program, this is exactly the process that one goes through mentally.

Verifying that a program will operate as expected is a complex and difficult task. Instruction step simulation (mentally or with pencil and paper) is only the first pass at this task. It is sufficient only for the simplest programs.

Program verification for complex programs requires computer assistance. Modern microprocessor development systems provide the capability of observing a program as it executes. The program can be single-stepped, and

Table 1.9 Instruction step simulation

Step	Instruction	A	C	B(hex)	Z
		00000101	x	xx	x
1	CLRB	00000101	0	00	1
2	LSRA	00000010	1	00	0
3	BCC EXTST				(no branch)
4	INCB	00000010	1	01	0
5	TSTA	00000010	0	01	0
6	BNE LOOP				(branch)
7	LSRA	00000001	0	01	0
8	BCC EXTST				(branch)
9	TSTA	00000001	0	01	0
10	BNE LOOP				(branch)
11	LSRA	00000000	1	01	1
12	BCC EXTST				(no branch)
13	INCB	00000000	1	02	0
14	TSTA	00000000	0	02	1
15	BNE LOOP				(no branch)

selected registers displayed after each step. The program can be run in real time or slow time while particular registers are observed. The system bus can be monitored for particular events (e.g., writes to a particular memory region; instruction fetches from a region); these events or events around them can be stored for later perusal.

Computer assistance, however, is not a substitute for the ability to do instruction step simulation mentally and with facility. This is a basic skill required in reading and writing programs.

Example 6. Clear a block of 50 memory registers.

A flowchart for this program is shown in Figure 1.13. Before entering the loop, the address of the block is loaded into *IX*, and accumulator *B* is initialized to 50. *IX* will be used as a pointer to the next byte of the block on each pass through the loop; *B* will be used as the loop pass counter.

```
          ORG   $5000
BLK       RMB       50
          ORG   $2000
START     LDX   #BLK
          LDAB  #50
LOOP      CLR   0,X
          INX
          DECB
          BNE   LOOP
```

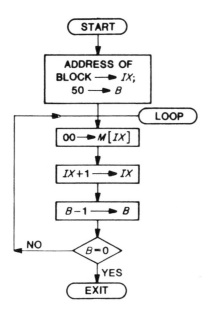

Figure 1.13   Flowchart for Example 6

Origin statements are included to make clear the use of labels with immediate addressing in the LDX instruction. Since BLK represents address 5000, BLK could be replaced by $5000 in the LDX instruction. When executed, $5000 \rightarrow IX$.

Note that LDX BLK would not be correct. This would load $M2[5000]$ into IX.

Since ↕ is indicated in the Z column of the DECB instruction, $1 \rightarrow Z$ if $B = 0$ after DECB is executed. Hence, it is not necessary to use TSTB to set up the exit test.

Subroutines

It frequently happens that the same computation must be performed at several different points in a program. It is possible to include the instructions that perform this computation at each such point. Alternatively, these instructions may be included in the program at one place only, and terminated with a return from subroutine instruction. The subroutine can then be "called" by executing a branch (or jump) to subroutine at each point where the computation is desired.

Example 7.   Count the number of 1's in accumulator A and return from the subroutine with the result in B.

```
ONES    CLRB
LOOP    LSRA
        BCC     EXTST
        INCB
EXTST   TSTA
        BNE     LOOP
        RTS
```

This is exactly the same as the program of Example 5, with a label added at the subroutine entrance and an RTS added at the end.

Example 8. Use the subroutine ONES to compare the number of ONES in $M[3000]$ and $M[3001]$. If they are the same, then branch to SAME; otherwise continue.

```
        ORG  0
WR      RMB  1                  Working Register
        ORG  $2000
        LDAA $3000
        JSR  ONES
        STAB WR
        LDAA $3001
        JSR  ONES
        CMPB WR
        BEQ  SAME
```

Example 9. A subroutine to clear a block of memory. Enter the subroutine with the address of the block to be cleared in IX and the length of the block in B.

```
CLRBLK  CLR   0,X
        INX
        DECB
        BNE   CLRBLK
        RTS
```

This subroutine may be used to clear any block of memory up to 256 bytes in length. For example, to clear the block defined in Example 6 the subroutine is called as follows:

```
        LDX   #BLK
        LDAB  #50
        JSR   CLRBLK
```

1.1.5 Input-Output Operation

One of the most important and difficult aspects of computer operation is the transfer of information between primary memory and IO devices. The fundamental concepts involved are illustrated in this section, using a printer as an example IO device. The same principles apply to other types of IO devices, including secondary memory devices.

In Chapter 6, the circuits that implement the operation discussed here are designed. Specifically, the printer IO controller, the DMA controller, and the 6800 processor are all designed.

A Printer Interface

Figure 1.14 shows the connection of a printer to the system bus. The printer is equipped with a *parallel port*, which allows it to receive all bits of a character at once (as compared with a *serial port*, which would receive a character one bit at a time).

When the printer is ready to receive a character, it holds $RDY = 1$. The parallel output controller (POC) must then hold a character at PD (parallel data) and produce a pulse at TR (transfer request). The printer will change RDY to 0, take the character at PD, and then set $RDY = 1$ again when it is ready to receive the next character.

The maximum rate at which characters can be transferred is controlled by the printer via the RDY signal. The simplest printers have only a one-charac-

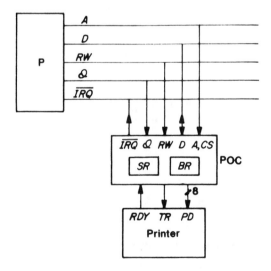

Figure 1.14 Printer connection

ter "buffer" register, so that each character must be printed before the next
character is sent. Such printers typically print 100 or 200 characters per second, so this is the rate at which characters can be transferred to the printer.
After a character is received, RDY is held at 0 until the character has been
printed [e.g., 5 or 10 milliseconds (ms)].

Other printers have a buffer memory that is large enough to hold one or
more lines of characters. While the buffer is being filled, characters can be
transferred to the printer at a high rate. RDY is held at 0 only briefly for each
character (e.g., a few microseconds). After the buffer is filled, there is a
longer delay while the characters in the buffer are being printed. Even at a
very high print rate this delay will be large relative to the system bus clock
(e.g., at 1200 lines per minute, the delay is 50 ms per line, enough time for
100,000 bus cycles with a 2-megahertz clock).

The function of the POC is to "interface" the printer to the system bus, so
that the printer can be controlled via system bus read and write operations.
The POC contains two registers: a buffer register $BR\langle 7:0\rangle$ and a status register $SR\langle 7:0\rangle$. Particular addresses are assigned to these registers when the
POC chip address and chip select inputs are connected to the A bus (see Section 6.3.1). Communication with these registers is then possible via system
bus read and write cycles.

The buffer register BR is used to hold a character that has been sent via the
system bus while that character is being transferred to the printer. The status
register is used for two control functions: SR_7 serves as a ready flag for system
bus transfers to BR (like the printer RDY signal for transfers from POC to
the printer), and SR_0 is used to enable or disable interrupt requests from
POC. If $SR_0 = 1$, then POC will interrupt when it is ready to receive a character (i.e., when $SR_7 = 1$). If $SR_0 = 0$, then POC will not interrupt. The other
bits of SR are not used.

The transfer of a character to POC via the system bus proceeds as follows.
POC indicates that it is ready by setting SR_7. The processor reads SR and,
finding $SR_7 = 1$, writes a character to BR. The POC clears SR_7 when it loads
this character into BR to indicate that another character should not be sent
for the moment. POC then proceeds to transfer the character in BR to the
printer by generating a pulse at TR as described above. The processor, in the
meantime, continues to fetch and execute instructions. If it should happen to
read SR, it will find $SR_7 = 0$ and hence will not attempt to send another
character to the printer (if it is programmed properly). When the printer is
ready to receive another character, POC sets SR_7. The transfer cycle can now
repeat.

Print Character Subroutine.   The subroutine PRCHAR below will send one
character to the printer. Upon entrance into the subroutine, the character is
in accumulator A.

```
PRCHAR  TST   PSR      SR₇ → N
        BPL   PRCHAR   if N = 0, wait.
        STAA  PBR      A → BR; 0 → SR₇
        RTS
```

PBR and PSR are labels for the addresses of the POC registers BR and SR. The instructions TST and BPL test the "ready flag," SR_7. These instructions are executed repeatedly until $SR_7 = 1$ (this is called a "wait loop").

When $SR_7 = 1$, the STAA instruction writes the byte in accumulator A to POC register BR. In addition to loading BR, this instruction also clears SR_7 and activates the POC circuitry that transfers the byte in BR to the printer.

Block IO Transfers

Communication between IO devices and primary memory is normally done in blocks (e.g., 128 or 256 bytes per block) rather than a single character at a time. There are three standard ways to control block IO transfers: direct control, interrupt control, and direct memory access (DMA) control.

Each of these techniques is illustrated below, using the printer as the example IO device. The same techniques are used for other devices, including secondary memory devices (e.g., disk and tape).

Direct Control. Direct control is used when the processor can be devoted completely to controlling the block transfer while the transfer is in progress. The subroutine PRBLK below transfers a block under direct control. The subroutine is entered with the address of the block in IX and the block length in accumulator B. The POC interrupt is assumed disabled (i.e., $SR_0 = 0$).

```
PRBLK  LDAA  0,X
       JSR   PRCHAR
       INX
       DECB
       BNE   PRBLK
       RTS
```

The first two instructions set up and call the PRCHAR subroutine to print one character. The processor will wait in the PRCHAR wait loop if the printer is not ready.

Upon return from PRCHAR, IX is incremented to point to the next character to be printed, and B is decremented. This loop is repeated until B reaches 0, and then RTS is executed.

The following program calls the subroutine PRBLK to print a block of 200 characters stored in memory at address 3000.

```
LDX   #$3000
LDAB  #200
JSR   PRBLK
```

Interrupt Control.   Under direct control, a great deal of processor time can be wasted in wait loops. If the real-time constraints of an application are met in spite of this, then there is no disadvantage in squandering processor time in this fashion. If this is not the case, however, then it is desirable to avoid wait loops and allow the processor to work on some other computation while a block transfer is in progress.

This is exactly the purpose of the interrupt mechanism. Rather than waiting in a loop for an IO device, the processor can work on an independent task. When the IO device is ready, it interrupts, forcing control of the processor to be transferred to an interrupt service routine (ISR). The ISR transfers the next character to/from the IO device, and then returns control to the interrupted program.

An ISR for the IRQ interrupt of the 6800 is written below. It is assumed that several IO devices are connected to IRQ. Hence, the ISR begins by checking the ready flag of each device to see which one has interrupted. This is called *polling*. It is assumed that the printer has highest priority, and hence it is polled first.

```
          ORG  $5000
IRQISR    TST  PSR          Poll printer
          BPL  POLLTERM     If PSR₇ = 1,
          BRA  PRINT        branch to PRINT

POLLTERM  TST  TSR
....                        Poll other devices,
                            beginning with the
                            terminal
PRINT     LDX  BA           Byte address → IX
          LDAA 0,X          Get next character
          STAA PBR          Send it to BR
          INX               Increment byte
                            address
          STX  BA
          DEC  BC           Decrement byte count
          BNE  RETURN
          CLR  PSR          0 → SR₀ if block
                            transfer complete
```

```
RETURN     RTI

BA         RMB  2               Reserve memory for
BC         RMB  1               byte address and
                                byte count

TERM       ....                 Routines to service
                                interrupts from
                                other devices

           ORG  $FFF8
           FDB  IRQISR          IRQ interrupt vector
```

The interrupt service routine cannot expect to know what is in the processor registers when it begins executing, because another program has been using them. The ISR must, therefore, use its own memory registers rather than *IX* and *B* to hold the address of the next byte, and the number of bytes left in the block. These are memory registers *BA* and *BC*, reserved by the RMB directives.

The ISR begins at IRQISR by polling the printer. If the printer has interrupted, then $SR_7 = 1$ and control will branch to PRINT. If the printer has not interrupted, then $SR_7 = 0$ and the program proceeds to check the ready flags of the lower priority devices. The next three statements transfer the next byte of the block to the printer. Then *BA* and *BC* are updated and the return from interrupt is executed. If $BC = 0$, the POC interrupt is disabled by clearing SR_0 before RTI.

When an IRQ interrupt occurs, the processor gets the address of the ISR from $M2$[FFF8] (see Figure 1.9). The last two statements of the program put the address of IRQISR into $M2$[FFF8].

In order to print a block under interrupt control, it is necessary only to initialize the *BA* and *BC* registers of the ISR and enable the POC interrupt. The following program does this for a block of length 200 at address 3000. It is assumed that the 6800 IRQ interrupt is enabled (i.e., I = 0).

```
           LDX   #$3000
           STX   BA
           LDAA  #200
           STAA  BC
           LDAA  #$01
           STAA  PSR      1  →  SR₀
```

DMA Control.   Block transfer under DMA control requires another device, a DMA controller (DMAC). The connection of the DMAC into the system is illustrated in Figure 1.15.

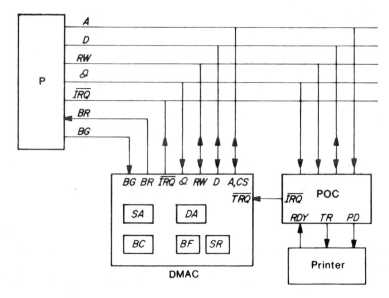

Figure 1.15 DMAC connection

The POC is still required. All POC connections are as in Figure 1.14, except that the POC *IRQ* output is connected to the DMAC transfer request input (*TRQ*) rather than to the processor IRQ input.

When the POC is ready to receive a character, it will assert its *IRQ* output, which is the DMAC *TRQ* input. The DMAC will then request control of the bus by asserting its *BR* output. After the processor relinquishes the bus (indicated by $BG = 1$), DMAC will read the next character from memory and then write it to the *BR* register in POC (two consecutive bus cycles). The DMAC will then return control of the bus to the processor, which it indicates by clearing the *BR* output (see Figure 1.9).

The DMAC that we will design in Chapter 6 will be capable of controlling block transfers from input device to memory, from memory to memory, and from input device to output device, as well as from memory to output device. Two address registers are provided: a source address register $SA\langle 15:0\rangle$ and a destination address register $DA\langle 15:0\rangle$. In our case, SA will hold the next byte address in memory and DA will hold the address of the buffer register *BR* in POC (do not confuse this *BR* register with the *BR* output of DMAC). SA will be incremented after each byte transfer, but DA will not be incremented.

The DMAC byte count register *BC* is 16 bits, allowing block lengths up to 64K. The buffer register $BF\langle 7:0\rangle$ receives the byte that the DMAC reads, and during the subsequent write cycle *BF* is sent out.

The status register $SR\langle7:0\rangle$ includes a ready flag SR_7 and an interrupt enable bit SR_0. Writing a 0 to SR_7 initiates a block transfer. When the DMAC completes a block transfer, it sets SR_7. The DMAC generates an interrupt request when the ready flag is set and the DMAC interrupt is enabled (i.e., $SR_7 = 1$ and $SR_0 = 1$).

The type of block transfer is selected by writing to $SR\langle2:1\rangle$. $SR\langle2:1\rangle =$ 10 selects the transfer from memory to output device.

Addresses are assigned to the DMAC registers by the connection of the chip select input CS to the A bus (see Chapter 6). Each 16-bit register is assigned two addresses, one to the high half and the next consecutive address to the low half. The LDX and STX instructions can be used to read and write these registers.

The following program sets up the DMAC to print a block of 200 characters starting at address 3000.

```
LDX    #$3000
STX    DSA
LDX    #200
STX    DBC
LDX    #PBR
STX    DDA
LDAA   #$04
STAA   DSR
LDAA   #$01
STAA   PSR
```

The labels DSA, DBC, DDA, and DSR represent the addresses of DMAC registers SAH, BCH, DAH, and SR. PBR and PSR represent the addresses of the BR and SR registers in POC. The first six instructions initialize SA, BC, and DA. The next two instructions write 04 to SR, which does each of the following: disables DMAC interrupts; selects memory to output transfer; initiates the block transfer. The last two instructions enable the POC interrupt.

After this program executes, the processor may go on to execute some other program. The DMAC will handle the block transfer with no further assistance from the processor.

Comparison. The three techniques of controlling a block transfer may be compared by noting the amount of processor time that is used for each type of transfer. To be specific, suppose that the block is 200 characters and the printer prints 200 characters per second. Suppose that the period of clock ϕ is 1 microsecond (μs).

The direct control technique will use essentially 1 second of processor time, since the processor is tied up for the duration of the block transfer.

For the interrupt control technique, the processor makes one pass through the interrupt service routine for each character transferred. Using the instruction execution times from Table 1.3, one pass through the interrupt service routine will require 59 μs. In addition, 9 bus cycles are required for the hardware interrupt response. Hence, a total of 13,600 μs of processor time is used to transfer the block, versus 1 million μs for direct control.

For the DMA control technique, two bus cycles are required to transfer each character. Since the processor is idle during these bus cycles, it is appropriate to say that 2 μs of processor time is used for each character transferred. The processor time used in transferring the block is then about 400 μs.

Another dimension for comparison is *response time*. That is, after POC sets SR_7, how much time elapses before the next character is written to BR? Response time is not important for a printer, but it may be important for some devices. For example, data may be arriving at an input port at a fixed rate; each byte must be taken before the next byte arrives or it is lost. Secondary memory interfaces are frequently of this sort. It is left as an exercise to compute the response times for the printer example.

1.1.6 Exercises

1. Represent each of the following integers by an 8-bit word using B2 code: 6, 23, 75, 168, 223.

2. For each of the following, specify the final contents of any processor or memory registers that change during one processor cycle (i.e., fetch and execute one instruction). In each case, assume that the contents of processor and memory registers before the cycle begins are: $A = 12$, $B = 34$, $CC = $ FF, $IX = 5678$, $SP = 2468$, $PC = 4567$, and $M[\alpha] = $ last two digits of the hex address reversed (e.g., $M[1234] = 43$), except for $M3[4567]$, which are specified for each case, as follows:

(a) 86 C2 41 (i.e., $M[4567] = 86$, $M[4568] = $ C2, and $M[4569] = 41$)
(b) 6A 05 27
(c) 76 52 16
(d) 97 A6 B8
(e) 25 04 C6
(f) BD 65 43

3. Specify the machine code for the program of Example 2.

4. Specify the sequence of bus operations that will occur when the processor fetches and executes the program of Example 2 (like Table 1.8).

5. Do an instruction step simulation of Example 2 (like Table 1.9).

6. Write programs to do each of the following:

(a) Move a block of length 50 from address 3000 to address 4000.

(b) Move one line of text from address 3000 to address 4000 (one line = all characters up to first $\textcircled{CR}$).

(c) Compare two strings of length 20 starting at 3000 and 4000 (branch to MATCH if strings match).

7. Write subroutines to do each of the tasks in Problem 6. Addresses and lengths should be variable, however, to be specified when calling the subroutine.

8. Compute the response time of the processor to a printer request for each of the three ways of controlling a block transfer. (That is, how much time elapses after POC sets SR_7 before the next character is written to BR?)

9. Modify the block transfer subroutines for direct control and interrupt control to allow block lengths up to 64K (like the DMAC).

10. How much processor time is used per character transferred for the programs of Exercise 9? What is the response time for each?

1.2 COMPUTER DESIGN [6-19]

1.2.1 Models
1.2.2 Modular Design Procedures
1.2.3 The Levels of Computer Design
1.2.4 Exercises

Computers are complex systems. A typical computer contains hundreds of thousands of transistors and other electronic components. The complexity arises primarily from the enormous amount of detail associated with the interconnection of these components. In order to manage this complexity, it is necessary for the computer designer to use systematic modular design techniques. Systems that are designed by these techniques have a characteristic multilevel structure. An appreciation of this multilevel structure is essential for a proper understanding of computers and other complex systems.

In this section we will discuss the multilevel nature of complex systems, using computers as the primary example. The evolution of systematic procedures for designing such systems is discussed, and the role of abstract models in the design process is emphasized.

1.2.1 Models [9-13]

A *model* of a system is an abstract representation of the complete reality of the system. Any system, whether natural or manufactured, is infinitely complex. No model can represent all of the details of structure and operation, nor is it desirable to do so. The very purpose of the model is to provide a representation that is as simple as possible, consistent with the needs of the user of the model. Only those aspects of structure and operation that are of interest to the user are represented in the model. All other details are suppressed.

It follows that a system may be represented by different models, depending upon the needs of the user. To an electrical engineer, for example, a television is a cathode-ray tube (CRT) and associated electronic circuitry, represented by a collection of diagrams and equations of considerable complexity. To someone repairing the television, the schematic diagrams alone provide a sufficient model. To the average owner/operator, the television is represented by the controls for tuning and adjusting the set, as described in the owner's manual. To an interior decorator, the same television is simply a cabinet of particular dimensions and color, to be hidden among other pieces of furniture.

The models that are used in engineering and science are usually mathematical in nature. A model is constructed by identifying the important system variables and representing the relationships between variables, and the evolution of variables in time, by mathematical functions, relations, and equations of various sorts.

In addition to formal mathematical constructions, a model frequently involves a collection of notations that are used in constructing graphs and diagrams that provide visual representations of the structure and operation of the system. Also included in a model are the symbolic names and the terminology used to identify and describe important concepts.

Models play a central role in almost all areas of engineering and science. Not only do they provide a precise and unambiguous language for communication and documentation, but they facilitate conceptualization as well. In fact, in areas such as atomic physics and electromagnetics, where the human senses are so inadequate for observation, models provide essentially the only vehicle for communication and conceptualization.

Some of the difficulty in understanding computers is a result of the unobservability of system structure and operation, as in atomic physics. A source of even greater difficulty, however, is the management of the enormous amount of detail associated with a computer system. A computer of moderate size may contain hundreds of thousands of electronic devices, and be controlled by programs consisting of a similar number of individual "machine instructions." Understanding the interconnection and interaction of all of these components is the major obstacle to a deep and complete understanding of the computer.

Models play a crucial role in overcoming this obstacle. By employing a hierarchy of models, with each higher level suppressing much of the detail of lower levels, this "complexity of many components" can be managed. Techniques for doing so are discussed in Section 1.2.2, "Modular Design Procedures."

Time

Perhaps the most fundamental characteristic of real physical systems is that they exist in time and some of their most interesting behavior consists of events that occur sequentially in time. Since time plays such an important role in the behavior of a system, it must have some representation in the model of the system. Usually time is represented as a variable over a linearly ordered set (e.g., the real numbers or the integers). Furthermore, the time variable is thought of as *independent*, meaning that it is not a function of any other variable, but rather that it changes (evolves) independently, taking on successive values in the time set. In addition to time there may be other variables associated with a system (e.g., voltages, currents, forces, temperatures, spatial positions, velocities). Each of these is represented in the model by an abstract variable and an associated set of values over which the variable may range. These are all *dependent* variables of time; if v is such a variable, then at any time t, v has a particular value $v(t)$. Such variables are said to *vary with time* and are called *time variables*.

These variables may also be variables in another sense: at any particular time their value is unknown or, for some reason, unspecified. For example, the value of a voltage v at time 0 [i.e., $v(0)$] may be a variable. In this second sense, some of these variables may be *inputs* (which are independent variables) and others may be *outputs* (which are dependent variables). An *input variable* for a system is a variable whose value is in no way determined by the system itself; it is independent of the system. An *output variable* is one whose value is in some way determined by the system; usually it is some function of the input variables, and possibly of some internal variables.

Notice that the concepts of "dependent variable" and "function" are closely related. The existence of a dependent variable implies the existence of a function that specifies the value of the dependent variable, given the values of all variables upon which it depends. Hence we use the standard functional notation $v(t)$ to refer to the value of v at time t. Similarly, system output variables are related to system input variables via functions of some sort, since the outputs "depend upon" the inputs in some way.

There are two basic types of deterministic systems: *static* and *dynamic*. Both types of system exist in time. A static system, however, is one for which time may be ignored in modeling the system. Specifically, a static system can be modeled by a set of input variables $\{x_1, x_2, \ldots, x_n\}$, a set of output variables $\{y_1, y_2, \ldots, y_m\}$, and a function f such that for any time t,

$$(y_1(t), \ldots, y_m(t)) = f(x_1(t), \ldots, x_n(t)); \tag{1.11}$$

that is, the outputs of a static system at any time are a function only of the inputs to the system at that time. A static digital system is called a *combinational network*.

In general, the outputs of a system at any time are a function not only of the inputs at that time but also of the inputs at previous times. Such systems are called *dynamic* systems; they are said to possess *memory* since they remember something about past input values. The crucial question for such systems is: How much information about past inputs is actually remembered by the system? This leads to the concept of state. The *state* of a dynamic system is that information about the system which summarizes all the relevant history of the system; it is exactly what the system remembers. Knowledge of the state of a system at a particular time, together with the input values at the present and all future times, is sufficient to determine the output values for the present and all future times.

Consider now the case of a *discrete time* system: the time set is the set of integers. If s is the state of the system, x is the input, and y is the output, then there exist two functions f and g called the *next state* and *output* functions, respectively, such that

$$s(t + 1) = f(s(t), x(t)) \qquad (1.12)$$

and

$$y(t) = g(s(t), x(t)) \qquad (1.13)$$

It is common to speak about "properties of systems" rather than "properties of models," even when the second would be more appropriate. For example, we have been discussing "discrete time systems" as opposed to "continuous time systems." In fact, all systems exist in continuous time. The discrete/continuous dichotomy is one that exists only for models. Discrete time models are frequently simpler; they are used in preference to their continuous time counterparts whenever the simpler model provides an adequate approximation to the real system for the purpose at hand. By extension, a system is called a discrete time system if it submits (for the purposes at hand) to description by a discrete time model. In similar fashion the static/dynamic dichotomy already discussed is actually a property of models. Finally, the deterministic/random dichotomy as encountered by engineers is more a property of models than of real systems. The engineer is not interested in the philosophical question of whether the inherent nature of a system is fundamentally deterministic or random. The choice of a deterministic versus a random model is based on utility for the purpose at hand.

1.2.2 Modular Design Procedures [8, 15–17]

Consider the general design problem. The designer has a specified goal (a system to be designed) and a set of components that may be used to construct the goal system. If the goal is similar in nature to the components, then the designer may be able to approach the problem directly. For example, the design of an amplifier from transistors and other electronic components is such a problem. A transistor itself is a primitive amplifier. It is only necessary to find ways to enhance this natural behavior in order to solve the design problem.

On the other hand, if the goal system is very different in nature from the components to be used, then the design problem is more difficult. For example, consider the problem of using electronic components to construct a machine that can solve equations or sort a list of numbers. The disparity between the goal system and the components is so great that a direct design approach is not easily devised.

Bottom-Up and Top-Down Design

There are two general methods for attacking a design problem where the components and the goal system are very different: *bottom-up design* and *top-down design*.

The top-down approach begins by decomposing the goal system into simpler subsystems. If these subsystems are still not simple enough to be constructed directly from the available components, then they are further decomposed into yet simpler subsystems. The process continues in this fashion until the subsystems can be designed directly from the components available.

Bottom-up design is the reverse process. The designer begins with the available primitive components and constructs another set of components that are more suitable for the design task. A new component, for example, may exhibit some behavior that is desired in the goal system. If these new components are not sufficient to allow direct design of the goal system, then yet another level of components may be constructed, and so forth.

Multilevel Structure

The bottom-up and top-down design techniques may be used either separately or together. They both result in the same sort of multilevel system structure.

A level is defined primarily by the components that are used to design systems at that level. In general, the systems that are designed at any level are components at the next higher level.

A level is also characterized by the type of models that are used to describe the components, the interconnection of components, and the resulting systems. In general, models at lower levels are more detailed than models at higher levels. That is, when a system at a lower level (i.e., an interconnection of components) is used as a component at a higher level, the model at the higher level suppresses many of the details of the lower level. Only those details are preserved that are relevant to system design problems at the higher level. Typically, the details of the internal construction of a component are suppressed, and the representation of variables is simplified.

It is this controlled suppression of detail that makes the modular/multilevel approach so effective in the design of complex systems. It provides a systematic way to manage the details associated with an arbitrarily large number of interconnections.

1.2.3 The Levels of Computer Design

After many systems of the same type have been designed, the multilevel structure associated with that type of system may become standardized. The potential benefits of standardization provide continuous pressure in this direction. For example, the existence of standard components makes available the advantages of mass production; the adoption of standard models facilitates communication and reduces the costs of education.

There is a more or less standard multilevel structure of this sort associated with computers. This structure is illustrated in Table 1.10. Some of the levels are less distinct or less mature than others, and the entire structure is subject to change as the field evolves, but this is a reasonable description of the multilevel structure of computers at the present time.

Table 1.10. The levels of computer design

Level	Components	Models
Software	Machine instructions	Computer architecture; flowcharts; data structures; algorithms; all types of variables
PMS (processor-memory-switch)	Processors; memories; IO devices; IO controllers; interconnection networks	Concurrent processes; graph theory; queueing theory; petri nets; integer variables
Register transfer	Registers; combinational networks; RAM; sequential networks	Binary word variables; RT operations; sequential machines; timing diagrams
Logic design	Gates; flip-flops; switches	Binary variables; switching functions; Boolean algebra
Electronics	Transistors; resistors; capacitors; voltage sources	Real variables of time; v-i curves; algebraic and ordinary differential equations
Physics	Semiconductors; conductors; insulators	Real variables of time and space; partial differential equations

Physics [23, 28, 56]

The physics level deals directly with the raw materials and basic phenomena of nature. The models at this level provide the most detailed and accurate representation of the actual "computer hardware."

The processor, main memory, and IO controllers of a computer are constructed from electronic devices: diodes, transistors, resistors, capacitors, inductors, and wires. These devices are constructed from the basic electrical materials: conductors, semiconductors, and insulators. These materials are the primitive components at the physics level. The electronic devices are the "systems" designed at the physics level.

In the early days of computers, each electronic component was produced as a separate device (i.e., "discrete components"). Today it is possible to put hundreds of thousands of electronic components (primarily transistors) on a single *integrated circuit chip*. Such a chip is a wafer of silicon, usually less than 1 centimeter square. It is mounted in the familiar integrated circuit (IC) package, as illustrated in Figure 1.16.

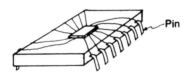

Figure 1.16   Integrated circuit packages

The physics level is concerned with the fabrication of IC chips. This involves producing the silicon wafer and then, in a series of processing steps, depositing on or diffusing into the surface of the wafer various materials. The result is several layers of conductors, semiconductors and insulators in intricate patterns on the surface of the wafer.

The models at the physics level must represent the fundamental electrical and mechanical properties of materials. These models are drawn from quantum mechanics, electromagnetic field theory, thermodynamics, atomic physics, and so on. The important variables (e.g., electric fields; positions, velocities, and accelerations of particles) vary with both space and time. These variables are typically related by partial differential equations, which tend to be complex and difficult to solve (e.g., Maxwell's equations, Schrödinger's wave equation, equations describing diffusion processes).

Simplified models that are derived from these equations are frequently used to provide a more intuitive conceptual representation of these complex phenomena. These models involve "mechanical" representations of charged particles moving among stationary atoms and molecules, under the influence of electrical and mechanical forces.

The physics level is discussed further in Sections 1.3 and 2.3. Section 1.3 provides an introduction to the mechanics of the IC fabrication process, and Section 2.3 discusses the implementation and operation of IC transistors. Considerations at the physics level also arise necessarily in the discussions of radiated noise and transmission line effects in Chapter 7, because these are both forms of electromagnetic radiation.

Electronics [19]

The principal components at the electronics level are diodes, transistors, resistors, capacitors, inductors, and voltage sources. Devices that are designed at this level include logic gates, flip-flops, one-shots, oscillators, and power supplies.

Models at this level are simpler than those at the physics level. The major simplification is the suppression of the details associated with parameter variation in space, leaving only time as an independent variable. Ordinary differential equations replace the partial differential equations of the physics level. For example, the voltage v and current i at the terminals of a capacitor are related by the equation $i = C \, dv/dt$. Similarly, an inductor is modeled by the equation $v = L \, di/dt$. The resulting electric circuit models are referred to as "lumped parameter" models, as distinguished from the "distributed parameter" models of the physics level.

Frequently, even time variation is suppressed at the electronics level, resulting in "static" models. For example, a resistor is modeled by an algebraic equation $v = iR$, and diodes and transistors are modeled by v-i curves.

Digital system design at the electronics level is discussed in Chapter 2.

Logic Design [30]

The basic components at the logic design level are logic gates and flip-flops. Transistors may also be used directly as components at this level, in which case they are used simply as switches.

Logic design level models are even simpler than electronic level models. Component inputs and outputs are voltages. At the electronics level these voltages are represented by real (i.e., continuous) variables, but at the logic design level they are represented as binary variables. The details of the transition from real to binary variables are described in Section 5.1.

There are two basic types of systems designed at this level: combinational networks and sequential networks. Combinational network design is presented in Chapter 3 and sequential network design in Section 5.5.

Register Transfer [46–49]

At the register transfer level the concept of information representation and manipulation first emerges. The variables involved in register transfer level models are binary word variables. Components are modeled essentially by the register transfer operations that they can perform. At this level it becomes possible to directly design devices that can store and process information (e.g., processors, memories, IO controllers).

The principal components for design at this level are registers, random access memories, combinational networks, and sequential networks. Registers are used to provide fast access storage for small numbers of words. Random access memory provides somewhat less accessible storage for larger numbers of words. Combinational networks implement primitive word operations. Sequential networks serve as control units that decide when register transfer operations should be performed, and generate the control signals required to evoke them. These components are described in Chapter 5. Systematic techniques for designing register transfer level systems are presented in Chapter 6.

Processor-Memory-Switch [14, 16, 17]

The major components at the processor-memory-switch (PMS) level are processors, memories, IO controllers, and IO devices. The first three of these are supplied by the RT level. Some IO devices may also be supplied by the RT level, for example, a light-emitting diode (LED) display or a magnetic bubble memory. Most IO devices, however, involve nonelectrical components, and hence are not designed entirely at the RT level. The design of such devices is not discussed in this book. Systems designed at the PMS level include general-purpose computers and special-purpose computers of all sorts (e.g., computers used to control machines, or to provide intelligence in instruments and toys).

Interconnections between PMS level components are established by data paths and switches. The use of switches to allow different devices to communicate over the same data paths is of central importance at this level.

The simplest computers are constructed around a single bus, as illustrated in Figure 1.3. The power of a single-bus computer can be increased by adding more memory, more IO devices, and so on. Eventually, however, performance is limited by the bus itself. Only one pair of devices at a time can communicate over the bus; other devices wishing to use the bus must queue up and wait their turn. The bus becomes a bottleneck that prevents concurrent operation of the many devices in the system. Recall in Section 1.1 that the processor was required to wait while the DMAC had control of the system bus. Hence, although the advantage of increased storage capacity is gained by adding more primary memory or secondary memory, the full potential benefit of concurrent operation is not achievable with the single-bus structure.

In addition to multiple memory modules and multiple IO devices, the PMS designer may use multiple processors. An example of the PMS structure of a multiprocessor system is shown in Figure 1.17. There are two types of processors in this system: general-purpose computational processors, P, and input-output processors, P_{io}. The programs to control both of these are in the memory modules in the center.

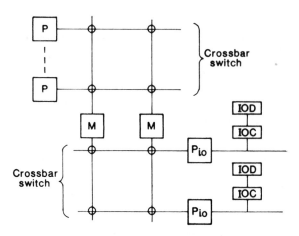

Figure 1.17   A multiprocessor system

An input-output processor is a natural extension of a DMA controller. In addition to being able to transfer a block of words from M to an IOD, an IO processor can perform various formatting and error detection/correction operations. A program that describes the block(s) to be transferred and the nature of the transfer is stored in a memory module by a computational processor. The IO processor fetches and executes the program. Note that the computational processor need not communicate directly with the IO processor, as it did with the DMAC. Communication is indirect, through M. This simplifies the interconnection structure.

The system of Figure 1.17 is constructed around two "crossbar switches." Each open circle identifies a switch that may be used to connect a processor and a memory module. Each memory module has two ports. This implies that within each module there is a switch that can connect either the north port or the south port to the internal memory. If the internal memory itself is composed of two or more modules, then both connections may be established concurrently, provided there is no conflict (i.e., both ports do not require access to the same internal module).

The interconnection structure of Figure 1.17 is by no means the only possible multiprocessor structure. If the number of the processors and memories is large, it is, in fact, a prohibitively expensive structure. The cost of the crossbar switch grows as the square of the number of processors and memories. Also, this structure does not allow direct communication between processors, which may be desirable in some cases.

A much simpler multiprocessor system is shown in Figure 1.18. This sort of interconnection is usually referred to as a *network*. Each processor has its own private memory and IO devices. Hence the system consists of a number of essentially independent computers that can share certain IO devices. For example, the shared devices might be a high-speed line printer and a large high-speed disk memory. Random access memory could also be shared, as shown.

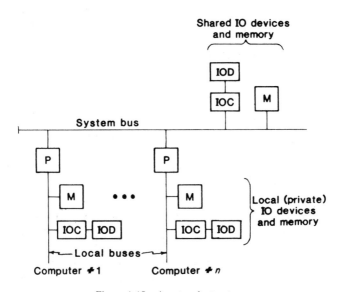

Figure 1.18 A network structure

The network offers the economic advantage of allowing expensive resources to be shared, and the operational advantage of allowing communication between computers via shared memory. Thus, for example, several computers could work simultaneously on the same data base stored in a shared disk; they could leave messages for each other in a shared RAM.

Many other multiprocessor system structures are possible. The major complexities that arise in designing such systems involve providing data paths and switches to interconnect the components, and developing mechanisms for coordinating the operation of multiple processors. Multiprocessor system design is perhaps the most promising and challenging area of research and development in computer design today.

Software [15]

As discussed in Section 1.1, the operation of a computer is controlled by a program. The lower levels of Table 1.10 are concerned with the design of computer hardware (i.e., the physical devices that comprise the computer). The software level is concerned with the design of programs to control the computer hardware.

The primitive components at the software level are the machine instructions of the computer's processor(s). The model of the computer hardware that is required by the software designer is called the *architecture* of the computer. It includes primarily a description of the instruction set(s), a description of the automatic operation of each PMS level device (e.g., Figure 1.9 for a processor), and a description of how each device may be controlled by the available instructions.

A complex program may be constructed from hundreds of thousands of machine instructions, just as the hardware of a complex computer may be constructed from hundreds of thousands of transistors. The modular design principles that apply to computer hardware design apply to software design as well. The rigorous application of modular techniques in software design is called *structured programming*.

The top-down design of a large program might begin with a high-level flowchart. Each block of this flowchart might then be represented by a more detailed flowchart, and so on. Eventually a level is reached where each flowchart block may be implemented directly by a small program.

Bottom-up design of a large program would begin by writing a set of small programs that perform operations that are expected to be useful. Each of these "modules" is then represented by a simple model, which suppresses the details of internal operation and retains only the information that is required to use the module (e.g., data provided to the program, and results returned by the program). Higher level modules may then be constructed using these modules as components, and so on.

In Table 1.10, software design is represented as a single level. This may be the case for a very simple special-purpose computer. However, as discussed above, software design for a complex application necessarily involves multiple levels. Only the lowest level of software design is encountered in this book.

Programs at this level directly control the computer hardware and do simple processing tasks.

Progressively higher levels of software design are further and further removed from the hardware. More and more details of the hardware are necessarily suppressed, and the computer appears more and more like a machine that can directly perform the operations that are required in the application environment.

A general-purpose computer is normally equipped with a collection of programs called the *system software*. The purpose of the system software is to facilitate the development of programs for a variety of applications, perhaps by many different users. These "application programs" are usually written in a high-level language (e.g., Pascal or COBOL). The system software includes *compilers* that can translate such programs into machine language. The system software also includes an *operating system*, which handles input and output operations for the users, manages system resources (perhaps sharing these among many simultaneous users), provides file-handling services, and makes available a library of "canned" programs for various computations and processing services.

The idea of information representation, which was introduced at the register transfer level, is developed at the software level into a major discipline of computer science called *data structures*. At the register transfer level, information is represented by binary words. The information that is represented is relatively simple: numbers, characters, and machine instructions. At the software level more complex data structures emerge: arrays, lists, trees, graphs, records, files, functions, sets, and so on. The atoms of these complex structures are simple entities (e.g., numbers, characters) that are represented by binary words, as at the register transfer level. The emphasis at the software level, however, is on the relationships between atoms.

As the complexity and amount of information to be represented grow, yet a higher level of information representation emerges called *data base management*. Data base management deals with very large files. The problems involve representing information and storing it in secondary memory devices in such a fashion that convenient and efficient access is possible.

The concept of an "algorithm," like the idea of "information representation," emerges at the register transfer level and is developed into a major discipline at the software level. An *algorithm* is procedure for performing a complex task by the sequential and/or parallel execution of simple operations. At the register transfer level simple algorithms appear, for example multiplication by a sequence of shifts and adds, or conversion from a base 2 to a base 10 code by a sequence of divisions. At the software level, very complex algorithms are developed for a variety of computations, for example, searching a large file for a particular sort of information, sorting a long list of numbers, minimizing a function, etc.

Summary

In Table 1.10, six distinct levels of computer design are described. Although there may be some disagreement about the boundaries between levels, or perhaps the distinctness of some level in a particular computer, this multilevel structure accurately represents computer design as it is practiced today. Each level in this hierarchy represents essentially a separate engineering discipline.

For systems involving large programs, the software level should itself have a significant multilevel structure. It is not possible, however, to identify a typical structure that would apply to all, or even to most, large programs. This may be due in part to less clearly perceived advantages of standardization at the software level. It is mostly due, however, to a greater inherent flexibility and variability of software relative to hardware. Most of the variation in applications is accommodated by software rather than hardware. In fact, this is the very basis for the idea of a general-purpose computer.

The difference in flexibility between the hardware and software levels is decreasing, however. Hardware costs are falling while software costs are rising. This may lead to more standardization at the software level and less standardization at the hardware level. The design of custom hardware for particular applications may become much more common than it is today. It is unlikely, however, that general-purpose computers will become significantly less important, or that hardware will ever be as flexible as software.

1.2.4 Exercises

1. Explain why computers have a multilevel structure.

2. Name the major levels of computer structure, and list the principal components that are used to design systems at each level.

3. Illustrate the controlled suppression of detail that occurs in moving upward in the multilevel structure by describing the nature of the models that are used at each level.

1.3 COMPUTER PACKAGING AND PRODUCTION [16-20]

1.3.1 Microcircuits
1.3.2 Macrocircuits
1.3.3 Independence of Design Levels
1.3.4 The Future

Three of the four major subsystems of a computer (P, M, and IOC) are constructed entirely from electronic components, primarily transistors, resistors, diodes, and capacitors. IO devices also contain electronic components, in addition to other sorts of physical and mechanical parts. In this section we consider the production and packaging of electronic components.

Nearly all of the individual electronic components in computers today are microscopic in size. Many such components can be connected together into a complex *microcircuit* and packaged as a single intergrated circuit chip. It is possible today to put the three major subsystems (P, M, and IOC) of a small computer on a single chip. Most computers, however, are constructed by interconnecting many IC chips into a complex *macrocircuit*.

A computer designer today should understand the fundamentals of both microcircuit and macrocircuit design. Both are considered in this text. In this section, the mechanical aspects of microcircuit and macrocircuit packaging and production are discussed.

1.3.1 Microcircuits

In the early days of the computer industry, each electronic component (i.e., each resistor, transistor, capacitor, etc.) was contained in a separate package. Today these are referred to as *discrete components*. The cost of manufacturing a computer was high primarily because all connections between electronic components were made by mechanical processes, either manual or automatic. The enormous numbers of mechanical connections resulted not only in high manufacturing costs, but also in high maintenance costs, since these connections were subject to high failure rates.

In the early 1960s a manufacturing process was developed that allowed several electronic components to be fabricated and interconnected on the surface of a single small chip of silicon. The process allowed many such chips to be produced simultaneously at low cost, and the interconnections on the chip proved to be very reliable. This device was called an *integrated circuit*.

During the past 20 years, enormous resources have been devoted to research and development in IC fabrication technology. Never has a production technology been developed and improved at such a rate. The history of this development can be traced by noting the increase in the number of electronic components that could be implemented on a single chip [19].

1960—Small-scale integration (SSI), several tens of components per chip

1965—Medium-scale integration (MSI), several hundred components per chip

1970—Large-scale integration (LSI), several thousand components per chip

1975—Very large-scale integration (VLSI), several tens of thousands of components per chip

1983—Grand-scale integration, several hundred thousand components per chip

Development of IC fabrication technology, more than any other single factor, is responsible for the computing revolution that is upon us. The cost and size of computing machines have decreased to the point where it has become physically and economically feasible to include information processing capability in virtually every machine, instrument, or system that can use it. Applications are limited only by the imagination and understanding of designers.

There are two types of transistors commonly used in integrated circuits today: *bipolar* transistors and *metal oxide semiconductor field effect transistors* (MOSFETs, or simply MOS transistors). There are several integrated circuit "logic families" that employ each of these transistor types. The bipolar families include: resistor–transistor logic (RTL), diode–transistor logic (DTL), transistor–transistor logic (TTL), emitter–coupled logic (ECL), and integrated injection logic (I^2L). The MOS families include: n-channel MOS (nMOS), p-channel MOS, and complementary MOS (CMOS). Each of these logic families is distinguished by the basic structure of the "logic gates" in the family (see Chapter 2).

The IC fabrication process for each logic family is different. In fact, there may be substantial differences in the fabrication processes used by different manufacturers of ICs in the same family.

In this text we will not study all of the logic families. In fact, we will study only two families: TTL and nMOS. In Chapter 2 the construction and operation of the basic transistor and gates for each of these families are discussed, and a simple nMOS IC fabrication process is presented.

In this section, we will discuss the basic mechanics of IC fabrication processes that apply to all logic families. The mechanics of IC fabrication are conceptually simple, even though the implementation of these mechanics with the precision that has been achieved today is extremely sophisticated. Our objective in this discussion is to provide a sufficient background in the fundamental aspects of IC fabrication to allow a proper appreciation of the role that this technology plays in computer design.

IC Fabrication [19, 26–28]

An IC chip is a thin rectangular slice of silicon with electronic components implemented and interconnected on its surface. The basic materials for constructing the electronic components are n-type and p-type semiconductors. Silicon itself is an "intrinsic semiconductor." An *npn* bipolar transistor can be created on the surface of a silicon chip by converting three adjacent areas on the chip surface to n-type, p-type, and n-type semiconductors, respectively. (The nature of n- and p-type semiconductors and the operation of transistors will be discussed in Chapter 2.) The transistor can be made very small by making the n- and p-type regions small. Diodes, resistors, and MOS transistors can be created in similar fashion.

Components can be interconnected by depositing narrow paths of metal on the surface of the chip. The metal paths must be separated from the components over which they pass by a layer of insulation. Connections to selected components are made through "contact cuts" in the insulation. Connections may also be made by n-type or p-type paths in the chip surface, although these paths have higher resistance. A capacitor can be created by sandwiching insulation between semiconductor or metal plates. "Stray" (i.e., unintentional) capacitance is introduced unavoidably in this fashion.

The n- and p-type regions in the chip surface are created by injecting impurity atoms into the silicon (e.g., boron atoms for p-type, phosphorus atoms for n-type), a process known as *doping*. Doping may be accomplished either by *diffusion* or by *ion implantation*. Diffusion involves exposing the silicon surface to a gas containing the impurity atoms at a high temperature. The thickness of the doped region can be precisely controlled by the temperature and the time of exposure. Ion implantation involves bombarding the surface with high-energy impurity atoms.

In either case, the areas of the chip surface that are to be exposed for doping must be precisely controlled. For example, an area of a few square "microns" (a micron is 10^{-6} meter) may be separated from a nearby area by only a micron. This precise exposure control is accomplished by a process known as *photolithography*. The areas to be exposed are defined by a *mask*, that is, a glass plate upon which the desired pattern is printed (e.g., the mask is clear where exposure is desired and opaque elsewhere, or the reverse). The surface of the chip is coated with a "photoresist" material, and then exposed to ultraviolet light through the mask (a "contact printing" process). The chip is then immersed in a solution that will dissolve the photoresist that has been exposed, and leave the unexposed resist intact (or the reverse). The surface of the chip is then exposed to the diffusion process, which will affect the chip only where there is no resist. The remaining photoresist is then dissolved with another solution.

Masks are used in a similar fashion in "deposition processes," which deposit thin layers of material (e.g., insulation or metal) on the surface of the chip.

The exact sequence of diffusion and deposition steps that are involved in producing a chip varies from one fabrication process to another. The steps involved in an nMOS process are described in Section 2.3.

In addition to the diffusion and deposition steps, there are several other steps involved in a complete fabrication process. These are illustrated in Figure 1.19. The first step is to "grow" an ingot of silicon from a small "seed crystal." Ingots 3 or 4 inches in diameter and several feet long can be pro-

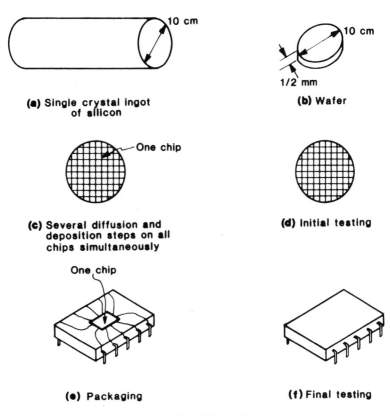

(a) Single crystal ingot of silicon

(b) Wafer

(c) Several diffusion and deposition steps on all chips simultaneously

(d) Initial testing

(e) Packaging

(f) Final testing

Figure 1.19   IC fabrication

duced. Impurity atoms can be added to the silicon as the ingot is produced if it is desired to have a doped "substrate" (the chip itself is called the *substrate*). An area on the surface of a doped substrate can be converted to a semiconductor of the opposite type by adding enough impurities of the opposite type.

The ingot is machined to the desired shape and then cut into wafers about 1 millimeter thick with a diamond saw (step b). The wafer surface is ground smooth and polished.

The electronic components are created and interconnected in the diffusion and deposition steps that follow (step c). Each wafer is large enough to be cut into many chips (typically 100 to 400). The masks that are used are the same size as the wafer and bear the same pattern repeated many times (once for each chip).

While still part of the wafer, the individual chips are subjected to initial tests (step d). Those found to be defective are marked.

In step e the wafer is cut into individual chips, and each chip is mounted in a plastic or ceramic carrier. The most common carrier is the "dual in-line package" (DIP) shown in Figure 1.20. The carrier is equipped with "pins" (i.e., terminals) that are large enough and sturdy enough for convenient macrocircuit interconnections. The carrier pins are connected within the package to large metal "bonding pads" on the chip, which were provided by a metal deposition step within step c.

Each package is then subjected to final testing (step f).

Chip size. The *yield* of the IC fabrication process is the number of good chips produced per wafer. The primary cause of faulty chips is defects on the surface of the wafer. Such defects may be created at any step of the process: chemical impurities in the original ingot, scratches on the surface produced while polishing the wafer or in handling the wafer at any point, faults in one of the layers on the surface due to particles of foreign material between the mask and the wafer.

A defect need not be large to ruin a chip. A scratch or particle of dust only a few microns long can break a signal path. Since a chip cannot be repaired, a single such defect can ruin a chip.

In spite of the most extraordinary precautions in the production process, defects are inevitably scattered over the surface of every wafer. For a given defect density, the number of good chips obtained from a wafer (i.e., the yield) is determined by the size of the chips. If the chips are very large then every chip is certain to include a defect. If the chips are small enough, most chips will avoid surface defects.

Chip cost. The cost of manufacturing a chip is proportional to the size of the chip, for a number of reasons.

As already noted, yield is inversely proportional to chip size. Furthermore, steps a, b, and c of the fabrication process (Figure 1.20) are independent of chip size, and hence the cost of these steps per chip is inversely proportional to yield, thus directly proportional to chip size.

The cost of bonding the chip into its package (step e) is also proportional to chip size, since larger chips normally have more pins.

Finally, testing costs (steps d and f) are proportional to chip size since larger chips contain more complex circuits, which tend to be more difficult to test thoroughly.

The manufacturing costs associated with the six steps of Figure 1.20, however, do not represent all of the cost of producing a chip. To these must be added the cost of making the masks and the costs of designing the chip circuit. These costs are also proportional to chip size, and in fact tend to grow more than linearly with chip size. Since the costs are distributed over all of the chips that are produced, the volume of production becomes a crucial factor.

Finally, the cost of the fabrication equipment must be distributed over all of the chips of all types that are produced over the life of the equipment.

Component size and density. The number of components that can be placed on a chip is determined not only by the size of the chip, but also by the size of the components and the distance between components. Component size is limited by the *resolution* of the fabrication process, that is, the precision with which desired patterns can be created on the chip surface. The masks that define the various patterns are not perfect, and the patterns that are actually replicated on the chip surface are even less perfect. A signal path that is intended to be of constant width actually varies in width. In order to prevent the path from shrinking to zero width at some point, a minimum path width with ample tolerance for error must be observed. For typical commercial fabrication process, this is about 1 to 2 microns (1984).

Resolution is also affected by *mask alignment error* and *distortion* of the silicon wafer to due to high-temperature processing. These errors tend to affect the distance between features on different levels.

Since it limits the distance between features, process resolution limits not only component size but also component density. A related factor that also affects component density is the amount of wiring required to interconnect components. Since wires (signal paths) have a minimum width and a minimum separation, the chip area occupied by wiring can be significant. The amount of wiring required can be dramatically affected by the placement of components on the chip, as we shall see. In fact, wiring considerations are crucial in microcircuit design not only at the electronics level, but at higher levels as well. Logic designers and register transfer level designers must consider chip layout directly, in order to minimize the amount of chip area that will be required for wiring.

The same comments apply to macrocircuit design. The fact is that wiring costs are important at every level of computer design and tend to become increasingly important at higher levels. At the PMS level, wiring costs (i.e., interconnection costs) are perhaps the single most important design consideration.

Minimum-size transistors are used wherever possible. The maximum current that can be supplied through a minimum transistor, however is limited. This current may not be sufficient for some purposes. In such cases, the size of the transistor must be increased. For example, transistors that generate signals to be sent off the chip are usually much larger than minimum-size transistors.

Also associated with off-chip signals, either inputs or outputs, are large metal bonding pads. These pads must be large (e.g., 100 μm^2) to allow mechanical connection to the IC package pins. The size of these pads and the fact that they are most conveniently located around the perimeter of the chip limit the number of pins that can conveniently be provided on an IC package. The largest packages commercially available at this time (1984) have 68 pins (Intel's 80186 and 80286 microprocessors).

1.3.2 Macrocircuits [18, 20]

Microcircuit design is the design of a system (circuit) to be implemented on a single IC chip. *Macrocircuit design* is the design of a system using ICs as components. The various levels of packaging for macrocircuit systems are illustrated in Figure 1.20.

PC cards

The first level of macrocircuit packaging is the printed circuit (PC) board/ card. A PC board is a sheet of tough insulating material (e.g., fiberglass) about 1/8 inch thick, ranging in size from a few to a few hundred square inches. The IC packages are mounted on the board by drilling holes into which the IC pins may be inserted and secured by solder. Alternatively, sockets may be mounted on the board, allowing easy insertion and removal of ICs.

The IC packages are interconnected by metal paths deposited on either the front or the back surface of the PC card, or both. These paths are deposited by a photolithographic process, similar to that used in IC fabrication but on a macroscopic scale. Solder is used to connect IC pins (or socket pins) to the metal paths electrically, as well as to establish a solid mechanical connection. Signal paths that must cross without touching are routed on different sides of the card. A signal may be transferred from one side of a card to the other via a "plated through" hole.

For very high speed ICs, connections between packages on a PC card must be treated as transmission lines (see Chapter 7). Multilayer cards are frequently used in such systems. Internal layers are used to distribute power. For example, a four-layer card might use the top and bottom surfaces for signal paths, one internal layer as a ground plane, and the other internal layer for +5 volts. Each internal layer is essentially a solid sheet of copper, with openings cut where connections must be made between the adjacent surface layer and the other internal layer or the other surface layer. Such connections are made via plated through holes in the surface layer. The use of internal layers in this fashion establishes a good transmission line environment; signal paths have uniform characteristics, and noise problems due to "cross talk" and electromagnetic interference are minimized (see Chapter 7).

Signals for off-card communication are routed to the edge of the card, where an *edge connector* may be attached. An edge connector has spring-

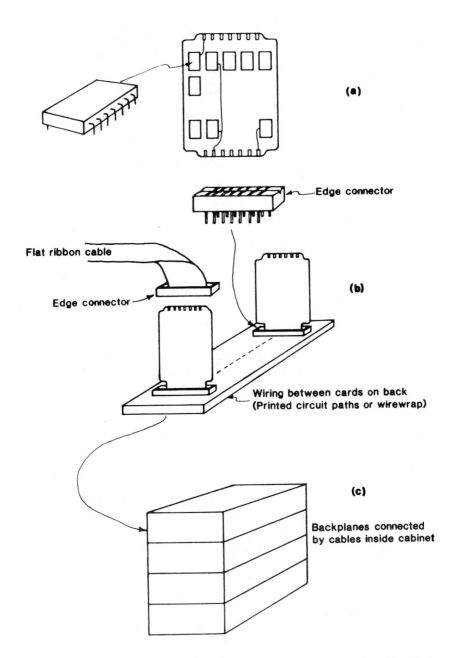

Figure 1.20   Macrocircuit packaging: (a) printed circuit card; (b) backplane; (c) cabinet

loaded contacts that press against the metal paths at the edge of a card that is pushed into the connector. On the other side of the connector are pins, which may be connected to wires of a cable or inserted into holes in another PC card (e.g., a backplane).

Wire-wrap cards are sometimes used as alternatives to PC cards. A wire-wrap card is similar in appearance to a PC card. ICs are plugged into sockets that are mounted on the card. Interconnections are made by open wiring between socket pins. There are wire-wrap machines that can be programmed to make these connections automatically. There are also various hand tools available for wire-wrapping. Wire-wrap cards are particularly suitable for one-of-a-kind systems and for *breadboarding* (i.e., building a portotype of system for testing).

Backplanes

If a system has too many ICs to be mounted on a single PC card, then multiple PC cards mounted on a backplane may be used. A *backplane* is a heavy PC card with several edge connectors mounted on the card in the same fashion that IC sockets are mounted on a PC or wire-wrap card. PC cards can be plugged into the edge connectors. Usually the backplane is the bottom of a box, and along the sides of the box are card guides that provide vertical support for the cards. PC cards are interconnected by printed paths on the bottom side of the backplane, or by open wiring between the pins of the backplane edge connectors.

Backplanes are frequently a foot or more in length. Signal paths are "terminated" to minimize transmission line reflections and noise, even in relatively low-speed systems. For high-speed systems the backplane should be provided with a good ground plane, for example, by making one side of the backplane a solid metal layer.

Communication between PC cards that are plugged into the backplane and devices that are not connected to the backplane is normally accomplished by cables connected to the top edges of the cards.

Cabinets

Systems that are too large for a single backplane may be packaged as several backplanes mounted in a cabinet or rack. Each drawer of the cabinet contains one backplane. Backplanes are interconnected by cables.

Systems too large for a single cabinet are packaged in multiple cabinets. Communication delays can be a crucial factor limiting the performance of systems packaged in multiple cabinets.

1.3.3   Independence of Design Levels

An important characteristic of the multilevel structure of Table 1.10 is that each level is, to a large extent, independent and self-contained. Information from lower levels that is relevant to design at any level is included in the models of components for that level. Upper-level considerations are included in the specifications for the systems to be designed.

Because of this independence of levels, it is not necessary for a designer to be familiar with all levels in order to participate in the design process. Similarly, the student need not study computer design from the bottom up. It is just as reasonable to begin at the top level and work down, or to begin in the middle and work toward the outer levels.

The independence of levels is illustrated nicely by the packaging history of the computer industry. In the early days, before integrated circuits, discrete electronic components were produced by certain companies, and entirely separate companies built computers from these components. The independence of the physics level from higher levels was very clear at that time.

Later, with the development of small-scale integrated circuits, the independence of the electronics level from levels above was exploited in the same fashion. The IC manufacturers produced logic design level components, and separate companies used these "off-the-shelf" components to build computers.

With the development of medium- and large-scale ICs, the independence of the register transfer level was similarly exploited. The introduction of very large scale integrated (VLSI) circuits is now illustrating the independence of the PMS level. Similarily, the independence of the programming level has long been evident from the existence of "software houses" that design only software.

The above discussion illustrates clearly that the various levels of computer design *can* be completely independent. However, complete independence of levels does not usually produce optimal designs. The types of components produced by IC manufacturers are not necessarily the most useful components for the designer at the next level. The computer hardware produced by the register transfer and PMS level designers is not necessarily the ideal hardware for the programmer. There are considerations that cut across levels, and better systems can be designed by establishing better communication between levels.

Progress in IC fabrication technology has made it possible to put sophisticated processors on a single IC chip. Soon it will be possible to put multiple processors and memories on one chip. It will be interesting to notice to what extent the potential independence of levels is exploited in this environment, and to what extent independence is abandoned in the interests of optimization.

1.3.4   The Future

Computer design is a broad and dynamic field. Students entering the field, and even professionals already working in the field, may well wonder where their time and energies should be directed in learning and staying abreast with the state of the art. What will the role of the computer designer be in the future? Where will the research activity be? To what extent will the design process be automated? Will design work be primarily at the software and PMS levels, or will the lower levels continue to be active? Will smaller scale ICs eventually disappear? Will the steady increase in microcircuit size eventually slow and then stop at a point of diminishing returns? Will a catalog of "standard" microcircuits eventually be generated that will be sufficient for all applications, and then evolve thereafter very slowly? (This would essentially eliminate microcircuit design as a significant job area.) Or will microcircuit size continue to increase, until all "local" systems are implemented as microcircuits? (This would limit the role of the macrocircuit designer essentially to communications, with most of the actual computer design being done by microcircuit designers.)

Any serious attempt to answer these questions reveals a wealth of complexity due to a variety of interrelated factors. We will not attempt a comprehensive analysis here, but will simply point out some of the important factors. Speculation about the future will be left to the reader.

Microcircuit size

At present, component size and density are limited primarily by the resolution of the IC fabrication process. Continued improvements can be expected from continued investment in research and development. Such improvements cannot continue indefinitely, however. There are physical limits to component size and density. For example, it is predicted theoretically that the minimum channel length for an MOS transistor is about $1/2$ micron.

Chip size is limited by defect density. Unlike component size, there is no fundamental limit to reduction of defect densities. Even if practical limits are encountered, it may be possible to develop techniques that will tolerate defects on chips (fault-tolerant design). Hence, chip size is potentially unlimited. Consequently, even though component size and density are limited, microcircuit size is potentially unlimited.

Economies of scale

For a given chip size and complexity, chip cost is determined by the number of chips produced. This is a result of overhead such as design cost, mask production, and equipment cost. It is possible to provide a low-cost chip only if many chips are produced; that is, the market for the chip must be large.

The economies of scale also apply to macrocircuit systems, but not so dramatically. The overhead for macrocircuit production rivals that for microcircuit production only for the very largest systems. For most systems the overhead is far less. In addition, the macrocircuit manufacturing cost per unit is higher; for large macrosystems it is much higher.

Programmability

Most of the ICs produced today are general-purpose ICs, that is, ICs that have broad applicability and are used by macrocircuit designers in a wide variety of systems. To ensure broad applicability, a large-scale IC must be *programmable*; that is, it must be possible to tailor the chip in some fashion to fit different situations. Memory chips, programmable logic arrays, and standard IO controller chips are all programmable (see Chapters 5 and 8). Microprocessor chips are not themselves programmable, but are used in conjunction with memory chips that hold programs which control their operation.

The necessity for broad applicability, of course, is dictated by the economies of scale. The same considerations apply to macrocircuit systems. This is the very idea of the general-purpose digital computer. It is possible to sell computers at low prices only because they are programmable and therefore have a large market.

An IC that is designed for a specific application is called a *custom* IC. In the past the use of custom ICs was limited to a few very high volume applications. Recently, however, some IC manufacturers have been offering custom IC services that make custom ICs feasible in volumes as small as a few thousand chips.

Various types of *gate arrays* are commonly used for custom IC applications. Gate arrays extend the concept of programmability to include the register transfer and logic design level structure of a chip. The layout of the components (gates and transistors) is essentially fixed, and the designer can "program" (i.e., specify) the interconnections.

Programmability may be extended even further in the future. Ultimately the "programmer" may specify the system to be implemented in a suitable high-level language, and a "compiler" will convert this specification into a microcircuit layout. It should not be expected, however, that such a process will make microcircuit design costs insignificant; the cost of standard software produced in this fashion is certainly not insignificant.

Summary

Because of the advantages of miniaturization (low manufacturing costs, reliability, low power consumption, small size), there will always be incentives to put larger circuits on a single chip. Hence microcircuit design is likely to remain important.

On the other hand, no matter how large a circuit can be put on a single chip, it will always be possible to build larger and more powerful systems by interconnecting chips. Hence, the continued importance of macrocircuit design is also assured.

Both microcircuit and macrocircuit design are covered in this book. The same fundamental design principles apply to both, and we will emphasize these principles. However, there are important considerations that are unique to each that will be dicussed as well. A good understanding of computer design requires familiarity with the fundamentals of both microcircuit design and macrocircuit design, and the interface between the two.

Chapter 2

DIGITAL ELECTRONICS

2.1 Electric Circuit Review
2.2 Digital Circuits
2.3 Integrated Circuits

In Section 2.1 the fundamentals of electric circuit analysis are reviewed. Only direct current (DC) analysis is considered, since this is sufficient for modeling digital circuits.

In Section 2.2 the principal digital system component, the transistor, is introduced. Electric circuit models of digital circuits are presented, and the construction of various types of logic gates is discussed.

In Section 2.3 the implementation of digital circuits by integrated circuit fabrication is discussed.

2.1 ELECTRIC CIRCUIT REVIEW [11, 21–24]

2.1.1 Resistor Circuits
2.1.2 Capacitance
2.1.3 Inductance
2.1.4 Power Supplies
2.1.5 Informal Circuit Analysis
2.1.6 Power and Energy
2.1.7 Exercises

The basic two-terminal devices that are used to construct and model electric circuits are shown in Figure 2.1. The fundamental techniques for analyzing circuits constructed from these components are reviewed in this section.

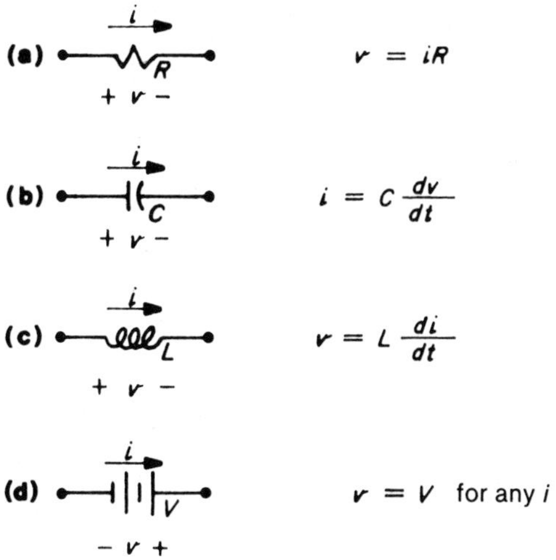

(a) $v = iR$

(b) $i = C \dfrac{dv}{dt}$

(c) $v = L \dfrac{di}{dt}$

(d) $v = V$ for any i

Figure 2.1   Two-terminal circuit elements: (a) resistor; (b) capacitor; (c) inductor; (d) constant-voltage source

2.1.1   Resistor Circuits

Consider the circuit of Figure 2.2. A complete set of equations for the circuit is written using Kirchhoff's voltage law (the sum of the voltage drops around a closed loop is zero), Kirchhoff's current law (the sum of the currents flowing into a node is zero), and the circuit element equations. This set of seven equations in seven unknowns can be solved to determine the unique value for each voltage and current in the circuit.

Since the circuit element equations are so simple, it is usually easy to eliminate these equations even before writing them by including them implicitly when writing Kirchhoff's equations. In this way, Kirchhoff's equations could have been written directly as follows:

$$V = iR_4 + i_1R_1 + i_1R_2 \qquad (2.1)$$
$$V = iR_4 + i_2R_3 \qquad (2.2)$$
$$i = i_1 + i_2 \qquad (2.3)$$

The problem is thus reduced immediately to solving a set of three equations in three unknowns.

It is frequently useful in analyzing circuits to be able to replace several components by a single equivalent component. For resistors, such simplifications are based upon the series and parallel equivalent circuits illustrated in Figure 2.3. The notation $R_1 \| R_2$ is sometimes used to represent the parallel combination resistance $R_1R_2/(R_1 + R_2)$, as shown.

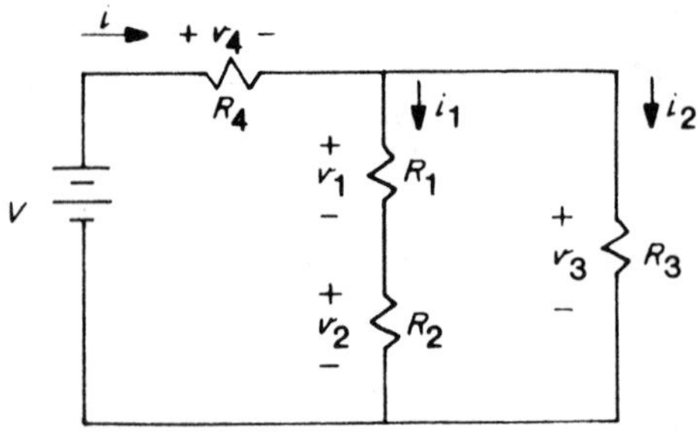

Kirchhoff's voltage equation around 2 loops:

$$V = v_4 + v_1 + v_2 \text{ (inner loop)}$$
$$V = v_4 + v_3 \text{ (outer loop)}$$

Kirchhoff's current equation at one node:

$$i = i_1 + i_2$$

Circuit element equations:

$$v_4 = iR_4$$
$$v_1 = i_1 R_1$$
$$v_2 = i_1 R_2$$
$$v_3 = i_2 R_3$$

Figure 2.2   A simple circuit

The current i in the circuit of Figure 2.2 càn quickly be determined by using parallel and series equivalents, as shown in Figure 2.4. This approach is usually easier than solving the equations directly.

A simple resistor circuit that is used frequently in digital systems is called a *voltage divider*, shown in Figure 2.5. The input voltage is divided between the resistors R_1 and R_2. The fraction of the total voltage dropped across R_2 is $R_2/(R_1 + R_2)$. If R_2 is very large relative to R_1, then $V_{out} \simeq V_{in}$; if R_2 is very small relative to R_1, then $V_{out} \simeq 0$.

2.1.2   Capacitance

Capacitance is an important characteristic of all digital circuits. Occassionally capacitors are intentionally included in a digital circuit, but more often capacitance is an unwanted but unavoidable component. Specifically, associated with any input terminal of a digital device (e.g., a logic gate), there is a capacitance. In order to change the voltage at the terminal, this capacitance must be charged or discharged. The larger the capacitance, the greater the amount of charge that must be moved for a given voltage change: $C = q/v$.

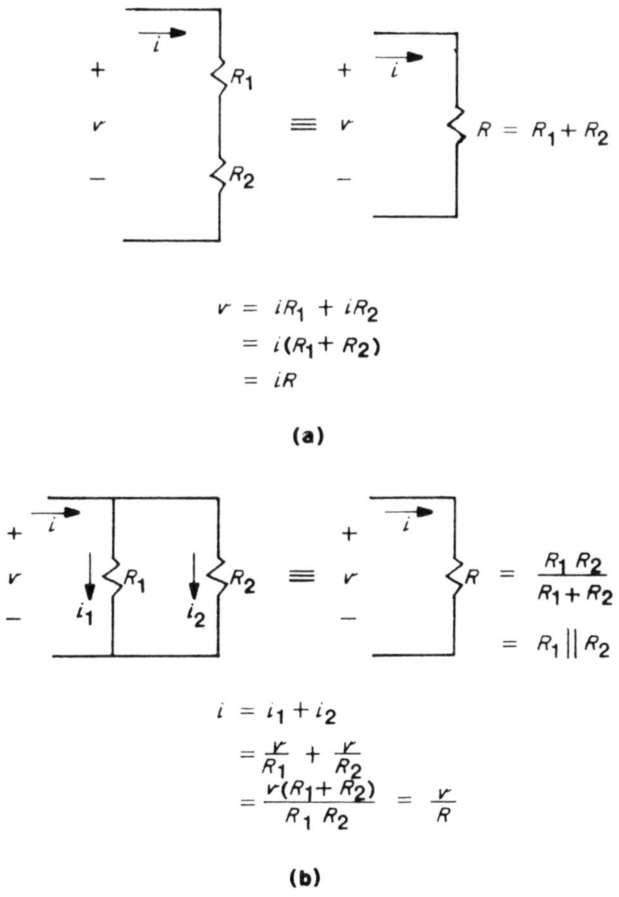

$$v = iR_1 + iR_2$$
$$= i(R_1 + R_2)$$
$$= iR$$

(a)

$$i = i_1 + i_2$$
$$= \frac{v}{R_1} + \frac{v}{R_2}$$
$$= \frac{v(R_1 + R_2)}{R_1 R_2} = \frac{v}{R}$$

(b)

Figure 2.3 Equivalent circuits: (a) series combination; (b) parallel combination

In an electric circuit model of a digital circuit, these unwanted "parasitic" or "stray" capacitances are represented by capacitors, just as intentional capacitors are. The speed of a digital circuit is determined by the size of these stray capacitances and by the size of the resistances through which they must charge and discharge.

Figure 2.6 is representative of the switching operations that occur in digital systems. The capacitor C represents the parasitic capacitance at an input terminal, and R is the resistance through which it must charge or discharge. The voltage v is the voltage that appears at the terminal. The two voltage sources represent the two voltage levels (low and high) that in turn represent the binary values 0 and 1. The switch is moved to the left or right to establish a 0 or

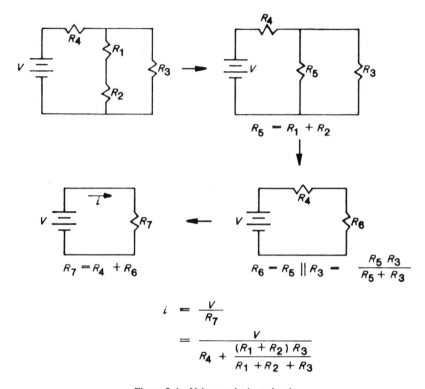

Figure 2.4   Using equivalent circuits

1 at the input. The switch is usually implemented using one or more transistors (see Section 2.2), but mechanical switches are also sometimes used.

The timing diagram shows the voltage $v(t)$ during a time interval in which the switch changes from left to right and then back to the left. It is assumed that the switch was in the left position for a long time before $t = T$.

The two equations for $v(t)$ in Figure 2.6 may be derived by writing the circuit equations with the switch in each position, and then solving the resulting differential equations. Rather than go through this process twice, however, we will analyze the circuit of Figure 2.7, which includes both Figure 2.6 situations.

In Figure 2.7, the switch closes at time $t = 0$. The capacitor voltage at that time is $v(0) = V_I$. (It is irrelevant how this voltage was established.) This corresponds to the left-to-right switch of Figure 2.6 if $V_I = V_L$ and $V_F = V_H$. It corresponds to the right-to-left switch if $V_I = V_H$ and $V_F = V_L$. In both cases the time scale is shifted so that the switch occurs at $t = 0$. This

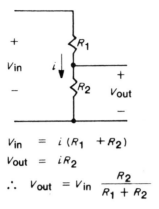

$$V_{in} = i(R_1 + R_2)$$
$$V_{out} = iR_2$$
$$\therefore V_{out} = V_{in} \frac{R_2}{R_1 + R_2}$$

Figure 2.5 Voltage divider

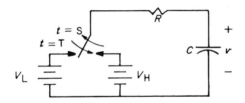

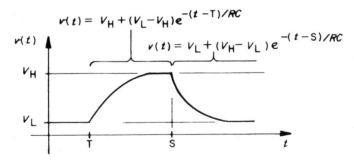

$$v(t) = V_H + (V_L - V_H)e^{-(t-T)/RC}$$
$$v(t) = V_L + (V_H - V_L)e^{-(t-S)/RC}$$

Figure 2.6 An RC circuit: typical digital operation

does not change the solution (except for the time shift), but it does simplify the equations.

The circuit equations for $t \geq 0$ in Figure 2.7 are

$$V_F = iR + v \qquad (2.4)$$
$$i = C(dv/dt) \qquad (2.5)$$

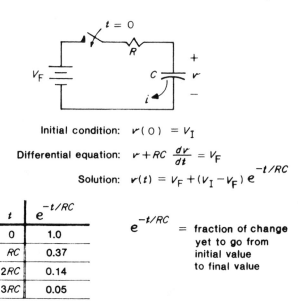

Figure 2.7   RC circuit analysis

These can be combined into the first order differential equation given in the figure. The solution for the specific initial condition $v(0) = V_I$ is also given in the figure [21]. The correctness of this solution may be verified by direct substitution. First, differentiate the solution to obtain dv/dt:

$$\frac{dv}{dt} = \frac{-(V_I - V_F)}{RC} e^{-t/RC} \tag{2.6}$$

Then substitute v and dv/dt into the original equation to verify that the equation is satisfied. To verify that the initial condition is satisfied, evaluate the solution for $t = 0$.

This solution deserves careful attention. Notice that whether $V_I < V_F$ or $V_I > V_F$, the solution begins at V_I (at time $t = 0$) and approaches V_F asymptotically as t increases. The total change in v is $v(\infty) - v(0) = V_F - V_I$. As t increases, the term $(V_I - V_F)e^{-t/RC}$ gets smaller so that $v(t)$ gets closer to its final value V_F.

The rate at which $v(t)$ approaches V_F is determined by RC, called the *time constant* for the circuit. The quantity $e^{-t/RC}$ may be interpreted as the fraction of the total change yet to go in moving from the initial value V_I to the final value V_F. The table given in Figure 2.7 specifies this fraction for several values of t.

If R is given in ohms and C in farads, then RC is in seconds:

$$RC = \text{ohms} * \text{farads}$$

$$= \frac{\text{volts}}{\text{amps}} * \frac{\text{coulombs}}{\text{volts}}$$

$$= \frac{\text{coulombs}}{\text{coulombs/second}}$$ (2.7)

$$= \text{seconds}$$

Unit Prefixes. The unit prefixes, pico-, nano-, micro-, milli-, kilo-, mega-and giga-, represent the factors 10^{-12}, 10^{-9}, 10^{-6}, 10^{-3}, 10^3, 10^6 and 10^9, respectively. With the abbreviation for a unit name, these prefixes are abbreviated: p, n, μ, m, K, M and G, respectively. For example, 5pF = 5 pico-farads = $5 * 10^{-12}$Farads. If R is in Kilohms and C is in picofarads, then RC is in nanoseconds.

2.1.3 Inductance

Associated with current in a wire, there is a magnetic field in the space around the wire. A changing magnetic field exerts a force on electric charges, just like an electric force (voltage). When the current in a wire changes, the magnetic field around the wire changes, creating a voltage that opposes the change in current. The size of this voltage is proportional to the rate of change of current, that is, $v = L \, di/dt$. L is called the (*self-*) *inductance* of the wire.

Just as every circuit has capacitance, so every circuit also has inductance. In digital circuits, however, inductance can almost always be ignored. We will not discuss it again until Chapter 7, where it arises in connection with transmission lines and noise.

2.1.4 Power Supplies

A voltage source that maintains a constant voltage between its output termi-nals is called a *DC voltage source* (DC stands for direct current). The circuit symbol for a DC voltage source is shown in Figure 2.1(d).

A voltage source that produces a sinusoidally varying voltage [$v(t) = V$ sin wt] is called an *AC voltage source* (AC is for alternating current). The voltage that is supplied by public electric power companies is AC. In the United States, AC power is supplied at 60 hertz (hertz is cycles per second). Analog communication circuits involve high-frequency AC voltage sources. These AC voltages are used as "carriers" to transmit information over com-munication channels of various sorts.

Digital systems always use DC voltage sources to supply power. Batteries are used as voltage sources in some systems (e.g., portable instruments, airborne systems). Most digital systems, however, use a device known as a *DC power supply*. A DC power supply, or power supply for short, is an electronic circuit that converts AC voltage to DC voltage. A power supply is rated by the amount of current that it can supply at a particular constant voltage (e.g., 4 amps at 5.0 volts).

A single integrated circuit chip may contain thousands of electronic circuits (e.g., gates), each of which requires a voltage source. For most digital chips, only one voltage level is required, the most common being 5.0 volts; a few chips require two or three voltage levels. For simplicity, we will confine this discussion to chips requiring only a 5.0-volt supply and systems constructed entirely from such chips.

Two pins are provided on each chip for connection to a DC power supply. One pin is referred to as "ground" and is assigned the voltage level 0 volts. The other pin is 5.0 volts. The symbol $\perp$ is used in circuit diagrams to identify the ground pin, or any point connected to the ground pin by a low-resistance wire. The other power supply pin is denoted V_{DD} for nMOS circuits or V_{CC} for bipolar circuits.

The double subscript is a standard convention for power supply terminals. The D in V_{DD} stands for drain; the drain terminal of each nMOS transistor is normally connected to V_{DD}, either directly or through some other circuitry. The C in V_{CC} stands for collector; the collector terminal of each bipolar transistor is usually connected to V_{CC}, either directly or through some other circuitry.

The "source" terminal of an nMOS transistor is usually connected to ground, either directly or via some other circuitry. And the "emitter" terminal of a bipolar transistor is usually connected to ground, directly or otherwise. The ground pin is thus sometimes referred to as V_{EE} for a bipolar chip or V_{SS} for an nMOS chip.

The 5.0 volts and ground are made available to all the circuits on a chip via a grid of wires on the metal level of the chip, as shown in Figure 2.8. Each small square represents an essentially independent electronic circuit (e.g., a gate) that must be connected to 5.0 volts and ground. Each of these circuits is designed and analyzed separately at the electronics level. No one attempts to write a single set of simultaneous equations such as those of Figure 2.2 for the entire chip. There are loading effects and noise effects that tend to couple the individual circuits to each other, but these can be handled separately (see Section 2.2.5 and Chapter 7).

The individual circuits communicate with each other via wires, shown dashed in Figure 2.8. The circuits are designed so that the current flowing in these signal wires is small, and hence the loading effects are small.

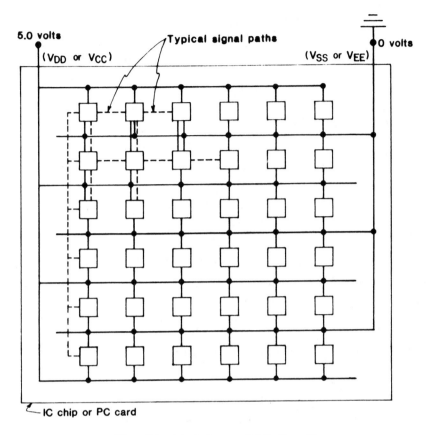

Figure 2.8 A typical power distribution grid

Information on the signal wires is represented by voltage levels (see Chapter 5). These signal voltages are all measured relative to ground. Hence, it is extremely important that the potential at all points of the ground grid be the same (see Chapter 6). As chips become bigger and circuits smaller, this becomes more and more difficult to accomplish, and it may eventually be necessary to recognize limitations to the size of an "equipotential region."

In Chapter 1, packaging levels above the chip are discussed. At each of these levels, power distribution plays an important role. On a printed circuit card, power is distributed to the individual chips by a grid similar to the chip grid of Figure 2.8. Distribution on a backplane is also similar.

2.1.5   Informal Circuit Analysis

We will frequently encounter circuits with several resistors and capacitors (inductors will seldom be involved). Complete solution of the circuit equations may be quite difficult. It is frequently useful in such cases to be able to reason informally about the circuit operation.

Usually the operation of interest is the response of the circuit to a sudden change somewhere in the circuit (e.g., a switch opening or closing; a transistor turning on or off). The following steps may serve to guide an informal analysis in such cases. Assume that the change occurs at time $t = 0$.

Step 1. Determine the steady-state value of voltages and currents at time $t = 0-$ (i.e., just before the change). Steady state in such circuits means that all voltages and currents have stopped changing.

Step 2. Determine values at $t = 0+$ (i.e., just after the change).

Step 3. Determine the steady state that will eventually be reached.

Step 4. Reason about the shape of the curves between initial values and steady state.

Step 5. Estimate the time required to reach steady state.

For example, consider the circuit of Figure 2.9(a). The informal analysis might proceed as follows.

Step 1. At $t = 0-$, all voltages and currents are zero.

Step 2. Voltage across a capacitor cannot change instantaneously, since it takes time to transfer charge, and $v = q/C$. Hence, $v_2(0+) = v_4(0+) = 0$. The voltage across R_1 is $V - v_2$, hence $i_1(0+) = V/R_1$. The voltage across R_3 is $V_2 - V_4$, hence $i_3(0+) = 0$.

Step 3. At steady state, the voltage across each capacitor will be constant, hence the current through each capacitor will be zero. Consequently, capacitors can be removed from the circuit at steady state without changing any steady-state voltages or currents. When this is done in Figure 2.9(a), there is no closed loop and all currents will be zero. Hence at steady state $v_2 = v_4 = V$ and $i_1 = i_2 = i_3 = 0$.

Step 4. Current i_2 will decrease as capacitor C_2 charges and v_2 increases. Current i_3 will increase initially as v_2 increases but will reach a peak and then decrease as capacitor C_4 charges. Approximate curves are shown in Figure 2.9(b).

Step 5. If R_3 is very large, the time constant for v_2 and i_2 will be R_1C_2. If R_3 is very small then the time constant for i_2 and v_2 will be $R_1(C_2 + C_4)$.

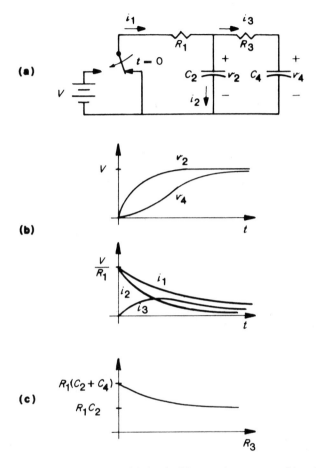

Figure 2.9   Informal circuit analysis: (a) circuit; (b) approximate curves; (c) v_2 time constant

Hence this time constant as a function of R_3 will probably look something like Figure 2.9(c).

Voltage v_4 will follow voltage v_2 with a time constant $R_3 C_4$. Hence if $R_3 C_4$ is much larger than $R_1 C_2$, v_4 will lag considerably behind v_2. But if $R_3 C_4$ is small, then v_4 will follow v_2 closely.

It is helpful to develop the ability to analyze circuits informally in this way. This sort of reasoning provides a conceptual model, an intuition, that is invaluable in guiding analysis and design efforts. Of course, informal analysis does not replace more formal analysis, which frequently must be used to confirm and extend intuitive understanding.

2.1.6 Power and Energy

The power (i.e., the energy per unit time) that is being supplied to a two-terminal device at time t is $p(t) = v(t)i(t)$, where $v(t)$ is the voltage between the device terminals at time t and $i(t)$ is the current that is flowing through the device from the high-voltage terminal to the lower voltage terminal. The unit of power is the watt; 1 watt $=$ 1 volt $*$ 1 amp.

If current is flowing through a device from the lower to the higher voltage terminal, then negative power is being delivered to the device; that is, the device is actually supplying power. A power supply normally supplies power. A resistor cannot supply power; it can only absorb power. A capacitor absorbs power while charging and supplies power while discharging.

The power that is absorbed by a resistor is dissipated as heat. Capacitors do not dissipate power. The energy that is supplied to a capacitor while charging is stored in the capacitor and is later returned to the circuit when the capacitor is discharged.

The heat that is generated by power dissipation in resistors is an important consideration in electronic circuits. This heat must be removed from the system so that it does not raise the temperature of the electronic components above rated limits. This is one of the considerations that limits the density of electronic components on the surface of a chip, and also the density of components in a cabinet.

The power dissipated in a resistor R carrying a current i is

$$p = vi = (iR)i = i^2R \tag{2.8}$$

In digital circuits, two types of power dissipation in resistors are distinguished: *static* (or *steady state*, or *quiescent*) and *dynamic*. Static power dissipation refers to the power absorbed by a resistance at steady state, that is, when the current through the resistance is constant. Dynamic power dissipation refers to power absorbed by resistors when a circuit is changing from one steady state to another, that is, while capacitors are charging or discharging.

Consider the circuit of Figure 2.6. There is no static power dissipation since steady state current is 0 when the switch is in either position. The power that is dissipated in the resistor while the capacitor is charging or discharging is dynamic power. If the switch moves from left to right at $t = 0$, then for $t > 0$,

$$v(t) = V_H + (V_L - V_H)e^{-t/RC} \tag{2.9}$$

The current through C, and hence through R, is

$$i = C(dv/dt)$$
$$= (V_H - V_L)e^{-t/RC}/R \tag{2.10}$$

The power supplied to R thus is

$$p = i^2R = \frac{(V_H - V_L)^2}{R}e^{-2t/RC} \tag{2.11}$$

The total energy dissipated in the resistance, assuming that the switch stays at the right until C is fully charged, is

$$W = \int_0^\infty p\,dt$$

$$= \left.\frac{-C}{2}(V_H - V_L)^2\,e^{-2t/RC}\right|_0^\infty \tag{2.12}$$

$$= \frac{C(V_H - V_L)^2}{2}$$

Notice that W does not depend upon R. The energy dissipated in R while charging C from V_L to V_H is $\frac{1}{2}C(V_H - V_L)^2$, regardless of the value of R.

Similarly, the energy dissipated in R while discharging from V_H to V_L is $\frac{1}{2}C(V_H - V_L)^2$. Hence the total energy required for one cycle (charging and discharging) is $C(V_H - V_L)^2$. The dynamic power dissipation of a circuit that charges and discharges a capacitance C at an average of f cycles per second is $p = fC(V_H - V_L)^2$. If C is in farads, $(V_H - V_L)$ in volts, and f in cycles per second, then p is in watts:

$$p = fC(V_H - V_L)^2$$

$$= \frac{\text{cycles}}{\text{second}} * \frac{\text{farad volt}^2}{\text{cycle}}$$

$$= \frac{\text{coulomb volt}}{\text{second}} \tag{2.13}$$

$$= \text{amp volt}$$

$$= \text{watt}$$

2.1.7 Exercises

1. In Figure 2.2, suppose $R_1 = 10\ \Omega$, $R_2 = 20\ \Omega$, $R_3 = 30\ \Omega$, $R_4 = 40\ \Omega$, and $V = 5$ volts. Determine i, i_1, i_2, v_1, v_2, v_3 and v_4.

2. In Figure 2.5, choose R_1 and R_2 such that $R_1 + R_2 = 15$ KΩ and $V_{out} = 0.7\ V_{in}$.

3. In Figure 2.6, suppose $C = 10$ pF and $R = 2000\ \Omega$. Starting at time $t = 0$, suppose that the switch is alternately moved left and then right, 100 ns

in each position. At $t = 0$, $v = V_L$. Sketch $v(t)$ versus t for 500 ns. What is v at $t = 120$ ns?

4. What is the equivalent capacitance of two capacitors in series? Of two capacitors in parallel? Do an analysis similar to that of Figure 2.3.

5. In Figure 2.9(a), suppose that a resistor R_5 is connected in parallel with C_4. Analyze the circuit response informally. Sketch the approximate evolution of important variables with time. Estimate time constants.

6. Suppose that a 50 pF capacitance is charged to five volts and discharged to zero 10^6 times a second through a resistance of 100 ohms. What will be the average power dissipated in the resistance?

7. If R is in Kilohms and i is in milliamps, in what units is the power, $i^2 R$?

2.2 DIGITAL CIRCUITS [11, 19, 24-26]

     2.2.1 **Diodes and Transistors**
     2.2.2 **Logic Gates**
     2.2.3 **Gate Interconnections**
     2.2.4 **CMOS Logic**
     2.2.5 **Exercises**

In digital circuits, voltages are used to represent binary variables. A low voltage usually represents the binary value 0, and a high voltage the value 1. Power is supplied by a DC voltage source. The negative terminal of the voltage source is normally used as the *signal ground*; that is, all signal voltages in the circuit are measured with respect to this terminal; it is the zero voltage reference. As shown in Figure 2.8, the power terminals (ground and $+V_{DD}$) are made available to all parts of a digital circuit by a network of conductors.

Digital circuits are constructed from electronic components, primarily resistors, diodes, and transistors. In this section we introduce diodes and transistors and show how they are used to construct logic gates. In later chapters we show how logic gates are used to construct more complex digital circuits.

2.2.1 Diodes and Transistors

A resistor is a two-terminal device for which the relationship between v and i is linear; that is, a graph of v versus i would be a straight line. The slope of the line dv/di is the resistance R.

A diode is a *nonlinear* resistance; that is, the graph of v versus i for a diode is not a straight line. A transistor is a three-terminal device for which one of the terminals is used to control the resistance between the other two terminals. This resistance is also nonlinear.

Nonlinear resistances can be represented by equations. For example, a diode is approximately represented by the equation

$$i = I_0(e^{v/c} - 1) \qquad (2.14)$$

where I_0 and c are constants.

However, in most situations a nonlinear resistance is represented by a graph of v versus i, called the *v-i characteristic* or the *v-i curve* for the device. Graphical techniques can be used to find the point on the *v-i* curve where the device will operate in a particular circuit. This is called the *operating point*.

Diodes

The *v-i* curve for a diode is shown in Figure 2.10, along with the standard circuit symbol for the device. A diode is constructed by juxtaposing a p-type semiconductor material and an n-type semiconductor material (see Section 2.3). If the semiconductor material is silicon, which is usually the case in modern digital circuits, then $V_T = 0.7$ volt. The slope dv/di of the diode curve is nearly horizontal for voltages less than zero and nearly vertical for voltages above V_T.

Diodes are most often used to block current from flowing in one direction while allowing current to flow in the other direction. The "rectifier" circuit of Figure 2.11(a), for example, converts an input voltage that is alternately positive and negative to an output voltage that is always positive (see Exercise 1).

Diodes are also used to "clip" or "limit" a voltage to the value V_T. For example, the circuit of Figure 2.11(b) will convert a sinusoidal input voltage to an output voltage that is nearly a square wave (see Exercise 2).

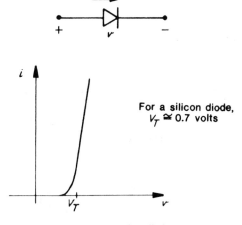

For a silicon diode,
$V_T \cong 0.7$ volts

Figure 2.10   The diode

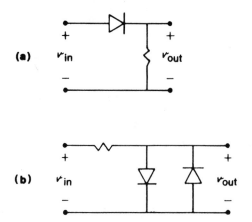

Figure 2.11   Diode circuits: (a) rectifier; (b) clamping circuit

Combining v-i Curves

When devices are connected in parallel or in series, the v-i curve for the combination is easily obtained from the individual v-i curves. The technique is illustrated in Figure 2.12.

For a series combination, Figure 2.12(a), the same current flows through each device. For any current value, the corresponding voltage value for the combined curve is the sum of the voltages for the individual curves at that current value.

For a parallel combination, Figure 2.12(b), the same voltage is across each device. For any voltage value, the corresponding current value for the combined curve is the sum of the current values at that voltage for the individual curves.

Operating Point

When nonlinear devices are included in a circuit, the operating point on the v-i curve may be determined graphically, as illustrated in Figure 2.13. First the circuit is decomposed into two two-terminal subcircuits such that the parallel interconnection of the two subcircuits is the circuit of interest. In Figure 2.13, one subcircuit is the diode and the other is the series combination of V and R. The v-i curve for each of the subcircuits is then plotted on the same v-i graph. In Figure 2.13, the v-i curve for the V-R combination may be obtained by writing the equation $V = iR + v$ (Kirchhoff's voltage law) and plotting v versus i. Alternatively, the curves for the two devices V and R may be com-

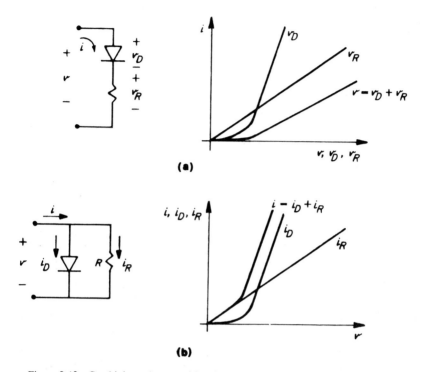

Figure 2.12   Combining *v-i* curves: (a) series combination; (b) parallel combination

bined as described in Figure 2.12(a). In this case, however, the R curve is subtracted from the V curve since $v = V - v_R$.

The operating point for each subcircuit must lie on the *v-i* curve for that subcircuit. Hence, the operating point for the circuit must be at a point where the two curves intersect.

MOS Transistors

A transistor is a three-terminal device, formed by juxtaposing three semiconductor regions (*n-p-n* or *p-n-p*; see Section 2.3). There are two basic types of transistors: *bipolar* and *metal oxide semiconductor* (MOS). Transistors of both types are used primarily as switches in digital systems. They differ in the manner in which the switch operation is controlled. *n*MOS transistors will be considered first.

There are two types of MOS transistors: *n*MOS (two *n*-regions with a *p*-region between) and *p*MOS (two *p*-regions with an *n*-region between). The

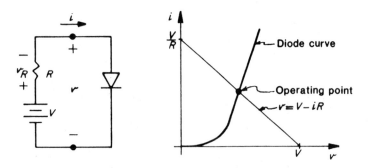

Figure 2.13   Operating point determination

operating characteristics of nMOS and pMOS transistors are essentially the same, except that the directions of voltages and currents are reversed.

The circuit symbol of an nMOS transistor is shown in Figure 2.14(a). The three terminals are called the *gate* (g), the *drain* (d), and the *source* (s). Physically, the source and drain terminals are identical; the terminal at the higher potential is called the drain. In some applications the voltage between these two terminals changes sign during operation, so that the terminals change roles.

The drain-source path through the transistor is essentially a resistance, the value of which is controlled by the gate-source voltage v_{gs}. For low values of gate-source voltage, the drain-source resistance R_{ds} is high; for high v_{gs} values, R_{ds} is low. The v-i characteristics of a typical nMOS transistor are shown in Figure 2.14(b). Note that in addition to varying with v_{gs}, R_{ds} also varies with v_{ds} (i.e., R_{ds} is a nonlinear resistance). For a fixed value of v_{gs}, the current i_{ds} increases linearly with v_{ds} for small values of v_{ds}, but beyond a certain point (called "saturation" or "pinchoff") further increases in v_{ds} produce essentially no increase in i_{ds}.

A circuit model for the nMOS transistor is shown in Figure 2.14(c). The gate-source path is modeled as a capacitance C_{gs}. It is the amount of charge that must be moved between gate and source to effect a 1-volt change in v_{gs}. Actually, C_{gs} varies with v_{gs} (i.e., it is nonlinear), but this variation is of secondary importance and will be ignored. There is also some capacitance between drain and gate, which we can ignore.

The drain-source path is represented by a resistance R_{ds}, the value of which is controlled by the gate-source voltage v_{gs}. In digital applications, v_{gs} is usually a binary signal voltage with stable values in either a high range (binary 1) or a low range (binary 0). Typical ranges for nMOS circuits are shown in Figure 2.14(c). When v_{gs} is in the low range ($v_{gs} = L$), the transistor is said to be "turned off," and the drain-source path is a high resistance, $R_{ds} = R_{off}$.

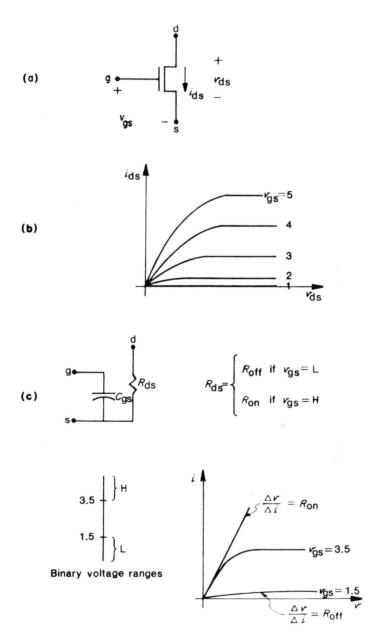

Figure 2.14 nMOS transistor (enhancement): (a) circuit symbol; (b) v-i characteristics; (c) digital circuit model

When v_{gs} is in the high range, the transistor is "turned on" and the drain-source resistance is much lower, $R_{ds} = R_{on}$.

The values of R_{off}, R_{on}, and C_{gs} depend upon many parameters associated with the fabrication process (see Section 2.3). For a given process, R_{off} and R_{on} are proportional to L/W and C_{gs} is proportional to $L * W$, where L and W are the length and width of the "channel" region (i.e., the p-type material below the gate; see Section 2.3). For a typical nMOS process, a transistor with $L = W = 6 * 10^{-6}$ meters will have $R_{on} \cong 10^4$ ohms, $R_{off} \cong 10^{10}$ ohms, and $C_{gs} \cong 0.015$ pF [26]. This is a minimum-size transistor for a process with a resolution of 3 microns (a micron is 10^{-6} meters). We will use these values in examples.

It is possible to reduce the value of gate-source voltage for which the nMOS transistor turns on by injecting n-type impurities into the p-type "channel" region below the gate (see Section 2.3). The resulting transistor is called a *depletion mode* nMOS transistor. The ordinary nMOS transistor with no injected channel impurities (Figure 2.14) is called an *enhancement mode* transistor.

The circuit symbol for a depletion mode transistor is shown in Figure 2.15(a). It is the same as the enhancement mode symbol, except that the line representing the gate is broader.

The v-i characteristics of the depletion mode transistor are essentially the same as those of the enhancement mode transistor, except for the values of v_{gs}. In particular, for $v_{gs} = 0$ the transistor is turned on, as shown in Figure 2.15(b).

If the gate of a depletion mode transistor is connected to the source, then v_{gs} is held at zero. The transistor is thus converted into a two-terminal device, a nonlinear resistance. The v-i curve describing the device is the $v_{gs} = 0$ curve for the transistor, as shown in Figure 2.15(c). Resistors in nMOS circuits are implemented in this way. To emphasize its role as a resistor, the depletion model transistor with gate tied to source is often represented by the alternative symbol in Figure 2.15(d). We might even use the standard resistor symbol.

The resistance value of a depletion resistor may be controlled either by the amount of impurity injection into the channel region or by the length-to-width ratio L/W of the channel region. Usually, all depletion mode transistors in a circuit receive the same impurity injection. Resistance values are then controlled by varying L/W. In our examples, we will assume that the impurity injection is such that a depletion mode transistor with $v_{gs} = 0$ is turned on about the same as an enhancement mode transistor with $v_{gs} = 3.5$. Hence, a minimum-size depletion resistor in the linear region (small v_{ds}) will have a resistance of about 10^4 ohms ($= R_{on}$ for a minimum-size enhancement transistor).

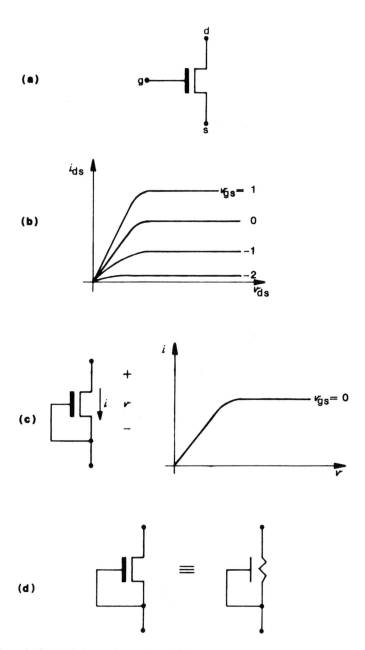

Figure 2.15   Depletion mode transistor (a) circuit symbol; (b) $v\text{-}i$ characteristics; (c) resistor implementation; (d) alternative symbol

Bipolar Transistors

There are two types of bipolar transistors: the *npn* transistor (two *n* regions with a *p* region between) and the *pnp* transistor (two *p* regions with an *n* region between). The *npn* transistor is described in Figure 2.16. The *pnp* transistor is identical except that currents and voltages are opposite in direction.

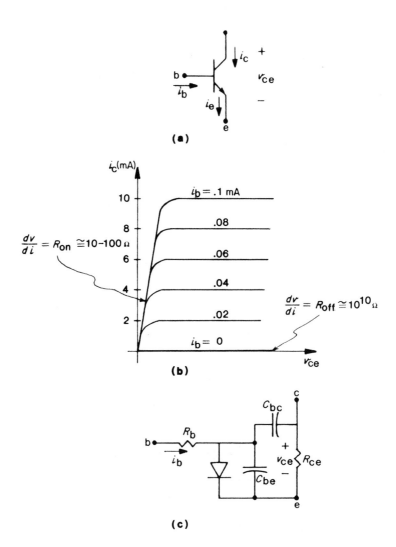

Figure 2.16   Bipolar transistor: (a) circuit symbol; (b) *v-i* curves; (c) circuit model

The symbol for the *npn* transistor is given in Figure 2.16(a). The three terminals are called the *base* (b), *collector* (c), and *emitter* (e). The *pnp* symbol is the same except that the emitter arrow is in the opposite direction.

The *v-i* curves are almost identical to the *n*MOS curves, except for two major differences:

1. The collector-emitter path (which corresponds to the drain-source path) is controlled by the base current i_b (rather than by v_{be}, which corresponds to v_{gs}); and

2. The turned-on resistance of the collector-emitter path is orders of magnitude less than the drain-source resistance of a turned-on *n*MOS transistor of comparable size (typical values are given in Figure 2.16).

The circuit model for a bipolar transistor is given in Figure 2.16(c). The base-emitter path is a diode in series with a relatively small resistance (e.g., a few hundred ohms). The collector-emitter path is a resistance, the value of which is controlled by i_b. Both the base-emitter capacitance and the base-collector capacitance are significant.

2.2.2 Logic Gates

The basic building blocks from which digital circuits are constructed are logic gates and flip-flops. Both are constructed from electronic components. Logic gates are discussed in this section, and flip-flops in Section 5.4.

A logic gate is an electronic circuit that accepts binary voltage signals as inputs and generates a binary voltage signal as an output. A binary voltage signal represents the binary value 1 when it is high and the value 0 when it is low.

Many different families of logic devices are available. Each family is characterized by the type of circuit used to implement gates and flip-flops. Bipolar families (i.e., families using bipolar transistors) include transistor-transistor logic (TTL), emitter-coupled logic (ECL), and integrated injection logic (I^2L). The MOS families include *n*MOS, *p*MOS, and complementary MOS (CMOS). Each family, moreover, may have several subfamilies (e.g., standard TTL, Schottky TTL, low-power Schottky TTL). The families and subfamilies differ from each other in various ways, including:

1. Speed (i.e., how fast outputs change in response to input changes);

2. Logic levels (i.e., what voltage ranges represent 0 and 1);

3. Power consumption;

4. Noise immunity;

5. Density (i.e., how many components can be placed on one chip); and

6. Power supply level(s).

In this text, we will use two logic families as examples: *n*MOS and TTL. The structure of the logic gates in each of these families is described in this section.

The three basic types of logic gates in the *n*MOS and TTL families are shown in Figure 2.17. For each type of gate a symbol representing the gate is given as well as a table defining the operation of the gate. An *inverter* generates a high voltage at its output when the input voltage is low and a low output when the input is high. A *NOR gate* generates a high output if all inputs are low and a low output otherwise. The NOR gate shown has only two inputs, but the definition applies to any number of inputs. A *NAND gate* generates a low output if all inputs are high, and a high output otherwise. The NAND gate may also have any number of inputs.

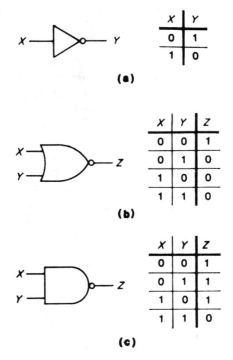

Figure 2.17   Logic gates: (a) inverter; (b) NOR gate; (c) NAND gate

General Structure

The logic gates in many families, including TTL and *n*MOS, have the general structure illustrated in Figure 2.18. The gate output is connected to the positive power supply terminal V_{DD} through a "pull-up circuit" and to the ground terminal through a "pull-down circuit." The gate inputs are used to turn transistors on and off in the pull-up and/or pull-down circuits.

The principle of operation for the gate is that of the voltage divider. When a low output is required, the pull-down circuit provides a low-resistance path to ground while the pull-up circuit provides a much higher resistance path to V_{DD}. Conversely, when a high output is required, the pull-down resistance is made high relative to the pull-up resistance.

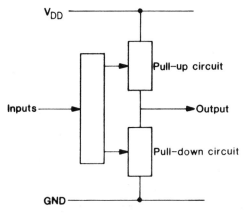

Figure 2.18 General gate structure

nMOS Gates

The standard nMOS gate circuits are presented in Figure 2.19. For each gate the pull-up circuit is simply a resistor, implemented by using a depletion mode transistor. The pull-down circuits are constructed with enhancement mode transistors. A 5-volt power supply is used.

The pull-down circuit for the inverter is a single transistor. The L/W ratios of the pull-up and pull-down transistors are adjusted so that $R_{pu} \cong 4R_{on}$, where R_{on} is the resistance of the turned-on pull-down transistor. For example, if a minimum-size pull-down transistor is used ($L_{pd} = W_{pd} = $ minimum), then $R_{on} = 10^4$ ohms. If the pull-up transistor is minimum width ($W_{pu} = W_{pd}$), then $L_{pu} \cong 4W_{pu}$.

When the inverter input X is high (>3.5 volts), the pull-down transistor is turned on, so that the gate divides the supply voltage in a 4-to-1 ratio. The output Y is 1.0 volt, which represents logic 0 (<1.5 volts).

When the inverter input is low, the pull-down transistor is turned off and the pull-down resistance is several orders of magnitude greater than the pull-up resistance. The output is essentially 5.0 volts, which represents logic 1.

Figure 2.19(b) shows a two-input NOR gate. The pull-down circuit consists of two transistors in parallel, each controlled by one of the inputs. If either input is high, the corresponding transistor is turned on and the gate output is pulled low. The output remains high only if both inputs are low, and hence both pull-down transistors are turned off.

NOR gates with many inputs may be constructed in this fashion. Each input controls a separate pull-down transistor. If any input is high the corresponding transistor pulls the output low. If all inputs are low, the pull-down resistance is the parallel combination of all the turned-off transistors. For example, if $R_{off} = 10^{10}$ ohms, then a NOR gate with 100 inputs will have a pull-down resistance of 10^8 ohms when all inputs are low. If $R_{pu} = 4R_{on} = 4 * 10^4$ ohms, the output is still near 5.0 volts, just as it is for a two-input gate.

A two-input NAND gate is shown in Figure 2.19(c). The pull-down circuit consists of two transistors in series, each controlled by one of the inputs. The output is pulled low only when both inputs are high. In this case both input transistors are turned on and the pull-down resistance is $2R_{on}$. In order to keep the low output at 1.0 volt, the pull-up resistor must be $8R_{on}$.

NAND gates with n inputs may be constructed by putting n transistors in series for the pull-down circuit, each controlled by one input. The pull-up resistance for an n-input NAND gate, however, must be around $n * 4 * R_{on}$ in order to keep the low output at 1.0 volt. We shall see later that it is disadvantageous to make R_{pu} very large. This makes nMOS NAND gates with many inputs impractical.

Bipolar Gates

The same basic structure that is used for nMOS gates (Figure 2.19) may be used for bipolar gates. An inverter, for example, may be constructed as shown in Figure 2.20. This type of gate construction is called resistor-transistor logic (RTL).

The value of the input resistance R_I is chosen so that the resulting base current for a high input voltage is sufficient to turn the transistor on and pull the output low, but the base current for a low input will not turn the transistor on and the output will remain high.

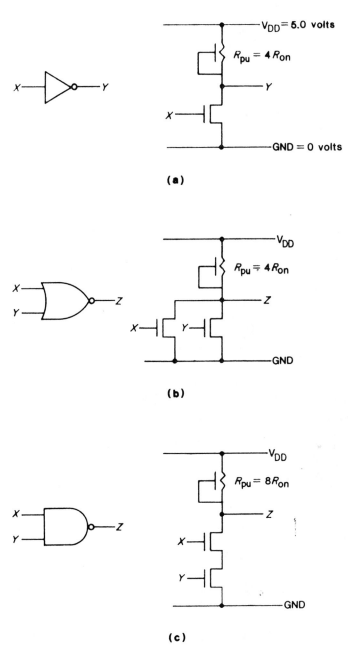

Figure 2.19 nMOS logic gates: (a) inverter; (b) NOR gate; (c) NAND gate

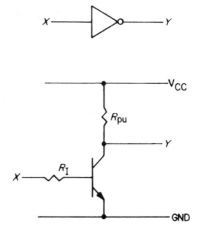

Figure 2.20   RTL inverter

The gates of the TTL (transistor-transistor logic) family are more elaborate. The additional complexity is used to increase the speed of the gates and to provide more "output drive" capability (see Section 2.2.3).

The basic TTL NAND gate is shown in Figure 2.21. The pull-up circuit consists of a transistor Q_3, a diode, and a resistor in series. The pull-down circuit is one transistor, Q_4. The middle transistor Q_2 is used to control the pull-up and pull-down transistors; when Q_2 is off, Q_3 is on and Q_4 is off, hence the output is high; when Q_2 is on, Q_3 is off and Q_4 is on, hence the output is low.

The input transistor Q_1 is used to control Q_2. Q_1 has two emitters, one for each input. Q_1 is turned on when sufficient base current flows in either emitter, hence when either input is low. When both inputs are high, Q_1 is turned off.

When both inputs are high, current actually flows from the base to the collector of Q_1, and into the base of Q_2. (This reverse collector current is not represented in Figure 2.16.) This turns on Q_2, which turns Q_3 off and Q_4 on, thus establishing a low output.

When either emitter is low, Q_1 is turned on. Any charge on the base of Q_2 is quickly removed and Q_2 is turned off. This turns off Q_4 and turns on Q_3, thus pulling the output high. The "active" pull-up through Q_3 (rather than the "passive" pull-up through a resistance, as for RTL) allows a faster low-to-high transition (see Section 2.2.3).

The diodes at the inputs are used to limit negative voltage swings to -0.7 volt. Such swings may occur as a result of transmission line reflections (see Section 7.2).

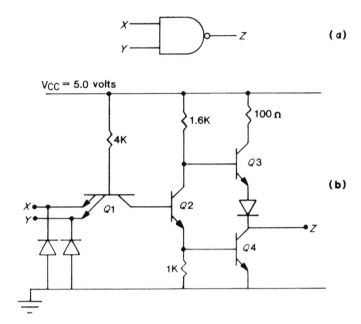

Figure 2.21 7400 series TTL NAND gate: (a) logic symbol; (b) circuit

Gate Input and Output Characteristics

The technique described above for combining v-i curves can be applied to the nMOS gate circuits to obtain the v-i characteristics at the gate output, as illustrated in Figure 2.22. In Figure 2.22(a) v and i are defined. In Figure 2.22(b) the gate circuit is drawn in the usual way, and then redrawn to emphasize its structure as an nMOS transistor in parallel with a voltage source and resistor in series. Two i_{ds} curves are shown, one for $v_{gs} = 1.0$ and one for $v_{gs} = 5.0$. The curve for $v_{gs} = 1.0$ is on the horizontal axis. The curve labelled i_s is for the series combination of V_{DD} and R_{pu}. (A linear R_{pu} is assumed for simplicity.) The curve for i(output low) is obtained by subtracting $i_{ds}(1)$ from i_s, and i(output high) by subtracting $i_{ds}(5)$ from i_s.

The input characteristic for an nMOS gate coincides with the horizontal axis, since the input path is simply a capacitance (the input resistance is essentially infinite). Note that the v-i curves represent the steady-stage v-i relationship, that is, the values of v and i when all capacitances have been charged or discharged and both v and i are steady.

The v-i input and output characteristics for a TTL gate can be constructed as above, with considerable effort. They may also be obtained by direct measurement. The curves are shown in Figure 2.23.

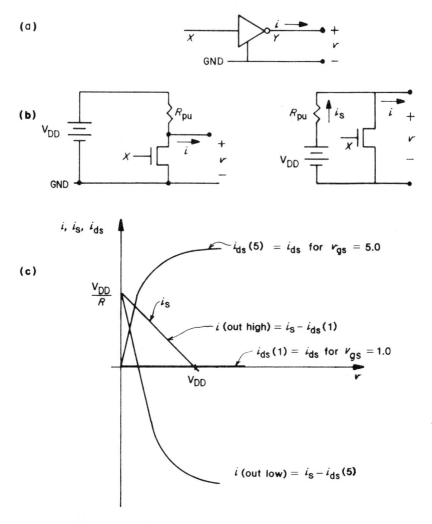

Figure 2.22 nMOS gate output characteristics: (a) output variables; (b) electronic circuit; (c) v-i curves

Transfer Curves

A graph of v_{in} versus v_{out} for a gate is called the gate *transfer characteristic*. This curve can be obtained by superimposing the v-i curve of the pull-up transistor on the v-i curves of the pull-down transistor, as illustrated in Figure 2.24. The gate is assumed unloaded, so the drain-source current is the same through both transistors. The v-i curves for the pull-down transistor are the

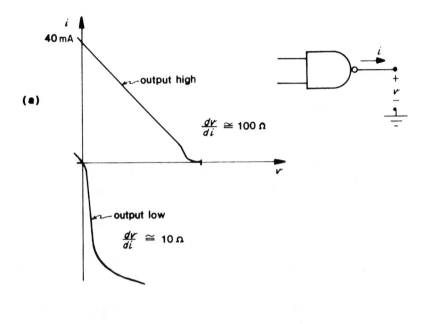

(a)

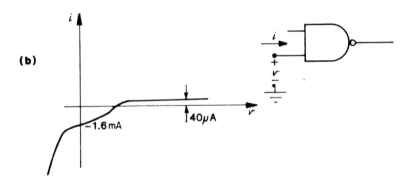

(b)

Figure 2.23   TTL v-i characteristics: (a) output; (b) input

curves of Figure 2.14 with $v_{gs} = X$ and $v_{ds} = Y$. The v-i curve for the depletion mode pull-up in series with V is the same as the i_s curve of Figure 2.22,
with the nonlinearity represented.

Each intersection of the pull-up curve with a pull-down curve gives one
point on the transfer curve, as illustrated in Figure 2.24. The gate threshold
voltage V_t is the input voltage that produces an equal output voltage. This
point is designed to be midway between the logic 0 and logic 1 regions.

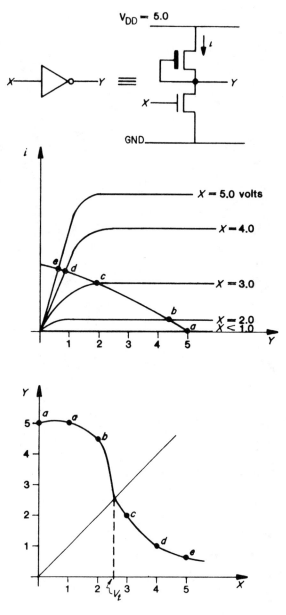

Figure 2.24   nMOS transfer curve

Schmitt Trigger Gates

The transfer curve of a *Schmitt trigger* gate is designed to have a double threshold, as illustrated in Figure 2.25. If the input to a Schmitt trigger inverter has been low, the output will not switch from high to low until after the input has reached the high threshold, V_{tH}. After switching low, the output will not switch high again until after the input has reached the low threshold, V_{tL}.

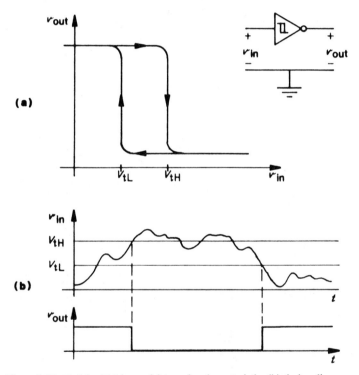

Figure 2.25   A Schmitt trigger: (a) transfer characteristic; (b) timing diagram

Schmitt trigger gates are used to convert noisy signals or signals that do not make "monotonic" transitions between high and low into good digital signals (i.e., signals that make sharp, well-defined transitions), as illustrated in Figure 2.25(b).

2.2.3   Gate Interconnections

Complex digital circuits are constructed by interconnecting gates, output terminals to input terminals (see Chapter 3). Figure 2.26(a) shows such an inter-

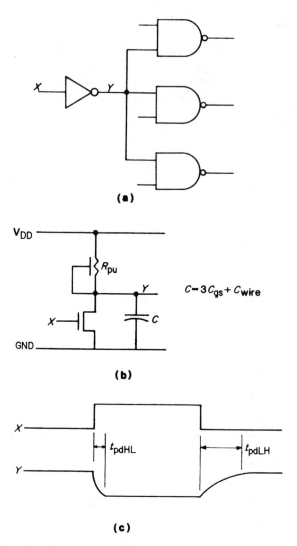

Figure 2.26   Gate interconnections: (a) logic diagram; (b) circuit model; (c) timing diagram

connection for one output. The circuit model for this interconnection is shown in Figure 2.26(b), assuming nMOS gates. The capacitance C is the sum of the input capacitances for all of the gate inputs and the wiring connecting the output to inputs.

In order to change the voltage at the gate output, the capacitance C must be charged or discharged. The time that it takes to charge or discharge C is determined by the time constant RC, where R is the resistance through which the capacitance charges or discharges. When the inverter input is low, the pull-down transistor is turned off and C charges through the pull-up resistance, $R_{pu} = 4R_{on}$.

When the inverter input is high, the pull-down transistor is turned on and C discharges through $R_{pd} = R_{on}$. Actually, C discharges through $R_{pd} \| R_{pu} = 0.8R_{on}$, although this is not obvious without writing the equations.

The time constant for a low-to-high transition of the output is thus about five times as large as the time constant for a high-to-low transition, as illustrated in Figure 2.26(c).

Propagation Delay

The propagation delay of a gate is the time required for the output to change after an input has changed. Suppose we say that the output has changed whenever it has gone 95% of the way from its initial value to the final value that it approaches asymptotically. Then the propagation delay is approximately $3RC$, since $e^{-3} = 0.05$ (see Section 2.1.2).

Suppose, for example, that $C = 0.2$ pF, $R_{on} = 10^4$ ohms, and $R_{pu} = 4 * 10^4$ ohms. Then the propagation delay from low to high is approximately $3R_{pu}C = 24$ ns and the propagation delay from high to low is about 4.8 ns.

The conflict involved in selecting the value of R_{pu} for nMOS gates is now apparent. It is desirable to make R_{pu} much larger than R_{on} so that the logic 0 voltage will be low (e.g., if R_{pu} were 10^7 ohms, then the low output would be approximately 0.0 volts and the high output would still be approximately 5.0 volts). On the other hand, it is desirable to make R_{pu} low in order to reduce the low-to-high propagation delay. As a compromise, $R_{pu} = 4R_{on}$ is selected.

Power

An nMOS gate with its output high will dissipate very little power. For $V_{DD} = 5.0$ volts, the current supplied to the gate will be $5.0/(R_{pu} + R_{off}) \cong 0.5$ nanoamps. Hence the power supplied is 2.5 nanowatts, which is negligible.

If the output is low, however, there is a significant steady-state power dissipation. The current supplied to the gate is $5.0/(R_{pu} + R_{on}) \cong 0.1$ milliamps. Hence the power is 0.5 milliwatt.

Dynamic power dissipation is harder to estimate. As noted in Section 2.1, the energy required to charge and discharge a capacitor once is CV^2. If a capacitance of 5 picofarads (e.g., a long data path on a chip) is charged and discharged between 1 and 5 volts once every microsecond, then the average power required is

$$\frac{5 \text{ picofarads} * 4 \text{ volts}^2}{10^{-6} \text{ seconds}} = \frac{80 * 10^{-12}}{10^{-6}} \text{ watts}$$

$$= 80 * 10^{-6} \text{ watts}$$

$$= 0.08 \text{ milliwatts} \qquad (2.15)$$

Most of the gates on a typical chip will be driving loads much smaller than this. Hence in most cases dynamic power dissipation in nMOS circuits will be much less significant than static power dissipation.

2.2.4   CMOS Logic

Two shortcomings of standard nMOS logic are:

1. The long low-to-high switching time due to the relatively large pull-up resistance; and

2. The steady-state power dissipation when a gate output is low.

The complementary MOS (CMOS) logic family eliminates both of these problems. CMOS gates use pMOS transistors for pull-up circuits and nMOS transistors for pull-down circuits. The CMOS inverter is shown in Figure 2.27.

A pMOS transistor operates like an nMOS transistor except that low gate-source voltages turn the transistor on and high gate-source voltages turn it off. In Figure 2.27, where $X = $ L, the nMOS pull-down is off and the pMOS pull-up is on. Hence Y is connected through a low resistance to V_{DD}. When $X = $ H, the nMOS pull-down is on and the pMOS pull-up is off; Y is connected through a low resistance to ground.

The speed problem is solved since the value of R_{pu} is low when the output is high and high when the output is low. Conversely, the value of R_{pd} is low when the output is low and high when the output is high.

The power problem is also solved, since at steady state there is never a low-resistance path between V_{DD} and ground. At steady state, either the pull-up transistor is turned off or the pull-down transistor is off, and since R_{ds} is extremely large for an off transistor, the steady-state power dissipation is negligible. The power consumed by a CMOS gate is just the dynamic power, fCV^2, where f is the number of times per second that the gate output switches be-

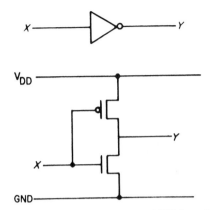

A circle at the gate indicates a pMOS transistor.

X	R_{pd}	R_{pu}	Y
L	R_{off}	R_{on}	V
H	R_{on}	R_{off}	GND

Figure 2.27   CMOS inverter

tween H and L, V is the voltage difference between H and L ($V = H - L$), and C is the capacitance driven by the gate.

Since R_{ds} is very large for an off transistor, H $\cong V_{DD}$ and L $\cong 0$. Hence V in the above formula for CMOS power dissipation is V_{DD}. The greater separation between H and L is another advantage of CMOS over nMOS (H $-$ L $\cong$ $0.8 V_{DD}$ for nMOS).

A disadvantage of CMOS is that multiple input gates require a pull-up circuit of the same complexity as the pull-down circuit. CMOS NOR and NAND gates are shown in Figures 2.28 and 2.29.

The pull-up and pull-down circuits can each be regarded as implementing directly a logic function with voltages as inputs and resistance as "output" ($R_{on} = 0$ and $R_{off} = 1$). Under this interpretation, the pull-down circuit implements the desired gate function, and the pull-up circuit implements the inverse of that function, as illustrated in the truth tables of Figures 2.28 and 2.29.

When analyzing nMOS gates, we noted that the NAND gate was inferior to the NOR gate because the series transistors in the pull-down circuit increased the value of R_{on}. The same problem exists in CMOS for both NAND gates (in the pull-down circuit) and NOR gates (in the pull-up circuit). If minimum-size transistors are used, the low-to-high switching time of the NOR gate and

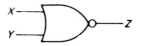

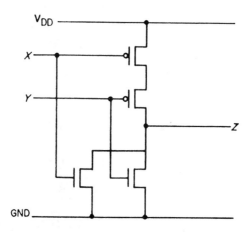

X	Y	R_{pd}	R_{pu}	Z
L	L	R_{off}	R_{on}	V_{DD}
L	H	R_{on}	R_{off}	GND
H	L	R_{on}	R_{off}	GND
H	H	R_{on}	R_{off}	GND

Figure 2.28   CMOS NOR gate

the high-low switching time of the NAND gate are both proportional to the number of gate inputs.

CMOS gates with many inputs are unattractive, both because of the slow switching times and because of the chip area that they occupy. When many-input gates are required, the standard nMOS NOR gate or some similar structure may be used.

Another technique that is useful for gates with very many inputs, either in CMOS or in nMOS, is *precharging*. This technique, illustrated in Fig. 2.30, requires use of a two-phase clock. The gate output line is charged to V_{DD} during phase 1 and inputs are applied during phase 2. The gate output is valid only during phase 2.

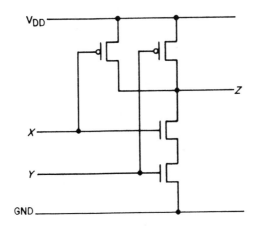

X	Y	R_{pd}	R_{pu}	Z
L	L	R_{off}	R_{on}	V_{DD}
L	H	R_{off}	R_{on}	V_{DD}
H	L	R_{off}	R_{on}	V_{DD}
H	H	R_{on}	R_{off}	GND

Figure 2.29   CMOS NAND gate

In this text we will use nMOS logic to illustrate system design ideas at the electronics level. In most cases, however, the same ideas apply equally well to CMOS logic.

2.2.5   Exercises

1. Sketch the waveform v_{out} for the circuit of Fig. 2.11(a) with $v_{in} = V \sin wt$.

2. Sketch v_{out} for the circuit of Fig. 2.11(b) with $v_{in} = V \sin wt$, $V = 5$ volts, and $R = 1000$ ohms. Assume $dv/di \cong 20$ ohms for the diode when $v > V_T = 0.7$ volt.

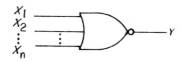

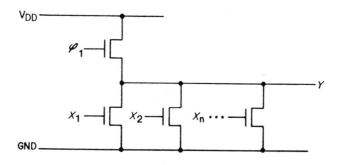

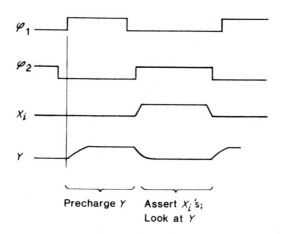

Figure 2.30   Precharged gate

3. Sketch the *v-i* curve for each of the following circuits:

   (a)

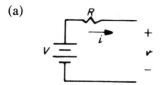

(b)

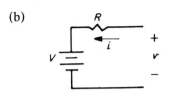

(c)

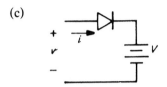

4.

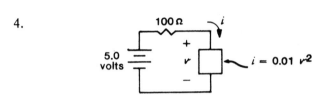

Find the operating point of the above circuit: (a) by solving equations; (b) graphically.

5.

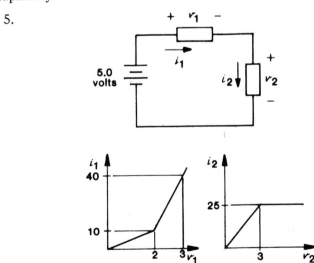

Find the operating point for the above circuit: (a) graphically; (b) by writing and solving equations.

6. Specify the output v_z of the NOR gate of Figure 2.19(b) for each of the input conditions: $(X, Y) = $ (L, L); (L, H); (H, L); and (H, H). Assume that each pull-down resistance is R_{on} or R_{off} for $v_{gs} = $ H or L, respectively, where $R_{on} = 10^4$ ohms and $R_{off} = 10^{10}$ ohms. Specify v_z in volts (not just L or H).

7. Repeat Exercise 6 for the NAND gate of Figure 2.19(c).

8. Suppose that the NOR gate of Figure 2.19(b) drives a capacitance of 0.5 pF [e.g., Figure 2.26(b)]. Plot the output voltage v_z to scale for the following input waveforms: $X = Y = H$ for $t < 0$; X switches to L at $t = 0$; Y switches to L at $t = 80$ ns; X switches to H at $t = 160$ ns. Assume $R_{on} = 10^4$ ohms and $R_{off} = 10^{10}$ ohms.

9. The following are approximate equations for the nMOS transistor [26]:

$$I_{ds} = 0 \quad \text{for} \quad V_{gs} < V_{th}$$

$$I_{ds} = \frac{\mu \xi W}{LD}(V_{gs} - V_{th})V_{ds} \quad \text{for} \quad V_{ds} < \frac{V_{gs} - V_{th}}{2}$$

$$I_{ds} = \frac{\mu \xi W}{LD} \frac{(V_{gs} - V_{th})^2}{2} \quad \text{for} \quad V_{ds} > \frac{V_{gs} - V_{th}}{2}$$

where L and W are channel length and width, D is insulation thickness (Figure 2.31), μ is electron mobility, and ξ is insulator permittivity.

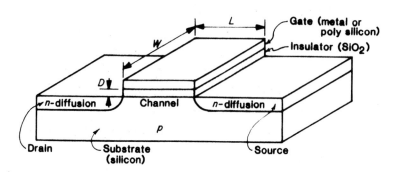

Figure 2.31 nMOS transistor structure

For a typical nMOS process, $D/\mu\xi = 3 * 10^4$ ohm·volts and $V_{th} = 1.0$ volt.

(a) Plot the v-i characteristics of Figure 2.14(b) using these equations for a square transistor ($L = W$).

(b) Plot the $V_{gs} = 4$ curve for a transistor with $L = 4W$. (This is approximately the depletion mode curve with $V_{gs} = 0$.)

(c) Using the curves of (a) for the pull-down and (b) for the pull-up, plot the nMOS gate output characteristics (Figure 2.22).

(d) Plot the gate transfer curve (Figure 2.24).

10. For the NOR gate and load of Exercise 8:

(a) What is the static power dissipation for each of the four possible input conditions: LL, LH, HL, and HH?

(b) What is the dynamic power dissipation assuming $X =$ L and Y oscillates between L and H with a period of 200 ns (i.e., Y switches every 100 ns).

11. Sketch the nMOS implementation of the following circuit:

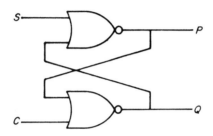

2.3   INTEGRATED CIRCUITS [11, 19, 26–29]

2.3.1   **Materials Review**

2.3.2   *n***MOS Transistors**

2.3.3   **Parameter Values**

2.3.4   **Exercises**

In this section, integrated circuit implementation of digital circuits is discussed. The geometric structure and operation of nMOS transistors are described, a typical nMOS fabrication process is discussed, and some typical nMOS circuit layouts are presented.

2.3.1   Materials Review [11, 23]

A *metal* is a material that has a large number of "free electrons," that is, electrons that are loosely bound to their associated atomic nuclei. Free electrons can move through the metal under the influence of an electric field; such motion constitutes electric current.

A *semiconductor* is a material that has some free charge carriers, but not nearly so many as a metal. The charge carriers may be either electrons or holes. A *hole* is not actually a charged particle. Rather it is a space in the atomic structure of a semiconductor material that can readily accept an electron from a neighboring atom. This "space" or "hole" can move through the semiconductor material under the influence of an electric field just as though it were a free, positively charged particle.

An *intrinsic* semiconductor has an equal number of holes and electrons that are free to carry current. Pure silicon is an intrinsic semiconductor. In an *n-type* semiconductor, most of the free charge carriers are electrons (the *n* stands for negative). In a *p-type* semiconductor, most of the carriers are holes.

An intrinsic semiconductor can be converted to an *n*-type semiconductor by adding *donor* atoms, which contribute free electrons to the material. An intrinsic semiconductor can be converted to *p*-type by adding *acceptor* atoms, which contribute holes. Similarly, *n*-type or *p*-type can be converted to the opposite type by adding enough impurity atoms of the proper type. The process of adding impurity atoms is called *doping*.

An *insulator* has essentially no free carriers, either holes or electrons. It does not conduct current, except in an extremely high electric field, which can tear electrons away from the atoms to which they are bound.

When a metal or a semiconductor is subjected to an electric field, the free charges accelerate under the influence of the field. The free charges that are accelerated by the field will suffer frequent collisions with atoms that occupy fixed positions in the material. At steady state, the free carriers have an average velocity v that is proportional to the field strength E. The proportionality constant $\mu = v/E$ is called the *mobility* of the charge carriers in the material.

The *resistance* of a conductor or semiconductor path is determined by the number of charge carriers available, the mobility of the carriers, and the geometry of the path. Specifically, $R = L/n\mu A$, where L and A are the length and cross-sectional area of the path and n is the density of charge carriers. The constant $1/n\mu$ is called the *resistivity* of the material, usually denoted ρ.

2.3.2   *n*MOS Transistors

The structure of an *n*MOS transistor is illustrated in Figure 2.31. The chip itself, called the *substrate*, is a *p*-type semiconductor. The *n*MOS transistor is created on the surface of the substrate as follows:

1. Deposit a layer of insulation and then a layer of metal or polycrystalline silicon directly over the insulation to form the transistor gate.

2. Diffuse donor atoms into the surface of the chip on both sides of the gate, converting the material on the chip surface to *n*-type semiconductor. The substrate under the gate, called the *channel*, remains *p*-type.

Operation

Suppose that we ground the substrate, the source, and the drain of the transistor in Figure 2.31. A positive voltage applied to the gate will attract free electrons in the p-substrate toward the gate. These electrons are minority carriers in the substrate, supplied either by thermal generation or by diffusion from the drain and source regions.

As the gate voltage is increased, more electrons are attracted toward the gate. Eventually the concentration of electrons below the gate is sufficient to effectively convert a thin layer of the substrate from p-type to n-type. The gate voltage at which this happens is called the threshold voltage, V_{th}. The thickness of this "n-channel" below the gate is proportional to ($V_{gs} - V_{th}$).

If a positive voltage is now applied to the drain, current will flow from drain to source, since there is effectively a continuous path of n-type material from drain contact to source contact. The magnitude of the current I_{ds} will be proportional to V_{ds} for small values of V_{ds}. However, as drain potential increases, the gate-to-drain potential decreases, causing the n-channel near the drain to become thinner. Eventually the channel is "pinched off" and further increases in V_{ds} produce only small increases in I_{ds}. This is the knee of the V_{ds} versus I_{ds} curve for a fixed V_{gs}.

For values of V_{ds} below pinchoff, the drain-source resistance $R_{ds} = V_{ds}/I_{ds}$ is inversely proportional to the thickness of the n-channel, which is proportional to V_{gs}. Hence, as V_{gs} increases, R_{ds} decreases.

The threshold voltage V_{th} can be adjusted in various ways during fabrication, for example, by controlling the doping level of the substrate. For enhancement mode nMOS transistors, V_{th} is adjusted to about $0.2 V_{DD}$.

Depletion mode transistors are characterized by a negative threshold voltage. This is accomplished by adding sufficient donor impurities to the channel region to convert the p-type substrate to a slightly n-type material. Such a transistor will conduct (i.e., is turned on) for $V_{gs} = 0$, since a continuous n-channel is supplied during fabrication. In order to turn the transistor off, a negative gate voltage must be applied to repel the free electrons, effectively converting the channel region back to p-type material.

Fabrication

In Section 1.3 the general aspects of integrated circuit fabrication were discussed. The details of the deposition and diffusion steps, which actually create the electronic devices on the chip surface, were omitted because they vary considerably from one process to another. The following discussion will provide those details for a typical nMOS fabrication process.

The three-dimensional structure of a nMOS transistor is illustrated in Figure 2.31. Plan and elevation views of this structure are shown in Figure 2.32.

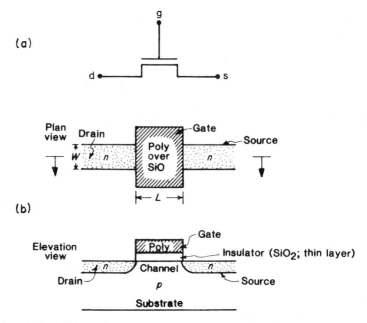

Figure 2.32   MOS transistor structure: (a) circuit symbol; (b) chip layout, plan view, and elevation view

The chip layout of an *n*MOS inverter is shown in Figure 2.33. The symbolic representation of the circuit (i.e., electronics level) is shown in Figure 2.33(a) and the plan view of the chip layout in Figure 2.33(b). The resistance of a turned-on transistor is determined by the length-to-width ratio of the channel, L/W. The pull-up resistance of an inverter must be about four times the pull-down resistance for proper operation (see Section 2.1). Power (V_{DD} and GND) is distributed on the metal level, because paths on this level have the least resistance. Signals may be routed on the metal level, or on the poly or *n*-diffusion levels. Signal A is shown coming in on the poly level, which simply becomes the gate of the pull-down transistor. Signal B goes out on the *n*-diffusion level, an extension of the drain of the pull-down transistor and the source of the pull-up.

Connections between levels are made by contact cuts, shown in the plan view by heavily shaded regions. V_{DD} is connected to the drain of the pull-up transistor and GND to the source of the pull-down transistor in this fashion. Also, the gate and source of the pull-up transistor are connected in this fashion. Since gate and source are not vertically adjacent, this cut is longer.

The masks that are used to produce this circuit are shown in Figure 2.33(c).

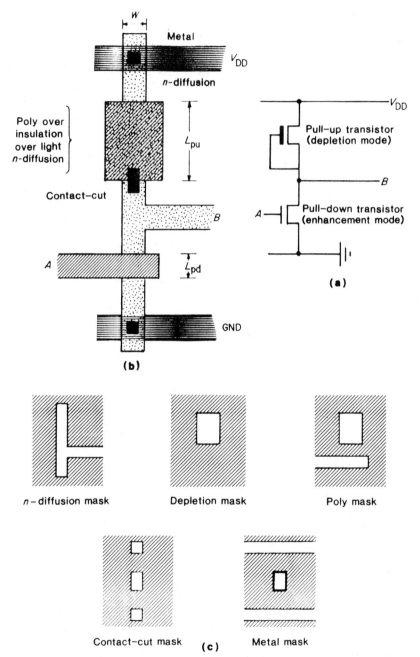

Figure 2.33   Chip layout of an nMOS inverter: (a) symbolic circuit; (b) plan view of chip area;
(c) masks

The fabrication sequence is as follows:

1. The n-diffusion mask is used to deposit a thick layer of SiO_2 where the mask is opaque (i.e., where n-diffusion is not to be located). This layer will separate signal paths on the poly level from the substrate.

2. The depletion mask is then used to diffuse donor impurities into the channel of depletion mode transistors. This is a lighter doping than the n-diffusion doping of step 6.

3. A very thin layer of SiO_2 is deposited over the entire surface.

4. The poly mask is used to deposit polysilicon in the desired areas. Poly areas that will be used for gates are separated from the substrate by the thin layer of SiO_2. Poly areas that serve as signal paths are separated by the thicker layer deposited in step 1.

5. The thin oxide layer is removed from all areas not covered by poly.

6. The n-diffusion mask is used to diffuse n-type impurities into the substrate. The previously deposited poly protects the gate areas from this diffusion. Hence n-diffusion areas result only where there is a mask opening *and* there is no poly.

7. A thick SiO_2 layer is deposited over the entire surface.

8. The contact-cut mask is used to remove the SiO_2 from those areas where contact between layers is required.

9. The metal mask is used to deposit metal on the surface.

The vertical structure of the MOS transistor is illustrated in the elevation views of Figure 2.34.

2.3.3 Parameter Values [26]

The *resolution* of an IC fabrication process is the accuracy of the process in creating the desired geometric patterns on a chip surface. Resolution is characterized by the maximum variation that can occur in the distance between two geometric features on the chip surface as a result of process inaccuracies. This distance is denoted λ.

For commercial processes in 1984, λ ranges from about 1 micron to several microns. Each process has its own set of geometric "design rules" that specify minimum acceptable dimensions for various features. Mead and Conway [26] give a typical set of nMOS design rules, abstracted from a number of processes with different λ values. The most important of these rules are shown in Figure 2.35. They may be used to estimate the chip area needed for specific

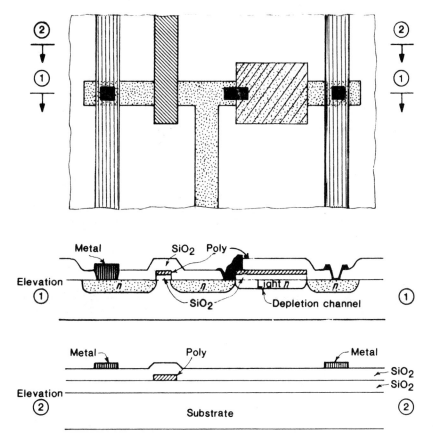

Figure 2.34   Plan and elevation views of inverter

microcircuits (assuming a particular process resolution) and also to estimate the values of electrical parameters.

Table 2.1 (also from Mead and Conway) specifies the resistances and capacitances of a typical nMOS process with $\lambda = 3$ microns. The resistance of poly paths varies considerably from one process to another, and thus is given as a range. The other numbers may be considered representative of a typical nMOS process with $\lambda = 3$ microns.

Resistance is specified in "ohms per square of surface area." The resistance of a path of length L and constant width W is the resistance per square times L/W. The thickness of the path and the resistivity are included in the "resistance per square" value.

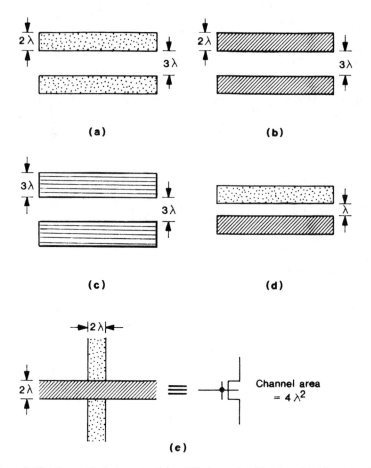

Figure 2.35   Geometric design rules: (a) n-diffusion paths; (b) poly paths; (c) metal paths; (d) parallel poly and n-diffusions paths; (e) minimum-size transistor

Capacitance is specified in picofarads per square micron of surface area. All capacitances are relative to the underlying substrate, except for the poly over thin oxide with $V_{gs} > V_{th}$. This capacitance is relative to the channel of the turned-on transistor.

The n-diffusion capacitance is a *pn* junction capacitance. The metal capacitance is similar to a junction capacitance since the charges in the substrate that produce the E field are uncovered impurity atoms in a depletion region. The insulation between the substrate and the metal serves to decrease the capacitance by increasing the distance through which the E field acts.

Three poly capacitances are specified. The poly over thin oxide values are for transistor gate regions. The poly over thick oxide value is for poly signal paths.

Table 2.1. Resistance and capacitance ($\lambda = 3$ μm)

Material	Resistance (ohms per square)	Capacitance (pF/μm^2)
Metal	0.03	$0.3 * 10^{-4}$
n-diffusion	10	$1 \quad * 10^{-4}$
Poly	15–100	$0.4 * 10^{-4}$ (over thick SiO$_2$) $0.8 * 10^{-4}$ (over thin SiO$_2$, $V_{gs} <$ V_{th}) $4 \quad * 10^{-4}$ (over thin SiO$_2$, $V_{gs} >$ V_{th})
Drain-source path of a turned-on transistor (i.e., channel)	10^4	$1 \quad * 10^{-4}$

The capacitances for poly over thick oxide and poly over thin oxide with $V_{gs} < V_{th}$ (i.e., turned-off transistor) are similar to the metal-to-substrate capacitance. The poly over thin oxide capacitance with $V_{gs} > V_{th}$ is quite different. This corresponds to a turned-on transistor, for which there is a channel of electrons immediately below the gate. The E field between the gate and the underlying substrate terminates in the channel. The capacitance is thus similar to parallel-plate capacitance. The E field acts only through the thin oxide layer rather than through a wide depletion layer. The capacitance is thus significantly larger than a junction capacitance to the lightly doped substrate.

The gate-to-source capacitance C_{gs} that must be charged and discharged in turning a transistor on and off varies with gate-to-source voltage and with drain-to-source voltage. To a first-order approximation, however, C_{gs} may be represented by the value for poly over thin oxide with $V_{gs} > V_{th}$.

The capacitance of the drain-source path of a turned-on transistor is a pn junction capacitance, since the channel is effectively an n-type semiconductor. The value is about the same as n-diffusion capacitance.

To get a feeling for the operation of $\lambda = 3$ circuits (Table 2.1), let us consider two examples.

Example 1

A small inverter driving a nearby small inverter. The circuit is shown in Figure 2.36(a). A rough geometric layout of the circuit is shown in Figure 2.36(b). The total n-diffusion area (including the channel) driven by the first inverter is $20\lambda * 2\lambda = 40\lambda^2$. The total poly over thick SiO$_2$ area is $10\lambda * 2\lambda = 20\lambda^2$. The poly gate area is $2\lambda * 2\lambda = 4\lambda^2$. Hence the total capacitance driven

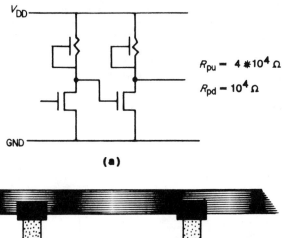

(a)

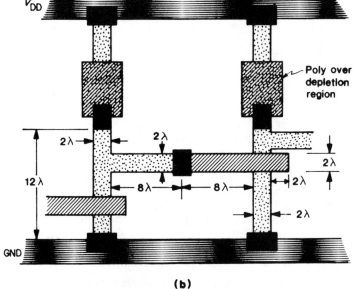

(b)

Figure 2.36   Example 1: (a) circuit diagram; (b) geometric layout

by the inverter is $C = 40\lambda^2 * 10^{-4} + 20\lambda^2 * 0.4 * 10^{-4} + 4\lambda^2 * 4 * 10^{-4} =$
0.0576 pF. The signal path resistances are negligible relative to R_{pu} and R_{pd}.
The propagation delay for a low-to-high-output transition is thus $R_{pu}C = 40$
$* 0.0576 = 2.3$ ns.

The static power dissipation when the output is low is $v \cdot i = V_{DD} * V_{DD}/$
$(R_{pu} + R_{pd}) = 0.5$ milliwatts.

The dynamic power dissipation, assuming a frequency of 1 MHz, is CV^2f
$= 0.0576 * 10^{-12} * 4^2 * 10^6 = 0.92 * 10^{-3}$ milliwatts.

Example 2

A minimum-size NOR gate with 100 inputs, as illustrated in Figure 2.37. The total metal area of the pull-down circuit is $1000\lambda * 3\lambda = 3000\lambda^2$. This area plus the drain area of each transistor $(200\lambda * 2\lambda = 400\lambda^2)$ must charge and discharge between H and L. The total capacitance is $C = 27,000 * 0.3 * 10^{-4} + 3600 * 10^{-4} = 1.17$ pF. (We are ignoring ground path capacitance since the voltage swings are much less.)

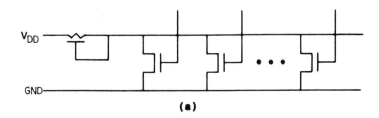

(a)

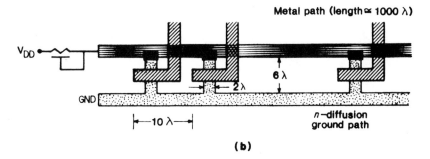

(b)

Figure 2.37 Example 2: (a) circuit diagram; (b) geometric layout of pull-down circuit

The resistance of the metal path is $(1000\lambda/3\lambda) * 0.03 \cong 9$ ohms, which is negligible relative to R_{pu} or R_{pd}. The propagation delay for a low-to-high transition is approximately $R_{pu} * C = 40 * 1.17 = 46.8$ ns.

The static power dissipation is about 0.5 milliwatts, as for Example 1.

The dynamic power dissipation, assuming a 1-MHz frequency, is $CV^2f = 1.17 * 10^{-12} * 4^2 * 10^6 \cong 0.02$ milliwatts.

2.3.4 Exercises

1. The n-diffusion mask defines paths that are continuous through the gate regions of transistors, and yet there is no n-diffusion desired in the gate regions (i.e., where a poly path crosses an n-diffusion path).

(a) How does the fabrication sequence accomplish this selective n-diffusion?

Consider an alternative nMOS process in which the n-diffusion mask is opaque in all desired gate regions.

(b) Describe the fabrication sequence that would then be used.

(c) Compare with the fabrication sequence described in the text.

2. The SiO_2 layer between the poly and the substrate is not of uniform thickness across the chip.

(a) Where is it thick and where is it thin?

(b) Why is this varying thickness desirable?

(c) Describe how the fabrication process accomplishes this variation.

3. Draw the set of masks for the nMOS fabrication of the NAND gate of Figure 2.19

4. Using the design rules of Figure 2.35, sketch the geometric layout of the circuit of Exercise 11 in Section 2.2.

Chapter 3

LOGIC DESIGN: COMBINATIONAL NETWORKS

3.1 **Switching Functions**
3.2 **Gate Networks**
3.3 **Switch Networks**
3.4 **Elementary Word Operations**

The logic design level is concerned with the design of two types of networks: *combinational networks*, represented by static models, and *sequential networks*, represented by dynamic models. The fundamentals of combinational network design are presented in this chapter. Sequential network design is discussed in Section 5.5.

Two types of combinational networks are discussed in this chapter: gate networks, which are constructed from logic gates, and switch networks, which are constructed from switches (e.g., transistor switches). Both types are represented by the same sort of mathematical model, based upon a particular type of function called a *switching function*. The chapter begins with a discussion of switching functions.

Notation

The set consisting of two elements, 0 and 1, will be denoted $\mathbf{B}$. That is, $\mathbf{B} = \{0, 1\}$. $\mathbf{B}^n$ will denote the set of binary words of length n. For example, $\mathbf{B}^3 = \{000, 001, 010, 011, 100, 101, 110, 111\}$. The notation $f: \mathbf{X} \to \mathbf{Y}$ is shorthand for "f is a function that maps the set $\mathbf{X}$ into the set $\mathbf{Y}$." That is, for any element x in the set $\mathbf{X}$, the value of the function $f(x)$ is a unique element in the set $\mathbf{Y}$.

If we do not wish to name a function, but simply specify the input and output sets, we might say "a function $\mathbf{X} \to \mathbf{Y}$".

The abbreviation "iff" will be used for the phrase "if and only if."

3.1 SWITCHING FUNCTIONS [12, 13, 30-34]

3.1.1 Specification of Switching Functions
3.1.2 Properties of Logic Operations
3.1.3 Exercises

A combinational network is a system with binary input variables and binary output variables such that the value of the output variables at any time of interest is a function only of the input variables at that time. Hence, a combinational network with n inputs and m outputs may be represented by a function $f: \mathbf{B}^n \to \mathbf{B}^m$. Such a function is called a *switching function*.

The inputs to a combinational network may be n individual binary variables, or n bits of a single binary word variable, or any collection of bit and word variables. The "input word" (i.e., the element of $\mathbf{B}^n$) is formed by concatenating the individual input bits and words. The same comments apply to the output word.

Most of the discussion in this chapter assumes $m = 1$ for simplicity (i.e., a single-bit output variable). The extension to multiple-bit output words is considered in Sections 3.2.3 and 3.4.

3.1.1 Specification of Switching Functions

Truth Tables

Since the set $\mathbf{B}^n$ is finite (it has 2^n elements), it is possible to specify (i.e., define) a switching function simply by listing in a table the value of the output word for each value of the input word. Such a table is called a *truth table*. This term originated with the mathematical study of correct reasoning, involving statements that have two possible "values": true (1) or false (0). The subject is called mathematical logic, and from it also comes the name for the subject that we are discussing, logic design.

In Table 3.1 are shown truth tables for four different switching functions. The first is an arbitrary switching function with three inputs and two outputs. The next three are well-known functions from mathematical logic. The AND function has output value 1 iff both inputs have value 1; that is, the statement "A and B" is true iff the statements A and B are both true. Similarly, "A OR B" is true iff either A is true or B is true, or both A and B are true. Finally, "NOT A" is true iff A is false.

These functions are called logic operations, and the "operation symbols" $\cdot$, $+$, and $\neg$ (or $\overline{}$) are used to represent them, as shown in the table. These

TABLE 3.1. Truth tables

(a) A three-input, two-output switching function

Inputs			Outputs	
A	B	C	D	E
0	0	0	0	1
0	0	1	1	1
0	1	0	1	0
0	1	1	1	1
1	0	0	0	0
1	0	1	1	0
1	1	0	0	0
1	1	1	1	1

(c) The OR operation

A	B	$A + B$
0	0	0
0	1	1
1	0	1
1	1	1

(d) The NOT operation

A	$\bar{A}$ or $\neg A$
0	1
1	0

(b) The AND operation

A	B	$A \cdot B$
0	0	0
0	1	0
1	0	0
1	1	1

logic operations play a central role in combinational network design, as we shall see.

The operator symbol for the OR operation is the same as the standard symbol for numerical addition. We will depend upon the context to indicate the correct interpretation. We will avoid this sort of ambiguity with the AND operation by using "$*$" to denote numerical multiplication.

Common alternative names for the NOT operation are INVERT and COMPLEMENT.

The most important thing to understand about a truth table is this: *a truth table completely and uniquely defines a switching function.*

Formulas

Another way to define a switching function is by providing a formula or expression that specifies how to compute the value of the function by operating on the function variables using the basic logic operations AND, OR, and NOT. For example,

$$F(A, B, C) = (A \cdot C) + ((A \cdot B) + (B \cdot \bar{A}))$$

defines a switching function F of three variables A, B, and C. Notice that parentheses are used to uniquely define the order in which the specified operations are to be carried out, just as with arithmetic expressions. The number of parentheses required in such expressions can be reduced if an *operator precedence* convention is adopted. The standard convention is that when the order of applying two operations is not specified by parentheses, then AND takes precedence over OR, and NOT takes precedence over both AND and OR.[1] We will use this convention. Hence, the expression defining F may be simplified:

$$F(A, B, C) = A \cdot C + (A \cdot B + B \cdot \bar{A})$$

The truth table for the function F may be constructed by evaluating this expression for each combination of input variables. This is done in Table 3.2. Intermediate variables V, W, X, Y, and Z are defined for simplicity.

TABLE 3.2. Truth table for $F(A, B, C) = A \cdot C + (A \cdot B + B \cdot \bar{A})$

A	B	C	$V =$ $A \cdot C$	$W =$ $A \cdot B$	$X =$ $\bar{A}$	$Y =$ $B \cdot X$	$Z =$ $W + Y$	$F =$ $V + Z$
0	0	0	0	0	1	0	0	0
0	0	1	0	0	1	0	0	0
0	1	0	0	0	1	1	1	1
0	1	1	0	0	1	1	1	1
1	0	0	0	0	0	0	0	0
1	0	1	1	0	0	0	0	1
1	1	0	0	1	0	0	1	1
1	1	1	1	1	0	0	1	1

[1] This applies when NOT is represented by $\neg$. When NOT is represented by $\bar{}$, the length of the bar indicates what is to be complemented. Hence $\bar{A} + B = \neg A + B$ while $\overline{A + B} = \neg(A + B)$.

TABLE 3.3. Truth table for $B + (A \cdot \bar{B}) \cdot C$

A	B	C	$\bar{B}$	$A \cdot \bar{B}$	$(A \cdot \bar{B}) \cdot C$	$B + (A \cdot \bar{B}) \cdot C$
0	0	0	1	0	0	0
0	0	1	1	0	0	0
0	1	0	0	0	0	1
0	1	1	0	0	0	1
1	0	0	1	1	0	0
1	0	1	1	1	1	1
1	1	0	0	0	0	1
1	1	1	0	0	0	1

It is possible that two different expressions may define the same switching function. Consider, for example, the expression $B + (A \cdot \bar{B}) \cdot C$. The truth table for this expression is developed in Table 3.3. Comparing Tables 3.2 and 3.3, notice that the expressions $A \cdot C + (A \cdot B + B \cdot \bar{A})$ and $B + (A \cdot \bar{B}) \cdot C$ do indeed define the same switching function. That is, for any values of the variables A, B, and C,

$$A \cdot C + (A \cdot B + B \cdot \bar{A}) = B + (A \cdot \bar{B}) \cdot C$$

In general, we will say that two expressions are equal if and only if they define the same switching function; that is, they specify the same value for any values of the variables involved in the expressions.

3.1.2 Properties of Logic Operations

Several important properties of the OR and AND operations are stated below. Each of these may be verified using truth tables.

$A \cdot (B \cdot C) = (A \cdot B) \cdot C$	($\cdot$ is associative)	(3.1)
$A + (B + C) = (A + B) + C$	($+$ is associative)	(3.2)
$A \cdot B = B \cdot A$	($\cdot$ is commutative)	(3.3)
$A + B = B + A$	($+$ is commutative)	(3.4)
$A \cdot (B + C) = A \cdot B + A \cdot C$	($\cdot$ is distributive over $+$)	(3.5)
$A + (B \cdot C) = (A + B) \cdot (A + C)$	($+$ is distributive over $\cdot$)	(3.6)

$$A \cdot A = A \tag{3.7}$$

$$A + A = A \tag{3.8}$$

$$A \cdot 1 = A \tag{3.9}$$

$$A + 1 = 1 \tag{3.10}$$

$$A \cdot 0 = 0 \tag{3.11}$$

$$A + 0 = A \tag{3.12}$$

$$A \cdot \bar{A} = 0 \tag{3.13}$$

$$A + \bar{A} = 1 \tag{3.14}$$

$$\overline{A \cdot B} = \bar{A} + \bar{B} \tag{3.15}$$

De Morgan's theorems

$$\overline{A + B} = \bar{A} \cdot \bar{B} \tag{3.16}$$

$$A \cdot (A + B) = A \tag{3.17}$$

$$A + A \cdot B = A \tag{3.18}$$

$$A \cdot (\bar{A} + B) = A \cdot B \tag{3.19}$$

$$A + \bar{A} \cdot B = A + B \tag{3.20}$$

$$\bar{\bar{A}} = A \tag{3.21}$$

Since AND and OR are associative (properties 3.1 and 3.2) it is not necessary to specify the order in which a sequence of AND's or a sequence of OR's is to be carried out. Hence we can omit parentheses in such situations and simply write, for example, $A \cdot B \cdot C$ to mean either $(A \cdot B) \cdot C$ or $A \cdot (B \cdot C)$; or we can write $A + B + C$ for either $(A + B) + C$ or $A + (B + C)$. In fact, it is easy to see that

$$A_1 \cdot A_2 \cdot \ \cdots \ \cdot A_n = 1 \quad \text{iff} \quad A_i = 1 \quad \text{for all } i, \quad 1 \le i \le n \tag{3.22}$$

and

$$A_1 + A_2 + \cdots + A_n = 1 \quad \text{iff} \quad A_i = 1 \quad \text{for some } i, \quad 1 \le i \le n \tag{3.23}$$

When confronted with two expressions, there are two general ways to determine whether the expressions are equal. The most straightforward way is simply to construct the truth table for both expressions. If the switching functions specified by both expressions (as indicated by the truth tables) are the same, then the expressions are equal. Otherwise, they are not. In some cases, however, it may be quicker to manipulate one or both of the expressions by substituting known equivalent expressions for subexpressions within the given expression(s). The list of equivalences 3.1–3.21 is useful for this purpose. For example, consider the expressions $A \cdot B \cdot (\bar{C} + D)$ and $A \cdot \bar{B} + A \cdot C \cdot \bar{D}$. We will show that these expressions are equal by manipulating the first expression. Each step in the manipulation will use one of the properties 3.1–3.21, as indicated on the right.

$$\overline{A \cdot B \cdot (\overline{C} + D)} = A \cdot (\overline{B} + \overline{(\overline{C} + D)}) \quad \text{using} \qquad 3.15$$

$$= A \cdot (\overline{B} + \overline{\overline{C}} \cdot \overline{D}) \qquad \text{using} \qquad 3.16$$

$$= A \cdot (\overline{B} + C \cdot \overline{D}) \qquad \text{using} \qquad 3.21$$

$$= A \cdot \overline{B} + A \cdot C \cdot \overline{D} \qquad \text{using} \qquad 3.5$$

Formulas for specifying switching functions are called *Boolean* formulas or expressions, after the mathematician George Boole. The mathematical theory of Boolean expressions is called Boolean algebra. Boolean algebra has much in common with the familiar algebra of numbers. For example, properties 3.1–3.5 correspond exactly to properties of numerical algebra, with " + " and " · " representing addition and multiplication, respectively. These similarities facilitate algebraic manipulations such as the one performed above.

There are also differences, however, between numerical and Boolean algebra. For example, property 3.6 is *not* true for numerical algebra—numerical addition does not distribute over numerical multiplication [e.g., $5 + (2 \cdot 3) \neq (5 + 2) \cdot (5 + 3)$]. When manipulating Boolean expressions, a special effort should be made to recognize opportunities to apply these unfamiliar properties of Boolean algebra.

Not all of the properties 3.1–3.23 are independent axioms. Some properties can be derived from others. For example, property 3.19 is easily derived from 3.5, 3.12, and 3.13, as follows.

$$A \cdot (\overline{A} + B) = A \cdot \overline{A} + A \cdot B$$

$$= 0 + A \cdot B$$

$$= A \cdot B$$

Another mathematician, E. V. Huntington, identified a set of seven axioms from which all the properties of Boolean algebra can be derived (Huntington's postulates). Other sets of axioms were subsequently proposed by others. We will not study the axiomatic theory of Boolean algebra.

3.1.3 Exercises

1. Prove De Morgan's theorems (equations 3.15 and 3.16). Interpreting A and B as "statement variables" that may be either true (1) or false (0), formulate a prose statement of each of these theorems.

2. Prove the distributive properties (equations 3.5 and 3.6). Provide "statement logic" interpretations of these, as in Exercise 1.

3. Provide generalized versions of De Morgan's theorems:

$$\overline{A_1 + A_2 + \cdots + A_n} =$$

$$\overline{A_1 \cdot A_2 \cdot \cdots \cdot A_n} =$$

Prove your generalizations for three variables. Use mathematical induction to prove each for any n.

4. Is the operation $\odot$ defined below associative? Prove your answer.

A	B	$A \odot B$
0	0	0
0	1	0
1	0	1
1	1	0

5. State and prove whether each of the following is true or not.

(a) $(A \cdot B) + (A \cdot \bar{B}) = A$
(b) $(A \cdot \bar{B} + \bar{A} \cdot B) \cdot C = (A \cdot C + B \cdot C) \cdot \overline{(A \cdot B)}$
(c) $\bar{A} \cdot (\bar{B} + C) = A \cdot (B + C) + B \cdot (A + \bar{C})$

6. Which of the properties of Boolean algebra (3.1–3.23) are also properties of numerical algebra?

7. Derive properties 3.17, 3.18, and 3.20 using other given properties, by algebraic manipulation.

3.2   GATE NETWORKS [24, 30–36]

3.2.1   Logic Gates
3.2.2   Gate Interconnections
3.2.3   Optimal Design
3.2.4   Exercises

In this section, systematic techniques are presented for designing gate networks to implement switching functions.

3.2.1 Logic Gates

The inputs and outputs of logic gates are voltages. A high voltage usually represents logic 1, and a low voltage logic 0. The manner in which voltage ranges are selected to represent logic 0 and logic 1 is discussed in Section 5.1. Until then it is sufficient to understand that it is possible to construct gates that reliably implement the basic logic operations, and that these gates may be interconnected to implement any switching functions.

In Chapter 2, nMOS gates to implement the operations INVERT, NAND, and NOR were presented. These are the easiest operations to implement in nMOS circuits and most other circuit types as well. Standard symbols to represent these gates, together with equations defining their operation, are presented in Figure 3.1. In words, the operation of the NAND gate may be described as follows: the output is 0 (i.e., low voltage) if all inputs are 1 (high voltage). Similarly, the output of a NOR gate is 1 (high) if all inputs are 0 (low).

Also shown in the figure are the symbols for AND and OR gates. Notice the similarity in the gate symbols for NAND and AND and for NOR and OR. The

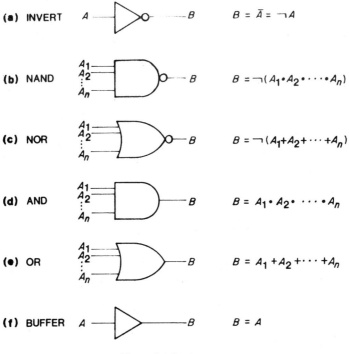

Figure 3.1 Logic gates

only difference is the small circle at the output. This small circle may be thought of as representing inversion.

The last gate in the figure, called a buffer, implements the identity function. Buffers are used in logic circuits for electrical reasons (e.g., to shift from one voltage range to another when transferring signals from one type of logic circuit to another type; to provide additional current drive capability).

An AND gate may be implemented as a NAND gate followed by an inverter, and an OR gate as a NOR followed by an inverter. AND and OR gates are thus slower and more expensive than NAND and NOR gates. For this reason it is usually desirable to design circuits directly using NAND and NOR gates rather than AND and OR gates. However, the AND and OR operations are more convenient and natural to use than NAND and NOR. We will first consider design techniques based upon the AND and OR operations, and then show how these techniques may be converted for use with NAND and NOR gates.

3.2.2 Gate Interconnections

Gate networks are constructed by connecting the outputs of some gates to the inputs of other gates. Figure 3.2 shows a gate network that generates an output variable D as a function of input variables A, B, and C. This network can be directly represented by a logic equation, as shown in the figure. The value of output D for any values of A, B, and C is given by the equation.

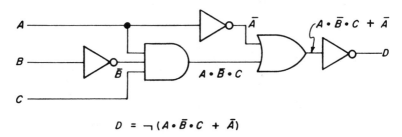

$$D = \neg (A \cdot \bar{B} \cdot C + \bar{A})$$

Figure 3.2 A logic expression and corresponding gate network

Conversely, given a logic equation such as the one in Figure 3.2, it is possible to directly construct a gate network that implements the switching function represented by the equation. When a switching function is specified by an equation, this is the most straightforward implementation technique, although it may not be the best.

A switching function may alternatively be specified by a truth table. It is possible to construct a "sum of minterms" equation directly from the truth table. A gate network can then be constructed directly from this equation.

A *minterm* for variables A_1, A_2, $\ldots$, A_n is a product, $L_1 \cdot L_2 \cdot \cdots \cdot L_n$, where for each i, $L_i = A_i$ or $L_i = \bar{A}_i$. That is, a minterm is a product in which each input variable appears exactly once, either complemented or uncomplemented. There are exactly 2^n minterms associated with n input variables, and each minterm has value 1 for exactly one combination of values for these variables. The eight minterms for variables A, B, and C are shown in Table 3.4. Each minterm is shown opposite the unique combination of input values for which the minterm has value 1. It is obvious that any switching function may be represented as a sum of minterms, as illustrated in Figure 3.3.

The sum of minterms implementation of a switching function is in general not the least costly implementation. The direct implementation of a switching function from an equation likewise may be more costly than necessary and/or slower than necessary. Optimal design techniques are discussed in the next section.

Before finishing our discussion of gate interconnections, however, we should consider the type of interconnection illustrated in Figure 3.4. In this network, the output Q serves as an input to the gate network that generates Q. This is called a *feedback interconnection*.

Notice that the logic equation that represents the network specifies the output Q as a function of Q itself. Given values for the network inputs (S and R in this case), such an equation may have a unique solution, or it may have no solution, or it may have multiple solutions.

Compare this with the equation for a gate network with no feedback, such as in Figure 3.2. In this case, the equation has a unique solution for any given input values. That is, the value of the output is determined uniquely by the value of the inputs. This is the defining characteristic of a "combinational network" (or, in a more general context, a "static system").

TABLE 3.4. Minterms for A, B, C

A	B	C	Minterms
0	0	0	$\bar{A} \cdot \bar{B} \cdot \bar{C}$
0	0	1	$\bar{A} \cdot \bar{B} \cdot C$
0	1	0	$\bar{A} \cdot B \cdot \bar{C}$
0	1	1	$\bar{A} \cdot B \cdot C$
1	0	0	$A \cdot \bar{B} \cdot \bar{C}$
1	0	1	$A \cdot \bar{B} \cdot C$
1	1	0	$A \cdot B \cdot \bar{C}$
1	1	1	$A \cdot B \cdot C$

A	B	C	D
0	0	0	0
0	0	1	1
0	1	0	0
0	1	1	0
1	0	0	1
1	0	1	0
1	1	0	1
1	1	1	0

$$D = \bar{A} \cdot \bar{B} \cdot C + A \cdot \bar{B} \cdot \bar{C} + A \cdot B \cdot \bar{C}$$

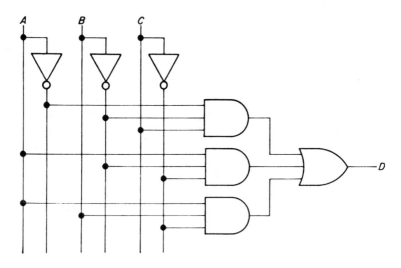

Figure 3.3   Sum of minterms implementation

A gate network with feedback is called an *asynchronous sequential network* (ASN) [35]. Such networks will not be studied in this chapter. They are not combinational networks. They will be encountered again in Sections 5.3 and 5.4. When the defining equation of an ASN has multiple solutions, the circuit can serve as a memory device (e.g., bistable circuits, Section 5.4); when the equation has no solution, the circuit may serve as an oscillator (e.g., a clock, Section 5.3).

It is possible to use ASNs as control units for computers, but synchronous sequential networks (SSNs) are usually used instead. SSNs are easier to design and, in general, more reliable. ASNs, however, have a potential speed advantage, and they may be more widely used in the future. The general theory of ASN design is not covered in this text.

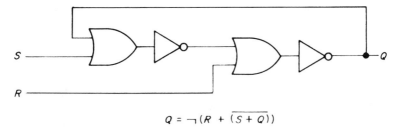

$$Q = \neg (R + \overline{(S + Q)})$$

Figure 3.4   Gate network with feedback

3.2.3   Optimal Design

We have shown that any switching function can be represented by a sum of minterms expression, which can be converted directly into a gate network. We have seen, however, that more than one expression might represent the same switching function. Each such expression corresponds to a gate network that implements the function. The question arises: How does one find the "best" gate network implementation for a switching function? The answer to this question will depend upon what is meant by best. Two criteria that are frequently important in evaluating digital systems of any kind are speed and cost. Speed for a combinational network is simply the inverse of the time required for an input change to propagate through the network. For ideal gates, changes are propagated from input to output instantaneously. For real gates, there is a finite *propagation delay* associated with each gate. The speed of a gate network is inversely proportional to the number of *gate levels* of the network—that is, the maximum number of gates that a signal must pass through from any input to any output. For the network of Figure 3.3, there are three gate levels. The network of Figure 3.2 has four levels. In addition, if the signal paths connecting the gates are long, then the propagation delay along these paths may be nonnegligible.

The criterion of cost is somewhat more complex. In addition to the cost associated with the components themselves (i.e., gates and signal paths to connect them) there is the cost of actually making the connections.

A comprehensive optimal design procedure for gate networks would allow the establishment of an optimality criterion that involves a weighted combination of various speed and cost factors that could be adjusted to suit the situation at hand. Such a general procedure does not exist. The basic design procedures of classical combinational network theory use the following criterion: *an optimal gate network implementation of a switching function is one that has at most three gate levels, and, within this constraint, has the fewest number of gates, and finally, within both of these constraints, has the fewest gate inputs.* The restriction to three gate levels allows one level to generate the complements of all inputs. If all inputs are available in both complemented and uncomplemented form, then the maximum number of gate levels in the criterion becomes two instead of three. We have already shown that there always exists at least one 2-level (3 with invert) gate network to implement any switching function, namely the sum of minterms network. It follows that there always exists an optimal network according to the classical criterion, although the optimal network may not be unique. It should be noted that this discussion is based on the assumption that AND gates and OR gates are available with any number of inputs. If this is not the case, then there may not exist a 2-level network to implement some switching networks. It should also be noted that, although the emphasis in this criterion may seem to be on cost (in fact, the optimization procedure is normally referred to as *gate minimization*), nevertheless the major emphasis is on speed, since only networks of three levels or less are considered. It is generally possible to find implementations with fewer gates if more than three gate levels are allowed. This is emphatically the case for functions of many variables, as we shall see. In fact, the classical optimization techniques are practical only for small networks, if applied directly. They can be extended to larger networks by decomposing a large switching function into smaller functions, and applying the minimization techniques to the smaller functions. We shall see examples of this procedure in Chapters 4 and 5.

AND-OR Design

Let us proceed now to describe the classical optimization algorithm. The algorithm is based upon the fact that a single product term can "cover" more than one minterm. For example, in the network of Figure 3.3, the minterms $A \cdot \bar{B} \cdot \bar{C}$ and $A \cdot B \cdot \bar{C}$ can be covered by the single product term $A \cdot \bar{C}$, that is,

$$A \cdot \bar{B} \cdot \bar{C} + A \cdot B \cdot \bar{C} = A \cdot \bar{C} \cdot \bar{B} + A \cdot \bar{C} \cdot B$$
$$= A \cdot \bar{C} \cdot (\bar{B} + B)$$
$$= A \cdot \bar{C} \cdot 1$$
$$= A \cdot \bar{C}$$

Hence, $D = \bar{A} \cdot \bar{B} \cdot C + A \cdot \bar{C}$. This, in fact, is an optimal expression.

The optimization algorithm simply involves identifying a minimial set of product terms that exactly covers the minterms of the switching function. The most useful implementation of the algorithm for small networks involves representing the switching function in a special table called a *Karnaugh map*, or simply a *K-map*. A Karnaugh map for *n* variables is a table containing 2^n squares, one square for each possible combination of values for the variables, and hence one square for each minterm. The table is arranged in such a way that physical adjacency of squares in the table corresponds to *logical adjacency* of the associated minterms. Two minterms are logically adjacent if and only if they differ only in one term: $A \cdot B \cdot \bar{C}$ and $A \cdot \bar{B} \cdot \bar{C}$ are logically adjacent, while $A \cdot \bar{B} \cdot C$ and $\bar{A} \cdot B \cdot C$ are not. A Karnaugh map for three variables, A, B, and C, is shown in Figure 3.5. The minterm associated with each square of the map is shown by writing it into the square. We are interested in logical adjacency because any two minterms that are logically adjacent can be exactly covered by a single product term consisting of all the "literals" that are common to both minterms. A *literal* is a binary variable, either complemented or uncomplemented. Associated with a variable A there are two literals, A and $\bar{A}$.

A	0	0	1	1
B	0	1	1	0
C				
0	$\bar{A}\bar{B}\bar{C}$	$\bar{A}B\bar{C}$	$AB\bar{C}$	$A\bar{B}\bar{C}$
1	$\bar{A}\bar{B}C$	$\bar{A}BC$	ABC	$A\bar{B}C$

Figure 3.5 A Three Variable K-map

The "physical adjacency of squares" also requires definition. Two squares are considered physically adjacent if they are horizontally adjacent or vertically adjacent; diagonal adjacency does not count. Furthermore, a square on the left edge of the K-map is considered physically adjacent to the square in the same row on the right side of the K-map. If one imagines the K-map formed into a cylinder by joining together the left edge and the right edge, then the concept of logical adjacency of minterms corresponds exactly to the concept of physical adjacency of squares on the K-map. That is, two minterms are logically adjacent if their corresponding squares are physically adjacent. In Figure 3.6, all pairs of adjacent minterms are shown for this K-map. For each pair, the single product term that covers that pair is given. Note that the literals that appear in this product term are all the literals that are the same for both minterms.

The concept of logical adjacency can be applied to any products, not just to minterms. In particular, it can be applied to the products of Figure 3.6 that cover adjacent minterms. It is easily seen that logical adjacency of these products corresponds to physical adjacency of the pairs of minterms on the K-map. Two such adjacent products can be covered by a single term, which

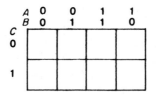

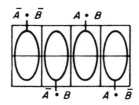

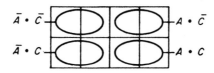

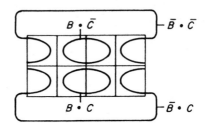

Figure 3.6   Pairs of adjacent minterms

hence covers four minterms. All groups of four minterms that can be covered by a single term are shown in Figure 3.7.

Using the K-map, one can quickly identify all product terms that exactly cover some group of minterms of a function to be implemented. It is a simple matter then to select the smallest set of such product terms that cover the function; this is an optimal implementation. Figure 3.8 shows the implemen-

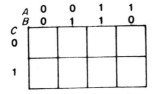

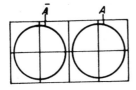

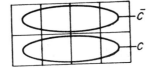

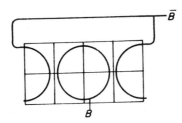

Figure 3.7 Pairs of adjacent pairs

tation of several functions, the first of which is the function of Figure 3.3. In the second example, $E(A, B, C)$, note that there is a third product that covers two minterms, $\bar{A} \cdot B$, but this product is not used in the final implementation. A good rule of thumb when selecting product terms is to cover first those minterms that can be covered by only one product term; these product terms *must* be present. In this example, $B \cdot \bar{C}$ must be present to cover $A \cdot B \cdot \bar{C}$, and $\bar{A} \cdot C$ must be present to cover $\bar{A} \cdot \bar{B} \cdot C$. Hence $\bar{A} \cdot B$ is not needed.

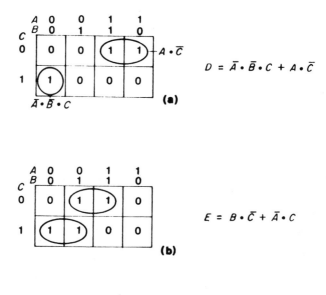

$$D = \bar{A} \cdot \bar{B} \cdot C + A \cdot \bar{C}$$

(a)

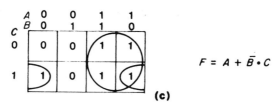

$$E = B \cdot \bar{C} + \bar{A} \cdot C$$

(b)

$$F = A + \bar{B} \cdot C$$

(c)

Figure 3.8   Minimization using K-maps

In the third example, $F(A, B, C)$, note that the minterm $A \cdot \bar{B} \cdot C$ is covered twice, once by A and once by $\bar{B} \cdot C$. We could have used $A \cdot \bar{B} \cdot C$ in place of $\bar{B} \cdot C$, and thus $A \cdot \bar{B} \cdot C$ would have been covered only once. But this would have required one additional gate input and the same number of gates as the given implementation. Since there is no harm in covering a minterm twice, the given implementation is better.

A K-map for four variables is shown in Figure 3.9. For this map, physical adjacency of squares corresponds exactly to logical adjacency of minterms, provided that physical adjacency of squares is interpreted to mean horizontal or vertical adjacency on the toroid (doughnut) formed from the K-map by joining the right edge to the left (forming a cylinder) and the top edge to the

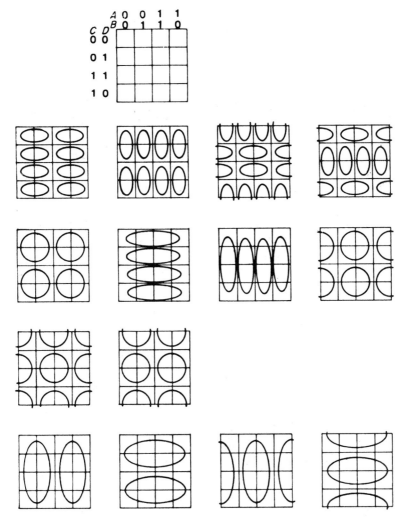

Figure 3.9   Four-variable K-map

bottom (forming the toroid). Also indicated in Figure 3.9 are all adjacent pairs of minterms. Each of these is covered exactly by a single product of three literals, but the products are not shown. Also indicated are the adjacent pairs of adjacent pairs (four-minterm groups), each covered by a product of two literals, and the adjacent pairs of these minterm groups (i.e., eight-minterm groups), each covered by a single literal.

In Figure 3.10 the four-variable K-map is used to implement three switching functions.

OR-AND Design

The design technique that we have been describing always leads to an expression of the same form, a sum of products. If the same technique is applied to

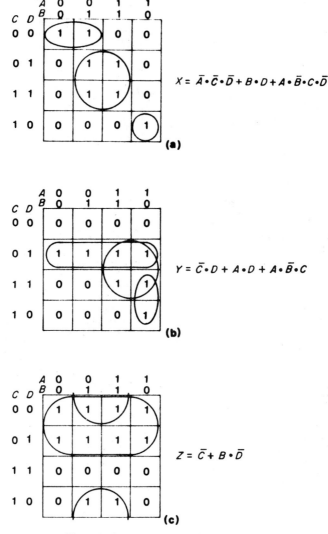

Figure 3.10   Four-variable minimization

the inverse of the function, and De Morgan's theorems are applied to the result, a product of sums expression is obtained. Both approaches result in a three-level gate network, and both must be considered in the search for an optimal implementation. In the example of Figure 3.11, a product of sums expression is optimal.

The design procedure described above can be extended to five- and six-variable functions, although five- and six-variable K-maps are somewhat

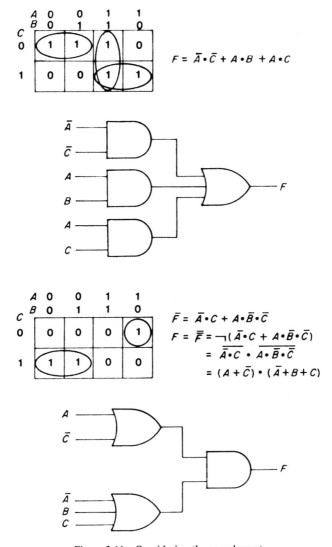

Figure 3.11   Considering the complement

more cumbersome. For more than six variables, there are tabular versions of this same algorithm. These techniques are somewhat tedious for hand calculation, but lend themselves readily to computer implementation [33].

NAND-NAND and NOR-NOR Design

An AND-OR network may be converted directly into a NAND-NAND network, and an OR-AND network into a NOR-NOR network. These conversions are most easily explained by using the "small circle convention" associated with logic gate symbols.

As noted previously, the small circle at the output of the NAND gate symbol or the NOR gate symbol may be thought of as an inverter. The NAND operation is equivalent to AND followed by INVERT; NOR is equivalent to OR followed by INVERT.

This convention may be extended to apply to gate inputs as well as to outputs, resulting in symbols to represent various nonstandard gates, and alternative symbols to represent standard gates. The small circle convention is illustrated in Figure 3.12. Notice in particular the alternative symbols for NOR and NAND gates.

The procedure for converting an AND-OR network into a NAND-NAND network is trivial: simply replace each AND gate, and also the OR gate, with a NAND gate (with one exception, noted below). The justification for this procedure is illustrated by the sequence of transformations in Figure 3.13. In step (a) the optimal AND-OR network is constructed. This is converted in (b) to an equivalent network by putting two inverters in series at each AND out-

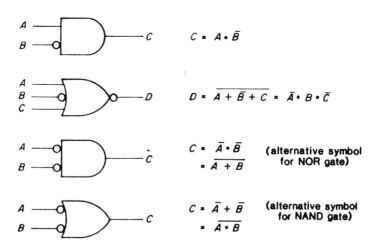

$$C = A \cdot \bar{B}$$

$$D = \overline{A + \bar{B} + C} = \bar{A} \cdot B \cdot \bar{C}$$

$$C = \bar{A} \cdot \bar{B} \qquad \text{(alternative symbol}$$
$$= \overline{A + B} \qquad \text{for NOR gate)}$$

$$C = \bar{A} + \bar{B} \qquad \text{(alternative symbol}$$
$$= \overline{A \cdot B} \qquad \text{for NAND gate)}$$

Figure 3.12   Small circle convention

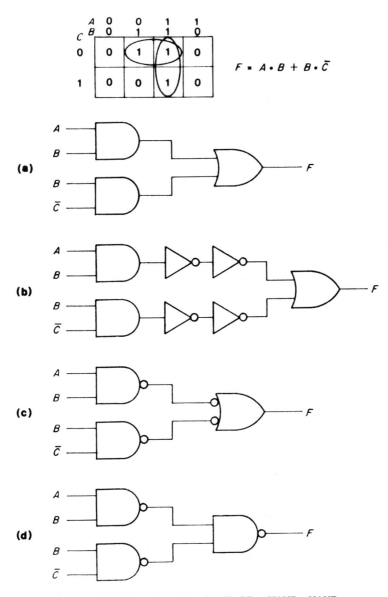

Figure 3.13 Transformation of AND-OR to NAND—NAND

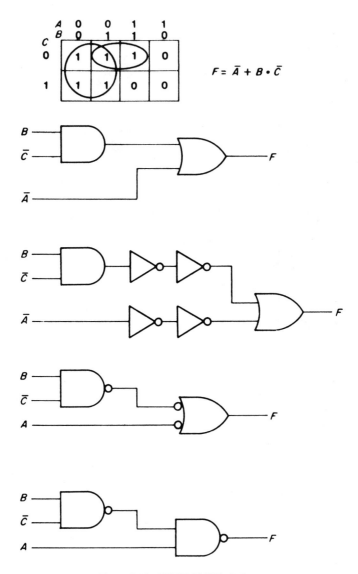

$$F = \bar{A} + B \cdot \bar{C}$$

Figure 3.14   NAND-NAND design

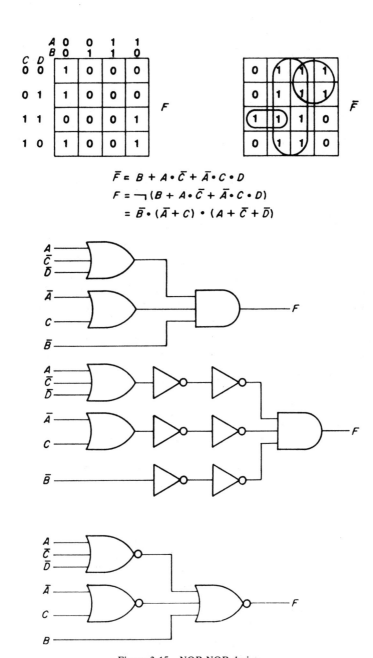

$$\bar{F} = B + A \cdot \bar{C} + \bar{A} \cdot C \cdot D$$
$$F = \neg (B + A \cdot \bar{C} + \bar{A} \cdot C \cdot D)$$
$$= \bar{B} \cdot (\bar{A} + C) \cdot (A + \bar{C} + \bar{D})$$

Figure 3.15 NOR-NOR design

put. In each case, the second inverter cancels the effect of the first, so that the OR input is unchanged (except for propagation delay). In step (c), inverters are replaced with small circles and associated with gate inputs and outputs. And in step (d), standard gate symbols replace the alternative symbols, using the equivalences of Figure 3.12.

This procedure always works, except when a network input serves directly as an OR gate input, without passing through an AND gate. The complement of that input must be used as the input to the final NAND in such a case. An example is given in Figure 3.14.

NOR-NOR design is similar. Begin with an optimal OR-AND network and replace each OR gate and the AND gate with a NOR gate, complementing any AND input that does not first pass through an OR gate. The procedure is illustrated in Figure 3.15.

Exclusive-OR Gates

The exclusive-OR operation, XOR, and the symbol for an XOR gate are defined in Figure 3.16(a). It is easy to prove that the two-input XOR operation is associative (i.e., $A \oplus (B \oplus C) = (A \oplus B) \oplus C$), which justifies the omission of parentheses in the notation $A_1 \oplus A_2 \oplus \cdots \oplus A_n$.

The XOR operation is not a "primitive" operation, like NAND or NOR, that can be easily implemented by an electronic circuit. It is more like the AND and OR operations, which are implemented by combining more primi-

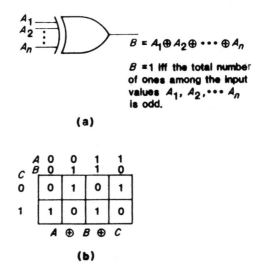

Figure 3.16   The XOR gate: (a) symbol and definition; (b) K-map for three-input XOR

tive gates (e.g., NAND is AND followed by INVERT). XOR, however, is much more difficult to implement than AND or OR. This is apparent from the K-map of the three-variable XOR operation in Figure 3.16(b). Since there are no logical adjacencies among the 1's, each 1 must be covered by a separate minterm.

It is clear from the "checkerboard" characteristic of the XOR K-map that the 2-level implementation of the n-variable XOR operation will be expensive. Because of the associativity of XOR, much cheaper (but slower) implementations of n-input XOR are possible using two-input XOR networks as components.

Any switching function of many variables will be expensive to implement as a 2-level network if it has the checkerboard characteristic over a large part of

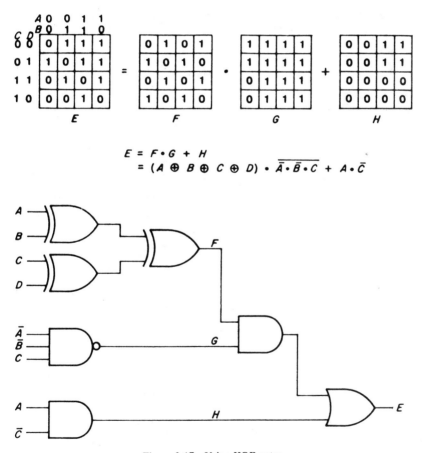

$$E = F \cdot G + H$$
$$= (A \oplus B \oplus C \oplus D) \cdot \overline{A} \cdot \overline{B} \cdot C + A \cdot \overline{C}$$

Figure 3.17   Using XOR gates

its K-map. Two-input XORs can be used as components in constructing a cheaper implementation with more gate levels. An example of the technique is given in Figure 3.17, though in this case the XOR implementation is actually more expensive. The function E is formed from the Exclusive-OR function F by: (1) forcing two 0's into the lower left corner of E by ANDing F with G and (2) forcing four 1's into the upper right corner of E by ORing H with $F \cdot G$.

Don't Care Conditions

It frequently happens that the value of a switching function to be implemented is irrelevant for certain values of the input word. These are commonly referred to as "don't care" values or "don't care conditions." When specifying a switching function, don't care values will be indicated by a small "x" (small "d" and "ϕ" are also sometimes used). A don't care value may be replaced by either 0 or 1 when implementing the function. The switching function F in Figure 3.18 has three don't care values, corresponding to input values $ABCD = 0011, 0101$, and 1011. If the don't care values corresponding to $ABCD = 0101$ and 1011 are made 1's and the remaining don't care is made 0, then the resulting function can be covered with two product terms as shown. The basic strategy is to choose values for the don't care that will allow the least costly implementation.

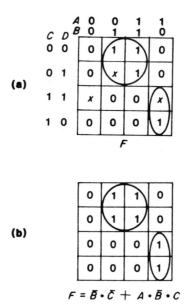

Figure 3.18   Don't care conditions: (a) specification of F with don't care values;
(b) possible implementation of F

Multiple-Output Minimization

Optimal 2-level implementation of multiple-output switching functions is essentially the same as for single-output functions, except that first-level terms (i.e., products for AND-OR, sums for OR-AND) may be shared among the various outputs to be generated.

An example is given in Figure 3.19. If functions E, F, and G are implemented separately, six product terms are required, as shown in Figure 3.19(a). If they are implemented together, sharing product terms whenever possible, only four product terms are required. Multiple-output minimization is important when using programmable logic arrays (PLAs), discussed in Section 5.2.

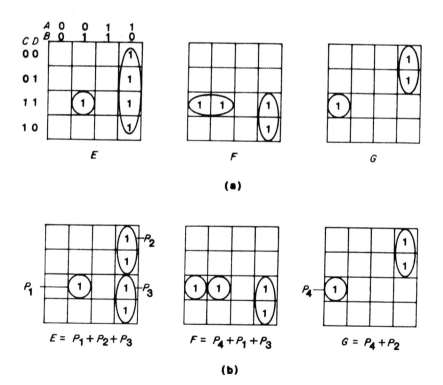

Figure 3.19   Multiple-output implementation: (a) separate; (b) combined

3.2.4 Exercises

1. For what value of inputs R and S does the equation of Figure 3.4 have more than one solution?

2. Implement the four-input AND operation using only two-input AND gates as components.

3. Repeat Exercise 2 for:

(a) OR gates
(b) NAND gates
(c) NOR gates

4. Are the NAND and NOR operations associative? Prove your answer.

5. Find an optimal NAND-NAND implementation of each of the functions in Figure 3.20 separately. (The arrangement of input variables on each K-map is the same.)

6. Repeat Exercise 5 for NOR-NOR.

7. Use two-input XOR gates to implement function M.

8. Find an optimal NAND-NAND implementation of the three functions G, H, and K together.

9. Repeat Exercise 8 for NOR-NOR.

10. Figure 3.15 illustrates the optimal NOR-NOR design technique. An alternative sequence of transformations is possible for NOR-NOR design, which involves starting with an optimal AND-OR implementation of $\overline{F}$ and then inserting an inverter at the OR output and double inverters at the AND inputs.

(a) Illustrate this technique using the function of Figure 3.15.

(b) In similar fashion, develop an alternative NAND-NAND design sequence that begins with an optimal OR-AND implementation of $\overline{F}$. Illustrate using the function F of Figure 3.14.

11. Prove that the two-input XOR operation is associative, that is, $A \oplus (B \oplus C) = (A \oplus B) \oplus C$.

12. Prove or disprove the following:

$$A \cdot (B \oplus C) = (A \cdot B) \oplus (A \cdot C)$$

That is, does AND distribute over $\oplus$?

13. How many gates will be required for a ⅔-level implementation of the n-variable XOR operation? Express your answer as a function of n. Assume gates with any number of inputs are available. Count an inverter as a gate. How many gate inputs are required?

14. Propose minimum-cost implementation of the n-input XOR operation using two-input XORs as components. How many gates are required? How many gate inputs? Count each XOR as five gates and eight gate inputs. Your design should be as fast as possible within the minimum-cost constraint (i.e.,

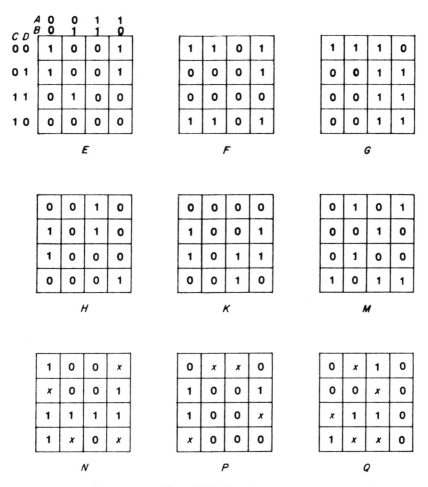

Figure 3.20 Exercises

minimize the number of gate levels). How many gate levels does your network have?

15. Figure 3.21 shows a standard seven-segment display. Each segment of the display is controlled by a binary signal (e.g., segment "a" is turned on when $A = 1$ and turned off when $A = 0$). The input signals (W, X, Y, Z) represent a decimal numeral (0, 1, 2, 3, 4, 5, 6, 7, 8, or 9) in base 2 code, with W the most significant bit and Z the least. The gate network generates the signals $(A, B, \cdots, G)$ so that the numeral represented by (W, X, Y, Z) is displayed. For example, if $WXYZ = 0010$ then $ABCDEFG = 1101101$. Design the gate network.

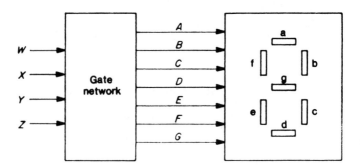

Figure 3.21   Seven-segment display

3.3   SWITCH NETWORKS [26, 30]

    3.3.1   **Formulas for Switch Networks**
    3.3.2   **Transistor Switches**
    3.3.3   **Tree Networks**
    3.3.4   **Pull-Down Networks**
    3.3.5   **Electrical Considerations**
    3.3.6   **Exercises**

A mechanical switch can be modeled by a binary variable: the value is 1 when the switch is closed and 0 when the switch is open. A network of switches connecting two points can be represented by a switching function of the variables that represent the switches. For a particular arrangement of switch positions, the value of the switching function is 1 iff there is a path (i.e., current can flow) from one point to the other through the switch network. This function is called the *transmission function* of the switch network.

    The transmission function of a switch network may be obtained directly by inspection. If there are n switches then there are 2^n possible arrangements of switch positions. For each of these, the network is simply examined for the existence of a path between the two terminals. An example is presented in Figure 3.22.

3.3.1   Formulas for Switch Networks

Another way to determine the transmission function of a switch network is to write a sum of products formula for the network. Each product represents one path through the network, and each path is represented by one product. For example, the formula for the network of Figure 3.22 is $A \cdot B + A \cdot C$. This

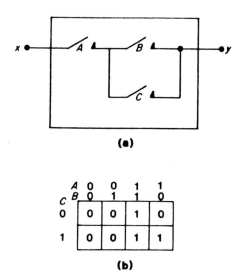

(a)

(b)

Figure 3.22   A switch network: (a) switch network; (b) transmission function

formula exactly represents the following statement: "there is a path (i.e., current can flow) from x to y through the network iff either A is closed and B is closed or A is closed and C is closed."

Another example is shown in Figure 3.23. An interesting aspect of this example is that current may flow in either direction through switch C to establish a current from x to y. This "bilateral" characteristic of switches can be used to advantage in constructing switch networks, but can also be a subtle source of errors. Note that because of the bilateral nature of switches, there is no "direction" associated with a switch network. By contrast, there *is* a direction associated with a combinational network constructed from logic gates:

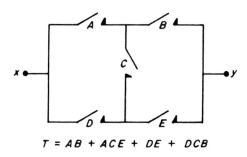

$$T = AB + ACE + DE + DCB$$

Figure 3.23   Transmission function formula

there are input terminals and output terminals, and information can flow only from input to output.

3.3.2 Transistor Switches

An MOS transistor is essentially a switch. The switch is controlled by the gate voltage. When the gate voltage is high the switch is closed and current can flow from drain to source. Either terminal may serve as drain or source; the device is symmetrical and hence bilateral. When the gate voltage is low the switch is open and current cannot flow through the transistor between drain and source.

The equivalence of the MOS transistor to the mechanical switch that we have been discussing is illustrated in Figure 3.24. The gate voltage of the transistor is represented as a binary variable A. When modeled as a switch it is this variable that represents the switch: when $A = 1$ the switch is closed; when $A = 0$ the switch is open.

Figure 3.24   The MOS transistor as a switch

Bipolar transistors are geometrically asymmetrical and hence are not bilateral. Parts of this discussion of switch networks do apply to bipolar as well as MOS transistor switches, but we will consider only nMOS transistors directly.

The major shortcoming of the MOS transistor used as a switch is the relatively high ON resistance. Ideally the resistance of a closed switch is zero, but the ON resistance of an MOS transistor may be several thousand ohms. This resistance limits the number of MOS transistor switches that can be connected in series (i.e., in the same path).

When used as a switch between an input signal and an output signal, an MOS transistor is frequently referred to as a *pass transistor* or a *transmission gate*.

3.3.3 Tree Networks

In some situations the use of switches in designing a combinational network is suggested by the specification of the network. Consider the network of Figure 3.25 for example. The output D is to be connected to A or B depending upon

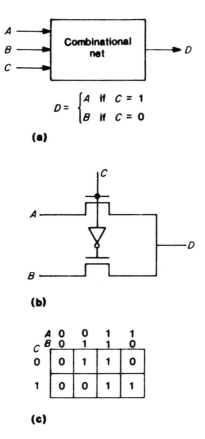

Figure 3.25 A combinational network: (a) specification; (b) implementation; (c) K-map

whether $C = 1$ or $C = 0$. This immediately suggests two switches controlled by C and $\bar{C}$ as shown in Figure 3.25(b).

The implementation of Figure 3.25(b) may not have been evident if the desired function had been specified as the K-map of Figure 3.25(c). However, after seeing this example, a general design technique may be suggested. This technique is based upon the following property of switching functions.

THEOREM. *For any switching function $F:\mathbf{B}^n \rightarrow \mathbf{B}$ there exist functions $G:\mathbf{B}^{n-1} \rightarrow \mathbf{B}$ and $H:\mathbf{B}^{n-1} \rightarrow \mathbf{B}$ such that $F(X_1, X_2, \ldots, X_n) = X_1 \cdot G(X_2, \ldots, X_n) + \bar{X}_1 \cdot H(X_2, \ldots, X_n)$.*

This theorem suggests the implementation of Figure 3.26. The functions G and H may be implemented using gate networks, or the theorem can be ap-

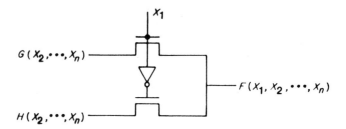

Figure 3.26   Tree theorem

plied again to either or both of these functions. If the theorem is applied repeatedly, a tree network results. In general (i.e., in the worst case) this implementation results in a switch network of $2^1 + 2^2 + \cdots + 2^{n-1}$ transistors (plus n inverters if the complements of input variables are not available).

For some functions the full tree network is not required, and this design technique leads to a particularly good implementation. Figure 3.25 is such an example. For other functions the full tree network is required, as illustrated in Figure 3.27.

Figure 3.27 also illustrates another important point. If the decomposition $F = X_1 \cdot G + \bar{X}_1 \cdot H$ is such that $H = 0$, it is nevertheless necessary to include the switch that connects 0 to F when $X_1 = 0$. In Figure 3.27 this occurs in the decomposition of Q.

This point is illustrated in simplest terms in Figure 3.28. An AND gate cannot be implemented with a single transistor as in Figure 3.28(a) because when Y goes low after having been high, the output Z will be isolated. The capacitance of the output Z and whatever it is connected to will hold Z at whatever value X was when Y changed to 0. Specifically, if X was 1 then Z will remain at 1, even though Y has changed to 0. The function of the second transistor in Figure 3.28(b) is to pull Z low when $Y = 0$. Similar comments apply to the tree theorem when $G = 0$ or when $G = 1$ or $H = 1$.

The tree network of Figure 3.27 was derived by applying the tree theorem directly to the K-map. Alternatively, a tree network may be developed from a sum of products formula by "factoring out" each variable in succession. For example, the function D of Figure 3.27 may be factored as follows:

$$D = \bar{A} \cdot B \cdot \bar{C} + \bar{A} \cdot \bar{B} \cdot C + A \cdot B \cdot C$$
$$= \bar{A} \cdot (B \cdot \bar{C} + \bar{B} \cdot C) + A \cdot (B \cdot C)$$
$$= \bar{A} \cdot (B \cdot (\bar{C}) + \bar{B} \cdot (C)) + A \cdot (B \cdot (C) + \bar{B} \cdot (0))$$

This tree network design technique is most effective when n is small. For large n, a tree may be combined with gate networks to construct fast and economical combinational networks.

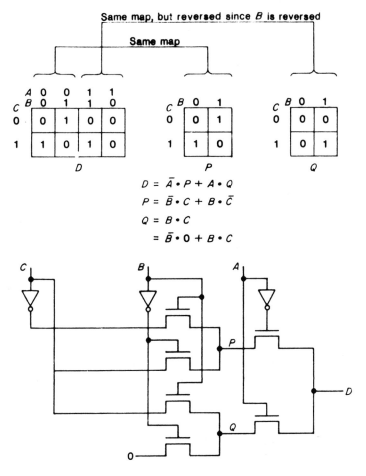

Figure 3.27 Tree network

3.3.4 Pull-Down Networks

Another general technique for using switch networks in the design of combinational networks is illustrated in Figure 3.29. The function to be implemented is defined by the K-map. Using classical 2-level minimization techniques, a minimal sum of products expression is found which covers the 0's of the function. In this case the sum of products is $AC + A\bar{B}$. A series-parallel switch network can be constructed from this formula. Each product is a separate series path through the network, and these series paths are connected in parallel. The resulting network will provide a path exactly when the output must be 0. The function may then be implemented as shown in Figure 3.29(a)

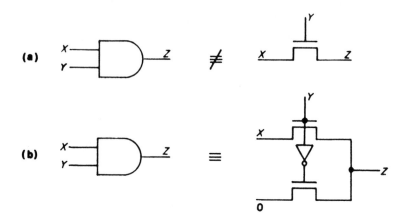

Figure 3.28   Switch network AND

by using a pull-up resistor to hold the output at 1 except when there is a path through the switch network that pulls the output low. The pull-up resistance must be large relative to the turned-on resistance of any path through the switch network, and small relative to the turned-off resistance of the network.

The minimal series-parallel switch network can frequently be further simplified, although we will suggest no systematic technique for doing so. For example, one transistor may be removed from the circuit of Figure 3.29(a) by using the same transistor in both of the paths AC and $A\bar{B}$. This corresponds to factoring out the A term: $AC + A\bar{B} = A(C + \bar{B})$. In gate network design, factoring out common subproducts in this fashion will in general result in a network that is more than two levels. But no such disadvantage results from factoring in switch network design.

This "sharing of switches" by factoring can result in significant savings. For example, consider the function $\bar{F} = AD + ACE + BE + BCD$. This is a minimal sum of products expression for this function. It is implemented directly in Figure 3.30(a). In Figure 3.30(b) the same function is implemented using a simpler switching network which shares switches between paths when possible.

The pull-down design technique should be recognized as the same technique that was used to construct logic gates in Chapter 2.

3.3.5 Electrical Considerations

We have seen two fundamentally different ways to implement switching functions by using MOS transistors. One way uses pull-up resistors/transistors and pull-down transistors. The other uses *pass transistors*, that is, transistors

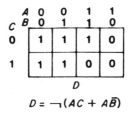

	A	0	0	1	1
C	B	0	1	1	0
0		1	1	1	0
1		1	1	0	0

$$D$$

$$D = \neg(AC + A\bar{B})$$

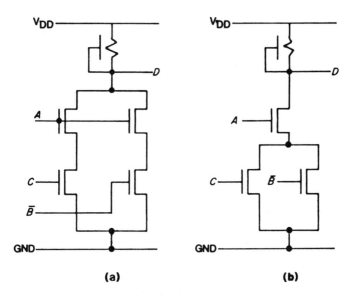

(a)　　　　　　　**(b)**

Figure 3.29　Pull-down design

that pass signals along the drain-source path, as in the tree networks. Which technique is more suitable for a given situation and how the techniques may be used together depend upon a few electrical and timing considerations.

The high and low logic levels for pull-up/pull-down logic (Figure 3.31(a)) are determined by the relative resistances of the pull-up and pull-down paths. The discussions of Section 2.2 for standard logic gates apply as well to "nonstandard gates," such as in Figure 3.29. To provide a satisfactory low output, the ratio $R_{\text{pu}}/R_{\text{pd}}$ must be 4 or greater, where R_{pd} denotes the low pull-down resistance. At the same time, R_{pu} must be small enough so that low-to-high transitions are not too slow. Hence $R_{\text{pu}}/R_{\text{pd}} = 4$ is normally used, giving a low logic level of $0.2\,V_{\text{DD}}$. The high logic level for pull-up/pull-down logic is essentially V_{DD}, since when the pull-down path is off, $R_{\text{pd}} \gg R_{\text{pu}}$.

The logic levels of a pass transistor output (Figure 3.31(b)) are determined differently. When V_g is high the pass transistor is turned on, and V_{out} (ide-

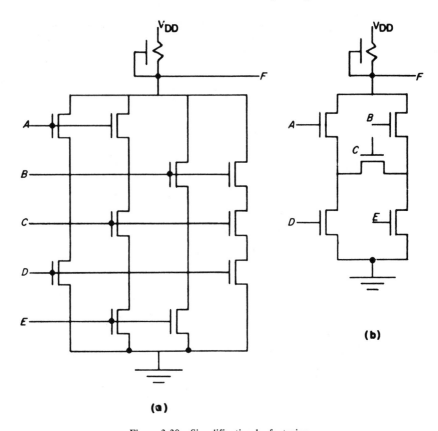

Figure 3.30   Simplification by factoring

ally) follows V_{in}. If V_{in} is low, then the output capacitance C will discharge through the pass transistor to the same value as V_{in}. Hence, V_{out} (low) $= V_{in}$ (low). If V_{in} is high, then the output capacitance will charge through the pass transistor toward V_{in}. However, as V_{out} rises, the gate-source voltage (the output is the source terminal now) decreases. When V_{out} reaches $V_g - V_{th}$, the transistor turns off and V_{out} increases no further. V_{th} is the threshold voltage of the pass transistor. V_{th} is designed to be about $0.2 V_{DD}$ for transistors used to build logic gates, as described in Chapter 2. These same transistors are used as pass transistors.

Hence, if V_g is driven by a standard logic gate then V_g (high) $\cong V_{DD}$. The high output of a pass transistor will thus be about $0.8 V_{DD}$ rather than the full V_{DD}. For this reason a pass transistor output should not drive the gate of another pass transistor, since this would bring the high output of the second transistor down to about $0.6 V_{DD}$, which is not an acceptable high level.

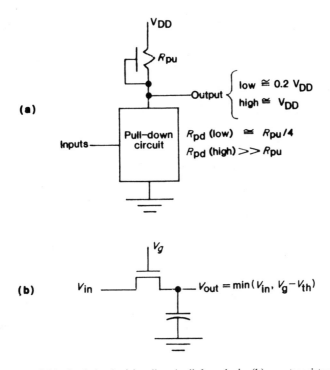

Figure 3.31   Logic levels: (a) pull-up/pull-down logic; (b) pass transistor

This same phenomenon also affects pull-up/pull-down logic whenever a pull-down transistor's source terminal is not connected to ground (e.g., a standard NAND gate). This must be taken into account in determining the size of transistors to use in the pull-down circuit, since the transistors not connected to ground will not turn on as fully for a high input (and hence R_{pd} will be larger).

Also, since the high-output level of a pass transistor is much less than V_{DD}, any logic gate driven by a pass transistor will not pull down as hard (i.e., R_{pd} will be higher than it would be if the input were supplied by a logic gate). Consequently, the pull-down transistors must be made wider (or the pull-ups longer) to maintain the desired $R_{pu} \cong 4R_{pd}$.

Pass transistor logic and pull-up/pull-down logic may be combined in the same circuit. In fact, this is necessary when using pass transistors, since the gate of a pass transistor may not be driven by a pass transistor due to logic level considerations, as discussed above.

Switching speed is another consideration in combining the two types of logic. The delay in propagating a signal through a pass transistor is proportional to RC, where R is the drain-source resistance of the turned-on transistor and C is the channel-to-substrate capacitance plus any capacitance driven by the output. A pessimistic approximation of the delay through n pass transistors in series is $(nR)(nC) = n^2RC$ (i.e., charge all capacitance through all of the resistance). An optimistic approximation is nRC (i.e., each C charges only through one R). The actual case is closer to n^2RC, that is, proportional to n^2.

The delay through a logic gate is proportional to RC, where R is R_{pu} or R_{pd} and C is the gate-to-source capacitance plus any capacitance driven by the gate output. The delay through n logic gates is the sum of the gate delays; that is, it is proportional to n. Each capacitance actually does charge or discharge through a single R (not through the sum of R's for all gates).

When many logic levels are required to implement a function, pull-up/ pull-down logic is preferable to pass transistor logic because propagation delay is proportional to n rather than n^2. However, pass transistor logic is preferable from a power standpoint because there is no steady-state power dissipation. Also, a pass transistor stage has a smaller R and a smaller C than a standard logic gate stage, and less chip area is required since no pull-up is needed. Consequently, an optimal implementation of a many-level combinational network usually involves a combination of pass transistor and pull-up/ pull-down logic.

3.3.6 Exercises

1. Implement the function F of Figure 3.15 using both tree network and pull-down design techniques. Minimize the number of transistors required. Count a pull-up resistor as one transistor.

2. Implement the two-input XOR operation. Minimize the number of transistors.

3. Implement the three-input XOR operation using a minimum number of transistors.

4. The mechanical switches that we have considered (e.g., Figure 3.22) are the simplest possible, having only a single contact and two terminals. This switch is shown in Figure 3.32(a), along with its nMOS transistor equivalent. Some other common mechanical switches are shown in Figure 3.32(b), (c), and (d).

- Suggest an nMOS equivalent for the switch of Figure 3.32(d).

- Design a switch network to control a single light from two different locations. Two type (b) switches will suffice.

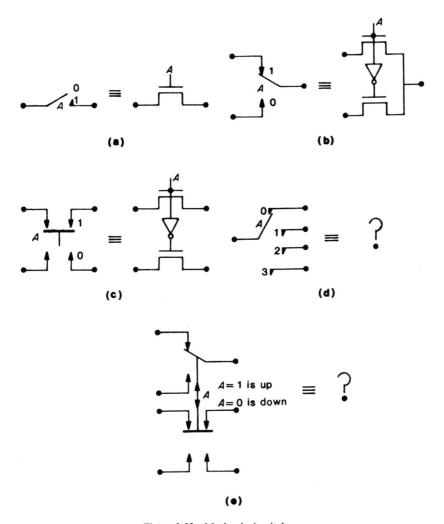

Figure 3.32   Mechanical switches

Hint: The XOR operation models the desired network. Changing the position of either switch will complement the transmission function.

• Simple binary switches of types (a), (b), and (c) can be combined into more complex binary switches by having one switch control the contact arms on multiple simple switches. Switch (e) is an example. Show the nMOS equivalent of this switch.

• Design a switch network to control a single light from three locations. Two type (b) switches and one combination switch [two type (b)'s] will suffice.

3.4 ELEMENTARY WORD OPERATIONS [33, 48]

3.4.1 Logic Operations on Words
3.4.2 Other Operations
3.4.3 Exercises

In register transfer (RT) systems, information is represented by binary words, and information is manipulated by doing operations on words. The primitive word operations that a register transfer system can perform are usually very simple. Complex information processing tasks are accomplished by doing long sequences of primitive word operations. Primitive word operations are implemented by combinational networks. Sequential networks are used to select and control the sequence of operations performed.

In this section a number of simple word operations are defined and gate network implementations are presented. Also, 6800 instructions that implement some of these word operations are discussed and a few example programs are written.

3.4.1 Logic Operations on Words

Logic operations can be extended to operations on words in several ways. Three common extensions are illustrated in Figure 3.33 for the AND operation. The first extension takes two n-bit input words and produces an n-bit output word ($n = 4$ in the figure). The output word is generated by ANDing together bits of the input words in corresponding positions, as defined in the last column: $Z_i = X_i \cdot Y_i$.

The gate network implementation for this operation is shown in the second column, using standard logic design level notation. The implementation is simply a bank of two-input AND gates. In the first column, an equivalent RT level notation for the same network is shown. A single line represents each word, with the number of bits specified by using the "slash" notation.

The notation $\mathbf{B}^n \times \mathbf{B}^n \to \mathbf{B}^n$ in the third column indicates that this operation takes two n-bit input words and produces an n-bit output word. The set $\mathbf{B}^n \times \mathbf{B}^n$ is essentially the same as the set $\mathbf{B}^{2n}$. The $\mathbf{B}^n \times \mathbf{B}^n$ notation simply emphasizes that the $2n$-bit input word consists of two n-bit words.

The second row of the figure defines a second extension of the AND operation. This extension takes an n-bit word and a 1-bit word and produces an n-

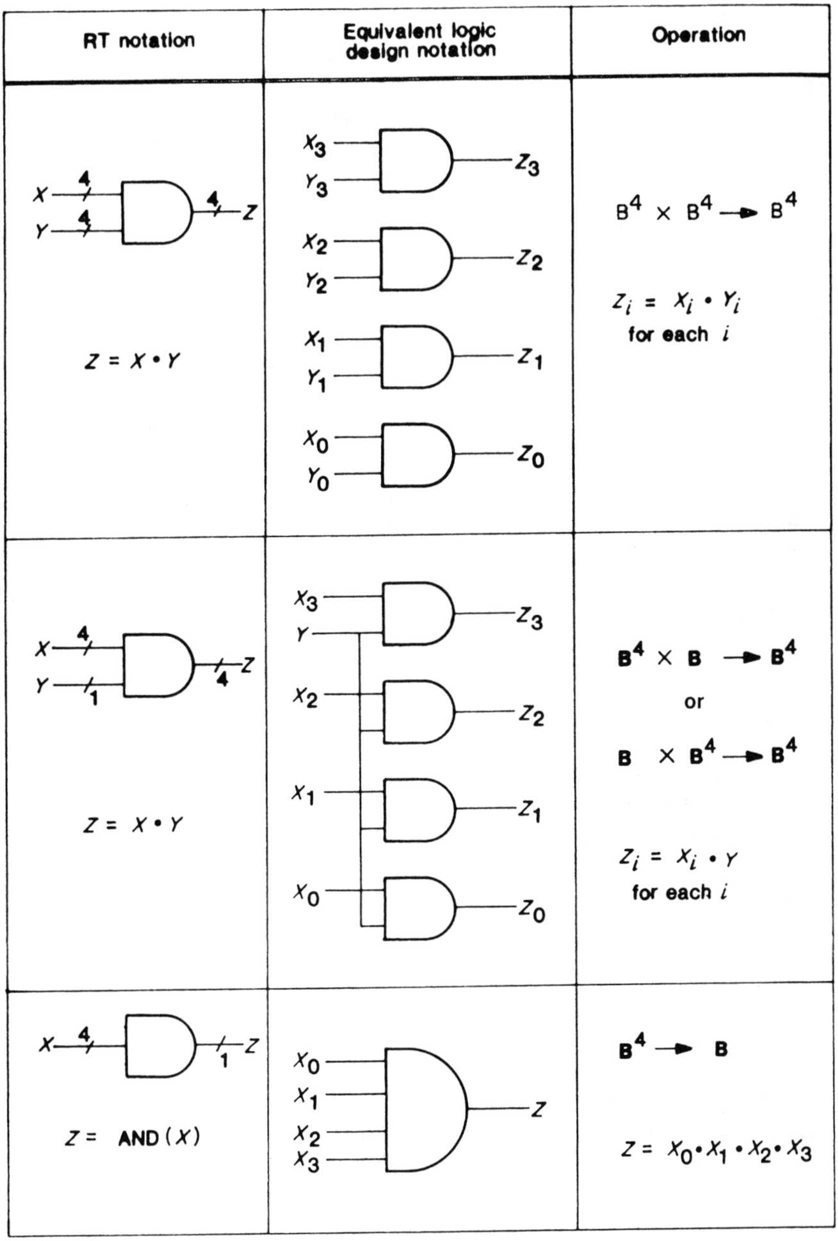

RT notation	Equivalent logic design notation	Operation
$X \xrightarrow{4}$ $Y \xrightarrow{4}$ $\xrightarrow{4} Z$ $Z = X \cdot Y$	X_3 Y_3 → Z_3 X_2 Y_2 → Z_2 X_1 Y_1 → Z_1 X_0 Y_0 → Z_0	$B^4 \times B^4 \longrightarrow B^4$ $Z_i = X_i \cdot Y_i$ for each i
$X \xrightarrow{4}$ $Y \xrightarrow{1}$ $\xrightarrow{4} Z$ $Z = X \cdot Y$	X_3 Y → Z_3 X_2 → Z_2 X_1 → Z_1 X_0 → Z_0	$B^4 \times B \longrightarrow B^4$ or $B \times B^4 \longrightarrow B^4$ $Z_i = X_i \cdot Y$ for each i
$X \xrightarrow{4}$ $\xrightarrow{1} Z$ $Z = \text{AND}(X)$	X_0 X_1 X_2 X_3 → Z	$B^4 \longrightarrow B$ $Z = X_0 \cdot X_1 \cdot X_2 \cdot X_3$

Figure 3.33   Extended logic operations

bit output word. The third row defines a third extension of AND, which is simply the generalization of the 2-bit AND operation to an n-bit AND operation. This operation takes one n-bit input word and produces a 1-bit output word.

Any two-input logic operation can be extended to a word operation in each of the ways shown in Figure 3.33. For example, the OR, NOR, NAND, and XOR operations can each be extended in these ways.

The NOT operation can be extended to word operation $\mathbf{B}^n \to \mathbf{B}^n$ by complementing each bit of the input word to generate the output (i.e., a bank of inverters). Hence, $Y = \bar{X}$ iff $Y_i = \bar{X}_i$ for each i.

Logic operations on words can be used to implement other useful operations on words. In Figure 3.34, for example, a simple switch is implemented. The switch connects either X or Y to output Z depending upon whether $C = 0$ or $C = 1$. The utility of the compact RT notation is evident in comparing Figure 3.34(b) and (c).

The 6800 instruction set includes instructions to implement several logic operations on words. The COM instructions (COM, COMA, and COMB) implement the extended NOT operation. The AND, ORA (i.e., OR Accumulator), and EOR instructions implement the first type of extension (Figure 3.33) for the AND, OR, and XOR operations. The BIT instructions also implement the AND operation, but no destination register is loaded.

The following examples illustrate the use of these logic instructions.

Example 1

Branch to JESSE if $A\langle 7:4 \rangle = 0011$.

```
ANDA  #$F0
EORA  #$30   1 → Z if A⟨7:4⟩ = 0011
BEQ   JESSE
```

The AND operation is used to "mask" bits $A\langle 3:0 \rangle$ so that they will not be involved in the comparison. The XOR operation is used for comparison. (The subtract operation could also have been used.)

Example 2

Complement bit 2 of the word in output buffer register SQOUT. Leave other bits unchanged. (SQOUT might be generating eight square-wave outputs of different frequencies, for example. This operation would be done on different bits at different times.)

```
LDAA  SQOUT
EORA  #$04
STAA  SQOUT
```

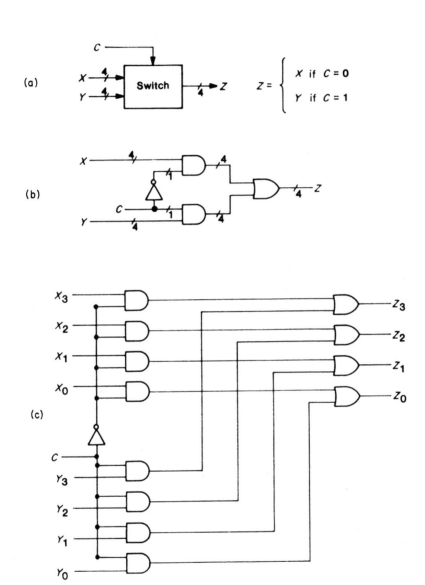

Figure 3.34   A switch: (a) definition; (b) implementation (RT notation); (c) implementation (logic notation)

Example 3

Clear all bits of memory register KATIE except bits $\langle 4:3 \rangle$, which should be complemented.

```
LDAA  KATIE
ORAA  #$E7
COMA
STAA  KATIE
```

Example 4

Branch to DANNY if $A_5 = 1$, but do not change A

```
BITA  #$20      Ā₅ → Z
BNE   DANNY
```

$\bar{A}_5 \rightarrow Z$

3.4.2 Other Operations

There are important word operations that do not require any gates for implementation. One such operation is concatenation, represented by ∘. This operation takes any two words of length n and m as arguments and forms a word of length $n + m$ by chaining the two words together. Hence for any X in $\mathbf{B}^n$ and Y in $\mathbf{B}^m$, $X \circ Y = X_{n-1} \cdots X_0 Y_{m-1} \cdots Y_0$. This operation can be extended to have any number of arguments. The notation for representing concatenation in RT diagrams and the corresponding logic diagram representation are illustrated in Figure 3.35.

Shift and rotate operations also require no gates for implementation. Five of the most common shift and rotate operations are defined in equations 3.24–3.28.

$\text{LSR}(X) = 0 \circ X\langle n - 1:1 \rangle$	(logical shift right)	(3.24)
$\text{ASL}(X) = X\langle n - 2:0 \rangle \circ 0$	(arithmetic shift left)	(3.25)
$\text{ROR}(X) = X_0 \circ X\langle n - 1:1 \rangle$	(rotate right)	(3.26)
$\text{ROL}(X) = X\langle n - 2:0 \rangle \circ X_{n-1}$	(rotate left)	(3.27)
$\text{ASR}(X) = X_{n-1} \circ X\langle n - 1:1 \rangle$	(arithmetic shift right)	(3.28)

Implementations of these operations are shown in Figure 3.36. As with concatenation, these operations require no gates for their implementation. They simply involve rearranging bit positions.

The 6800 instruction set includes instructions for each of these shift and rotate operations. For each of these instructions, the same 9-bit register

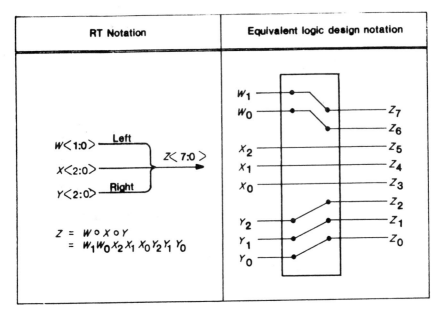

RT Notation	Equivalent logic design notation

Figure 3.35   Concatenation

serves as both source and destination for the instruction. This register is $C \circ R$ for the ROL, ROR, and ASL instructions and $R \circ C$ for the ASR and LSR instructions. In each case R may be A or B or M.

The shift and rotate instructions are used in processing tasks that require bit manipulation. In Example 5 of Section 1.1.4, for example, the LSR instruction was used to move each successive bit of A into C, where it could be tested.

These instructions are also useful in implementing arithmetic operations, as we shall see in Chapter 4. Specifically, shifting left corresponds to multiplication by 2 and shifting right corresponds to division by 2. Whether the "logical" shift or the "arithmetic" shift is used depends upon whether the code involved is B2 or 2C. The ASL operation is used for both B2 and 2C multiplication; it could just as well have been called LSL.

3.4.3   Exercises

1. Suppose that A and B are n-bit word variables. State whether each of the following is true (for all values of A and B) or false (for at least one value of A and B). Draw a gate representation of each expression.

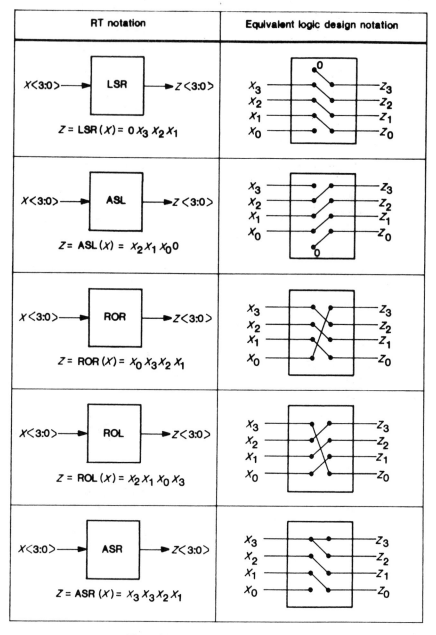

Figure 3.36   Shift and rotate operations

(a) $A \oplus 0 = A$
(b) $A \oplus 1 = \bar{A}$
(c) $+(A \cdot B) = (+A) \cdot (+B)$
(d) $\cdot (A + B) = (\cdot A) + (\cdot B)$
(e) $\overline{(+A)} = +(\bar{A})$
(f) $\overline{(\cdot A)} = +(\bar{A})$

2. Design the SWITCH of Figure 3.34 using only NAND gates. Use RT notation.

3. Provide a gate implementation for each of the following operations.

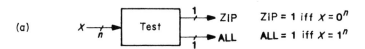

(a) $X \xrightarrow{n}$ Test $\longrightarrow$ ZIP   ZIP = 1 iff $X = 0^n$
                  $\longrightarrow$ ALL   ALL = 1 iff $X = 1^n$

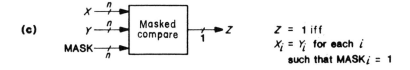

(b) $X \xrightarrow{n}$, $Y \xrightarrow{n}$ Compare $\xrightarrow{1}$ Z $Z = 1$ iff $X = Y$

(c) $X \xrightarrow{n}$, $Y \xrightarrow{n}$, MASK $\xrightarrow{n}$ Masked compare $\xrightarrow{1}$ Z $Z = 1$ iff $X_i = Y_i$ for each i such that $MASK_i = 1$

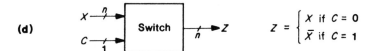

(d) $X \xrightarrow{n}$, $C \xrightarrow{1}$ Switch $\xrightarrow{n}$ Z $Z = \begin{cases} X & \text{if } C = 0 \\ \bar{X} & \text{if } C = 1 \end{cases}$

     1. Use only AND, OR, and NOT operations.
     2. Use XOR operation only.

4. Consider the following sequence of RT operations involving registers X and Y:

     1. $X \oplus Y \rightarrow X$
     2. $X \oplus Y \rightarrow Y$
     3. $X \oplus Y \rightarrow X$

If $X = \alpha$ and $Y = \beta$ before this sequence of operations is performed, what will be in X and Y after it is done?

5. Write 6800 programs to do each of the following tasks:

(a) $M[\alpha]\langle 6:5\rangle \rightarrow M[\beta]\langle 6:5\rangle$ (don't disturb other bits of $M[\beta]$ or any bits of $M[\alpha]$)

(b) The ASCII character in $M[\alpha]$ is known to be a hexadecimal numeral (i.e., 0, 1, ..., F). Branch to DECNUM if it is a decimal numeral.

(c) Swap the left and right halves of $M[\alpha]$; that is, $M[\alpha]\langle 7:4\rangle \leftrightarrow M[\alpha]\langle 3:0\rangle$.

Chapter 4

DIGITAL ARITHMETIC

4.1 Integer Codes
4.2 Addition
4.3 Subtraction
4.4 Multiplication
4.5 Division
4.6 Real Arithmetic

Numbers are represented within a computer by binary words. Arithmetic operations are performed by doing operations on words. In this chapter we discuss word operations that represent the four basic arithmetic operations, and design combinational networks to implement these operations.

This chapter is more formal than previous chapters. Definitions of concepts associated with arithmetic word operations are stated precisely, and important properties that follow from these definitions are stated as theorems. The proofs, which are straightforward but not always obvious, are included for completeness. They may be omitted on a first reading, if desired. It is essential only that the statement of each theorem be clearly understood.

It is important, particularly in introductory discussions of computer arithmetic, to distinguish between a binary word and the number that is represented by that word under a particular code. Failure to do so is a common source of confusion. Similarly, a binary word operation must be distinguished from the arithmetic operation that it represents. We have introduced a few special notations to make explicit these distinctions. The improved clarity that results should more than compensate for the additional burden of using these notations.

A few general notations will be used in this chapter that have not been encountered before. If X is a set of any sort (e.g., a set of numbers), then "$x \in X$" means "x is a member of the set X" and "$x \notin X$" means "x is not a member of the set X." The notation $\langle i:j \rangle$ represents the set of all integers between i and j, inclusive. For example, $\langle -2:3 \rangle = \{-2, -1, 0, 1, 2, 3\}$.

Hence, $2 \in \langle -2:3 \rangle$, but $4 \notin \langle -2:3 \rangle$. The notation 0^n represents an n-bit word, all zeros. Similarly, 1^n is an n-bit word, all ones. For example, $0^3 1^5 =$ 00011111.

4.1   INTEGER CODES [30–34, 36, 37, 39]

4.1.1   Definitions: B2 and 2C Codes
4.1.2   Fundamental Properties
4.1.3   Other Codes
4.1.4   Exercises

In order for a computer to store and process numerical information, it is necessary to define a code that specifies the number that is represented by each binary word. Most codes in use today are derived from the fundamental base 2 code (B2 code) for representing "unsigned integers" (i.e., 0, 1, 2, ...). This code is the binary (i.e., base 2) version of the familiar decimal (i.e., base 10) "weighted-position" code.

The most widely used code for representing "signed integers" (i.e., 0 ± 1, ± 2, ...) is the two's complement code (2C code). The B2 and 2C codes are defined in this section and some of the fundamental properties of these codes are derived.

4.1.1   Definitions: B2 and 2C Codes

If X is a binary word, then $[X]_2$ will denote the integer represented by X under the base 2 code.

Definition (base 2 code)

If $X \langle n-1:0 \rangle$ is a binary word, then $[X]_2$ is defined as follows:

$$[X]_2 = \sum_{i=0}^{n-1} X_i * 2^i \tag{4.1}$$

Examples:

(a) $[1101]_2 = 1*2^3 + 1*2^2 + 0*2^1 + 1*2^0$
$ = 8 + 4 + 0 + 1$
$ = 13$

(b) $[00101101]_2 = 45$

Notice that on the right of each equation above we have integers and integer expressions represented using the familiar decimal notation and familiar operations on integers. *No special notations are used for integer expressions.* For example, we do not write "45_{10}" to indicate that "45" should be interpreted as a decimal (i.e., base 10) representation. Decimal representation is assumed by default. Nor do we write $+_1$ or $+_{10}$ to indicate that the addition involved is integer addition (rather than a word operation representing addition), or base 10 addition (rather than base 8, or whatever).

We will never mix binary words and integers in the same expression. For example, $25 + 101$ can only mean the sum of integers twenty-five and one hundred one (i.e., 126). If we had meant the sum of integer twenty-five and the integer represented by the word 101 under the base 2 code, we would have written $25 + [101]_2$.

Definition (two's complement code)

If $X\langle n - 1:0\rangle$ is a binary word, then the integer represented by X under the two's complement code, denoted $[X]_{2C}$, is defined by:

$$[X]_{2C} = [X]_2 \qquad \text{if} \quad X_{n-1} = 0$$
$$\quad\quad\quad = [X]_2 - 2^n \qquad \text{if} \quad X_{n-1} = 1 \tag{4.2}$$

Examples:
(a) $[1101]_{2C} = [1101]_2 - 2^4 \qquad \text{since} \quad X_3 = 1$
$$\quad\quad\quad\quad = 13 - 16$$
$$\quad\quad\quad\quad = -3$$
(b) $[01101]_{2C} = [01101]_2 \qquad \text{since} \quad X_4 = 0$
$$\quad\quad\quad\quad\; = 13$$

Both the B2 code and the 2C code are presented for $n = 4$ in Table 4.1. The words are listed in ascending order under the B2 code. The patterns in this "B2 counting sequence" should be studied, and compared to the decimal counting sequence. Note that this same ordering applies to the 2C code, except for the discontinuity at 1000.

4.1.2 Fundamental Properties

The *range* of an integer code is the set of integers that may be represented under the code. The range of the B2 code is the set of all nonnegative integers, and the range of the 2C code is the set of all integers (in each case, considering words of all lengths).

In most applications, the number of bits to be used in representing an integer is fixed in advance (usually some multiple of the memory register length). An important consideration then is: What is the *range* of a code (i.e., the set

TABLE 4.1 Two integer codes

$X\langle 3:0\rangle$	$[X]_2$	$[X]_{2C}$
0000	0	0
0001	1	1
0010	2	2
0011	3	3
0100	4	4
0101	5	5
0110	6	6
0111	7	7
1000	8	-8
1001	9	-7
1010	10	-6
1011	11	-5
1100	12	-4
1101	13	-3
1110	14	-2
1111	15	-1

of integers represented) when restricted to words of this fixed length? We will let **RANGE__B2(n)** and **RANGE__2C(n)** denote the ranges of the B2 and 2C codes respectively when restricted to words of length n.

THEOREM   (code ranges) (4.3)

(a) **RANGE__B2(n)** $= \langle 0 : 2^n - 1 \rangle$
(b) **RANGE__2C(n)** $= \langle -2^{n-1} : +(2^{n-1} - 1) \rangle$

Proof.   Every bit of a word under the B2 code is weighted positively. Hence the smallest integer is represented by the word 0^n and the largest by 1^n. It is easy to see that $[1^n]_2 = 2^n - 1$ since the next count after 1^n in the B2 counting sequence is 10^n. QED(a).

When $X_{n-1} = 1$, $[X]_{2C} = [X]_2 - 2^n$. This integer will be most negative when $[X]_2$ is as small as possible, that is, when $X = 1 \circ 0^{n-1}$. In this case, $[X]_{2C} = 2^{n-1} - 2^n = 2^{n-1}(1 - 2) = -2^{n-1}$. Hence the left end point of the n-bit 2C range is -2^{n-1}.

The right end point is the largest that $[X]_2$ can be when $X_{n-1} = 0$, which is $[0 \circ 1^{n-1}]_2 = 2^{n-1} - 1$. QED.

Another important property of the 2C code is that the leftmost bit of a word is the "sign bit." This property is stated precisely as follows.

THEOREM   (2C sign bit) (4.4)

$$[X]_{2C} < 0 \text{ if and only if } X_{n-1} = 1$$

Proof. If $X_{n-1} = 0$ then $[X]_{2C} = [X]_2 \geq 0$. If $X_{n-1} = 1$ then $[X]_{2C} = [X]_2$ $- 2^n$. But from Theorem 4.3, $[X]_2 \leq 2^n - 1$. Hence $[X]_{2C} \leq (2^n - 1) - 2^n$ $= -1$. QED.

Sometimes it is necessary to increase the length of a word without changing the integer that is represented. For example, an analog-to-digital converter might generate a 12-bit word which you would like to use as input to a computer that represents integers as 16-bit words.

Under the B2 code, one would simply append 0's at the left end of the word to make it longer. This does not work for the 2C code, however (e.g., $[1101]_{2C}$ $= -3$ while $[01101]_{2C} = 13$). Instead, the word should be lengthened by extending the sign bit left. The "extend left" operation is defined as follows.

$$EL(X\langle n - 1:0\rangle) = X_{n-1} \circ X$$

The integer represented by a word under the 2C code is unaffected by this operation. That is,

THEOREM   (extend left operation)   (4.5)

$$[EL(X)]_{2C} = [X]_{2C}$$

Examples:

(a) $[1011]_{2C} = [1011]_2 - 2^4 = -5$
    $[11011]_{2C} = [11011]_2 - 2^5 = -5$
(b) $[0110]_{2C} = [00110]_{2C} = 6$

Proof.   The proof is obvious when $X_{n-1} = 0$. When $X_{n-1} = 1$,

$$
\begin{aligned}
[EL(X)]_{2C} &= [EL(X)]_2 - 2^{n+1} \\
&= 2^n + [X]_2 - 2^{n+1} \\
&= [X]_2 - 2^n \\
&= [X]_{2C} \\
&\quad QED
\end{aligned}
$$

A slightly different statement of this theorem is the following.

COROLLARY   (4.6)

$$[X\langle n:0\rangle]_{2C} = [X\langle n - 1:0\rangle]_{2C} \text{ if and only if } X_n = X_{n-1}$$

From the corollary it is clear that this property of the 2C code can be used both to lengthen a word and, when the leftmost bits are the same, to shorten a word.

Yet another important property of the 2C code is the following.

THEOREM   (alternative definition)   (4.7)

$$[X]_{2C} = -X_{n-1}*2^{n-1} + \sum_{i=0}^{n-2} X_i*2^i$$

Example: Using Definition 4.2:

$$[1010]_{2C} = [1010]_2 - 2^4 = -6$$

Using Theorem 4.7:

$$[1010]_{2C} = -2^3 + [010]_2 = -6$$

Proof   (left as an exercise).

From the theorem it is seen that the 2C code is a weighted-position code, just like the B2 code. The weight associated with position i is $+2^i$ for $i = 0, 1, \ldots, n-2$, and -2^i for $i = n-1$.

4.1.3   Other Codes

Although the B2 and 2C codes are the most widely used integer codes, there are other codes in use. Some of these are described briefly below.

One's Complement Code

This code has properties similar to the 2C code. The definition is:

$$\begin{aligned}[X]_{1C} &= [X]_2 & \text{if} \quad X_{n-1} = 0 \\ &= [X]_2 - (2^n - 1) & \text{if} \quad X_{n-1} = 1\end{aligned} \qquad (4.8)$$

One drawback of this code is that 0 is represented by two different words, 0^n and 1^n. The principal advantage is that the "negate" operation is easy:

$$[\bar{X}]_{1C} = -[X]_{1C} \qquad (4.9)$$

Signed-Magnitude Codes

An alternative to complement codes for representing signed integers is simply to use the leftmost bit of a word as the sign bit and use the remaining bits to represent the magnitude under an unsigned integer code. For example, if the B2 code is used for the magnitude then the word 1101 represents -5 and 0101 represents $+5$. This is called the B2-signed-magnitude code. The precise definition is:

$$[X]_{2SM} = [X\langle n - 2:0\rangle]_2 \qquad \text{if} \quad X_{n-1} = 0$$
$$\qquad\quad = -[X\langle n - 2:0\rangle]_2 \qquad \text{if} \quad X_{n-1} = 1 \qquad (4.10)$$

BCD Codes

The basic unsigned binary coded decimal (BCD) code is defined as follows. Divide a word into groups of 4 bits each, starting at the right, and let each group represent a numeral between 0 and 9 using the B2 code. The string of numerals then represents an integer in decimal notation. For example,

$$[01011001]_{BCD} = 59$$

Signed integers may be represented by making the leftmost bit a sign bit, or by using base 10 versions of the two's or one's complement codes (called ten's and nine's complement codes).

Excess Codes

These codes offer another alternative for representing signed integers. The Excess-m B2 code is defined as follows:

$$[X]_{Em} = [X]_2 - m \qquad (4.11)$$

Examples:

(a) $[0000]_{E8} = -8$
(b) $[1100]_{E8} = 4$

This code is frequently used to represent the exponent of a floating-point number (see Section 4.6).

4.1.4 Exercises

1. Fill in the blanks in the following table.

$X\langle 7:0\rangle$	$[X]_2$	$[X]_{2C}$	$[X]_{E128}$	$[X]_{2SM}$
01010111				
	219			
		−105		
			−7	
				−56

2. Specify the n-bit range of each of the following codes: B2, 2C, excess -2^{n-1}, B2-signed-magnitude, BCD. Also give the range in each case for $n = 8$.

3. Design a 2-level network to perform the following code translations for $n = 4$:
   (a) 2SM to 2C
   (b) 2C to excess-8
   (c) Excess-8 to 2C
   (d) 1C to 2SM

4. Design a combinational network to do each of the following translations for any n:
   (a) 2C to excess-2^{n-1}
   (b) Excess-2^{n-1} to 2C
   (c) 1C to 2SM
   (d) 2SM to 1C

5. Write 6800 programs to do each of the translations in Exercise 4 for $n = 8$.

6. Four decimal numerals in ASCII code are stored in $M4[\alpha]$, most significant digit first. Write a 6800 program to put the BCD code for the number represented into $M2[\beta]$.

4.2   ADDITION [30–34, 36, 37, 39]

   4.2.1   B2 Addition
   4.2.2   Overflow
   4.2.3   2C Addition
   4.2.4   Addition Instructions
   4.2.5   Exercises

In this section we discuss word operations that represent addition under the B2 and 2C codes. The integer addition operation is represented by the standard symbol, $+$. The word operations that represent addition under the B2 and 2C codes are denoted $+_2$ and $+_{2C}$, respectively.

Capital letters will be used to represent binary word variables. Lowercase letters will be used to represent integer variables. This convention will help to maintain a distinction between words and the integers that they represent.

The B2 addition operation, $+_2$, is the most fundamental arithmetic operation. As we shall see, all other arithmetic operations under the B2 and 2C codes can be implemented from the $+_2$ operation.

4.2.1   B2 Addition

Consider the problem of designing a combinational network to represent the integer addition operation under the B2 code. Suppose that the integers to be added, x and y, are represented by n-bit words X and Y. That is, $[X]_2 = x$ and $[Y]_2 = y$. Then x and y are both in the range $\langle 0:2^n - 1\rangle$, and thus $x + y$ must be in the range $\langle 0:2^{n+1} - 2\rangle$. Hence any result may be represented by an $(n + 1)$-bit word. We will design a combinational network with two n-bit inputs and an $(n + 1)$-bit output, as illustrated in Figure 4.1.

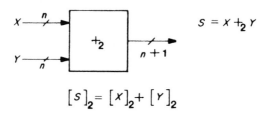

$$[S]_2 = [X]_2 + [Y]_2$$

Figure 4.1   A base 2 adder

Two-Level Implementation

The combinational network to be designed is uniquely specified by Figure 4.1. That is, for any n-bit input words X and Y, there is a unique output word $S\langle n:0\rangle$ that satisfies the equation $[S]_2 = [X]_2 + [Y]_2$. For small values of n, the desired combinational network can be designed by classical techniques. The design is carried out in Figure 4.2 for $n = 2$.

Three K-maps are constructed, one for each output. The arrangement of input variables is the same for each map, but for simplicity is shown only on the first. To see how the K-maps are constructed, consider the last square in the third row of each map. This square corresponds to inputs $X = 10$ and $Y = 11$. The integers represented are 2 and 3. The correct sum is $5 = [101]_2$. Hence $S\langle 2:0\rangle$ must be 101. The switching functions represented by these three K-maps may be implemented as a 2-level network using the techniques of Chapter 3.

Ripple Carry Implementation

As n increases, the classical combinational network design technique rapidly becomes impractical. The number of gates required grows exponentially. A more economical implementation is possible, based upon the familiar pencil and paper algorithm for adding integers that are represented by using a posi-

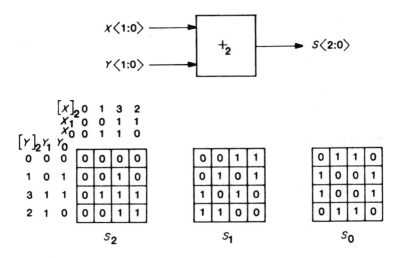

Figure 4.2   Base 2 adder design for $n = 2$

tional notation. This algorithm is illustrated in Figure 4.3. Notice that each of the numbers to be added is represented in its expanded form, as a sum of powers of 2. The addition algorithm is begun, starting at START in Figure 4.3, by adding the 2^0 terms in the two expansions, and expressing the result as a sum of two terms:

$$X_0*2^0 + Y_0*2^0 = C_1*2^1 + S_0*2^0$$

The factors S_0 and C_1 are each either 0 or 1. S_0 is called the "sum bit for stage 0" and C_1 is called the "carry out from stage 0" or the "carry in to stage 1." Next the carry in to stage 1 is added to the X and Y bits at stage 1, resulting in a carry out from stage 1 and a sum bit for stage 1. This process continues through stage $n - 1$. The addition carried out at each stage is identical in form:

$$X_i*2^i + Y_i*2^i + C_i*2^i = C_{i+1}*2^{i+1} + S_i*2^i \qquad (4.12)$$

where C_{i+1} and S_i are both binary variables; $i = 0, 1, \ldots, n - 1$; $C_0 = 0$.

Note that by making $C_0 = 0$, equation 4.12 describes stage 0 as well as subsequent stages. It should also be noted that X_i, Y_i, C_i, C_{i+1}, and S_i in the above equation are all binary variables; that is, they assume values from the set **B**. Coincidentally, the symbols used to represent the elements of **B** (i.e., 0 and 1) also represent integers, since these are numerals in standard decimal notation which we are using to represent integers. Hence in equation 4.12, X_i, Y_i, C_i, C_{i+1}, and S_i represent integers.

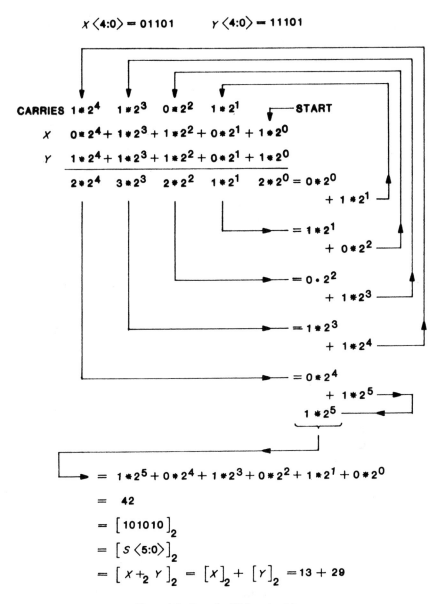

Figure 4.3   Base 2 addition algorithm

Now, notice that equation 4.12 uniquely defines the values of C_{i+1} and S_i for any given values of X_i, Y_i, and C_i (assuming that these are all binary variables). A combinational network that generates outputs C_{i+1} and S_i from inputs X_i, Y_i, and C_i, as defined by equation 4.12, is called a *full adder*. The design of a full adder is shown in Figure 4.4.

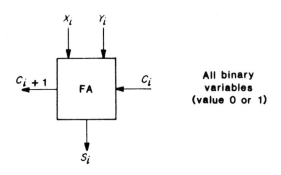

Integer equations

$$(X_i + Y_i + C_i) * 2^i = C_{i+1} * 2^{i+1} + S_i * 2^i$$

Or simply

$$X_i + Y_i + C_i = C_{i+1} * 2 + S_i$$

Resulting K-maps and logic equations

$$C_{i+1} = X_i \cdot Y_i + X_i \cdot C_i + Y_i \cdot C_i$$

$$S_i = X_i \oplus Y_i \oplus C_i$$

Figure 4.4   Full adder

An n-bit adder can be constructed by interconnecting n full adders, as shown in Figure 4.5. Notice that in addition to the two n-bit inputs X and Y, the adder has a third input, a single bit, C_0. This is called the "carry-in" to the adder. If C_0 is set to 0 then the adder directly implements the two-operand addition operation (i.e., $S\langle n:0\rangle = X +_2 Y$ when $C_0 = 0$).

If C_0 is set to 1 then $[S\langle n:0\rangle]_2 = [X]_2 + [Y]_2 + 1$. Note that $n + 1$ bits is sufficient to represent this sum since $x \leq (2^n - 1)$ and $y \leq (2^n - 1)$ implies $x + y + 1 \leq 2^{n+1} - 1$.

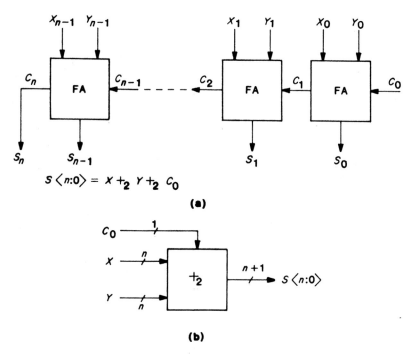

$$S\langle n{:}0\rangle = X +_2 Y +_2 C_0$$

(a)

(b)

Figure 4.5 Parallel adder: (a) construction from full adders; (b) block diagram symbol.

If C_0 is treated as a variable, then the adder actually implements the 3-operand B2 addition operation where two operands are in the range $\langle 0{:}2^n - 1\rangle$ and one is in the range $\langle 0{:}1\rangle$.

The adder defined in Figure 4.5 is called a *parallel adder*, in contrast to a *serial adder*, which consists of one full adder and a 1-bit register to hold the carry out. Sum bits are generated and sent to the destination register one at a time. Serial adders are used in special purpose computers (e.g., STARAN), in which words move through the system serially (i.e., one bit at a time) rather than in parallel.

The particular implementation of $+_2$ in Figure 4.5 is called the *ripple carry* adder, because a carry-in at C_0 must "ripple" through all stages before reaching C_n. This long path from input to output limits the speed of the ripple carry adder. Faster implementations of $+_2$ are available, most of which make use of some form of "carry look ahead." We will not discuss these other implementations.

4.2.2 Overflow

The word operation $+_2$ takes two n-bit words (and a single-bit carry-in) and produces an $(n + 1)$-bit word. We will call this the *extended-range* B2 addition operation, because the range of the result extends beyond the operand range.

It is convenient to define a slightly different operation $\hat{+}_2$ which takes two n-bit words (and a single-bit carry-in) and produces an n-bit result. This n-bit result is obtained from the $(n + 1)$-bit result generated by $+_2$ simply by dropping the leftmost bit, which happens to be the carry-out from the addition. That is, $X\langle n - 1:0\rangle \hat{+}_2 Y\langle n - 1:0\rangle = S\langle n - 1:0\rangle$. We will call $\hat{+}_2$ the *fixed-range* B2 addition operation.

In most applications, all integer variables are represented by words of the same length. When two words of this length are added, the result is normally stored in a register of the same length. Hence, it is the fixed-range result that is stored. Overflow is said to occur if the integer represented by the fixed-range result is not correct, that is, is not the same as the integer represented by the extended-range result.

The fixed- and extended-range results represent the same integer under the B2 code if and only if $S_n = 0$. Hence, overflow occurs if and only if the carry-out C_n is 1 (recall that $S_n = C_n$). C_n is thus called the *overflow detect* bit for B2 addition.

The concepts of fixed-range B2 addition and overflow are illustrated in Figure 4.6.

Notice that the fixed-range result is correct if and only if the correct result is in the range of the n-bit B2 code. That is, if $C_n = 1$ then the correct result is outside the n-bit B2 range (and hence the fixed-range result cannot be correct), and if $C_n = 0$ then the fixed-range result is correct.

The concepts of overflow and fixed- and extended-range representations are very general. We will encounter them again when implementing other arithmetic operations.

Most arithmetic instructions in most computers generate a fixed-range result which is loaded into a specified destination register. If overflow occurs, either a "flag bit" is set to indicate that fact, or (in a few cases) an interrupt is generated. Instructions are available that allow the programmer to check the flag bits. Some arithmetic instructions may generate the extended-range result and load it into an extended register (integer multiplication is usually done in this way). The program may then truncate to obtain the fixed-range result, if desired, and compare with the extended result to determine whether overflow has occurred.

4.2.3   2C Addition

Suppose that X and Y are n-bit words representing integers x and y under the 2C code. Since x and y are both in the set **RANGE__2C(n)** $= \langle -2^{n-1}: + (2^{n-1} - 1)\rangle$, the sum $x + y$ must be in the set $\langle -2^n: + (2^n - 2)\rangle$, which is

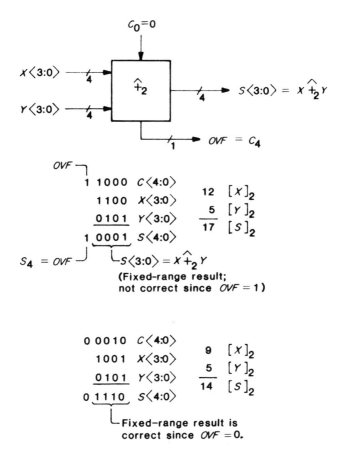

Figure 4.6   Fixed-range B2 addition

included in **RANGE__2C(n + 1)** $= \langle -2^n: +(2^n - 1)\rangle$. Hence, $n + 1$ bits are sufficient to represent the result $x + y$ under the 2C code.

The extended-range 2C addition operation, $+_{2C}$, is defined in Figure 4.7. It takes two n-bit words X and Y and produces an $(n + 1)$-bit word T that represents the correct sum under the 2C code. Theoretically, we could design a 2/3-level combinational network to implement $+_{2C}$ using the techniques of Chapter 3. This is practical, however, only for very small values of n. For larger values of n we must find a less costly implementation. Theorem 4.13 below suggests a practical implementation, based upon the use of a B2 adder. The heart of the theorem, part (a), states that the fixed-range 2C addition operation (which generates $T\langle n - 1:0\rangle$) is identical to the fixed-range B2 addition operation (i.e., $\hat{+}_{2C} = \hat{+}_2$). The theorem also states how an over-

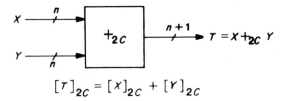

$$[T]_{2C} = [X]_{2C} + [Y]_{2C}$$

Figure 4.7   Extended-range 2C addition

flow detect bit may be produced, as well as how to produce the extended sum bit T_n.

THEOREM   (2C addition)   4.13

(a) The fixed-range sum $T\langle n - 1{:}0\rangle = X \stackrel{\wedge}{+}_{2C} Y$ may be generated using the base 2 adder as follows:

$$T\langle n - 1{:}0\rangle = X \stackrel{\wedge}{+}_2 Y$$

(b) The overflow detect bit may be generated in either of the following ways when doing the above addition:

$$OVF = C_n \oplus C_{n-1}$$

or

$$OVF = (X \cdot Y \cdot \bar{T} + \bar{X} \cdot \bar{Y} \cdot T)_{n-1}$$

(c) The extended-range sum may be formed by concatenating one bit on the left of the fixed-range result. This bit is:

$$T_n = OVF \oplus T_{n-1}$$

Implementation.   The theorem is illustrated in the combinational network implementation of Figure 4.8. The carry-in to the base 2 adder is set to 0 in the figure. However, as mentioned above, $C_0 = 1$ is permissible and would generate $x + y + 1$. The proof of the theorem that follows can easily incorporate this modification, but we have kept $C_0 = 0$ for simplicity.

In part (b) of the theorem, two tests for overflow are given. The second test is specified using a shorthand notation: the subscript $n - 1$ applies to all variables within parentheses.

Several examples of the theorem are given in Figure 4.9. In each case the two 4-bit words are added using the base 2 addition operation. OVF is then generated by exclusive-ORing the two leftmost carry bits, and then T_4 is generated by exclusive-ORing T_3 and OVF.

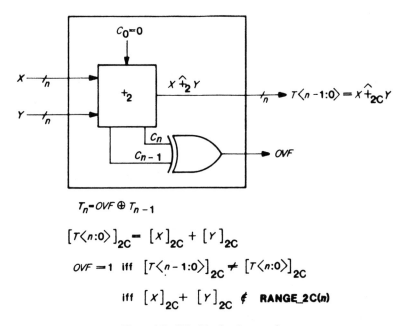

$$[T\langle n:0\rangle]_{2C} = [X]_{2C} + [Y]_{2C}$$

$$OVF = 1 \;\; \text{iff} \;\; [T\langle n-1:0\rangle]_{2C} \neq [T\langle n:0\rangle]_{2C}$$

$$\text{iff} \;\; [X]_{2C} + [Y]_{2C} \notin \textbf{RANGE\_2C}(n)$$

Figure 4.8   2C adder implementation

Proof. A proof of this theorem is outlined in Figure 4.10. The words X and Y to be added are expanded in Figure 4.10(a) via Theorem 4.7, and corresponding positions are added. Clearly the first $n - 1$ stages are the same as for B2 addition since all weights are positive. Hence $T_i = S_i$ for $i = 0, \ldots,$ $n - 2$.

The last stage, however, is different. The carry-in, C_{n-1}, is positive since it is generated by a B2 stage. X_{n-1} and Y_{n-1} are negative, by Theorem 4.7. T_{n-1} is positive since it is *not* the leftmost bit of the extended-range result, and T_n is negative because it *is* the leftmost bit. The resulting equation is given in Figure 4.10(b). The table of Figure 4.10(b) gives the unique binary solution of this equation for each possible value of k.

Figure 4.10(c) shows the equation and corresponding solution table for the last stage of the B2 adder. For the B2 adder, S_{n-1} and C_n are determined uniquely by $C_{n-1}, X_{n-1},$ and Y_{n-1}. Similarly, for the 2C adder, T_n and T_{n-1} are functions of $C_{n-1}, X_{n-1},$ and Y_{n-1}. The truth table for all six of these functions and the proposed overflow tests are shown in Figure 4.10(d).

The theorem follows directly from this truth table. By construction, $T\langle n:0\rangle$ is the correct 2C sum. We have already shown that $T_i = S_i$ for $i = 0,$ $\ldots, n - 2$. Now by comparing columns T_{n-1} and S_{n-1}, $T_{n-1} = S_{n-1}$. This proves that $T\langle n - 1:0\rangle = X \hat{+}_2 Y$.

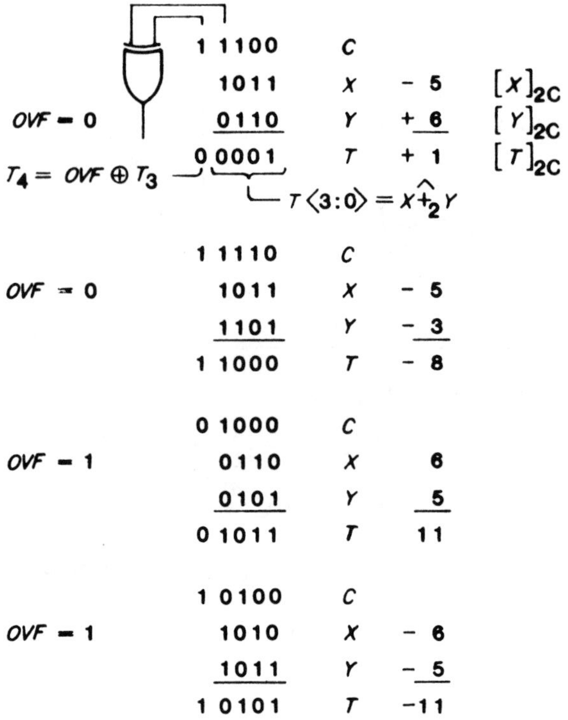

$$
\begin{array}{llll}
\text{1 1100} & C & & \\
\text{1011} & X & -\ 5 & [X]_{2C} \\
\text{0110} & Y & +\ 6 & [Y]_{2C} \\
\text{0 0001} & T & +\ 1 & [T]_{2C}
\end{array}
$$

$OVF = 0$

$T_4 = OVF \oplus T_3$

$T\langle 3:0 \rangle = X \hat{+}_2 Y$

$$
\begin{array}{lll}
\text{1 1110} & C & \\
\text{1011} & X & -\ 5 \\
\text{1101} & Y & -\ 3 \\
\text{1 1000} & T & -\ 8
\end{array}
$$

$OVF = 0$

$$
\begin{array}{lll}
\text{0 1000} & C & \\
\text{0110} & X & 6 \\
\text{0101} & Y & 5 \\
\text{0 1011} & T & 11
\end{array}
$$

$OVF = 1$

$$
\begin{array}{lll}
\text{1 0100} & C & \\
\text{1010} & X & -\ 6 \\
\text{1011} & Y & -\ 5 \\
\text{1 0101} & T & -11
\end{array}
$$

$OVF = 1$

Figure 4.9   Examples of Theorem 4.13

To prove part (b) of the theorem, note that overflow occurs iff $[T\langle n:\emptyset\rangle]_{2C}$ $\neq [T\langle n-1:0\rangle]_{2C}$. But by the extend left theorem, $[T\langle n:0\rangle]_{2C} \neq [T\langle n-1:0\rangle]_{2C}$ iff $T_n \neq T_{n-1}$. And from the truth table $T_n \neq T_{n-1}$ iff $C_n \oplus C_{n-1} =$ 1 iff $(X \cdot Y \cdot \overline{T} + \overline{X} \cdot \overline{Y} \cdot T)_{n-1} = 1$. This proves part (b) of the theorem. Furthermore, since $0 \oplus T_{n-1} = T_{n-1}$ and $1 \oplus T_{n-1} = \overline{T}_{n-1}$, part (c) follows immediately. QED

An intuitive feeling for Theorem 4.13 can be obtained by studying Figure 4.11. The 16 binary words of length 4 are arranged in a circle, along with the integers that they represent under the B2 and 2C codes. Notice that for both codes the numbers increase in the clockwise direction, except for one point of discontinuity (15 to 0 for B2 and 7 to -8 for 2C). By construction, the operation $\hat{+}_2$ corresponds to stepping clockwise around the circle. A carry-out is generated (and discarded) when stepping from 15 to 0. Since 2C numbers are also increasing clockwise, adding a positive number under the 2C code is clearly accomplished by the same operation [e.g., $(-7) + 3 =$ start at (-7) and take 3 steps clockwise].

$$+ C_n 2^n + C_{n-1} 2^{n-1} + C_{n-2} 2^{n-2} \bullet \bullet \bullet + 0\ 2^0$$
$$- X_{n-1} 2^{n-1} + X_{n-2} 2^{n-2} \bullet \bullet \bullet + X_0 2^0$$
$$- Y_{n-1} 2^{n-1} + Y_{n-2} 2^{n-2} \bullet \bullet \bullet + Y_0 2^0$$
$$\overline{- T_n 2^n + T_{n-1} 2^{n-1} + T_{n-2} 2^{n-2} \bullet \bullet \bullet + T_0 2^0}$$

(a)

same as for base 2;

hence $T_i = S_i$ for $i = 0, \bullet \bullet \bullet, n-2$

$$C_{n-1} 2^{n-1} - X_{n-1} 2^{n-1} - Y_{n-1} 2^{n-1} = - T_n 2^n + T_{n-1} 2^{n-1}$$

dividing by 2^{n-1}, this becomes:

$$\underbrace{C_{n-1} - X_{n-1} - Y_{n-1}}_{k} = - T_n \bullet 2 + T_{n-1}$$

k	T_n	T_{n-1}
0	0	0
1	0	1
-1	1	1
-2	1	0

(b)

$$\underbrace{C_{n-1} + X_{n-1} + Y_{n-1}}_{m} = C_n \bullet 2 + S_{n-1}$$

m	C_n	S_{n-1}
0	0	0
1	0	1
2	1	0
3	1	1

(c)

Figure 4.10   2C addition theorem: (a) addition algorithm; (b) last stage; (c) last stage of base 2 adder; (d) truth tables

C_{n-1}	X_{n-1}	Y_{n-1}	k	T_n	T_{n-1}	m	C_n	S_{n-1}	$C_n \oplus C_{n-1}$	$(X Y \bar{T} + \bar{X} \bar{Y} T)_{n-1}$
0	0	0	0	0	0	0	0	0	0	0
0	0	1	-1	1	1	1	0	1	0	0
0	1	0	-1	1	1	1	0	1	0	0
0	1	1	-2	1	0	2	1	0	1	1
1	0	0	1	0	1	1	0	1	1	1
1	0	1	0	0	0	2	1	0	0	0
1	1	0	0	0	0	2	1	0	0	0
1	1	1	-1	1	1	3	1	1	0	0

(d)

Figure 4.10   (Continued)

Since the numbers are in a circle, adding a negative number $-x$ can be done either by stepping counterclockwise x times, or by stepping clockwise $16 - x$ times. The 2C code represents $-x$ by the same word that represents $16 - x$ under the B2 code. Hence $\hat{+}_2$ also works for adding negative numbers [e.g., $6 + (-3) = $ start at 6 and step $16 - 3$ steps clockwise].

We have proved part (a) of Theorem 4.13 informally by using the number circle of Figure 4.11. The same sort of reasoning applies directly to other complement codes and provides an intuitive understanding of complement codes in general. The number circle is not very helpful in proving parts (b) and (c) of the theorem, however.

4.2.4   Addition Instructions

The basic 6800 addition instructions are ADDA, ADDB, and ABA. These instructions differ from each other only in the identity of the source and destination registers. The operation that is performed in each case is 8-bit fixed-range B2 addition, $\hat{+}_2$.

All bits of the CC register (except I) are affected in the standard fashion. Notice in particular that after an addition, $CC_0 = C$ indicates B2 overflow and $CC_1 = V$ indicates 2C overflow. That is, $C_8 \to C$ and $C_8 \oplus C_7 \to V$.

The H bit of the CC register is used in conjunction with the DAA instruction (decimal adjust accumulator) for BCD addition. Specifically, if accumulator A and $M[\alpha]$ each contain a two-digit BCD number, then these numbers may be added as follows:

```
ADDA  ALPHA
DAA
```

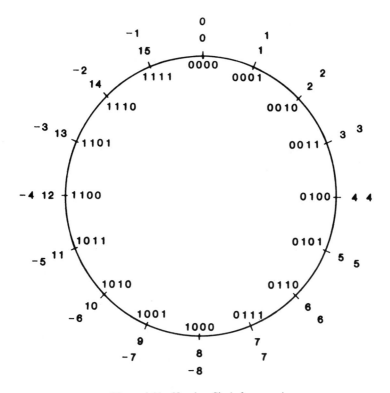

Figure 4.11 Number Circle for $n = 4$

After execution of these two instructions, $C \circ A$ will contain the correct BCD sum. That is, A contains the fixed-range BCD sum and C indicates BCD overflow.

The DAA instruction adjusts the result of the ADDA instruction by adding one of the words 00, 06, 60, or 66 to A. Which word is added depends upon the contents of H, C, and A when DAA is executed. (See Exercise 7.)

In many applications, more than 8 bits are required to represent an integer. Two-byte representation of integers is commonly referred to as "double precision," three-bytes representation as "triple precision," and so on. These are actually misnomers, however, since it is range rather than precision that is increased. Nevertheless, we will use these terms.

The add with carry instructions, ADCA and ADCB, are useful for adding multiple-precision integers. These instructions are identical to ADDA and ADDB except that the carry flag C is included in the addition, so the operation performed is $A \mathbin{\hat{+}_2} M \mathbin{\hat{+}_2} C \to A$ or $B \mathbin{\hat{+}_2} M \mathbin{\hat{+}_2} C \to B$.

The following program does the double-precision addition $M2[\alpha] \; \hat{+}_2$ $M2[\beta] \rightarrow M2[\alpha]$:

```
LDDA   ALPHA+1
ADDA   BETA+1
STAA   ALPHA+1
LDAA   ALPHA
ADCA   BETA
STAA   ALPHA
```

The first two instructions add the low bytes and set C to 1 or 0 depending upon whether there is a carry-out or not. The STAA and LDAA instructions do not affect C, so that ADCA adds the high bytes plus the carry from the low-byte addition. After ADCA, the C and V bits of CC indicate B2 and 2C overflow for the double-precision addition.

4.2.5 Exercises

1. Design a 2-level gate network to implement each of the following operations:

(a) Extended-range 2C adder for $n = 2$:

$$T\langle 2:0\rangle = X\langle 1:0\rangle +_{2C} Y\langle 1:0\rangle$$

(b) Extended-range 2C incrementer for $n = 3$:

$$Y\langle 3:0\rangle = X\langle 2:0\rangle +_{2C} 1$$

(c) Extended-range 2C subtract-5 network:

$$[Y\langle 3:0\rangle]_{2C} = [X\langle 2:0\rangle]_{2C} - 5$$

2. Using full adders and gates as components, design a combinational network to implement each of the following operations:

(a) $[S\langle ?:0\rangle]_2 = [X\langle n - 1:0\rangle]_2 + 5$
(b) $[T\langle ?:0\rangle]_{2C} = [X\langle n - 1:0\rangle]_{2C} - 5$
(c) $S\langle ?:0\rangle = X\langle n - 1:0\rangle +_2 Y\langle n - 1:0\rangle +_2 Z\langle n - 1:0\rangle$
(d) $T\langle ?:0\rangle = X\langle n - 1:0\rangle +_{2C} Y\langle n - 1:0\rangle +_{2C} Z\langle n - 1:0\rangle$

3. (a) Using gates as components, design a "half-adder" network that can add two bits of the same weight and generate a carry-out and a sum bit. The equation for the half-adder is

$$C_i + X_i = 2*C_{i+1} + S_i$$

(Half-adder accepts C_i and X_i as inputs and generates C_{i+1} and S_i.)
(b) Use half-adders and gates to design

- An extended-range B2 incrementer:

$$Y\langle n:0\rangle = X\langle n - 1:0\rangle +_2 1$$

- An extended-range 2C incrementer:

$$Y\langle n:0\rangle = X\langle n - 1:0\rangle +_{2C} 1$$

4. Design n-bit adders for the following codes:
(a) B2-signed-magnitude
(b) Excess-2^{n-1}
(c) one's complement
Use the B2 adder and gates as components.

5. Write 6800 programs to do each of the following additions:
(a) $M3[\alpha] +_2 M3[\beta] \rightarrow M3[\alpha]$
(b) $[M2[\alpha]]_{2C} + [M[\beta]]_{2C} \rightarrow [M2[\alpha]]_{2C}$; provide overflow detection.
(c) Same as (b) except $M[\beta]$ is B2.
(d) Add a list of single-precision 2C integers and produce the correct double-precision result. Write as a subroutine. Enter with address of list in IX and length in B; exit with result in $B \circ A$.

6. Suppose that the add with carry instructions were not available. Write a program to do double-precision addition. Do C and V indicate B2 and 2C overflow upon exit?

7. Let $D\langle 7:0\rangle$ denote the word that is added to accumulator A by the DAA instruction.
(a) Specify $[DL]_2$ (either 0 or 6) as a function of $[AL]_2$ and H.
(b) Specify $[DH]_2$ (either 0 or 6) as a function of $[AH]_2$, C, and $[AL]_2$.

4.3 SUBTRACTION [30–34, 36, 37, 39]

4.3.1 The 2C Negate Operation
4.3.2 2C Subtraction
4.3.3 B2 Subtraction
4.3.4 Subtraction Instructions
4.3.5 Ordering Relations and Branch Instructions
4.3.6 Exercises

Integer subtraction is a two-operand operation: given two integers x and y, it produces another integer $x - y$. It is closely related, however, to a single-operand operation, the negate operation (sometimes called "unary subtract"). The negate operation takes a single integer x and produces another integer neg(x). The negate operation is defined in terms of the addition operation by the equation $x + \text{neg}(x) = 0$. [The result of the negate operation is usually denoted "$-x$". We are using neg(x) to avoid confusion with two-operand subtraction.] The two-operand subtract operation may be defined in terms of the negate and addition operations by the equation $x - y = x + \text{neg}(y)$.

In this section we will implement the subtract operation under the B2 and 2C codes, and the negate operation under the 2C code. Notice that there is no negate operation under the B2 code, since negative numbers are not represented under B2.

4.3.1 The 2C Negate Operation

Let NEG denote the fixed-range 2C negate operation. That is, for any $X\langle n - 1:0\rangle$, NEG will generate a word $Y\langle n - 1:0\rangle$ such that $[Y]_{2C} = -[X]_{2C}$, if the negative of $[X]_{2C}$ is in the n-bit 2C range. If not, then an overflow detect bit is set. This operation is illustrated in Figure 4.12.

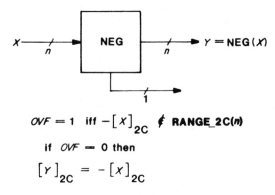

$$OVF = 1 \quad \text{iff} \quad -[X]_{2C} \notin \text{RANGE\_2C}(n)$$

if $OVF = 0$ then

$$[Y]_{2C} = -[X]_{2C}$$

Figure 4.12   Fixed-range 2C negate

A practical implementation for the NEG operation is suggested by the following theorem.

THEOREM   (2C negate)   (4.14)

(a) $\text{NEG}(X) = \bar{X} \mathbin{\hat{+}}_2 1$
(b) $OVF = 1$ if and only if $X = 1 \circ 0^{n-1}$
(c) $OVF = C_n \oplus C_{n-1}$

Examples:
(a) $X = 1101;\ \bar{X}\ \hat{+}_2\ 1 = 0011$
$[X]_{2C} = -3;\ [\bar{X}\ \hat{+}_2\ 1]_{2C} = +3$
(b) $X = 1000;\ \bar{X}\ \hat{+}_2\ 1 = 1000$
$[X]_{2C} = -8;\ -(-8) = +8 \neq \textbf{RANGE\_2C(4)}$ (overflow)

Implementation. An implementation based upon this theorem is shown in Figure 4.13. A B2 adder is used to implement the increment operation. Alternatively, the incrementer of Exercise 3, Section 4.2 could be used.

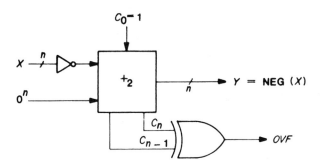

Figure 4.13 Negate implementation

Proof. Part (b) is obvious, since -2^{n-1} is the only point in the n-bit 2C range that does not have its negative in the same range.

To see that part (a) is correct, note that $X\ \hat{+}_2\ \bar{X} = 1^n$ (e.g., $1001\ \hat{+}_2\ 0110 = 1111$). Therefore,

$$X\ \hat{+}_2\ (\bar{X}\ \hat{+}_2\ 1) = (X\ \hat{+}_2\ \bar{X})\ \hat{+}_2\ 1$$
$$= 1^n\ \hat{+}_2\ 1$$
$$= 0^n$$

It follows that $\bar{X}\ \hat{+}_2\ 1$ must be NEG(X), since $\hat{+}_2 = \hat{+}_{2C}$ by Theorem 4.13.

Part (c) is obvious since $0 \circ 1^{n-1}$ is the only word that can produce $C_n \neq C_{n-1}$ when incremented. QED.

4.3.2 2C Subtraction

The extended-range 2C subtract operation is defined in Figure 4.14. The following theorem suggests a practical implementation.

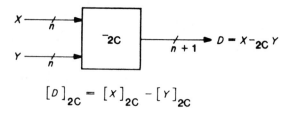

$$[D]_{2C} = [X]_{2C} - [Y]_{2C}$$

Figure 4.14   2C subtracter

THEOREM   (2C subtraction)   (4.15)

(a) The fixed-range difference $D\langle n - 1{:}0\rangle = X \doteq_{2C} Y$ may be generated using the base 2 adder as follows:

$$D\langle n - 1{:}0\rangle = X \mathbin{\hat{+}_2} \bar{Y} \mathbin{\hat{+}_2} 1$$

(b) The overflow detect bit may be generated as part of the above addition in either of the following ways:

$$OVF = C_n \oplus C_{n-1}$$

or

$$OVF = (X \cdot \bar{Y} \cdot \bar{D} + \bar{X} \cdot Y \cdot D)_{n-1}$$

(c) The extended-range difference may be generated by concatenating one bit on the left of the fixed-range result. That bit is

$$D_n = OVF \oplus D_{n-1}$$

Implementation.   A combinational network to perform extended- or fixed-range subtraction may be implemented using a B2 adder as shown in Figure 4.15. This implementation is a direct application of the theorem.

The carry-in to the base 2 adder is set to 1 to compute $x - y$. If instead $C_0 = 0$ then the operation $x - y - 1$ would be implemented. By setting $y = 0$, the decrement operation $x - 1$ is obtained. The hardware of Figure 4.14 may thus be regarded as implementing the operation $x - y - \bar{C}_0$.

Several examples of the theorem are given in Figure 4.16.

Proof.   The proof follows directly from Theorems 4.14 and 4.13, except when $Y = 1 \circ 0^{n-1}$, which causes the negate operation to overflow. This difficulty may be avoided by using the extend left theorem to convert X and Y to $(n + 1)$-bit words at the outset. QED.

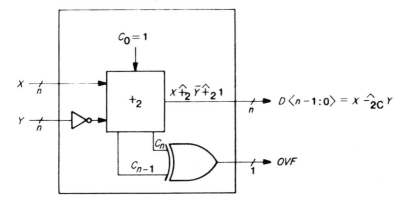

$$D_n = OVF + D_{n-1}$$
$$\left[\, D\langle n:0\rangle\,\right]_{2C} = \left[\,X\,\right]_{2C} - \left[\,Y\,\right]_{2C}$$
$$OVF = 1 \text{ iff } \left[\, D\langle n-1:0\rangle\,\right]_{2C} \neq \left[\, D\langle n:0\rangle\,\right]_{2C}$$
$$\text{iff } \left[\,X\,\right]_{2C} - \left[\,Y\,\right]_{2C} \; \epsilon \; \textbf{RANGE\_2C}(n)$$

Figure 4.15   2C subtracter implementation

4.3.3   B2 Subtraction

Since the B2 code cannot represent negative numbers, an extended-range representation of subtraction under the B2 code is not possible. Fixed-range representation, however, is possible, and is sometimes useful (e.g., for address arithmetic within a processor). The fixed-range representation of B2 subtraction is defined in Figure 4.17.

The following theorem suggests a practical implementation of B2 subtraction.

THEOREM   (B2 subtraction)   (4.16)

(a) $X \stackrel{\triangle}{-}_2 Y = X \stackrel{\wedge}{+}_2 \bar{Y} \stackrel{\wedge}{+}_2 1$
(b) $OVF = \bar{C}_n$

A combinational network that implements B2 subtraction is shown in Figure 4.18. Except for overflow detection, it is identical to the fixed-range 2C subtract implementation.

Two examples of B2 subtraction are given in Figure 4.19.

$X = 1011$
$Y = 1101$

$[X]_{2C} \quad -5$

$-[Y]_{2C} \quad -(-3)$

$\overline{[D]_{2C} \quad -2}$

$OVF = 0$

$$\begin{array}{ll} 0 \;\; 0111 & C\langle 4{:}0\rangle \\ \;\;\;\, 1011 & X\langle 3{:}0\rangle \\ \;\;\;\, \underline{0010} & \bar{Y}\langle 3{:}0\rangle \\ 1 \;\; 1110 & D\langle 4{:}0\rangle \end{array}$$

$D\langle 3{:}0\rangle = X \,\hat{+}_2\, \bar{Y} \,\hat{+}_2\, 1$

$D_4 = OVF \oplus D_3$

$X = 0111$
$Y = 1010$

$[X]_{2C} \quad 7$

$-[Y]_{2C} \quad -(-6)$

$\overline{[D]_{2C} \quad 13}$

$OVF = 1$

$$\begin{array}{ll} 0 \;\; 1111 & C\langle 4{:}0\rangle \\ \;\;\;\, 0111 & X\langle 3{:}0\rangle \\ \;\;\;\, \underline{0101} & \bar{Y}\langle 3{:}0\rangle \\ 0 \;\; 1101 & D\langle 4{:}0\rangle \end{array}$$

$D\langle 3{:}0\rangle = X \,\hat{+}_2\, \bar{Y} \,\hat{+}_2\, 1$

$D_4 = OVF \oplus D_3$

Figure 4.16   Examples of Theorem 4.15

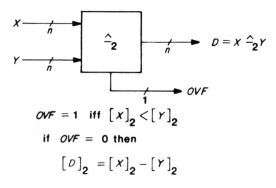

$OVF = 1$ iff $[X]_2 < [Y]_2$

if $OVF = 0$ then

$$[D]_2 = [X]_2 - [Y]_2$$

Figure 4.17   Fixed-range B2 subtraction

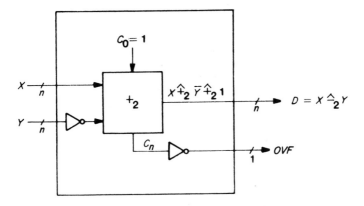

Figure 4.18   B2 subtract implementation

Proof.   Apply Theorem 4.15 to the $(n + 1)$-bit words $0 \circ X$ and $0 \circ Y$. Both (a) and (b) follow directly. QED

4.3.4   Subtraction Instructions

The 2C negate operation is implemented by the instructions NEG, NEGA, and NEGB. The CC bit V indicates 2C overflow following the negate operation. The C bit is also affected (see Table 1.3), but since negate is not a B2 operation it is not useful.

There are three straight subtract instructions (SUBA, SUBB, and SBA) and two subtract with carry instructions (SBCA and SBCB). The subtract with carry instructions are used for multiple-precision subtraction, in the same fashion that ADCA and ADCB are used for multiple-precision addition.

All of the CC bits (except I) are affected in the standard fashion by each of the subtract instructions. In particular, notice that C and V indicate B2 and 2C overflow. That is, $\bar{C}_8 \rightarrow C$ and $C_8 \oplus C_7 \rightarrow V$, where C_7 and C_8 are the carries produced by the addition that is performed (e.g., $A \; \hat{+}_2 \, M \; \hat{+}_2 \, 1$ for SUBA and $A \; \hat{+}_2 \, \bar{M} \; \hat{+}_2 \, \bar{C}$ for SBCA).

4.3.5   Ordering Relations and Branch Instructions

It is frequently necessary to determine the numerical order of words under the B2 and 2C codes. This may be accomplished by doing a subtraction, and examining the result (e.g., $x < y$ iff $x - y < 0$, $x = y$ iff $x - y = 0$, etc.).

Notice, however, that it is the *correct* result (i.e., the extended-range result) that must be examined, not the fixed-range result. When working with fixed-

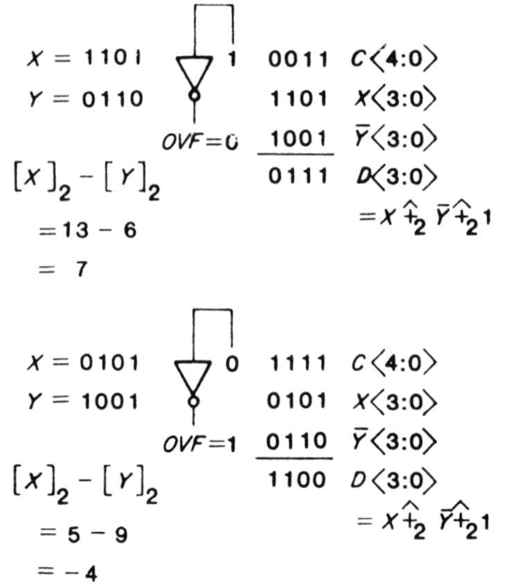

$$X = 1101 \qquad 1 \quad 0011 \quad C\langle 4:0\rangle$$
$$Y = 0110 \qquad\quad 1101 \quad X\langle 3:0\rangle$$
$$OVF = 0 \quad \underline{1001} \quad \bar{Y}\langle 3:0\rangle$$
$$[X]_2 - [Y]_2 \qquad\quad 0111 \quad D\langle 3:0\rangle$$
$$= 13 - 6 \qquad\qquad = X \hat{+}_2 \bar{Y} \hat{+}_2 1$$
$$= 7$$

$$X = 0101 \qquad 0 \quad 1111 \quad C\langle 4:0\rangle$$
$$Y = 1001 \qquad\quad 0101 \quad X\langle 3:0\rangle$$
$$OVF = 1 \quad \underline{0110} \quad \bar{Y}\langle 3:0\rangle$$
$$[X]_2 - [Y]_2 \qquad\quad 1100 \quad D\langle 3:0\rangle$$
$$= 5 - 9 \qquad\qquad = X \hat{+}_2 \bar{Y} \hat{+}_2 1$$
$$= -4$$

Figure 4.19   B2 subtraction examples

range subtraction, appropriate "flags" must be set during a subtraction to allow subsequent determination of ordering relations. This is exactly what is done by most modern processors, including the 6800. The flag bits for the 6800 are the CC register bits N, Z, V, and C. The following theorem specifies the tests for ordering relations under the B2 and 2C codes using these bits.

A numerical relation symbol ($<$, $=$, $\leq$, etc.) with a subscript 2 or 2C refers to the corresponding relation on words under the B2 or 2C code. For example, $X <_{2C} Y$ means $[X]_{2C} < [Y]_{2C}$.

THEOREM.   (Ordering relations) $\hspace{4cm}$ (4.17)

Suppose $X\langle n-1:0\rangle$ and $Y\langle n - 1:0\rangle$ are any words, and let

$$D\langle n - 1:0\rangle = X \hat{+}_2 \bar{Y} \hat{+}_2 1$$
$$N = D_{n-1}$$
$$Z = \text{NOR}\,(D\langle n - 1:0\rangle)$$
$$V = C_n \oplus C_{n-1}$$
$$C = \bar{C}_n$$

where $C\langle n:1\rangle$ are the carries generated by the above addition of X and $\bar{Y}$ with $C_0 = 1$.

Then

(a) $X <_{2C} Y$ iff $N \oplus V = 1$

(b) $X =_{2C} Y$ iff $Z = 1$

(c) $X \leq_{2C} Y$ iff $(N \oplus V) + Z = 1$

(d) $X <_{2} Y$ iff $C = 1$

(e) $X =_{2} Y$ iff $Z = 1$

(f) $X \leq_{2} Y$ iff $C + Z = 1$

This theorem follows directly from the previous theorems. The proof is left as an exercise.

The name "C" is used both to denote the carry word $C\langle n:0 \rangle$ and the single bit C of the CC register, which is equal to $\overline{C}_n$ after a subtraction. The C that appears in (d) and (f) is the single bit $C = \overline{C}_n$.

Each of the statements (a)–(f) is "if and only if." Hence, the opposite of any relation can be tested simply by reversing the test condition. For example, reversing (a) yields: $X \geq_{2C} Y$ iff $N \oplus V = 0$.

In the 6800, any one of the subtract instructions (SUBA, SUBB, or SBA) may be used to establish the conditions of the hypothesis of Theorem 4.17. The compare instructions (CMPA, CMPB, CBA) may also be used for this purpose. The only difference between the compare instructions and the subtract instructions is that the fixed-range result $D\langle n - 1:0 \rangle$ is not loaded into a destination register for the compare instructions.

The 6800 has conditional branch instructions for each of the tests specified in Theorem 4.17, and for the converse of each test. BLT and BGE correspond to (a), BEQ and BNE to both (b) and (e), BLE and BGT to (c), BCS and BCC to (d), and BLS and BHI to (f).

There are also conditional branch instructions to test directly for 2C overflow (BVS and BVC) and for the sign bit of the fixed-range result (BMI and BPL). These instructions, however, are *not* used to test for numerical ordering under the B2 or 2C codes.

A few examples of program fragments using branch instructions follow. In these examples, ABC and XYZ are names for memory registers. Assume that these are single-byte registers unless otherwise mentioned. These same names are assumed to be labels for the statements that define these registers (e.g., ABC RMB 1). We will use italics when such a name is used as variable, and no italics when used as a label.

Example 1

Branch to KAY if $ABC \leq_{2C} XYZ$.

```
LDAA  ABC
SUBA  XYZ
BLE   KAY
```

This program operates correctly whether or not overflow occurs when SUBA is executed. CMPA could be used in place of SUBA if it is desired to have ABC in accumulator A rather than $ABC \doteq_{2C} XYZ$.

Example 2

Branch to JIM if $ABC \geq_2 XYZ$.

```
LDAA  ABC
CMPA  XYZ
BCC   JIM
```

Unlike the BLE mnemonic in the previous example, the BCC mnemonic does not suggest the numerical test that is being performed. In general it is wise to avoid relying too heavily on the mnemonics when selecting a branch instruction.

Example 3

Branch to TONY if $[ABC +_{2C} XYZ]_{2C} < 0$.

```
LDAA  ABC
ADDA  XYZ
BLT   TONY
```

This is not an application of Theorem 4.17(a), since the hypothesis of the theorem is not satisfied (an addition rather than a subtraction is done). However, by Theorem 4.13, the sign bit of the extended-range result after an addition is $N \oplus V$, so the BLT instruction can be used to determine whether $[ABC +_{2C} XYZ]_{2C} < 0$. The program works whether or not there is overflow.

Example 4

Branch to AL if $[ABC]_{2C} + [XYZ]_{2C} = 0$

```
       LDAA  ABC
       ADDA  XYZ
       BVS   CONT
       BEQ   AL
CONT   :
       :
```

It is not sufficient to test Z only, since it is possible to add two numbers and get a fixed-range result of 0^n and an extended-range result of $1 \circ 0^n$. Hence, V must be tested as well to ensure that the correct result is 0^{n+1}.

With subtraction it is sufficient to test Z since $1 \circ 0^n$ cannot be the result of an n-bit subtract operation.

Example 5

Branch to TOM if $ABC <_{2C} XYZ$, where ABC and XYZ are 16-bit words.

```
LDAA  ABC+1
SUBA  XYZ+1
LDAA  ABC
SBCA  XYZ
BLT   TOM
```

4.3.6 Exercises

1. Using full adders and gates as components, design combinational networks to implement each of the following operations. The inputs are of different lengths: $W\langle 4:0 \rangle$, $X\langle 3:0 \rangle$, and $Y\langle 2:0 \rangle$. The output in each case is $Z\langle n - 1:0 \rangle$. Make n as small as possible, while retaining the capability to represent the correct result for any inputs.

   (a) $[Z]_{2C} = [X]_{2C} - [Y]_{2C}$
   (b) $[Z]_{2C} = [X]_{2C} + ([Y]_{2C} - [W]_{2C})$
   (c) $[Z]_2 = [Y]_2 * 2 + [X]_2$
   (d) $[Z]_{2C} = [Y]_{2C} * 2 - [X]_{2C}$
   (e) $[Z]_{2C} = [X]_{2C} + [Y]_2$ (Y is base 2)
   (f) $[Z]_{2C} = [Y]_{2C} - 1$
   (g) $[Z]_2 = |[W]_{2C}|$ (absolute value)

2. Write 6800 programs to do each of the following:

   (a) $M3[\alpha] \triangleq_{2C} M3[\beta] \rightarrow M3[\alpha]$
   (b) $[M2[\alpha]]_{2C} - [M[\beta]]_{2C} \rightarrow [M2[\alpha]]_{2C}$; detect overflow
   (c) Same as (b) except $M[\beta]$ is B2

3. (a) Design a 2·level "full subtracter" that satisfies the integer equation

$$X_i - Y_i - B_i = -B_{i+1} \cdot 2 + D_i$$

(X_i, Y_i, and B_i are inputs; B_{i+1} and D_i are outputs).

   (b) Use n full subtracters to construct an n-bit fixed-range B2 subtracter.

4. Design n-bit subtracters for each of the following codes, using the B2 adder and gates as components.
   (a) B2 signed-magnitude
   (b) Excess-2^{n-1}
   (c) One's complement

5. Using full adders and gates as components, design a network that will generate three single-bit outputs EQ, GT, and LT from two input words $X\langle n - 1:0\rangle$ and $Y\langle n - 1:0\rangle$ such that:

$$EQ = 1 \quad \text{iff} \quad [X]_{2C} = [Y]_{2C}$$

$$GT = 1 \quad \text{iff} \quad [X]_{2C} > [Y]_{2C}$$

$$LT = 1 \quad \text{iff} \quad [X]_{2C} < [Y]_{2C}$$

6. Repeat Exercise 5 using B2 instead of 2C code.

7. Design an iterative gate network that implements B2 comparison directly (rather than by doing a subtract). The network should have two inputs, $X\langle n - 1:0\rangle$ and $Y\langle n - 1:0\rangle$, and two output bits, EQ and GT:

$$EQ = 1 \quad \text{iff} \quad X = Y$$

$$GT = 1 \quad \text{iff} \quad [X]_2 > [Y]_2$$

Your network should identify the leftmost bit position where $X_i \neq Y_i$. The iterative cell should be cheaper than either a full adder or a full subtracter.

8. Write 6800 programs to do each of the following:
   (a) Branch to MARY if $[ABC]_{2C} + [XYZ]_{2C} \leq 0$.
   (b) Branch to JESSE if $[ABC]_2 + [XYZ]_2 = 0$.
   (c) Branch to HANK if $ABC \leq_{2C} XYZ$
   where ABC and XYZ are 16-bit memory registers.
   (d) Branch to GAIL if $[ABC]_{2C} + [XYZ]_{2C} - [DEF]_{2C} > 0$.

9. Below are listed a number of simple tasks that are frequently done by computers as part of some larger computation. For each of these, many variations are possible, some of which are the following:

• Write as a subroutine, or as a dedicated program for specific input values.

• If a subroutine, consider different modes of communication; call subroutine for specific task.

• Code for data (e.g., 2C, B2, BCD)

• Check for overflow or not.

• Single- or multiple-precison data.

• Block length (≤ 255, > 255).

Other variations may also be possible, depending upon the task. The tasks are:

    (a) Find the largest number in a list.
    (b) Multiple-precision increment.
    (c) Multiple-precision decrement.
    (d) Sort a list of numbers (i.e., arrange in ascending order).

4.4 MULTIPLICATION [7, 33, 34, 37, 39]

    4.4.1 Unsigned
    4.4.2 Signed
    4.4.3 Programs
    4.4.4 Exercises

4.4.1 Unsigned

The familiar pencil and paper algorithm for multiplication of decimal numbers is easily converted for B2 or 2C multiplication. The conversion is based upon the following theorem.

THEOREM. (Multiplication by 2)   (4.18)

For any $X\langle n - 1:0\rangle$,

$$[X]_2 * 2^m = [X \circ 0^m]_2$$

$$[X]_{2C} * 2^m = [X \circ 0^m]_{2C}$$

The proof follows directly from the definitions of the codes.

    Using this property, and the definition of the B2 code, the B2 multiplication algorithm is derived as follows.

$$[X]_2 * [Y]_2 = [X]_2 * (Y_{n-1} * 2^{n-1} + Y_{n-2} * 2^{n-2} + \cdots + Y_0 * 2^0)$$

$$= [X]_2 * Y_{n-1} * 2^{n-1} + [X]_2 * Y_{n-2} * 2^{n-2}$$

$$+ \cdots + [X]_2 * Y_0 \qquad (4.19)$$

Since Y_i is either 0 or 1, multiplication by Y_i is simply the AND operation. Multiplication by 2^i is accomplished by adding i zeros.

    This general multiplication algorithm is illustrated in Figure 4.20 for $n = 4$. In Figure 4.20(a), the four words to be added are written in the famil-

$$
\begin{array}{ll}
1101 & X\langle 3{:}0\rangle \\
\underline{1011} & Y\langle 3{:}0\rangle \\
1101 & X \cdot Y_0 \\
1101 & X \cdot Y_1 \circ 0 \\
0000 & X \cdot Y_2 \circ 00 \\
\underline{1101} & X \cdot Y_3 \circ 000 \\
10001111 & P\langle 7{:}0\rangle = B2 \text{ sum of above words}
\end{array}
$$

(a)

$$
\begin{array}{ll}
1101 & X\langle 3{:}0\rangle \\
\underline{1011} & Y\langle 3{:}0\rangle \\
+_2\left\{\begin{array}{l} 1101 \\ 1101 \end{array}\right. & \begin{array}{l} X \cdot Y_0 = S0 \\ X \cdot Y_1 \circ 0 \end{array} \\
+_2\left\{\begin{array}{l} 100111 \\ 0000 \end{array}\right. & \begin{array}{l} S0 +_2 X \cdot Y_1 \circ 0 = S1 \\ X \cdot Y_2 \circ 00 \end{array} \\
+_2\left\{\begin{array}{l} 0100111 \\ 1101 \end{array}\right. & \begin{array}{l} S1 +_2 X \cdot Y_2 \circ 00 = S2 \\ X \cdot Y_3 \circ 000 \end{array} \\
10001111 & S2 +_2 X \cdot Y_3 \circ 000 = S3 = P\langle 7{:}0\rangle
\end{array}
$$

(b)

Figure 4.20   B2 multiplication algorithm: (a) pencil and paper algorithm; (b) modified for machine implementation

iar format used for decimal pencil and paper multiplication. Each word of the form $X \cdot Y_i \circ 0^i$ is written with trailing zeros omitted, in the usual fashion. The four words are then added in one operation to produce the desired product.

The combinational network multiplier of Figure 4.21 implements this algorithm directly. The manner in which it adds the n words to be added, however, is not quite the way in which people do this operation. A person will start in column 0 and add all bits, then go to column 1, and so on. The carry that is produced in adding the bits in column i may be greater than 1 (although this does not happen in the example of Figure 4.20). Representing such nonbinary carries is a problem.

To avoid this problem, the multiplier of Figure 4.21 does only two operand additions, as illustrated in Figure 4.20(b). First, $X \cdot Y_0$ and $X \cdot Y_1 \circ 0$ are added to produce a sum $S1$. Then $X \cdot Y_2 \circ 0^2$ is added to $S1$ to produce $S2$, and so on. Notice that at any stage i, only an n-bit addition is required, because the word being added (e.g., $X \cdot Y_i \circ 0^i$) has only n nonzero bits. Notice also

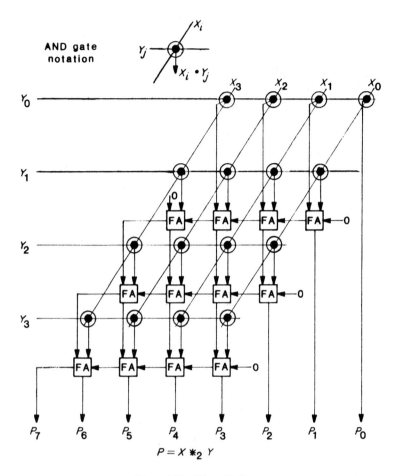

Figure 4.21   B2 multiplier

that this addition produces an $(n + 1)$-bit result, so that $S(i + 1)$ is one bit longer than Si.

4.4.2   Signed

Multiplication under the 2C code may be done in a similar fashion, as indicated by the following derivation:

$$[X]_{2C} * [Y]_{2C} = [X]_{2C} * (-Y_{n-1} * 2^{n-1} + Y_{n-2} * 2^{n-2} + \cdots + Y_0 * 2^0)$$

$$= -[X]_{2C} * Y_{n-1} * 2^{n-1} + [X]_{2C} * Y_{n-2} * 2^{n-2}$$

$$+ \cdots + [X]_{2C} * Y_0 * 2^0 \qquad (4.20)$$

Multiplication by 2^i may still be performed by adding i zeros and multiplication by Y_i by the AND operation. The notable differences from B2 multiplication are two:

1. At each stage the correct 2C result rather than the correct B2 result must be produced.

2. At the last stage, a subtraction rather than an addition must be performed, since Y_{n-1} is weighted by -2^{n-1}.

The 2C algorithm is illustrated in Figure 4.22 for $n = 4$, and a combinational network implementation is given in Figure 4.23.

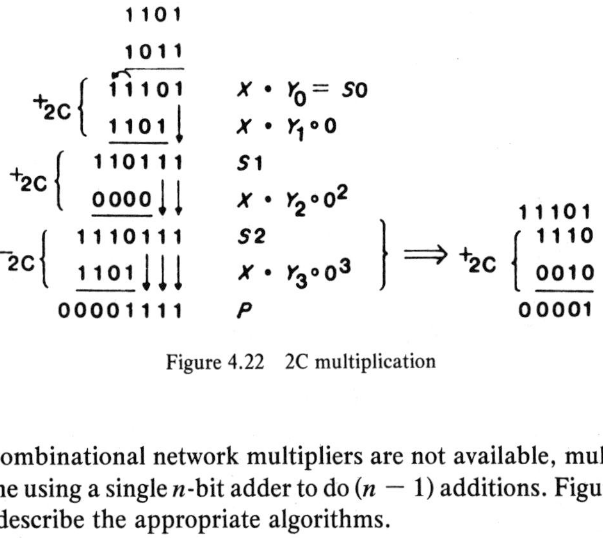

$$
\begin{array}{lll}
& 1101 & \\
& 1011 & \\
{}^{+}2C \left\{ \begin{array}{l} 11101 \\ 1101 \downarrow \end{array} \right. & \begin{array}{l} X \cdot Y_0 = S0 \\ X \cdot Y_1 \circ 0 \end{array} & \\
{}^{+}2C \left\{ \begin{array}{l} 110111 \\ 0000 \downarrow\downarrow \end{array} \right. & \begin{array}{l} S1 \\ X \cdot Y_2 \circ 0^2 \end{array} & \\
{}^{-}2C \left\{ \begin{array}{l} 1110111 \\ 1101 \downarrow\downarrow\downarrow \end{array} \right. & \begin{array}{l} S2 \\ X \cdot Y_3 \circ 0^3 \end{array} & \\
& 00001111 \quad P &
\end{array}
$$

Figure 4.22   2C multiplication

When combinational network multipliers are not available, multiplication can be done using a single n-bit adder to do $(n - 1)$ additions. Figures 4.20(b) and 4.22 describe the appropriate algorithms.

For very high speed combinational network multipliers, the algorithm of Figure 4.20(a) may be implemented differently. For example, the full adder may be abandoned in favor of a component that can add more than 3 bits simultaneously.

4.4.3   Programs

The 6800 does not have a multiply instruction. The 6800 architecture, however, was designed so that efficient B2 multiplication is possible, using a sequence of shift and add operations. The algorithm is presented in Figure 4.24. It is the same basic algorithm as in Figure 4.20.

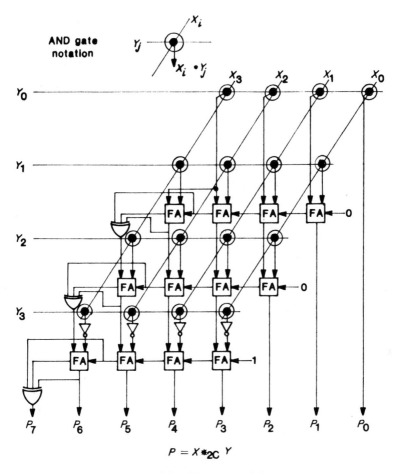

Figure 4.23   2C array multiplier

The reader should simulate the algorithm using 4-bit words to verify its operation. The algorithm is a little bit tricky in that rather than shifting the multiplicand left to multiply by 2, the accumulated partial product in $A \circ B$ is shifted right. Also, B is used for two purposes: it holds the multiplier initially, and it holds the low half of the result upon exit. On each pass through the loop, a new product bit is shifted into the left end of B, and a multiplier bit is shifted out the right of B into C (where it can be tested, and then discarded). The subroutine follows.

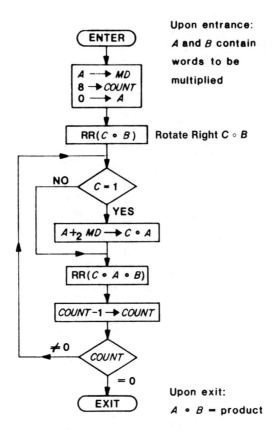

Upon entrance:
A and B contain
words to be
multiplied

Upon exit:
$A \circ B$ = product

Figure 4.24   B2 multiply flowchart

B2 Multiply Subroutine

Upon entrance: words to be multiplied are in A and B.

Upon exit: product is in $A \circ B$.

```
MULB2  STAA  MD
       LDX   #8        Use IX for COUNT
       CLRA
       RORB
LOOP   BCC   SHIFT
       ADDA  MD
SHIFT  RORA             RR(C∘A∘B)
       RORB
       DEX              COUNT − 1 → COUNT
```

```
            BNE  LOOP
            RTS
      MD    RMB  1
```

The calling program can easily test for B2 overflow with two instructions after JSR MULB2: TSTA and BNE OVF.

Multiple Precision

The single-precision subroutine MULB2 can easily be extended to a multiple-precision subroutine. The subroutine MB216 below is such an extension to double precision.

The product generated by MB216 is 32 bits long, denoted $P\langle 31:0\rangle$. PH will denote the high half of this product and PL the low half; that is, $PH = P\langle 31:16\rangle$ and $PL = P\langle 15:0\rangle$. The subroutine will use $A \circ B$ for PH and a double memory register for PL. Another double memory register is used for MD. A more general flowchart for the shift-add algorithm of Figure 4.24 is shown in Figure 4.25. The subroutine MB216 implements this flowchart.

Upon entrance: 16-bit words to be multiplied are in double memory registers MD and PL at the end of the subroutine

Upon exit: the 32-bit product is in $A \circ B \circ PL$

```
MB216  LDX  #16      Use IX for COUNT
       CLRA          0 → PH
       CLRB
       ROR  PL        Rotate Right C∘PL
       ROR  PL+1
LOOP   BCC  SHIFT
       ADDB MD+1     PH +₂ MD → C∘PH
       ADCA MD
SHIFT  RORA          RR(C∘P)
       RORB
       ROR  PL
       ROR  PL+1
       DEX           COUNT − 1 → COUNT
       BNE  LOOP
       RTS
PL     RMB  2
MD     RMB  2
```

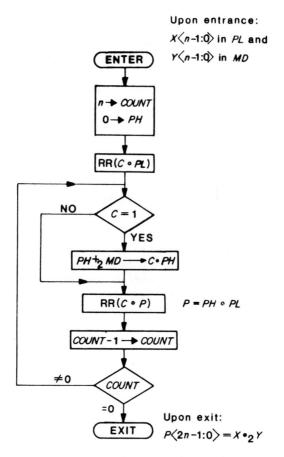

Figure 4.25   General B2 multiply algorithm

4.4.4   Exercises

1. Using full adders and gates as components, design a combinational network to implement each of the following operations.

(a) $[P]_2 = [X\langle 3:0\rangle]_2 * [Y\langle 2:0\rangle]_2$

(b) $[P]_{2C} = [X\langle 3:0\rangle]_{2C} * [Y\langle 2:0\rangle]_{2C}$

(c) $[P]_{2C} = [X\langle 3:0\rangle]_{2C} * [Y\langle 3:0\rangle]_2$

(d) $[P]_2 = [X\langle 3:0\rangle]_2 * 5$

2. Design a combinational network to do n-bit 2C multiplication, using as components: an n-bit B2 multiplier, fixed-range B2 incrementers, and gates.

3. Write 6800 programs to do each of the following:

(a) Multiply a double-precision B2 number by a single-precision B2 number.

(b) Single-precision 2C multiplication (convert to B2, multiply, and convert to 2C).

(c) Multiply a 2C number by a B2 number (result in 2C).

4.5 DIVISION [7, 33, 34, 37, 39]

4.5.1   Unsigned
4.5.2   Signed
4.5.3   Programs
4.5.4   Exercises

Division is different from the other operations that we have considered in that the set of integers is not closed under division. That is, if x and y are integers then $x + y$, $x - y$, and $x * y$ are all integers, but x/y need not be an integer. If we are using a code that represents only integers then we must express the result of a division operation in terms of integers. A way to do this is suggested by the following: for any integers $x > 0$ and $y > 0$, there exist unique integers $q \geq 0$ and $r \geq 0$ such that

$$x = q * y + r \tag{4.21}$$

and

$$r < y$$

The integer q is called the *quotient* and r the *remainder*. (Integers x and y are called the *dividend* and *divisor*, respectively.) We will express the result of an integer division by these two integers, quotient and remainder. If it is necessary to approximate the result by a single integer then we may either:

1. Drop the remainder (i.e., use q alone), or

2. Round to the nearest integer (i.e., use q if $r/y < \frac{1}{2}$ and $q + 1$ if $r/y \geq \frac{1}{2}$).

If negative as well as positive integers are involved then definition 4.21 is unsatisfactory because neither q nor r is defined uniquely. For example, if $x = -21$ and $y = +5$ then

$$-21 = (-5) * 5 + 4$$
$$-21 = (-4) * 5 + (-1)$$
$$-21 = (-3) * 5 + (-6)$$

etc.

Additional constraints are necessary to define q and r uniquely. The following definition provides these constraints, and reduces to definition 4.21 when restricted to nonnegative integers:

$$x = q * y + r \qquad (4.22)$$

$$\text{where } |r| < |y|$$
$$\text{sign}(r) = \text{sign}(x)$$

Equation 4.22 uniquely defines integers q and r for any integers x and y except when $y = 0$. Division by 0 is normally considered to be undefined, and is treated as an overflow condition.

Dividing equation 4.22 by y yields

$$\frac{x}{y} = q + \frac{r}{y} \qquad (4.23)$$

which relates the real number quotient x/y to the integer quotient and the fraction r/y. Since $\text{sign}(x) = \text{sign}(r)$, it follows from equation 4.23 that

$$\text{sign}\left(\frac{x}{y}\right) = \text{sign}\left(\frac{r}{y}\right) \qquad (4.24)$$

Furthermore, since $|r/y| < 1$, it also follows that

$$\text{sign}(q) = \text{sign}\left(\frac{x}{y}\right) \qquad \text{if } q \neq 0 \qquad (4.25)$$

4.5.1 Unsigned

The B2 version of the pencil and paper decimal division algorithm is illustrated in Figure 4.26. The algorithm may be applied to words of different lengths. In most computers, the divisor, the quotient, and the remainder are each of length n, and the dividend is of length $2n$. Overflow occurs when the correct quotient cannot be represented by n bits. The example in Figure 4.26 illustrates overflow, since the correct quotient requires 4 bits and $n = 3$.

The quotient bits are generated one at a time as follows. $Q_i = 1$ if $2^i * [Y]_2$ is less than the "remaining dividend" at that point. Initially the remaining dividend is X. The dividend is reduced by subtracting $2^i * [Y]_2$ whenever $Q_i = 1$. Quotient bits are generated starting with the most significant bit. The remaining dividend after generating Q_0 is the remainder R.

Another example of B2 division is shown in Figure 4.27. This example does not produce overflow.

A combinational network divider is pictured in Figure 4.28. Each row of the array is a B2 subtracter plus a switch. The subtracter is implemented by

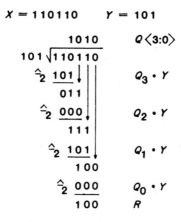

Figure 4.26   Binary division

using full adders, as in Figure 4.18, except that the carry-out from the last stage is *not* complemented. Hence, the horizontal output from the leftmost cell will be 1 if the subtraction did *not* produce overflow. The subtracter in the top row thus indicates divide overflow if $[Y]_2 < [X\langle 7:4\rangle]_2$, hence $2^4 * [Y]_2 < [X]_2$, hence $Q_4 = 1$.

In addition to indicating overflow, this bit also controls the switch that passes the "remaining dividend" to the next stage. If $OVF = 0$ then $X\langle 7:4\rangle$ is passed to the next subtracter.

The next row subtracts Y from $X\langle 6:3\rangle$. If the final carry-out from this subtracter is 1, then $[Y]_2 < [X\langle 6:3\rangle]_2$, hence $[Y]_2 * 2^3 < [X]_2$, hence $Q_3 =$

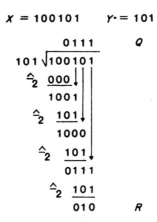

Figure 4.27   Another example of B2 division

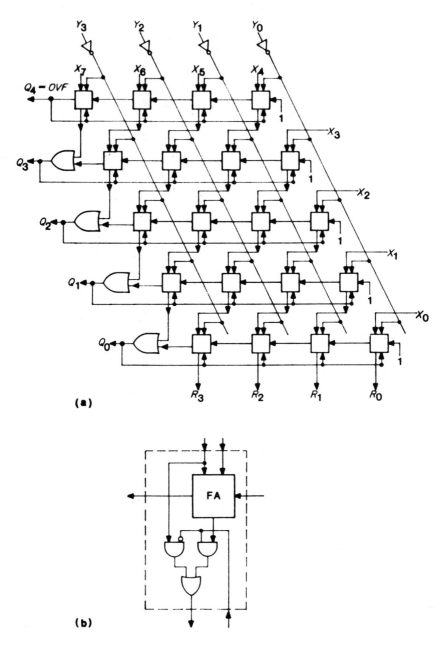

Figure 4.28   B2 array divider: (a) array; (b) array cell

1. It is also possible that $X_7 = 1$, in which case also $[Y]_2 * 2^3 < [X]_2$, and hence $Q_3 = 1$. This accounts for the OR gate that generates Q_3. Q_3 controls the switch that passes the remaining dividend (either $[X]_2 - 2^3 * [Y]_2$ or $[X]_2$) to the next stage.

The next three rows of the array work in the same fashion. The remaining dividend from the bottom row is the final remainder $R\langle 3:0 \rangle$.

4.5.2 Signed

Division under the 2C code is normally done by converting negative numbers to positive numbers and then doing B2 division. This will produce a quotient Q and remainder R of the correct magnitudes, but not necessarily of correct signs. If the sign of Q or R is incorrect, then the word is negated. Specifically, if $X_{2n-1} = 1$ then $\bar{R} \hat{+}_2 1 \rightarrow R$ (from equation 4.22, and if $X_{2n-1} \neq Y_{n-1}$ then $\bar{Q} \hat{+}_2 1 \rightarrow Q$ (from equation 4.25).

4.5.3 Programs

The 6800 processor does not have a division instruction. A flowchart for doing unsigned division as a sequence of subtract and rotate operations is shown in Figure 4.29. This is essentially the same algorithm that is implemented by the combinational network of Figure 4.28. After discussing the flowchart, we will implement this algorithm as a 6800 subroutine.

The dividend X is stored initially in the double-length register DD and the divisor in register DR. After initializing a counter, an overflow test is performed: overflow iff $DR \leq DDH$. This test may be understood by comparing the examples of Figures 4.26 and 4.27. Notice that there is overflow in Figure 4.26 since $Q_3 = 1$ but not in Figure 4.27.

After the overflow test, the flowchart enters the loop. C is cleared so that DD_0 will be 0 after the rotate-left operation. The rotate left of DD in the flowchart corresponds to shifting $DR = Y$ to the right in the pencil and paper algorithm.

After the rotate, if $C = 1$ then the next Q bit is definitely 1 since the 1 in C corresponds to a bit of higher weight than the current leftmost DR bit, as in Figure 4.27. In this case the subtraction is performed. The Q bit is set to 1 by putting 1 in DD_0.

If $C = 0$ then the next bit of Q may still be 1 and a subtraction performed, but only if $DR < DDH$. For example, see the third subtract in Figure 4.27.

After subtracting or not, $COUNT$ is decremented and tested for 0. If $COUNT \neq 0$, another pass through the loop is made.

The following subroutine implements this algorithm for the 6800 processor with $n = 8$.

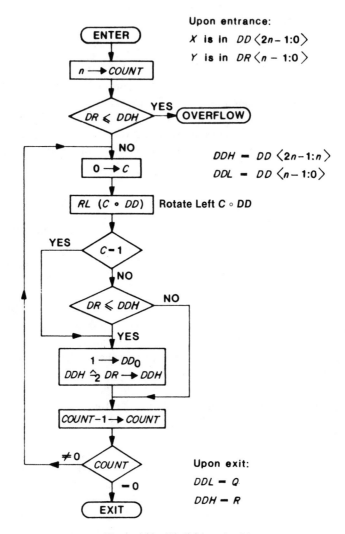

Figure 4.29   B2 division algorithm

Upon entrance:
$$A \circ B = X \quad (A \circ B \text{ is } DD)$$
$$DR = Y \quad (DR \text{ is a memory register})$$

Upon exit:

if overflow, $C = 1$;
if no overflow: $C = 0$, $B = Q$, $A = R$
where $[X]_2 = [Q]_2 \cdot [Y]_2 + [R]_2$

```
DIVB2  LDX   #8        Use IX for COUNT
       CMPA  DR        DDH − DR
       BCC   OVF       Overflow if DDH ≥ DR
LOOP   CLC
       ROLB            RL(C ∘ DD)
       ROLA
       BCS   SETQ
       CMPA  DR        DDH − DR
       BCS   NEXT
SETQ   ORAB  #$01      1 → DD₀
       SUBA  DR        DDH − DR → DDH
NEXT   DEX             COUNT − 1 → COUNT
       BNE   LOOP
       CLC
       RTS             No overflow
OVF    SEC
       RTS             Overflow
DR     RMB   1
```

4.5.4 Exercises

1. Let q and r be the quotient and remainder upon division of x by y, as defined by equation 4.22. Give examples of integers x, y, q, and r such that:
   (a) $\text{sign}(x) = \text{sign}(q)$, x positive
   (b) $\text{sign}(x) \neq \text{sign}(q)$, x positive
   (c) $\text{sign}(y) = \text{sign}(r)$, x negative
   (d) $\text{sign}(y) \neq \text{sign}(r)$, x negative

2. Design a combinational network to do n-bit 2C division, that is, generate Q and R from X and Y. Use as components: an n-bit B2 divider, fixed-range B2 incrementers, and gates.

3. Write a 6800 subroutine to do 2C division, with a 16-bit dividend and 8-bit divisor.

4. Write a 6800 subroutine to do double-precision B2 division (32-bit dividend and 16-bit divisor).

4.6   REAL ARITHMETIC [37–40]

4.6.1   Fixed-Point Representation
4.6.2   Floating-Point Representation
4.6.3   Fixed- Versus Floating-Point Arithmetic
4.6.4   Exercises

It is frequently necessary to represent not only integers, but other real numbers as well. There are many binary codes available for this purpose. The most popular of these are known as *fixed-point* and *floating-point* codes.

Both fixed-point and floating-point codes are based upon codes for integers, such as the base 2 and two's complement codes. Arithmetic under these codes is performed by using integer arithmetic operations. But there is a fundamental difference between machine representation of real arithmetic and machine representation of integer arithmetic. Integer arithmetic is *exact*, while real arithmetic is *approximate*. A binary integer code represents every integer in the range covered by the code. The result of a chain of calculations is exact, provided only that there is no overflow (i.e., neither in the final result nor in any of the intermediate results).

A binary code for representing real numbers, however, cannot represent every real number in the range covered by the code, even though the range may be finite in extent. Between any two real numbers there are infinitely many real numbers. In fact, the number of real numbers in such an interval is uncountably infinite (i.e., the real numbers within the interval cannot be put into 1 : 1 correspondence with the integers, hence cannot be counted).

Consider the machine representation of a chain calculation (i.e., a sequence of operations where the result of each operation is used in the next operation). The initial data, in general is not exact, but has some representational error. Furthermore, each operation may introduce further error into the computation. The error in the final result may be much larger than the representational error in the original data.

There are techniques for estimating and controlling the propagation of errors in chain calculations. Such techniques, however, are beyond the scope of this text. We will discuss the implementation of real arithmetic operations, and the error introduced by each operation, but will not consider the propagation of errors in a sequence of operations.

4.6.1   Fixed-Point Representation

Real numbers are commonly represented in pencil and paper computations by a sequence of decimal digits with a *base point* inserted at some point in the sequence. (The "base point" for decimal notation is usually called the "decimal point," but we will prefer the more general term in this discussion.) For example, the sequence 537.29 represents the real number $5 \cdot 10^2 + 3 \cdot 10^1 + 7 \cdot 10^0 + 2 \cdot 10^{-1} + 9 \cdot 10^{-2}$.

There are countably many real numbers that may be represented exactly by such sequences. There are uncountably many real numbers, however, that can be represented only approximately by any finite sequence of this sort.

If the number of digits to the right of the base point is restricted to m, then any real number may be represented with an error less than $10^{-m}/2$ by such a sequence. That is, for any real number x there is a decimal representation $d = d_{n-1}d_{n-2} \cdots d_0 d_{-1}d_{-2} \cdots d_{-m}$ such that $|x - d| \leq 10^{-m}/2$. The actual difference $(x - d)$ is called the *representation error*.

In similar fashion, a real number may be represented by a sequence of binary digits (bits) with an inserted base point. If the number of bits in the sequence is fixed for the representation of all numbers, and the position of the base point in the sequence is fixed, then the resulting binary code is called a *fixed-point code*.

The major advantage of a fixed-point code over a floating-point code (to be defined later) is simplicity of implementation. In fact, fixed-point arithmetic operations are exactly the same as integer operations. The only additional complexity that arises is in the placement of the base points for multiplication and division.

Fixed-Point B2 and 2C Codes

Both the B2 and the 2C codes are easily generalized to fixed-point codes. For example, if we put the base point 2 bits from the right, the two codes are interpreted as in the following examples:

$$[1101.01]_2 = 1 * 2^3 + 1 * 2^2 + 0 * 2^1 + 1 * 2^0 + 0 * 2^{-1} + 1 * 2^{-2}$$
$$= 8 + 4 + 0 + 1 + 0 + \frac{1}{4}$$
$$= 13\frac{1}{4}$$
$$= 13.25$$

$$[1101.01]_{2C} = -1 * 2^3 + 1 * 2^2 + 0 * 2^1 + 1 * 2^0 + 0 * 2^{-1} + 1 * 2^{-2}$$
$$= -8 + 4 + 0 + 1 + 0 + \frac{1}{4}$$
$$= -2\frac{3}{4}$$
$$= -2.75$$

Fixed-Point Operations

Fixed-point addition under both the B2 and 2C codes is illustrated in Figure 4.30. Notice that the word operations performed are the integer word opera-

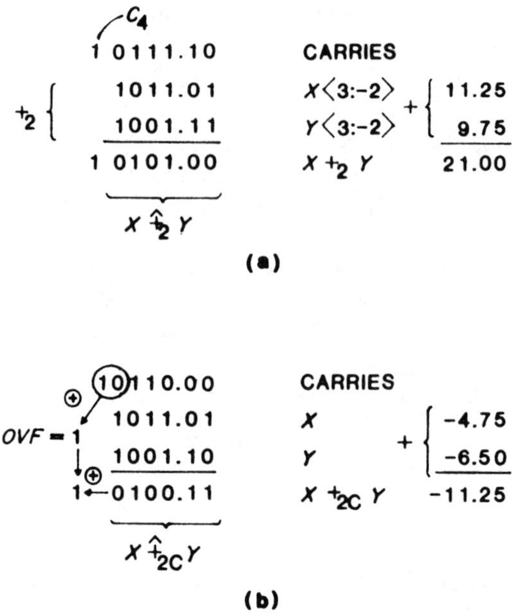

$$
\begin{array}{ll}
\quad\; \overset{\displaystyle c_4}{\overbrace{}} \\
+_2\Bigg\{ \begin{array}{l} 1\;0\;1\;1\;1.1\;0 \\ 1\;0\;1\;1.0\;1 \\ \underline{1\;0\;0\;1.1\;1} \\ 1\;0\;1\;0\;1.0\;0 \end{array}
& \begin{array}{l} \text{CARRIES} \\ X\langle 3\text{:-}2\rangle \\ Y\langle 3\text{:-}2\rangle \\ X +_2 Y \end{array}
\; + \Bigg\{ \begin{array}{r} 11.25 \\ 9.75 \\ 21.00 \end{array}
\end{array}
$$

$$X \overset{\wedge}{+_2} Y$$

(a)

$$
\begin{array}{ll}
OVF = 1 & \begin{array}{l} \overset{\displaystyle \oplus}{} \underset{\oplus}{\overset{\boxed{1\,0}}{}}1\,1\,0.0\,0 \\ 1\;0\;1\;1.0\;1 \\ \underline{1\;0\;0\;1.1\;0} \\ 1\leftarrow 0\;1\;0\;0.1\;1 \end{array}
& \begin{array}{l} \text{CARRIES} \\ X \\ Y \\ X +_{2C} Y \end{array}
\; + \Bigg\{ \begin{array}{r} -4.75 \\ -6.50 \\ -11.25 \end{array}
\end{array}
$$

$$X \overset{\wedge}{+_{2C}} Y$$

(b)

Figure 4.30   Fixed-point addition: (a) B2 code; (b) 2C code

tions. The position of the base point affects only the interpretation (i.e., the numbers represented). In both examples there is overflow. Note that it is detected exactly as for the integer operations, and the extended result bit is also generated in the same way as for integers. Finally, notice that the index range for each word is $\langle 3: -2\rangle$ corresponding to the weights assigned each bit position.

Subtraction is illustrated in Figure 4.31. Again, all operations are exactly as for integers.

Multiplication is illustrated for the B2 fixed-point code in Figure 4.32. The extended-range result, $X *_2 Y$, is exactly correct. The fixed-range result, $X \overset{\wedge}{*_2} Y$, is extracted from the extended result by positioning the base point the same as for the operands. Overflow is then detected by examining the remaining bits to the left. Remaining bits on the right represent the error in the fixed-range result that is introduced by the operations.

Fixed-point B2 division is illustrated in Figure 4.33. Word X is to be divided by word Y. The double-length dividend is formed from Y by concatenating n zeros on the left and m zeros on the right, where n and m are the numbers of integer bits and fraction bits in the operand format. The division is performed exactly as for integers, producing a quotient of the same format

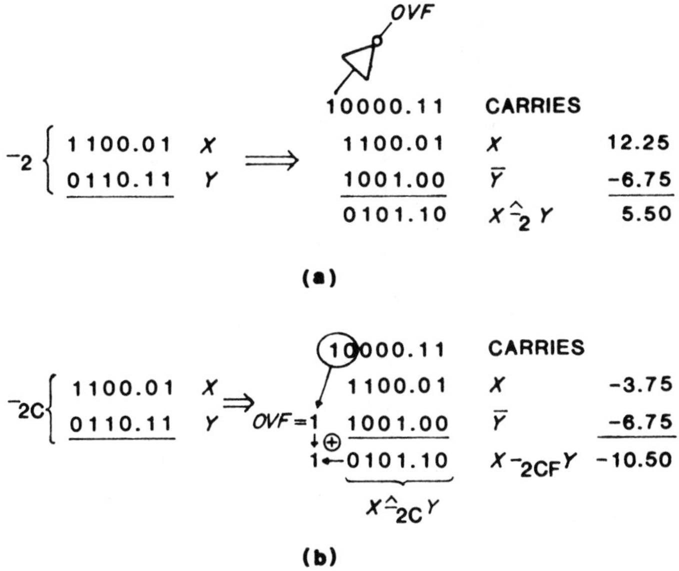

Figure 4.31 Fixed-point subtraction: (a) B2 code; (b) 2C code

as the operands (i.e., n integer bits and m fraction bits). The error in the quotient will be less than 2^{-m}, since there are m fraction bits.

4.6.2 Floating-Point Representation

Consider the representation of the three real numbers .0319, 4380, and 65.7, using a fixed-point decimal code. Central to the notion of a fixed-point code is the constraint that the base point is in the same position in all numbers represented. Stated another way, the number of integer digits is the same in all numbers represented, and the number of fraction digits is the same in all numbers.

Subject to these constraints, a decimal fixed-point code to represent the numbers .0319, 4380, and 65.7 must have at least four integer digits and four fraction digits. Using this minimal code, the numbers are represented as follows: 0000.0391, 4380.0000, and 0065.7000.

A *floating-point* code allows the base point position to vary from one number to another. The floating-point representation of a number consists of a sequence of digits with the base point assumed to be in some zero position, together with another sequence of digits that specify how far the base point should be moved from the zero position. Using such a code, the above three numbers may be represented as follows: (319, −1); (438, 4); (657, 2). The

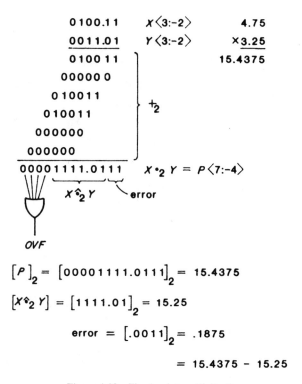

$$[P]_2 = [00001111.0111]_2 = 15.4375$$

$$[X^\wedge_2 Y] = [1111.01]_2 = 15.25$$

$$\text{error} = [.0011]_2 = .1875$$

$$= 15.4375 - 15.25$$

Figure 4.32   Fixed-point multiplication

zero position of the base point is immediately to the left of the first digit in the sequence before the comma. The single-digit sequence after the comma (with sign) indicates the position of the base point with respect to the zero position.

Since multiplication by 10 corresponds to moving the base point one position to the right, and division by 10 to moving one position left, floating-point decimal notation is often represented in the form $c * 10^e$.

Using this notation, the three numbers are represented $.319 * 10^{-1}$, $.438 * 10^4$, and $.657 * 10^2$. In this notation, c is called the *coefficient* (or *mantissa*) and e is the *exponent* (or *characteristic*). The number 10 is called the *floating-point base*.

Binary Floating-Point Codes

There are many different floating-point codes possible, depending upon: the codes used to represent the coefficient and the exponent; the zero position of the base point; and the choice of a floating-point base. (The choice of the codes to represent the coefficient and the exponent includes specification of the number of bits to be used for each.)

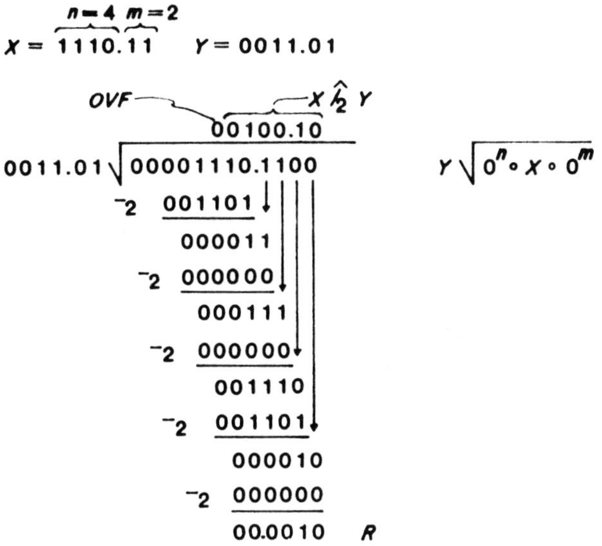

$$\overbrace{X = 1110.11}^{n-4\ m=2} \qquad Y = 0011.01$$

$$OVF \underset{}{\overbrace{}} \overset{-X\,\hat{/}_2\,Y}{}$$

$$00100.10$$

$$0011.01\,\overline{)00001110.1100} \qquad Y\sqrt{0^n \circ X \circ 0^m}$$

$$\begin{array}{r} {}^-2\quad 001101 \downarrow \\ \hline 000011 \\ {}^-2\quad 000000 \downarrow \\ \hline 000111 \\ {}^-2\quad 000000 \downarrow \\ \hline 001110 \\ {}^-2\quad 001101 \downarrow \\ \hline 000010 \\ {}^-2\quad 000000 \\ \hline 00.0010 \quad R \end{array}$$

$$[X]_2 \,/\, [Y]_2 \;=\; 14.75 \,/\, 3.25 \;=\; 4.5384615$$

$$[X \,\hat{/}_2\, Y]_2 \;=\; 4.5$$

$$4.5384615 - 4.5 = .0384615 < .25 = 2^{-m}$$

Figure 4.33   Fixed-point division

The most natural floating-point base is 2, since multiplying or dividing by 2 corresponds to shifting the base point right or left one place. Other bases have also been used, however. For example, if the floating-point base is 16 then increasing or decreasing the exponent by 1 corresponds to shifting the base point 4 places right or left since $16^1 = 2^4$.

A natural choice for the zero position of the base point would be to the right of the rightmost bit of the coefficient. The coefficient would then represent an integer. This choice is seldom used, however. Instead, the zero position is usually either to the left of the leftmost bit (making the coefficient a fraction), or between the two leftmost bits (making the coefficient an integer, 0 or 1, plus a fraction).

Since the 2C code is a de facto standard for representation of signed integers and fixed-point reals, it would seem the natural choice for representation of the coefficient and the exponent. A more popular choice, however, has been base 2 signed-magnitude code for the coefficient and the excess-m code for the exponent (see Section 4.1.3). This choice allows a simpler determination of ordering relations, as will be demonstrated below.

Because there are so many choices involved in selecting a floating-point code, with pros and cons for each choice or combination of choices, there are many different codes in current use. To continue this discussion we must select a particular code to use as an example. This code is described next.

IEEE Standard

Recently, the Institute for Electrical and Electronics Engineers (IEEE, pronounced "I triple E") proposed a comprehensive floating-point standard [40]. The standard covers not only the code to be used, but various choices involved in implementing arithmetic operations and responding to overflow conditions. The basic code proposed by the IEEE standard is defined in Figure 4.34. We will use this code as an example in our discussion.

Under the IEEE code, a floating-point word X has three fields: a sign bit S; an exponent field E; and a fraction field F. The standard allows three formats (single, double, and quad), to accommodate applications with different precision requirements. The number of exponent and fraction bits for each is indicated in the figure. The number represented by X is $[X]_{FL} = (-1)^s * c * 2^e$. The exponent e is represented by the field E under the excess-m code, where m depends upon the number of exponent bits, as shown. The coefficient is represented by the B2 fixed-point word with a single integer bit (always 1) and the entire F field as the fraction part. The integer bit, since it is always a 1, need not be represented in X; it is called the *hidden bit*[1].

The IEEE standard defines $[X]_{FL}$ as in Figure 4.34 for all values of the exponent except the smallest and the largest ($E = 00 \cdots 0$ and $E = 11 \cdots 1$). These exponents are reserved to represent special operands, to be discussed later.

Examples:

Suppose $n_e = 3$ and $n_f = 3$.
  (a) $[1001110]_{FL} = -[1.110]_2 * 2^{1-3}$
  $\qquad\qquad\qquad = -1.75 * 2^{-2}$
  $\qquad\qquad\qquad = -0.4375$
  (b) $[0111110]_{FL} = [1.110]_2 * 2^{7-3}$
  $\qquad\qquad\qquad = 1.75 * 2^4$
  $\qquad\qquad\qquad = 28$

---

[1] Exception: The quad precision format uses the leading bit of the F field as the integer bit of the coefficient instead of the hidden bit. The advantage of the hidden bit is that it provides an extra bit of precision, but it also complicates the representation of very small numbers (see Table 4.2).

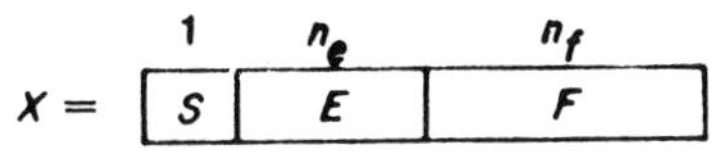

$$X = \boxed{\begin{array}{c|c|c} S & E & F \end{array}}$$

with labels: 1, n_e, n_f — number of bits

$$[X]_{FL} = c * 2^e \qquad \text{(see exception 1)}$$

$$\text{where} \quad e = [E]_2 - m$$

$$c = (-1)^S * [1.F]_2 \qquad \text{(see exception 2)}$$

Precision	n_e	n_f	$m = 2^{n_e - 1} - 1$
Single	8	23	127
Double	11	52	1023
Quad	15	112	16383

Exceptions:

1. This definition does not apply exactly when $E = 00 \cdots 0$ or $E = 11 \cdots 1$ (see text).

2. Quad precision uses the leading bit of F as the integer bit (see text).

Figure 4.34   IEEE standard code

Code Range

Figure 4.35 shows the range of the coefficient c for the IEEE code. The coefficient can exactly represent 2^{n_f} real numbers between 1 and 2. Specifically, it represents the numbers $1, 1 + 1/D, 1 + 2/D, \ldots, 1 + (D - 1)/D$, where $D = 2^{n_f}$.

For each value of the exponent e, the IEEE code represents each of these same numbers times 2^e. Hence for $e = 1$ the numbers represented are $2, 2 +$

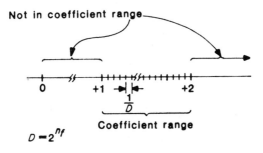

Figure 4.35   Range of the coefficient (unsigned)

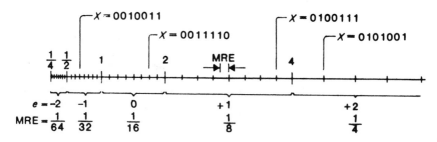

Figure 4.36   Partial range of $[X]_{FL}$ with $n_e = n_f = 3$

$2/D$, $2 + 4/D$, $\ldots$, $2 + 2(D - 1)/D$, and for $e = -1$ the numbers represented are $1/2$, $1/2(1 + 1/D)$, $\ldots$, $1/2(1 + (D - 1)/D)$. Note that the length of the interval covered for a fixed exponent e is 2^e, and the distance between numbers represented is $2^e/2^{n_f}$. The positive numbers represented by the IEEE code with $n_e = n_f = 3$ for a few values of the exponent are represented in Figure 4.36. The 7-bit words that represent a few of these points are specified.

The maximum representation error (MRE) for numbers in the range of exponent e is half the distance between exactly representable points in that range. Hence, MRE $= 2^{e-n_f-1}$.

Only numbers from the positive range are illustrated in Figure 4.36. $S = 0$ for all of these. The negative range ($S = 1$) is the mirror image of the positive range.

Ordering Relations

Since all the numbers with exponent e have smaller magnitude than all numbers with exponent $e + 1$, it is easy to see that numerical order under this floating-point code is the same as numerical order under the base 2 signed-magnitude code. That is,

THEOREM   (4.26)
$$[X]_{FL} < [Y]_{FL} \text{ if and only if } [X]_{2SM} < [Y]_{2SM}$$

Floating-Point Operations

Addition.   Floating-point addition of numbers with the same sign or subtraction of numbers with different signs is accomplished in five steps:

1. Align base points
2. Add unsigned coefficients (B2 addition)

3. Normalize

4. Round

5. Attach sign of X to result

The process is illustrated in Figure 4.37 using the IEEE code with $n_e = n_f = 3$.

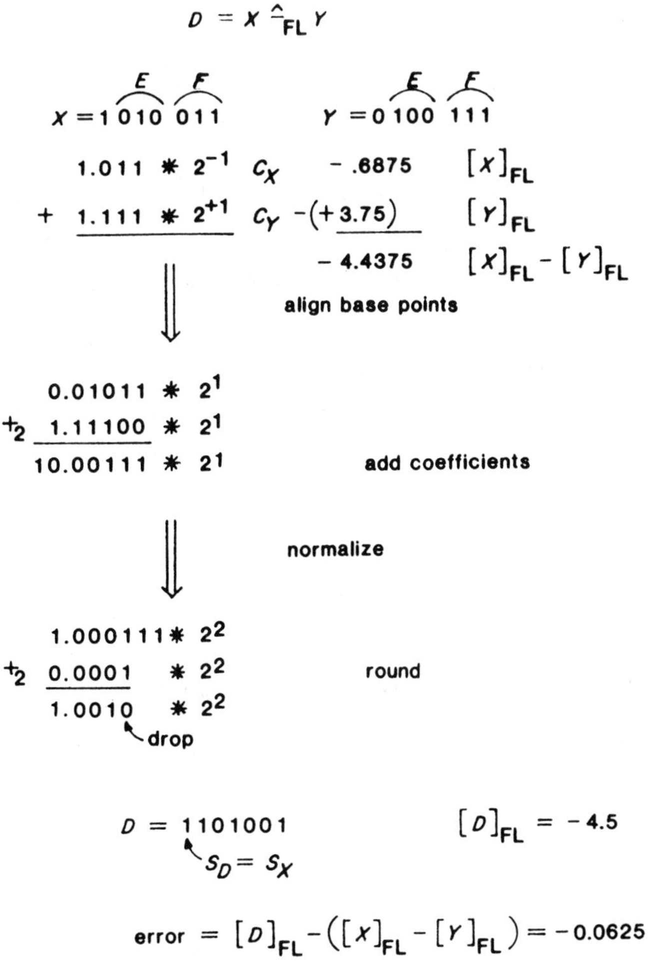

$$D = X \overset{\wedge}{-}_{FL} Y$$

$$X = 1\,\overbrace{0\,1\,0}^{E}\,\overbrace{0\,1\,1}^{F} \qquad Y = 0\,\overbrace{1\,0\,0}^{E}\,\overbrace{1\,1\,1}^{F}$$

$$
\begin{array}{llll}
& 1.011 \ast 2^{-1} & c_X & -.6875 & [X]_{FL} \\
+ & 1.111 \ast 2^{+1} & c_Y & -(+3.75) & [Y]_{FL} \\
\hline
& & & -4.4375 & [X]_{FL} - [Y]_{FL}
\end{array}
$$

align base points

$$
\begin{array}{ll}
& 0.01011 \ast 2^1 \\
+_2 & 1.11100 \ast 2^1 \\
\hline
& 10.00111 \ast 2^1
\end{array}
$$

add coefficients

normalize

$$
\begin{array}{ll}
& 1.000111 \ast 2^2 \\
+_2 & 0.0001 \ast 2^2 \\
\hline
& 1.0010 \ast 2^2
\end{array}
$$

round

↖ drop

$$D = 1101001 \qquad\qquad [D]_{FL} = -4.5$$

↖ $s_D = s_X$

$$\text{error} = [D]_{FL} - ([X]_{FL} - [Y]_{FL}) = -0.0625$$

Figure 4.37   Floating-point addition/subtraction ($n_f = n_e = 3$)

Base points are aligned by shifting the coefficient with the lesser exponent right and increasing its exponent. Error is avoided at this step by using long registers so that bits are not lost in the right shift. Register length $1 + n_f + 3$ is required by the standard, where the rightmost bit is a "sticky bit"—that is, the OR of all bits shifted through it. This ensures that the representation error of the final result will be $\leq$ the MRE for the range of the final exponent (i.e., the only error is that of the rounding step).

Coefficients are added using the B2 addition operation. If there is a carry-out, then the result must be "normalized" and "rounded," that is, the coefficient must be put in the form $1.F$. Normalization is accomplished by shifting right once, so that there is a single 1 to the left of the base point. The fraction part must then be "rounded" to the correct number of bits. Rounding is accomplished by adding $0.0^{n_f} 1$ to the normalized result (and shifting right if there is a carry-out). Only n_f bits are retained for F. This rounds to the nearest exactly representable point, and gives an average error of 0.

Subtraction. Addition of numbers with different signs, or subtraction of numbers with like signs, is a six-step process.

0. Determine ordering of coefficients by B2 comparison
1. Align base points
2. Subtract smaller coefficient from larger (B2 subtraction)
3. Normalize
4. Round
5. Attach sign

Steps 1–5 are as in Figure 4.37, except that B2 subtraction is done rather than addition, and normalization, if necessary, involves shifting left rather than right.

Multiplication. Multiplication is accomplished in five steps:

1. Multiply coefficients
2. Add exponents
3. Normalize
4. Round
5. Attach sign

The process is illustrated in Figure 4.38. Step 1 is fixed-point extended-range B2 multiplication. Hence no error is introduced at this step.

$$\left(c_x \ast 2^{e_x}\right) \ast \left(c_y \ast 2^{e_y}\right) = \left(c_x \ast c_y\right) \ast 2^{e_x + e_y}$$

$$X = 1110110 \qquad Y = 0001101$$

$$P = X \ast_{FL} Y$$

1.110 $\ast 2^3$	$c_x \ast 2^{e_x}$	-14.0
$\ast$ 1.101 $\ast 2^{-2}$	$c_y \ast 2^{e_y}$	$\ast$ 0.40625
1 110		-5.6875
00 00		
111 0		
1110		

$$\overline{\text{10.110 110}} \ast 2^1 \qquad \left(c_x \ast c_y\right) \ast 2^{e_x + e_y}$$

⇓ normalize

1.0110	$\ast 2^2$	
$+_2$ 0.0001	$\ast 2^2$	round
1.0111	$\ast 2^2$	

↖drop

Hence $P = 1101011$ $\qquad [P]_{FL} = -5.5$

↖ $S_P = S_X \oplus S_Y$

$$\text{error} = [P]_{FL} - \left([X]_{FL} \ast [Y]_{FL}\right) = +0.18$$

Figure 4.38 Floating-point multiplication ($n_e = n_f = 3$)

Normalization may be necessary to put the result in the form $1.F$. After normalization, F need only be $n_f + 1$ bits (i.e., bits further to the right may be dropped).

Rounding is accomplished, as for addition, by adding $0.0^{n_f} 1$ (and shifting right if there is a carry-out), then retaining n_f bits for F.

A minus or plus sign is attached to the result, depending upon whether the operand signs were different or the same.

Division. Division is similar to multiplication, except that: step 1 is fixed-point B2 division with quotient bits generated until an $(n_f + 2)$-bit normalized result is obtained (integer bit, plus n_f fraction bits, plus one extra bit for rounding); and exponents are subtracted rather than added. The process is illustrated in Figure 4.39. Note that the dividend is formed by adding $n_f + 3$ zeros to the X coefficient. This is always sufficient to produce an $(n_f + 2)$-bit normalized result, since both dividend and divisor begin with integer bit 1.

$$\frac{c_x * 2^{e_y}}{c_y * 2^{e_y}} = \frac{c_x}{c_y} * 2^{e_x - e_y} = q \cdot * 2^{e_q}$$

$$X = 0101010 \qquad Y = 1110101 \qquad Q = X \div_{FL} Y$$

$$[X]_{FL} = 5 \quad [Y]_{FL} = -13 \quad [X]_{FL} \div [Y]_{FL} = -0.3846153$$

$$
\begin{array}{r}
c_q \\
c_y \sqrt{c_x}
\end{array}
\qquad
\begin{array}{r}
0.110001 \\
1.101 \overline{)1.010000000} \\
{}^-2 \quad 1101 \downarrow \\
\hline
01110 \\
{}^-2 \quad 1101 \downarrow \\
\hline
00010000 \\
{}^-2 \quad 1101 \\
\hline
0011
\end{array}
\qquad
\begin{array}{l}
\text{add } n_f + 3 \text{ 0's to } c_x \\
\text{to maintain precision}
\end{array}
$$

$$
\begin{array}{lll}
0.110001 & * 2^{-1} & c_q + 2^{e_q} \\
1.10001 & * 2^{-2} & \text{normalize} \\
+ 0.00010 & * 2^{-2} & \\
\hline
1.10011 & * 2^{-2} & \text{round}
\end{array}
$$

$$Q = 1001100 \qquad\qquad [Q]_{FL} = -0.375$$
$$\quad\ ^{\backslash} S_Q = S_X \oplus S_Y$$

$$\text{error} = [Q]_{FL} - \left([X]_{FL} \div [Y]_{FL}\right) = +0.0096153$$

Figure 4.39   Floating-point division ($n_f = n_e = 3$)

Overflow and Underflow.   There are two types of "overflow" conditions in floating-point arithmetic, referred to as overflow and underflow. These conditions are illustrated in Figure 4.40. Overflow occurs when representation of the correct result of a floating-point operation has a magnitude that requires an exponent that is greater than emax (the most positive exponent that can be represented). Underflow occurs when representation of the correct result requires an exponent less than emin (the most negative exponent that can be represented). The term "correct" here means the correct rounded result, not the exact result (which may not be representable).

Overflow is the more serious condition. When overflow occurs, the correct result is truly beyond the range of the code and cannot be represented. Underflow is less serious. The correct result can be represented with an error less than 2^{emin} by $+$xmin or $-$xmin (or by 0 if there is an exact representation of 0).

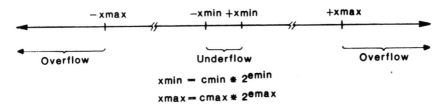

Figure 4.40   Overflow and underflow

The IEEE code reserves the exponents $E = 00 \cdots 0$ and $E = 11 \cdots 1$ to represent special operands. These are not considered part of the exponent range for purposes of determining overflow and underflow. Hence, the emin and emax of Figure 4.39 correspond to $E = 0^n1$ and $E = 1^n0$, respectively, where $n = n_e - 1$.

The special operands represented by the exponents $E = 00 \cdots 0$ and $E = 11 \cdots 1$ are specified in Table 4.2. $E = 00 \cdots 0$ and $F = 00 \cdots 0$ is an exact representation of 0. $E = 00 \cdots 0$ and $F \neq 00 \cdots 0$ provides an exact representation for numbers beyond the range of the standard code (i.e., numbers in the underflow region) by allowing coefficients with integer bit 0. This is sometimes called *gradual underflow*.[2]

The combination $E = 11 \cdots 1$ and $F = 00 \cdots 0$ provides representations for $+\infty$ and $-\infty$. The IEEE standard includes specifications for infinity arithmetic, which we will not discuss. The combination $E = 00 \cdots 0$ and $F \neq 00 \cdots 0$ provides for the representation of things that are not numbers. The F field may represent system-dependent information (e.g., special codes for storage initialization by the operating system; pointer to an "extended range" correct result).

TABLE 4.2   IEEE special operands

	E	F	$[X]_{FL}$
*	$00 \cdots 0$	$00 \cdots 0$	$(-1)^s * 0$ (exact 0)
*	$00 \cdots 0$	$\neq 00 \cdots 0$	$(-1)^s * 2^{emin}\,[0.F]_2$
	$11 \cdots 1$	$00 \cdots 0$	$(-1)^s * \infty$
	$11 \cdots 1$	$\neq 00 \cdots 0$	NaN (Not a Number)

*Exception: Special treatment of $E = 00 \cdots 0$ is not necessary for quad precision (see text).

---

[2] Treating $E = 00 \cdots 0$ as a special case is necessary only because the "hidden bit" does not allow the coefficient to have a 0 integer part. The quad precision format does not use the hidden bit. Instead, the leading bit of the fraction field is used as the integer bit. This makes special treatment of $E = 00 \cdots 0$ unnecessary.

4.6.3 Fixed- Versus Floating-Point Arithmetic

To be specific, we will compare the IEEE code with the B2-signed-magnitude fixed-point code. This is for convenience only, however. The results of the comparison have general validity.

These two codes are most easily compared if the leading bit of the F field is used as the integer part of the coefficient, as in the quad precision format (rather than the hidden bit, as in the single- and double-precision formats), and if $n_f = n + m$, where n and m are the integer and fraction parts of the fixed-point code. If this is the case, then the same number of bits is used directly to represent a number in both codes. The exponent bits of a floating-point code are used to specify the position of the base point, and do not directly provide additional precision.

When the value of the exponent is $e = n - 1$, then both codes have exactly the same number of integer bits (hence the same range) and the same number of fraction bits (hence the same precision). In fact, they represent exactly the same real numbers.

Taking this as a starting point, the advantages of having a variable exponent, which can effectively move the base point, are apparent. Specifically, they are the following.

1. The problem of overflow is greatly reduced. When an operation produces a result that would be out of range for the fixed-point code, the exponent is simply increased (and the coefficient shifted right). This effectively increases the number of integer bits and decreases the number of fraction bits, thus increasing the range of the code at the expense of precision. In most cases this is a desirable trade-off, because increased representational error is usually preferable to overflow.

2. Representation error for small numbers is reduced. Under a fixed-point code, when an operation produces too many fraction bits (e.g., Figure 4.32), the extra bits on the right must always be dropped, even when the leading integer bits are zeros. Under a floating-point code, the leading zeros can be discarded by decreasing the exponent (and shifting the coefficient left), thus making room for the fraction bits on the right.

The costs of enjoying these advantages are the following:

1. Need to use bits to represent the exponent

2. Increased complexity of implementation

3. Decreased execution speed (particularly if floating-point operations must be implemented in software)

4. Possibility of very large representation errors in computed results

All of the above considerations are involved in selecting a code to represent real numbers in a particular application. Also, the precision requirements of the application must be considered. If the same precision is required throughout the range that must be covered, fixed-point arithmetic is more suitable. If greater precision is required for smaller numbers, or if the natural constraint on precision is "number of significant digits" rather than "maximum representation error (MRE)," then floating-point arithmetic is more suitable.

4.6.4 Exercises

1. What is the range of the fixed-point 2C code with 24 integer bits and 16 fraction bits? What is the maximum representation error (MRE)?

2. In a particular application you need to represent real numbers in the range -10^9 through $+10^9$ with an MRE less than 10^{-7}. Using the fixed-point 2C code, how many bits are required?

3. Consider the fixed-point 2C code with 8 integer bits and 4 fraction bits. Let $X = 000011011011$ and $Y = 111101110101$. Compute $S = X \hat{+}_{2C} Y$, $D = X \hat{-}_{2C} Y$, $P = X \hat{*}_{2C} Y$, and $Q = X \hat{\div}_{2C} Y$. In each case, indicate whether there is overflow, and specify the error introduced by each operation.

4. Consider the IEEE floating-point code with $n_e = 4$ and $n_f = 7$. Let $X = 111000110111$ and $Y = 010001101011$.

   (a) Compute $S = X \hat{+}_{FL} Y$. Specify the error introduced by this operation (i.e., error $= [S]_{FL} - ([X]_{FL} + [Y]_{FL})$.

   (b) Repeat (a) for $\hat{-}_{FL}$.

   (c) Repeat (a) for $\hat{*}_{FL}$.

   (d) Repeat (a) for $\hat{\div}_{FL}$.

5. For the application described in Exercise 2, how many bits will be required using the IEEE floating-point code? (n_e and n_f may be any values. Choose them so that the sum is as small as possible.)

6. Specify the range and maximum representation error for $e = 0$ for each of the IEEE formats, Figure 4.34. Repeat for $e = 50$, 100, and -50.

7. Compare the single-precision IEEE floating-point code with the 32-bit fixed-point 2C code that uses 16 integer bits and 16 fraction bits.

   (a) What is the range of each code?

   (b) Identify the portions of the real line for which each code is more precise (i.e., smaller representational error).

8. How many bits must a fixed-point code use to provide the same range as the single-precision IEEE code, with the same precision as the IEEE code between numbers 1 and 2 on the real line?

9. (a) How many exponent bits (n_e) must an IEEE-type code have to cover the same range as the fixed-point 2C code with 16 integer bits and 16 fraction bits?

(b) How many fraction bits (n_f) must this code have to provide the same precision or better for this entire range?

(c) With n_e and n_f as determined in (a) and (b), for what part of the real line is the IEEE code more precise than the fixed-point code?

(d) How much can the range be extended by adding 4 more exponent bits? What will be the maximum representation error for the largest exponent value?

10. Design combinational networks to do the four basic arithmetic operations under the IEEE format. You may use integer adders, multipliers, and dividers as components. You may also define other high-level components (e.g., a shifter).

11. Write a "floating-point package" for the 6800, that is, a set of subroutines to do floating-point operations.

Chapter 5

REGISTER TRANSFER LEVEL COMPONENTS

5.1 **Digital Signals**
5.2 **Combinational Networks**
5.3 **Pulse Generators**
5.4 **Memory Components**
5.5 **Sequential Networks**

In this chapter, the major classes of register transfer level components are presented. Both microcircuit and macrocircuit design of these components are discussed. The chapter begins with a discussion of the representation of digital signals, which are used for communication between components.

5.1 DIGITAL SIGNALS [36, 42]

5.1.1 **Logic Levels and Noise Margins**
5.1.2 **Modeling Digital Signals**
5.1.3 **Signal Paths**
5.1.4 **Exercises**

Information in computers is represented by binary words. Each bit of a binary word within a computer is represented by a voltage, usually with high voltages representing logic 1 and low voltages representing logic 0. Information is processed by doing long sequences of register transfer operations, which are evoked by control signals (also voltages).

In this section, the fundamental characteristics of the voltage signals that are used to represent information and to control information processing are discussed. Also, electrical paths for transmitting signals in microcircuits and macrocircuits are studied.

5.1.1   Logic Levels and Noise Margins

In order to use a continuous variable (such as a voltage) to represent a binary variable, it is necessary to partition the range of the continuous variable into distinct regions representing 0 and 1. So that the two regions are clearly distinguished, there should be a gap between them, as illustrated in Figure 5.1.

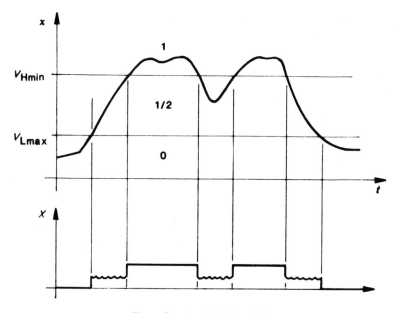

Figure 5.1   Logic level partition

A voltage signal that makes sharp transitions between 0 and 1 can be regarded as a "binary signal." If the time spent in the transition region is not negligible, however, and if dynamic rather than just steady-state operation is important, then a ternary (i.e., three-level) representation is necessary. A fundamental responsibility of the digital system designer is to assure that information signals are not "looked at" while they are in the transition region. In timing diagrams we will sometimes use a wiggly line to represent a signal transition, as illustrated in Figure 5.1.

Noise

All digital systems are afflicted to some extent by *noise*, that is, by undesired changes in signal voltages. Techniques for limiting the amount of noise in a system are studied in Section 7.3. It is never possible to eliminate noise entirely, however, and digital systems are built to tolerate a certain amount of noise. The mechanism for providing this noise tolerance is simple and elegant; gate outputs are required to satisfy a different logic level partition than the inputs, as illustrated in Figure 5.2. At steady state, gate outputs are guaranteed to be at correct levels according to the output partition provided that inputs are at correct levels according to the input partition. The difference between the minimum acceptable high output and the minimum acceptable high input, $V_{OHmin} - V_{IHmin}$, is called the high-level *noise margin*, denoted N_H in Figure 5.2. Similarly, $V_{ILmax} - V_{OLmax} = N_L$ is the low-level noise margin. A signal that is contaminated by noise in transmission from output to input will not cause the system to fail if the noise is smaller than the noise margin.

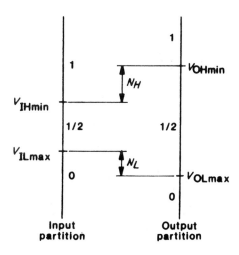

Figure 5.2   Dual logic level partitions

Logic levels and noise margins for a logic family are determined by the transfer curves for the gates in the family, as illustrated in Figure 5.3. First a *transfer band* is constructed which includes the transfer curve of every noninverting gate in the family and every pair of inverting gates in series. This band allows for all variations that may occur from gate to gate within the family (e.g., parameter variations during manufacture, differences in loading within specified limits). V_{ILmax} is that value of V_{in} such that the distance of the transfer band below the $V_{in} = V_{out}$ curve is maximized. This maximizes N_L. V_{IHmin} is determined in similar fashion to maximize N_H.

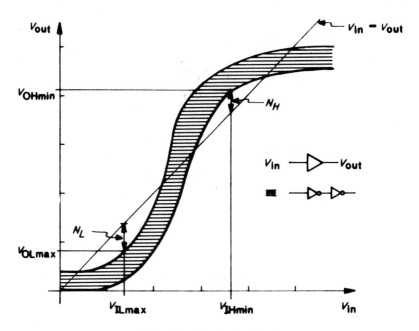

Figure 5.3   Choosing logic levels

Standard Logic Levels

The standard logic levels for transistor-transistor logic (TTL) devices are specified in Figure 5.4. For compatibility with TTL, nMOS devices use the same logic levels externally. The nMOS buffers that transfer signals between internal circuits and external terminals make the necessary changes in logic levels, so that the internal circuitry can operate at levels appropriate for nMOS while external terminals conform to TTL standards.

This compatibility is important because nMOS is not a complete logic family. Because of the simplicity and low power consumption of nMOS gates, very high density is possible (i.e., many gates per unit chip area). Hence nMOS is appropriate for large-scale devices such as processors, memories, and input-output (IO) controllers. However, because of the high resistance of nMOS transistors, nMOS devices are relatively slow and have limited drive capability. TTL devices are used when these characteristics are required. Also, since a complete family of small-scale devices is available in TTL (e.g., buffers, individual registers, logic gates), these functions are not duplicated in nMOS. Instead TTL devices are used when small-scale functions are required. This mixing of nMOS and TTL devices in the same system is facilitated by designing nMOS devices to use TTL logic levels externally.

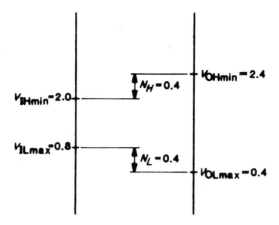

Figure 5.4   TTL logic levels

5.1.2   Modeling Digital Signals

In this section notations are developed for representing digital signals that vary with time, and concepts associated with such signals are identified.

The distinction between the input and output logic partitions is ignored in this discussion, and henceforth. Only one partition (the input partition) is represented for the purpose of modeling digital signals at the register transfer (RT) level. The output partition serves its function of providing noise tolerance automatically, and need not be represented explicitly. Each digital signal is thus modeled as a three-valued continuous time variable. When representing such signals in timing diagrams, we may use the notation of Figure 5.5. A line at 1 indicates that X is stable in the logic 1 region; a line at 0 indicates that X is stable in the 0 region. A sharp transition between the 0 and 1 regions is represented by a steeply sloped or vertical line. A line at $\frac{1}{2}$ (which may be wiggly for emphasis) indicates that X is in transition.

As discussed previously, the unit of information at the RT level is the binary word, which is an n-tuple of bits. A word is represented in digital sys-

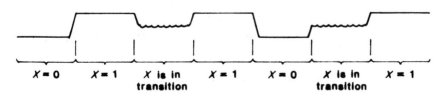

Figure 5.5   Timing diagram notation for single-bit signals

tems by an n-tuple of signals. We could represent each of these n signals as a separate line in a timing diagram, as in Figure 5.6(a). However, such a diagram contains much more information than is necessary at the RT level. In fact, it is normally sufficient to represent the entire word by a single line in a timing diagram. We will use the notation of Figure 5.6(b). Note that only two general conditions are indicated by this notation: double lines (at 0 and 1) indicate that X is stable (i.e., each bit of X is stable at either 0 or 1); and a single line at $\frac{1}{2}$ indicates that X is unstable (i.e., some bit of X is in transition). When X is stable, the stable value may be written between the double lines. In many cases, however, it is not desired to specify any particular stable value, but only that X is stable. In such cases the notation of Figure 5.6(b) is more suitable than the notation of Figure 5.6(a), in addition to being simpler, since the particular stable value need not be specified.

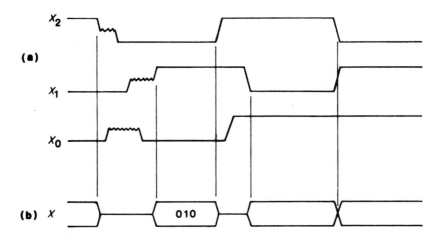

Figure 5.6   Timing diagram notation for level signals

A sharp transition of X (i.e., all bits involved in the tansition change sharply at the same time) is indicated by crossing the double lines. A transition is not sharp unless all bits involved change at the same time. Note that in the second transition of Figure 5.6 all bits change sharply, but at different times, so that X is unstable for a significant time (e.g., consider the output of a parallel adder; the upper bits may not change until long after the lower bits). Of course, time duration is a relative matter. Hence, it may be suitable to represent a transition as sharp in one situation, and unsuitable to represent the same transition as sharp in another situation.

Signal Types and Events

At this point it is useful to separate digital signals into two functional classes: *edge* signals and *level* signals. A *level* signal is a signal that is used to represent information (either data or control information) by the value (or level) of the signal. A level signal carries information only when it is stable at 0 or 1. An *edge* signal is a signal that is used to identify specific points in time. It does so by making sharp transitions, either from 0 to 1 or from 1 to 0, at such times.

Edge signals will be represented in timing diagrams by using the notation of Figure 5.5, but only sharp transitions (steeply sloped lines) will occur. Level signals normally occur in words and are represented by using the notation of Figure 5.6(b). There are only five different types of *events* that occur in digital systems: two types for edge signals and three types for level signals. These are illustrated in Figure 5.7. C is an edge signal, and X is a level signal. The two types of events for C are a positive transition, denoted $C\uparrow$, and a negative transition, denoted $C\downarrow$. The three types of events for X are a transition from unstable to stable, denoted $X<$; a transition from stable to unstable, denoted $X>$; and a sharp transition of X, denoted $X\updownarrow$.

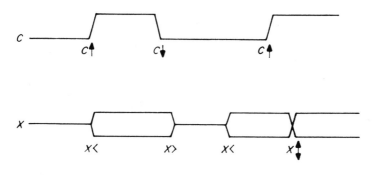

Figure 5.7 Events

Interval Types

Timing specifications for digital systems are normally given in terms of the lengths of time intervals between events. Square brackets will be used to represent time intervals. Specifically, $[t_1, t_2]$ denotes the interval between t_1 and t_2. We will denote the time that an event occurs with the same notation used to denote the event itself. Hence, $[X<, C\uparrow]$ will denote the time interval between a transition of X to a stable value and a positive transition of C. The same notation will be used to represent the length of an interval, that is, the elapsed time between the first event and the second.

Setup and Hold.   Standard names have emerged for certain types of intervals that appear frequently in timing specifications. A *setup* interval is an interval bounded on the left by the time that a level signal word becomes stable and on the right by the time that an edge signal makes a transition. Hence, $[X<, C\uparrow]$, $[X<, C\downarrow]$, $[X\updownarrow, C\uparrow]$, and $[X\updownarrow, C\downarrow]$ are setup intervals. It is understood that X remains stable throughout the setup interval. A *hold* interval is an interval that is bounded on the left by a transition of an edge signal and on the right by a transition from stable to unstable of a level signal (i.e., $[C\uparrow, X>]$, $[C\downarrow, X>]$, $[C\uparrow, X\updownarrow]$, $[C\downarrow, X\updownarrow]$). Setup and hold intervals are illustrated in Figure 5.8.

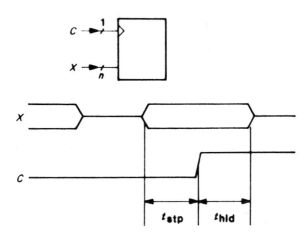

Figure 5.8   Setup and hold intervals

Setup and hold intervals are normally involved with the transfer of information into a device. In Figure 5.8, the level input X carries the information to be transferred and the edge input C indicates when the device may look at X.

In order for the device to perceive the information at X, X must be stable for a sufficiently long time. This time during which X must be stable is expressed in terms of setup and hold times measured with respect to the active edge of the timing input. Essentially all input transfers are specified by minimum acceptable values for setup and hold intervals as illustrated here.

The small triangle at the C input in Figure 5.8 indicates that C is an edge-sensitive input. This notation is frequently used at the logic design level, and occasionally at the register transfer level as well. However, in register transfer diagrams this level of detail is frequently not required and the triangles are not included.

A small circle is frequently used in conjunction with the small triangle to indicate the direction of the active transition. Absence of the circle, as in Figure 5.8, indicates that the positive edge is active; presence of the circle, as in Figure 5.9, indicates that the negative edge is active.

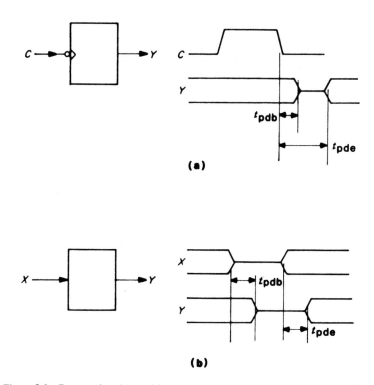

Figure 5.9   Propagation delays: (a) initiated by $C\downarrow$; (b) initiated by change in X

Propagation Delay.   A *propagation delay* is an interval that is bounded on the left by an event that causes, or contributes to causing, the event that bounds the interval on the right. The events on either side of the interval may be any of the five types.

In Figure 5.9(a), the event C causes Y to change value. The interval t_{pdb} is the propagation delay to the beginning of the transition, and t_{pde} is the propagation delay to the end (or completion) of the transition.

Complete specifications for the device of Figure 5.9(a) should include a guaranteed minimum value for t_{pdb} [i.e., $Y>$ is guaranteed not to occur until at least $(t_{pdb})_{min}$ after $C\downarrow$] and a guaranteed maximum value for t_{pde} [i.e., $Y<$ is guaranteed to occur before $(t_{pde})_{max}$ after $C\downarrow$].

Frequently, however, the distinction between the beginning and end of the transition will not be made explicitly, and only one propagation delay, t_{pd}, will be mentioned. In this case, t_{pd} is normally t_{pde}, and the only specification that will be given is $(t_{pd})_{max} = (t_{pde})_{max}$. If both minimum and maximum values are given for t_{pd}, then these are $(t_{pdb})_{min}$ and $(t_{pde})_{max}$.

For some devices the propagation delay of a single-bit output for transitions from high to low may be significantly different from that for transitions from low to high. Separate specifications may then be given. When several such outputs are grouped together into a word, the worst of the individual specifications should be used. For example, if $5 \le t_{HL} \le 10$ and $7 \le t_{LH} \le 15$ for each individual bit, then for the word, $5 \le t_{pd} \le 15$ (i.e., $t_{pdb} \ge 5$ and $t_{pde} \le 15$).

In Figure 5.9(b), a change in the value of X causes a change in the value of Y. For example, the device might be a combinational network. Complete device specifications include minimum and maximum values for t_{pdb} and t_{pde}, respectively.

Timing Specifications

Timing specifications for digital components at the logic design level and above are given as minimum and maximum values for intervals of the types described above. For macrocircuit components, the necessary specifications are given in a "data sheet." We will look at the specifications for some typical macrocircuit components later in this chapter.

Maximum propagation delays for outputs of macrocircuit components always have an associated load capacitance. If the specified load capacitance is exceeded, the specified propagation delay may also be exceeded.

For microcircuit design, timing specifications must be determined by analysis of RC delays, or by simulation. Some microcircuit design procedures are very similar to macrocircuit design in that libraries of standard "cells" are used as components. Timing specifications for these cells are given in the same fashion as for macrocircuit components.

For the purpose of converting existing macrocircuit designs to microcircuit designs, cell libraries frequently include microcircuit versions of standard macrocircuit components. Such cells are also useful for new designs, because designers are familiar with their characteristics.

5.1.3 Signal Paths

Signals are transferred from one point to another within a computer (and between computers) via signal paths of some sort. In an nMOS microcircuit, a signal path may be any of the following: a thin trace of metal on the chip surface; a thin trace of polysilicon on the chip surface (polysilicon is the material used for transistor gates); a narrow n-diffusion path in the chip surface (n-diffusion regions of the substrate are used for transistor drain and source terminals); any combination of the above. In a macrocircuit system, a signal path may be a narrow trace of metal on the surface of a printed circuit card or backplane, or it may be a wire of some sort (e.g., an open wire such as those used with wire-wrap cards; a wire bundled together with other wires into a cable; the signal wire in a coaxial cable).

Ideally, a signal path is a "perfect conductor" with no resistance, capacitance, or inductance. When a gate output is connected via a signal path to a gate input, a change in output voltage will (ideally) appear instantly and without modification at the input. In practice, this is not the case. Any signal path has some resistance, capacitance, and inductance. Voltage changes do not propagate instantaneously along a signal path, nor are pulse shapes unmodified by transmission over a signal path. These matters will be discussed in Chapter 7. Until then, signal paths will be represented as ideal conductors, perhaps with some capacitance. This is the appropriate model for short paths.

Buses

System components communicate with each other via signal paths. At the register transfer level the unit of information is the word, and data paths between components are normally wide enough to transfer all bits of a word simultaneously. The "width" of a data path is the number of separate signal paths that constitute the data path.

As the number of components grows, it quickly becomes impractical to provide a separate data path between each pair of components that must communicate. Instead, shared data paths, called *buses*, are used.

Buses may be implemented in several ways. In RT level diagrams we will frequently use the generic notation of Figure 5.10 to represent a bus. No particular implementation is implied by this notation. An open circle denotes an input connection, and a solid dot an output connection. Arrow directions also distinguish inputs from outputs. The bus shown in Figure 5.10 has two inputs and two outputs, though in general there may be more of either or both.

The open circles at bus inputs represent switched connections. The control signals that operate these switches may be shown, if necessary, as in Figure

5.10. We will usually use the following mnemonic convention in naming bus control signals: if x is the name of the bus and y the name of an input, then the control signal that puts input y onto bus x is denoted yTx (the "T" stands for "to").

The operation of the generic bus represented in Figure 5.10(a) is described by the table of Figure 5.10(b). This operation is easily generalized to any number of inputs and outputs. An input is placed on the bus by asserting the corresponding control signal and holding all other input controls unasserted. While an input is on the bus it is simultaneously available at all bus outputs.

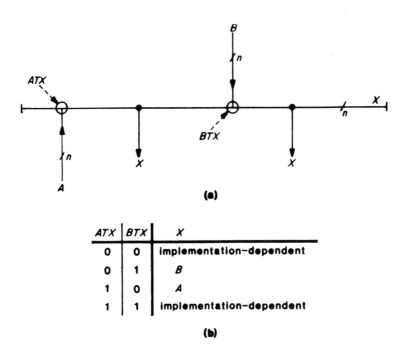

Figure 5.10   Generic bus representation: (a) generic notation; (b) operation

When there are no bus control signals asserted, the value carried by the bus depends upon the specific implementation of the bus. Likewise, when more than one input control is asserted, the bus value depends upon the implementation.

Bus Implementations

Several possible implementations of the generic bus of Figure 5.10 are presented next. Outputs are not shown unless special circuitry is required to take words from the bus. Usually the signal paths that constitute the bus can simply be extended and connected to an input port of a device that needs to read the bus.

The simplest nMOS implementation of the bus is shown in Figure 5.11(a), using register transfer diagram notation. In Figure 5.11(b) the same bus is shown in more detail. The operation of the bus is shown in Figure 5.11(c). The transistors that are controlled by the bus control signals are called *bus*

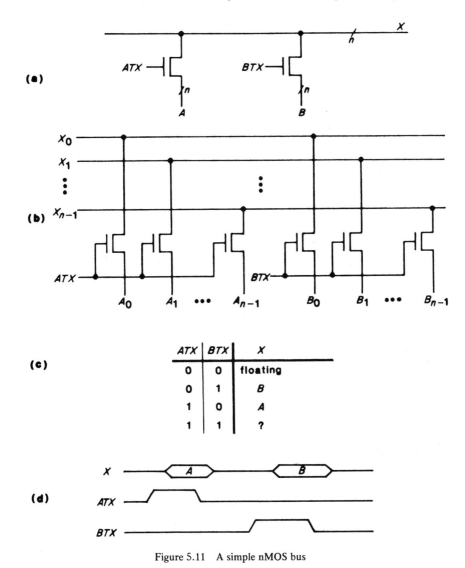

Figure 5.11   A simple nMOS bus

drivers. When no control signals are asserted, the bus drivers are all turned off and the bus is left floating. The term "floating" means that there does not exist a low-resistance path either to V_{DD} or to ground. When a signal line is floating, the voltage on the line is uncertain. Due to capacitance, the value that was last established on a line before it was left floating will linger momentarily. But it may drift to an uncertain value in a short time. Hence, when a bus is left floating, the word carried by the bus must be assumed unknown. The timing diagram of Figure 5.11(d) illustrates the operation of the bus.

When more than one bus control input is asserted, then the enabled drivers may be trying to establish different values on the bus simultaneously. This situation is illustrated for a single bus line in Figure 5.12. The bus drivers for both input A and input B are turned on. The A driver is trying to put $A_i = 0$ on bus line X_i, while the B driver is trying to put $B_i = 1$ on the same line. The resulting voltage on X_i will be somewhere between the A_i and B_i levels.

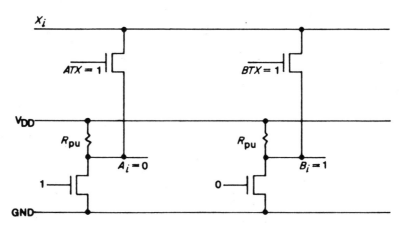

Figure 5.12   Bus line with two drivers on

The bus structure of Figure 5.11 allows implementation of a bus using minimum chip area, but it may be too slow if the bus capacitance is large. The speed problem is clear from Figure 5.12. Consider the case where $ATX = 1$ and $BTX = 0$. If the bus was previously at 1, it must discharge to 0 through *both* the bus driver *and* the A_i pull-down transistor. Even worse, if ATX changes to 0 and BTX to 1, then the bus must charge to 1 through both R_{pu} and the bus driver.

This bus can be made faster by making the bus drivers and the gates that generate bus inputs larger than minimum size. A better solution, however, is to use a *tristate bus*, illustrated in Figure 5.13(a). The output stage of the tristate driver, Figure 5.13(b), provides a connection to either V_{DD} or ground,

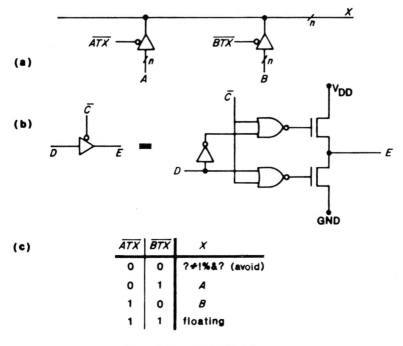

$\overline{ATX}$	$\overline{BTX}$	X
0	0	?≠!%&? (avoid)
0	1	A
1	0	B
1	1	floating

Figure 5.13 nMOS tristate bus

each through a single transistor. The control input to the driver is asserted low (indicated by the small circle and by the bar over the signal name). When not asserted ($\overline{C} = 1$) both output transistors are turned off and the output E is left floating. When the control input is asserted ($\overline{C} = 0$), one of the output transistors is enabled and the other disabled, as selected by the data input D.

The operation of the bus is described in Figure 5.13(c). The bus floats if no control input is asserted. If more than one control input is asserted then there may be one driver attempting to pull a bus line low, and another trying to pull the same line high, as in Figure 5.12. The situation is worse than in the simple bus case, however, because the path from V_{DD} to ground is through only two turned-on transistors. This results in a large steady-state current, which is undesirable.

Tristate drivers are frequently used to drive integrated circuit (IC) package pins, to provide the capability of constructing a macrocircuit bus simply by interconnecting chips. The driving transistors in this case must be very large, in order to drive the large capacitance of the external bus. It is crucial to avoid enabling multiple drivers simultaneously in this case, because the resulting large currents could damage the drivers.

There sometimes arise situations where bus control inputs are generated by devices operating independently and asynchronously. (Interrupt request lines are a common example.) Multiple drivers can be enabled simultaneously during normal operation, and hence a tristate bus should not be used.

In such cases, it is necessary to use a form of bus driver that can only pull in one direction. Enabling multiple drivers can then do no harm. Such a bus is illustrated in Figure 5.14. The driver is a NOR gate followed by an inverter with the pull-up resistor removed. A pull-up resistor is provided externally to hold the bus at 1 when no driver is pulling it low. Hence, when no driver is enabled, $X = 1^n$. If multiple drivers are enabled, then the bus will be pulled low if any of the enabled inputs is low, hence X is the AND of the enabled inputs.

With a pull-up resistor added, this type of driver is an OR gate. Since the pull-up is missing it is sometimes called an *open-drain* OR gate.

The TTL version of the open-drain OR gate is the open-collector NAND gate. It is formed from the basic TTL gate of Figure 2.21 by removing the pull-up circuit (resistor, transistor and diode) from the output.

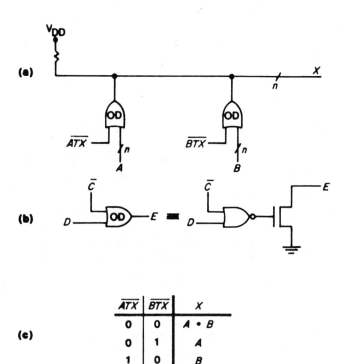

Figure 5.14   Open-drain bus

A bus constructed from open-collector NAND gates is shown in Figure 5.15. This bus is different in that the data path Z actually carries the complement of the data provided to the driver. Hence an inverter must be used when reading the bus to recover the original data. Alternatively, the data could be complemented when provided to the driver. An open-collector driver used in this fashion is compatible with the open-drain drivers of Figure 5.14.

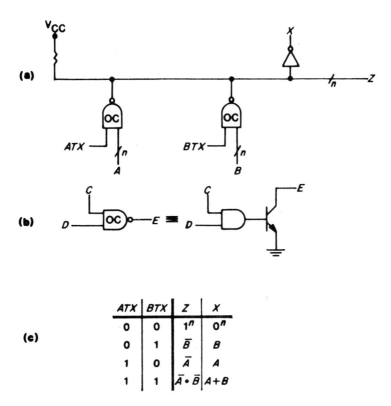

Figure 5.15   Open-collector bus

Open-collector gates are also used as high-voltage and/or high-current peripheral drivers, as illustrated in Figure 5.16. The output transistor is constructed to tolerate high voltages and/or high currents (e.g., 80 volts and 300 mA for the 75471 chip).

The open-collector and open-drain buses are slower than the tristate bus because they must charge through a relatively large pull-up resistor (e.g., for nMOS it is about four times the pull-down resistance). Speed can be increased by removing the pull-up resistor and precharging the bus to V_{DD} just

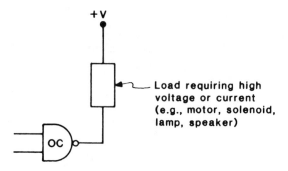

Figure 5.16   Open-collector peripheral driver

before using it. The bus drivers need only pull down those lines that should be low. Such a bus is illustrated in Figure 5.17. The bus is precharged by setting $P = 1$, which is done just prior to asserting ATX or BTX. Precharging is most often used with a two-phase clock (see Section 5.3). The bus is precharged during one phase and used to transfer information during the next. Precharging can also be used with the simple bus of Figure 5.11.

For completeness we should mention one other implementation of the generic bus of Figure 5.10, the multiplexer. Multiplexers will be discussed in the next section, and it will be seen that a bus is essentially a "distributed multiplexer."

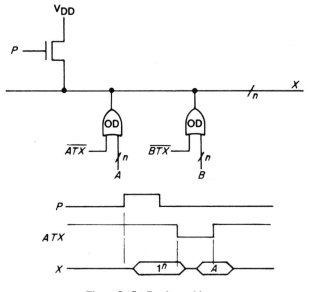

Figure 5.17   Precharged bus

5.1.4 Exercises

1. (a) Given the transfer curve for an inverter, construct the transfer curve for two inverters in series.

(b) Given the "transfer band" for a family of inverting gates, construct the "transfer band" of two gates in series (i.e., the band of Figure 5.3).

2. Suppose that the transfer band of Figure 5.3 lies entirely below the $V_{in} = V_{out}$ line, except near the origin. What effect will this have on the operation of a gate network with many levels (e.g., a ripple-carry adder)?

3. What will be the voltage on bus line X_i in Figure 5.12 if $R_{pu} = 40$ KΩ, $R_{ds} = 5$ KΩ for a turned-on bus driver, and $R_{ds} = 10$ KΩ or 10^7 KΩ for a turned-on or turned-off pull-down transistor?

4. Suppose that all gates of a particular logic family have a guaranteed minimum propagation delay of 2 ns and maximum propagation delay of 10 ns. That is, an input change is guaranteed *not* to affect the output for at least 2 ns, and guaranteed to have reached steady state within 10 ns.

(a) Specify $(t_{pdb}^{X-Y})_{min}$ and $(t_{pde}^{X-Y})_{max}$ for the network below

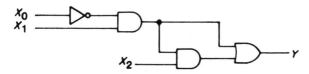

(b) Specify $(t_{pdb})_{min}$ and $(t_{pde})_{max}$ for the n-bit ripple-carry adder of Figures 4.4 and 4.5. Assume that the full adder is implemented as a ⅔-level network.

5.2 COMBINATIONAL NETWORKS [19, 24, 26, 30–36]

5.2.1   Decoders
5.2.2   Multiplexers
5.2.3   Read Only Memory (ROM)
5.2.4   Programmable Logic Array (PLA)
5.2.5   Arithmetic Logic Unit (ALU)
5.2.6   Exercises

A general model for a combinational network is illustrated in Figure 5.18. There may be multiple input and output ports, as indicated by the "dots." For each output there is a switching function that relates that output to the inputs. This relationship may be expressed either as an equation, $Y = f(X, \ldots)$, or as a register transfer operation, $f(X, \ldots) \rightarrow Y$. The register transfer

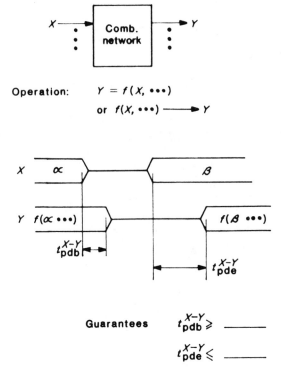

Figure 5.18   Combinational network

notation is actually more appropriate, since the equality holds only after the inputs have been stable for a sufficient time. We will use both notations.

The timing diagram in the figure assumes that all input variables except X remain stable. A change in X produces a corresponding change in Y. The relevant propagation delays and the associated timing specifications are shown. Frequently the first specification, $(t_{pd}^{X-Y})_{\min}$, is not provided.

In Section 3.2 classical techniques for designing 2-level combinational networks were presented. In Chapter 4 the classical techniques were extended to the design of iterative arrays used to implement the basic arithmetic operations. In this section, several other combinational networks that are frequently useful at the RT level are described. For each of these we will consider microcircuit as well as macrocircuit implementations.

5.2.1 Decoders

Information in normally "encoded" for efficient storage and transmission in digital systems; n bits may be used to represent 2^n different values. If this information is to be used for control purposes, "decoding" is frequently necessary. For example, in order to access a register, a memory must decode the supplied address and assert the single control bit that enables the selected register. Similarly, the processor must decode machine instructions to evoke the appropriate register transfer operations.

The most widely used type of decoder is the n-to-2^n decoder, described in Figure 5.19. Exactly one of the 2^n decoder output bits is asserted at any time, the one that is selected by X as shown. The outputs of the decoder in Figure 5.19 are asserted high. A simple variation is to have outputs asserted low, that is, $Y_i = 0$ iff $[X]_2 = i$.

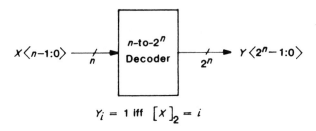

Figure 5.19 The n to 2^n decoder

Gate Implementation

A straightforward implementation of the decoder is shown in Figure 5.20 for $n = 2$. This implementation is easily extended to higher values of n. The numbers of gates and gate inputs required for this implementation are specified as functions of n. These will be used later in comparing the complexity of this implementation with others.

In the nMOS technology, NOR and NAND are the natural gate structures. It is desirable, therefore, to have an implementation that uses only these gates. For most people it is easier to think terms of AND and OR gates. It is usually possible, with the assistance of De Morgan's theorems and the "small circle convention" (i.e., a small circle at an input or output represents inversion), to convert an AND-OR network into a network involving only NAND and NOR gates. This conversion process is illustrated in Figure 5.21. In Figure 5.21(a), an AND gate is shown to be equivalent to a NOR gate with inputs inverted. In Figure 5.21(b) this equivalence is used to convert the AND decoder to a NOR decoder. Note that the NOR input connections are complemented (at no extra cost). For example, $Y_0 = \overline{X_1 + X_0} = \overline{X_1} \cdot \overline{X_0}$. Figure 5.22 illustrates the process for NAND gates. Note that the decoder outputs are asserted low.

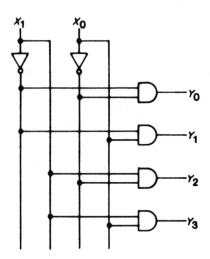

Component count with n inputs:

n Inverters

2^n AND gates

$n \cdot 2^n$ AND gate inputs

Figure 5.20   One-level decoder

Microcircuit Layout

It is possible to convert the gate implementations of Figure 5.21 and 5.22 directly into microcircuit designs. For example, the gate network of Figure 5.21(b) could be laid out on a chip exactly as it appears in the diagram, with each gate located on the chip surface in the position it occupies in the diagram.

It is generally possible to do better, however, by distributing components over the surface of the chip rather than implementing them in one position as in the logic diagram. This can result in a significant reduction in the amount of chip area devoted to wiring.

This technique is illustrated in Figure 5.23, which shows a microcircuit implementation of the decoder of Figure 5.21. The NOR gates in this implementation are distributed across the chip. Each NOR input transistor is placed adjacent to the appropriate input wire. It is thus sufficient to have a single wire crossing the array of input wires for each NOR gate, rather than a separate wire for each NOR input, as in Figure 5.21. To appreciate the advantage of this layout, picture the situation for an input $X\langle n - 1 : 0 \rangle$. The localized layout of Figure 5.21 must allow sufficient space vertically for each NOR gate

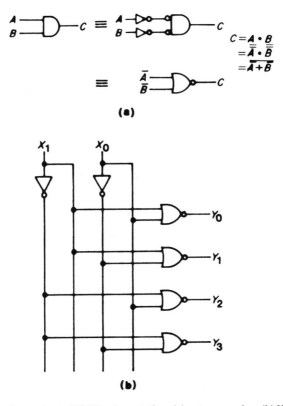

$$C = A \cdot B$$
$$= \overline{\overline{A} \cdot \overline{B}}$$
$$= \overline{\overline{A} + \overline{B}}$$

Figure 5.21 Conversion to NOR implementation: (a) gate conversion; (b) NOR decoder

to accommodate n horizontally running wires. Since each wire has a minimum width, and there is a minimum spacing between wires, this uses a great deal of chip area. If a transistor occupies the same distance vertically as a wire (this is approximately true for nMOS) then the localized structure of Figure 5.21 requires about $n/2$ times the chip area required by the distributed structure of Figure 5.23. Figure 5.24 shows the distributed layout of the NAND decoder of Figure 5.22.

The advantage of *distributed components* does not apply only to decoder implementations. It applies to the microcircuit implementation of any network or system. In fact, as the systems to be implemented become larger, the problem of chip layout becomes more difficult, and the advantages to be gained by the careful distribution of components over the chip become greater.

When we discuss microcircuit implementation, the primary focus of our attention will be chip layout and, in particular, the distribution of compo-

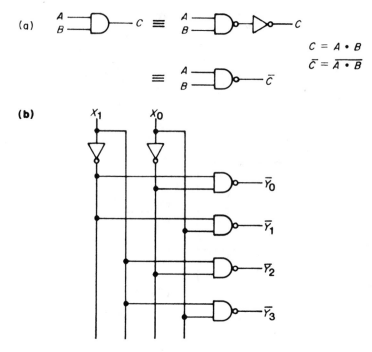

Figure 5.22   Conversion to NAND implementation: (a) gate conversion; (b) NAND decoder

nents over the chip. These considerations apply to any type of circuit (MOS or bipolar) and any fabrication process. The details of electronic component structure (i.e., transistors, resistors, etc.) will vary, as will the specific interconnection details (e.g., number of levels available for signal paths; techniques for connecting between levels). However, the advantages of distributing higher level components over the chip are largely independent of these details.

It is not always necessary to show the electronic structure of every component in a microcircuit diagram. If the purpose is to show how components are to be distributed over the chip surface, which is frequently the case, then the internal structure of components that are localized need not be shown. For example, the inverters in Figure 5.23 and 5.24 are represented by the usual gate symbols. In general, the details in any part of a diagram can be suppressed in order to focus attention on the desired structural details.

Chip layout affects not only the area occupied by a circuit, but also the speed of the circuit. This will become increasingly important as chip size increases and feature size decreases. Wires (signal paths) on the chip will become longer and narrower (as well as more numerous). Wire propagation de-

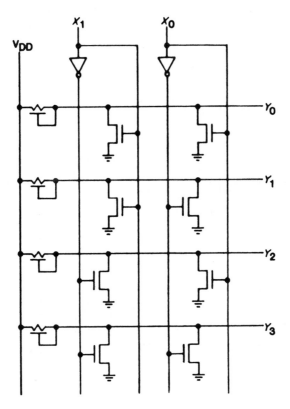

Figure 5.23   Microcircuit layout of NOR decoder

lays will thus become increasingly important. The current conventional practice of separating processor and memory may be abandoned when it becomes possible to put both on the same chip. It may prove advantageous to interlace the processor and the memory together over the chip, thereby saving both chip area and communication delays.

Two-Level Decoder

The one-level decoder structure of Figures 5.20 to 5.22 is suitable for small values of n, but for larger values it becomes very expensive. For nMOS gates, each gate has one load transistor plus one transistor for each gate input. Hence for $n = 16$, the one-level decoder requires 1,114,144 transistors.

The two-level decoder of Figure 5.25 is considerably better. For $n = 16$ only 201,248 transistors are required, fewer than 20% of the number required

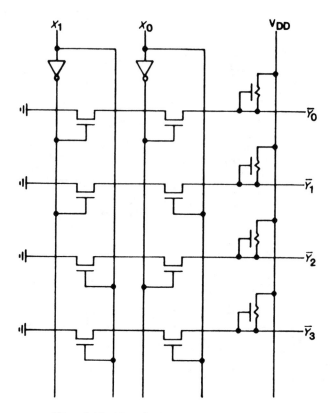

Figure 5.24   Microcircuit layout of NAND decoder

for the one-level decoder. Furthermore, in the design of memories, the most common application of large decoders, it is usually possible to combine the final AND stage of the decoder with the memory cell itself, thereby saving at least another 2^n transistors.

Note, however, that the advantage of the two-level structure is lost if it is necessary to bring all 2^n outputs outside the array. The two-level decoder *must* be distributed (interlaced) with the component that uses the decoder output.

Macrocircuit Implementation

It is frequently necessary to implement decoders at the macrocircuit level. For example, suppose it is necessary to construct a $2^{22} \times 8$ memory from $2^{16} \times 8$ chips. The lower 16 address bits may be decoded on each chip. The upper 6 address bits must then be decoded externally with a macrocircuit decoder.

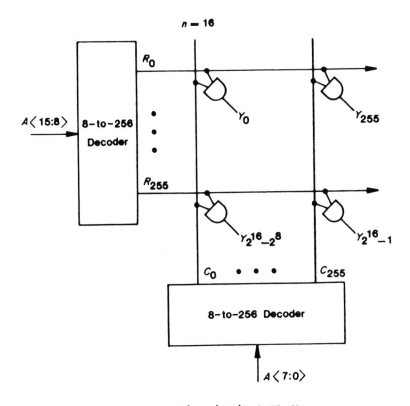

Component count for n inputs, even n:

$$\begin{aligned}
\text{Inverters:} \quad & n \\
\text{AND gates:} \quad & 2^{n/2} + 2^{n/2} + 2^n \\
\text{AND gate inputs:} \quad & \frac{n}{2}(2^{n/2} + 2^{n/2}) + 2 \cdot 2^n
\end{aligned}$$

Figure 5.25   Two-level decoder

Although it is no problem to fit a 6-to-64 decoder on one chip, such chips are not available as standard parts because of the expense of providing so many pins on an IC package. The largest decoder that is available as a standard IC package is a 4-to-16 decoder; 3-to-8 decoders, two to a package, are also available.

The operation of a typical decoder package with n inputs is defined in Figure 5.26. In addition to the usual n inputs, there is an "enable" input provided to facilitate expansion. When the enable input is asserted, the package operates as a decoder. When not enabled, all outputs of the package are un-

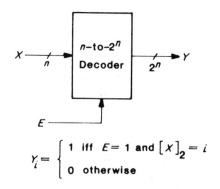

$$Y_i = \begin{cases} 1 & \text{iff } E = 1 \text{ and } [X]_2 = i \\ 0 & \text{otherwise} \end{cases}$$

Figure 5.26   A standard IC decoder package

asserted. In Figure 5.27, nine 3-to-8 decoders are interconnected to form a 6-to-64 decoder.

5.2.2 Multiplexers

Another combinational network that is frequently used in register transfer level design is the *multiplexer* (or *data selector*), defined in Figure 5.28(a). The multiplexer is a switch. It connects one of the 2^n inputs $X\langle 2^n - 1 : 0 \rangle$ to the single output Y. The input that is so connected is selected by the input $S\langle n - 1 : 0 \rangle$. MUX is a common abbreviation for multiplexer.

Implementation

An AND-OR implementation of the multiplexer for $n = 2$ is shown in Figure 5.28(b). In Figure 5.29(a) and AND-OR implementation is converted to a NOR-NOR implementation by applying De Morgan's theorem as in Figure 5.21(a) and replacing the OR gate by a NOR-INVERT pair. In Figure 5.29(b) the NOR implementation is further simplified by noting that the inverters at the X inputs and the Y output can be removed. The microcircuit layout is left as an exercise.

Application in Implementing Switching Functions

Multiplexers can be used instead of gates to implement switching functions. This design technique is illustrated in Figure 5.30. A function of three variables is implemented using an 8-to-1 MUX. The K-map of the function is given. To the right of the K-map is a map showing the correspondence of the squares in the K-map to $[A\langle 2:0 \rangle]_2$. $A\langle 2:0 \rangle$ is used as the select input to the

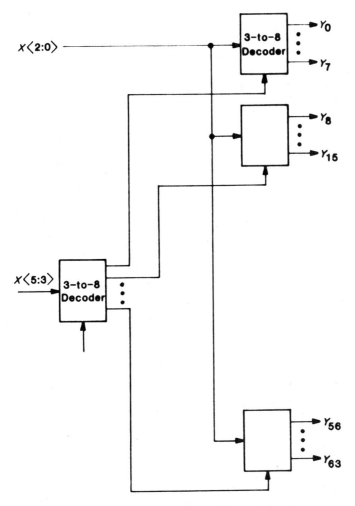

Figure 5.27   A 6-to-64 decoder from 3-to-8 decoders

MUX. Each data input to the MUX is connected to either 0 or 1. When $[A]_2$ = 0, the MUX connects input 0 to the output, B. But when $[A]_2 = 0$ we want $B = 0$, since square 0 of the K-map specifies value 0. Hence we connect input 0 to value 0. In general, input i of the MUX is connected to the value (0 or 1) specified by square i of the K-map.

If a switching function of $n + m$ variables is to be implemented using a 2^n-to-1 MUX, then n variables are connected to S, and the data inputs of the MUX are connected to appropriate functions of the remaining m variables.

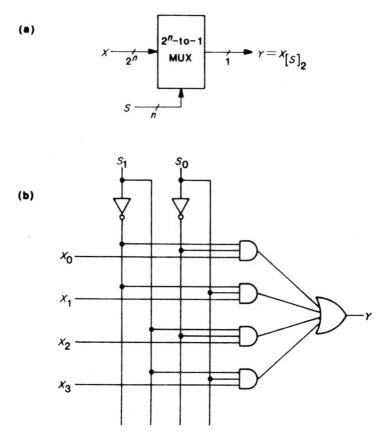

Figure 5.28   The multiplexer (data selector): (a) definition; (b) AND-OR implementation

These functions may be implemented using gates, or perhaps another level of multiplexers. Figure 5.31 illustrates the technique. A four-variable switching function is implemented in two ways: using an 8-to-1 MUX, and using a 4-to-1 MUX. When using an 8-to-1 MUX there is only one variable not connected to S. There are only four functions of a single variable X: 0, 1, X, and $\bar{X}$. Each MUX data input is connected to one of these. The map in Figure 5.31(b) shows the squares of the K-map that correspond to each value of S.

The implementation using the 4-to-1 MUX in Figure 5.31(c) has only two variables connected to S. The data inputs of the MUX are connected to functions of the remaining variables, A_1 and A_0. The K-map of one of these subfunctions is shown.

The designer is free to choose which variables should be connected to S. This decision may well affect the cost of the resulting implementation.

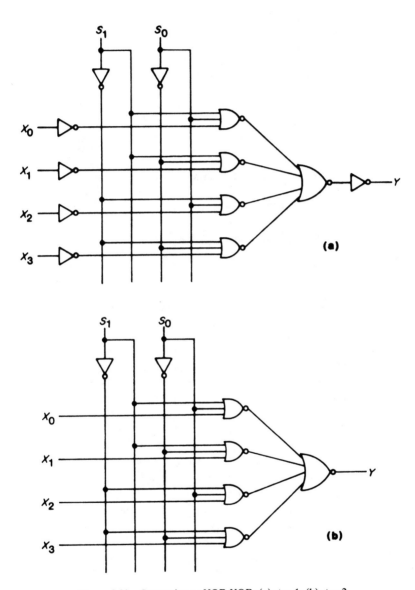

Figure 5.29 Conversion to NOR-NOR: (a) step 1; (b) step 2

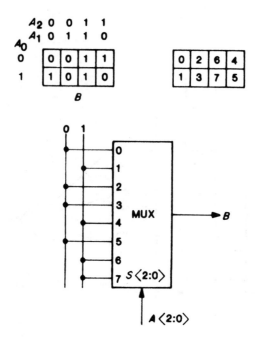

Figure 5.30   MUX implementation of switching functions

The use of multiplexers to implement arbitrary switching functions is practical in macrocircuit design because frequently a lower package count (or, more precisely, pin count) can be obtained than is possible using only small-scale IC gate packages. The technique may also be useful in microcircuit design due to the regularity of the resulting circuit.

The major use of multiplexers in both microcircuit and macrocircuit design is for switching, specifically for input switching in a time-sharing context. For example, it may be desirable to use a single adder at different times to add words in several pairs of registers. Hence it is necessary to connect different registers to the adder inputs at different times. Multiplexers may be used for this purpose. Used in this fashion, a multiplexer is similar to a bus (Section 5.1); it provides the "switching" function of a bus, but not the shared data path. Note, however, that if a multiplexer is distributed over the chip surface, then the multiplexer output effectively becomes a shared data path. Hence, a distributed multiplexer is essentially a bus with encoded control inputs.

5.2.3   Read Only Memory (ROM)

A *read only memory* (ROM) is a combinational network that can be *programmed* to implement any switching function $f: \mathbf{B}^m \to \mathbf{B}^n$, where m is the

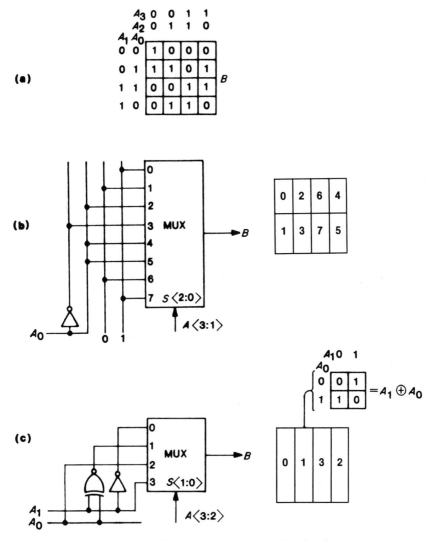

Figure 5.31   MUX implementation of switching functions

number of ROM inputs and n the number of outputs. A ROM may also be regarded as a memory (i.e., a set of registers) that contains a fixed word in each register. The word contained in each register is fixed at the time the device is programmed. This dual nature of ROM is illustrated in Figure 5.32. The ROM input port is normally labeled A (for address) and the output port D (for data).

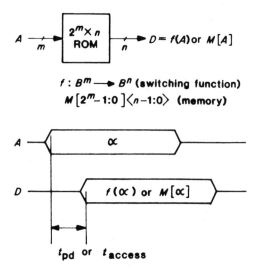

$f : B^m \longrightarrow B^n$ (switching function)
$M[2^m-1:0]\langle n-1:0\rangle$ (memory)

Figure 5.32   Read only memory

Gate Implementation

An AND-OR implementation of a $2^2 \times 3$ ROM is shown in Figure 5.33. Programmable connections are marked by "$\times$". Each output is generated by a four-input OR gate. When the device is programmed, each of the four inputs is either made or broken. A broken connection results in a "floating" input to the OR gate, that is, an input that is not connected to anything. For proper operation of the ROM, a floating OR input must act like a 0 input. Hence breaking a connection effectively removes that input from the OR gate.

It is obvious from the implementation of Figure 5.33 that ROM is a combinational network. Each output is a sum of products. The products that are included in the sum for each output are established at programming time.

The products that are available to form sums are minterms (see Section 3.2). In fact, the bank of AND gates generates all of the minterms of the input variables. Since any switching function can be represented as a sum of minterms, it is clear that the ROM can be programmed to implement any function $f:\mathbf{B}^m \rightarrow \mathbf{B}^n$. In terms of K-maps, each minterm covers exactly one square of a map; a function is thus implemented by covering each 1 of a function individually.

The bank of AND gates of Figure 5.33 should be recognized as a decoder. In Figure 5.34 a $2^3 \times 4$ ROM is shown, with the bank of AND gates represented by a decoder. The figure also illustrates the notation that will be used to represent a programmed ROM. This ROM has been programmed to implement the four functions defined in the K-maps. A heavy dot over a "$\times$" or

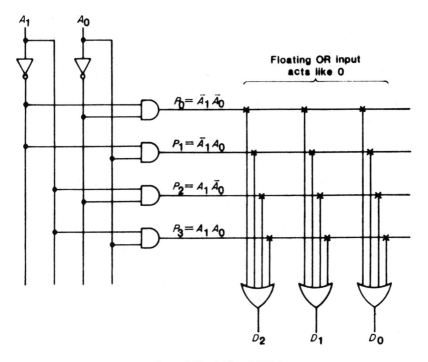

Figure 5.33   A $2^2 \times 3$ ROM

alone indicates a connection that is "made" during the programming process. A "$\times$" without a heavy dot indicates a connection that is "broken" during the programming process.

Figure 5.34 also illustrates the dual nature of ROM. In Figure 5.34(a) the ROM is represented as a combinational network implementing a switching function $f: \mathbf{B}^3 \rightarrow \mathbf{B}^4$. In Figure 5.34(b) the same ROM, programmed identically, is represented as a memory of eight registers, 4 bits per register. The words stored in the register were fixed by the programming process.

Programming Mechanisms

The first ROMs to be introduced, and still perhaps the most widely used, are *mask programmed*. These ROMs are programmed during fabrication. A mask is created that defines where connections are to be made or broken. When the mask is used, the appropriate connections are made or broken on the surface of the chip.

For example, programming may be done at the metal level by cutting slits in the mask between points that are to be connected and not cutting slits be-

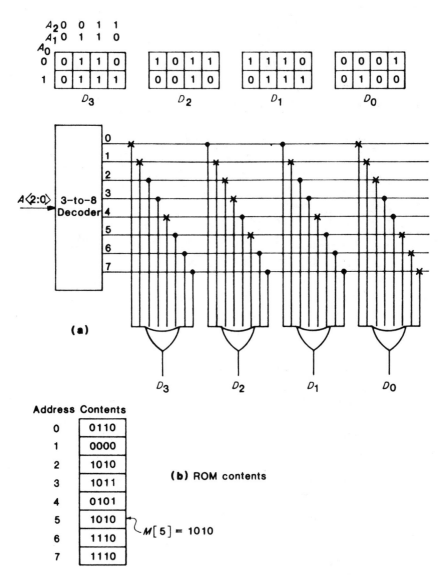

(a)

Address Contents

0	0110
1	0000
2	1010
3	1011
4	0101
5	1010
6	1110
7	1110

(b) ROM contents

$M[5] = 1010$

Figure 5.34   Programmed ROM

tween points not to be connected (i.e., broken connections). Alternatively, the programmable connections may be connections between layers. The programming would then be done by the contact cut mask.

Exactly which mask will be used for programming depends upon the fabrication process. It is even possible that more than one mask might be involved in the programming process.

In some IC technologies it may be possible to mask program more than just a connection; entire components may be inserted or removed by mask programming. For example, in the nMOS technology described in Chapter 1, transistors can be easily inserted or removed by programming the "poly" level mask. Including a poly path over an n-diffusion path creates a transistor; not including the poly path leaves a continuous n-diffusion path with no transistor. For simplicity, however, we will continue to represent the programming process as applying to "connections" only, and not to "components."

Field programmable ROMs (PROMs) were introduced later. These devices are manufactured with "fusible links" in signal paths where programmable connections are desired. The links function as normal connections at normal current levels. If a large current is passed through a fusible link, however, the connection is destroyed.

These devices are delivered with all programmable connections "made." Selected connections may be broken by providing the appropriate address at the usual address input, providing the desired data word at the data output port (now used as an input), and supplying a large voltage pulse (e.g., 25 volts) at a special programming terminal.

Still later *erasable ROMs* (EROMs) were introduced. These devices are not only field programmable, but are erasable as well. One such device uses an nMOS transistor with an "isolated gate" to make or break a connection. By providing an appropriate large voltage pulse, charge can be injected onto the isolated gate. When the voltage is removed, the charge is trapped on the gate, and the transistor remains on (i.e., the drain-source connection is made). The gate is isolated well enough so that charge will not leak away for a long time (e.g., 10 years). The ROM is erased by exposing the chip to ultraviolet light through a window in the package, which results in a photoelectric current that removes any charge on the isolated gates.

Microcircuit Layout

The AND-OR implementation of a ROM in Figure 5.33 is converted to a NOR-NOR implementation in Figure 5.35(a). Using De Morgan's theorem, each AND is replaced by a NOR, with inputs inverted. Each OR is also replaced by a NOR followed by an inverter. The output inverter may be re-

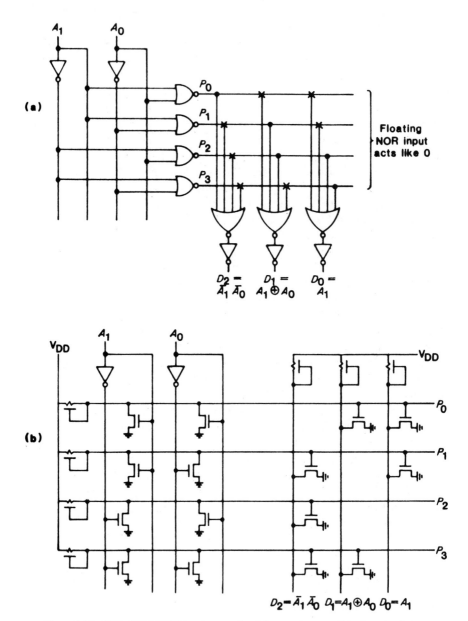

Figure 5.35   NOR-NOR ROM implementation (a) gate structure; (b) microcircuit layout

moved if the programmed inputs to the output NOR are reversed (i.e., the inverse function is programmed).

Figure 5.35(b) shows the microcircuit layout of this ROM. In both (a) and (b) the ROM is programmed to implement the same three functions. Note that programmed connections are reversed in (b) since the output inverters have been removed.

Two-Dimensional Implementation

For large values of n, two-dimensional decoders may be used to reduce component count. A two-dimensional 16×1 ROM is shown in Figure 5.36. At each intersection of a row and column there is a cell consisting of two transistors. These two transistors implement the final AND operation of the decoder and also serve together as an input to a distributed NOR gate, which generates the ROM output. (The inverter at the output could be removed, as discussed previously.) The distributed NOR gate is redrawn in Figure 5.37. The ROM is shown programmed to implement the function specified in the figure.

In comparing this implementation with the one-level implementation, note that in addition to the savings realized by using a two-level decoder, there are further savings achieved by combining the final AND operation of the decoder with the required input to the distributed NOR. The one-level implementation of a $2^m \times 1$ ROM requires about $(m + 2)2^m$ transistors for large m, compared with about 2^{m+1} for the implementation of Figure 5.36.

An implementation requiring even fewer transistors is illustrated in Figure 5.38. The column decoder is replaced by a multiplexer. The multiplexer uses more transistors than the decoder, but for large values of m this difference is insignificant relative to the 2^m transistors that are saved in the array, since each cell uses only one transistor. For large values of m, the total number of transistors required is about 2^m.

The structure of Figure 5.38 also has the advantage of not requiring the single large NOR gate to generate the output. For large m, the capacitance of the long NOR output path may make the ROM too slow.

Figure 5.39 illustrates how the same basic structure may be extended to implement ROMs with word length $n > 1$. By using $\log_2 n$ fewer column address bits than row address bits, a square memory array is maintained.

Macrocircuit Implementation

ROMs that are supplied as IC packages are normally equipped with an "enable" or "chip select" input. This input is used to control a tristate buffer that

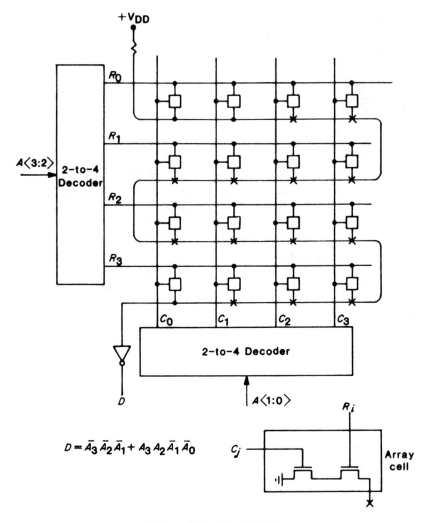

Figure 5.36   16 × 1 ROM

is inserted at the chip output, as shown in Figure 5.40. The tristate buffer is described in Figure 5.13.

The chip select inputs facilitate the interconnection of ROM packages to construct larger ROMs. In Figure 5.41, eight $2^{12} \times 4$ packages are interconnected to form a $2^{14} \times 8$ ROM. D outputs may be connected directly together because only one of the packages so connected is "selected" at any time. This package establishes the value of the D output. The outputs of the 2-to-4 decoder are asserted low.

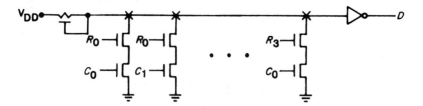

Figure 5.37   The distributed NOR of the 16 × 1 ROM

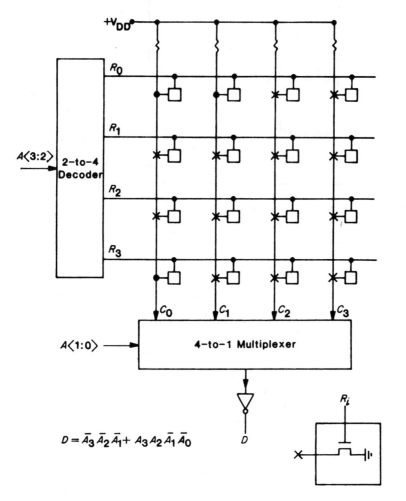

$$D = \bar{A}_3 \bar{A}_2 \bar{A}_1 + A_3 A_2 \bar{A}_1 \bar{A}_0$$

Figure 5.38   16 × 1 ROM

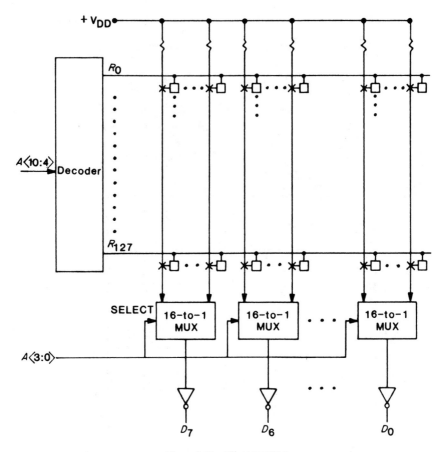

Figure 5.39 $2^{11} \times 8$ ROM

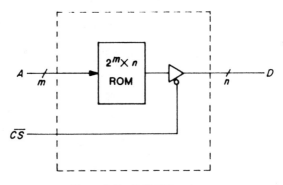

Figure 5.40   ROM IC package

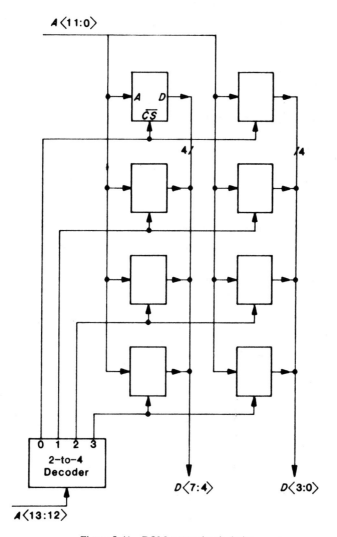

Figure 5.41   ROM macrocircuit design

5.2.4   Programmable Logic Array (PLA)

A weakness of ROM when used to implement switching functions is that no attempt is made to cover multiple minterms with a single product term. Any function is implemented as a sum of minterms. Since a ROM generates all minterms of the input variables, the size of a ROM more than doubles with the addition of each input. Hence the number of inputs that may be provided on a ROM will always be severely limited. This makes ROM unsuitable for implementing functions with many inputs.

The programmable logic array (PLA), Figure 5.42, is more suitable for implementing functions with many inputs. Rather than providing 2^m AND gates (where m is the number of inputs) fewer gates are provided, but the gate inputs are programmable. This allows a single product to cover multiple minterms. Each AND gate can be programmed to represent *any* of the 3^m possible products of the input variables.

A PLA may be characterized by the number of inputs, the number of product terms, and the number of outputs. The circuit of Figure 5.42 is a $3 \times 4 \times 2$ PLA. A typical commercially available bipolar PLA, the 82S100, is $16 \times 48 \times 8$. Microcircuit PLA dimensions may be selected to suit the application.

Since each PLA output is implemented as a sum of products, the classical theory of gate minimization (Section 3.2) applies directly. Efficient use of the PLA requires sharing of product terms among the outputs. In the classical theory this is known as multiple output minimization.

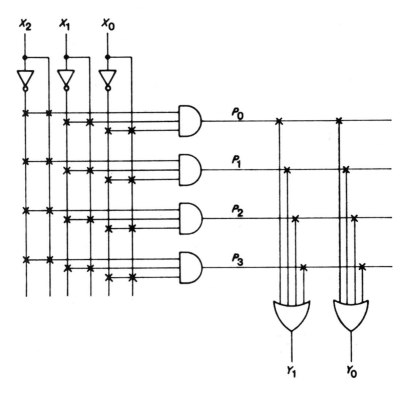

Figure 5.42   Programmable logic array

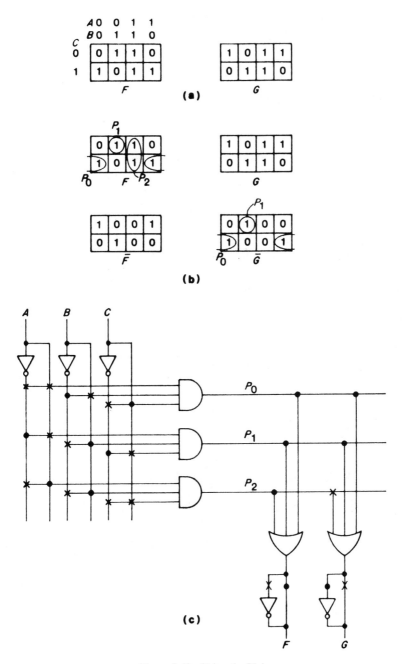

Figure 5.43   Using the PLA

The ability to share products is enhanced considerably by including inverters at the PLA outputs. This allows the designer to implement the complement of a function in the AND-OR structure and then complement the OR output to produce the desired function. All 2^n combinations of output functions and their inverses should be considered for implementation in the AND-OR array. The design process is illustrated in Figure 5.43.

Note that product terms P_0 and P_1 are shared by F and $\overline{G}$, making it possible to implement both functions with three products. Direct implementation of F and G would require five products.

PLAs that are available as IC packages are normally provided with chip select inputs and tristate outputs or open-collector outputs to facilitate interconnection of packages to form large PLAs. Since it is not possible to share product terms between packages, much of the advantage of the PLA over the ROM in implementing switching functions is lost in the macrocircuit expansion of PLAs. In the worst case, adding one input will double the number of PLA packages, just as for ROM. At the microcircuit level, however, it is always possible to share product terms, so the PLA retains its advantage over ROM for any number of inputs.

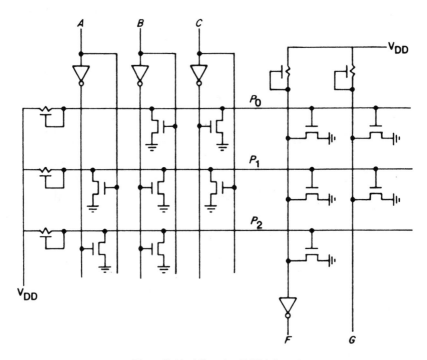

Figure 5.44   Microcircuit PLA layout

Another disadvantage of macrocircuit PLAs with respect to macrocircuit ROMs is that the number of product terms is fixed, and this number is not large enough for some functions. That is, for a typical $n \times k \times m$ macrocircuit PLA, there are functions with n inputs and m outputs that cannot be implemented because k is too small.

A microcircuit layout of the PLA of Figure 5.43 is shown in Figure 5.44. A "stick diagram" of the same PLA is shown in Figure 5.45. A stick diagram is a microcircuit layout which shows the material used for the signal paths. In Figure 5.45 a metal path is a solid line, a poly path is dashed, and an n-diffusion path is dotted. A transistor is formed where a poly path crosses an n-diffusion path, as discussed in Section 2.4. When colors are available, stick diagrams are commonly drawn using blue for metal, red for poly, and green for n-diffusion paths [26, 50].

The next level of detail below the stick diagram is the geometric layout, which shows the actual dimensions of all elements of the chip surface. Examples of geometric layouts are given in Section 2.4. In this text we will usually

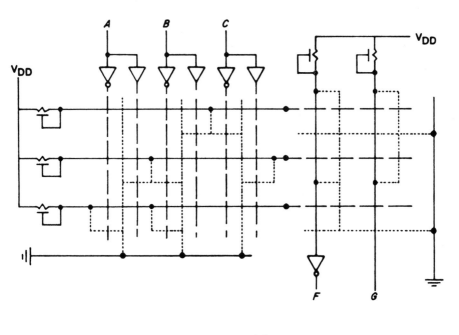

———————— metal

— — — — poly

·················· n–diffusion

Figure 5.45   PLA stick diagram

ignore details below the level of the microcircuit layout (e.g., Figure 5.44). The microcircuit layout shows the relative positions of all elements on the chip surface, but does not indicate exactly how the elements are implemented (i.e., materials used for signal paths, and dimensions).

5.2.5 Arithmetic Logic Unit (ALU)

One final type of combinational network component that is frequently used in computer design is the ALU. An ALU is a device that is capable of performing a number of different operations on its inputs. The specific operation that is to be performed at any time is selected by a control word input. A typical small ALU is shown in Figure 5.46. This ALU is capable of performing any one of eight operations, as determined by the select input $S\langle 2:0 \rangle$. The input CIN and the outputs $COUT$ and OVR are used for the three arithmetic operations. They are not used for the other five operations, and in fact $COUT$ and OVR are defined in the figure only for the three arithmetic operations. Note that OVR is the 2C overflow indicator for all arithmetic operations, $COUT$ is

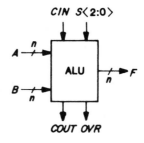

$S\langle 2:0 \rangle$	F
000	0^n
001	$B \stackrel{\wedge}{+}_2 \bar{A} \stackrel{\wedge}{+}_2 CIN$
010	$A \stackrel{\wedge}{+}_2 \bar{B} \stackrel{\wedge}{+}_2 CIN$
011	$A \stackrel{\wedge}{+}_2 B \stackrel{\wedge}{+}_2 CIN$
100	$A + B$
101	$A \oplus B$
110	$A \cdot B$
111	1^n

$$COUT = C_n \text{ and } OVR = C_n \oplus C_{n-1}$$

Figure 5.46   A typical ALU

the B2 overflow for addition, and $\overline{COUT}$ is the B2 overflow for subtraction (see Chapter 4).

ALU "slices" are available as standard IC components. In fact, the ALU of Figure 5.46 with $n = 4$ is a 74382 IC package. ALU slices can be cascaded by connecting COUT of each stage to CIN of the next higher stage. For example, four 74382 packages can be cascaded to form a 16-bit ALU. The reader is referred to the 74382 data sheet for the internal implementation of this ALU at the logic design level. The ALU on a microprocessor chip would be interlaced with other components and buses (see Section 7.3). An example of another ALU, and an interesting microcircuit implementation using multiplexers and pass transistors, may be found in [26].

5.2.6 Exercises

1. (a) Do the microcircuit layout of the NOR-NOR multiplexer circuit of Figure 5.29(b).

(b) Try using a two-level structure (like Figure 5.25). When will this be useful?

2. Do a macrocircuit implementation of a 32-to-1 multiplexer using 8-to-1 multiplexers as components.

3. Program the ROMs of Figures 5.36 and 5.38 to implement the function

$$D = (\bar{A}_1 + A_2 \cdot \bar{A}_3) \cdot (A_0 + \bar{A}_2)$$

4. (a) Use an 8-to-1 multiplexer to implement the function of Exercise 3.

(b) Use a 4-to-1 multiplexer.

5. Construct a microcircuit ROM like Figure 5.35(b) to implement the functions $D_2 = \bar{A}_1 A_0$, $D_1 = A_1 \bar{A}_0$, and $D_0 = A_1 \bar{A}_0 + \bar{A}_1 A_0$.

6. (a) Construct a $2^2 \times 3$ NAND-NAND ROM, like Figure 5.35(b). Be careful to have the "broken connections" in the second bank of gates act like logic 1 inputs to the NAND gates. Explain how to program the ROM.

(b) Program the ROM to implement the functions of Exercise 5.

7. (a) Sketch the microcircuit layout of a $3 \times 4 \times 3$ PLA (like Figure 5.44), programmed to implement the functions $Y_2 = \bar{X}_2\bar{X}_0 + \bar{X}_1 X_0$, $Y_1 = X_2\bar{X}_0 + \bar{X}_2\bar{X}_1 X_0$, and $Y_0 = X_0 + X_2 \cdot \bar{X}_1$.

(b) Sketch a stick diagram of this PLA (like Figure 5.45).

8. Sketch a stick diagram (like Figure 5.45) of the ROM of Figure 5.35.

9. Using the geometric design rules of Figure 2.3.5, estimate the length and width of the PLA of Figure 5.45. Assume $\lambda = 1$ micron. Write general expressions for the length and width of a PLA with n inputs, m outputs, and k product terms.

10. For a macrocircuit $n \times k \times m$ PLA, how large must k be to allow implementation of *any* n-input, m-output function?

5.3   PULSE GENERATORS [19, 24, 26, 36, 49]

5.3.1   Clocks
5.3.2   One-Shots
5.3.3   Switches and Reset Circuits
5.3.4   Exercises

A typical computer performs millions of register transfer operations every second. For each of these operations, a destination register must be loaded. One of the tasks of the computer designer is to generate pulses to load destination registers at the proper times. In this section we discuss devices that may be used to generate pulses for this and other purposes.

The two most common types of pulse generators are *clocks* and *one-shots* (also called *monostables*). There are many variations of each of these devices. We will look at a few typical examples of each.

5.3.1   Clocks

A clock is a device that generates a string of pulses. The most frequently used clocks are free-running and periodic. Such a clock generates a continuous sequence of equally spaced pulses, as illustrated in Figure 5.47. There are no inputs to such a clock. As long as power is on, a steady stream of pulses is generated.

A free-running clock may be used to generate pulses at selected times, as illustrated in Figure 5.48. The signal LOADY need not be crisp clean signal, making the decision hardware easier to design. LOADY need only be stable while $\phi = 1$. CLKY is a clean pulse that loads register Y (see Section 6.2).

There are many electronic oscillator circuits that may be used as clocks. The analysis and design of such circuits are beyond the scope of this text. An example of such a circuit is shown in Figure 5.49.

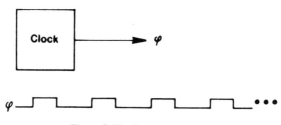

Figure 5.47   Free-running clock

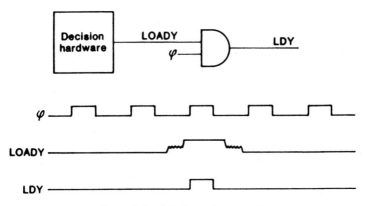

Figure 5.48 Selective pulse generation

The frequency of a crystal oscillator, such as the circuit in Figure 5.49, is established by the natural resonant frequency of the piezoelectric crystal. Crystal oscillators are widely used because they have extremely good frequency stability. Typically frequency will be stable to within a few thousandths of 1% for temperature variations from 0° to 70°C and power supply variations of ±5%.

Ring Oscillators

There are many situations where very good frequency stability is not essential. In these cases a variety of other types of oscillator circuits may be used as

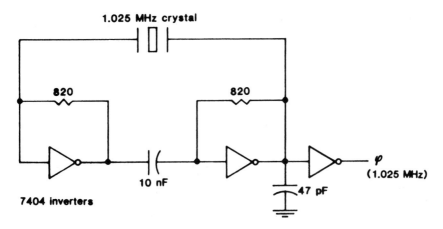

Figure 5.49 A crystal oscillator

clocks. One such example is the *ring oscillator*, the simplest version of which is shown in Figure 5.50.

The device in the feedback path around the NOR gate is a delay element with delay δ. One way to implement a delay, as a string of inverters, is shown in the figure. Other ways are also possible. If a long delay is desired, then an *RC* network might be used together with the inverters, or with some other threshold device.

The operation of the clock is illustrated in the timing diagram. Both the NOR gate and the delay element are modeled as pure delays. The period of the clock is $2(\Delta + \delta)$ where Δ is the delay through the NOR gate.

Actually, however, it is not desirable for the delay element to be a pure delay. If a noise pulse is introduced into the clock loop in some way, it will continue to circulate around the loop if the delays are pure delays. It may be desirable to insert an *RC* network in the loop to prevent this if the inherent capacitance of the circuit is not sufficiently large.

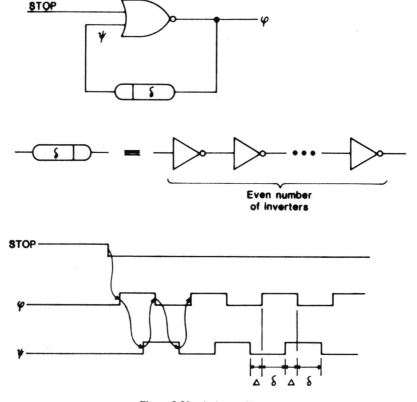

Figure 5.50   A ring oscillator

One might consider removing the STOP input and replacing the NOR gate with an inverter. However, there may be some difficulty in starting the clock properly if this is done. Power does not come up everywhere in the circuit simultaneously, and it does not come up sharply but very slowly. The waveform that ends up circulating around the loop after power-up may not be a suitable clock waveform.

Ideally, this clock should be started by holding STOP = 1 while power is coming up, and then pulling STOP low after power is stable everywhere in the circuit. Circuits for generating such initializing signals are discussed in Section 5.3.3.

In addition to providing a means for starting the clock properly after power-up, the STOP input also makes it possible to stop the clock at any time. This is important in some situations. In the next section we will see how it is useful in synchronizing inputs.

More elaborate versions of the ring oscillator are possible. For example, by providing more inputs on the NOR gate and different feedback paths, one can provide a clock with an adjustable frequency.

Gate delays vary considerably with temperature and with power supply voltage. Consequently, the ring oscillator of Figure 5.50 does not have very good frequency stability. This and similar circuits are thus unattractive in many situations.

There is at least one situation, however, where these circuits may be preferable, specifically, when providing an onboard clock for a microcircuit. All of the devices on the chip will be subjected to essentially the same variations in power supply voltage and temperature. A clock of the type in Figure 5.50 will automatically adjust its frequency to adapt itself to these changes.

Multiphase Clocks

A multiphase clock has several outputs oscillating at the same frequency. The output waveforms may have different shapes, or they may have the same shape and simply be displaced with respect to each other. Since all outputs are at the same frequency, the relative phase of the outputs with respect to each other remains unchanged.

Figure 5.51 shows a simple circuit that may be used to generate a nonoverlapping two-phase clock from a single-phase clock. "Nonoverlapping" means that ϕ_1 and ϕ_2 are never at 1 simultaneously, that is, $\phi_1 \cdot \phi_2 = 0$. This characteristic is guaranteed by the structure of the circuit: $\phi_1\downarrow$ causes (and hence must precede) $\phi_2\uparrow$, and $\phi_2\downarrow$ causes (hence must precede) $\phi_1\uparrow$.

A similar circuit using NAND gates can generate ϕ_1 and ϕ_2 such that $\phi_1 + \phi_2 = 1$, that is, ϕ_1 and ϕ_2 are never at 0 simultaneously.

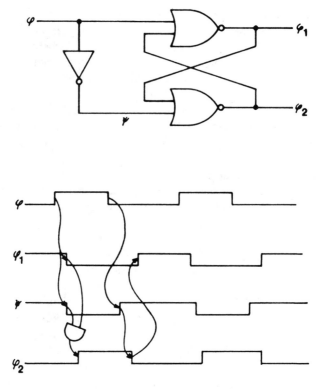

Figure 5.51   Nonoverlapping two-phase clock

5.3.2   One-Shots

A *one-shot* (or *monostable multivibrator*) is a device that generates a pulse at its output in response to an edge at its input. Normally only input transitions in one direction produce output pulses, although a one-shot could be designed to respond to transitions in either direction. To be specific, we will describe a one-shot that is sensitive to negative edges at its input and produces positive pulses at its output.

Such a device is represented in Figure 5.52(a). The small triangle at the input terminal is a standard notation for identifying an edge-sensitive input. The small circle is used in conjunction with the triangle to specify the active edge: presence of the circle indicates negative edge sensitive; absence of the circle indicates positive edge sensitive. A standard notation is also used at the output: the letter Q denotes an output terminal that produces a positive pulse, $Q\uparrow\downarrow$; $\bar{Q}$ is used to identify an output terminal that produces a negative pulse, $\bar{Q}\downarrow\uparrow$.

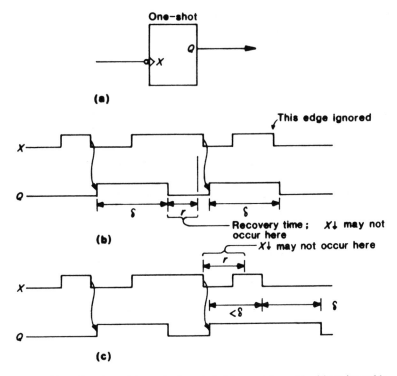

Figure 5.52   One-shots: (a) standard symbol; (b) nonretriggerable; (c) retriggerable

There are two standard types of one-shots: *retriggerable* and *nonretriggerable*. The operation of the nonretriggerable type is illustrated in Figure 5.52(b). There are two major timing parameters involved: *pulse width* δ and *recovery time* r. An edge $X\downarrow$ that occurs while $Q = 0$ will produce a pulse $Q\uparrow\downarrow$. An edge $X\downarrow$ that occurs while $Q = 1$ will be ignored. After $Q\downarrow$, the one-shot reinitializes itself to prepare for the next $X\downarrow$. The time required to do this is the recovery time r. $X\downarrow$ transitions are not permitted to occur during this interval.

The recovery time specification is a minimum acceptable value for the interval $[Q\downarrow, X\downarrow]$. Complete timing specifications would include a maximum propagation delay from $X\downarrow$ to $Q\uparrow$, and minimum requirements for X pulse widths.

A retriggerable one-shot, Figure 5.52(c), operates in the same fashion, as long as $X\downarrow$ transitions occur only while $Q = 0$. If an $X\downarrow$ occurs while $Q = 1$, however, a retriggerable one-shot will respond by reinitializing its timing circuitry and extending the output pulse for an additional time δ. The recovery time for this type of one-shot is measured with respect to $X\downarrow$. It may be specified as a minimum acceptable value for $[X\downarrow, X\downarrow]$, or more likely as minimum values for both $[X\downarrow, X\uparrow]$ and $[X\uparrow, X\downarrow]$. There must also be a limit on $[Q\uparrow, X\downarrow]$ for an $X\downarrow$ transition to be recognized in time to hold $Q = 1$.

IC One-Shots

There are many electronic circuits that might be used to implement one-shots. The analysis and design of such circuits are beyond the scope of this text.

One-shots are available as standard ICs, for example, the TTL packages 74121, 74122, and 74123. In order to make these ICs broadly applicable, the value of δ is programmable; it is normally established by a simple RC network connected to specified pins of the IC. The value of δ as a function of R and C values is given by formulas or graphs. The range of values that δ may assume is typically very large, from nanoseconds to seconds.

In general, the parameter δ is difficult to control precisely. It tends to vary from one IC to another, as well as with temperature, power supply voltage, and aging. Synchronous sequential networks (Section 5.5) can generate pulses with much more precisely controlled widths, and hence are used in preference to one-shots whenever possible.

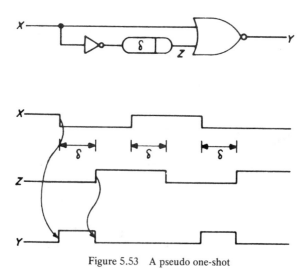

Figure 5.53   A pseudo one-shot

Similar Devices

The circuit of Figure 5.53 is similar to a one-shot; it generates a positive pulse at the output in response to a negative transition at the input. The timing diagram assumes that the gate delays are small relative to δ.

This circuit is not quite a bona fide one-shot because the output pulse may be affected by nonactive input transitions. After an output pulse has been initiated by $X\downarrow$, if $X\uparrow$ occurs before time δ has elapsed then the output pulse will be curtailed.

Nevertheless, circuits of this sort can frequently be used when short pulses must be generated in response to transitions.

5.3.3   Switches and Reset Circuits

Switches of various sorts are often used to generate input signals. In some cases the simple connection shown in Figure 5.54(a) will suffice. However, due to a phenomenon known as *contact bounce*, the input generated in this way may not be acceptable. The phenomenon is illustrated in Figure 5.54(b). The name "contact bounce" originated in relay switching circuits in which the spring-loaded contacts would actually bounce when changing position.

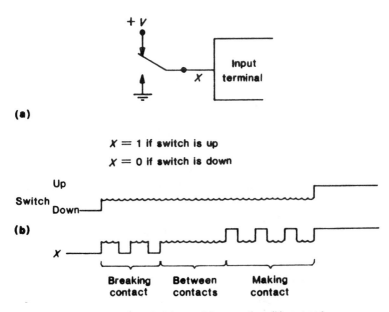

Figure 5.54   Simple switch input: (a) connection; (b) contact bounce

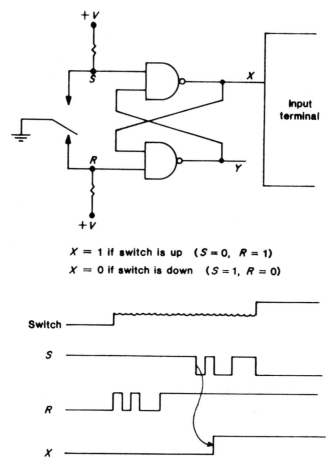

$X = 1$ if switch is up $(S = 0, \; R = 1)$

$X = 0$ if switch is down $(S = 1, \; R = 0)$

Figure 5.55   Debouncing the switch

Any mechanical switch exhibits similar behavior, however, because contacts are imperfect and they do not make or break cleanly. The "bounce time" is relatively long since changing the position of a switch is a mechanical operation, and hence the time required is large relative to electronic speeds (i.e., milliseconds rather than nanoseconds).

In Figure 5.54(b), the wiggly level in the "switch" time line indicates the duration of the switch operation (perhaps 20 ms). The wiggly level in the X line indicates that the contact is broken or partially broken, and the value of X is uncertain. The actual value will depend not only upon the nature of the contact but also upon the internal circuitry connected to terminal X.

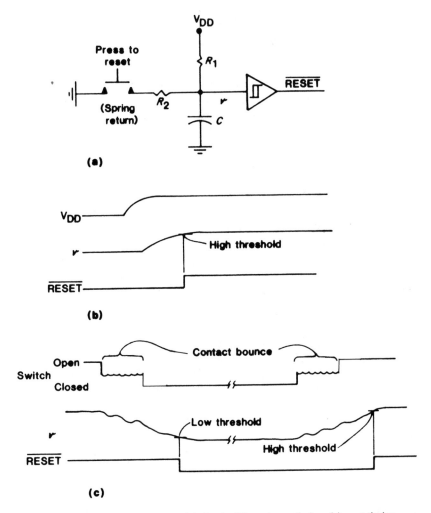

Figure 5.56 Reset operation: (a) circuit; (b) power-up timing; (c) reset timing

If the input X is looked at only when the switch is known to be stationary, then contact bounce is no problem, and the simple connection of Figure 5.54(a) is suitable. For example, the switch may be used to select an operating mode; the switch is set before operation begins and then remains set.

If a "clean" input signal is needed from a switch, then the connection of Figure 5.54 is inadequate. In such cases a circuit such as the one in Figure 5.55 may be used to "debounce" the switch. The two NAND gates connected in this fashion are called a *latch circuit*. This circuit can be used as a storage cell for registers and will be considered for that application in the next section. Its operation as a switch debouncer is illustrated in Figure 5.55. When the switch is in the down position, $R = 0$ and $S = 1$, hence $Y = 1$ and $X = 0$. When the lower contact begins to break, R oscillates between 0 and 1 due to contact bounce. But Y is held at 1 by $X = 0$, so this oscillation has no effect. When the upper contact begins to make, S oscillates between 0 and 1. When it first goes to 0, X changes to 1 and (since $R = 1$ now) Y changes to 0. When S bounces back to 1 momentarily, X does not change again because $Y = 0$ holds X at 1. The switch from up to down is similar. The signal X thus produced is a clean digital signal.

One application where a clean pulse is needed from a switch input is the *system reset* function. Most systems have a *reset* button which can be pressed when it is desired to put the system in some initial state. When the reset button is released, the fetch execute operation begins. The circuit of Figure 5.55 can be used for a reset switch.

In most systems, the reset circuit generates a pulse automatically when power is turned on as well as in response to a reset switch being pressed. A circuit such as the one in Figure 5.56 may be used for this purpose.

This circuit uses RC delays both to detect power coming up and to debounce a reset switch. Consider the power detect circuit first. The R_1C time constant is chosen large enough so that V_{DD} is at its specified level several milliseconds before v reaches the high threshold of the Schmitt trigger buffer. Hence $\overline{RESET} = 0$ for several milliseconds after all circuits are powered up, and this level forces the system into the desired initial state (usually by clearing selected control registers).

If the reset button is pressed while the system is running, the capacitor will discharge to $V_{DD}R_2/(R_1 + R_2)$. R_2 is chosen small enough so that this level is below the low threshold of the Schmitt buffer, and hence $\overline{RESET}$ will go to 0, but large enough so that the switch bounce is smoothed by the RC delay.

5.3.4 Exercises

1. Design a circuit similar to the one in Figure 5.51 using NAND gates. The circuit should generate two clock phases ϕ_1 and ϕ_2 such that $\phi_1 + \phi_2 = 1$ at all times. Draw a timing diagram illustrating the operation of the circuit.

2. Design a "frequency doubler" using pseudo-one-shots such as the one in Figure 5.53. The input is a square wave of frequency f_0. The output is a square wave (approximately) of frequency $2f_0$.

3. Using two inverters, a resistor and a capacitor, design a delay element $\boxed{\text{\small$\bigtriangleup$}\delta}$. Will your circuit delay positive transitions and negative transitions by the same amount? Can this be controlled? How will the size of R and C, as well as RC, affect the operation of the circuit?

4. The network below will "stretch" positive pulses.
   (a) Draw a timing diagram to illustrate the operation of this circuit.

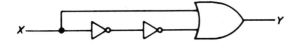

   (b) Design a similar circuit to stretch negative pulses.

5.4   MEMORY COMPONENTS

5.4.1   Immediate Access Registers
5.4.2   Random Access Memory (RAM)
5.4.3   Sequential Access Memory (SAM)
5.4.4   Exercises

There are a number of different mechanisms that may be used to store information in digital systems. For example, a bit may be stored in any of the following ways:

1. By the presence or absence of charge on a capacitor

2. By the state of a "bistable" circuit (i.e., a circuit with two stable states)

3. By the alignment of magnetic dipoles (i.e., flux direction) in a magnetic material

Each of these mechanisms will be discussed in this section.

In addition to the type of storage mechanism used, memory components are also classified according to the type of "access" that is provided to the stored information. The major types are *immediate access, random access,* and *sequential access.* An immediate access register provides storage for a single word, which is continuously available at an output port for reading and may be written at any time via an input port. A random access memory (RAM) is a set of registers that are all equally accessible for reading or writing, but only one of which may be accessed at a time. This type of access is called "random" in contrast to the type of access provided by a sequential access memory (SAM). The words stored in a SAM are arranged sequentially in some fashion (e.g., magnetic tape or disk). A word is made accessible by moving the stored words in sequence past a read/write position. The time required to access a word depends upon its distance from the read/write position. Hence words are not "randomly" (i.e., "equally") accessible as in a RAM.

We have already seen one type of memory component, the read only memory (ROM). The term "read only" refers to the lack of a write operation, and not to the type of access. The words in a ROM are randomly accessible as in a RAM.

In this section we examine memory components using each type of storage mechanism and each type of access described above.

5.4.1 Immediate Access Registers

The most accessible form of storage is the *immediate access* register. Such a register provides storage for one binary word. It has an output port, at which the word stored in the register is continuously available. It has an input port through which a word may be *loaded* (*stored*, *written*, *entered*) into the register at any time. The operation of storing a word in the register is called the *parallel load operation*. In addition to the parallel load operation, an immediate access register may have other operations (e.g., increment, decrement, shift).

In the discussion to follow we will first present register transfer level models of typical immediate access registers, and then discuss microcircuit and macrocircuit implementations of these registers.

Register Models

In RT level block diagrams, an immediate access register is usually represented by a rectangle, as illustrated in Figure 5.57. In operational models, the register is represented by a binary word variable (variable Y in Figure 5.57). The value of the variable at any time is the word stored in the register at that time. The input port of the register is represented by another binary word

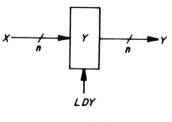

Operation: $X \longrightarrow Y$ (evoked by LDY)

Figure 5.57   Immediate access register

variable (X in Figure 5.57). The output port is represented by the same variable as the register itself, since the word stored in the register is continuously available at the output port.

The register pictured in Figure 5.57 has only one operation, the parallel load operation $X \rightarrow Y$. This operation is evoked by the control input LDY. There are two general ways to control a register operation: edge control and level control. These are discussed next.

Edge Control

An *edge-controlled* parallel load operation is illustrated in Figure 5.58. The operation is evoked by the edge $LDY\downarrow$ (i.e., by the 1 to 0 transition of LDY). For proper execution of the operation, certain input requirements must be met. The word to be loaded into the register must be stable at X for some minimum acceptable setup time before $LDY\downarrow$, and for some minimum acceptable hold time after $LDY\downarrow$. Also, the pulse $LDY\uparrow\downarrow$ must have a minimum acceptable width, and so must the pulse $LDY\downarrow\uparrow$.

If the input requirements are met, then certain events are guaranteed to occur within other specified limits. The output Y is guaranteed not to begin changing until some minimum time after $LDY\downarrow$ (the subscript "pdb" means

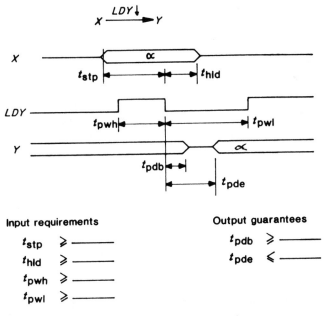

Figure 5.58   Edge-controlled operation

"propagation delay to the beginning of the transition"). The output Y is guaranteed to be stable at its new value before some maximum specified time after $LDY\!\downarrow$ (the subscript "pde" means "propagation delay to the end of the transition").

The blanks in Figure 5.58 represent timing specifications. For a register of a particular type, they are "worst case" minimum and maximum values. That is, the "worst" register of that type is guaranteed to meet the output specifications provided that the input specifications are met. (Notice that $LDY\!\uparrow$ may precede $X\!<$ since there is no requirement to the contrary.)

A register operation may also be evoked by a positive edge, as illustrated in Figure 5.59 for the parallel load operation. All timing specifications are measured with respect to $LDY\!\uparrow$ rather than $LDY\!\downarrow$.

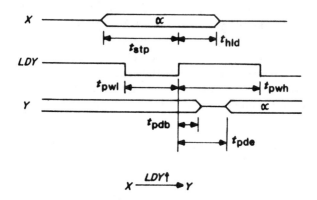

Figure 5.59   Positive-edge-triggered

To avoid unnecessary repetition, timing specifications are not listed explicitly in Figure 5.59. In this figure, as in others to follow, timing specifications may be assumed to be similar to those of Figure 5.58.

Level Control

The other general way to control a register operation is *level control*, illustrated in Figure 5.60 for the parallel load operation. As with edge control, the word to be loaded is held at input port X and a pulse is produced at input LDY. The pulse is positive (i.e., $LDY\!\uparrow\!\downarrow$) if LDY is "asserted high," as in Figure 5.60. If LDY is "asserted low" then a negative pulse, $LDY\!\downarrow\!\uparrow$, is used. Setup and hold times are measured with respect to the transition of LDY to its unasserted level.

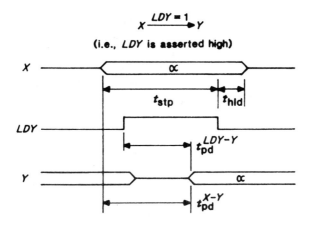

Figure 5.60 Level-controlled operation

The difference between edge control and level control is reflected in the propagation delay specifications. For level control, propagation delay is measured both from the transition of LDY to its asserted level, and from $X<$. The load operation begins when LDY goes to its asserted level, and continues as long as LDY remains asserted. If X changes while LDY is asserted, the register will follow the change and load the new value.

Figure 5.60 illustrates how the register is normally used. The input X remains stable while LDY is asserted (or possibly $LDY\uparrow$ precedes $X<$, but then X remains stable until after $LDY\downarrow$). Figure 5.61 illustrates how the register behaves if X changes from one stable value to another while LDY is asserted. Notice how Y follows the input change; the register loads α first and then β.

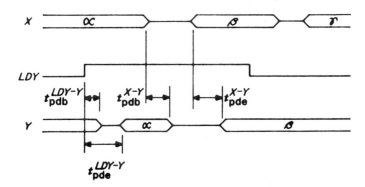

Figure 5.61 Propagation delays for level control

An edge-controlled register, by contrast, would load only one of these values (α if positive-edge-triggered; β if negative-edge-triggered).

Figure 5.61 also identifies all of the propagation delay parameters for the level-controlled operation. In Figure 5.60, only the propagation delays to the *end* of the Y transition are identified.[1] In Figure 5.61, propagation delays to the *beginning* of the Y transition are also identified. Complete timing specifications for the operation would include guaranteed minimum values for the intervals $[LDY\uparrow, Y>]$ and $[X>, Y>]$, and guaranteed maximum values for $[LDY\uparrow, Y<]$ and $[X<, Y<]$.

Multioperation Registers

A register with multiple operations is represented in Figure 5.62. Operations are initiated by positive transitions of the timing input $CLKY$. The specific

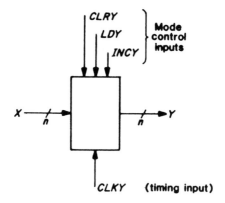

CLRY	LDY	INCY	Operation (on $CLKY\uparrow$)
1	—	—	$0^n \longrightarrow Y$
0	1	—	$X \longrightarrow Y$
0	0	1	$Y \stackrel{\wedge}{+_2} 1 \longrightarrow Y$
0	0	0	$Y \longrightarrow Y$

— = don't care

Figure 5.62   Multiple operation register

---

[1] The timing parameter t_{pd} will always denote t_{pde} rather than t_{pdb}. The parameter t_{pdb} is less important, in general, and is frequently not even specified. There are situations, however, where $(t_{pdb})_{min}$ is needed. If it is not specified, then 0 must be assumed. (It could not be less than 0 since the events bounding the interval are related by cause and effect.)

operation that is evoked by a particular occurrence of $CLKY\uparrow$ is determined by the mode control inputs as shown in the table. To evoke a desired operation, mode control inputs are first established and then an active transition of $CLKY$ is produced.

Timing specifications for such a register would be similar to those of Figure 5.59. Inputs $CLRY$, LDY, and $INCY$ would all have setup and hold requirements measured with respect to $CLKY\uparrow$. The load operation would also have setup and hold requirements for X. All operations would have propagation delay guarantees, also measured with respect to $CLKY\uparrow$.

Register Implementation

The simplest nMOS implementation of a register is illustrated in Figure 5.63. This implementation uses the capacitance of the inverter pull-down transistor gate as the storage mechanism, as illustrated in Figure 5.63(c).

A 1 is stored in cell i by establishing $X_i = 1$ and then producing a pulse $LDY\uparrow\downarrow$. While $LDY = 1$, the gate of the pull-down transistor charges through the "pass transistor" to about $V_{DD} - V_{th} \cong 4$ volts (assuming LDY is at V_{DD}, $V_{th} = 0.2\ V_{DD}$, and $V_{DD} = 5.0$ volts). After $LDY\downarrow$, the charge that was stored on the pull-down gate is isolated, since the pass transistor controlled by LDY is turned off. As long as the gate remains charged, the pull-down transistor is turned on and $\overline{Y}_i = 0$ (hence $Y_i = 1$).

A 0 is stored in cell i be establishing $X_i = 0$ and then producing $LDY\uparrow\downarrow$. If the gate of the pull-down had previously been charged, it will discharge through the pass transistor while $LDY = 1$. After $LDY\downarrow$ the pull-down gate is again isolated, so the pull-down transistor remains turned off and $\overline{Y}_i = 1$ (hence $Y_i = 0$).

The output of this register is $\overline{Y}$ rather than Y. If necessary, an additional bank of inverters may be provided to generate Y.

The load operation for this register is level-controlled, since the charge on the gate of cell i will follow X_i as long as $LDY = 1$. The setup requirement is determined by the time constant $R_{ds}C_{gs}$, where R_{ds} is the drain-source resistance of the pass transistor and C_{gs} is the gate-source capacitance of the pull-down transistor. The hold requirement is 0. The propagation delays are determined by the resistances of the pull-up, pull-down, and pass transistors, and by the gate-source capacitance of the pull-down transistor, as well as by the resistance and capacitance driven by the output.

A fundamental characteristic of this implementation is that it will store a word only for a short time. This is because the storage capacitance C_{gs} will "leak" through the turned-off pass transistor. Hence if a 1 has been stored, C_{gs} will slowly discharge to 0 while $LDY = 0$ if $X_i = 0$. Or if a 0 has been

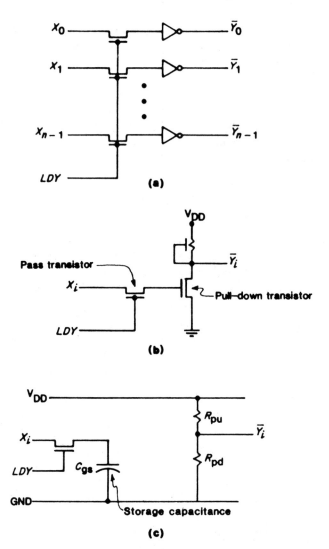

Figure 5.63   A dynamic nMOS register: (a) an n-bit register; (b) one cell; (c) cell model

stored, C_{gs} will slowly charge to 1 while $LDY = 0$ if $X_i = 1$. Hence, after LDY has been at 0 for some time, the word stored in the register is uncertain.

A register is said to be *dynamic* if it can store a word only for a short time, as described above. A register that can store a word indefinitely is called *static*. As always, the terms "dynamic" and "static" refer roughly to "changing" and "unchanging" with time.

If it is desired to use a dynamic register to store information over long periods of time, the register must be *refreshed* periodically; that is, the word stored in the register must be written back into the register periodically. Figure 5.64 shows the basic dynamic nMOS cell of Figure 5.63(b) with the capability to refresh added. The cell is loaded by putting the desired value at the data input D and producing a positive pulse at the gate input G. The cell is refreshed by producing a positive pulse at the refresh input R. The bit stored is continuously available at output Q, and the complement at $\bar{Q}$. (The letter Q is traditionally used to denote the output of a storage cell, though the mnemonic reference, if any, is obscure.) The R and G inputs are never asserted simultaneously (i.e., $R \cdot G = 0$).

In Figure 5.65, two registers constructed from the basic cell of Figure 5.64 are shown. The first retains the refresh input. The second drives the refresh inputs with the complement of LDY, effectively creating a static register. This register is continuously refreshed while $LDY = 0$.

Bistable Circuits

The register implementations described above for nMOS circuits are not easily converted to bipolar circuits for two reasons: (1) the storage mechanism is

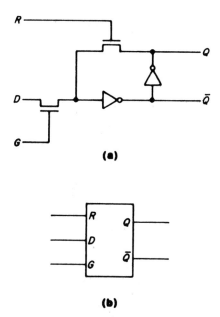

(a)

(b)

Figure 5.64   Dynamic cell with refresh: (a) the circuit; (b) logic diagram symbol

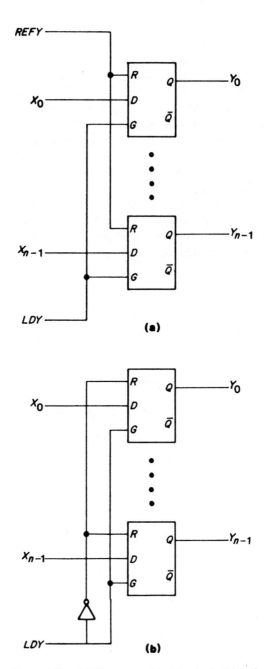

Figure 5.65   nMOS registers: (a) with refresh; (b) static

gate capacitance, for which there is no bipolar counterpart, and (2) the loading and refreshing operations utilize the pass transistor, which likewise has no bipolar counterpart.

A general type of circuit that may be used to construct registers in either bipolar or MOS technologies is the bistable. A *bistable circuit* (or simply, a *bistable*) is a circuit that has exactly two stable states (for some fixed input condition). If a mechanism is provided for switching a bistable circuit from one stable state to another, then it may be used as a storage cell in constructing registers.

Such a circuit may be constructed from two NOR gates, as shown in Figure 5.66. This particular circuit is called a *latch*. The latch is an example of an

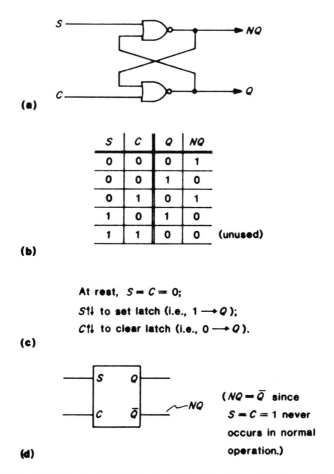

(a)

S	C	Q	NQ	
0	0	0	1	
0	0	1	0	
0	1	0	1	
1	0	1	0	
1	1	0	0	(unused)

(b)

At rest, $S = C = 0$;

$S\!\Uparrow$ to set latch (i.e., $1 \longrightarrow Q$);

$C\!\Uparrow$ to clear latch (i.e., $0 \longrightarrow Q$).

(c)

(d)

($NQ = \bar{Q}$ since $S = C = 1$ never occurs in normal operation.)

Figure 5.66   The latch circuit: (a) latch circuit; (b) stable states; (c) latch operation; (d) block diagram symbol

asynchonous sequential network. These circuits are characterized by the existence of "feedback" interconnections. They were discussed briefly in Section 3.2. An analysis of the latch circuit follows.

The latch is in a stable state if all inputs and outputs are steady at legitimate logic levels (i.e., not in the $1/2$ region). This can be the case only if both NOR gate equations are satisfied. For example, $(S, C, Q, NQ) = (0, 1, 0, 0)$ is not a stable state because the equation for the top NOR gate is not satisfied; this gate will try to change NQ to 1. When NQ reaches 1, the state will be stable at $(0, 1, 0, 1)$.

Figure 5.66(b) shows all the stable states for the latch. Note that there are two stable states for $(S, C) = (0, 0)$. This is the bistable configuration of the latch. The state $(S, C, Q, NQ) = (0, 0, 0, 1)$ is the 0 state and $(0, 0, 1, 0)$ is the 1 state. Hence when $(S, C) = (0, 0)$, the value of Q denotes the state of the latch.

The inputs S and C are used to *set* and *clear* the latch. (The term "set" means to put the latch in the 1 state; "clear" means to put it in the 0 state. The term "reset" is frequently used as a synonym for "clear".) Suppose for example, that the latch is in the 0 state, $(S, C, Q, NQ) = (0, 0, 0, 1)$. If S is changed to 1 then one input to the top NOR gate will be 1 and the output NQ will change to 0, which in turn will cause the bottom gate to change its output Q to 1. The change in Q will produce no further change since the state $(S, C, Q, NQ) = (1, 0, 1, 0)$ is stable. If S now returns to 0, the latch will be in the 1 state $(0, 0, 1, 0)$, where it will remain as long as $(S, C) = (0, 0)$ since this is also a stable state. Hence a pulse $S\uparrow\downarrow$ will switch the latch from the 0 state to the 1 state. In similar fashion, a pulse $C\uparrow\downarrow$ will switch the latch from the 1 state to the 0 state.

A pulse at S or C must be wide enough to allow for the propagation delay through two gates in order to switch the state of the latch reliably. If an S or C pulse terminates too soon, the operation of the latch is unpredictable. Usually it will stabalize quickly to either the 0 state or the 1 state. However, there is a small but nonzero probability that it will hang up in a "metastable" state between 0 and 1.

It is also possible that the latch will begin to oscillate in a quasi-stable fashion if the S or C pulse terminates prematurely. This is also a form of metastable operation. Our simple model of the latch circuit predicts this behavior. Suppose, for example, that the S pulse terminates after NQ has changed to 0, but before Q changes to 1. Then the state of the latch will be $(0, 0, 0, 0)$. This is not a stable state. Both Q and NQ will tend to change to 1. The next state will thus be $(0, 0, 1, 1)$. This state is not stable either, and Q and NQ will both tend to change back to 0. Hence the latch will oscillate between states $(0, 0, 0, 0)$ and $(0, 0, 1, 1)$.

A thorough analysis of metastable operation requires a more detailed model of the latch circuit and will not be attempted here. In Section 5.5, however, the system design problems associated with metastable operation are discussed.

During normal operation, inputs S and C are never asserted simultaneously, hence the state $(1, 1, 0, 0)$ is never entered. In all other stable states, $NQ = \bar{Q}$. Hence the NQ output of a latch is normally labeled $\bar{Q}$, and is used as the complement of Q.

The NOR latch of Figure 5.66 can be transformed into a NAND latch by using De Morgan's theorem and the "small circle convention" (Figure 3.12), as shown in Figure 5.67. Inverters are inserted at the S and C inputs of the NOR latch initially, forming a latch with S and C inputs asserted low. The first step applies De Morgan's theorem directly: $\overline{A + B} = \bar{A} \cdot \bar{B}$.

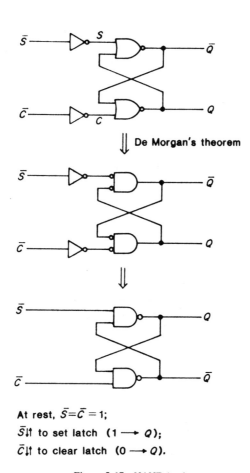

At rest, $\bar{S} = \bar{C} = 1$;

$\bar{S}\!\downarrow\!\uparrow$ to set latch $(1 \longrightarrow Q)$;

$\bar{C}\!\downarrow\!\uparrow$ to clear latch $(0 \longrightarrow Q)$.

Figure 5.67   NAND latch

The next step removes the small circle and inverter combination at the S and C inputs, and moves the other input circle for each gate to the output of the other gate, thus reversing the Q and $\bar{Q}$ outputs.

Registers can be constructed from bistable circuits in many ways. A very simple register, which requires a two-step load operation, is shown in Figure 5.68. The register cell, shown in Figure 5.68(a), is simply a NAND latch together with a gate that is used to generate the pulse to set the latch. The register, shown in Figure 5.68(b), has two control inputs, LDY and $\overline{CLR}$. Input $\overline{CLR}$ is normally held high. It is pulsed low to clear the register. Loading the

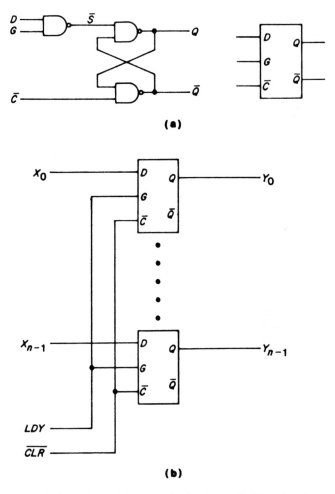

(a)

(b)

Figure 5.68   Register with two-step load: (a) one cell; (b) static register

register requires a pulse $\overline{CLR}\downarrow\uparrow$ to clear, followed by a pulse $LDY\uparrow\downarrow$ that will set each bit Y_i for which $X_i = 1$. The other Y_i bits will remain at 0.

With two additional gates, a one-step load operation can be provided, as illustrated in Figure 5.69. The register cell, shown in Figure 5.69(a), is sometimes called a "gated D-type flip-flop." "Flip-flop" is a general term describing a circuit consisting of a bistable plus other circuitry that is used to generate the pulses that switch the bistable. There are several different types of flip-flops, depending upon the types of inputs that are provided. The timing of the load operation of the register in Figure 5.69 is exactly as in Figure 5.60.

All of the registers that we have constructed thus far are level-controlled. Edge-controlled registers are more expensive but are simpler to use, as we shall see. We will look at the implementation of one such register, constructed from an edge-triggered SR flip-flop (Figure 5.70).

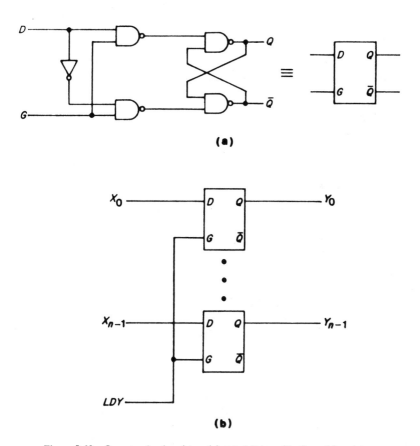

(a)

(b)

Figure 5.69 One-step load register: (a) gated D-type flip-flop; (b) register

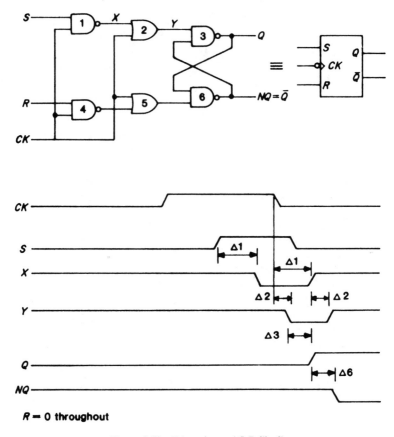

R = 0 throughout

Figure 5.70   Edge triggered S-R flip-flop

The operation of this flip-flop is illustrated in the timing diagram. The notation Δi represents the propagation delay through gate i. Illustrated is the operation of setting the flip-flop. This is accomplished by holding $S = 1$ and $R = 0$ while producing a negative transition at CK. $S\uparrow$ must occur at least $(\Delta 1)_{max}$ before $CK\downarrow$ (setup requirement). Similarly $R\downarrow$ (not shown) must occur $(\Delta 4)_{max}$ before $CK\downarrow$. The transition $CK\downarrow$ produces a pulse $Y\downarrow\uparrow$, which sets the latch. The pulse is produced because the change $CK\downarrow$ affects Y via two paths: $CK-2-Y$ and $CK-1-2-Y$. Since $X = 0$ when $CK\downarrow$ occurs, $CK\downarrow$ first causes $Y\downarrow$ via the short path, and then causes $Y\uparrow$ (after causing $X\uparrow$) via the long path. This is the "pseudo-one-shot" idea of Figure 5.53.

The width of the pulse $Y\downarrow\uparrow$ is $\Delta 1$. Hence this delay must be made large enough for the latch to switch reliably.

The circuit of Figure 5.70 may be transformed into the alternative form shown in Figure 5.71 by the usual technique (e.g., Figure 5.67). The resulting circuit operates in the same way as the original circuit. The two gate paths from CK to Y are $CK—10—3—Y$ and $CK—10—9—1—2—3—Y$. The difference is the three-gate delay $\Delta 9 + \Delta 1 + \Delta 2$. This will be the width of the pulse $Y\downarrow\uparrow$.

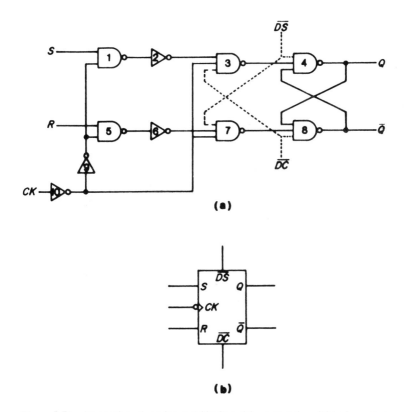

Figure 5.71   Alternative edge-triggered flip-flop: (a) construction; (b) logic symbol

By removing gate 10 the circuit is converted to a positive-edge-triggered SR flip-flop. Since gate 10 is in both paths from CK to Y, the width of the $Y\downarrow\uparrow$ pulse is unaffected. This change is reflected in the block diagram symbol by removing the small circle at the CK input.

In general, the small triangle in a logic symbol identifies an edge-sensitive input. A small circle in conjunction with the triangle means negative-edge-sensitive; the absence of a circle indicates positive-edge-sensitive.

Also shown in Figure 5.71 (dashed lines) are two additional inputs, direct set (*DS*) and direct clear (*DC*), that are sometimes provided. These inputs override all other inputs. When *DS* is asserted (i.e., $\overline{DS} = 0$), *Q* is forced to change to 1 and $\overline{Q}$ to 0, regardless of the values or changes that may be occurring at the *R*, *S*, or *CK* inputs. Likewise, when *DC* is asserted, $\overline{Q}$ is forced to 1 and *Q* to 0. These inputs are normally driven by a $\overline{\text{RESET}}$ pulse (see Section 5.3.3).

A *D*-type edge-triggered flip-flop is easily constructed from an edge-triggered *SR* flip-flop, as shown in Figure 5.72(a). A register with an edge-controlled load operation may be constructed from these, as in Figure 5.72(b).

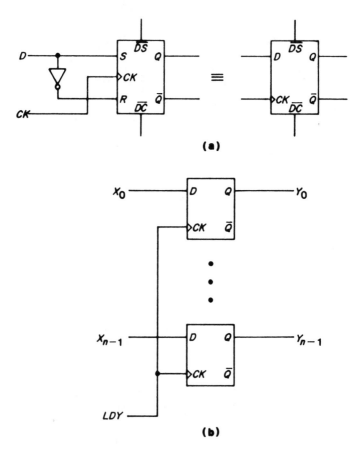

Figure 5.72   Edge-controlled register

Master-Slave Registers

A general type of register construction that may be used either with bistable cells or with capacitive storage cells is illustrated in Figure 5.73. This is known as master-slave construction. A single master-slave register consists of two level-controlled registers, the first of which is called the *master* and the second the *slave*. The master is loaded while $LDY = 1$ and the slave while $LDY = 0$. Setup, hold, and propagation delay are all measured with respect to $LDY\downarrow$. Hence this is an edge-controlled register.

Macrocircuit Registers

Registers of various types are available as separate IC packages. A typical example is the TTL register 74273, shown in Figure 5.74. The package contains an 8-bit edge-triggered immediate access register with parallel load and direct clear operations. The load operation is evoked by $CK\uparrow$, and the clear operation by $\overline{DC} = 0$. Typical timing specifications for low-power Schottky (LS) versions of this and other macrocircuit registers are given later.

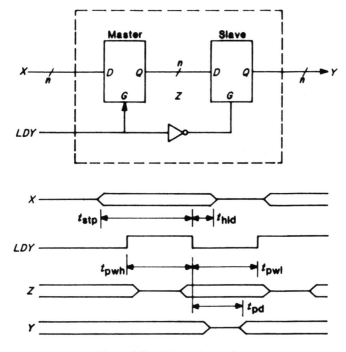

Figure 5.73   Master-slave register

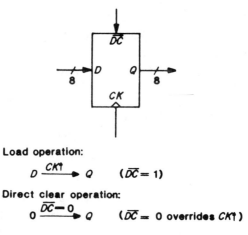

Load operation:

$$D \xrightarrow{CK\uparrow} Q \quad (\overline{DC} = 1)$$

Direct clear operation:

$$0 \xrightarrow{\overline{DC}=0} Q \quad (\overline{DC} = 0 \text{ overrides } CK\uparrow)$$

Figure 5.74   74273 register

The 74163 IC, Figure 5.75, is a 4-bit multioperation register. This IC is designed to allow direct construction of longer registers by simple interconnection of 74163 packages. This is also possible with 74273 packages, of course. But providing this capability for the 74163 package is more difficult because of the necessity of passing carries between stages to implement the increment operation. Notice that $COUT = 1$ if and only if $CIN = 1$ and all four register bits, $Q\langle 3:0 \rangle$, are 1. In the operation table, notice that the increment operation is evoked only when $COUNT = 1$ and $CIN = 1$ (and $CLEAR$ and $LOAD$ are at their unasserted levels).

The multioperation register of Figure 5.62 with $n = 16$ is implemented using four 74163 packages as in Figure 5.76. Notice that the increment operation of any package is enabled only if $INCY = 1$ (and $LDY = CLRY = 0$) and the bits stored in all less significant packages are all ones.

The 74169 IC, Figure 5.77, is similar to the 74163. The clear operation is replaced by a decrement operation. When $COUNT$ is asserted, the UD input (up-down) selects the increment or decrement operation. $COUT$ is asserted when all bits are 0 if $UD = 0$ and when all bits are 1 if $UD = 1$. The asserted level for CIN and $COUT$ is low rather than high as for the 74163.

The 74198 register, Figure 5.78, has right and left shift operations, in addition to parallel load and direct clear. Shift registers longer than 8 bits may be constructed by interconnecting 74198 ICs.

Typical timing specifications for low-power Schottky (LS) versions of these and other 7400 series TTL registers are given in Figure 5.79.

Pinouts

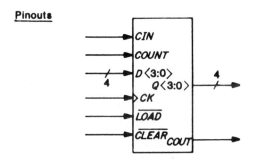

Operation

$\overline{CLEAR}$	$\overline{LOAD}$	COUNT	CIN	Operation (on CK↑)
0	–	–	–	$0 \xrightarrow{4} Q$ (clear)
1	0	–	–	$D \longrightarrow Q$ (load)
1	1	1	1	$Q \xrightarrow{+}_2 1 \longrightarrow Q$ (increment)
1	1	0	–	$Q \longrightarrow Q$
1	1	–	0	

$$COUT = CIN \cdot Q_3 \cdot Q_2 \cdot Q_1 \cdot Q_0$$

Figure 5.75   74163 register

5.4.2   Random Access Memory (RAM)

A random access memory (RAM) is a set of registers, each with a unique address. We will assume that a RAM has a "single port" unless otherwise mentioned. That is, it is possible to access (i.e., read or write) only one register in the RAM at a time.

A RAM may be constructed either from bipolar or MOS transistors. In bipolar RAMs, bits are stored via bistable circuits. MOS RAMs use both bistable circuits and capacitance for storage. The terms "static" and "dynamic," defined previously for immediate access registers, apply also to RAM. A RAM that uses capacitance for storage is called dynamic; every bit stored must be rewritten or "refreshed" periodically. A RAM that uses bistables is static; refreshing is not necessary.

Static RAM

The register transfer model of a basic static RAM is given in Figure 5.80. The $M[\alpha]$ notation for the RAM registers has already been defined. The device

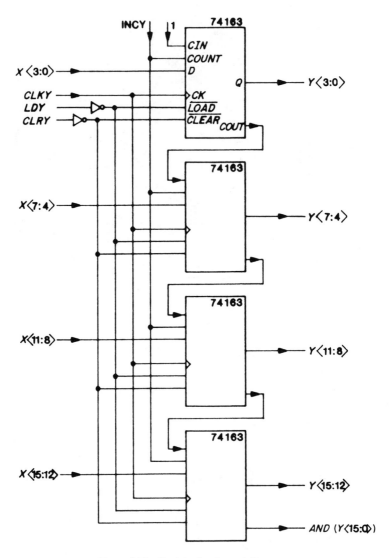

Figure 5.76   Register implementation

Pinouts

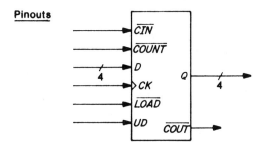

Operation

$\overline{LOAD}$	$\overline{CIN}$	$\overline{COUNT}$	UD	Operation (on CK↑)
0	–	–	–	$D \longrightarrow Q$ (load)
1	0	0	1	$Q \stackrel{+}{_2} 1 \longrightarrow Q$ (increment)
1	0	0	0	$Q \stackrel{-}{_2} 1 \longrightarrow Q$ (decrement)
1	1	–	–	$Q \longrightarrow Q$
1	–	1	–	$Q \longrightarrow Q$

$$\overline{COUT} = \neg (UD \cdot Q_3 \cdot Q_2 \cdot Q_1 \cdot Q_0 \cdot \overline{CIN}$$
$$+ \overline{UD} \cdot \overline{Q}_3 \cdot \overline{Q}_2 \cdot \overline{Q}_1 \cdot \overline{Q}_0 \cdot \overline{CIN})$$

Figure 5.77   74169 register

terminals, pictured in the block diagram, are: address input port, A; data input port, DI; data output port, DO; and write strobe terminal, WS.

Only two operations are possible; *read* and *write*. Typical timing descriptions are given in the figure. For the read operation, the RAM acts like a combinational network (in particular, like a ROM). The address of the desired register α is held stable at A, and after a time t_{access} the word stored in $M[\alpha]$ appears at DO. DO remains stable for a time t_{dhld} after A is released. The read access time, t_{access}, and the data hold time, t_{dhld}, are propagation delays. Specifically, $t_{access} = t_{pde}$ and $t_{dhld} = t_{pdb}$, using our standard notation. The alternative notation is used in the figure because the terms "access" and "data hold" are more commonly used in practice.

The write timing should be recognized as the basic level-controlled load operation, with the additional constraint on the address setup time $t_{AS} \geq (t_{AS})_{min}$. The minimum address setup time $(t_{AS})_{min}$ is the difference between the maximum delay from $A <$ to the select input of any internal register and the minimum delay from $WS\uparrow$ to any internal register. Data is written into the selected internal register while $WS = 1$ at that register. The minimum address setup time assures that an internal register will not be modified acci-

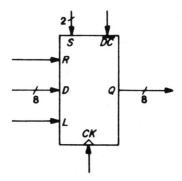

$S\langle 1{:}0\rangle$	Synchronous operation, on $CK\uparrow$ ($\overline{DC}$ = 1)
0 0	$Q \longrightarrow Q$ (no operation)
0 1	$L \circ Q\langle 7{:}1\rangle \longrightarrow Q\langle 7{:}0\rangle$ (shift right)
1 0	$Q\langle 6{:}0\rangle \circ R \longrightarrow Q\langle 7{:}0\rangle$ (shift left)
1 1	$D \longrightarrow Q$ (parallel load)

Direct clear operation:

$$0 \xrightarrow{\overline{DC}} Q \quad (\overline{DC} = 0 \text{ overrides } CK\uparrow)$$

Figure 5.78   74198 register

dentally by *WS* coming up before the desired register has been selected and the others deselected.

The data setup time t_{DS} and data hold time t_{DH} are measured with respect to *WS*↓. The specified minimum values for t_{DS} and t_{DH} depend not only on the characteristics of the internal registers, but also on the relative delays from *WS* and *DI* to the internal register.

There is also a minimum acceptable address hold time $(t_{AH})_{min}$, which depends upon the minimum delays from *WS* and *A* to the internal register. (The address setup requirement depends upon the maximum delays from *WS* and *A* to the internal registers.)

Microcircuit Implementation.   A random access memory may be implemented as part of a microcircuit involving other components such as processors or IO controllers, or it may be implemented as a separate microcircuit. The discussion that follows applies to either situation. It does not, however, consider the possibility of distributing the RAM over the surface of a chip intermingled with other components. This is not ordinarily done at the

Direct clear operation

Requirement: **Guarantee:**

$[\overline{DC}{\downarrow}, \overline{DC}{\uparrow}] \geqslant$ 20 ns $\quad$ $[\overline{DC}{\downarrow}, Q<] \leqslant$ 25 ns

Synchronous operations

Requirements:

$[x<, CK{\uparrow}] \geqslant$ 20 ns (setup) $\quad\Big\}$ $x =$ any data or control

$[CK{\uparrow}, x>] \geqslant$ 0 ns (hold) $\qquad$ input involved in the operation

$[CK{\uparrow}, CK{\downarrow}] \geqslant$ 15 ns

$[CK{\downarrow}, CK{\uparrow}] \geqslant$ 20 ns

$[\overline{DC}{\uparrow}, CK{\uparrow}] \geqslant$ 15 ns (recovery time after direct clear)

Guarantees:

$[CK{\uparrow}, Q<] \leqslant$ 20 ns

$[CK{\uparrow}, y<] \leqslant$ 30 ns $\quad\Big\}$ $x = C/N$ for 74163 or $\overline{C/N}$ for 74169

$[x<, y<] \leqslant$ 20 ns $\qquad$ $y = COUT$ for 74163 or $\overline{COUT}$ for 74169

Figure 5.79 Typical timing specifications for 74163, 169, 198 and 273 registers

present time, but in the future this may become more common, as a way to reduce wire length and communication delays between memory and other components.

The microcircuit structure of RAM is very similar to the two-dimensional ROM structures of Section 5.2. The difference is in the cells of the array, and in the control circuitry for accessing the cells; it is necessary to write as well as read from each cell.

Figure 5.81 shows a two-dimensional decoder type of organization, similar to the ROM of Figure 5.36. This organization may be used either with bipolar or MOS RAMs. It is especially well suited for bipolar because of the efficiency of implementing the required second-level AND operation. This can be done simply by using multiple emitters on the transistors of the bistable of each cell, as shown in Figure 5.82.

This memory cell is designed so that when one or more of the emitters are low for each transistor, the cell must be in one of two stable states: transistor Q_0 saturated and transistor Q_1 turned off (logic 0); or Q_1 saturated and Q_0

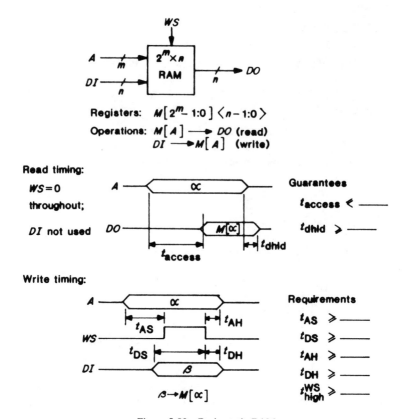

Figure 5.80   Basic static RAM

turned off (logic 1). If cell ij is in state 0 it may be forced to change to state 1 by holding all emitters of Q_0 high and holding emitter W_1 of Q_1 low. This will cause Q_0 to turn off and Q_1 to saturate; that is, the cell switches to state 1. The cell will remain in state 1 even after the emitters of Q_0 are returned low. To switch the cell to state 0, the emitters of Q_1 are held high and the W_0 emitter of Q_0 is held low.

The operation of the RAM is as follows. To read cell ij, WS is held low, CS is held high, and the appropriate address is held at A (i.e., $[A\langle 11:6\rangle]_2 = i$ and $[A\langle 5:0\rangle]_2 = j$). This will cause X_i and Y_j to be asserted high, while all other X and Y bits will be low. Only one cell in the memory array, cell ij, will have both its X and Y emitters high. Every other cell will have either its X emitters low or its Y emitters low, or both. The memory cell, the read/write circuit, and the decoders are designed in such a fashion that the W_i emitter will sink very little current unless Q_i is saturated and *both* the X and Y emitters of Q_i are high; if either the X or the Y emitter is low, then this emitter

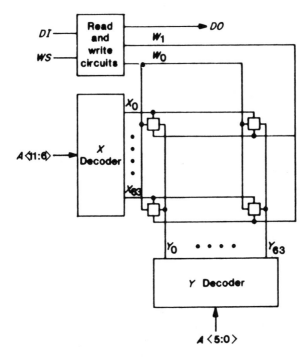

Figure 5.81   A $2^{12} \times 1$ RAM

will sink essentially all of the current through Q_i, even though W_i may also be low. Since only cell ij has both its X and Y emitters high, this cell will establish the W_1 and W_0 currents to ground through the read circuitry. The read circuits are designed to output 1 if the W_1 current is larger than the W_0 current, and 0 if W_0 is larger than W_1.

To write into cell ij, CS is held high, the appropriate address is held at A, and the bit to be written is held at DI. After the decoder outputs X and Y have stabilized, WS is pulsed high. If $DI = 1$ the W_0 will go high with WS. This will cause cell ij to switch to state 1 since all the emitters of Q_0 will be high for cell ij and the W_1 emitters of Q_1 will be low. No other cell will change state, since only cell ij has both its X and Y emitters high. In similar fashion, if $DI = 0$ then cell ij will be forced into state 0.

The RAM of Figure 5.81 uses a two-level decoder. Each cell of the memory array, in addition to providing one bit of storage, also implements the two input AND function required for the second level of decoding. An alternative organization that does not require the cells to provide the decoding function is shown in Figure 5.83. This is similar to the ROM organization of Figure 5.38. Half of the address bits are decoded to select a row of the memory array. The

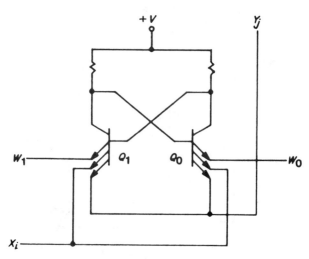

Figure 5.82   Bipolar RAM cell ij

bidirectional multiplexer selects one cell within that row for reading or writing, as determined by the other half of the address bits.

The bipolar RAM cell of Figure 5.82 may be modified for use with this organization: simply remove the Y emitter from each of the transistors, Q_0 and Q_1. These two emitters represent the total cost of implementing the AND function within the cell, since the X emitters must be present in any case in order to select the cell and the W emitters must be present in order to read and write.

MOS memories may be constructed by using either of the organizations shown in Figures 5.81 and 5.83. A typical nMOS cell for the organization of Figure 5.83 is shown in Figure 5.84. The bistable operation of the cell is essentially the same as for the bipolar cell of Figure 5.82. The cell of Figure 5.84 may be modified for use with the organization of Figure 5.81 by adding two transistors to be controlled by Y. These are inserted in series with the transistors controlled by X_i.

The $2^n \times 1$ RAM organizations that we have discussed may be easily extended to $2^n \times m$ organizations. Figure 5.39 shows the extension of the decoder/multiplexer organization for ROM. The extension for RAM is similar. The extension of the two-level decoder implementation is the same, except that the Y decoder need not be repeated for each bank as is the case for the multiplexer; the Y decoder outputs are simply routed to each bank just as the X decoder outputs.

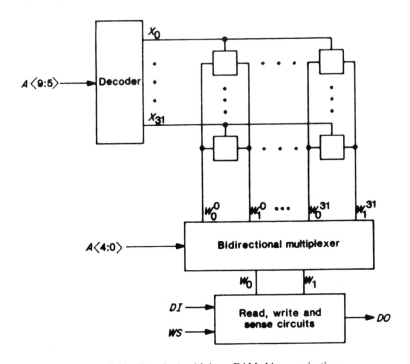

Figure 5.83   Decoder/multiplexer RAM chip organization

Macrocircuit Implementation.   There are many RAM chips available as standard IC packages that may be used to construct large RAMs. They offer a broad range of choices over several important parameters including speed, cost per bit, words per package, bits per word, bits per package, pins per package, voltage levels, and power consumption. There are also many variations in the way read and write operations are controlled.

Every RAM chip provides either tristate buffers or open collector/drain buffers (see Section 5.1) at the data output port. These buffers make it possible to connect the data out ports of several chips directly together. Standard ROM chips also have this capability, and it is possible to connect ROM and RAM chips together in the same memory.

Every RAM chip also provides one or more chip select or chip enable inputs. Selected bits of the full memory address are connected to these inputs, either directly or through a decoder. When all chip select inputs to a chip are asserted, the chip will perform read and write operations as requested by the control inputs. If one or more chip select inputs are unasserted, the chip will perform no operation, regardless of the requests of control inputs. Hence chip

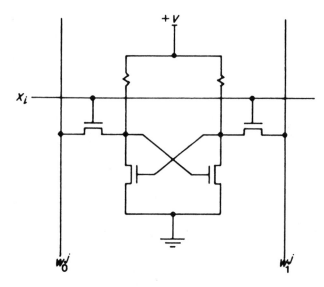

Figure 5.84   MOS RAM cell

select inputs must participate in controlling the data output buffers and in generating the internal write strobe pulse that loads the selected register during a write operation. A chip select input may even be used directly to determine write timing, that is, to determine when the internal WS signal will change.

Two common RAM chip configurations are shown in Figure 5.85. The configuration of Figure 5.85(a) has separate ports for data input and output, while the configuration of Figure 5.85(b) has one shared port. The advantage of the shared port is that it reduces the number of pins required on the chip. The disadvantage is that it may be more difficult to use, since extra care must be taken to avoid conflicts on the D bus, and this may result in slower operation in some circumstances.

In Figure 5.80, the RAM register load operation during a write cycle was described as being level-controlled; the selected internal register follows the data input as long as $WS = 1$. In order to make the chip easier to use, the timing generator can use an edge of RW to generate $WS\uparrow\downarrow$. Hence to the user the write operation appears to be edge-controlled. Earlier in this section a similar situation was discussed with respect to the latch circuit. The latch itself is level-controlled, but by providing appropriate circuitry to generate the level pulses that set and clear the latch, it was possible to construct an edge-triggered flip-flop (Figure 5.71). In the RAM, this additional circuitry is shared by many cells, making it possible to use the simplest circuitry within each cell.

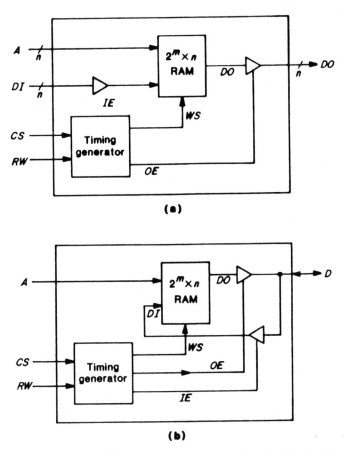

Figure 5.85   RAM chip organizations: (a) separate ports for data input and output; (b) shared port for data input and output

There is considerable variation among standard RAM chips in the control of the write operation. In addition to direct level control ($WS = RW$) and edge control ($RW\downarrow$ generates $WS\uparrow\downarrow$) it is possible to provide variations of level control by delaying the leading and trailing edges of the RW pulse by different amounts in generating WS. Yet another possibility is to let RW be a level input that is established at the beginning of a cycle to indicate read or write. A separate strobe input could be supplied to provide timing (e.g., WS and OE could be generated by this strobe input). A CS input is sometimes used for this purpose.

Large memories can be constructed by interconnecting RAM and ROM chips. For RAM chips with a shared data port, the interconnection is as illustrated in Figure 5.41. For RAM chips with separate data ports, the *DI* ports are connected together and the *DO* ports are connected together.

In order to conserve power, the chip select input of a RAM chip may be used to control power to the decoder and multiplexer circuits. In a large memory, most of the chips at any time will be deselected, so that considerable savings in power can be achieved in this fashion. The same idea can be used with ROM chips.

Dynamic RAM

The general organization of a dynamic RAM is essentially the same as that of the static RAM of Figure 5.81. The major difference is that each cell stores a bit of information by the presence or absence of charge on a capacitor rather than by the state of a bistable. This difference has important consequences in the operation of dynamic RAMS.

It is desirable to isolate the storage capacitor of a cell when it is not being written, so that any charge stored on the capacitor will remain there. Perfect isolation, however, is not possible. A fully charged storage capacitor in a typical dynamic RAM cell will discharge in about 2 or 3 ms.

It is possible, as illustrated in Figure 5.64, to include additional circuitry with each cell that provides the capability of "refreshing" the stored charge (i.e., restoring to full charge a capacitor that is partially discharged). But this would increase the chip area required by a cell, so that the advantage of dynamic over static RAM would be lost. In fact, as shown in Figures 5.64 and 5.65, this additional circuitry is essentially what is required to convert a dynamic storage cell into a static cell.

The alternative is to share the refresh circuitry among many cells. This is the approach taken with dynamic RAM. The major constraint in designing this shared refresh circuitry is that the required refresh operation should not significantly interfere with the normal read and write operation of memory. For example, the most obvious refresh technique is to read the contents of each word by using the usual read operation, and then write the contents back by using the normal write operation. Assuming that a read and a write operation each require 50 ns, this would allow refreshing 10 words per microsecond, or 10^4 cells per millisecond. If it is necessary to refresh each cell every 2 ms, then a 2^{14}-word RAM would have to spend 80% of its time refreshing, leaving only 20% available for reading and writing. A 2^{15}-word RAM could not keep all words refreshed even if it devoted all of its time to refresh operations. A better refresh technique is described below.

Microcircuit Implementation

A dynamic RAM cell using three transistors is shown in Figure 5.86, and a RAM that uses this cell is shown in Figure 5.87. A bit is stored in cell *ij* by

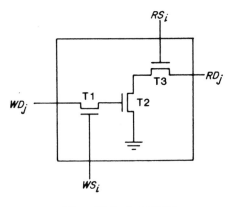

T1 = Write transistor
T2 = Storage transistor
T3 = Read transistor

Figure 5.86   Three-transistor dynamic RAM cell

holding the desired bit at WD_j and pulsing WS_i. The gate of T2 will be charged or discharged through T1 to the level of WD_j, and then isolated when WS_i returns to 0. The read, write, and refresh operations for the whole RAM are described below.

Read Operation.   The read operation proceeds as follows. First a "precharge" pulse is supplied at PCH. While $PCH = 1$ each of the RD_j lines is charged to V_{DD}. That is, each RD_j is connected to V_{DD} through a pass transistor controlled by PCH. $PCH\uparrow\downarrow$ is wide enough so that $RD_j = V_{DD}$ for each j. When PCH returns to 0, the RD_j lines are isolated and hence remain at V_{DD}.

After $PCH\uparrow\downarrow$, a pulse is supplied at RD. While $RD = 1$ the decoder will hold $RS_i = 1$, where $i = [A\langle 15:8\rangle]_2$. This will turn on the read transistor of every cell in row i. If cell j currently stores a 1, then T2 is on and RD_j discharges through T2. If cell j currently stores a 0, T2 is off and RD_j remains at V_{DD}.

During RD all the bits stored in row i become available at $RD_0, \ldots, RD_{255}$ in inverted form. The multiplexer holds $\overline{RD}_j$ at DO while $RD = 1$, where $j = [A\langle 7:0\rangle]_2$. Hence, after DO stabilizes, $DO = M[A]$.

It is clear that the decoder and multiplexer of Figure 5.87 are more complex than the standard devices. Their design is left as an exercise.

Refresh Operation.   An entire row is refreshed in one operation. Hence only 256 refresh operations are required during each refresh period. If the refresh

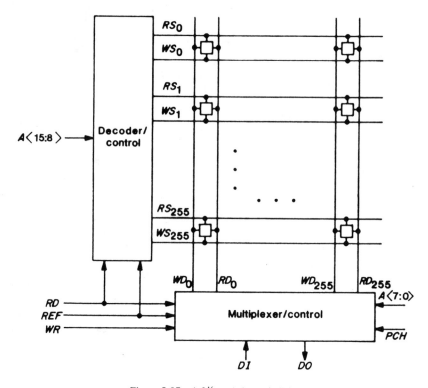

Figure 5.87   A $2^{16} \times 1$ dynamic RAM

period is 1 ms, and the refresh operation requires 100 ns, then less than 3% of the memory's time is required for refreshing.

The refresh operation proceeds as follows. First a $PCH\uparrow\downarrow$ pulse precharges each RD_j, as in the read operation. Then an $REF\uparrow\downarrow$ pulse is supplied. During REF, the multiplexer charges or discharges each WD_j to the level $\overline{RD_j}$. That is, if RD_j is in the logic 0 region then WD_j is connected to V_{DD}; if RD_j is in the logic 1 region, then WD_j is connected to ground.

Also during REF, the decoder holds $WS_i = 1$. Hence the gate of transistor T2 in every cell of row $i = [A\langle 15:8\rangle]_2$ is either charged to V_{DD} or discharged to 0, depending upon whether T2 was in the logic 1 or logic 0 region initially.

Write Operation.   The write operation is identical to the refresh operation except that WR is asserted during the refresh pulse $REF\uparrow\downarrow$. The multiplexer uses the input DI rather than the level of $\overline{RD_j}$ to determine whether to charge or discharge WD_j for $j = [A\langle 7:0\rangle]_2$. Hence 255 cells of row i are refreshed, and one cell, the one selected by $A\langle 7:0\rangle$, is loaded with the value presented at DI.

Precharging. The technique of precharging the RD_j lines at the beginning of each operation (read, write, or refresh) is an alternative to the use of a NOR gate for RD_j. The NOR gate technique was used in the ROM of Figure 5.36. To compare the techniques, note first that RD_j lines can be precharged in parallel with decoding the address. After the address is decoded, then each RD_j is pulled low or not according to the bit stored in cell ij. For the NOR gate technique, RD_j is charged or discharged *after* the address is decoded. The initial level of RD_j may be either 0 or 1.

The pull-up resistance for a NOR gate must be about four times as large as the pull-down resistance of one input. Hence, it will take the NOR gate about four times as long to pull RD_j up to 1 as to pull it down to 0. For the precharge technique, only the pull-down will occur after address decode, and this will be through the same path as the NOR gate (i.e., two turned-on transistors in series to ground). But the resistance of this path will be somewhat less, since the current level is lower than for the NOR pull-down (because there is no current supplied from V_{DD}, but only from the precharged line). Furthermore, the precharge technique will pull RD_j down further, again because there is no current from V_{DD}.

From the above discussion it is clear that the precharge technique is better than the NOR technique in three ways. It is faster, particularly in establishing a high level on RD_j after address decoding, but even in establishing a low level. It pulls RD_j lower for 0 and higher for 1, since there is no steady-state current from V_{DD}. And it consumes less power, again because there is no steady-state current.

The disadvantage of the precharge technique is that the timing for the read and write operations is more complex.

Single-Transistor Cell. An even simpler dynamic RAM cell, consisting of one transistor and a capacitor, is shown in Figure 5.88. A 1 is stored by charging the capacitor C_s to V_{DD}; a 0 is stored by discharging C_s.

The RAM organization is essentially the same as in Figure 5.85, except that there is only one line per row and one line per column. The read operation is more difficult with this cell. Sense amplifiers must be provided at each column. These amplifiers must be sensitive enough to detect the small current pulse that results when C_s is discharged from around V_{DD} to ground. There is a design trade-off here. If C_s is made larger then it becomes easier to build reliable sense amplifiers, but the cell becomes larger and slower.

Another difficulty with this cell is that the read operation is destructive. Hence a read operation must be followed by a write to restore the lost data. This results in slower operation and additional complexity. Nevertheless, because of the cell's simplicity, and because there is only one wire per row and

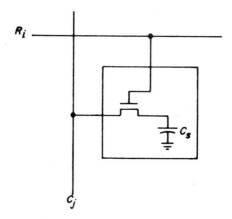

Figure 5.88   Single-transistor dynamic RAM cell

per column, this cell offers the possibility of greater bit density than the three-transistor cell.

Macrocircuit Design

The general organization of a dynamic RAM chip is essentially the same as for a static RAM chip, as illustrated in Figure 5.83. The differences are that the timing generator must generate more signals to control the dynamic array (e.g., *RD*, *WR*, *REF*, and *PCH* versus *WS* only), and different signals may be supplied to the timing generator.

These differences are related to an important design trade-off. At one extreme the timing generator can be made very simple by requiring that all control signals (*RD*, *WR*, *REF*, and *PCH*) be supplied via input pins. The timing generator in this case is eliminated altogether. The chip is very hard to use, however, because the macrocircuit designer is required to generate all timing signals.

At the other extreme, the chip inputs may be essentially the same as for a static RAM, with perhaps one more input to evoke the refresh operation, and with simple timing requirements. The responsibility of generating the required internal signals is then transferred to the timing generator. The chip is easier to use, but more complex and more costly to design and fabricate.

5.4.3   Sequential Access Memory (SAM)

A SAM is a storage device in which bits are stored sequentially in some fashion. There is one "read-write position," and the stored words are rotated through this position in sequential order. At any time, only the word that is in the read-write position is accessible. There is a *latency time* associated with accessing any other word. This is the time required to move that word into the read-write position.

With SAM, information is usually transferred in blocks consisting of many consecutive words (e.g., blocks of 128 or 256 8-bit words are typical). There is a latency time associated with accessing the first word only. Thereafter, words are accessed in sequential order, allowing the highest possible transfer rate.

SAMs are normally used as secondary memories in computers, as discussed in Section 1.1. The most common types of SAMs in use today are magnetic tape, magnetic disk, and long shift registers. In general, shift registers have the smallest latency time and the highest transfer rate. Disk memories are intermediate in both respects, and tape memories have the largest latency times and lowest transfer rates. Cost per bit of storage follows the same order.

Shift Register Memory

In a shift register memory, bits are stored in a long register that has a single-bit input port and a single-bit output port. The register is capable of doing a shift operation in which all bits are moved right one position, a new bit is shifted in at the left, and a bit is lost at the right. By connecting the output to the input, the shift operation is converted to a rotate operation and the output bit is saved rather than lost.

To access a word, the register is rotated (i.e., shifted, with output port connected to input port) until the first bit of the desired word is at the output port. The next n bits to be rotated through the output port will be the desired word. A write operation is accomplished at this point by shifting the bits of the new word in at the input port rather than bits from the output port.

A long shift register memory is illustrated in Figure 5.89(a). The shift register itself is $m \cdot n$ bits (m words, n bits per word). Also included is an n-bit input register and an n-bit output register. The shift register input is taken either from the input register, or from the output port of the long shift register. The switch that controls this selection is shown in Figure 5.89(b).

Not shown in the figure are the timing inputs that determine when the long register shifts right, and when the input and output registers are loaded or shifted. Also not shown is the address register that keeps track of the address of the word that is currently at the output port. This register counts up with each pulse that shifts the long shift register.

A faster shift register memory can be constructed by putting n long shift registers in parallel, as shown in Figure 5.89(c). A word is stored across the n registers, so that all bits of the word may be accessed simultaneously (in one bit time) after the word is rotated into position.

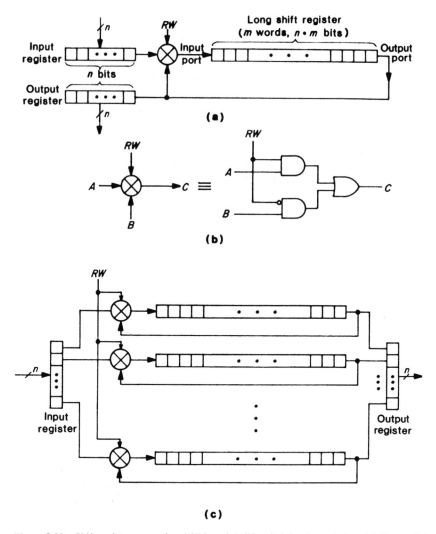

Figure 5.89 Shift register memories: (a) bit-serial; (b) switch implementation; (c) bit-parallel

There are many ways to implement long shift register memories. Currently the most popular implementations are charge-coupled device (CCD) memory and magnetic bubble memory (MBM).

Magnetic Disk and Tape

The storage medium for tape and disk memories is a thin coating of magnetic material on the surface of a plastic or metallic tape or disk. Bits are stored by recording "flux patterns" in the magnetic surface. This is accomplished by moving the tape or disk past a read-write head and applying a write voltage v_W as illustrated in Figure 5.90. The voltage v_W produces a current i and an associated magnetic field, represented by magnetic flux lines Φ. The flux lines are concentrated in the magnetic material of the read-write head, as shown. At the gap in the head some of the flux lines pass through (and thus magnetize) the magnetic material on the disk/tape surface. By reversing the polarity of the write voltage, the direction of magnetization of the surface is reversed.

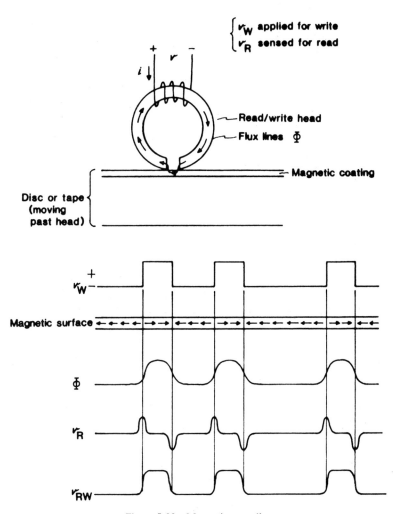

Figure 5.90   Magnetic recording

The flux pattern thus recorded can be later "read back" by passing the surface under the head again. But, instead of applying a voltage at v, the voltage pulses that are produced there by the flux changes in the magnetic surface are detected (v_R in Figure 5.90). The original write waveform v_W can be recovered from the read waveform v_R, since every transition of v_W is marked by a pulse at v_R. The recovered waveform is denoted v_{RW}.

The density of recorded flux transitions is limited by the electrical, mechanical, and magnetic characteristics of the disk/tape drive and the recording medium. If the transitions are too close together, the read circuitry will be unable to recover the write waveform v_W from the read waveform v_R.

When recording data, a clock of some sort must be used to determine the record rate. The most straightforward way to generate the write waveform is simply to let v_W in each clock period represent one bit, as illustrated in Figure 5.91(a). To recover the bit stream stored in this fashion, the write waveform must be reconstructed *and* a clock of appropriate frequency must be used to sample the waveform. The major difficulty to be overcome is the unavoidable variation in disk rotation rate or tape speed. The recovered data waveform v_{RW} will follow this variation, and hence the clock must also follow.

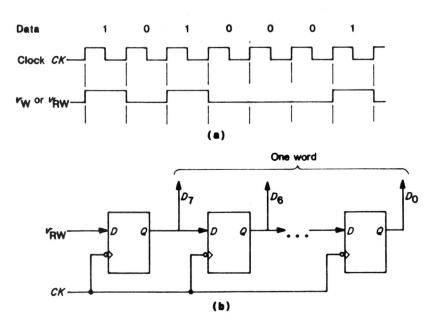

Figure 5.91   A simple recording scheme: (a) waveforms; (b) read circuit

One way to produce a suitable clock for use with this simple recording scheme is to generate the clock from a flux pattern stored permanently on a "clock track" of the recording medium. The clock as well as the data will then follow the disk speed variations.

A read circuit for this simple recording scheme is shown in Figure 5.91(b). The falling edge of CK is used to sample v_{RW}, since this occurs in the center of each "bit cell." Each $CK\downarrow$ clocks a new data bit into a shift register and shifts other bits right one place. After a full word is assembled (8 bits in this case), the disk IO controller takes the word (at $D\langle 7:0\rangle$).

The use of a clock track to produce a clock pulse for writing and reading is not suitable for single-track magnetic tape drives. Nor is it suitable for a low-cost disk drive because of the extra cost of providing a separate head to read the clock track.

A variety of other techniques have been developed for magnetic recording without requiring a clock track. We will describe the two standard techniques that are used with floppy disk drives. Both techniques involve mixing clock and data pulses together in some way to produce v_W, and then separating the two in some fashion when processing the recovered waveform v_{RW} in order to extract the data.

The first technique, used for "single-density" recording, is illustrated in Figure 5.92. Time is divided into "bit cells" of 4 μs each. Each bit cell represents one data bit. If the bit is 1 then a pulse is produced in the middle of the bit cell; if the bit is 0 there is no pulse. Every bit cell begins with a clock pulse. The v_W waveform for a particular bit stream is shown in Figure 5.92(b).

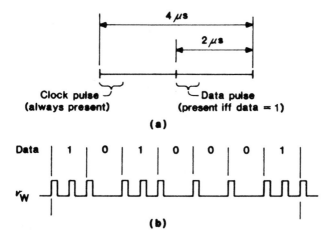

Figure 5.92   Single-density format: (a) one bit cell; (b) write waveform

A simple circuit that might be used to extract the data from the recovered waveform, v_{RW}, is shown in Figure 5.93. The one-shot is nonretriggerable. It generates a pulse $CK\!\uparrow\!\downarrow$ in every bit cell such that $CK\!\downarrow$ occurs near the middle of the data slot in each bit cell. The 8 flip-flops form a shift register which is used to assemble an 8-bit word for transfer to an IO controller. Each $CK\!\downarrow$ loads a new data bit into D_7 and shifts other bits right. After the 8th $CK\!\downarrow$, the IO controller has 4 μs to take the assembled word.

In order for this circuit to work properly, it must be assured that the one-shots begin triggering on a clock pulse and not a data pulse. This is usually arranged by preceding each block of data with a sequence of bit cells having no data pulses. This is usually followed by a "synchronizing sequence," which is followed by the data words of the entire block. The synchronizing sequence provides "character synchronization"; after detecting the synchronizing se-

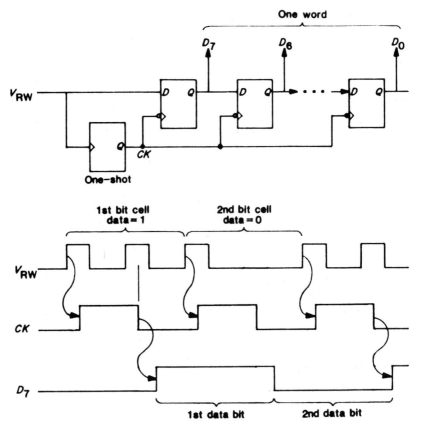

Figure 5.93   Recovering the data

quence, the read circuitry knows that the next bit cell contains the first data bit. Synchronization techniques will be discussed further in Section 6.3.4.

The double-density recording format is defined in Figure 5.94. Notice that the minimum distance between pulses is the same as for single density (2 μs between rising edges). Hence the density of recorded flux transitions is the same, so the waveform can be recorded and recovered using the same disk drive as for single-density recording.

The price paid for double density is the complexity of extracting the data from the recorded waveform. The problem is that the clock pulse is not present in every bit cell, so the simple one-shot circuit of Figure 5.93 will not suffice.

This problem is normally solved by using a phase-locked loop (PLL). The PLL is used to generate a waveform that has a clock pulse and a data pulse in every bit cell. That is, it takes the recovered waveform v_{RW}, which has missing clock pulses and missing data pulses, and it supplies all the missing pulses. This waveform can then be used to generate a data window, and the data can be extracted by a simple mechanism such as in Figure 5.93.

The required PLL circuit is shown in Figure 5.95. It consists of a voltage-controlled oscillator (VCO), a phase comparator (PC), and an analog network that can add two voltages. The VCO generates a pulse stream v_P, the frequency of which is determined by its input voltage v_C. It is desired that v_P should track the bit cells of v_{RW}, putting a clock pulse in every clock slot and a data pulse in every data slot. Hence when both v_P and v_{RW} have a pulse, they

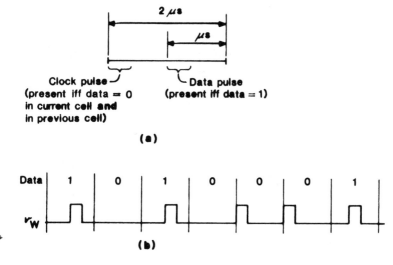

Figure 5.94 Double-density format: (a) bit cell; (b) write waveform

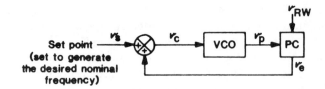

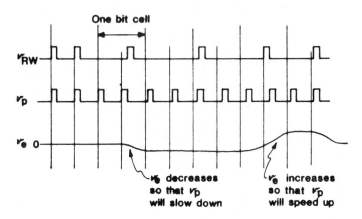

Figure 5.95   Phase-locked loop

should coincide exactly. The PC will generate an error voltage v_e; v_e will be positive if the v_{RW} pulses are occurring before corresponding v_P pulses (thus causing VCO to increase the frequency of v_P); v_e will be negative if v_P pulses are ahead of v_{RW} pulses (thus causing VCO to decrease the frequency of v_P). The magnitude of v_e will be proportional to the amount that the v_P and v_{RW} pulses are displaced. Missing v_{RW} pulses do not affect v_e.

A PLL can accurately track the bit cells on a disk provided that the variations in rotation rate are not too great. A thorough analysis of PLL operation, however, requires a background in the theory of servomechanisms (i.e., feedback controllers), and will not be attempted here. Nor are we equipped to discuss the implementation of the PLL components, which requires a background in analog electronics.

5.4.4   Exercises

1. Construct a table of all the stable states, like Figure 5.66(b), for the NAND latch of Figure 5.67.

2. Construct a 24-bit shift register using 74198 ICs as components.

3. Use edge-triggered D flip-flops and gates to construct:
   (a) The 74198 circuit
   (b) The 74163
   (c) The 74169

4. Assuming the timing specifications for gates and flip-flops given in Figure 5.102, determine the timing specifications (as in Figure 5.79) for the circuits you designed in Exercise 3.

5. Draw a timing diagram (like Figure 5.70) illustrating the "reset" operation of Figure 5.71 (i.e., $R \uparrow \downarrow$ to evoke $0 \rightarrow Q$).

6. The timing generators of Figure 5.85 can be very simple, or fairly complex. The advantages to be gained in more complex implementations are simplifications of the constraints in using the chip.

   (a) Design a simple timing generator for the RAM chip of Figure 5.85(a).

   (b) Derive complete timing specifications for the chip from specifications on the internal RAM (Figure 5.80) and the gates used in constructing the timing generator.

   (c) Suppose $m = 14$ and $n = 4$. Use your chip to build a $2^{16} \times 8$ RAM. Give timing specifications for the memory in terms of the specifications of the components used. Be careful of bus contention (on DO bus) and generating the internal WS signals too soon.

   (d) Discuss how a more complex timing generator might make the chip easier to use.

7. What difficulties might be encountered in using a RAM chip of type (b) (Figure 5.85) that are not encountered with chips of type (a). Be specific.

8. Design the decoder/control and multiplexer/control blocks of Figure 5.87.

9. Consider designing a RAM chip around the dynamic RAM of Figure 5.87.

   (a) Use the basic structure of Figure 5.85(a). Make the timing generator as simple as possible; PCH, RD, WR, and REF should be chip inputs. Specify the form of the timing constraints for using the chip, as in Figure 5.80. Include specifications for the refresh operation.

   (b) Discuss the timing and refresh circuitry that will be required when constructing a memory from these chips.

   (c) Consider the possibility of providing a more complex timing generator to make the chip easier to use.

10. For proper operation of the circuit of Figure 5.93, $CK \downarrow$ must occur during the data slot of each bit cell so that the setup and hold requirements of D_7 are satisfied. If the data pulse is narrow, this constraint may be difficult to meet in the face of the disk speed variations and one-shot pulse width variations. Suggest modifications to overcome this difficulty.

5.5   SEQUENTIAL NETWORKS [24, 30-36]

5.5.1   The Sequential Machine
5.5.2   The Synchronous Sequential Network (SSN)
5.5.3   Sequential Machine Construction
5.5.4   Input Synchronization
5.5.5   Exercises

A register transfer system is capable of performing complex computations by doing long sequences of simple register transfer operations. The subsystem of the register transfer system that decides what operations should be performed at each point in the computation and generates the control signals that evoke these operations is called the *control unit*. The heart of the control unit is a very important device called a *sequential network*. In this section we will study the operation, modeling, and design of sequential networks.

5.5.1   The Sequential Machine

The model for a sequential network is called a *sequential machine*. The sequential machine is an important model. In addition to modeling digital sequential networks, it can be used to represent many other types of systems and processes in all fields of engineering and science. It is a general model for discrete time dynamic systems.

A sequential machine consists of a set of inputs **IN**, a set of outputs **OUT**, a set of states **S**, and output function $\lambda:\mathbf{S} \times \mathbf{IN} \to \mathbf{OUT}$, and a next state function $\delta:\mathbf{S} \times \mathbf{IN} \to \mathbf{S}$. The model is illustrated in Figure 5.96. The input variable in the figure is denoted x, the output variable is y, and the internal state variable is q. Time is represented by the integers. At any time t the value of the input variable is denoted x^t. This value, x^t, must be some element of the input

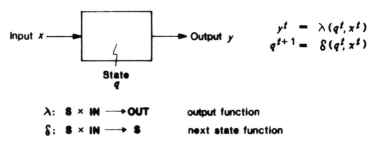

$$y^t = \lambda(q^t, x^t)$$
$$q^{t+1} = \delta(q^t, x^t)$$

$$\lambda: \mathbf{S} \times \mathbf{IN} \longrightarrow \mathbf{OUT} \qquad \text{output function}$$
$$\delta: \mathbf{S} \times \mathbf{IN} \longrightarrow \mathbf{S} \qquad \text{next state function}$$

Figure 5.96   Sequential machine

set **IN**. Similarly the output and the state at time t, denoted y^t and q^t, are elements of **OUT** and **S**.

The functions λ and δ completely define the operation of the sequential machine in the following sense:

> Given any initial state q^0 in **S** and any sequence of input values from **IN**, $x^0, x^1, x^2, \ldots$, the functions δ and λ will generate a unique sequence of states $q^0, q^1, q^2, \ldots$ and a unique sequence of outputs y^0, $y^1, y^2, \ldots$.

A simple example of a sequential machine is given in Figure 5.97. The next state and output functions are completely defined by the table in Figure 5.97(a). These functions could alternatively have been defined by a type of graph called a *state diagram*. The state diagram for this sequential machine is shown in Figure 5.97(b). Each state of the sequential machine is represented by a node of the graph. The branches of the graph represent the next state

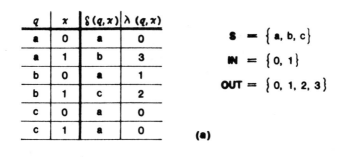

q	x	$\delta(q,x)$	$\lambda(q,x)$
a	0	a	0
a	1	b	3
b	0	a	1
b	1	c	2
c	0	a	0
c	1	a	0

$$\mathbf{S} = \{a, b, c\}$$
$$\mathbf{IN} = \{0, 1\}$$
$$\mathbf{OUT} = \{0, 1, 2, 3\}$$

(a)

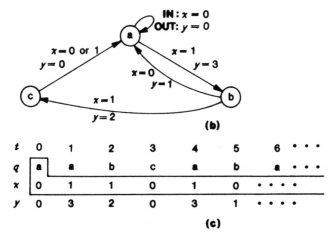

(b)

t	0	1	2	3	4	5	6	• • •
q	a	a	b	c	a	b	a	• • •
x	0	1	1	0	1	0	•	• • •
y	0	3	2	0	3	1	•	• • •

(c)

Figure 5.97   A simple sequential machine: (a) definition; (b) state diagram; (c) operation

function, and the output designations adjacent to the branches define the output function. The operation of the sequential machine is illustrated in Figure 5.97(c). If the initial state and the sequence of input values are given (shown boxed in) the sequence of states and outputs can be generated as shown.

If the output variable y does not depend upon the input variable [i.e., for any q in **S**, $\lambda(q, x) = \lambda(q, x')$ for any x and x' in **IN**] then the sequential machine is called a *Moore machine*. If there exists a state q such that $\lambda(q, x) \neq \lambda(q, x')$ for some x and x' in **IN**, then it is a *Mealy machine*. The output of a Moore machine depends only upon the state, that is, $\lambda: \mathbf{S} \to \mathbf{OUT}$. The output of a Mealy machine may depend upon both the input and the state. The Mealy machine is more powerful since it can respond more quickly to input changes. But there are times when it is advantageous to use Moore machines. In this discussion, we will deal with the more general Mealy machine. Our discussions will apply to Moore machines as well, since the Moore machine is a special case of the Mealy machine.

5.5.2   The Synchronous Sequential Network (SSN)

As we have mentioned, a sequential machine can represent many different types of discrete time dynamic systems. Another way of saying this, from the point of view of a designer, is that there are many ways to implement the behavior represented by a sequential machine. We are interested in implementing this behavior with a particular type of digital system called a *synchronous sequential network* (SSN).

A particular form of SSN is illustrated in Figure 5.98(a). It consists of a combinational network and a state register driven by a single-phase clock. X, Y, and Q are binary coded representations of variables x, y, and q. The state register is a simple parallel load register. W is the binary word representing the next state. W is loaded into Q with each falling edge of the clock. The combinational network implements the next state and output functions.

Relation to the Sequential Machine

The exact relationship between the sequential machine and the SSN that it represents is illustrated in Figure 5.98(b). The timing diagram describes the operation of a SSN that implements the sequential machine of Figure 5.97. The initial state and input sequence are those used in Figure 5.97(c). Hence the sequential machine operation of Figure 5.97(c) is the abstract representation of the SSN operation of Figure 5.98(b).

Time is represented by the clock. Clock period i of Figure 5.98(b) corresponds to discrete time i of Figure 5.97(c). The falling edge of the clock at the

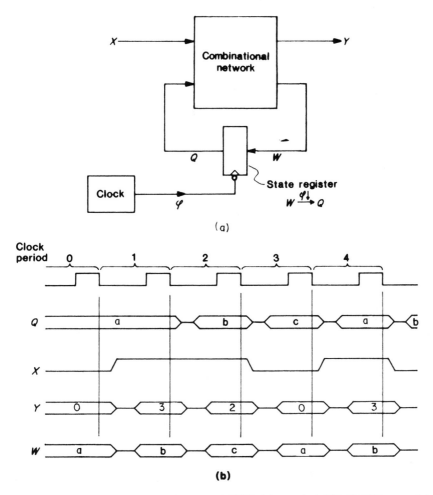

Figure 5.98   Synchronous sequential network (SSN): (a) canonical SSN; (b) SSN-sequential machine relationship

beginning of clock period i loads the value w^i into the state register. There is some propagation delay associated with this operation, so Q is in transition at the beginning of the clock period. Q eventually stabilizes to q^i and remains at q^i for the rest of the clock period. Changes in the input X must also occur at the beginning of the clock period. This is a constraint that the SSN designer must observe. After Q and X stabilize at q^i and x^i there is a propagation delay through the combinational network, after which Y and W stabilize at $y^i = \lambda(q^i, x^i)$ and $w^i = \delta(q^i, x^i)$. Hence, the variables Q, X, Y, and W are stable during the latter part of clock period i at values q^i, x^i, $y^i = \lambda(q^i, x^i)$, and $w^i = \delta(q^i, x^i)$.

Any sequential machine may be implemented with a SSN in the canonical form of Figure 5.98. Some variations from this canonical form are useful in certain situations. These will be discussed later. The basic nature of the SSN remains the same regardless of the variations. For the moment we will consider only the basic canonical SSN of Figure 5.98.

Design Procedure

The process of designing a SSN may be decomposed into four steps:

1. Construct a sequential machine that exhibits the desired sequential behavior.

2. Code the sequential machine.

3. Design a combinational network to implement the next state and output functions.

4. Establish timing.

Sequential Machine Construction. There is no mechanical procedure (algorithm) for defining a sequential machine. This is the most creative step of the design process. Because it is so difficult to formalize, consideration of this step will be postponed until the other design steps are understood. The sequential machine of Figure 5.97 will be used to illustrate these straightforward steps.

Coding the Sequential Machine. This step involves defining binary codes to represent the abstract states, inputs, and outputs of the sequential machine. This is done in Figure 5.99 for our example machine.

q	$Q\langle 1{:}0\rangle$
a	11
b	00
c	10

y	$Y\langle 1{:}0\rangle$
0	00
1	01
2	10
3	11

x	X
0	0
1	1

Figure 5.99   Coding the sequential machine

The base 2 code is used to represent the output variable y (i.e., $[Y]_2 = y$). The input variable x is already a binary variable (i.e., $X = x$). The code that is used to represent the state variable q was chosen arbitrarily.

In some cases there may be reason for choosing one code over another. Specifically, the choice of the codes may affect the speed or the cost of the SSN. There is a considerable body of theory associated with the selection of state codes. This is known as the *state assignment* problem. Most of this theory is aimed at selecting state codes that reduce the cost of the SSN. In our applications these considerations are of minor importance and will not be discussed.

Combinational Network Design. The coded versions of the next state and output functions are given in Figure 5.100. The K-maps were constructed directly from the sequential machine definition of Figure 5.97. For example, the upper right square of the K-maps corresponds to the situation $q = c$ and $x = 0$. From Figure 5.97, the next state should be $q = a$, and the output should be $y = 0$. Hence $W\langle 1{:}0 \rangle = 11$ (the code for state a) and $Y\langle 1{:}0 \rangle = 00$ (the code for output 0). Hence, the upper right corners of the maps for W_1, W_0, Y_1, and Y_0 are marked 1, 1, 0, and 0, respectively. The squares corresponding to $Q\langle 1{:}0 \rangle = 01$ are "don't cares" since that state code is not used.

Optimal two-level equations are written for W_1, W_0, and Y_0. Y_1 is implemented as the complement of W_0.

Timing. Timing the network of Figure 5.100(b) is the last step of the design process. This involves determination of timing constraints on the clock ϕ to guarantee proper operation of the network. We will consider first the timing of the general SSN structure of Figure 5.98. The results of this analysis will then be applied to the specific SSN of Figure 5.100(b).

A timing diagram for one clock period of SSN operation is shown in Figure 5.101. The output Y is not shown in the figure; it will be discussed subsequently. We will assume that the state register has an edge-triggered load operation, with setup and hold requirements measured with respect to $\phi\downarrow$.

The state register is loaded at the beginning of each clock period. In order to guarantee satisfaction of the state register setup requirement, the clock period must be sufficiently long to allow for the slowest possible state register change, and to allow that change to propagate along the slowest path through the combinational network to W, with enough time left to satisfy the minimum setup requirement. That is,

$$T_\phi \geq (t^Q_{\text{pde}})_{\text{max}} + (t^{Q-W}_{\text{pde}})_{\text{max}} + (t^W_{\text{stp}})_{\text{min}} \qquad (5.1)$$

The input X may also change at the beginning of each clock period. There is a similar inequality to guarantee that this change will have to propagate through to W.

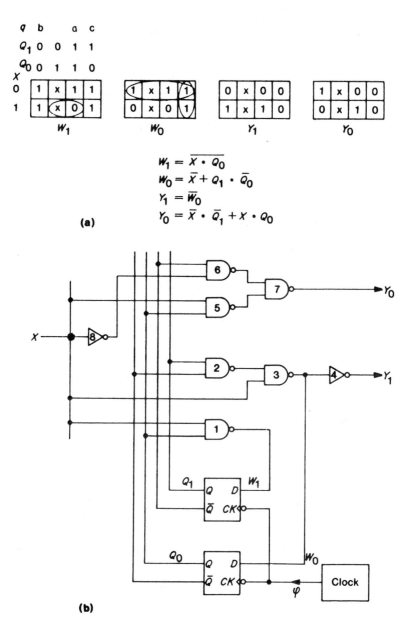

Figure 5.100   Combinational network design: (a) K-maps and equations; (b) logic circuit

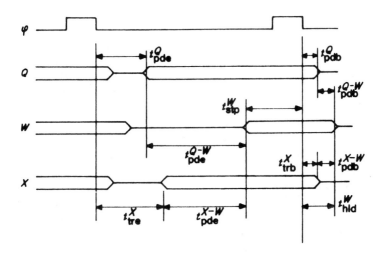

Figure 5.101   SSN state change timing

$$T_\phi \geq (t_{tre}^X)_{max} + (t_{pde}^{X-W})_{max} + (t_{stp}^W)_{min} \tag{5.2}$$

If there is a greater than zero hold requirement at W, then we must ensure that the changes at Q and X that occur at the beginning of each clock period do not propagate to W too quickly. This results in two additional inequalities:

$$(t_{pdb}^Q)_{min} + (t_{pdb}^{Q-W})_{min} \geq (t_{hld}^W)_{min} \tag{5.3}$$

$$(t_{trb}^X)_{min} + (t_{pdb}^{X-W})_{min} \geq (t_{hld}^W)_{min} \tag{5.4}$$

Satisfaction of these four inequalities guarantees that the setup and hold requirements of the state register will be met. In addition to the setup and hold requirements, the state register will also have direct constraints on the width and frequency of the clock. If these direct requirements as well as the above setup and hold inequalities are satisfied, then the state register is guaranteed to operate properly.

The SSN output Y also must have requirements for proper operation. In our applications these are usually setup and hold requirements measured with respect to $\phi\downarrow$. If Y were included in the timing diagram of Figure 5.101, it would look essentially the same as W. Associated with the setup and hold requirements for the output there will be four inequalities similar to those for the state register.

$$T_\phi \geq (t_{pde}^Q)_{max} + (t_{pde}^{Q-Y})_{max} + (t_{stp}^Y)_{min} \tag{5.5}$$

$$T_\phi \geq (t_{tre}^X)_{max} + (t_{pde}^{X-Y})_{max} + (t_{stp}^Y)_{min} \tag{5.6}$$

$$(t_{\text{pdb}}^{Q})_{\min} + (t_{\text{pdb}}^{Q-Y})_{\min} \geq (t_{\text{hld}}^{Y})_{\min} \tag{5.7}$$

$$(t_{\text{trb}}^{X})_{\min} + (t_{\text{pdb}}^{X-Y})_{\min} \geq (t_{\text{hld}}^{Y})_{\min} \tag{5.8}$$

This completes the timing analysis of the general SSN of Figure 5.98. Proper operation is guaranteed by ensuring that these inequalities are satisfied.

Consider now the particular SSN of Figure 5.100(b), assuming the timing specifications of Figure 5.102. The input and output specifications in the figure were chosen arbitrarily. The gate and flip-flop specifications were taken from data sheets for typical Schottky TTL devices.

The propagation delay specifications for a device depend upon the load driven by the device. The capacitive load assumed specified in most Schottky TTL data sheets is 15 pF. If the actual load is greater than the specified load, then the maximum propagation delay should be increased for a correct worst-case analysis. If the load is less, then the minimum propagation delay should be decreased.

Minimum propagation delays are frequently not given in data sheets. For a worst-case hold analysis in this case, either a 0 minimum delay must be assumed, or an appropriate value determined by analysis, simulation, or exper-

Requirements: $t_{\text{stp}}^{W} \geqslant 3$ ns $t_{\text{hld}}^{W} \geqslant 0$ ns

                      $t_{\text{high}}^{CK} \geqslant 6$ ns $t_{\text{low}}^{CK} \geqslant 7$ ns

Guarantees: $3 \leqslant t_{\text{pd}}^{Q} \leqslant 10$ ns

(a)

Guarantees: 2 ns $\leqslant t_{\text{pd}}^{\text{gate}} \leqslant 6$ ns

(b)

Guarantees: $t_{\text{trb}}^{X} \geqslant 4$ ns $t_{\text{tre}}^{X} \leqslant 20$ ns

(c)

Requirements: $t_{\text{stp}}^{Y} \geqslant 10$ ns $t_{\text{hld}}^{Y} \geqslant 5$ ns

(d)

Figure 5.102 Timing specifications: (a) flip-flop specifications; (b) gate specifications; (c) input specifications; (d) output specifications

imentation. When a minimum propagation delay is specified, it is usually between one-fifth and one-half of the maximum propagation delay.

If the delays along different paths through the combinational network are different then each of the inequalities 5.1 to 5.8 may actually represent several inequalities, one for each path of the appropriate type. For example, inequality 5.1 actually represents three inequalities corresponding to the paths $Q_1 \rightarrow$ gate 2 $\rightarrow$ gate 3 $\rightarrow W_0$; $Q_0 \rightarrow$ gate 1 $\rightarrow W_1$; and $\bar{Q}_0 \rightarrow$ gate 2 $\rightarrow$ gate 3 $\rightarrow W_0$.

Consider first the setup inequalities: 5.1, 5.2, 5.5, and 5.6. The clock period must be large enough to satisfy all of these for all possible paths. Let us first identify the longest path of each type. They are: $\bar{Q}_0 \rightarrow$ gate 2 $\rightarrow$ gate 3 $\rightarrow W_0$ for 5.1; $X \rightarrow$ gate 1 $\rightarrow W_1$ for 5.2; $Q_0 \rightarrow$ gate 2 $\rightarrow$ gate 3 $\rightarrow$ gate 4 $\rightarrow Y_1$ for 5.5; and $X \rightarrow$ gate 8 $\rightarrow$ gate 6 $\rightarrow$ gate 7 $\rightarrow Y_0$ for 5.6. The inequality corresponding to the X-to-Y_0 path is the worst case. It requires $T_\phi \geq 20 + 6 + 6 + 6 + 10 = 48$ ns.

Consider now the hold inequalities. For these it is the shortest path that is the worst. The shortest paths are: $Q_0 \rightarrow$ gate 1 $\rightarrow W_1$ for 5.3; $X \rightarrow$ gate 1 $\rightarrow W_1$ for 5.4; $Q_1 \rightarrow$ gate 6 $\rightarrow$ gate 7 $\rightarrow Y_0$ for 5.7; and $X \rightarrow$ gate 5 $\rightarrow$ gate 7 $\rightarrow Y_0$ for 5.8. The corresponding inequalities are: $3 + 2 \geq 0$; $4 + 2 \geq 0$; $3 + 2 + 2 \geq 5$; and $4 + 2 + 2 \geq 5$. Since all of these are satisfied, the hold requirements of the state register and the output are satisfied. If any of the hold inequalities had not been satisfied, it would have been necessary to insert delay in the offending path (e.g., an RC delay or two inverters in series).

To summarize, the network of Figure 5.100(c) is guaranteed to operate properly if $T_\phi \geq 48$ ns and $t_{high}^\phi \geq 6$ ns. The second of these is a direct requirement on the flip-flop clock input.

This completes our discussion of the general SSN design procedure. Most presentations of SSN design would have included another step in the design procedure. This step, called state reduction, would come between steps 1 and 2. It involves converting the sequential machine of step 1 into an "equivalent" machine with a minimal number of states. There exist systematic techniques for performing this "state reduction" (see Kohavi [30]).

State reduction is of secondary importance for our applications. If a machine is constructed carefully at the outset, then the savings that may be obtained by state reduction are usually slight, and the reduced machine may not be as readily understandable as the original machine.

5.5.3 Sequential Machine Construction

The first step in designing an SSN is the definition of a sequential machine that exhibits the required sequential behavior. There is no general systematic procedure for construction of a sequential machine. The following comments, however, may be helpful.

A sequential machine specifies outputs and next states on a clock period by clock period basis. It is sometimes effective to assume a particular input sequence and initial state, and specify a machine that will produce correct outputs for this sequence. Then go back and try to define the next state and output functions for alternative inputs at each state.

The "state" of the machine at any time represents all of the relevant information about the input sequence since beginning in the initial state. Introduce a new state only if there is no existing state that represents the required information. It is sometimes helpful to carefully define the information that is represented by each state.

We are particularly interested in using sequential networks to control register transfer systems. Examples of sequential machine definition for such applications will be presented in detail in Chapter 6.

Sequential networks are also used, however, for a multitude of smaller tasks. Three such examples are presented here, and several others are suggested in the exercises.

A Ones Counter

The machine defined in Figure 5.103 counts the 1 bits that appear at the input X. A new bit (either 0 or 1) arrives at X at the beginning of each clock period (i.e., just after $\phi\downarrow$). The output $Y\langle 1{:}0\rangle$ indicates the total number of 1's among the current input bit and the past two input bits. An example input-output sequence is given in the figure.

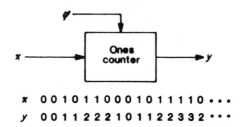

x 0 0 1 0 1 1 0 0 0 1 0 1 1 1 1 0 $\cdots$
y 0 0 1 1 2 2 2 1 0 1 1 2 2 3 3 2 $\cdots$

Figure 5.103   A ones counter

A sequential machine that exhibits this behavior is defined in Figure 5.104. This machine was constructed by noting what must be remembered by the state at any time: the state must remember what the past two input bits were, and their order. Since there are four possible two-bit sequences, there must be four states. In Figure 5.104 these states are labeled q_0, q_1, q_2, and q_3. The "interpretation" for each state is given in the table.

Present state q^t	State interpretation x^{t-2} x^{t-1}
q_0	0 0
q_1	0 1
q_2	1 0
q_3	1 1

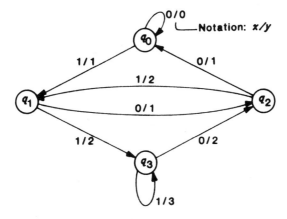

Figure 5.104   Ones counter sequential machine

The sequential machine is easily constructed, given the interpretation of each state. The initial state is q_0.

A Synchronization Detector

Consider the problem of designing an SSN to detect a particular sequence of 0's and 1's in a serial bit stream, as illustrated in Figure 5.105. The bit stream arrives at X, synchronized with clock ϕ as shown. The sequence to be found is 10010110 (the ASCII SYN character with even parity). The detector begins looking for SYN in the clock period after START = 1. It asserts Y during the clock period when the final bit of a correct sequence arrives. After detecting SYN, it ignores X until START is asserted again.

The SYN character will be sent just before a sequence of data characters is sent. Hence $Y = 1$ is an indication to the data-receiving circuits that it should begin accepting data bits in the next clock period.

The sending circuit will hold $X = 0$ before the SYN character is sent. However, due to noise, there is a small probability that X will be 1 in some of these clock periods. The probability that noise will produce exactly the SYN se-

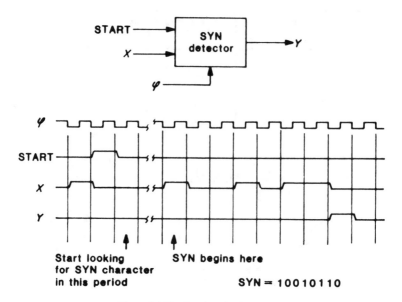

Figure 5.105   Synchronization detector

quence, however, is extremely small. Hence, it is extremely unlikely that the SYN detector will give a false $Y = 1$ indication. Even a "noise pulse" that is correct in the first 7 bits but wrong in the last bit will be rejected.

A sequential machine for this synchronization detector is defined in Figure 5.106. This machine was constructed by starting in state q_0 and defining an appropriate response to the input sequence: START $= 1$, $X = 1$, $X = 0$, $X = 0$, etc. (i.e., the sequence to be detected).

State q_0 represents the fact that $START = 1$ has not yet occurred. It is the initial state. State q_1 represents the occurrence of $START = 1$, with the first bit of SYN yet to arrive. State q_i for $i = 2, 3, \ldots, 8$ represents the occurrence of $i - 1$ correct bits.

After constructing the entire sequence through q_8, alternative inputs were considered. In q_2, the initial 1 has been received and the correct next bit is 0, which will lead to state q_3. If a 1 occurs instead, then this is not the correct second bit so it is necessary to go to a state other than state q_2. Since it *is* the correct first bit, it is appropriate to go to state q_2, since this may be the first bit of SYN.

The other input conditions are handled in the same way. For example, $q = q_6$ means that the last 5 bits received were 10010. If the next bit is 0 it is not the correct sixth bit, but it *is* the correct third bit. Hence q_4 is the next state (i.e., the SYN character could have started three clock periods earlier).

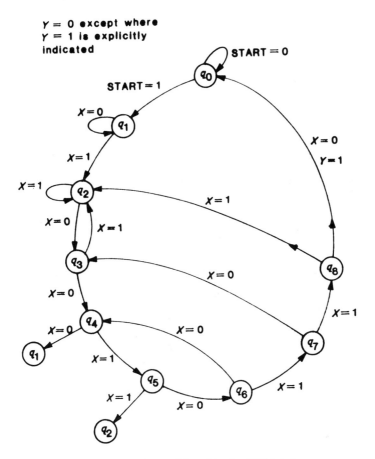

Figure 5.106　Sequential machine for SYN detector

A Synchronous One-Shot

Figure 5.107 illustrates the operation of a synchronous one-shot with a select-able pulse width. The one-shot produces a pulse $Y{\uparrow}{\downarrow}$ of width $[P]_2$ in response to $X{\uparrow}$. The one-shot is to be nonretriggerable, with a recovery time of one clock period. Inputs X and P are synchronized with ϕ as illustrated; any changes will occur immediately after $\phi{\downarrow}$. P will be looked at only during a clock period when $X{\uparrow}$ occurs. After an $X{\uparrow}$ initiates a pulse $Y{\uparrow}{\downarrow}$, X is ignored until $Y{\downarrow}$, after which X must be 0 for at least one clock period before another output pulse can be produced.

A sequential machine for this synchronous one-shot is defined in Figure 5.108. This machine was constructed by first defining the state sequence that

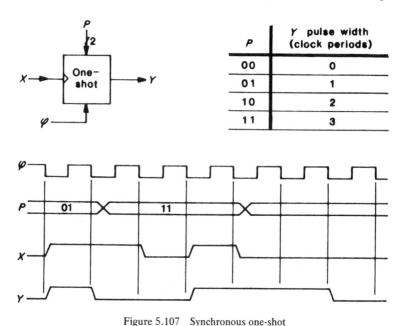

Figure 5.107   Synchronous one-shot

produces the longest pulse. Other branches out of state q_0 simply tap into this sequence at the appropriate point. Neither X nor P is looked at while $Y = 1$, so q_1, q_2, and q_3 each have a single branch out, which applies for any input condition.

5.5.4   Input Synchronization [26, 45, 49]

In the examples of sequential networks discussed above, we assumed that all inputs were synchronized with the clock. Specifically, we assumed that input changes occurred only at the beginning of each clock period.

The assumption of input synchronization is more than a convenience. It is a necessity. If inputs are not synchronized with the clock, then it is impossible to guarantee satisfaction of the setup and hold requirements of the state register inputs or the network outputs. In this section we discuss the problem of unsynchronized inputs in more detail and suggest ways to solve synchronization problems.

The Problem with Unsynchronized Inputs

If the SSN input X is not synchronized with the SSN clock ϕ, then X may change at any time during the clock period. If this is the case then it is not

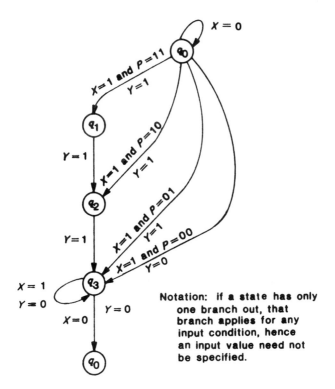

Notation: If a state has only one branch out, that branch applies for any input condition, hence an input value need not be specified.

Figure 5.108 One-shot sequential machine

possible to guarantee satisfaction of the setup and hold requirements of the state register and the output, regardless of how large T_ϕ is made, or how much delay is inserted in the signal paths.

But what exactly happens when the setup and hold requirements of the state register and output are not satisfied? Since we do not know what the output is used for, let us confine our attention to the state register. Similar comments will apply to the output in most situations.

Suppose that the data input to a D-type flip-flop changes during the required setup and hold interval, as shown in Figure 5.109. In this case one of three things may happen:

1. The flip-flop may remain in state 0.

2. The flip-flop may change to state 1.

3. The flip-flop may enter a prolonged period of transition, where it either remains in the $\frac{1}{2}$ region or oscillates between the 0 and 1 regions, before resolving to 0 or 1.

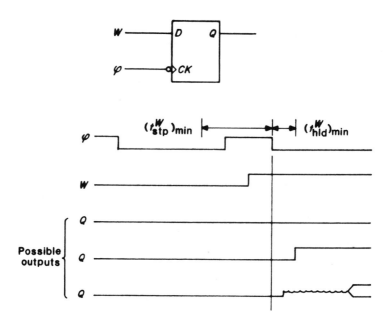

Figure 5.109   Flip-flop operation with asynchronous input

The third possibility is referred to as *metastable operation* of the flip-flop. The probability of its occurrence is very small, so small in fact that in most conventional systems it can be ignored. The probability is not zero however, and in systems where there are many flip-flops with high-frequency asynchronous inputs, metastable operation may be a significant problem.

Even if the probability of metastable operation is negligible (e.g., one occurrence every 10 years), the SSN of Figure 5.97 will in general be subject to frequent failure if X is not synchronized with ϕ. The failure mechanism is this. If X changes at a time that causes W to change during the required setup and hold interval, then some bits of Q may respond to the old value of W and some to the new value. This may result in a completely erroneous state change, as illustrated in Figure 5.110. Suppose that X changes from 0 to 1 while this system is in state 01, but the change occurs at such a time that the first bit of the state register responds to the old value of X, while the second bit responds to the new value. The SSN would then make a transition to state 00. This is correct for neither the old value of X nor the new value. Hence, although no flip-flop exhibits metastable operation, the SSN fails catastrophically. In general, the entire state sequence and output sequence will be in error after such a failure. In this example, the SSN goes to state 11 in the next clock period, but it should have gone to, or stayed in, state 10.

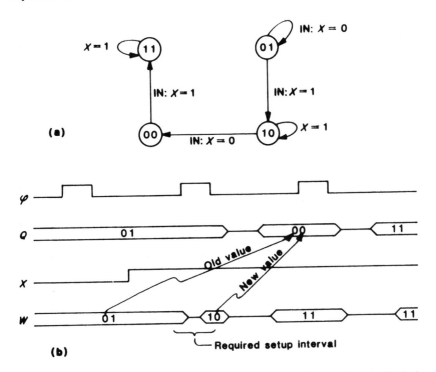

Figure 5.110   SSN failure due to asynchronous input: (a) partial state diagram; (b) timing diagram

Failures of this sort occur because of the differences in setup and hold requirements between any two flip-flops, and the differences in propagation delay along different paths to W. These failures can sometimes be prevented by a proper choice of the state assignment, and by careful design of the combinational network. But this is not always possible. And even when it is possible, it is usually simpler to prevent these failures by synchronizing the input to the clock before it enters the SSN.

A Simple Synchronizer

In many situations a simple D flip-flop may serve adequately as a synchronizer. The operation of a D flip-flop as a synchronizer is illustrated in Figure 5.111. $X(u)$ is the unsynchronized input and $X(s)$ is the synchronized version of $X(u)$. Illustrated in the timing diagram are two possible responses of the synchronizer to a positive transition of $X(u)$ that occurs during the required setup or hold interval of the flip-flop. $X(s)$ may go to 1 immediately, or the transition to 1 may be delayed by one clock period. Either of these must be considered acceptable. We are assuming that the probability of metastable operation is insignificantly small.

Every transition of $X(u)$ will produce a like transition of $X(s)$, provided that $X(u)$ transitions are separated by at least $T_\phi + (t_{stp})_{min}$. The delay from an $X(u)$ transition to the corresponding $X(s)$ transition depends upon when during the clock period the $X(u)$ transition occurs. The longest and shortest delays occur for $X(u)$ transitions near $\phi\downarrow$. If such a transition occurs too late to be recognized the delay will be more than $T_\phi + t_{pd}^Q$. If it occurs just in time to be recognized, the delay may be little more t_{pd}^Q.

In any case, $X(s)$ transitions are synchronized with $\phi\downarrow$ and $X(s)$ may be used directly as an SSN input. The varying delays from $X(u)$ transitions to $X(s)$ transitions can cause the width of $X(s)$ pulses to differ from the width of the original $X(u)$ pulses by more than T_ϕ. If such a variation represents a change in the information carried by X, then the input synchronizer of Figure 5.111 will not work. Otherwise, this synchronizer represents a good solution to the synchronization problem, if metastable operation can be neglected.

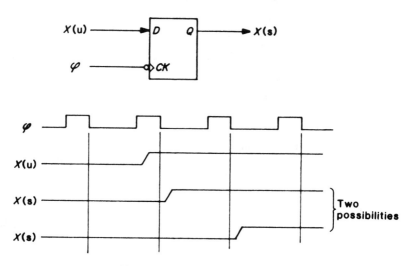

Figure 5.111   A simple synchronizer

Metastable Operation

We have ignored the possibility of metastable operation in this discussion. The SSN can still fail if metastable operation of the synchronizer flip-flop occurs. The probability of failure depends both on the frequency of $X(u)$ and the frequency of ϕ. If $X(u)$ changes infrequently then there are few opportunities for metastable operation and hence the probability of failure is low. For this reason, D flip-flops serve as reliable synchronizers for inputs that are generated manually (e.g., switches, pushbuttons) or by electromechanical devices.

If the frequency of ϕ is low then even if metastable operation of the synchronizing flip-flop does occur, the clock period is long enough to allow the flip-flop to resolve to a stable state long before the next $\phi\downarrow$. There is no delay after which a metastable flip-flop is guaranteed to resolve to a stable state, but the probability of remaining unresolved decreases rapidly with increasing time.

Because of the dependence of metastable failure on clock rate, systems with very high clock rates sometimes use two-stage synchronizers, illustrated in Figure 5.112. The period of ϕ' is n times the period of ϕ. The first flip-flop has a long interval, more than $(n - 1)T_\phi$, in which to resolve to a stable state if metastable operation occurs. This reduces the probability that the second flip-flop will exhibit metastable operation. Of course, changes in $X(u)$ must be separated by more than nT_ϕ if their recognition is to be guaranteed.

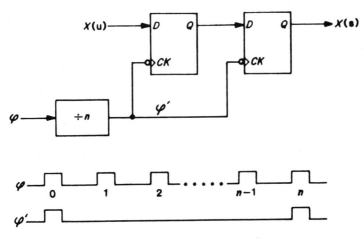

Figure 5.112   Two-stage synchronizer

Stoppable Clock-Synchronizer

For SSNs that have both a high-frequency clock and high-frequency inputs, metastable operation can be a significant problem. The two-stage synchronizer of Figure 5.112 cannot be used because it does not allow the SSN to respond quickly enough to input changes. A reliable solution to the synchronization problem for such systems is provided by the combined stoppable clock-synchronizer of Figure 5.113.

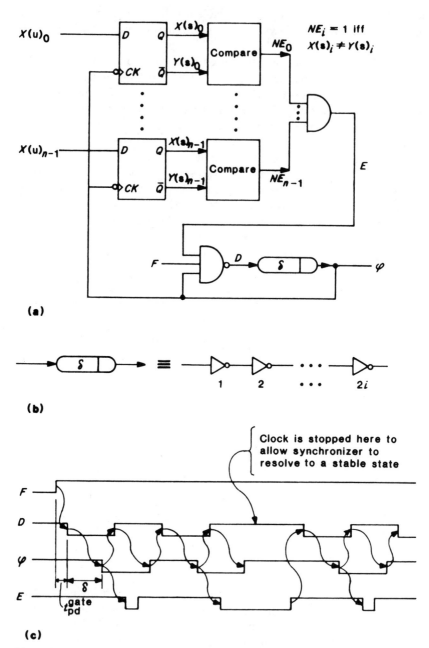

(a)

(b)

(c)

Figure 5.113 Stoppable clock-synchronizer: (a) stoppable clock-synchronizer circuit; (b) possible delay element implementation; (c) timing diagram

The clock in this circuit is a simple ring oscillator. The oscillator may be disabled by either of two inputs, E or F. Input F is generated externally. Input E is generated by a bank of synchronizers and compare circuits. The output of the compare circuit is 1 if the two inputs are at opposite logic levels. This will be the case except when the driving flip-flop exhibits metastable operation. Metastable operation is characterized by the two flip-flop outputs both hanging up in the $\frac{1}{2}$ region, or the two outputs oscillating in phase between 0 and 1. In either case, the output of the associated compare network will be 0. Hence $E = 0$ when any synchronizer flip-flop exhibits metastable operation. When all flip-flops have resolved to stable states, $E = 1$.

When power comes up, $F = 0$ and $E = 1$. F is raised to 1 to start the clock. As long as none of the synchronizer flip-flops becomes metastable, E remains at 1 and the clock output ϕ is periodic. The period is $2(\delta + t_{pd}^{NAND})$, where δ is the delay of the delay element, which may simply be a series of inverters as shown in Figure 5.113(b).

The asynchronous inputs are sampled by the synchronizing flip-flops with each $\phi\downarrow$. If any flip-flop becomes metastable, E goes to 0 and remains there until the flip-flop resolves to a stable state. If E returns to 1 before $\phi\uparrow$ then the metastable operation does not affect the clock. However, if E is still at 0 when $\phi\uparrow$ occurs, then the clock stops; ϕ remains at 1 until $E\uparrow$. A timing diagram illustrating the operation of this circuit is shown in Figure 5.113(c).

For proper operation, the delay in the oscillator loop must be large enough so that $E\downarrow$ will occur before $\phi\uparrow$. That is,

$$(t_{pd}^{NAND} + \delta)_{min} \geq (t_{pd}^{flip\text{-}flop} + t_{pd}^{compare} + t_{pd}^{AND})_{max} \qquad (5.9)$$

If this is not the case, then the sequence $\phi\uparrow$, $E\downarrow$, $E\uparrow$ may occur. This will produce a sequence of three transitions at D, $D\downarrow\uparrow\downarrow$, which will produce a like sequence at ϕ, $\phi\downarrow\uparrow\downarrow$. The interval $[\phi\downarrow, \phi\downarrow]$ may be very short. For this short clock period, setup and hold requirements of the SSN state register and output may not be met.

If inequality 5.9 is satisfied then metastable operation cannot produce short clock periods. It can only produce longer clock periods. It is guaranteed that the SSN inputs $X(s)_i$ and $\overline{X(s)}_i$ $(i = 0, \ldots, n - 1)$ will be stable for at least $(t_{pd}^{NAND} + \delta + t_{pd}^{compare} + t_{pd}^{AND})_{min}$ before each $\phi\downarrow$. Also, $X(s)_i$ and $\overline{X(s)}_i$ are guaranteed stable for at least $(t_{pd}^{flip\text{-}flop} + t_{pd}^{compare})_{min}$ after $\phi\downarrow$.

Using the clock-synchronizer circuit of Figure 5.113, the SSN can be designed in the standard fashion. Metastable operation is automatically handled by this circuit and may be ignored in the SSN design process. The clock period is treated as if it were fixed at

$$T_\phi = 2(t_{pd}^{NAND} + \delta) \qquad (5.10)$$

although in reality it may be stretched occasionally.

The clock period $T_\phi = 2(t^{NAND} + \delta)$ may vary considerably with temperature, supply voltage, aging, and component variations due to variations in the
IC fabrication process. For this reason, the stoppable clock-synchronizer is
not very well suited to central clock macrocircuit designs, where the clock
synchronizer is constructed from one or more IC packages, and the clock
pulse is routed to all other packages in the system. For such systems a clock
with a very stable fixed frequency is desirable (e.g., a crystal clock). Some
other technique for dealing with metastable operation may be preferable
(e.g., designing synchronizer flip-flops with very low probability of prolonged
metastable operation).

However, for microcircuit design, where the entire system including the
clock-synchronizer is on a single chip, these "disadvantages" become advantages since all circuit elements are affected by these same variations. The
clock in effect adapts to changing conditions, and hence is better than a fixed-
frequency clock.

One way to deal with metastable operation in large high-speed macrocircuit designs is to have a separate clock-synchronizer on each chip in the system. This not only eliminates the problems of metastable operation, but also
eliminates the problems of distributing clock pulses such as clock skew and
transmission line effects. These problems will be discussed later. The normal
practice at the present time is to use a central clock of very stable frequency.

. 5.5.5 Exercises

1. Design an SSN to implement each of the following sequential machines:
   (a) The ones counter (Figure 5.104)
   (b) The synchronization detector (Figure 5.106)
   (c) The synchronous one-shot (Figure 5.108)
2. Design a synchronization detector like the one of Figure 5.105 to detect
the character 10110110 (the leftmost bit arrives first).
3. Design a Moore machine version of the one-shot of Figure 5.107.
Change the specifications only where necessary.
4. Design a retriggerable synchronous one-shot, similar to the one-shot of
Figure 5.107 but with no P input. The output pulse should be four clock periods wide, unless retriggered. The recovery time should be one clock period,
measured from $X\downarrow$.
5. Design a selectable frequency clock. It should have a two-bit input F, a
clock input ϕ, and a single-bit output Y. The output should be a square wave
with a period $2[F]_2$, as long as F remains constant. Look at F (and change
frequency if necessary) only during the first ϕ clock period of a Y clock
period.

6. Design a synchronous "pure delay." The network has a clock input ϕ, a data input X, and an output Y. The output should be identical to X, but delayed three clock periods (i.e., $Y^{t+3} = X^t$ for $t \geq 0$; $Y^0 = Y^1 = Y^2 = 0$).

7. Design another version of the pure delay for which the delay is selectable by a two-bit input D.

8. Design an "inertial delay," which is the same as the delay in Exercise 7 except that changes in X of duration less than three clock periods are ignored.

9. Design a Moore machine version of the ones counter. It should output $y^t = $ number of 1's among $x^{t-3}, x^{t-2}, x^{t-1}$.

Chapter 6

REGISTER TRANSFER DESIGN

6.1 Fundamentals
6.2 A Synchronous One-Shot
6.3 IO Controllers
6.4 DMA Controllers
6.5 Processors
6.6 Control Unit Variations

A systematic technique for designing systems at the register transfer level is developed in this chapter. The technique is introduced via the design of a simple RT system, a synchronous one-shot. The technique is then applied to the design of the major subsystems of a computer: IO controllers, DMA controllers, and processors.

6.1 FUNDAMENTALS [26, 41, 46–51]

6.1.1 RT System Structure
6.1.2 The Design Process

6.1.1 RT System Structure

Register transfer systems are naturally decomposed into two types of modules, which we will call data units and control units. A *data unit* (DU) is a collection of RT level components (i.e., registers, RAMs, combinational networks) interconnected by data paths. It is capable of storing words and performing various operations on these words. However, a DU is a passive module in the sense that it does not initiate any operation. It performs an operation only in response to control signals that are generated externally.

Associated with a data unit there is always a *control unit* (CU). The CU decides when the DU should perform an RT operation, and generates the control signals that evoke the operation.

A simple RT system consisting of a single DU-CU pair is pictured in Figure 6.1. Information to be processed is brought into the system via input ports on the DU. The information is stored and processed within the DU, and results are made available at DU output ports.

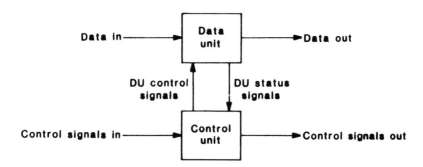

Figure 6.1   Register transfer system decomposition

The transfer of information into the DU, the internal processing, and the transfer of results out of the DU are controlled by the CU. Input and output transfers involve communication with external devices. Ports on the CU are used for signals to control this communication. Also, CU input signals may be used to control the overall operation of the system. Hence the processing that is performed may depend upon control signals that are received by the CU from external devices. External devices cannot directly control DU operations. This is the responsibility of the CU. But external devices can control the operation of the overall system by influencing the decisions of the CU.

Status signals from the DU are used to inform the CU of the current state of the computation being performed in the DU. The CU decides what operations to initiate next on the basis of these status signals, signals from external devices, and the current internal state of the CU. The CU is a sequential network.

Complex RT systems may have multiple CUs and/or DUs. This sort of structure arises naturally when the task to be performed by a system consists of subtasks that are independent of each other to a large extent. The relationships between subtasks are then represented by communication between separate CUs and/or DUs.

6.1.2   The Design Process

Designing a complex system involves making a large number of interrelated decisions. Since a designer can make only one decision at a time, the problem of deciding "what to do next" arises repeatedly. Because of the interrelationships between decisions, this problem is of central importance. It directly affects the amount of iteration that will be necessary to converge on a good design.

It is helpful to have a systematic design procedure which decomposes the design problem into a sequence of steps. A reasonable decomposition for RT system design is as follows:

1. System specification
2. Data unit
3. Control unit structure
4. Sequential operation
5. CU combinational network
6. Timing

Each of these steps will be illustrated in the next section via a simple example.

6.2   A SYNCHRONOUS ONE-SHOT

6.2.1   System Specifications and Data Unit
6.2.2   CU Structure
6.2.3   Sequential Operation
6.2.4   CU Combinational Network
6.2.5   Timing
6.2.6   Decomposition
6.2.7   Exercises

In Section 5.5 we designed an SSN to implement a synchronous one-shot with a dynamically selectable pulse width. Now consider designing a circuit of this sort with a pulse select input of 8 bits rather than 2.

We could extend the design of Section 5.5 to this case. The resulting SSN would be just as simple conceptually, but the number of states would be much larger (around 260). This large number of states would make the SSN more cumbersome and would complicate the design process (e.g., K-maps could not be used since there would be 10 input variables). Nevertheless, it is obviously possible to design an SSN to do the required job.

The SSN structure, however, does not seem quite appropriate for this application. Most of the SSN states are being used simply to count clock pulses, a function that could easily be performed by a separate counter. After some reflection, it should become clear that the RT system structure described in Section 6.1 is a more natural structure for this application. The counting function can be performed by a data unit under the supervision of a control unit, which initializes the count and evokes the decrement operation at appropriate times.

In this section, we will design an RT system to operate as a synchronous one-shot with a dynamically selectable 8-bit pulse width. We will follow the design procedure outlined in Section 6.1.

6.2.1 System Specification and Data Unit

Specifications for the one-shot operation have already been discussed in Section 5.5. The only difference is that P is now 8 bits rather than 2. Figure 6.2 summarizes these specifications.

The data unit consists of a single register T with a load operation and a decrement operation, as shown in Figure 6.3. The T register may be implemented by using two 74169 circuits (Figure 5.77), as illustrated in Figure 6.4.

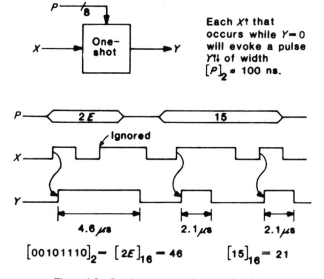

Figure 6.2   Synchronous one-shot specifications

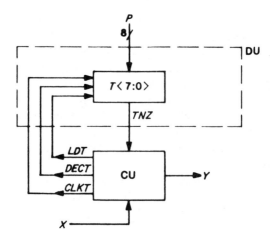

Figure 6.3   RT system one-shot

This implementation is similar to the counter implementation in Section 5.4 using 74163 circuits. The output TNZ (T not zero) is 1 if $T \neq 0^8$.

6.2.2   CU Structure

The structure of the control unit is shown in Figure 6.5. The heart of the CU is an SSN, consisting of a state register Q and a combinational network. The clock and reset circuit generates a reset pulse, as described in Section 5.3, and a clock. The clock frequency is chosen to be 10 MHz because the one-shot specification calls for output pulse widths that are multiples of 100 ns (i.e., one period of a 10-MHz clock). We will verify that the system can operate at this rate when we do a timing analysis.

The $\overline{RESET}$ signal is asserted (i.e., pulled low) when power comes up or when a reset button is pressed. This signal drives the direct clear (DC) input on the state register (see Figure 5.71). A $\overline{RESET}{\downarrow}{\uparrow}$ pulse will force all zeros into the state register, which will be the initial state q_0. $\overline{RESET}$ also initializes the other flip-flops in the control unit.

The flip-flop at the X input is used to synchronize X to the clock. Another synchronizing flip-flop must be included in the clock and reset box to synchronize $\overline{RESET}$ with ϕ. $\overline{RESET}$ must be synchronized with ϕ so that the first clock period of operation after $\overline{RESET}{\uparrow}$ will be a full clock period. That is, $\overline{RESET}{\uparrow}$ should occur just after $\phi{\downarrow}$.

The other CU flip-flop is used to generate the output Y. The purpose of this flip-flop may not be apparent. Why can we not generate output Y directly as a

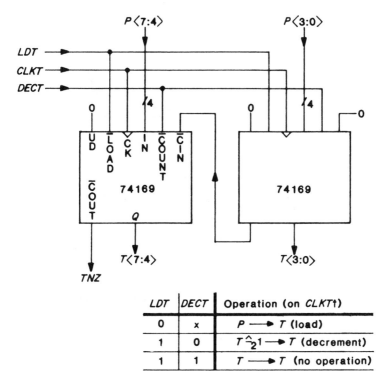

Figure 6.4 T register implementation

combinational network output (as we did in Section 5.5)? This question is answered in the following discussion of CU outputs.

CU outputs

There are three fundamental types of outputs that may be generated by the control unit: *direct*, *pulse*, and *extended*. These are illustrated in Figures 6.6 to 6.9. When it is necessary to indicate the "type" of a control unit output, the signal name will be followed by "d," "p," or "e" in parentheses, as shown in the figures. (The output y in the figures represents any CU output. It does not represent only the output Y of the one-shot network.)

A *direct output* is generated directly by the SSN combinational network. Direct outputs are characterized by the possibility of transients at the beginning of each clock period, as illustrated in Figure 6.6(b). These transients occur for two reasons. First, an output may be affected by an input change via two or more paths of different lengths. Hence in response to a single bit

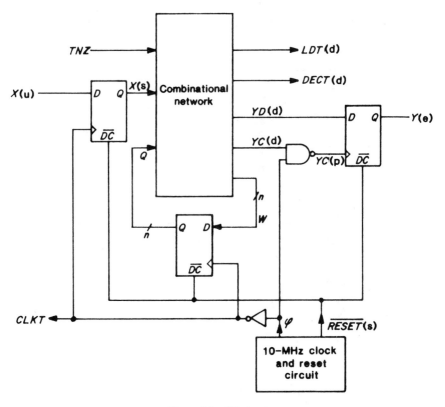

Figure 6.5   CU structure

change at X or Q, or multiple simultaneous bit changes at X and/or Q, an output can change two or more times.

Second, although Q and X change only at the beginning of a clock period, there is no assurance that individual bit changes will be simultaneous. Hence, even if all paths through the combinational network are of the same length, an output variable can nevertheless change two or more times at the beginning of a clock period.

Direct outputs are normally used only when output transients are acceptable. The LDT and $DECT$ signals are examples. These signals must be stable for a required setup time before $CLKT\uparrow$ (note that $CLKT = \bar{\phi}$, hence $CLKT\uparrow = \phi\downarrow$). However, after any $\phi\downarrow$ until the required setup interval before the next $\phi\downarrow$, these signals may change any number of times with no ill effects.

When an output must be transient-free, either a pulse output or an extended output is normally used. A *pulse output* is generated by using a gate to combine a direct output and a clock signal, as illustrated in Figure 6.7. The

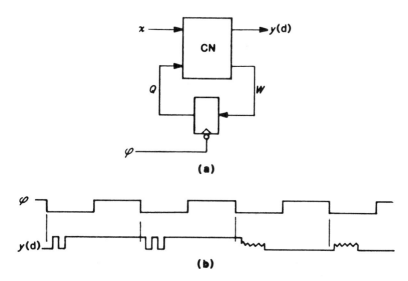

Figure 6.6 Direct output: (a) generation; (b) characteristic transients

network is designed so that any transients in the direct output will settle before the clock pulse occurs. The value of the direct output determines whether the pulse passes through the gate. Since the direct signal is stable throughout the clock pulse, there will be no transients at the pulse output in either case.

The pulse output of Figure 6.7 is generated by a NAND gate. The clock pulse is allowed to pass when $y(d) = 1$ and is inhibited when $y(d) = 0$. The pulse is inverted when it does pass.

Other types of gates may also be used to generate pulse outputs. A NOR gate, for example, will pass (and invert) negative clock pulses when the direct control signal is 0, and will inhibit pulses (holding the output low) when the control signal is 1. If $\bar{\phi}$ is used as the pulse input to the NOR, then positive pulses $\phi\uparrow\downarrow$ will be passed when $y(d) = 0$.

When a transient-free output is required that remains asserted for longer than one clock pulse width, then an *extended signal* is used. An extended signal is generated by a storage cell (e.g., a flip-flop). A simple extended signal implementation is shown in Figure 6.8. During each clock period, the combinational network generates at $y(d)$ the value desired at $y(e)$ during the next clock period. After any transients in $y(d)$ have died away, this value is loaded into the flip-flop $y(e)$.

In Figure 6.8, $\phi\downarrow$ is used to load $y(e)$. Hence the direct output $y(d)$ is delayed by about one clock period before reaching $y(e)$. This delay may be reduced by using a positive edge-triggered flip-flop to produce $y(e)$. Alternatively, a simple gated latch (Figure 5.69) may be used to generate $y(e)$.

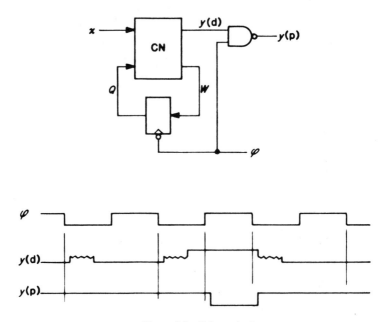

Figure 6.7   Pulse output

Another implementation of an extended output is shown in Figure 6.9. The flip-flop $y(e)$ is loaded only when it is necessary to change the value of $y(e)$. The direct output $yC(d)$ allows a pulse to pass to $yC(p)$ when $y(e)$ must change; otherwise the clock pulse is inhibited and the flip-flop is not loaded. The value that is loaded into $y(e)$ is determined by a second direct signal $yD(d)$.

The implementation in Figure 6.9 also delays the signal at $y(d)$ by about one clock period to $y(e)$. As with the implementation of Figure 6.8, this delay can be reduced by using $\phi\!\uparrow$ to load $y(e)$, or by using a gated latch which loads when $\phi = 1$.

Which of the two extended signal implementations is better depends upon the situation. If $y(e)$ changes infrequently it may be easier to generate $yD(d)$ and $yC(d)$ than the single output $y(d)$, which must be correct every clock period. If $y(e)$ is usually at one level and is only at the opposite level in a few situations, then $y(d)$ may be easier to implement than $yD(d)$ and $yC(d)$.

The output Y of the one-shot that we are designing should be an extended signal, because transients are unacceptable in a one-shot output. The implementation of Figure 6.9 was selected in order to have a pulse signal, $Y(p)$, included in the example. It is left as an exercise to try the extended signal implementation of Figure 6.8 for Y.

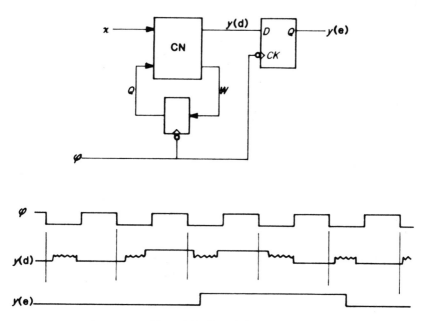

Figure 6.8 Extended output

6.2.3 Sequential Operation

We have proposed a data unit (Figure 6.4) and a control unit structure (Figure 6.5) for the desired RT system. The next step in the design process is to specify precisely the sequential operation of the system. This is done by constructing a sequential machine that specifies register transfer operations as outputs. The sequential machine is a complete specification of system operation. It indicates exactly the conditions under which any operation is to be performed, and no operation is performed by the system except as indicated by the sequential machine. Such a machine for our one-shot system is proposed in Figure 6.10.

In general, there may be many different sequential machines that satisfy the specifications for a given system. Selecting the "best" machine involves identifying the alternatives and comparing their characteristics. The machine of Figure 6.10 is only one of several machines that meet the general specifications for our one-shot system. After carrying the design of the one-shot through to completion for this machine, we will suggest two alternative machines. In the meantime, the reader may consider proposing his own alternatives.

Let us proceed now to describe the machine of Figure 6.10. When power comes up, or when a reset button is pushed, a RESET pulse forces q_0 into the

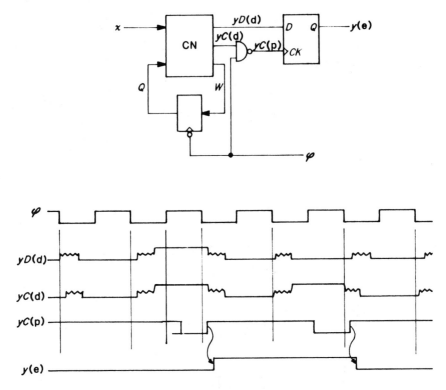

Figure 6.9   Alternative extended output

CU state register, where it remains as long as $X = 0$. The RESET pulse also clears the Y flip-flop and the X synchronizing flip-flop.

When X goes to 1, the system goes to state q_1 and loads P into T. In q_1 the DU status signal TNZ is checked to see if $T = 0$. If so, P was 0 when $X\uparrow$ occurred, hence no pulse should be generated. The system goes to q_2 and waits for X to return to 0, then returns to q_0 and waits for the next $X\uparrow$.

If $T \neq 0$ in q_1 then the system sets Y, decrements T, and goes to state q_3. The system remains in q_3 until $T = 0$ (i.e., $TNZ = 0$). T is decremented each clock period while in q_3. When T reaches 0, the system clears Y and goes to q_2, where it waits for $X = 0$ (in case X has never returned to 0 after the $X\uparrow$ that initiated this Y pulse).

The sequential machine specifies exactly when the system should perform any operation. By implication, it therefore determines when the control signals that evoke these operations must be asserted. The timing diagram of Figure 6.11 illustrates the resulting operation of the system for several clock periods. The relationship between the sequential machine and the timing dia-

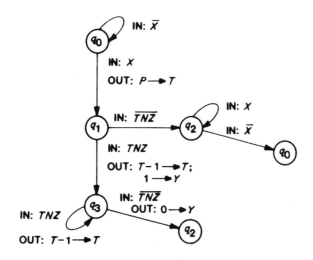

Figure 6.10   Sequential machine

gram should be carefully noted. Specifically, notice that *for any branch of the state diagram, the same clock edge that loads the next state into the state register also loads the destination register for any RT operation specified for that branch. The control signals that evoke the operations specified for a branch are asserted during the clock period in which the state at the tail of the branch is in the state register.*

The timing diagram of Figure 6.11 begins with the system in state q_0 and $X(s)$ making a positive transition. The state diagram specifies that P should be loaded into T and the next state should be q_1. *The intended interpretation is that the next occurrence of $\phi\downarrow$ should load q_1 into the state register and also load P into T.* To accomplish this, W (not shown) must change to q_1, and LDT must be held low (as shown) during clock period 1. P is not shown in the diagram, but is assumed to be 00000100 (04 hexadecimal) during the first clock period.

In clock period 2, q_1 is in the state register and 04 is in the T register. Since $T \neq 0$, the state diagram specifies next state q_3 and outputs $1 \rightarrow Y$ and $T - 1 \rightarrow T$. The intended interpretation (to repeat and emphasize) is that the next $\phi\downarrow$ should load q_3 into the state register, $T - 1$ into T, and 1 into Y. This is accomplished by: changing W to q_3 (not shown); holding LDT at 1 and $DECT$ at 0; and holding YD(d) and YC(d) at 1. YC(d) = 1 allows the next clock pulse to go through to YC(p) to load YD into Y.

In each of the next three clock periods, T is decremented and the system remains in q_3. In clock period 6, Y is cleared and the system goes to q_2.

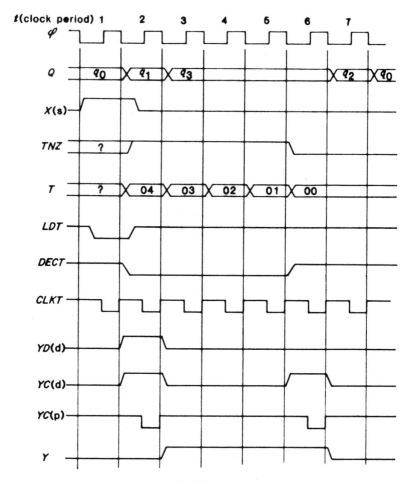

Figure 6.11   Timing diagram

6.2.4   CU Combinational Network

In order to evoke the operations specified by the sequential machine, the CU combinational network must assert each of its outputs at the appropriate times. In general, each output must be 0 under certain conditions, must be 1 under certain other conditions, and may be either 0 or 1 under any remaining conditions (called "don't care" conditions). The conditions for each of the one-shot outputs are listed in the output specification table, Table 6.1.

This table may be constructed directly from the sequential machine and the definition of operation for each control output. Consider *LDT* as an example.

TABLE 6.1. Output specification table

Direct output	Must be 0	Must be 1	Don't care
LDT	$q_0 \cdot X$	All others (i.e., $q_0 \cdot \bar{X}$, q_1, q_2, q_3)	None
$DECT$	$q_1 \cdot TNZ$, $q_3 \cdot TNZ$	All others	$q_0 \cdot X$
YD	$q_3 \cdot \overline{TNZ}$	$q_1 \cdot TNZ$	All others
YC	All others	$q_1 \cdot TNZ$, $q_3 \cdot \overline{TNZ}$	None
W_0*	All others	$q_0 \cdot X$, $q_1 \cdot TNZ$, $q_3 \cdot TNZ$	None
W_1*	q_0, $q_2 \cdot \bar{X}$	All others	None

*Conditions for W_1 and W_0 assume the following state assignment:

q	$Q\langle 1:0\rangle$
q_0	00
q_1	01
q_2	10
q_3	11

From the operation table of Figure 6.4 it is seen that LDT must be 0 when the load operation is to be performed, and must be 1 when the decrement operation or no operation is desired. From Figure 6.10, the load operation is to occur only in state q_0 when $X = 1$. Hence the only "must be 0" condition is $q_0 \cdot X$. For every other possible condition, either the decrement operation or no operation must occur. Hence the "must be 1" list covers all remaining possibilities. There are no don't care conditions.

The $DECT$ signal, from Figure 6.4, must be 0 to perform the decrement operation, must be 1 for no operation, and may be either 0 or 1 for the load operation. The conditions for "must be 0" and "don't care" are listed in the output specification table. For all other conditions, $DECT$ must be 1.

The signal YD(d) must be 1 when $1 \rightarrow Y$ is specified and must be 0 when $0 \rightarrow Y$ is specified. Each of these occurs only once in the state diagram, as indicated in Table 6.1. For all other conditions YD may be either 0 or 1, since the Y flip-flop is not being loaded and hence the D input is not looked at.

The clock input for the Y flip-flop, YC(d), must be 1 whenever the flip-flop is to be loaded (with either 0 or 1). When the flip-flop is not to be loaded, the clock pulse must be inhibited, hence YC(d) must be 0. There are no don't care conditions.

The next state variables (W_1 and W_0) may be included in the output specification table after a state assignment has been made. In Table 6.1, the natural state assignment, which uses the base 2 code for i to represent q_i, is assumed. W_0 must be 1 when the next state has an odd index number (i.e., q_1 or q_3); W_0 must be 0 for an even next state (i.e., q_0 or q_2). Similarly, W_1 must be 1 when the next state is q_2 or q_3 and 0 when the next state is q_0 or q_1.

Equations for the combinational network outputs may be written directly from the output specification table. Simply pick either the "must be 0" or the "must be 1" list of conditions, encode the state variables, and write the sum of products expression. If the "must be 0" conditions are picked, complement the sum. For the one-shot system the resulting equations are:

$$LDT = \neg \bar{Q}_1 \cdot \bar{Q}_0 \cdot X$$

$$DECT = \neg (\bar{Q}_1 \cdot Q_0 \cdot TNZ + Q_1 \cdot Q_0 \cdot TNZ)$$

$$YD(d) = \bar{Q}_1 \cdot Q_0 \cdot TNZ$$

$$YC(d) = \bar{Q}_1 \cdot Q_0 \cdot TNZ + Q_1 \cdot Q_0 \cdot \overline{TNZ}$$

$$W_0 = \bar{Q}_1 \cdot \bar{Q}_0 \cdot X + \bar{Q}_1 \cdot Q_0 \cdot TNZ + Q_1 \cdot Q_0 \cdot TNZ$$

$$W_1 = \neg (\bar{Q}_1 \cdot \bar{Q}_0 + Q_1 \cdot \bar{Q}_0 \cdot \bar{X})$$

Implementing the CU combinational network directly from equations written in this fashion has two advantages:

1. Simplicity. These equations can easily be written by hand even for large systems with many variables.

2. Natural interpretation. These equations directly reflect the structure of the system and the sequential machine. Each term in each equation has a straightforward interpretation in terms of system operation.

The disadvantage of this implementation procedure is that it does not produce an "optimal" combinational network. In particular:

1. It may not produce an optimal sum of products to cover either the 0's or the 1's of a function.

2. It may not assign "don't cares" in an optimal fashion. It makes "don't cares" either all 0's (the "must be 1" equation) or all 1's (the "must be 0" equation).

3. It does not consider sharing of product terms (i.e., multiple output minimization).

4. It does not consider implementations of more than two levels (to reduce cost).

An optimal design procedure should take each of these factors into consideration. For a very small system, classical two-level design techniques may be applied directly. This is done for the one-shot system in Figures 6.12 and 6.13.

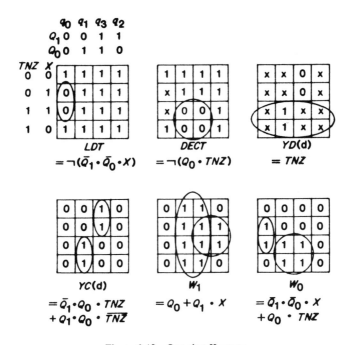

Figure 6.12 One-shot K-maps

As the number of variables grows, it quickly becomes impractical to optimize the combinational network design by hand. Computer assistance extends the range of systems for which optimal two-level solutions may be obtained. For yet larger systems, however, optimal two-level solutions become impractical to find and to implement. Computer-assisted heuristic techniques must be employed to find good suboptimal designs.

We will not consider the problem of implementing large control unit combinational networks further in this text. We will assume that a practical method is available for converting an output specification table, or perhaps even a sequential machine specification, into a good CU combinational network. For a survey of computer programs that have been developed for this application, as well as other aspects of computer-aided system design, see Ullman [50]. When we need to have a specific implementation for illustrative

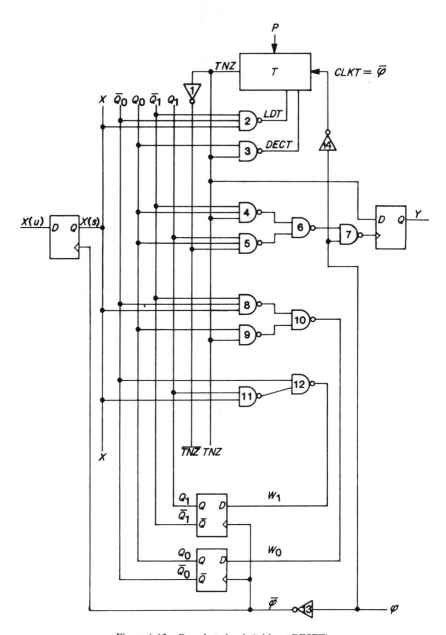

Figure 6.13   One-shot circuit (without RESET)

purposes, we will use equations written directly from the output specification table such as those above for the one-shot system.

6.2.5 Timing

The operation of a register transfer system is characterized by short bursts of activity (voltage and current changes) separated by short quiet periods. Each flurry of activity is initiated by a clock edge. Sufficient time is allotted before the next clock edge to allow this activity to subside and to allow the results of the activity to set up at the intended destination registers and output ports. These registers and ports may be in the data unit (e.g., the T register) or in the control unit (e.g., the state register or extended-output flip-flops). Timing of an RT system involves ensuring that the quiet period that follows each burst of activity is sufficient to satisfy the setup and hold requirements of all destination registers and ports.

For a complete timing analysis, every RT operation that a system performs must be analyzed to verify that the timing requirements of the destination register or port are satisfied. Consider, for example, the operation $T - 1 \rightarrow T$ that occurs in state q_1 when $T \neq 0$ (clock period 2 in Figure 6.11). Assume that each of the gates and flip-flops in Figure 6.13 satisfies the timing specifications given in Figure 5.102, and the T register specifications are those given in Figure 5.79. Assume also that wire delays are negligible.

To evoke the operation $T - 1 \rightarrow T$ reliably, LDT must be 1 and $DECT$ must be 0 for at least 20 ns before the $CLKT\uparrow$ at the end of the q_1 clock period (the 74169 setup requirement). The clock period must be long enough to allow for the propagation delay of Q (being loaded with q_1), the propagation delay of this new state value through one level of gates (gates 2 and 3 in Figure 6.13), and the required setup time at LDT and $DECT$. The resulting inequality is:

$$[\bar{\phi}\uparrow, CLKT\uparrow] \geq (t_{pd}^{Q})_{max} + (t_{pd}^{gate})_{max} + (t_{stp}^{74169})_{min}$$

$$= 10 + 6 + 20 = 36 \text{ ns} \qquad (6.1)$$

The path from TNZ to $DECT$ must also be considered, since T was loaded by the previous $CLKT\uparrow$.

$$[CLKT\uparrow, CLKT\uparrow] \geq (t_{pd}^{TNZ})_{max} + (t_{pd}^{gate})_{max} + (t_{stp}^{74169})_{min}$$

$$= 30 + 6 + 20 = 56 \text{ ns} \qquad (6.2)$$

Inequality 6.2 is a direct constraint on the clock period, since $[CLKT\uparrow, CLKT\uparrow] = T_{\phi}$. This constraint is easily satisfied by our assumed value, $T_{\phi} = 100$ ns.

If the delays through gates 13 and 14 are exactly the same, then $\bar{\phi}\uparrow$ and $CLKT\uparrow$ coincide, hence $[\bar{\phi}\uparrow, CLKT\uparrow] = T_\phi$. Inequality 6.1, then, is also a direct constraint on T_ϕ (which is also easily satisfied by $T_\phi = 100$ ns).

Clock Skew

If the delays through gates 13 and 14 are not the same, then $[\bar{\phi}\uparrow, CLKT\uparrow] \neq T_\phi$. This difference in propagation delays along paths that transmit clock signals is called *clock skew*. Maximum skew occurs when the delay along one path is the greatest that it could be, and the delay along the other is the least that it could be. That is,

$$(t_{skew})_{max} = (t_{pd}^{PATH\ 1})_{max} - (t_{pd}^{PATH\ 2})_{min} \qquad (6.3)$$

In our example, the paths are gate 13 versus gate 14 (since we are assuming negligible wire delay). From Figure 5.102, then, $(t_{skew})_{max} = 6 - 2 = 4$ ns. If the direction of skew is such that the edge that loads the state register is delayed more than the edge that loads T, then $[\bar{\phi}\uparrow, CLKT\uparrow] = T_\phi - t_{skew}$. Hence, inequality 6.1 becomes

$$T_\phi \geq (t_{pd}^Q)_{max} + (t_{pd}^{gate})_{max} + (t_{stp}^{74169})_{min} + (t_{skew})_{max} \qquad (6.4)$$

$$T_\phi \geq 40 \text{ ns}$$

In addition to the 74169 setup requirements on LDT and $DECT$, there are also hold requirements to be met. Specifically, $[CLKT\uparrow, y>] \geq 0$ ns, where $y>$ is $LDT\downarrow$ or $DECT\uparrow$. Although LDT remains at 1 and $DECT$ at 0 in state q_3, these hold requirements must be verified because transients are possible in direct outputs.

If there were no clock skew, satisfaction of these hold requirements would be automatic, since $y>$ is initiated by $\bar{\phi}\uparrow$ (which coincides with $CLKT\uparrow$ if there is no clock skew), hence $CLKT\uparrow$ must precede $y>$.

When clock skew is possible, however, satisfaction of these hold requirements is not automatic. If $\bar{\phi}\uparrow$ occurs before $CLKT\uparrow$ because of clock skew, then $y>$ (which is caused by $\bar{\phi}\uparrow$) may occur before $CLKT\uparrow$. We must verify that the minimum delay from $\bar{\phi}\uparrow$ to $y>$ is greater than the maximum clock skew. That is,

$$(t_{pd}^Q)_{min} + (t_{pd}^{gate})_{min} \geq (t_{skew})_{max} \qquad (6.5)$$

Using the specifications of Figure 5.102, inequality 6.5 becomes $3 + 2 \geq 4$, which verifies satisfaction of the 74169 hold requirement.

Clock skew is a significant consideration in both microcircuit and macrocircuit systems. In either case it is most important in large high-speed systems, in which clock pulses are distributed over long distances and wire delays are not negligible. In order to maintain a high clock rate, clock paths must be carefully matched so that skew is minimized.

The General Timing Procedure

The above analysis of the $T - 1 \rightarrow T$ operation illustrates the principles involved in verifying the timing requirements for any operation. A setup requirement is verified by starting at the clock edge with respect to which the setup is measured, and tracing each path back to a clock edge that initiates a change that affects the setup value. The distance between this initiating edge and the setup edge must be sufficiently large to allow for the maximum propagation delay along the path plus the minimum acceptable setup time. This will result in a constraint on the distance between two "derived" clock edges (e.g., $\bar{\phi}\uparrow$ or $CLKT\uparrow$). This is then converted into a constraint on the distance between "actual" clock edges (i.e., edges at the clock site) by adding the maximum clock skew between the two clock paths to the required distance between edges.

Associated with a single setup requirement there may be several such paths, which may begin at different clock edges. And associated with a single operation there may be several setup requirements.

Verification of a hold requirement is similar. Starting at the "derived" clock edge with respect to which the hold time is measured, trace a path back to an edge that will change the setup value being "held." The minimum delay along this path must be large enough to assure that the setup value is held beyond the required hold time, assuming maximum clock skew in the unfavorable direction.

Even for a small system such as our one-shot, timing analysis is a tedious job. We analyzed only the $T - 1 \rightarrow T$ operation. The operations $1 \rightarrow Y, 0 \rightarrow Y, P \rightarrow T$, and $W \rightarrow Q$ must be analyzed as well to complete the job.

For a large system, timing analysis is always done with the assistance of a computer. Usually simulation is used to verify correct operation and to identify critical timing paths. Detailed analysis as described above is applied only to critical paths.

Response Time

Response time is frequently an important timing consideration. It is the delay between the occurrence of an input event and the occurrence of a responding output event. For example, our one-shot system responds to $X\uparrow$ by generating a pulse $Y\uparrow\downarrow$. The response time (i.e., the delay from $X\uparrow$ to $Y\uparrow$) is approximately 210 to 300 ns, depending upon when $X(u)\uparrow$ occurs.

The synchronizing flip-flop introduces from about 10 to 100 ns of delay, depending upon where in the clock $X(u)\uparrow$ occurs. If $X(u)\uparrow$ occurs at the end of a clock period (i.e., just before $\phi\downarrow$) then $X(s)\uparrow$ will occur near the beginning of the next clock period (a delay of about 10 ns). If $X(u)\uparrow$ occurs near the beginning of a clock period (i.e., just after $\phi\downarrow$), then $X(s)\uparrow$ will not occur until the beginning of the next clock period (a delay of about 100 ns).

Another 200 ns of delay is introduced by the sequential machine structure: 100 ns in state q_0 after $X(s)\uparrow$ has occurred, and 100 ns in state q_1. The output response $Y\uparrow$ does not occur until the beginning of state q_3.

Consider the possibility of reducing response time of the one-shot. Since the synchronization requirement is unavoidable, there is no way to eliminate the synchronization delay. However, delays due to sequential machine structure may be avoidable.

In the sequential machine of Figure 6.10, we responded to $X\uparrow$ by first loading P into T and then checking TNZ to determine whether to set Y (if $T = 0$ then no output pulse is generated). We could respond to $X\uparrow$ sooner if we checked for $P = 0$ in state q_0 instead of waiting until q_1. An obvious way to do this is to use an eight-input NOR gate to test P directly. The cost of the NOR gate can be saved, however, if P is loaded into T in the clock period before $X\uparrow$ occurs, so that TNZ can be used. This idea is implemented in Figure 6.14. Response time is reduced by about 100 ns.

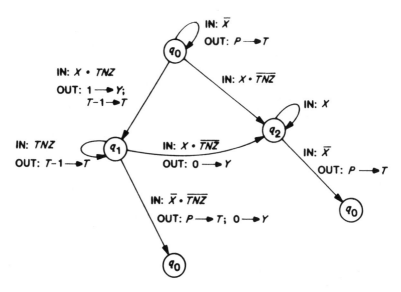

Figure 6.14   An improved one-shot

The machine of Figure 6.14 also eliminates the one clock period recovery time after $Y\downarrow$ by going directly to q_0 from q_1 after T goes to 0 when $X = 0$. This allows a quicker response to an $X\uparrow$ that occurs in the next clock period. This also eliminates the possibility that $X\uparrow$ will be missed, which could happen in the original design if X stayed at 1 for only one clock period in this situation.

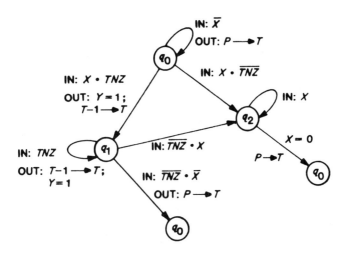

Y is a direct output. Y = 1 only where
specified explicitly; otherwise, Y = 0.

Figure 6.15   The fastest one-shot

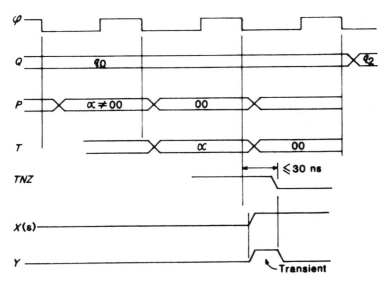

Figure 6.16   An output transient

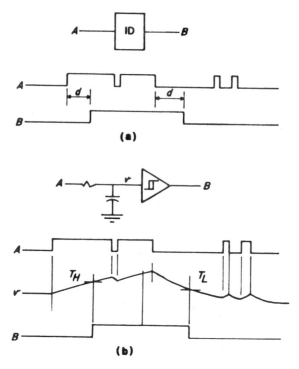

Figure 6.17   Inertial delay element: (a) ideal; (b) an approximation

Response time could be further improved if a direct output were used for Y (rather than an extended output), as illustrated in Figure 6.15. This machine responds to $X\uparrow$ by setting $Y = 1$ immediately (i.e., in the same clock period).

The problem with direct outputs, as discussed previously, is that transients can occur at the beginning of each clock period. One way in which a transient might occur at Y in this system is illustrated in Figure 6.16. The transient occurs because of the long transition time of TNZ. From Figure 5.79, the delay from $CLKT\uparrow$ to $TNZ<$ may be as large as 30 ns. If $P = 0$ in the clock period before $X\uparrow$, but $P \neq 0$ in the previous period, then TNZ and X will be 1 simultaneously for a while at the beginning of the $X\uparrow$ clock period.

Transients may occur at Y for other reasons as well. One approach to eliminating transients at a direct output is to identify each possible way in which a transient may occur, and then find a way to eliminate each of these. The state assignment, the combinational network implementation, and operating constraints placed upon inputs can all affect transient behavior at direct outputs. Elimination of transients in this fashion, however, may be difficult or even impossible.

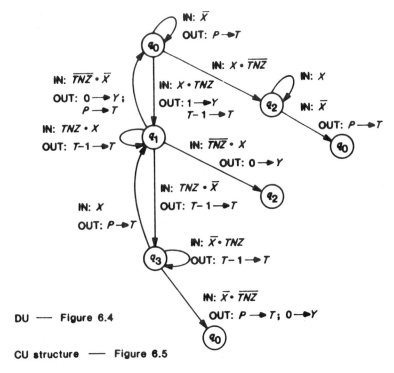

Figure 6.18   A retriggerable one-shot

A general technique for eliminating transients of any sort at an output is to insert an *inertial delay* in the output path. An ideal inertial delay element has a single binary input and a single binary output. The output follows the input with delay d, except that input changes of duration less than d are ignored, as illustrated in Figure 6.17(a).

A simple approximation to an inertial delay is shown in Figure 6.17(b). T_H denotes the high threshold of the Schmitt trigger buffer and T_L the low threshold. The delay d is determined by the RC time constant.

This circuit is not an ideal inertial delay. If input transients occur too frequently, the delay d is reduced, and eventually a transient may pass through to the output. For circuits that more closely approach the ideal inertial delay behavior, see Unger [35].

For the purpose of suppressing transients in a direct output, the inertial delay of Figure 6.17(b) is fine. Transients can occur only at the beginning of a clock period, allowing the circuit to recover in the latter part of each period. The delay d should exceed the maximum input transition time. For the one-shot system, this is the 30-ns transition time from $CLKT\uparrow$ to $TNZ<$. With

$d = 30$ ns, the improvement in response time over the system of Figure 6.14 is about 70 ns. The overall response time for the one-shot of Figure 6.15 from $X(\mathrm{u})\!\uparrow$ to $Y\!\uparrow$ is about 40 to 140 ns.

6.2.6 Decomposition

A sequential machine for a retriggerable version of the one-shot is defined in Figure 6.18. The data unit is the same as for the non-retriggerable one-shots. The sequential machine is similar to the machine of Figure 6.14. The additional complexity results from the necessity of continuously monitoring X while $Y = 1$, and reinitializing the timer when $X\!\uparrow$ occurs.

It is frequently the case that a system can be simplified and a better design produced by decomposing the task to be performed into subtasks. The retriggerable one-shot, for example, might be decomposed into two subsystems, as shown in Figure 6.19. System A is a simple non-retriggerable one-shot which, in response to each $X\!\uparrow$, generates a pulse $R\!\uparrow\!\downarrow$ that is one clock period wide. This relieves system B of the task of remembering the previous level of 1 so that it can detect 0-to-1 transitions. When system B sees $R = 1$ it either initiates or retriggers an output pulse, using the DU to measure the pulse duration, as before. Sequential machines for system A and system B are defined in Figure 6.20.

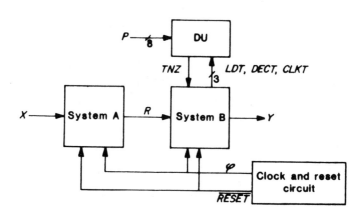

System A: Synchronize X with φ.
Set $R = 1$ for one clock period
in response to each $X(\mathrm{s})\!\uparrow$.

System B: Initiate or retrigger output
pulse $Y\!\uparrow\!\downarrow$ whenever $R = 1$.

Figure 6.19 Another retriggerable one-shot

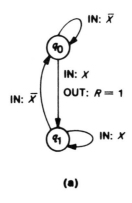

(a)

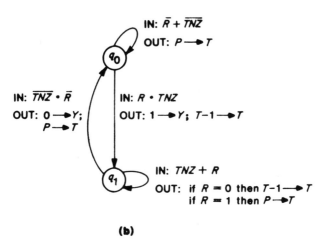

(b)

Figure 6.20   Sequential machines: (a) system A; (b) system B

6.2.7   Exercises

1. Modify Figure 6.5 by using the Figure 6.8-type extended output for Y. Carry this change through the design process. In particular, specify:
   (a) $Y(d)$ line of the timing diagram (Figure 6.11)
   (b) $Y(d)$ row of output specification table (Table 6.1)
   (c) $Y(d)$ K-map and equation

2. Complete the design of the one-shot described in Figure 6.14, following the same steps used to design the original system:
   (a) DU specification (already done, Figure 6.4)
   (b) CU structure design (already done, Figure 6.5)

(c) Timing diagram (use same inputs as Figure 6.11)
(d) Output specification table (like Table 6.1)
(e) K-maps (like Figure 6.12)
(f) Block diagram (like Figure 6.13)

3. Do Exercise 2 for the systems described in:
(a) Figure 6.15
(b) Figure 6.18
(c) Figures 6.19 and 6.20

4. Verify the setup and hold requirements for the $1 \rightarrow Y$ operation in state q_1 (Figure 6.10). What is the shortest that T_ϕ could be? Is it necessary to insert any delays?

5. What sort of synchronization requirement on P is required for proper operation of the one-shot of Figure 6.10? State such a requirement:
(a) Relative to $X(u)\uparrow$
(b) Relative to ϕ

6. Repeat Exercise 5 for the one-shot of Figure 6.14.

7. (Output transients.) Consider a Moore machine with a single-bit input and a single-bit output such that: $\delta(q_1, 1) = q_2$, $\lambda(q_1) = \lambda(q_2) = 1$, and $\lambda(q_0) = \lambda(q_3) = 0$.

(a) Show that the state assignment $q_0 = 00$, $q_1 = 01$, $q_2 = 10$, and $q_3 = 11$ makes the output susceptible to transients during transition from q_1 to q_2.

(b) Define a state assignment that eliminates this susceptibility.

8. Although a Moore machine does not guarantee that direct outputs will not be susceptible to transients [as illustrated in Exercise 7(a)], it sometimes makes it easy to eliminate this susceptibility by making an appropriate state assignment [as in Exercise 7(b)].

Design a Moore machine implementation of the one-shot which generates Y as a direct output, but is transient-free (without using an inertial delay). What is the response time? (Note: the machine must be Moore-type only for the Y output.)

9. Design the SYN detector of Section 5.5 as an RT system, using a 74198 register for the DU.

10. Design an RT system with two inputs, X and G, and a 4-bit output Y. While $G = 1$, $[Y']_2$ = number of 1's among the past 15 inputs (i.e., X^{t-15}, $X^{t-14}, \ldots, X^{t-1}$). $G\downarrow$ will clear $Y(0 \rightarrow Y)$. $G\uparrow$ will start the count anew, as though X had been 0 for the previous 15 clock periods.

11. Design a selectable frequency clock, with an 8-bit select input P, a clock input ϕ, a control input RUN, and an output Y. As long as $RUN = 0$, $Y = 0$. While $RUN = 1$ and P is constant, Y is a square wave with period $T_Y = 2([P]_2 + 1)T_\phi$. RUN and P are synchronized with ϕ. You should decide when to respond to changes in RUN and P.

12. Design an inertial delay, with selectable delay time D. D is an 8-bit input. It is synchronized with the clock input ϕ. The ID input X is also synchronized with ϕ. $Y^t = X^{t-[D]_2}$, except that a change in X of duration less than $[D]_2$ is ignored.

13. Design a pure delay, with selectable delay time D. D is a 4-bit input. It is synchronized with the clock input ϕ. The data input X is also synchronized with ϕ. The output during clock period t is $Y^t = X^{t-[D]_2}$.

6.3   IO CONTROLLERS [2, 3, 5, 44, 55]

6.3.1   The System Bus
6.3.2   A Programmable One-Shot
6.3.3   Parallel Port IOCs
6.3.4   Serial Port IOCs
6.3.5   Exercises

In this section, we design several IO Controllers. These IOCs are typical but simple examples of the IOC chips that are part of every microprocessor family. Our IOCs will be designed specifically for use with the system bus described briefly in Section 1.1.2 (i.e., 6800 and 6502 family processors). A more detailed description of this bus is provided in Section 6.3.1.

Although our IOCs will be designed specifically for use with the 6800-type system bus, these same chips can be used with other buses as well. In fact, it is not at all unusual to mix IOCs and microprocessors from different families in current system design practice. The maximum penalty that is paid for crossing family boundaries is the possible necessity of using a few small chips to generate the required timing signals.

It is possible to include IOCs together with a processor and even some memory on a single chip. Several of these "single-chip microcomputers" are currently available (e.g., Motorola 6801 and 6805, Intel 8048, Zilog Z8). Design of an IOC for such a context is somewhat different in that connection to an external system bus is not required. In all other respects, however, our IOC design examples will apply to this context as well.

Except in the very simplest cases, IOCs are RT systems. The design process described in Section 6.1 and illustrated in Section 6.2 may be applied directly. One additional consideration arises, however, in the particular case of IOC chip design: *the IOC chip must be controlled and monitored exclusively via system bus read and write operations.*

Deciding how this will be done is one of the most interesting parts of the IOC design problem. It includes the following considerations:

1. What "addressable" registers will be included on the chip?

2. How will these registers be used to control and monitor chip operation?

3. Exactly how will the chip respond to each system bus read or write operation involving the chip?

    This part of the IOC design will determine how the chip will look to the PMS level system designer and the IO programmer. It thus determines how easy (or difficult) it will be to use the chip.

    These considerations may be regarded either as part of the specification step or as part of the data unit step of the general RT system design process. Alternatively, we may represent them as new steps between these two steps. The resulting eight-step IOC design process is as follows:

1. System specification

2. Registers and terminals

3. System bus communication

4. Data unit

5. Control unit structure

6. Sequential operation

7. CU combinational network

8. Timing

6.3.1 The System Bus

A brief description of the 6800-type system bus was provided in Section 1.1.2. In this section, we provide a more comprehensive description of the bus, particularly those aspects that are related to connection of chips to the bus, and to control of IOC and DMAC chips via bus read and write operations.

    The standard single-bus system architecture is shown in Figure 6.21. For simplicity we will assume that there is only a single processor in the system, although multiple processors may be connected to the same bus (see Section 1.2.3).

    The IOD block in Figure 6.21 may represent any number of IO devices. Likewise, the IOC and M blocks may each represent multiple chips. We will assume for simplicity that the DMAC block represents a single DMA controller. It will be a simple matter, however, to remove this assumption later and allow multiple DMACs (see Exercise 5 in Section 6.4).

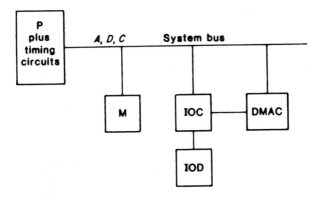

Figure 6.21   Single bus architecture

Bus Operations

The individual lines of the system bus are shown in Figure 6.22. There are 16 address lines (allowing a maximum of 2^{16} addressable registers), 8 data lines (each addressable register is 8 bits), and 7 control lines.

Two of the control lines (the clock ϕ and the *RESET* line) are generated by timing circuits. For the 6800 microprocessor, these timing circuits are exter-

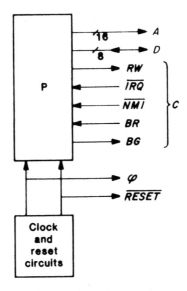

Figure 6.22   The system bus

nal to the processor chip. In fact, the external timing circuits generate two clock phases, denoted ϕ_1 and ϕ_2 in the 6800 data sheet. Both ϕ_1 and ϕ_2 are inputs to the 6800 chip, but only ϕ_2 is sent to external chips as part of the system bus. Since ϕ_1 is never involved in system bus operations, it is not shown in Figure 6.22. The signal ϕ in the figure is ϕ_2 of the 6800 data sheet.

Other processor chips in the 6800 family (e.g., the 6801 and 6809) have the clock circuitry on board. Internally these processors use a two-phase clock, just as the 6800. However, only a single clock phase (our ϕ) is sent off the processor chip as part of the system bus.

The processor communicates with the M, IOC, and DMAC blocks primarily via two types of bus operations or "cycles": read cycles and write cycles. A write cycle is used by the processor to store an 8-bit word (i.e., a byte) in an "external" register (i.e., a register in M, IOC, or DMAC). A read cycle is used to bring into the processor a copy of the word currently stored in an external register.

Each external register has an associated address (a 16-bit word). In general discussions we will use the name $M[\alpha]$ to denote the register with address α, although this register is not necessarily in M, but may be in any external block (M, IOC, or DMAC).

The timing for read and write cycles is specified in Figure 6.23. To perform a read cycle the processor places the address, α, of the register to be read on the A bus and holds $RW = 1$ for one clock period. The external devices monitor the A bus continuously. The device that contains register $M[\alpha]$ responds while $\phi = 1$ by placing a copy of the word in register $M[\alpha]$ on the D bus. The processor takes the word off the D bus during ϕ and stores it in an internal register.

The pulse $\phi\uparrow\downarrow$ is used by the external device to "strobe" data onto the D bus. The first part of the clock period, while $\phi = 0$, must be sufficiently long to allow transients on the A bus to subside [the maximum address delay is $(t_{AD})_{max} = 150$ ns] and to allow the external devices to "decode" the address to determine which device should respond. If $\phi\uparrow$ occurs too soon, more than one external device may attempt to place a word on the D bus, which may damage the tristate bus drivers (see Section 5.1). This is one of the factors that constrains the clock rate.

In addition, $\phi\uparrow\downarrow$ must be wide enough to allow data on the D bus to stabilize at the D input port of P for the required setup time, $(t_{DS})_{min}$. The particular timing specifications given in Figure 6.23 are for the 68B00 microprocessor.

Timing for a write cycle is similar. The processor puts the address on the A bus at the beginning of the clock period, and holds $RW = 0$ to indicate that a write operation is desired. The external devices decode the address, and the

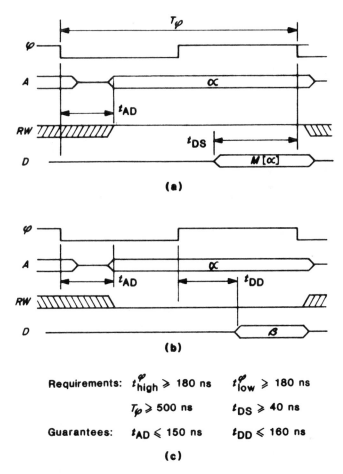

Figure 6.23   Bus cycle timing: (a) read cycle; (b) write cycle, $\beta \to M[\alpha]$; (c) timing specifications (68B00)

device containing register $M[\alpha]$ takes the data which is held on the D bus by the processor while $\phi = 1$ and loads it into register $M[\alpha]$.

In addition to its major function of providing the capability for read and write operations, the system bus also provides mechanisms for "interrupting" the processor, and for sharing "bus mastership" with DMACs in the system.

Any IOC or DMAC in the system may interrupt the processor by pulling the $\overline{\text{IRQ}}$ control line or the $\overline{\text{NMI}}$ control line low. Each of these lines is a single-bit open-collector type bus (see Section 5.1). The pull-up resistor for each is inside the processor.

Both of these interrupt request inputs are used for essentially the same purpose: to transfer control of the processor to another program (see Section 1.1). Requests at the *IRQ* input may be "masked" (i.e., disabled) by execution of the SEI instruction (set interrupt mask), or enabled by execution of the CLI instruction. Requests at the *NMI* input, however, cannot be disabled, hence the name nonmaskable interrupt (NMI). Details of the interrupt response are presented in Section 6.5.

The *BR* and *BG* signals are used for sharing bus mastership. Both the processor and the DMAC have the capability of initiating bus read and write operations. At any particular time, however, only one device is empowered to initiate bus operations. This device is called the *bus master*.

When power first comes up (i.e., after a *RESET* pulse), the processor is the bus master. A DMAC may gain control of the bus (i.e., become the bus master) by asserting the bus request input *BR*. The processor will respond to this request by disabling its *A*, *D*, and *RW* bus drivers (see Sections 1.1 and 5.1) and asserting bus grant *BG*. If more than one DMAC is included in the system, then circuitry must be provided to establish priority (see Exercise 6.4.5).

The companion term to "bus master" is "bus slave." A device that is operating as a bus slave must continuously monitor the *A* bus, and respond appropriately during any read or write operation that addresses one of its internal registers.

A DMAC must be able to operate either as a master or as a slave. When the processor is sending information to the DMAC to set up a block transfer, the DMAC must be a slave. When it is transferring a word during a block transfer, the DMAC must be the bus master.

The IOC and M blocks always operate as slaves, never as masters. Processors are normally designed to serve only as masters. Registers in the processor do not have assigned addresses, and hence other bus masters cannot access these registers. This is not a fundamental constraint, however, and processors in the future may be designed to operate as slaves as well as masters (e.g., this may be useful in multiprocessor systems).

The bus of Figure 6.22, which we have been discussing, is essentially the bus defined by the 6800 microprocessor. The names of the bus lines are the same, except for *BR* and *BG*, which are called *HOLD* and *BA* (bus available) in the 6800 data sheet. The read and write operations are as described above. In fact, the timing specifications of Figure 6.23 are taken from the 68B00 data sheet.

Three 6800 control lines are omitted from Figure 6.22, however, because they are of secondary importance. These lines are DBE (data bus enable), *TSC* (three state control), and *VMA* (valid memory address). *DBE* is normally driven by ϕ, but may be driven by a stretched version of ϕ to accommodate external chips with long setup and/or hold requirements. *TSC* is used to implement a bus request input with a faster response time than the *HOLD* input. *VMA* indicates when the processor has placed a valid address on the address bus. It is a peculiar signal which is necessary only because the processor sometimes puts "accidental addresses" on the A bus during idle bus cycles (i.e., when *P* is the bus master, but it is not using the bus), and certain IOC devices may be affected by such addresses. Specifically, reading certain IOC registers may set or clear IOC flip-flops as side effects. These signals are not worth further attention unless one is designing a 6800-based system.

Address Assignment

In most systems the primary memory M is not a single IC chip, but rather consists of multiple chips (some of which may be ROM and others RAM). Likewise, the IOC block of Figure 6.21 consists of multiple IOC chips, typically one IOC chip for each IO device.

The address that is assigned to each register in an external chip (whether in M, IOC, or DMAC) is determined by the manner in which the chip is connected to the *A* bus. Each external chip is equipped with one or more "chip select" or "chip enable" inputs, plus a sufficient number of "address" inputs to allow selection of registers within the chip. The address inputs to each chip are usually connected to consecutive bits of the *A* bus, starting with A_0. The chip select inputs are connected to upper address bits, either directly or via decoding circuitry of some sort. Hence, upper address bits are used to select chips, and lower address bits to select registers within chips.

A simple example is shown in Figure 6.24. There are 16 external chips, each with 12 or fewer address inputs. Address bits $A\langle 15:12 \rangle$ are decoded by using a 4-to-16 decoder. Each decoder output selects one of the external chips. Address bits $A\langle 11:0 \rangle$ (as many as necessary) are connected to the address inputs of each chip. The resulting "address map" is shown in Figure 6.24(b).

Usually IOC chips contain only a few registers. In the example of Figure 6.24, this would result in many addresses being wasted, since 2^{12} addresses are allocated to each chip. If it is necessary to add external chips to this system, then an address assignment that is less wasteful is required. Multiple chip select inputs on IOC chips are useful for this purpose. Other address assignment examples are considered in the exercises.

Address Sharing

Until now, we have assumed that each external register will be assigned a unique address. This, in fact, is true for registers in M, but it is not always true for registers in IOC chips. In order to reduce the number of address in-

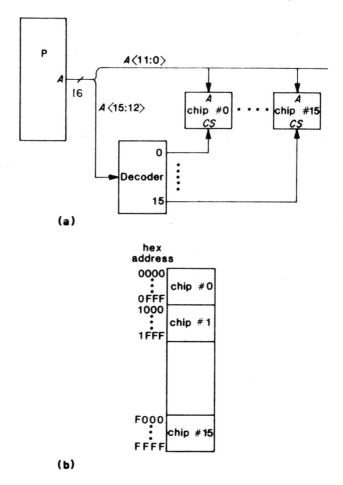

Figure 6.24   Address assignment: (a) bus connections; (b) address map

puts that must be provided (or to simplify chip operation, in some cases), IOC chips are sometimes designed such that multiple registers share the same address. Various techniques are used to determine which register is accessed by a particular read or write to a shared address. Some of these are:

1. One register is accessed for a read operation and another for write (i.e., one register is "read only" and the other is "write only").

2. Registers are accessed in a particular sequence after the access sequence is initialized in some way (e.g., by a reset pulse, or by an initialize command written to a command register).

3. The register to be accessed is selected by an address written previously to an internal address register. (The "address" enters the chip on the D bus.)

4. Bits of D may serve as address bits for a write operation (e.g., $D\langle 7:6\rangle$ may select one of four 6-bit registers to be written from $D\langle 5:0\rangle$).

In spite of this sharing of addresses by IOC registers, we will continue to use the notation $M[\alpha]$ in general discussions to denote "the" external register with address α, understanding that the register named $M[\alpha]$ may depend upon the situation.

Nonstandard Bus Operations

The operation of an IOC chip must be controlled and monitored by the processor via system bus read and write operations. It is usually possible for the designer to provide the desired control and monitoring capabilities using "standard" read and write operations (i.e., $M[\alpha] \rightarrow D$ for a read and $D \rightarrow M[\alpha]$ for a write). However, it is sometimes more convenient or efficient to use operations that are nonstandard in some respect.

For example, an IOC register may be fewer than 8 bits, so that reading or writing the register actually involves data transfer only on part of the D bus. Since the processor can do only the standard 8-bit operations, the IOC will normally put zeros on the unused data lines during a read (so that the processor does not read a floating bus), and it will ignore the unused data lines during a write (even though the processor sends something).

"Side effects" of various sorts are also used in nonstandard IOC bus operations. For example, an IOC chip may respond to a read request by clearing a flip-flop in the IOC in addition to putting a word on the D bus. Or it may respond to a write request by generating a pulse at an output terminal in addition to loading a register from the D bus.

Deciding how an IOC chip will be controlled and monitored by read and write operations is one of the most interesting steps in the design of IOCs. Nonstandard bus operations are an important aspect of this step.

More Complex Buses

All microprocessor buses provide essentially the same capabilities: read and write operations; processor interrupt control; a bus sharing mechanism; a RESET pulse; and a clock to drive IOC sequential circuits. The bus of Figure 6.22 is the simplest bus in common use. This bus, or some minor variation of it, is used by several microprocessors, including the 6800, 6502, and 6809 processors.

The additional complexities that are encountered with other microprocessor buses are usually associated with one or more of the following:

1. Use of a higher frequency clock, which allows more precise control of bus cycles (i.e., several clock periods per bus cycle)

2. Provision of a *READY* signal, which allows slow external chips to extend a bus cycle

3. Provision for more status information from the processor (e.g., instruction fetch; interrupt enabled)

4. Use of a wider data bus

5. Multiplexing (i.e., time-sharing) of processor pins to reduce processor pin count

We will use the bus of Figure 6.22 in our examples of IOC chip design. The fundamental design considerations are the same for this bus as for the more complex buses. In fact, IOC chips designed for use with the bus of Figure 6.22 can be used with other microprocessor buses as well, although a few extra gates may be required to generate the appropriate control signals.

6.3.2 A Programmable One-Shot

Consider the design of an IOC that will operate as a programmable one-shot. We will call this device the one-shot controller (OSC).

Specifications

We can use the same general specifications for OSC as for the "stand-alone" one-shot of Section 6.2. For simplicity, the non-retriggerable version will be designed.

The new aspect of this one-shot is that it must be controllable via system bus read and write operations. Specifically, it should be possible to send a word to OSC which determines the width of the one-shot output pulses, and it should be possible to enable or disable one-shot operation by appropriate write cycles. Also, the processor should be able to learn the current pulse width setting and the current status of OSC (enabled or disabled) via system bus read operations.

Registers and Terminals

Having specified what we would like OSC to do, the next step is to determine what internal registers and external terminals must be provided to implement the desired behavior. Our decisions for this step are illustrated in Figure 6.25.

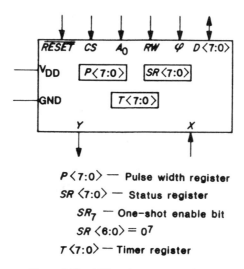

$P\langle 7:0\rangle$ — Pulse width register
$SR \langle 7:0\rangle$ — Status register
SR_7 — One-shot enable bit
$SR \langle 6:0\rangle = 0^7$
$T \langle 7:0\rangle$ — Timer register

Figure 6.25   OSC registers and terminals

The P register will be used to hold the word that specifies the width of the output pulses to be produced. The status register SR will be used to enable or disable the one-shot operation. When $SR_7 = 1$, the one-shot is enabled; when $SR_7 = 0$, it is disabled. The other bits of the register, $SR\langle 6:0\rangle$, are not used, and will not actually be implemented. The register is considered to be 8 bits long only for the purpose of communication over the 8-bit D bus. Reading the status register will always show $SR\langle 6:0\rangle = 0^7$. Writing to SR will actually write only to SR_7.

The T register will be used to measure the width of the output pulse, by counting clock pulses. It will be loaded from P when an output pulse begins, and decremented each clock period. When it reaches 0, the output pulse will be terminated. This register need not be accessible via the system bus.

There are only two terminals on the IO side of the OSC chip: an input terminal X and an output terminal Y. When enabled, the one-shot will detect positive transitions at input X and produce positive pulses at output Y.

On the system bus side of the OSC chip are the following terminals: an 8-bit bidirectional D port, to be connected directly to the D bus; an input RW, to be connected to bus line RW; a chip select input CS, to be connected to upper bits of the A bus in some way; a clock input ϕ, to be connected to the bus clock line; a single address input A_0, to be connected to line A_0 of the address bus; and the RESET input.

Also shown in Figure 6.25 are the power and ground terminals, VDD and GND, to be connected to the DC power supply. These terminals must be present on every chip, but are frequently omitted in block diagrams for simplicity.

System Bus Communication

The next step is to decide exactly how the OSC chip will respond during read and write operations to each chip address. This step is illustrated in Table 6.2.

TABLE 6.2. OSC system bus communication:
(a) Detailed specification

CS	A_0	RW	Operation
0	x	x	No operation
1	0	0	$D \xrightarrow{\phi\downarrow} P$
1	0	1	$P \xrightarrow{\phi} D$
1	1	0	$D_7 \xrightarrow{\phi\downarrow} SR_7$
1	1	1	$SR \xrightarrow{\phi} D$

(b) Abbreviated specification

A_0	Selected register
0	P
1	SR

$SR\langle 6:0 \rangle = 0^7$

Table 6.2(a) provides a detailed specification of system bus communication for the one-shot chip. When $CS = 0$, the chip is not selected and no operation is evoked. When $CS = 1$, $A_0 = 0$, and $RW = 0$ (a write to address 0), the chip loads the word at D into register P. Assuming that the load operation for register P is edge-controlled, the negative edge of ϕ should be used to load P, since the processor holds data on the D bus while $\phi = 1$. (The use of level-controlled registers will be considered in Section 6.6. Until then, we will consider only edge-controlled registers, which are a little easier to use.)

When $CS = 1$, $A_0 = 0$, and $RW = 1$ (a bus read from address 0), the one-shot chip should hold the word in register P at port D while $\phi = 1$. The processor will take the word from the D bus and load it into one of its internal registers.

The next two rows of the table are a read and a write at address 1. For the write operation, D_7 is loaded into SR_7. The other status register bits $SR\langle 6:0\rangle$ are actually not implemented as storage cells, and cannot be written to. For the read operation, the 8-bit word SR is held at D while $\phi = 1$. This word consists of SR_7 followed by seven zeros.

An abbreviated version of Table 6.2(a) is given in Table 6.2(b). This table indicates that address 0 is associated with register P and address 1 with register SR. This information is sufficient to specify system bus communication since the chip responds in the "standard fashion" during read and write operations at either address, except that bits $SR\langle 6:0\rangle$ are fixed at 0, as noted.

DU and CU Structure

The next steps in the design process are to construct the data unit and define the control unit structure. These are presented together in Figure 6.26.

Register T is a microcircuit version of the counter of Figure 6.4. The P register is a bank of 8 D-type flip-flops. Status register bit 7 is also a D-type flip-flop. SR_7 is concatenated with seven zeros to form the 8-bit word SR that can be placed on the D bus via a bank of eight tristate buffers. (Actually, tristate buffers need not be used for $SR\langle 6:0\rangle$. A bank of pull-down transistors controlled by $SRTD$ will suffice. Simplifications such as this are common in block diagrams.)

Sequential Operation

The sequential operation of OSC is defined by the sequential machine of Figure 6.27. The operation of this one-shot will be similar to the operation of the one-shots of Section 6.2, except in the way that the operation is enabled. The one-shots of Section 6.2 use the value $P = 0$ to disable the one-shot operation; a transition $X\uparrow$ that occurs while $P = 0$ is ignored (i.e., does not produce an output pulse). The IOC that we are now designing uses $SR_7 = 0$ for the same purpose. The value $P = 0$ can thus be used in some other way. We will use this value to specify an output pulse width of $2^8 * T_\phi$ (i.e., the widest possible pulse).

The one-shot remains in state q_0 as long as $SR_7 = 0$. While the one-shot is in q_0, transitions of X are ignored. After SR_7 is changed to 1 (by a system bus write operation), the one-shot remains in state q_0 as long as $X = 1$. When X changes to 0, the one-shot loads P into T and goes to state q_1.

In state q_1, the one-shot monitors X waiting for a transition to 1. It remains in q_1 as long as $SR_7 = 1$ and $X = 0$. While the one-shot is in q_1, the processor

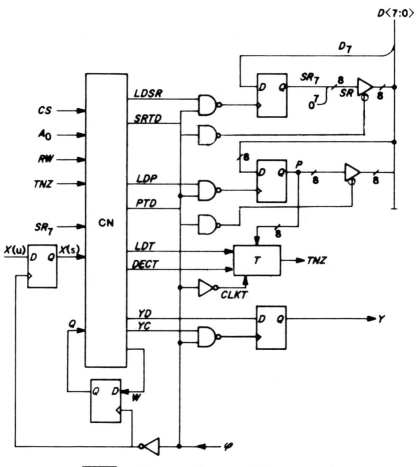

$\overline{RESET}$ = 0 (not shown) clears Q, Y, and SR_7.

Figure 6.26   OSC DU and CU structure

may write a new value into P. The one-shot thus loads P into T every clock period while waiting in q_1, so that the latest value of P is in T when $X\uparrow$ occurs. The processor may also write 0 to SR_7 while the one-shot is in q_1. If this happens, the one-shot returns to q_0, where it will not respond to $X\uparrow$ transitions.

If $X\uparrow$ occurs while the one-shot is in q_1, it sets Y, decrements T, and goes to q_2. While in q_2, the one-shot ignores changes in P and SR_7 and simply decrements T until $T = 0$. When $T = 0$ is reached, the one-shot clears Y and returns to either q_0 or q_1 depending upon SR_7 and X.

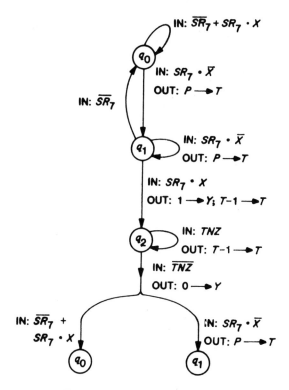

Figure 6.27   OSC sequential operation

The "split branch" out of state q_2 (a new notation) actually represents two branches: a branch with input condition $\overline{TNZ} \cdot (\overline{SR_7} + SR_7 \cdot X)$ and output $0 \to Y$, leading to state q_0, and a branch with input condition $\overline{TNZ} \cdot SR_7 \cdot \overline{X}$ and outputs $0 \to Y$ and $P \to T$, leading to state q_1. The split branch notation represents the factors that are common to both branches on the single branch out of q_2 (i.e., that for input $\overline{TNZ}$ the output $0 \to Y$ is generated, regardless of what the other input conditions may be).

Concurrent Operations

The sequential machine of Figure 6.27 does not completely describe the operation of the hardware of Figure 6.26. Specifically, it does not include the bus operations, which are described in Table 6.2(a).

At first, it may appear that this omission should be corrected by incorporating the bus operations into the sequential machine definition. However, in attempting to do so it is discovered that this may not be such a good idea. The difficulty is that the states of the sequential machine are associated with the one-shot behavior of the system, and the system bus operations are completely independent of this behavior. That is, the processor may read or write the *P* or *SR* register at any time, regardless of the state of the sequential machine. Hence, the bus operations are independent of the current state, and have no effect on the next state. Any attempt to merge the two will be clumsy and artificial.

The best way to model a system of this sort is to recognize the inherent independence of the two behaviors, and represent the system as two concurrently operating subsystems. Such a model for the one-shot IOC is shown in Figure 6.28.

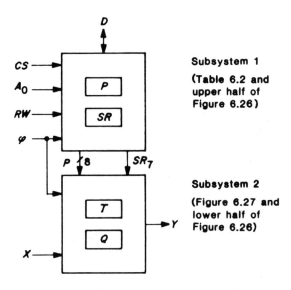

Figure 6.28   OSC concurrently operating subsystems

Subsystem 1 handles system bus communication, as described in Table 6.2(a). Subsystem 2 controls the one-shot behavior of the system, as described in Figure 6.27.

Each subsystem is a register transfer system. The data unit of subsystem 1 consists of registers *P* and *SR* and the associated tristate buffers and data paths. The control unit is simply a combinational network (which may be regarded as a sequential machine with a single state).

The details of the DU and CU structure for subsystem 1 are given in the upper half of Figure 6.26.

The data unit and control unit structure of subsystem 2 are shown in the lower half of Figure 6.26. The state register Q is part of this subsystem. The data unit is simply the T register.

CU Combinational Network

The output specification table for the CU combinational network is shown in Table 6.3. Notice that the top four rows, which correspond to subsystem 1 of Figure 6.28, do not involve the current state. These conditions are obtained from Table 6.2(a).

TABLE 6.3. OSC output specification table

Signal	Must be 0	Must be 1	Don't care
$LDSR$	All others	$CS \cdot A_0 \cdot \overline{RW}$	None
$SRTD$	All others	$CS \cdot A_0 \cdot RW$	None
LDP	All others	$CS \cdot \overline{A}_0 \cdot \overline{RW}$	None
PTD	All others	$CS \cdot \overline{A}_0 \cdot RW$	None
LDT	$q_0 \cdot SR_7 \cdot \overline{X}$ $q_1 \cdot SR_7 \cdot \overline{X}$ $q_2 \cdot \overline{TNZ} \cdot SR_7 \cdot \overline{X}$	All others	None
$DECT$	$q_1 \cdot SR_7 \cdot X$ $q_2 \cdot TNZ$	All others	Same as LDT "must be 0" conditions
YC	All others	$q_1 \cdot SR_7 \cdot X$ $q_2 \cdot \overline{TNZ}$	None
YD	$q_2 \cdot \overline{TNZ}$	$q_1 \cdot SR_7 \cdot X$	All others
$W_1{}^*$	All others	$q_1 \cdot SR_7 \cdot X$ $q_2 \cdot TNZ$	None
$W_0{}^*$	All others	$q_0 \cdot SR_7 \cdot \overline{X}$ $q_1 \cdot SR_7 \cdot \overline{X}$ $q_2 \cdot \overline{TNZ} \cdot SR_7 \cdot \overline{X}$	None

*Assuming the following state assignment:

q	$Q\langle 1:0 \rangle$
q_0	00
q_1	01
q_2	10

The other six rows of the table correspond to subsystem 2. The conditions for these signals are obtained from the sequential machine of Figure 6.27 (and from Figure 6.4 for *LDT* and *DECT*).

Timing

A timing analysis for OSC follows the general timing procedure outlined in Section 6.2. Consider, for example, the setup requirement for the *P* register load operation. The setup requirement is measured with respect to $\phi\downarrow$ at the end of a bus write operation to register *P*. The data at the *P* register *D* input is taken directly from the *D* bus. The processor puts data onto the *D* bus after $\phi\uparrow$. The delay from $\Phi\uparrow$ to $D<$ is denoted t_{DD} in Figure 6.23. The setup constraint associated with this operation is thus

$$t_{high}^{\phi} \geq (t_{DD})_{max} + (t_{stp}^{P})_{min} + (t_{skew}^{\phi})_{max}$$

The clock skew here is the amount that the edge $LDP(p)\uparrow$ that loads *P* may precede $\phi\downarrow$ at the processor input. In all likelihood, $\phi\downarrow$ will precede $LDP(p)\uparrow$, so this will be a negative number.

The timing constraints for other setup requirements are similar. Hold requirements are also similar, except that the concern is with shortest paths and minimum delays. Hold requirements are usually not a problem because of the inherent capacitance of all signal paths.

For the rest of this chapter we will assume that the clock is run slowly enough to satisfy all setup requirements, and there is sufficient capacitance to satisfy all hold requirements.

6.3.3   Parallel Port IOCs

Communication between an IO controller and an IO device may be either serial or parallel. These terms refer to the manner in which a word of information is transferred. The communication is parallel if all bits are transferred simultaneously and serial if the bits are transferred one at a time.

Most microprocessor families include at least one general-purpose parallel IOC chip and one general-purpose serial IOC chip. Simple versions of both types of IOC will be designed in this section and the next. First, we consider the design of a simple parallel output controller (POC) chip.

The POC chip that we will design here was used in Section 1.1.5 to control a printer. It may also be used to control other output devices.

POC Specifications

POC must be capable of receiving a byte via a system bus write cycle and transferring the byte to an output device "in parallel" (i.e., all 8 bits at once).

Communication with the output device should be controlled by the "hand-shake" protocol illustrated in Figure 6.29. *RDY* (ready) and *TR* (transfer request) are control signals. *PD* is the 8-bit parallel data port. The transfer of a single byte from POC to an output device proceeds as follows:

1. The output device indicates that it is ready to receive a byte by setting *RDY*.

2. POC holds the byte to be transferred at *PD* and sets $TR = 1$.

3. In response to *TR*↑, the output device takes the byte at PD and clears *RDY*.

4. In response to *RDY*↓, POC clears *TR*.

5. When it is ready to receive another byte, the output device sets *RDY*.

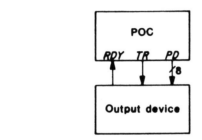

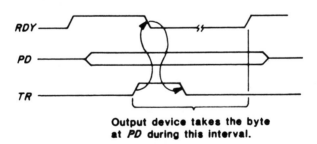

Output device takes the byte at *PD* during this interval.

Figure 6.29   POC-output device interface

POC must have the capability of interrupting the processor (i.e., pulling the bus line $\overline{IRQ}$ low) when it is ready to receive a byte. This will allow blocks to be transferred from memory to the output device under interrupt control, as described in Section 1.1.5.

It must also be possible for the processor to disable the IOC interrupt request, so that when there are no bytes to be transferred, or when a block is to be transferred under direct control, POC will not interrupt the processor. The processor must be able to determine, via a bus read operation, whether POC is ready to receive a byte. It also should be able to determine whether POC interrupt is enabled or disabled.

POC Registers and Terminals

Figure 6.30 specifies the registers and terminals for the POC chip. The terminals on the IO side of the chip have already been described. On the system bus side, a single address input is provided plus all the standard pins for system bus communication, including an $\overline{IRQ}$ output pin.

Only two registers are required: a buffer register BR, and a status register SR. The processor will send a byte to the IOC by writing to the buffer register. POC will hold the byte in BR while it is being transferred to the output device.

The status register is defined to be 8 bits for the purpose of communication over the system bus. Only 2 bits are actually used, however. SR_7 is the POC

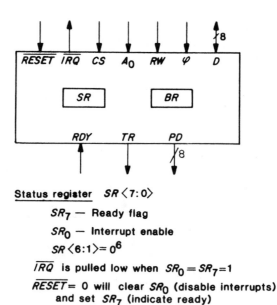

Status register $SR \langle 7:0 \rangle$

    SR_7 — Ready flag

    SR_0 — Interrupt enable

    $SR \langle 6:1 \rangle = 0^6$

    $\overline{IRQ}$ is pulled low when $SR_0 = SR_7 = 1$

    $\overline{RESET} = 0$ will clear SR_0 (disable interrupts) and set SR_7 (indicate ready)

Buffer register $BR \langle 7:0 \rangle$

    BR holds a byte that has been sent by the processor while it is being transferred to the output device.

Figure 6.30   POC registers and terminals

ready flag. It should be 0 when there is a byte in BR that has not yet been accepted by the output device. Otherwise, it should be 1 to indicate that the processor may send a byte.

SR_0 is the POC interrupt enable bit. This bit should be under program control. If a program wishes to be interrupted whenever POC is ready to receive a byte into BR, it should set $SR_0 = 1$. If the program does *not* wish to be interrupted, even though POC may be ready to receive, it should clear SR_0.

POC-System Bus Communication

Communication with the POC chip over the system bus is described in Table 6.4. Address $A_0 = 0$ is assigned to register SR. Reading from this address is a standard read operation; SR will be held on the D bus while $\phi = 1$. Bits $SR\langle 6:1\rangle$ will always be 0^6, as indicated by Figure 6.30. Writing to address $A_0 = 0$ will actually write only to SR_0. Assuming that SR_0 is an edge-triggered flip-flop, $\phi\downarrow$ loads D_0 into SR_0.

Address $A_0 = 1$ is assigned to register BR. Reading from this address is a standard read operation (BR is held at D while $\phi = 1$). Writing to $A_0 = 1$ evokes the standard write operation ($D \rightarrow BR$) plus an important "side effect" $0 \rightarrow SR_7$. Clearing SR_7 serves a double purpose: it indicates that there is a new byte in BR, and it activates the sequential circuitry that transfers the new byte to the output device.

POC DU and CU Structure

The DU and CU structure for the POC chip is shown in Figure 6.31. Most of this is similar to the DU and CU structure for the OSC chip (Figure 6.26) and should require no explanation. The only new feature is the connection to the $\overline{IRQ}$ line of the bus. An open-collector NAND gate is used rather than a gate with a standard output or a tristate output because there may be other IOCs driving the $\overline{IRQ}$ line as well. The open-collector NAND will pull $\overline{IRQ}$ low when $SR_7 \cdot SR_0 = 1$, but it will not attempt to hold $\overline{IRQ}$ high when $SR_7 \cdot SR_0 = 0$. Hence, another IOC is free to pull $\overline{IRQ}$ low. There is a pull-up resistor in the processor that holds $\overline{IRQ}$ high when no IOC is pulling low.

The BR register is connected to output port PD through a buffer that boosts drive capability. Hence $PD = BR$, except for the delay through the buffer.

As with the OSC system, POC may be regarded as two subsystems, one of which handles bus communication, and the other the sequential operation of transferring bytes to the output device. The first subsystem is the upper part of Figure 6.31 (above SR_7), and the second is the lower part (below SR_7). SR_7 may be considered part of either, since it is cleared by a bus operation and set by an IO port operation.

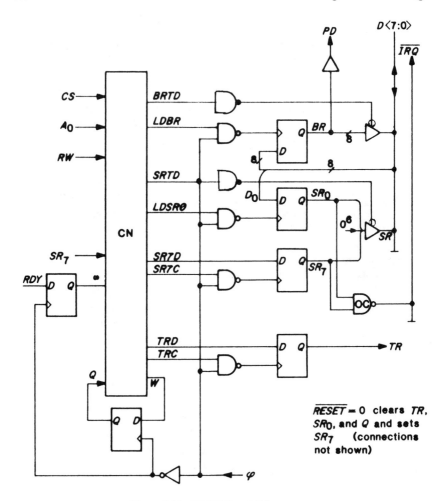

Figure 6.31   POC DU and CU structure

POC Sequential Operation

The process of transferring a byte from BR to the output device is a sequential operation. The sequential machine that controls this operation is defined in Figure 6.32. The transfer operation is initiated by $SR_7\downarrow$ (a side effect of a processor write to BR). The sequential machine responds to $SR_7\downarrow$ by setting TR and going to state q_1, where it waits for $RDY = 0$. When $RDY = 0$, the machine clears TR and goes to q_2, where it waits for $RDY\uparrow$. When $RDY\uparrow$ occurs, the machine sets SR_7 and returns to q_0 to wait for another byte from the processor.

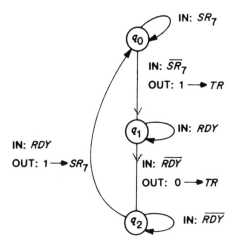

Figure 6.32   POC sequential operation

It is left as an exercise to construct the output specification table defined jointly by this sequential machine and the system bus communication table, Table 6.4.

The sequential machine of Figure 6.32 holds the byte at PD until the output device sets $RDY = 1$. The output device need not have a buffer register to hold the character.

An alternative is to assume that the output device has a buffer register which is loaded by $TR\uparrow$ or $TR = 1$ or $TR\downarrow$. This would allow a new character

TABLE 6.4.   POC system bus communication

CS	A_0	RW	POC operation
0	x	x	No operation
1	0	1	$SR \to D$
1	0	0	$D_0 \to SR_0$
1	1	1	$BR \to D$
1	1	0	$D \to BR; 0 \to SR_7$*

*$SR_7\downarrow$ activates a sequential machine that transfers the byte in BR to the output device and sets $SR_7 = 1$ when finished.

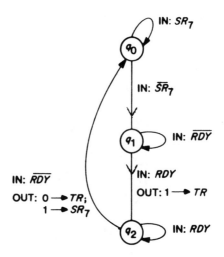

Figure 6.33   An alternative sequential machine

to be sent to *BR* before the output device is ready for the next *TR*↑. This alternative is implemented in Figure 6.33.

A Parallel Input Controller

Consider next the design of a parallel input controller (PIC) chip. The terminals on the PIC are the same as on the POC except that signal directions on the IO side are reversed, as shown in Figure 6.34.

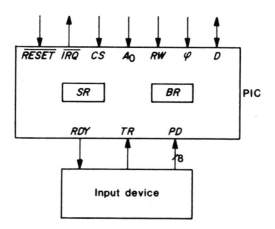

Figure 6.34   PIC registers and terminals

The PIC also has the same internal registers as the POC, SR and BR. The buffer register is loaded from the input port PD, and the processor reads BR via the system bus. SR_7 is 1 when there is a byte in BR waiting for transfer to the processor. It is cleared when the processor reads a byte.

The protocol for controlling communication between PIC and an input device is as follows:

1. PIC holds $RDY = 1$ to indicate that BR is empty.

2. The input device holds a byte at PD and sets $TR = 1$.

3. In response to $TR\uparrow$, PIC loads PD into BR and clears RDY.

4. The input device clears TR (this may be concurrent with 3).

5. After the processor reads BR, PIC sets $RDY = 1$ to indicate that it is ready to receive another byte.

This is exactly the same as the POC protocol described previously, with PIC playing the role of the output device in Figure 6.29, and the input device playing the role of POC.

System bus communication with PIC is defined in Table 6.5. It is the same as POC-bus communication (Table 6.4), except the side effect $0 \rightarrow SR_7$ occurs with a read from BR rather than a write to BR, and a write to BR does nothing. Also, of course, the sequential operation that is initiated by $SR_7\downarrow$ is an input transfer rather than an output transfer.

TABLE 6.5. PIC-system bus communication

CS	A_0	RW	PIC operation
0	x	x	No operation
1	0	1	$SR \rightarrow D$
1	0	0	$D_0 \rightarrow SR_0$
1	1	1	$BR \rightarrow D; 0 \rightarrow SR_7$*
1	1	0	No operation

*$SR_7\downarrow$ activates the sequential machine that controls the transfer of one byte from the input device into BR, and sets $SR_7 = 1$ when finished.

The DU and CU structure for the PIC chip is exactly the same as for the POC (Figure 6.31) except for three things:

1. BR is loaded from PD rather than from D, and BR does not drive PD.

2. RDY and TR must be interchanged (i.e., RDY is an extended output, and TR is an unsynchronized input).

3. $\overline{RESET} = 0$ clears SR_0, SR_7, and Q.

The sequential operation of PIC is defined in Figure 6.35. This sequential machine, together with Table 6.5, defines the CU combinational network. Construction of the output specification table is left as an exercise.

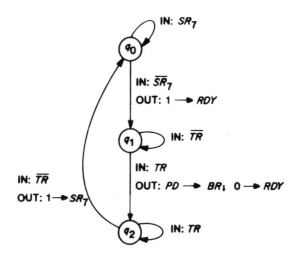

Figure 6.35   PIC sequential operation

6.3.4   Serial Port IOCs

A serial port IOC transfers characters to and/or from an IO device one bit at a time. In this section we discuss the "serial communication" in general terms. It is left as an exercise to design an IOC with a serial IO port.

The Synchronization Problem

The fundamentals of serial communication are illustrated in Figure 6.36. Data is transmitted 1 bit at a time via the transmit data terminal (TD), and received 1 bit at a time via the receive data terminal (RD). The clock input

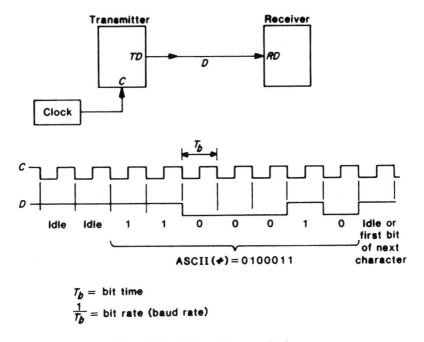

Figure 6.36   Basic serial communication

determines the bit transfer rate (i.e., 1 bit may be transferred during each clock cycle).

Each of these terminals (*TD*, *RD*, and *C*) is normally provided on a serial port IOC. Usually the IOC is capable of sending characters via *TD* and receiving characters via *RD* simultaneously (called "full duplex" operation).

If two devices are each equipped with a serial port (e.g., an IOC and an IOD, or IOCs from two different systems), they can communicate with each other if the *TD* terminal of each port is connected to the *RD* terminal of the other port. Synchronization of this communication may require other connections, however, as we shall see.

When a serial port IOC does not have a character to transfer, it holds the *TD* terminal at the *idle* level, which we will assume to be 1. When it does transfer a character, it transfers the bits in consecutive clock periods, rightmost bit first, as illustrated in Figure 6.36.

In order for the receiver to interpret the signal at *RD* properly, two problems must be solved:

1. The receiver must determine when to look at *RD* to obtain each bit that is sent (called "bit synchronization").

2. The receiver must determine where the idle bits end and the information bits begin (called "character synchronization").

In order to solve these problems, more information is required by the receiver. Depending upon how this information is supplied, several different types of serial communication are possible. We will describe three standard types: synchronous, isosynchronous, and asynchronous.

Synchronous Communication

Synchronous serial communication is illustrated in Figure 6.37. This type of communication is used whenever the transmitter can send a large number of information bits consecutively, with no intervening idle bits. For example, if ASCII characters are being transmitted, perhaps the transmitter would send 128 characters.

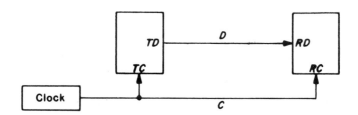

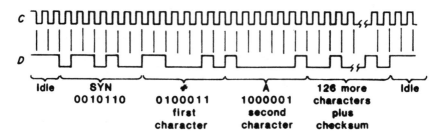

Figure 6.37 Synchronous serial communication

Bit synchronization is provided by using the same clock to drive the C input of both transmitter and receiver. The transmitter puts a new bit at TD with each $C\downarrow$, and the receiver samples RD with each $C\uparrow$.

Character synchronization is provided by a "synchronization character." In Figure 6.37 the ASCII SYN character is used. While the transmitter is waiting for a full block of characters to be ready for transfer, it holds $TD = 1$

(the idle level). When the block is ready, the transmitter sends SYN first, and then all the characters of the block with no break. Usually the information characters are followed by one or more "error control" characters. For example, a *checksum* is the sum of all the characters sent, with carries discarded.

The receiver looks at *RD* with each *C*↑. When it sees the last bit of the SYN character, it assumes that the bits to follow will be the information bits and then the checksum. It computes its own checksum while receiving the information characters and compares it with the checksum that it receives. If they do not match, it sets an error flag.

Isosynchronous Communication

Isosynchronous serial communication is illustrated in Figure 6.38. Bit synchronization is again provided by the clock *C*. Character synchronization, however, is provided for each character individually by "start" and "stop" bits.

This type of communication is used when characters may be transmitted at irregular intervals (i.e., "asynchronously") rather than in blocks. Each character transmission begins with a start bit (0 level) and ends with at least one stop bit (1 level). Between the stop bit(s) of one character and the start bit of

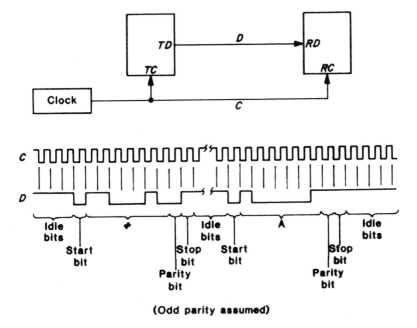

Figure 6.38   Isosynchronous serial communication

the next character, any number of idle bits may be inserted. Idle bits are inserted if the next character is not ready for transmission. If the next character is ready, no idle bits are inserted, but the stop bit is always required. A parity bit is normally added to each character for error detection (see Section 1.1).

Asynchronous Communication

Asynchronous serial communication is illustrated in Figure 6.39. This type has the advantage that it is not necessary to transmit the clock pulse with the data. Bit synchronization is provided by a high-frequency receiver clock in conjunction with the use of start and stop bits as in isosynchronous communication. The start and stop bits also provide character synchronization.

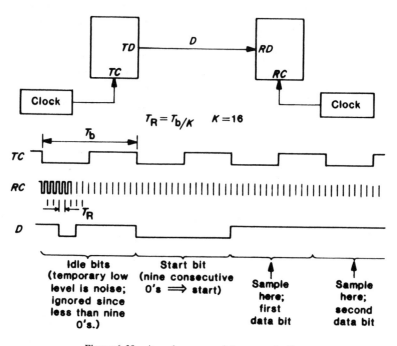

Figure 6.39   Asynchronous serial communication

The baud rate is agreed upon in advance by the transmitter and receiver. The frequency of the receiver clock is then adjusted to be K times this baud rate, that is, $T_R \simeq T_b/K$. Only "approximate equality" can be expected here, since the transmitter and receiver clocks are independent. For the same reason, the phase relationship is entirely random. A typical value for K is 16. This is the value used in Figure 6.39.

The transmitter operates exactly as in Figure 6.38, framing every character sent with a start bit and stop bit(s). The receiver detects the start bit by sampling RD with every trailing edge of the receiver clock. When $K/2$ consecutive 0's have been received, the receiver assumes that the middle of the start bit is at RD. K clock periods later the receiver samples RD again, assuming that the first data bit is present. It continues in this fashion, sampling RD every Kth clock period. Since the number of information bits per character is agreed upon in advance, the receiver knows where a stop bit should occur. (If a 0 occurs where a stop bit should be, character synchronization has been lost. This is sometimes called a "framing error.") After receiving the required stop bit(s), the receiver begins looking for the next start bit, and the process repeats.

Bit synchronization, as well as character synchronization, is renewed with every start bit. Hence even though T_R is not exactly T_b/K as desired, reliable communication is still possible. For example, suppose that the number of information bits (data plus parity) is 8. If $T_R = 1.05T_b/K$, then the receiver samples at about $0.55T_b$ for the first data bit, $0.6T_b$ for the second, etc. The stop bit is sampled at $0.95T_b$, almost too late. However, since the receiver will resynchronize on the next start bit, the frequency error does not accumulate further, and reliable communication is still achieved.

Usually an IOC does not have separate TC and RC terminals. Instead, a single clock input is provided which is used directly as RC, and is internally divided by K to obtain TC.

6.3.5   Exercises

1. (Address assignment.) Suppose that a system has seven memory chips, each $2^{13} \times 8$, and eight IOC chips, each with four or fewer address inputs. Propose an address assignment for the system (like Figure 6.24). Show the bus connections and the address map.

2. (Address assignment.) Suppose that a system has three memory chips, each $2^{12} \times 8$, and four IOC chips, each with four or fewer address inputs and two CS inputs. Propose an address assignment (like Figure 6.24) which does *not* use any chips other than those above. (It is permissible to have addresses that select more than one chip. These addresses must never be used, of course.)

3. (Complex buses.) Suppose that a bus cycle requires a minimum of four clock periods instead of one, so that the clock can be run about four times as fast. What additional processor pins will be required to control read and write operations?

4. (Complex buses.) Suppose that the processor has a READY input which can be pulled low to extend bus cycles that communicate with slow external chips. Draw timing diagrams to show how this might work.

(a) With a 6800-type bus

(b) With the bus of Exercise 3.

What advantage does the higher frequency clock have?

5. (Complex buses.) Suppose that 16 processor pins, $AD\langle 15:0 \rangle$, are shared for addresses and data. (For simplicity, suppose memory registers are 16 bits instead of 8 bits.) During the first part of a bus cycle, the address can be sent out on AD and "latched" into an external address register EAR. Data is transferred during the second part of the cycle. An address strobe output AS must be provided to load EAR.

(a) Draw a block diagram of such a system showing P, M, IOC, and EAR. Also show AD, A, D, and AS.

(b) Draw timing diagrams of read and write cycles. Assume four clock periods per cycle.

6. (OSC.) Explain how the design of the OSC must be modified to provide each of the following capabilities:

(a) Allow a 16-bit pulse width specification

(b) Allow program selection of: the active edge of X ($X\uparrow$ or $X\downarrow$); the sense of the output pulse ($Y\uparrow\downarrow$ or $Y\downarrow\uparrow$); retriggerable or non-retriggerable operation

7. Design a program-controlled IOC version of a selectable frequency clock (Exercise 11 in Section 6.2).

8. (POC.) Construct the output specification table for the IOC defined by Figures 6.29 to 6.32 and Table 6.4.

9. (POC.) Design an IOC with a parallel output port which generates a strobe pulse at TR in an "open loop" fashion rather than by "handshaking" with the IO device. Let the width of the TR pulse be determined by $SR\langle 4:1 \rangle$. Let the "sense" of the TR pulse be determined by SR_5.

10. (PIC-keyboard.) An ASCII keyboard has a 7-bit output port $OUT\langle 6:0 \rangle$ and a strobe output ST. When a key is pressed, the ASCII code for that key is held at OUT and a pulse $ST\uparrow\downarrow$ is generated.

(a) Use the PIC to interface the keyboard to the system bus.

(b) Write a subroutine to get one character from the keyboard.

(c) Write an interrupt service routine to respond to keyboard interrupts. Also, write a program to initialize interrupt operation.

11. (PIC-POC.) Connect computer A to computer B by connecting the POC of A to the PIC of B. Write programs to control the transfer of a block from the memory of A to the memory of B.

12. Study the data sheet of a commercially available parallel port IOC (e.g., Motorola 6820 or Intel 8255A).

(a) Use this chip to connect the printer of Section 1.1.5 to the system bus.

(b) Write programs to set up this interface and to transfer a block under direct control.

(c) Under interrupt control.

(d)-(f) Same as (a)-(c) but for the keyboard of Exercise 10 rather than the printer.

(g) Do an RT level design of the chip.

13. (Serial port IOC.)

(a) Design a serial port IOC that is capable of full-duplex asynchronous communication. Use the 74198 circuit for serial-parallel and parallel-serial conversion.

(b) Interface a terminal to the system bus using your IOC.

(c) Write programs to transfer characters to and from the terminal.

14. Study a commercially available serial IOC chip (e.g., Motorola 6850, Intel 8251A). Using this chip, repeat Exercise 13(b) and (c).

6.4 DMA CONTROLLERS [2, 3, 5, 44, 55]

6.4.1 **Specifications**
6.4.2 **Minimizing Chip Area**
6.4.3 **Data Unit**
6.4.4 **Control Unit**
6.4.5 **Chip Layout**
6.4.6 **Exercises**

In this section, a simple DMA controller is designed. This DMAC was described briefly in Section 1.1.5 and a program was written which sets up this DMAC to print a block of characters. It may be helpful to review Section 1.1.5 before proceeding.

In Section 6.3, we developed a general register transfer system design technique. We did not consider one important aspect of microcircuit design, however: minimization of chip area. We chose components on the basis of convenience rather than minimum size.

In this section, we will design an nMOS implementation of the DMAC with minimization of chip area in mind. Level-controlled rather than edge-controlled registers will be used for this reason, and this will lead to the use of a two-phase clock. The design technique of Section 6.3 will apply directly, but a few additional complexities will arise, primarily from the use of level-controlled registers and the two-phase clock.

6.4.1 Specifications

The general specifications for the operation of the DMAC that we will design were discussed in Section 1.1. Detailed specifications follow

Registers and Terminals

The DMAC registers and terminals are shown in Figure 6.40. Most of the terminals connect to the system bus as described in Section 6.3 for IO controllers. Note, however, that the A terminals are bidirectional for the DMAC, whereas they were input-only terminals for the IOCs. These terminals serve as inputs to the DMAC when the processor is bus master; specifically, they are used for internal register selection during bus cycles when the DMAC chip is selected. When the DMAC is bus master, the A terminals serve as outputs since the DMAC must supply the address for bus cycles that it initiates.

The transfer request terminal $\overline{TRQ}$ does not connect to the system bus. As noted in the figure, it will normally be driven by the $\overline{IRQ}$ output of an IOC. There are exceptions to this, however, which will be discussed later. A pull-up resistor is needed to hold $\overline{TRQ}$ high when the connected $\overline{IRQ}$ is not asserted, since $\overline{IRQ}$ is an open-collector output which can pull low but not high.

The status register contains a ready flag and an interrupt enable bit which operates in the standard fashion as described in Section 6.3 for IOCs. The "ready" condition is that the DMAC is free to transfer a block (i.e., it is not currently in the midst of a block transfer).

Two bits of the status register $SR\langle 2:1 \rangle$ are used to select one of four types of transfer, as indicated in the figure. In Section 1.1.5 an example was presented of the DMAC used for a memory-to-output-device type of transfer. The same DMAC may be used for each of the other types as well.

There are two address registers, SA and DA. When $SR_2 = 0$, SA holds the address of an "input port" (usually a buffer register in an IOC); when $SR_2 = 1$, SA holds the address of the next byte in the memory to be transferred. Hence, when $SR_2 = 1$, SA will be incremented after each byte transfer, but when $SR_2 = 0$, SA will remain fixed.

In similar fashion, DA may contain a memory address or an output port address, as determined by SR_1. DA is incremented after each byte transfer when $SR_1 = 1$, but remains fixed when $SR_1 = 0$.

For transfer types 01 and 10, $\overline{TRQ}$ is connected to $\overline{IRQ}$ of an IOC, as suggested in Figure 6.40. For an input-port-to-output-port transfer (type 00), the appropriate $\overline{TRQ}$ connection is less obvious. This input should be asserted (i.e., $\overline{TRQ} = 0$) when both the input IOC and the output IOC are ready for a byte transfer. Hence, the OR of the two $\overline{IRQ}$ outputs should be connected to $\overline{TRQ}$, so that $\overline{TRQ}$ is pulled low only when both $\overline{IRQ}$ outputs are low. In some cases it may be known that one device will always be ready before the other, so the $\overline{IRQ}$ of the slower device alone can drive $\overline{TRQ}$.

For a memory-to-memory type of transfer, the $\overline{TRQ}$ input can be ignored by the DMAC since the memory is always ready. In fact, rather than returning control of the bus after each byte transfer, the DMAC can retain control of the bus and transfer the entire block in consecutive bus cycles when doing a memory-to-memory transfer.

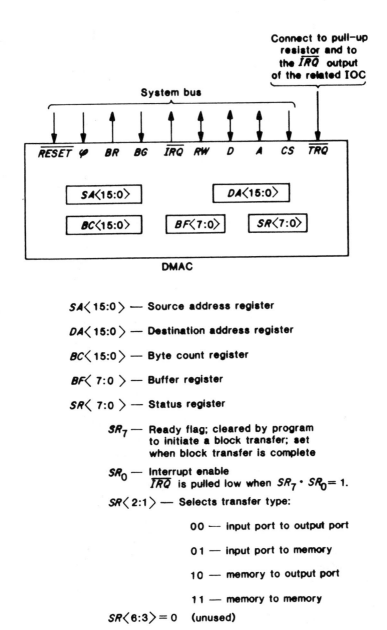

SA⟨15:0⟩ — Source address register

DA⟨15:0⟩ — Destination address register

BC⟨15:0⟩ — Byte count register

BF⟨7:0⟩ — Buffer register

SR⟨7:0⟩ — Status register

SR_7 — Ready flag; cleared by program to initiate a block transfer; set when block transfer is complete

SR_0 — Interrupt enable
$\overline{IRQ}$ is pulled low when $SR_7 \cdot SR_0 = 1$.

SR⟨2:1⟩ — Selects transfer type:

00 — input port to output port

01 — input port to memory

10 — memory to output port

11 — memory to memory

SR⟨6:3⟩ = 0 (unused)

Figure 6.40 DMAC registers and terminals

System Bus Communication

Table 6.6 specifies the operation of the DMAC during bus cycles when the DMAC acts as a bus slave. All operations are standard, except that bits $\langle 6:3 \rangle$ of SR are unused.

TABLE 6.6. DMAC system bus communication

$A\langle 2:0 \rangle$	Selected register
000	SAH ⎫
001	SAL ⎪
010	DAH ⎪
011	DAL ⎬ Write only
100	BCH ⎪
101	BCL ⎭
110	$SR*$
111	Unused

*A read from SR will always find $SR\langle 6:3 \rangle =$ 0. A write to SR will write only to 4 bits: $D\langle 2:0 \rangle \rightarrow SR\langle 2:0 \rangle$, $D_7 \rightarrow SR_7$. Writing 0 to SR_7 initiates a block transfer. Writing 1 to SR_7 terminates any block transfer in progress, except memory to memory. DMAC will automatically set SR_7 upon completion of any block transfer.

Clearing SR_7 by a write to SR initiates a block transfer. A block transfer in progress may be terminated by setting SR_7, except for memory-to-memory transfers, which cannot be terminated. Termination will take place between byte transfers, never in the middle of a transfer (i.e., after a byte has been read, but before it has been written). After termination, the same block transfer can be resumed from the point of termination by clearing SR_7.

Each 16-bit register is assigned two consecutive addresses, one for each half. The half-registers are thus accessible individually via 8-bit instructions, such as LDAA and STAA. Alternatively, the full 16-bit register can be accessed by using the address of the high half with the LDX and STX instructions.

The 16-bit registers are specified to be write only. The DMAC will leave the D bus floating during a read from any of these addresses. This is not a serious constraint on the user, but results in a considerable savings in circuitry.

6.4.2 Minimizing Chip Area

We could implement the DMAC just as we implemented the IOCs of Section 6.3. Three 16-bit registers are needed, two that can count up and one that can count down. The 74169 circuit can be used to implement these. Also needed are two simple registers, *BF* and *SR*, that may be implemented by using *D*-type flip-flops. Data paths must be provided for loading these registers from the D bus, and buffers for driving the *A* and *D* buses.

A design such as this could easily be implemented as a microcircuit. The 74169 circuit, the D flip-flops, and the buffers and gates needed could be implemented at the electronics level in the desired technology. The components could then be laid out and interconnected on the chip surface, either manually or with the help of programs that are available for this purpose.

The resulting design will not be very good, however, if minimization of chip area is a major concern. The principal components (i.e., the 74169, edge-controlled D-type flip-flops) are convenient to use and allow the design to be done quickly, but a high price is paid in chip area.

In this section, we will design an nMOS microcircuit implementation of the DMAC with minimization of chip area in mind. The design process will be essentially the same as in Section 6.3. However, due to the simplicity of the components used, timing and control considerations will be somewhat more complex.

Level-Controlled Registers

The registers and flip-flops that we used in Section 6.3 were convenient largely because they were edge-controlled. Level-controlled registers are simpler in construction (Section 5.4) and, hence, require less chip area. However, they are more difficult to use.

The principal difficulty with level-controlled registers is the *race condition* that exists when there is a "feedback loop" from register output to register input, as illustrated in Figure 6.41. Such a loop exists, for example, in a sequential network (e.g., a control unit) since the next state to be loaded into the state register is a function of the current state. A feedback loop also exists within the 74169 circuit in order to implement the count operations (e.g., $Y + 1 \rightarrow Y$).

Figure 6.41(b) shows the timing of the operation $f(Y) \rightarrow Y$, assuming that LDY↓ evokes the operation. It is desired to load the value $\beta = f(\alpha)$ into Y. Notice that X remains stable at value β until after *LDY↓* occurs, hence there is no difficulty in satisfying the setup requirement for the operation. X changes shortly after LDY↓, but since the hold requirement is typically very small, this is no problem either.

Figure 6.41(c) shows the timing of the same operation, assuming that the register is level-controlled. When *LDY* goes to 1, β is loaded into Y as desired. However, this change quickly races around to the input X, which then changes to $\gamma = f(\beta)$. Since LDY is still asserted, γ is now loaded into Y.

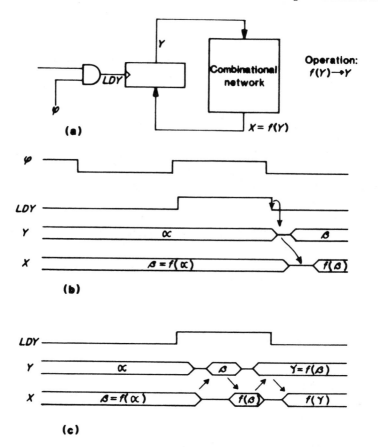

Figure 6.41   Race problem: (a) typical circuit; (b) timing if edge-controlled; (c) timing if level-controlled.

For example, if $f(\alpha) = \alpha + 1$ (as for the 74169 count operation), then the register will increment twice for the single LDY pulse shown. If the pulse were yet wider, Y would increment three times.

If the $LDY\downarrow$ pulse were just the right width, then Y would change only once and then remain stable. But it is impractical to use the register in this way. "Just the right width" for one register is not the right width for another. Hence, registers must be carefully matched and the clock pulse carefully adjusted to get the proper operation. But then when the temperature changes, or when components change with age or must be replaced, the circuit may no longer work properly.

In the circuit of Figure 6.41, X is a function of Y only. The same race problem exists in the more general situation where X is a function of other variables as well. For example, the combinational network may have another input Z, so that $X = f(Y, Z)$.

This is the case, for example, in a sequential network, where the next state is a function of both the current state and the network inputs.

Two-Phase Clocking

If it is desired to use level-controlled registers to conserve chip area, then two-phase clocking of some sort is normally used to manage the race problem. A two-phase clock may be generated from a single-phase clock using a circuit such as the one shown in Figure 5.51.

The idea of two-phase clocking is illustrated in Figure 6.42. In any feedback loop from the output of a register back to its input, there must be included a second register which is clocked by the opposite clock phase. The

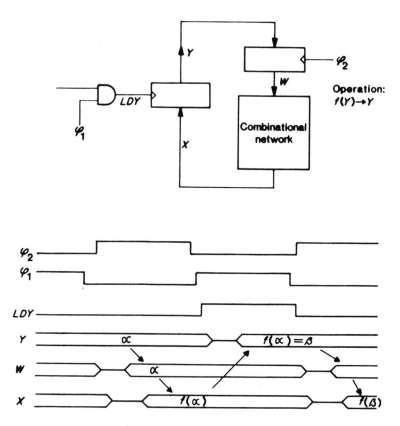

Figure 6.42   Two-phase clocking

circuit of Figure 6.42 is the circuit of Figure 6.41(a) with the necessary register inserted in the feedback loop.

The registers Y and W in Figure 6.42 are both level-controlled. The feedback register W is loaded each clock period during ϕ_2 (i.e., while $\phi_2 = 1$) with
the value in register Y. Register Y is loaded during ϕ_1. No race problem exists
because W holds the old value of Y stable during ϕ_1 while the new value is
being loaded.

6.4.3 Data Unit

A proposed data unit for the DMAC is shown in Figure 6.43. All registers are
level-controlled. Marked next to each register is the clock phase during which
the register is loaded.

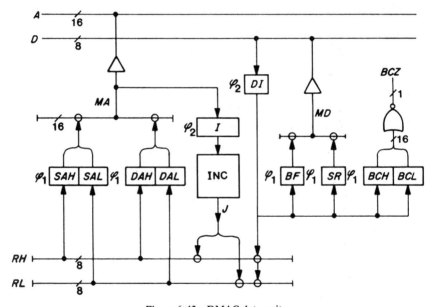

Figure 6.43   DMAC data unit

Each of the 16-bit registers has two load operations, one for the high half
and one for the low half. The BC register, in addition, has a 16-bit decrement
operation.

The SA and DA registers both need a 16-bit increment operation. To conserve chip area, the increment hardware is shared between the two. The feedback register I is also shared between SA and DA.

The *DI* register is used to "latch" data from the D bus during ϕ_2. This data may then be loaded into any of the other registers during ϕ_1.

The two clock phases are generated using the circuit of Figure 5.51. Notice that ϕ_2 corresponds to ϕ (i.e., $\phi_2 = 1$ when $\phi = 1$) except for two gate propagation delays. The gate propagation delays are exaggerated in Figure 5.51. At a frequency of 1 or 2 MHz, ϕ and ϕ_2 can be considered essentially identical.

Since the major DMAC registers are loaded during ϕ_1, the timing for this circuit will be similar to the timing of the circuits of Section 6.3. The falling edge of ϕ was used to load all registers in Section 6.3. Except for a few gate propagation delays, $\phi\downarrow$ corresponds to $\phi_2\downarrow$, which corresponds to $\phi_1\uparrow$.

Registers

To conserve chip area, all data unit registers are constructed using the nMOS dynamic register cell of Figure 5.64.

SA, DA, BF, SR, I, and DI. Figure 6.44 shows the implementation of the *SA* register. There are two load control inputs, *LDSAH* and *LDSAL*. The "(p1)" after these names indicates that these are pulse signals generated by ANDing a level signal with ϕ_1. Hence, *SAH* or *SAL* (or both) may be loaded during ϕ_1 from the high or the low half of the R bus (or both).

Every cell of the register is refreshed during every ϕ_2. (Refer to Section 5.4 if you do not recall why "refreshing" is necessary.)

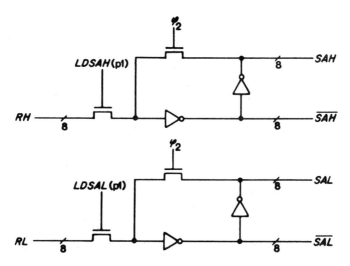

Figure 6.44 *SA* register implementation

The *DA* register is implemented in exactly the same fashion as *SA*. *BF* is also the same, except that it is only 8 bits and is loaded directly from *DI* rather than from the R bus. There is only one control input to *BF*, *LDBF*(p1).

The *I* and *DI* registers are shown in Figure 6.45. These registers are loaded during every ϕ_2, hence no control signals are required and no refreshing is required.

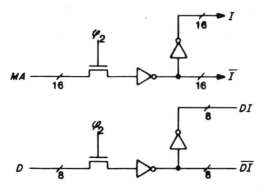

Figure 6.45   *I* and *DI* registers

Both *I* and *DI* are temporary registers. *I* is the feedback register in the increment *SA* and *DA* loops. *DI* holds the data from the D bus stable after ϕ_2 so that it can be loaded into destination registers during ϕ_1.

The *SR* register is shown in Figure 6.46. The standard dynamic register cell is used to implement 4 bits of this register, as shown. Bits $\langle 6:3 \rangle$ are tied to ground, so that $SR\langle 6:3 \rangle = 0$.

Two control signals are needed to operate *SR*. *LDSR* loads DI_7 into SR_7 and $DI\langle 2:0 \rangle$ into $SR\langle 2:0 \rangle$. $SETSR_7$ loads 1 into SR_7. The *RESET* connections are also shown. When $RESET = 1$ ($\overline{RESET} = 0$), $1 \rightarrow SR_7$ and $0 \rightarrow SR_0$.

BC Register.   *BC* is the most complex register in the DMAC. It must have a decrement operation as well as high and low load operations. An nMOS implementation of this register is shown in Figure 6.47.

To understand this implementation, examine the counting sequence for the base 2 code. Notice that to count down from any value to the next lower value, bit *i* should be inverted if bits $i - 1$ through 0 are all 0, but if any of these bits are 1, then bit *i* remains unchanged. For example, the next count down from $\alpha\langle 3:0 \rangle = 1100$ is 1011. Note that bits $\langle 2:0 \rangle$ are inverted since $\alpha\langle 1:0 \rangle = 00$. Bit 3 remains the same since $\alpha_2 = 1$.

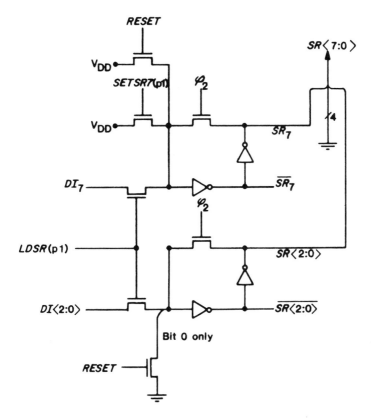

Figure 6.46 *SR* register

The iterative circuit of Figure 6.47(a) is based upon the above observation. The variable Z_i is 0 if bits $BC\langle i - 1:0 \rangle$ are all 0. If $Z_i = 0$, then BC_i should be complemented for the decrement operation. As noted in Figure 6.47(b), Z_{i+1} is easily formed from Z_i and BC_i. Hence, stage i of the BC register computes Z_{i+1} for the next stage using the value of Z_i passed to it by the previous stage.

The input Z_0 to stage 0 is 0 because stage 0 always inverts when decrementing. The output $\bar{Z}_{16}$ of the last stage is the single-bit output BCZ of Figure 6.43. This bit is 1 if and only if all bits of BC are 0.

The table of Figure 6.47(b) specifies the value to be loaded into BC_i during ϕ_1 for each BC register operation. The first two rows are the high and low load operations. The next two rows define the decrement operation: either BC_i or $\overline{BC_i}$ is loaded into BC_i, depending upon the value of Z_i, as discussed

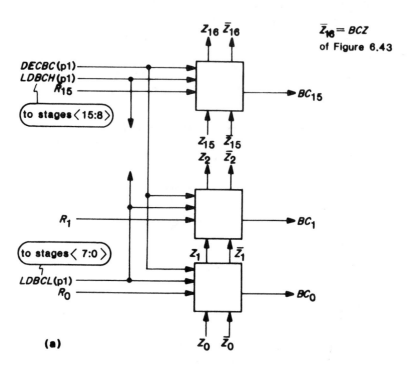

(a)

LDBCH	LDBCL	DECBC	Z_i	Value to load to BC_i during φ_1
1	0	0	x	R_i for $i = \langle 15{:}8 \rangle$
0	1	0	x	R_i for $i = \langle 7{:}0 \rangle$
0	0	1	0	$\overline{BC_i}$
0	0	1	1	BC_i
0	0	0	x	None

$Z_0 = 0$

for $i = 0, 1, \ldots, 15$

$Z_{i+1} = BC_0 + BC_1 + \cdots + BC_i$
$= Z_i + BC_i$

(b)

Figure 6.47   BC register: (a) iterative circuit; (b) cell operation; (c) cell circuit

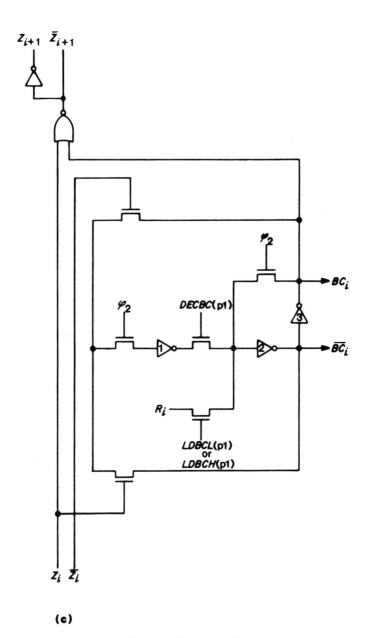

(c)

Figure 6.47   (continued)

above. The last row indicates that nothing is loaded into BC during ϕ_1 if no operation is requested.

The table does not specify what happens when multiple simultaneous operations are requested. We could define a priority structure as for the 74169, but this requires extra circuitry. We will simply make simultaneous requests illegal (i.e., operation undefined). The high and low load operations, however, can actually be done simultaneously.

Figure 6.47(c) shows the circuit for each cell of Figure 6.47(a). The heart of the circuit is the standard dynamic register cell (inverters 2 and 3). This cell is refreshed during each ϕ_2. It may be loaded during ϕ_1 with either R_i or the output of inverter 1. The pass transistor that loads R_i into BC_i is controlled by $LDBCL$ for $i = \langle 7:0 \rangle$ and by $LDBCH$ for $i = \langle 15:8 \rangle$.

The pass transistor that loads the output of inverter 1 into BC_i is controlled by $DECBC$. From the table of Figure 6.47(b), this should be either BC_i or $\overline{BC_i}$, depending upon the value of Z_i. Inverter 1, together with the pass transistor at its input, serves as the feedback register needed in this closed loop. This register is loaded during ϕ_2 with either BC_i or $\overline{BC_i}$ depending upon the value of Z_i. Z_i controls the pass transistor that loads $\overline{BC_i}$ and $\overline{Z_i}$ controls the pass transistor that loads BC_i. The complement of the loaded value appears at the output of inverter 1. This value will be loaded into BC_i during the next ϕ_1 if $DECBC = 1$.

Buses

To conserve chip area, the simple bus structure of Figure 5.11 will be used for all internal buses.

R, MD, and D.   The R, MD, and D buses are shown in Figure 6.48. The word in register DI may be placed on either the high half or the low half of the R bus. The control signals are $DITRH$ and $DITRL$. The 16-bit output of the increment network can also be placed on R, by the control signal JTR.

The registers that are loaded from the R bus (SA and DA) are always loaded during ϕ_1. Hence, the bus needs to carry information only during ϕ_1. The bus control signals, therefore, are ϕ_1 pulse signals. The bus is precharged during every ϕ_2. This allows faster operation since the bus is driven by ordinary gates (to conserve chip area), which can pull down faster than they can pull up (see Section 5.1).

The MD bus is used to supply the input to the external D bus driver. Since the D bus carries information during ϕ_2, MD must also carry information during ϕ_2. Hence, the control signals that put BF or SR onto the MD bus are ϕ_2 pulse signals, and the MD bus is precharged during ϕ_1.

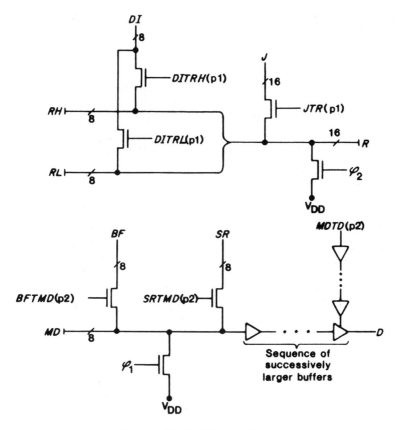

Figure 6.48   *R*, *MD*, and *D* buses

The capacitance of the external *D* bus may be several orders of magnitude larger than the capacitance of the internal *MD* bus (since the *D* ports of several chips may be connected to this bus). The *D* bus driver must, therefore, be capable of sourcing and sinking relatively large currents to charge and discharge this capacitance quickly (e.g., milliamps for the external bus compared with microamps for the internal bus).

The current drive capability of a buffer is made large by making the buffer very wide. The drain-source resistance of a minimum-size transistor is about 10^4 Ω (see Chapter 2). A transistor of the same length but 100 times as wide has a drain-source resistance of 100 Ω. Unfortunately, this transistor also has a gate capacitance 100 times that of a minimum-size transistor.

If a large output buffer is driven by a minimum-size buffer, then the small buffer will switch very slowly because of the large capacitance of the output buffer. Switching time is minimized if the large output buffer is driven by a sequence of buffers, with each buffer larger than the preceding buffer by a factor e, the base of the natural logarithms [26]. A factor of 4, however, is almost as good for speed and is much better for chip area.

In Figure 6.48, a sequence of successively larger buffers is shown from MD to D. If each buffer is four times larger than the preceding buffer and there are four buffers, then the output buffer will be 64 times larger than the first buffer.

The signal that controls the output buffer must itself drive a large capacitance. Hence, a sequence of successively larger buffers is used to generate this control signal also.

MA, A, and RW. The MA, A, and RW buses are shown in Figure 6.49. A and RW are external buses and hence each is driven by a sequence of successively larger buffers. The same signal, BE (bus enable), controls the final tristate buffer for each of these buses.

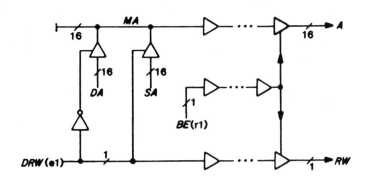

Figure 6.49 MA, A, and RW buses

BE is an "(r1)" type signal. This is a "register-extended" signal, which is generated by loading a refreshed dynamic register cell during ϕ_1 (see "CU Structure" below). BE is set when the DMAC assumes control of the system bus and cleared when it relinquishes control.

While $BE = 1$, MA is held on the A bus and DRW is held on the RW bus. DRW is an (e1)-type control signal. This is a simpler form of extended signal generated by loading a simple dynamic register cell every ϕ_1. DRW is loaded with a 1 for a read cycle and 0 for a write cycle.

In addition to driving the RW bus, DRW is used to select the address to be placed on MA, and hence A. The source address is held on MA for a read cycle, and the destination address for a write cycle.

The Increment Network

An implementation of the increment network is shown in Figure 6.50. The increment operation is similar to the decrement operation implemented previously. To count up from any word to the next higher word, bit i is complemented if all bits $i - 1$ through 0 are 1, otherwise bit i is unchanged. An iterative network based on this observation is shown in Figure 6.50(a). $C_i = 1$ if $I_j = 1$ for $j = \langle 0 : i - 1 \rangle$. $J_i = I_i$ if $C_i = 0$ and $J_i = \bar{I_i}$ if $C_i = 1$.

A standard logic gate implementation of the iterative network cell is shown in Figure 6.50(b). This implementation requires 15 transistors. An alterna-

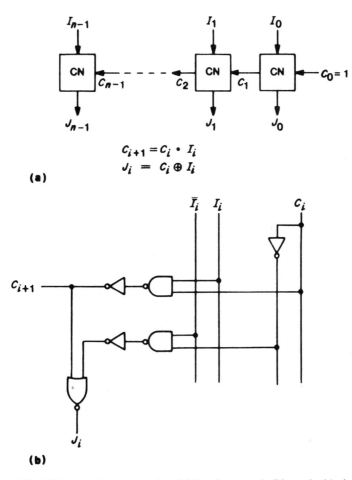

$$C_{i+1} = C_i \cdot I_i$$
$$J_i = C_i \oplus I_i$$

(a)

(b)

Figure 6.50 INC network implementation: (a) iterative network; (b) standard logic gate implementation of cell i; (c) another implementation of cell i; (d) iterative network with buffers

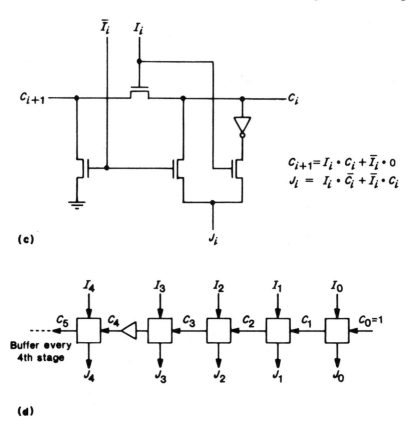

Figure 6.50   (continued)

tive implementation requiring only 6 transistors is shown in Figure 6.50(c). This implementation uses the tree network structure of Section 3.3.3.

An iterative network constructed directly from the cells of Figure 6.50(c) will be slow because C_{16}, in the worse case, must charge through a sequence of 16 pass transistors, each with a resistance of about 10^4 Ω (assuming minimum-size transistors). This propagation delay can be reduced significantly by including a buffer every few stages, as shown in Figure 6.50(d).

6.4.4   Control Unit

Control unit design is a bit more complex for a system using level-controlled registers and a two-phase clock than for a system using edge-controlled registers and a single-phase clock. The basic design procedure, however, remains the same.

Sequential Operation

The sequential operation of the DMAC is specified by the state diagram of Figure 6.51. Sequential operation is initiated by a system bus write operation to register SR which clears SR_7. When this happens, the CU leaves state q_0 and goes to either q_5 or q_1, depending upon whether the requested transfer is memory-to-memory or not.

If the requested block transfer is not memory-to-memory, the CU goes to q_1, where it waits for its $\overline{TRQ}$ input to be pulled low. $\overline{TRQ}$ is pulled low when the associated IOC(s) is (are) ready for a byte transfer. When this happens, the CU requests use of the system bus by setting $BR = 1$, and then waits in q_2 for $BG = 1$. When the processor has completed its current instruction cycle, it will relinquish control of the system bus and set $BG = 1$.

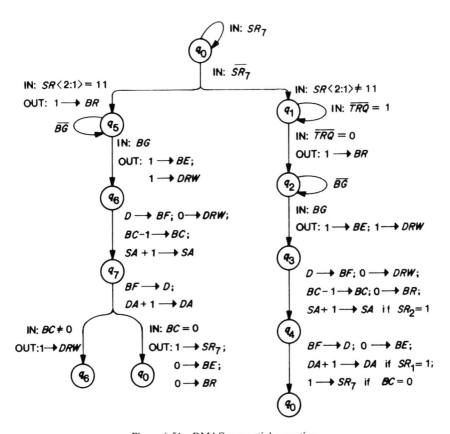

Figure 6.51   DMAC sequential operation

The DMAC CU responds by leaving q_2 and setting BE to enable its A and RW bus drivers, and setting DRW in preparation for a read operation during the next clock period.

In state q_3 the read operation occurs and the CU loads the data on the D bus into BF, via the temporary register DI. The DI register holds the data from D stable during ϕ_1 when BF is loaded. This is a necessary function since the data is stable on D only during ϕ_2. To be more specific, we could have written $D \rightarrow DI \rightarrow BF$ instead of just $D \rightarrow BF$. For the sake of brevity, however, we will usually not include intermediate registers such as DI and I when writing register transfer operations.

BR is cleared in state q_3 so that the processor will be notified one clock period in advance that it may resume control of the bus. This allows bus mastership to be transferred with no lost bus cycles.

SA is incremented in q_3 if the source of the block transfer is memory rather than an input device (see Figure 6.40).

DRW is cleared in preparation for a write operation during the next clock period.

In state q_4 a write operation is performed (since $DRW = 0$). BF is held on the D bus (via MD) during ϕ_2.

BE is cleared, so that the DMAC A and RW bus drivers will be disabled at the end of this clock period.

DA is incremented if the destination of the block transfer is memory rather than an output device.

SR_7 is set if the block transfer is complete.

The next state after q_4 is q_0. If SR_7 has been set, either by the CU itself in state q_4 or by a processor write to SR, then the CU remains in state q_0. If SR_7 is still 0, then the CU goes to q_1 where it waits to transfer the next byte (assuming $SR\langle 2:1 \rangle \neq 11$ still).

The state sequence q_1 through q_4 is used for any type of block transfer except memory-to-memory. For a memory-to-memory transfer ($SR\langle 2:1 \rangle = 11$), the CU goes to state q_5 from q_0 and immediately requests the bus (since there is no IO device to wait for).

After gaining control of the bus in state q_5 ($BG = 1$), the CU goes to q_6, where it reads a byte from memory into BF, decrements BC, and increments SA.

From q_6 the CU goes to q_7, where it writes the byte in BF to $M[DA]$, increments DA, and then checks BC. If $BC \neq 0$, it goes back to q_6 to transfer the next byte. If $BC = 0$, then the block transfer is complete. The CU sets SR_7, clears BR, clears BE, and returns to q_0.

CU Structure

The different types of control signals that can be generated using dynamic registers and a two-phase clock are illustrated in Figure 6.52. Noninverting

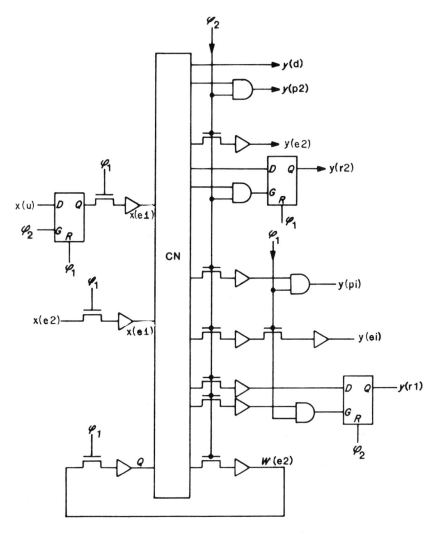

Figure 6.52   CU structure (functional)

gates are used in this figure to avoid the confusion associated with signal inversions. Representative timing diagrams are shown in Figure 6.53.

State Register

At the bottom of the figure, note that the feedback loop contains two dynamic registers clocked by opposite clock phases, to avoid a race condition. Timing for the state change operation is shown in lines 3–5 of Figure 6.53. Note that

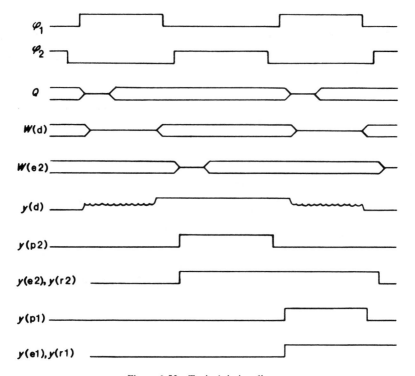

Figure 6.53   Typical timing diagrams

the timing for Q is essentially the same as for the single-phase systems of Section 6.3 with $\phi = \phi_2$: Q changes shortly after $\phi_2\downarrow$ and remains stable until the next $\phi_2\downarrow$.

Outputs

Direct outputs are generated directly by the CU combinational network, CN. As for single-phase systems, transients at the beginning of each clock period are unavoidable because the CN inputs are changing. See the y(d) line of Figure 6.53.

By making the interval $[\phi_1\uparrow, \phi_1\downarrow]$ long enough, we can assure that any transients in y(d) subside before $\phi_2\uparrow$. Hence, a clean pulse signal, y(p2), can be generated as shown.

Alternatively, a direct signal may be "extended" by loading the direct signal into a dynamic register. This type of signal is identified by the suffix "(e2)."

An (e2)-type signal can be held constant with no transients over any number of clock periods by loading the same value in each clock period. In single-phase systems, this corresponds to the extended signal implementation of Figure 6.8 (except that the signal changes after $\phi_2\uparrow$ rather than after $\phi_2\downarrow$).

The y(r2) output in Figure 6.52 shows another way to implement an extended signal, using a dynamic register cell with refresh (Figure 5.64). This

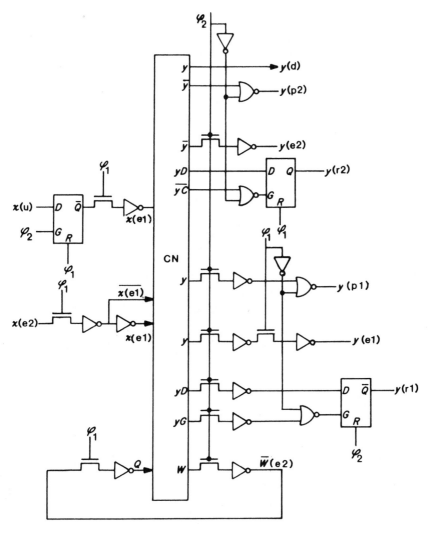

Figure 6.54   CU structure (nMOS)

corresponds to the extended-signal implementation of Figure 6.9. We will call this a "register-extended" signal.

A (p1)-type signal is formed by ANDing an (e2) signal with ϕ_1. An (e2) signal is stable throughout ϕ_1, hence a full-width pulse with no transients is produced.

An (e2) signal may be converted into an (e1) signal by loading the (e1) signal into a dynamic register during ϕ_1. Alternatively, an (e2) signal may be loaded into a dynamic register cell with refresh to produce an (r1) signal.

Inputs

An input that is asynchronous with respect to the clock may be synchronized as shown in Figure 6.52. The unsynchronized input, $x(u)$, is sampled during ϕ_2 by a refreshed register cell. During ϕ_1 the feedback path is enabled, resulting in the familiar bistable circuit (cross-coupled inverters). The bistable circuit may be unstable at $\phi_1\uparrow$ if $x(u)$ was changing near the end of ϕ_2. The circuit will resolve to a stable state soon after $\phi_1\uparrow$ (except when metastable operation occurs).

The CN requires an input that changes just after $\phi_1\uparrow$ and then remains stable through the next ϕ_2, like the state register output Q—i.e., an (e1)-type signal. The output of the sampling cell, however, changes during ϕ_2 since this is the sampling period. The proper type of CN input is produced by loading this output into a dynamic cell during ϕ_1, as shown. The output of the dynamic cell is the required (e1)-type signal.

If metastable operation is a significant problem, then one of the more elaborate synchronization schemes discussed in Section 5.5.4 will be necessary.

If an input is synchronized with the clock, but changes during ϕ_2 instead of ϕ_1—i.e., an (e2)-type signal—then the input may be loaded into a dynamic cell as shown to produce the desired (e1)-type signal. That is, only the second half of the general synchronizer is needed.

nMOS Structure

In the nMOS technology, inverters are easier to implement than noninverting buffers, and NOR gates are easier to implement than AND gates. We used noninverting buffers and AND gates in Figure 6.52 because most people find these gates easier to think about. The same control signal types, however, can be generated using the preferred nMOS gates, as shown in Figure 6.54.

Figure 6.54 was obtained from Figure 6.52 by replacing each noninverting buffer with an inverter and each AND gate with a NOR gate. Direct outputs, clock signals, and register cell outputs were inverted where necessary to ensure that the final control output would be unchanged. The "asserted level" of each direct output is indicated inside the CN box. For example, to produce a positive pulse at $y(p2)$, the direct output should be asserted low, indicated by the $\bar{y}$ in the CN box.

Reset Operation

The state register may be reset as shown in Figure 6.55(a). The *RESET* pull-down transistor must be large enough (i.e., have low enough resistance) to override the pass transistor enabled by ϕ_2.

Register-extended signals (r1) and (r2) may also be initialized by *RESET*, via direct set or direct clear inputs as shown in Figure 6.55(b). The *DS* and *DC* transistors must be large enough to override the *R* and *G* transistors.

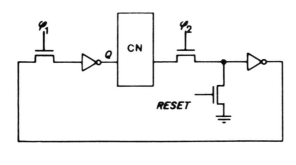

(a)

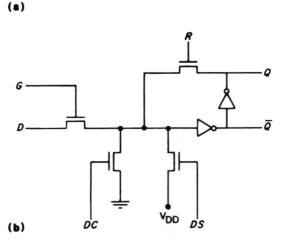

(b)

Figure 6.55   Reset operation: (a) state register; (b) direct set and direct clear

DMAC CU Structure

The CU structure for the DMAC specifically is shown in Figure 6.56. All CU inputs and outputs are shown.

None of the inputs to CN require synchronization since they are already (e1) or (r1) signals. The $\overline{RESET}$ input, however, is asynchronous, and requires full synchronization as shown. The synchronized signal $RESET$ (e1) is not a

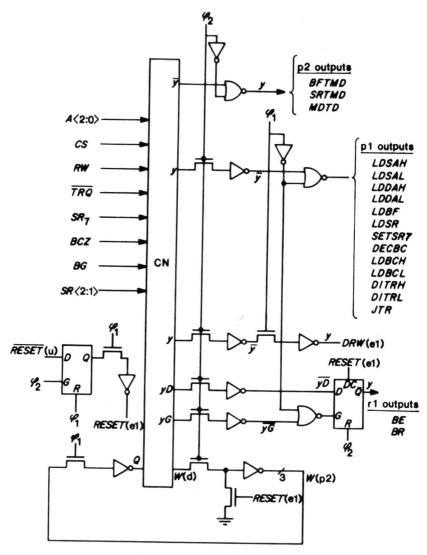

Figure 6.56   DMAC CU structure

CN input. Instead, it goes directly to the DC or DS inputs of the flip-flops that must be initialized, as well as to the state register.

Output Specification Table

The output specification table for the combinational network of the DMAC control unit is easily constructed from Figures 6.51 and 6.56 and Table 6.6. Several rows of the table are given in Table 6.7. It is left as an exercise to provide the missing rows.

Notice that the direct output for the $BFTMD$ signal is complemented since it is a (p2)-type output (see Figure 6.56). Hence, $BFTMD$(d) must be 0 when we want $BFTMD$(p2) $= 1$, and $\overline{BFTMD}$(d) must be 1 when we want $BFTMD$(p2) $= 0$.

TABLE 6.7. Partial output specification table

Direct output	Must be 0	Must be 1	Don't care
$LDSAH$	All others	$CS \cdot \bar{A}_2 \cdot \bar{A}_1 \cdot \bar{A}_0 \cdot \overline{RW}$, $q_3 \cdot SR_2$, q_6	None
$LDSAL$	All others	$CS \cdot \bar{A}_2 \cdot \bar{A}_1 \cdot A_0 \cdot \overline{RW}$, $q_3 \cdot SR_2$, q_6	None
$LDSR$	All others	$CS \cdot A_2 \cdot A_1 \cdot \bar{A}_0 \cdot \overline{RW}$	None
$SETSR_7$	All others	$q_4 \cdot BCZ$, $q_7 \cdot BCZ$	None
JTR	$CS \cdot \bar{A}_2 \cdot \overline{RW}$	$q_3 \cdot SR_2$, $q_4 \cdot SR_1$, q_6, q_7	All others
$\overline{BFTMD}$	q_4, q_7	$CS \cdot A_2 \cdot A_1 \cdot \bar{A}_0 \cdot RW$	All others
DRW	q_3, q_6	$q_2 \cdot BG$, $q_5 \cdot BG$, $q_7 \cdot \overline{BCZ}$	All others
BRG	All others	$q_1 \cdot TRQ$, q_3, $q_0 \cdot \overline{SR}_7 \cdot SR_2 \cdot SR_1$, $q_7 \cdot BCZ$	None
BRD	q_3, $q_7 \cdot BCZ$	$q_1 \cdot TRQ$, $q_0 \cdot \overline{SR}_7 \cdot SR_2 \cdot SR_1$	All others

Timing

A timing diagram illustrating the operation of the DMAC is shown in Figure 6.57. The diagram shows the control signals, buses, and registers involved in the $SA + 1 \rightarrow SA$ operation in state q_6.

Notice the similarity to single-phase timing, with the single-phase clock ϕ corresponding to ϕ_2. The same clock edge ($\phi_1\uparrow \cong \phi_2\downarrow \cong \phi\downarrow$) which loads the next state q_7 into the state register also loads the destination register SA.

Timing analysis for a two-phase system is straightforward if we insist that any signal that serves as a data or control input to an operation must be stable

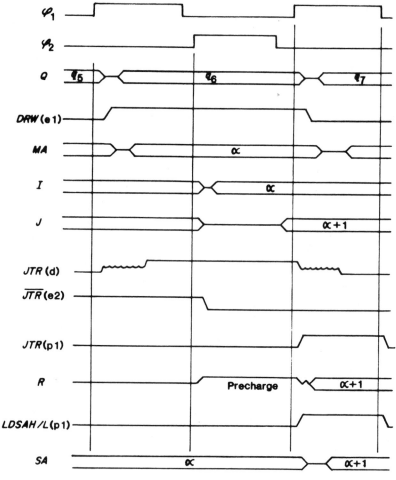

Figure 6.57   Timing diagram

before the pulse signal that evokes the operation goes to its asserted level. For the $SA + 1 \rightarrow SA$ operation, this means that J must be stable before the $LDSAH$ and $LDSAL$ signals go up at the beginning of q_7. The critical path is from $\phi_2\uparrow$ to $I<$ to $J<$. The delay along this path must be less than the time from clock edge $\phi_2\uparrow$ to the next $\phi_1\uparrow$ in order to ensure that J is stable before $LDSAH/L\uparrow$.

6.4.5   Chip Layout

In Chapter 5 we noted that the chip area devoted to wiring could be reduced considerably by distributing and interlacing components over the surface of a chip. We applied this principle at the logic design level in implementing decoders, PLAs, ROMs, etc. by distributing the transistors that comprise logic gates over the chip surface. In this section, we show how this distribution principle applies at the register transfer level.

DU Layout

Figure 6.43 is a functional block diagram of the DMAC data unit. If the DMAC chip were laid out in this way (i.e., with each component implemented on the chip surface in the position it occupies in Figure 6.43), there would be much more of the chip devoted to wiring than necessary. There also would be many more "crossovers" to deal with (i.e., wires that must cross without connecting or forming a transistor).

The distribution principle might be applied to the layout of this DU as illustrated in Figure 6.58. The MA and R bus lines are interlaced with each other across the top of the layout. The MD and DI lines are interlaced across the bottom half.

The MD and DI lines are duplicated on the left and right sides of the layout. This was not absolutely necessary. However, MD and DI are only 8 bits wide, while MA and R are 16 bits, and DI must connect to both halves of R. The duplication of the MD and DI lines produces a symmetrical layout, which makes the necessary connections convenient.

Interlaced among the data paths are the DMAC components. A typical cell of one component, the SA register, is shown as an example in Figure 6.59.

Control lines in general run perpendicular to the data lines. Control signals for the SA register are included in Figure 6.58, as an example. The signals that put DI onto RH and RL are also shown. Other control signals are not shown. Also not shown are the V_{DD} and ground lines that must go to every cell.

The DI register and the connections between the two sets of MD and DI lines are not shown. These would be at the bottom of the layout. Also not

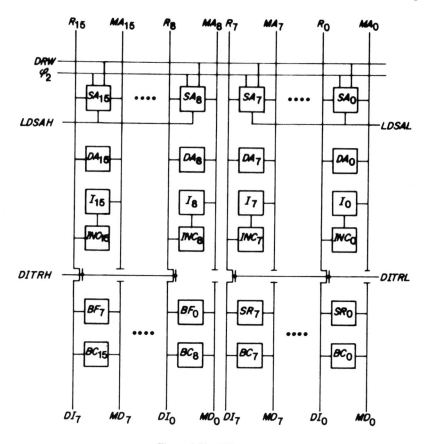

Figure 6.58   DU layout

shown are the buffers connecting *MA* to *A* and *MD* to *D*. These, and the large bonding pads to which they connect, would be around the perimeter of the chip.

CU Layout

The heart of the DMAC control unit, pictured in Figure 6.56, is the combinational network CN. This network may be implemented as a programmable logic array (Section 5.2.4) as illustrated in Figure 6.60.

Assuming that the state is represented by three state variables, the PLA has 15 inputs. Since both the inputs and their complements must be available to form products, there are 30 input lines running through the array across the product lines. Also running perpendicular to the product lines are 24 output

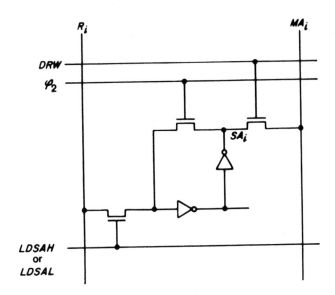

Figure 6.59   *SA* cell

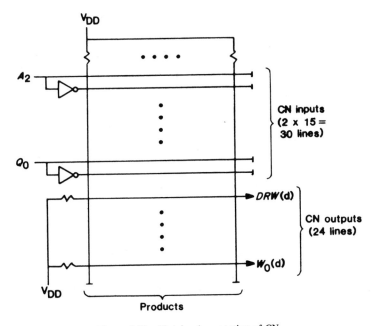

Figure 6.60   PLA implementation of CN

lines, including 3 next state variables. Not shown in the figure are the ground lines that must run through the array between input lines and between product lines, as shown in Figure 5.45.

The distribution principle can be applied in laying out the CU on the chip, as shown in Figure 6.61. Rather than keeping input lines and output lines in two separate groups as in Figure 6.60, inputs and outputs are interlaced. Outputs are generated where they are needed by the DU. Input lines are placed in spaces between output lines.

Input and output lines across from the *SA* register are shown as an example. Other inputs and outputs follow the same pattern.

The CSG block represents the circuitry that generates pulse and extended control signals from direct signals, as shown in Figure 6.56. The state register

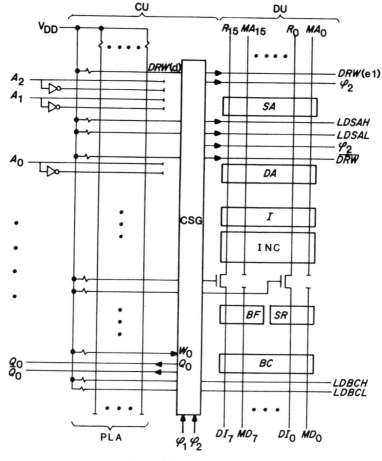

Figure 6.61   CU-DU layout

is included in this block, since W is a direct output and Q is an (e1)-type signal generated from W; that is, $W(e1) = Q$. At the bottom of Figure 6.61, notice that W_0 is a PLA output, an input to CSG; Q_0 and $\overline{Q}_0$ are outputs from CSG that extend across the product lines and, hence, serve as inputs to the PLA.

Not shown in Figure 6.61 are the DI register and the buffers from MD to D, from MA to A, and from DRW to RW. The buffers require a great deal of chip area. They can be placed around the perimeter of the circuitry in Figure 6.61 where chip area is available.

6.4.6   Exercises

1. Figure 1.15 shows the DMAC connected to allow DMA-controlled block transfers to the printer. Write a program to initiate a memory-to-memory block transfer using the same DMAC connections.

2. What will happen if $SR\langle 2:1 \rangle$ is changed while a block transfer is in progress?

3. Complete Table 6.7.

4. Redesign the OSC of Section 6.3.2, using level-controlled registers and a two-phase clock, as for the DMAC.

5. If there are multiple DMACs in a system, a more elaborate mechanism must be provided for sharing the system bus.

(a) One way to do this is to use a "priority encoder" to accept the BR signals from all DMAC chips and generate the BG signals to each DMAC. The priority encoder also accepts the BG output from the processor and generates the BR input to the processor. Design the required priority encoder, capable of handling up to four DMACs. Draw a block diagram of a system with four DMACs, and provide timing diagrams illustrating the operation of the priority encoder.

(b) Another way to do this is to "daisy chain" the bus grant signal from one DMAC to another. Each DMAC chip has a BGI (bus grant in) terminal and a BGO (bus grant out) terminal. The processor BG output is connected to BGI of the highest priority DMAC; BGO of this DMAC is connected to BGI of the next DMAC, etc. Modify the DMAC design to allow multiple DMACs connected in this fashion.

(c) Compare techniques (a) and (b) (i.e., discuss their relative advantages and disadvantages).

6. (Design exercises.) DMA-type controllers can be designed to perform tasks other than simple block transfers. Examples of tasks that might be useful are:

(a) Search a block for a specified character.

(b) Search a block for a specified string of characters (both the block and the string are in memory).

(c) Find the largest number in a list.

(d) Sort a list of numbers.

(e) Add a list of numbers.

(f) Add two vectors.

(g) Matrix multiply.

(h) Do floating-point arithmetic operations.

Many variations of (c) through (g) are possible, depending upon the codes used, the precision, the response to overflow, and so on.

Note to instructors: Exercises of varying complexity can be constructed around each of the tasks listed above, depending upon which design steps are to be completed. By allowing the basic components and CU structure of this section to be used directly, most of the low-level design details can be suppressed. The major effort can then be focused upon the more creative aspects of the design: the specifications (like Figure 6.40 and Table 6.6); the DU structure (like Figure 6.43); and the sequential operation (like Figure 6.51). Alternatively, macrocircuit-type components might be used, as in Section 6.3, with similar results.

Shorter exercises may be constructed by giving a partial design and asking for one or more parts to be completed. For example, given the specifications and DU structure, specify the sequential operation.

6.5 PROCESSORS [2-4, 14, 26, 46-51]

6.5.1 Fetch-Execute-Interrupt Operation
6.5.2 Data Unit and Chip Layout
6.5.3 CU Structure
6.5.4 Sequential Operation
6.5.5 Exercises

In this section a microcircuit implementation of the 6800 microprocessor is presented. This is a much more complex register transfer system than any we have encountered thus far. Producing a good implementation of a system of this size normally requires many man-months of design work, with computer assistance for optimization and simulation.

Motorola's implementation of the 6800 processor is proprietary. The implementation that is presented here was developed as an example for this text. It is not complete, nor is it optimal. It is intended only to illustrate how the basic design process developed in previous sections may be applied to the design of a large register transfer system. A commercially competitive design would require more attention to optimization, particularly to minimization of chip area. The implementation presented here, if carried to completion, would probably require significantly more chip area than is used by the actual 6800 processor.

We could have developed a microcircuit design that would be "pin compatible" with Motorola's 6800 chip. The differences in internal implementation would then be invisible to the chip user. That is, our chip could serve as a direct replacement for the Motorola chip.

For pedagogical reasons we have elected to design a chip that is not quite pin compatible. The major differences are these:

1. The number of clock periods required to fetch and execute an instruction may be different. In most cases, our implementation requires fewer clock periods.

2. Since the signals *TSC*, *DBE* and *VMA* are of secondary importance, these were not included in our design. They may be added as an exercise.

3. The RESET sequence is slightly different.

4. The interrupt response is slightly different.

5. The names *BR* and *BG* are used instead of *HALT* and *BA*.

6.5.1   Fetch-Execute-Interrupt Operation

The fetch-execute-interrupt operation of the 6800 is described in Figure 6.62. This is a more detailed version of a flowchart that was originally presented in Section 1.1 (Figure 1.9).

A low level at the $\overline{RESET}$ input overrides all other conditions and forces the processor into the *RESET* loop. When $\overline{RESET}$ is released, the *IRQ* interrupt response is disabled, the starting address is obtained from memory, and two flip-flops, *NMIFF* and *SWIFF*, are cleared. Neither of these flip-flops appeared in Figure 1.1.11. Their function will be discussed presently.

The fetch-execute-interrupt cycle begins at point $\textcircled{A}$ in the flowchart. The processor checks first for a bus request, as discussed in Section 1.1.2. Next it checks *INT*. *INT* is 1 if either $\overline{IRQ} = 0$ and $\mathbf{I} = 0$ (i.e., there is an unmasked *IRQ* interrupt request pending) or *NMIFF* = 1.

The $\overline{NMI}$ input is edge-sensitive, rather than level-sensitive like $\overline{IRQ}$. A negative transition at $\overline{NMI}$ will set *NMIFF*. *NMIFF* will remain set even if $\overline{NMI}$ returns to 1. *NMIFF* = 1 means that there is an *NMI* interrupt request pending.

Before looking at the interrupt response following *INT* = 1, let us trace the flowchart path for *INT* = 0. Byte 1 of the next instruction is fetched and put

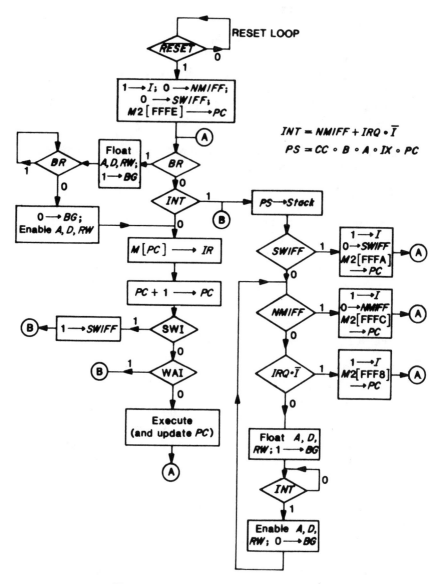

Figure 6.62   Fetch-execute-interrupt operation

into the instruction register IR. Then PC is incremented to point to the next instruction byte.

The next two decision boxes show the processor execution of the two instructions that can evoke the hardware interrupt response, which begins at point $\textcircled{B}$ in the flowchart. If register IR contains the opcode for SWI (IR = 3F), then the processor sets $SWIFF$ and then goes to point $\textcircled{B}$. If IR = 3E (the WAI instruction), the processor goes to point $\textcircled{B}$ directly.

Now examine the hardware interrupt response beginning at point $\textcircled{B}$. First the processor state is saved, as discussed in Section 1.1.2. Then the processor checks to find the source of the interrupt request. If more than one request is active, the first one checked will be honored.

$SWIFF$ will be set only if the SWI instruction is in the process of execution. In this case, the processor completes the interrupt sequence as follows:

1. Clear $SWIFF$. This flip-flop will not be set again until SWI is executed again.

2. Set the interrupt mask bit I. This disables interrupts at the IRQ level. SWI is thus designed to have a higher interrupt service priority than IRQ. Of course, the SWI service routine can override the hardware priority by clearing I. But unless this is done, IRQ interrupt requests will not be honored until after the SWI request is processed.

3. Load the address of the SWI service routine into PC. This address is obtained from the double memory register $M2[\text{FFFA}] = M[\text{FFFA}] \circ M[\text{FFFB}]$.

4. Return to $\textcircled{A}$. Note that an NMI interrupt request may take priority over SWI by causing an interrupt when INT is checked here. An IRQ request could not interrupt SWI, however, since I has been set.

If $SWIFF = 0$ and $NMIFF = 1$, then the NMI interrupt request is honored in similar fashion to the SWI request. If $SWIFF = 0$ and $NMIFF = 0$ and $IRQ \cdot \overline{I} = 1$, then the IRQ request is honored. Setting the interrupt mask bit here prevents a second response to the same IRQ interrupt request, and the possibility of an endless loop. For the same reason $SWIFF$ and $NMIFF$ are cleared in the SWI and NMI responses.

If $SWIFF = 0$, $NMIFF = 0$, and $IRQ \cdot \overline{I} = 0$, then the reason for entering the interrupt sequence can only be that the WAI instruction has been fetched. In this case, the processor responds just as though a bus request had occurred except that it monitors INT rather than BR to determine when to continue. The WAI instruction can thus be used as another way to initiate DMA activity.

Alternatively, WAI can be used simply to cause the processor to wait for an interrupt to occur, with no intention of using the bus for DMA. However, since the bus is floating and $BG = 1$, any bus request that might occur independently while the processor is waiting will be honored immediately.

After $INT = 1$, the processor resumes control of the bus and returns to respond to the IRQ or NMI request, whichever has occurred.

Most of the detail in this flowchart involves the interrupt response. This is only a relatively small portion of the processor operation, however. Most of the processor's activity actually takes place within one box of the flowchart, the execute box. This box represents the execution of all instructions except SWI and WAI. It includes fetching bytes 2 and 3 if they exist (and updating PC), computing the operand address or branch address, if any, and doing the RT operation specified by the instruction.

When any instruction byte is fetched, the processor always increments PC immediately. If the instruction is a branch and the branch condition (if any) is met, then the branch address will be loaded into PC in the execute box. Upon leaving the execute box, PC always contains the address of the next instruction to be fetched (unless an interrupt occurs).

6.5.2 Data Unit and Chip Layout

A block diagram of the DU is shown in Figure 6.63. The diagram shows all registers, combinational networks, and data paths. It also shows the intended layout of the chip. That is, the relative positions of the various components as they would be implemented on the chip are as shown in the diagram, except for distribution and interlacing of components.

General Description

There are three major combinational networks in the DU: the increment-decrement network IDN, the ALU, and the SHIFT network. IDN is capable of incrementing or decrementing a 16-bit word. The word to be incremented or decremented is first loaded into the feedback register ID, and after a propagation delay the result appears at L, from which it may be transferred to one of the 16-bit registers. IDN is also capable of passing a word unchanged to L, and hence provides a path from any 16-bit register to any other 16-bit register.

The ALU operates on two 8-bit words stored in feedback registers XR and YR. It is similar to the ALU of Section 5.2.

The SHIFT network is capable of performing various shift and rotate operations on the ALU output $Z\langle 7:0 \rangle$. These will be described later. We are using the name Z both for the 8-bit ALU output and for bit 2 of the CC register. The intended meaning should always be clear from the context.

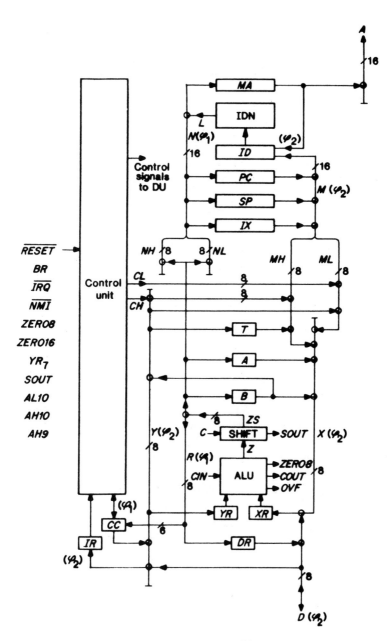

Figure 6.63   Data unit and chip layout

Each of the buses in the DU is active during one phase of the clock, and is precharged during the other phase. The active phase is indicated in parentheses beside the bus name. Any register that can be loaded from a bus must be loaded during the active clock phase for that bus.

Precharging the buses allows faster operation. However, since each bus is idle half of the time, more chip area than necessary is devoted to data paths. An alternative design might combine buses R and Y and buses M and N. This would save chip area, but would also require a decrease in clock rate. Otherwise the design would be essentially the same.

Bus R has only one input, ZS. Hence it need not be implemented as a bus; ZS could be connected permanently to R. Implementation as a bus, however, allows precharging of the data path and hence faster operation.

The DU has two independent parts, a 16-bit part and an 8-bit part. This allows a 16-bit operation and an 8-bit operation to be done in parallel during one clock period. Data may be exchanged between the 8- and 16-bit parts of the chip via several switches that connect the 8- and 16-bit buses.

The control unit can supply 8- and 16-bit words to the data unit via the CH and CL ports.

Component Implementation

Each register in the DU is a dynamic register. Figure 6.64 shows the implementation of a typical register SP. The implementation of other registers is similar. Registers XR, YR, T, DR, MA, and ID are simpler since they are never required to hold data over long periods, and hence refreshing is not required. PC and MA have separate load controls for upper and lower halves.

Notice in Figure 6.64(a) that the bus lines are interlaced with register cells, rather than run together beside the register as suggested in Figure 6.63. This reduces the amount of chip area that must be devoted to interconnections, and also reduces the number of crossovers. All registers as well as combinational networks are interlaced with buses in this fashion. The operation of the major combinational networks is defined in Figure 6.65.

The condition codes register is composed of six independent single-bit registers, as shown in Figure 6.66. The implementation of the V bit is shown in Figure 6.67. The other bits are implemented in similar fashion.

6.5.3 CU Structure

The general nMOS CU structure of Figure 6.53 is used.

Outputs

The CU outputs are listed in Table 6.8 according to type. Some of these signals have already appeared in Figures 6.64–6.69. Most of the others should be

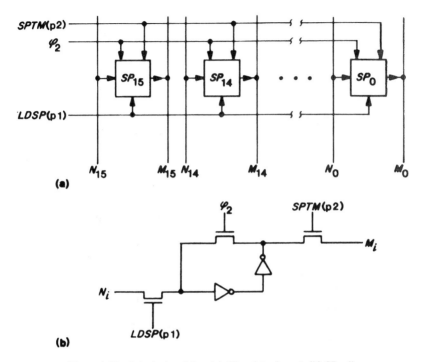

Figure 6.64   A typical register: (a) *SP* register layout; (b) *SP* cell

recognizable from the mnemonic convention used in constructing signal
names. If y is a bus, then a signal with the name "xTy" is used to put input x
onto bus y. If y is a multiple-input register, then signal xTy loads input x into
register y. If x is a single-input register, then the load control signal is LDx.

The (e1) signal PRW is the processor's RW signal. When the processor is
bus master, the processor holds PRW on the RW bus. The signal $\overline{BG}$ is used
by the processor to put PRW on RW, MA on A, and during a write cycle, DR
on D. As long as the processor is bus master, $BG = 0$ and $\overline{BG}$ thus enables
the RW and A bus drivers, and D during a write cycle. When the processor
gives up the bus it sets $BG = 1$, thus disabling all system bus drivers.

The CY signal is a "temporary carry" bit. It is used during indexed and
relative address computations to save the carry-out after adding the low bytes
of two 16-bit words. (The C bit of the CC register may not be used for this
purpose since it should change only as specified by the instructions.)

$NMIFF$ is not an ordinary (r1) signal. It is cleared by the CU at the points
indicated in Figure 6.62, but it is never set by the CU. It is set by negative
transitions of the $\overline{NMI}$ input. The implementation of $NMIFF$ is shown in Figure 6.68. The $\overline{NMI}$ input is synchronized as described in Section 6.4 (Figure
6.53), producing a synchronized signal $\overline{NMI}$(e1). The pseudo-one-shot circuit

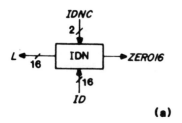

IDNC	L
0 x	ID
1 0	$ID \, \hat{+}_2 \, 1$
1 1	$ID \, \hat{-}_2 \, 1$

$ZERO16 = NOR(L)$

(a)

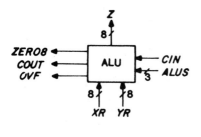

$COUT = c_8; \quad OVF = c_7 \oplus c_8$

$ZERO8 = NOR(Z)$

ALUS	Z
000	00
001	$\overline{XR} \, \hat{+}_2 \, YR \, \hat{+}_2 \, CIN$
010	$XR \, \hat{+}_2 \, \overline{YR} \, \hat{+}_2 \, CIN$
011	$XR \, \hat{+}_2 \, YR \, \hat{+}_2 \, CIN$
100	$XR + YR$
101	$XR \oplus YR$
110	$XR \cdot YR$
111	YR

(b)

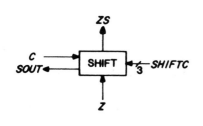

SHIFTC	SOUT ∘ ZS	Operation
000	$C \circ Z$	No shift
001	$Z_7 \circ Z\langle 6{:}0\rangle \circ C$	ROL
010	$Z_0 \circ C \circ Z\langle 7{:}1\rangle$	ROR
011	$Z\langle 7{:}0\rangle \circ 0$	ASL
100	$Z_0 \circ Z_7 \circ Z\langle 7{:}1\rangle$	ASR
101	$Z_0 \circ 0 \circ Z\langle 7{:}1\rangle$	LSR
110	Not used	
111	Not used	

(c)

Figure 6.65   Combinational network operation: (a) increment-decrement network; (b) ALU network; (c) shift network

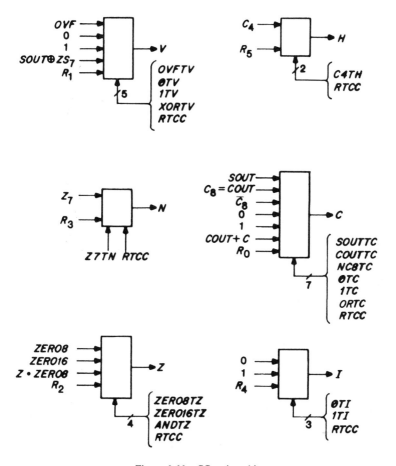

Figure 6.66   *CC* register bits

of Figure 5.53 is used to produce a *DS* pulse in response to an edge $\overline{NMI}$(e1)↓. This pulse generation, however, is disabled when *NMIFF* $= 1$. This prevents a direct set and a direct clear pulse from being produced simultaneously. The direct clear signal, *NMIDC*(p1), is generated by the CU combinational network during the hardware interrupt response.

Inputs

The CU inputs are shown in Figure 6.69, grouped according to the type of synchronization required.

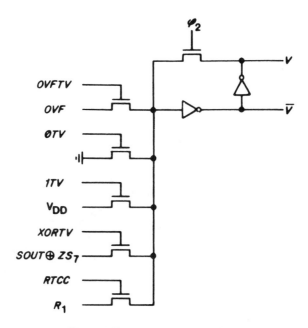

Figure 6.67   Implementation of the V bit

The first group requires no synchronization. These signals are already type (e1) or (r1) as required. All of these signals have been encountered previously, except *AL10*, *AL9*, and *AH10*. These are combinational functions of accumulator *A* which are used in the execution of the *DAA* instruction (see footnote 15 to the state table, Table 6.9).

The second group consists of (e2)-type signals (i.e., signals that change during ϕ_2). These signals must be converted to (e1)-type signals for input to CN. $IR\langle 7:0\rangle$ is the major input to the CU. More decisions are based upon these eight inputs than any others, since *IR* contains byte 1 of the instruction being executed. YR_7 is needed for sign extension during the relative address computation. *SOUT* is the bit shifted out of the shift network [Figure 6.65(c)]. It is needed during the execution of the shift and rotate instructions. *ZERO8* and *ZERO16* are outputs of the ALU and IDN networks, respectively (Figure 6.65). They are used as inputs to the *Z* bit of *CC* (Figure 6.67).

The last group consists of inputs that are unsynchronized with the clock. Full synchronization as discussed in Section 6.4 (Figure 6.52) is required.

6.5.4   Sequential Operation

In this section we define a sequential machine that represents the sequential operation of the 6800 processor.

TABLE 6.8. Control unit outputs.

(d) signals	(e2) signals	(p1) signals
$CL\langle 7:0\rangle$	$ALUS\langle 2:0\rangle$	Bus input controls:
$CH\langle 7:0\rangle$	$SHIFTc\langle 2:0\rangle$	LTN
(p2) signals	CIN	$RTNH$
	$IDNC\langle 1:0\rangle$	$RTNL$
Register load controls:		$ZSTR$
LDT	**(p1) signals**	
$LDXR$	Register load controls:	**(r1) signals**
$LDYR$	$LDMAL$	CY
$LDIR$	$LDMAH$	$SWIFF$
$MATID$	$LDPCL$	$NMIFF$
$MTID$	$LDPCH$	BG
Bus input controls:	$LDSP$	$(MATA = \overline{BG};$
$PCTM$	$LDIX$	$PRWTRW = \overline{BG};$
$SPTM$	LDA	$DRTD =$
$IXTM$	LDB	$\overline{BG} \cdot \overline{PRW} \cdot \phi_2)$
$CLTML$	$LDDR$	
$CHTMH$	$OVFTV$	**(e1) signal**
$YTML$	OTV	PRW
$TTMH$	ITV	
$MLTX$	$SOUTTC$	
$MHTX$	$COUTTC$	
ATX	$NC8TC$	
BTX	OTC	
DTX	$1TC$	
$CHTY$	OTI	
BTY	$1TI$	
$CCTY$	$C4TH$	
DTY	$Z7TN$	
$DRTD$	$ZERO8TZ$	
	$ZERO16TZ$	
	$RTCC$	
	$ORTC$	
	$XORTV$	
	$ANDTZ$	

Instruction Classes

It is convenient to identify classes of instructions that have common characteristics which enable them to be treated similarly at some point in the execution process. Each class of instructions will be represented by a binary variable that has value 1 when an instruction from that class is in *IR*. In the following, several instruction classes will be defined, and Boolean expressions for the corresponding binary variables will be given in some cases.

Each row of the instruction table, Table 1.3, defines a class of instructions that specify the same operation, but with different address modes. The in-

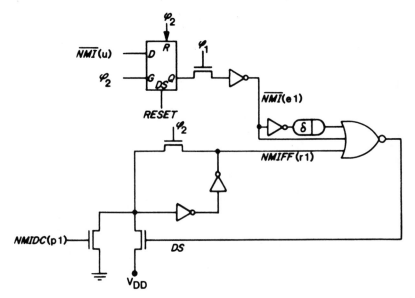

Figure 6.68   *NMIFF* implementation

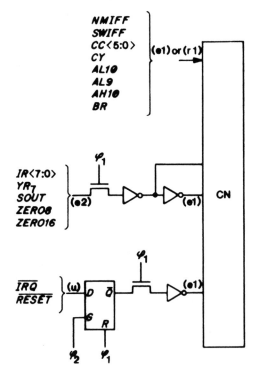

Figure 6.69   CU imputs

struction mnemonic will be used as the binary variable that represents such a class. For example, *ADDA* represents a class of four instructions having opcodes 8B, 9B, AB, and BB. Similarly, *STAB* represents a class of three instructions having opcodes D7, E7, and F7.

Boolean expressions for these instruction classes are easily obtained. Note that the second digit of the opcode is the same for all instructions in any row. Hence, when the opcode is in IR, $IR\langle 3:0\rangle$ is the same for all instructions in a class of this type. Boolean expressions are then obtained using a Karnaugh map, as illustrated in Figure 6.70 for *ADDA* and *STAB*.

Each address mode defines an instruction class. Binary variables *INH*, *DIR*, *IND*, *EXT*, *IMM*, and *REL* will be used to represent these classes. An examination of Figure 6.71 reveals that the first 4 bits of the opcode determine the address mode, with one exception (*BSR*).

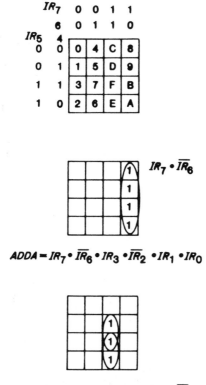

$$ADDA = IR_7 \cdot \overline{IR}_6 \cdot IR_3 \cdot \overline{IR}_2 \cdot IR_1 \cdot IR_0$$

$$TAB = (IR_7 \cdot IR_6 \cdot IR_5 + IR_7 \cdot \overline{IR}_6 \cdot IR_4) \cdot \overline{IR}_3 \cdot IR_2 \cdot IR_1 \cdot IR_0$$

Figure 6.70 Mnemonic classes: (a) hexadecimal minterm representation; (b) ADDA representation; (c) STAB representation

00	·		40	NEG	A	80	SUB	A	IMM	C0	SUB	B	IMM
01	NOP		41	·		81	CMP	A	IMM	C1	CMP	B	IMM
02	·		42	·		82	SBC	A	IMM	C2	SBC	B	IMM
03	·		43	COM	A	83	·			C3	·		
04	·		44	LSR	A	84	AND	A	IMM	C4	AND	B	IMM
05	·		45	·		85	BIT	A	IMM	C5	BIT	B	IMM
06	TAP		46	ROR	A	86	LDA	A	IMM	C6	LDA	B	IMM
07	TPA		47	ASR	A	87	·			C7	·		
08	INX		48	ASL	A	88	EOR	A	IMM	C8	EOR	B	IMM
09	DEX		49	ROL	A	89	ADC	A	IMM	C9	ADC	B	IMM
0A	CLV		4A	DEC	A	8A	ORA	A	IMM	CA	ORA	B	IMM
0B	SEV		4B	·		8B	ADD	A	IMM	CB	ADD	B	IMM
0C	CLC		4C	INC	A	8C	CPX	A	IMM	CC	·		
0D	SEC		4D	TST	A	8D	BSR		REL	CD	·		
0E	CLI		4E	·		8E	LDS		IMM	CE	LDX		IMM
0F	SEI		4F	CLR	A	8F	·			CF	·		
10	SBA		50	NEG	B	90	SUB	A	DIR	D0	SUB	B	DIR
11	CBA		51	·		91	CMP	A	DIR	D1	CMP	B	DIR
12	·		52	·		92	SBC	A	DIR	D2	SBC	B	DIR
13	·		53	COM	B	93	·			D3	·		
14	·		54	LSR	B	94	AND	A	DIR	D4	AND	B	DIR
15	·		55	·		95	BIT	A	DIR	D5	BIT	B	DIR
16	TAB		56	ROR	B	96	LDA	A	DIR	D6	LDA	B	DIR
17	TBA		57	ASR	B	97	STA	A	DIR	D7	STA	B	DIR
18	·		58	ASL	B	98	EOR	A	DIR	D8	EOR	B	DIR
19	DAA		59	ROL	B	99	ADC	A	DIR	D9	ADC	B	DIR
1A	·		5A	DEC	B	9A	ORA	A	DIR	DA	ORA	B	DIR
1B	ABA		5B	·		9B	ADD	A	DIR	DB	ADD	B	DIR
1C	·		5C	INC	B	9C	CPX		DIR	DC	·		
1D	·		5D	TST	B	9D	·			DD	·		
1E	·		5E	·		9E	LDS		DIR	DE	LDX		DIR
1F	·		5F	CLR	B	9F	STS		DIR	DF	STX		DIR
20	BRA	REL	60	NEG	IND	A0	SUB	A	IND	E0	SUB	B	IND
21	·		61	·		A1	CMP	A	IND	E1	CMP	B	IND
22	BHI	REL	62	·		A2	SBC	A	IND	E2	SBC	B	IND
23	BLS	REL	63	COM	IND	A3	·			E3	·		
24	BCC	REL	64	LSR	IND	A4	AND	A	IND	E4	AND	B	IND
25	BCS	REL	65	·		A5	BIT	A	IND	E5	BIT	B	IND
26	BNE	REL	66	ROR	IND	A6	LDA	A	IND	E6	LDA	B	IND
27	BEQ	REL	67	ASR	IND	A7	STA	A	IND	E7	STA	B	IND
28	BVC	REL	68	ASL	IND	A8	EOR	A	IND	E8	EOR	B	IND
29	BVS	REL	69	ROL	IND	A9	ADC	A	IND	E9	ADC	B	IND
2A	BPL	REL	6A	DEC	IND	AA	ORA	A	IND	EA	ORA	B	IND
2B	BMI	REL	6B	·		AB	ADD	A	IND	EB	ADD	B	IND
2C	BGE	REL	6C	INC	IND	AC	CPX		IND	EC	·		
2D	BLT	REL	6D	TST	IND	AD	JSR		IND	ED	·		
2E	BGT	REL	6E	JMP	IND	AE	LDS		IND	EE	LDX		IND
2F	BLE	REL	6F	CLR	IND	AF	STS		IND	EF	STX		IND
30	TSX		70	NEG	EXT	B0	SUB	A	EXT	F0	SUB	B	EXT
31	INS		71	·		B1	CMP	A	EXT	F1	CMP	B	EXT
32	PUL	A	72	·		B2	SBC	A	EXT	F2	SBC	B	EXT
33	PUL	B	73	COM	EXT	B3	·			F3	·		
34	DES		74	LSR	EXT	B4	AND	A	EXT	F4	AND	B	EXT
35	TXS		75	·		B5	BIT	A	EXT	F5	BIT	B	EXT
36	PSH	A	76	ROR	EXT	B6	LDA	A	EXT	F6	LDA	B	EXT
37	PSH	B	77	ASR	EXT	B7	STA	A	EXT	F7	STA	B	EXT
38	·		78	ASL	EXT	B8	EOR	A	EXT	F8	EOR	B	EXT
39	RTS		79	ROL	EXT	B9	ADC	A	EXT	F9	ADC	B	EXT
3A	·		7A	DEC	EXT	BA	ORA	A	EXT	FA	ORA	B	EXT
3B	RTI		7B	·		BB	ADD	A	EXT	FB	ADD	B	EXT
3C	·		7C	INC	EXT	BC	CPX		EXT	FC	·		
3D	·		7D	TST	EXT	BD	JSR		EXT	FD	·		
3E	WAI		7E	JMP	EXT	BE	LDS		EXT	FE	LDX		EXT
3F	SWI		7F	CLR	EXT	BF	STS		EXT	FF	STX		EXT

Notes: 1. Addressing Modes: A = Accumulator A   IMM = Immediate
                                B = Accumulator B   DIR = Direct
                               REL = Relative
                               IND = Indexed
        2. Unassigned code indicated by "·"

Figure 6.71   Instructions Listed by Opcode
(Courtesy of Motorola, Inc.)

Define $U\langle 15:0\rangle$ to be the decoded upper half of IR; that is, $U_i = 1$ if $[IR\langle 7:4\rangle]_2 = i$. Boolean expressions for the address mode classes are then easily written.

$$INH = U_0 + U_1 + U_3 + U_4 + U_5$$
$$DIR = U_9 + U_D$$
$$IND = U_6 + U_A + U_E$$
$$EXT = U_7 + U_B + U_F$$
$$IMM = (U_8 + U_C) \cdot \overline{BSR}$$
$$REL = U_2$$

(For convenience, BSR is not included in the REL group, although it does use relative addressing.) The subscript i is represented in hexadecimal rather than decimal for easy identification with machine code.

Using Karnaugh maps, the U_i variables are easily replaced by IR_i variables.

$$INH = \overline{IR_7} \cdot \overline{IR_5} + \overline{IR_7} \cdot \overline{IR_6} \cdot IR_4$$
$$DIR = IR_7 \cdot \overline{IR_5} \cdot IR_4$$
$$IND = IR_6 \cdot IR_5 \cdot \overline{IR_4} + IR_7 \cdot IR_5 \cdot \overline{IR_4}$$
$$EXT = IR_6 \cdot IR_5 \cdot IR_4 + IR_7 \cdot IR_5 \cdot IR_4$$
$$IMM = IR_7 \cdot \overline{IR_5} \cdot \overline{IR_4} \cdot \overline{BSR}$$
$$REL = \overline{IR_7} \cdot \overline{IR_6} \cdot IR_5 \cdot \overline{IR_4}$$

As we shall see later, the inherent address mode class consists of two sub-classes: those allowing fast execution, and those requiring slower execution. These subclasses are represented by $INHF$ and $INHS$.

$$INHF = (U_0 + U_1 + U_4 + U_5) \cdot \overline{INX} \cdot \overline{DEX}$$
$$= \overline{IR_7} \cdot IR_6 \cdot \overline{INX} \cdot \overline{DEX}$$
$$= \overline{IR_7} \cdot IR_6 \cdot (\overline{INX + DEX})$$
$$= \overline{IR_7} \cdot IR_6 \cdot (IR_7 + IR_6 + IR_5 + IR_4 + \overline{IR_3} + IR_2 + IR_1)$$
$$INHS = U_3 + INX + DEX$$
$$= \overline{IR_7} \cdot \overline{IR_6} \cdot IR_5 \cdot IR_4 + INX + DEX$$

The *IMM* class also consists of two subclasses, represented by *IMMF* and *IMMS*.

$$IMMF = (U_8 + U_C) \cdot (\overline{IR_3} + \overline{IR_2})$$

$$= IR_7 \cdot \overline{IR_5} \cdot \overline{IR_4} \cdot (\overline{IR_3} + \overline{IR_2})$$

$$IMMS = CPX + LDS + LDX$$

State Table

The complete sequential machine representing the sequential operation of the 6800 is specified in Table 6.9. The first column, q, represents the present state. The next column, IN, represents the input conditions. The next state is specified in column W, and the output in column OUT.

Outputs are represented by specifying the register transfer operations to be performed. Effects on the condition codes register are specified in the abbreviated notation suggested by the instruction table of Table 1.3. For example, $NZ\updownarrow$ means that N and Z are affected in the "standard fashion," as defined in Section 1.1; $V\downarrow$ means $0 \rightarrow V$; $V\uparrow$ means $1 \rightarrow V$.

The state table should be easy to read. A few of the output specifications require further explanation, which is provided in footnotes at the end of the table.

Bear in mind that this table is more than a general description of sequential operation. It is an exact specification, clock period by clock period, of the register transfer operations performed by the processor. Equations for the control unit outputs may be written directly from this table.

We have elected to use a state table rather than a state diagram because a complete state diagram would have been too cumbersome.

When reading the state table, if there is any doubt about whether the operations specified in any row can all be performed in one clock period, look back at the DU implementation and CU structure for verification. There are bound to be a few mistakes in this implementation. If you find one, try to fix it by modifying the DU, the CU structure, or the state table. Try not to introduce other errors by fixing the one you have found.

TABLE 6.9. State table

(a) Main table

	q	IN	W	OUT
①	r_0	*RESET*	r_0	Direct set and direct clear inputs are used to initialize registers as specified in ①
	r_0	$\overline{RESET}$	r_1	$FFFE \rightarrow MA$; $0 \rightarrow SWIFF$; $0 \rightarrow NMIFF$; $1 \rightarrow I$
	r_1	—	r_2	$D \rightarrow T$; $MA + 1 \rightarrow MA$ $\qquad (D = M[MA])$
	r_2	—	f_0	$T \circ D \rightarrow \begin{cases} MA \\ PC \end{cases}$
②	f_0	*BR*	h_0	$1 \rightarrow BG$; $D \rightarrow IR$; $PC + 1 \rightarrow \begin{cases} PC \\ MA \end{cases}$
③	f_0	$\overline{BR} \cdot INT$	i_0	$SP \rightarrow MA$
	f_0	$\overline{BR} \cdot \overline{INT}$	f_1	$D \rightarrow IR$; $PC + 1 \rightarrow \begin{cases} PC \\ MA \end{cases}$
	h_0	*BR*	h_0	—
	h_0	$\overline{BR}$	f_1	$0 \rightarrow BG$
④	i_0	—	i_1	$PCL \rightarrow DR$; $0 \rightarrow PRW$
	i_1	—	i_2	$PCH \rightarrow DR$; $MA - 1 \rightarrow \begin{cases} SP \\ MA \end{cases}$
	i_2	—	i_3	$IXL \rightarrow DR$; $MA - 1 \rightarrow \begin{cases} SP \\ MA \end{cases}$
	i_3	—	i_4	$IXH \rightarrow DR$; $MA - 1 \rightarrow \begin{cases} SP \\ MA \end{cases}$
	i_4	—	i_5	$A \rightarrow DR$; $MA - 1 \rightarrow \begin{cases} SP \\ MA \end{cases}$
	i_5	—	i_6	$B \rightarrow DR$; $MA - 1 \rightarrow \begin{cases} SP \\ MA \end{cases}$
	i_6	—	i_7	$CC \rightarrow DR$; $MA - 1 \rightarrow \begin{cases} SP \\ MA \end{cases}$
	i_7	—	i_8	$SP - 1 \rightarrow SP$; $1 \rightarrow PRW$

TABLE 6.9. *(continued)*
(a) Main table

q	IN	W	OUT
i_8	$WAI \cdot \overline{INT}$	i_8	$1 \to BG$
i_8	$\overline{WAI} + INT$	i_9	$IVA \to MA; 1 \to I; 0 \to BG;$ if $SWIFF = 1$ then $0 \to SWIFF;$ if $SWIFF = 0$ and $NMIFF = 1$ then $0 \to NMIFF$
i_9	—	i_{10}	$D \to T; MA + 1 \to MA$
i_{10}	—	f_0	$T \circ D \to \begin{cases} MA \\ PC \end{cases}$
f_1	$INHF \cdot BR$	h_1	$1 \to BA; D \to IR;$ $PC + 1 \to \begin{cases} MA \\ PC \end{cases};$ execute instruction in IR
f_1	$INHF \cdot \overline{BR} \cdot INT$	i_0	$SP \to MA;$ execute instruction in IR
f_1	$INHF \cdot \overline{BR} \cdot \overline{INT}$	f_1	$D \to IR; PC + 1 \to \begin{cases} PC \\ MA \end{cases};$ execute instruction in IR
h_1	BR	h_1	—
h_1	$\overline{BR}$	f_1	$0 \to BG$
f_1	$PSHA/B$	x_0	$A/B \to DR; SP \to MA; 0 \to PRW$
x_0	$PSHA/B$	x_1	$1 \to PRW; SP - 1 \to SP$
x_1	$PSHA/B$	f_0	$PC \to MA$
f_1	$PULA/B$	x_0	$SP + 1 \to \begin{cases} SP \\ MA \end{cases}$
x_0	$PULA/B$	f_0	$D \to A/B; PC + 1 \to \begin{cases} PC \\ MA \end{cases}$
f_1	DEX	f_0	$IX - 1 \to IX; Z\updownarrow$
f_1	DES	f_0	$SP - 1 \to SP$
f_1	INX	f_0	$IX + 1 \to IX; Z\updownarrow$
f_1	INS	f_0	$SP + 1 \to SP$

⑤ ⑥ ⑥ ⑥ ⑦

TABLE 6.9. *(continued)*
(a) Main table

q	IN	W	OUT
f_1	TXS	f_0	$IX - 1 \to SP$
f_1	TSX	f_0	$SP + 1 \to IX$
f_1	RTI	x_0	$SP + 1 \to \begin{cases} SP \\ MA \end{cases}$
x_0	RTI	x_1	$D\langle 5:0 \rangle \to CC;\ SP + 1 \to \begin{cases} SP \\ MA \end{cases}$
x_1	RTI	x_2	$D \to B;\ SP + 1 \to \begin{cases} SP \\ MA \end{cases}$
x_2	RTI	x_3	$D \to A;\ SP + 1 \to \begin{cases} SP \\ MA \end{cases}$
x_3	RTI	x_4	$D \to T;\ SP + 1 \to \begin{cases} SP \\ MA \end{cases}$
x_4	RTI	x_5	$T \circ D \to IX$
x_5	RTI	x_6	$SP + 1 \to \begin{cases} SP \\ MA \end{cases}$
x_6	RTI	x_7	$D \to T;\ SP + 1 \to \begin{cases} SP \\ MA \end{cases}$
x_7	RTI	f_0	$T \circ D \to \begin{cases} PC \\ MA \end{cases}$
f_1	RTS	x_0	$SP + 1 \to \begin{cases} SP \\ MA \end{cases}$
x_0	RTS	x_1	$D \to T;\ SP + 1 \to \begin{cases} SP \\ MA \end{cases}$
x_1	RTS	f_0	$T \circ D \to \begin{cases} PC \\ MA \end{cases}$
f_1	SWI	i_0	$SP \to MA;\ 1 \to SWIFF$
f_1	WAI	i_0	$SP \to MA$

TABLE 6.9. *(continued)*
(a) Main table

q	IN	W	OUT
⑧ f_1	IMMF	f_0	$PC + 1 \to \begin{cases} PC \\ MA \end{cases}$; execute instruction
⑨ f_1	CPX	im_0	$MA + 1 \to \begin{cases} PC \\ MA \end{cases}$; $IXH \mathbin{\hat{+}}_2 \bar{D} \mathbin{\hat{+}}_2 1$; $NZV\updownarrow$
im_0	CPX	f_0	$MA + 1 \to \begin{cases} PC \\ MA \end{cases}$; $IXL \mathbin{\hat{+}}_2 \bar{D} \mathbin{\hat{+}}_2 1$; $Z \cdot ZERO8 \to Z$
f_1	LDX	im_0	$PC + 1 \to \begin{cases} PC \\ MA \end{cases}$; $D \to T$; $N\updownarrow$; $V\downarrow$
im_0	LDX	im_1	$T \circ D \to IX$; $ZERO16 \to Z$
im_1	LDX	f_0	$PC + 1 \to \begin{cases} PC \\ MA \end{cases}$
f_1	LDS	im_0	$PC + 1 \to \begin{cases} PC \\ MA \end{cases}$; $D \to T$; $N\updownarrow$; $V\downarrow$
im_0	LDS	im_1	$T \circ D \to SP$; $ZERO16 \to Z$
im_1	LDS	f_0	$PC + 1 \to \begin{cases} PC \\ MA \end{cases}$
f_1	DIR	x_0	$0^8 \circ D \to MA$
f_1	$EXT \cdot \overline{JMP}$	e	$D \to T$; $PC + 1 \to \begin{cases} PC \\ MA \end{cases}$
e	$\overline{JSR}$	x_0	$T \circ D \to MA$
f_1	$IND \cdot \overline{JSR} \cdot \overline{JMP}$	ind	$D \mathbin{+}_2 IXL \to CY \circ MAL$
ind	—	x_0	$0^8 \mathbin{\hat{+}}_2 IXH \mathbin{\hat{+}}_2 CY \to MAH$
x_0	ADDA/B	f_0	$A/B \mathbin{\hat{+}}_2 D \to A/B$; $HNZVC\updownarrow$; $PC + 1 \to \begin{cases} PC \\ MA \end{cases}$
x_0	ADCA/B	f_0	$A/B \mathbin{\hat{+}}_2 D \mathbin{\hat{+}}_2 C \to A/B$; $HNZVC\updownarrow$; $PC + 1 \to \begin{cases} PC \\ MA \end{cases}$

TABLE 6.9. *(continued)*
(a) Main table

q	IN	W	OUT
x_0	$ANDA/B$	f_0	$A/B \cdot D \rightarrow A/B;\ NZ\updownarrow;\ V\downarrow;\ PC + 1 \rightarrow \begin{cases} PC \\ MA \end{cases}$
x_0	$BITA/B$	f_0	$A/B \cdot D;\ NZ\updownarrow;\ V\downarrow;\ PC + 1 \rightarrow \begin{cases} PC \\ MA \end{cases}$
x_0	CLR	x_1	$0^8 \rightarrow DR;\ NZVC\updownarrow;\ 0 \rightarrow PRW$
x_1	CLR	f_0	$1 \rightarrow PRW;\ PC + 1 \rightarrow \begin{cases} PC \\ MA \end{cases}$
x_0	$CMPA/B$	f_0	$A/B \hat{+}_2 \bar{D} \hat{+}_2 1;\ NZVC\updownarrow;\ PC + 1 \rightarrow \begin{cases} PC \\ MA \end{cases}$
x_0	COM	x_1	$0^8 \hat{+}_2 \bar{D} \rightarrow DR;\ 0 \rightarrow PRW;\ NZ\updownarrow;\ V\downarrow;\ C\uparrow$
x_1	COM	f_0	$1 \rightarrow PRW;\ PC + 1 \rightarrow \begin{cases} PC \\ MA \end{cases}$
x_0	NEG	x_1	$0^8 \hat{+}_2 \bar{D} \hat{+}_2 1 \rightarrow DR;\ 0 \rightarrow PRW;\ NZVC\updownarrow$
x_1	NEG	f_0	$1 \rightarrow PRW;\ PC + 1 \rightarrow \begin{cases} PC \\ MA \end{cases}$
x_0	DEC	x_1	$D \hat{+}_2 1^8 \rightarrow DR;\ NZV\updownarrow;\ 0 \rightarrow PRW$
x_1	DEC	f_0	$1 \rightarrow PRW;\ PC + 1 \rightarrow \begin{cases} PC \\ MA \end{cases}$
x_0	$EORA/B$	f_0	$A/B \oplus D \rightarrow A/B;\ NZ\updownarrow;\ V\downarrow;\ PC + 1 \rightarrow \begin{cases} PC \\ MA \end{cases}$
x_0	INC	x_1	$0^8 \hat{+}_2 D \hat{+}_2 1 \rightarrow DR;\ 0 \rightarrow PRW;\ NZV\updownarrow$
x_1	INC	f_0	$1 \rightarrow PRW;\ PC + 1 \rightarrow \begin{cases} PC \\ MA \end{cases}$
x_0	$LDAA/B$	f_0	$D \rightarrow A/B;\ NZ\updownarrow;\ V\downarrow;\ PC + 1 \rightarrow \begin{cases} PC \\ MA \end{cases}$
x_0	$ORAA/B$	f_0	$A/B + D \rightarrow A/B;\ NZ\updownarrow;\ V\downarrow;\ PC + 1 \rightarrow \begin{cases} PC \\ MA \end{cases}$

TABLE 6.9.   *(continued)*
(a) Main table

q	IN	W	OUT
x_0	STAA/B	x_1	$0^8 \hat{+}_2 A/B \to DR$; $NZ\updownarrow$; $V\downarrow$; $0 \to PRW$
x_1	STAA/B	f_0	$1 \to PRW$; $PC + 1 \to \begin{cases} PC \\ MA \end{cases}$
⑩ x_0	ROL/ROR/ASL/ ASR/LSR	x_1	$0^8 + D$; $0 \to PRW$; $SHIFTC = ROL/ROR/ASL/$ ASR/LSR; $SOUT \to C$; $SOUT \oplus ZS_7 \to V$; $ZERO8 \to Z$; $ZS_7 \to N$; $ZS \to DR$
x_1	ROL/ROR/ ASL/ASR/LSR	f_0	$1 \to PRW$; $PC + 1 \to \begin{cases} PC \\ MA \end{cases}$
x_0	SUBA/B	f_0	$A/B \hat{+}_2 \bar{D} \hat{+}_2 1 \to A/B$; $NZVC\updownarrow$; $PC + 1 \to \begin{cases} PC \\ MA \end{cases}$
x_0	SBCA/B	f_0	$A/B \hat{+}_2 \bar{D} \hat{+}_2 \bar{C} \to A/B$; $NZVC\updownarrow$; $PC + 1 \to \begin{cases} PC \\ MA \end{cases}$
x_0	TST	f_0	$D \hat{+}_2 0^8$; $NZ\updownarrow$; $VC\downarrow$; $PC + 1 \to \begin{cases} PC \\ MA \end{cases}$
⑨ x_0	CPX	x_1	$MA + 1 \to MA$; $IXH \hat{+}_2 \bar{D} \hat{+}_2 1$; $NZV\updownarrow$
x_1	CPX	x_2	$IXL \hat{+}_2 \bar{D} \hat{+}_2 1$; $Z \cdot ZERO8 \to Z$
x_2	CPX	f_0	$PC + 1 \to \begin{cases} PC \\ MA \end{cases}$
x_0	LDX/LDS	x_1	$D \to T$; $N\updownarrow$; $V\downarrow$; $MA + 1 \to MA$
x_1	LDX/LDS	x_2	$T \circ D \to IX/SP$; $ZERO16 \to Z$
x_2	LDX/LDS	f_0	$PC + 1 \to \begin{cases} PC \\ MA \end{cases}$
x_0	STX/STS	x_1	$IXH/SPH \hat{+}_2 0 \to DR$; $NZ\updownarrow$; $V\downarrow$; $1 \to PRW$
x_1	STX/STS	x_2	$MA + 1 \to MA$; $IXL/SPL \hat{+}_2 0 \to DR$; $Z \cdot ZERO8 \to Z$
x_2	STX/STS	f_0	$1 \to PRW$; $PC + 1 \to \begin{cases} PC \\ MA \end{cases}$

TABLE 6.9. *(continued)*
(a) Main table

q	IN	W	OUT
⑪ ⑫ f_1	$REL \cdot BCT$	rel_0	$PC + 1 \rightarrow PC$
rel_0	—	rel_1	$PCL +_2 D \rightarrow CY \circ \begin{cases} MAL \\ PCL \end{cases}$
rel_1	—	f_0	$PCH \hat{+}_2 (YR_7)^8 \hat{+}_2 CY \rightarrow \begin{cases} MAH \\ PCH \end{cases}$
⑫ f_1	$REL \cdot BCF$	f_0	$PC + 1 \rightarrow \begin{cases} PC \\ MA \end{cases}$
e	JSR	js_0	$PC + 1 \rightarrow PC$
⑬ f_1	$IND \cdot JSR$	js_0	$D \rightarrow YR; PC + 1 \rightarrow PC$
⑬ f_1	BSR	js_0	$D \rightarrow YR; PC + 1 \rightarrow PC$
js_0	—	js_1	$SP \rightarrow MA$
js_1	—	js_2	$0 \rightarrow PRW; PCL \rightarrow DR \, (ALUS = 111)$
js_2	—	js_3	$MA - 1 \rightarrow \begin{cases} MA \\ SP \end{cases}; PCH \rightarrow DR \, (ALUS = 111)$
js_3	—	js_4	$SP - 1 \rightarrow SP; 1 \rightarrow PRW$
js_4	IND	js_5	$YR +_2 IXL \rightarrow CY \circ \begin{cases} MAL \\ PCL \end{cases}$
js_5	IND	f_0	$IXH \hat{+}_2 0^8 \hat{+}_2 CY \rightarrow \begin{cases} MAH \\ PCH \end{cases}$
js_4	EXT	js_5	$PC - 1 \rightarrow MA$
js_5	EXT	f_0	$T \circ D \rightarrow \begin{cases} MA \\ PC \end{cases}$
js_4	BSR	rel_1	$PCL +_2 YR \rightarrow CY \circ \begin{cases} PCL \\ MAL \end{cases}$
f_1	$IND \cdot JMP$	jmp	$IXL +_2 D \rightarrow CY \circ \begin{cases} PCL \\ MAL \end{cases}$

TABLE 6.9. *(continued)*
(a) Main table

q	IN	W	OUT
jmp	IND	f_0	$IXH \mathbin{\hat{+}_2} 0^8 \mathbin{\hat{+}_2} CY \rightarrow \begin{cases} PCH \\ MAH \end{cases}$
f_1	$EXT \cdot JMP$	jmp	$D \rightarrow T;\ MA + 1 \rightarrow MA$
jmp	EXT	f_0	$T \circ D \rightarrow \begin{cases} MA \\ PC \end{cases}$

(b) *INHF* execution table

	IN	OUT
⑭	ABA	$A \mathbin{\hat{+}_2} B \rightarrow A;\ HNZVC\updownarrow$
	$CLRA/B$	$0^8 \rightarrow A/B;\ NVC\downarrow;\ Z\uparrow$
	CBA	$A \mathbin{\hat{+}_2} \bar{B} \mathbin{\hat{+}_2} 1;\ NZVC\updownarrow$
	$COMA/B$	$\overline{A/B} \rightarrow A/B;\ NZ\updownarrow;\ V\downarrow;\ C\uparrow$
	$NEGA/B$	$0^8 \mathbin{\hat{+}_2} \overline{A/B} \rightarrow A/B;\ NZVC\updownarrow$
⑮	DAA	$A \mathbin{\hat{+}_2} DA \rightarrow A;\ COUT + C \rightarrow C$
	$DECA/B$	$A/B \mathbin{\hat{+}_2} 1^8 \rightarrow A/B;\ NZV\updownarrow$
	$INCA/B$	$A/B \mathbin{\hat{+}_2} 0^8 \mathbin{\hat{+}_2} 1 \rightarrow A/B;\ NZVC\updownarrow$
⑯	rA/B	$D + 0^8;\ SHIFTC = ROL/ROR/ASL/ASR/LSR;\ SOUT \rightarrow C;$ $SOUT \oplus ZS_7 \rightarrow V;\ ZERO8 \rightarrow Z;\ ZS_7 \rightarrow N;\ ZS \rightarrow A/B$
	SBA	$A \mathbin{\hat{+}_2} \bar{B} \mathbin{\hat{+}_2} 1 \rightarrow A;\ NZVC\updownarrow$
	TAB	$A \mathbin{\hat{+}_2} 0^8 \rightarrow B;\ NZ\updownarrow;\ V\downarrow$
	TBA	$B \mathbin{\hat{+}_2} 0^8 \rightarrow A;\ NZ\updownarrow;\ V\downarrow$
	$TSTA/B$	$A/B \mathbin{\hat{+}_2} 0^8;\ NZ\updownarrow;\ VC\downarrow$
	CLC	$0 \rightarrow C$
	CLI	$0 \rightarrow I$
	CLV	$0 \rightarrow V$

TABLE 6.9. *(continued)*

(b) *INHF* execution table *(continued)*

IN	OUT
SEC	$1 \rightarrow C$
SEI	$1 \rightarrow I$
SEV	$1 \rightarrow V$
TAP	$A\langle 5:0 \rangle \rightarrow CC\langle 5:0 \rangle \; (A \rightarrow XR \rightarrow R \rightarrow CC)$
TPA	$0^2 \circ CC\langle 5:0 \rangle \rightarrow A$
⑰ NOP	—

(c) *IMMF* execution table

IN	OUT
⑱ ADDA/B	$A/B \hat{+}_2 D \rightarrow A/B; \; HNZVC\updownarrow$
ADCA/B	$A/B \hat{+}_2 D \hat{+}_2 C \rightarrow A/B; \; HNZVC\updownarrow$
ANDA/B	$A/B \cdot D \rightarrow A/B; \; NZ\updownarrow; \; V\downarrow$
CMPA/B	$A/B \hat{+}_2 \bar{D} \hat{+}_1 1; \; NZVC\updownarrow$
EORA/B	$A/B \oplus D \rightarrow A/B; \; NZ\updownarrow; \; V\downarrow$
LDAA/B	$D \hat{+}_2 0^8 \rightarrow A/B; \; NZ\updownarrow; \; V\downarrow$
ORAA/B	$A/B + D \rightarrow A/B; \; NZ\updownarrow; \; V\downarrow$
SUBA/B	$A/B \hat{+}_2 \bar{D} \hat{+}_2 1 \rightarrow A/B; \; NZVC\updownarrow$
SBCA/B	$A/B \hat{+}_2 \bar{D} \hat{+}_2 \bar{C} \rightarrow A/B; \; NZVC\updownarrow$

①$\overline{RESET} = 0$ initializes registers as follows: $r_0 \rightarrow Q; \; 1 \rightarrow PRW; \; 0 \rightarrow BG$. *MATA* and *PRWTRW* are initialized to 1 since $MATA = PRWTRW = \overline{BG}$.

②$1 \rightarrow BG$ disables the A, RW, and D bus drivers since $MATA = PRWTRW = \overline{BG}$ and $DRTD = \phi_2 \cdot \overline{BG} \cdot \overline{PRW}$.

③$INT = NMIFF + IRQ \cdot \bar{I}$. Hence $INT = 1$ iff there is an interrupt request pending.

④The register *PRW* is loaded with ϕ_1 of the clock period following the period in which the load operation is specified. Hence the memory write cycle occurs during state i_1.

⑤*IVA* is the interrupt vector address.

$$IVA = \begin{cases} FFFA & \text{if} \quad SWIFF = 1 \\ FFFC & \text{if} \quad SWIFF = 0 \quad \text{and} \quad NMIFF = 1 \\ FFF8 & \text{if} \quad SWIFF = 0 \quad \text{and} \quad NMIFF = 0 \end{cases}$$

IVA is provided to the DU via the $CH \circ CL$ port.

TABLE 6.9. *(continued)*

[6]The execution of the instruction in *IR* is accomplished as indicated in the *INHF* execution table.

[7]*A/B* represents either *A* or *B*. Hence *PSHA/B* represents either *PSHA* or *PSHB*, and $A/B \rightarrow DR$ represents either $A \rightarrow DR$ or $B \rightarrow DR$.

[8]The instruction execution is described in the *IMMF* execution table.

[9]*N* and *V* are affected by the comparison involving the upper half of *IX* only. *Z* is affected by the full 16-bit comparison.

[10]The "/", as in [7], denotes alternatives. Hence this row of the table actually represents five rows. All rows are identical, except for the value of *SHIFTC*. *SHIFTC* = 001 for *ROL*, 010 for *ROR*, etc.

[11]$PC + 1 \rightarrow PC$ is required here only because the 6800 branch address is specified to be $a(BYTE1) + [BYTE2]_{2C} + 2$. If this operation were omitted (and rel_0 removed) the branch address would be $a(BYTE1) + [BYTE2]_{2C} + 1$, and the branch would execute in three rather than four clock periods.

[12]*BCT* = 1 iff *REL* = 1 and the branch condition specified by the instruction in *IR* is met. *BCF* = 1 iff *REL* = 1 and the branch condition specified by the instruction in *IR* is not met. Specifically,

$$BCT = BRA + BCC \cdot \bar{C} + BCS \cdot C + BEQ \cdot Z + BGE \cdot \overline{(N \oplus V)} + BGT \cdot \overline{Z + (N \oplus V)} + BHI \cdot \overline{(C + Z)} + BLE \cdot (Z + (N \oplus V)) + BLS \cdot (C + Z) + BLT \cdot (N \oplus V) + BMI \cdot N + BNE \cdot \bar{Z} + BVC \cdot \bar{V} + BVS \cdot V + BPL \cdot \bar{N}.$$

$$BCF = BCC \cdot C + BCS \cdot \bar{C} + BEQ \cdot \bar{Z} + BGE \cdot (N \oplus V) + BGT \cdot (Z + (N \oplus V)) + BHI \cdot (C + Z) + BLE \cdot \overline{(Z + (N \oplus V))} + BLS \cdot \overline{(C + Z)} + BLT \cdot \overline{(N \oplus V)} + BMI \cdot \bar{N} + BNE \cdot Z + BVC \cdot V + BVS \cdot \bar{V} + BPL \cdot N.$$

[13]*YR* must hold data for five clock periods before it is used in this situation. The load pulse to *YR* must be inhibited.

[14]The *INHF* execution table specifies the operations that execute each of the *INHF*-type instructions during state f_1. The next state will be h_1, i_0, or f_1, as specified in the state table, depending upon the values of *BR* and *INT*. Other output operations are also performed, depending on *BR* and *INT*. The execution operations that are specified in the *INHF* table, however, do not depend upon *BR* and *INT*.

[15]$DA\langle 7:0 \rangle$ is supplied to the *ALU* via the *CH* port of the control unit.

$$DA\langle 3:0 \rangle = \begin{cases} 6 & \text{if } AL10 = 1 \text{ or } H = 1 \\ 0 & \text{otherwise} \end{cases}$$

$$DA\langle 7:4 \rangle = \begin{cases} 6 & \text{if } AH10 = 1 \text{ or } C = 1 \text{ or } (AH9 = 1 \text{ and } AL10 = 1) \\ 0 & \text{otherwise} \end{cases}$$

where

$$AL10 = 1 \quad \text{iff} \quad [A\langle 3:0 \rangle]_2 \geq 10$$
$$AH10 = 1 \quad \text{iff} \quad [A\langle 7:4 \rangle]_2 \geq 10$$
$$AH9 = 1 \quad \text{iff} \quad [A\langle 7:4 \rangle]_2 = 9$$

[16]*r* denotes any one of the following: *ROL*, *ROR*, *ASL*, *ASR*, or *LSR*. Thus this row actually represents 10 rows of the *INHF* execution table: one for each *rA* and one for each *rB*.

[17]Any unused opcode with left hexadecimal digit 0, 1, 4, or 5 will execute in the same way as *NOP*.

[18]The *IMMF* execution table specifies the operations that execute each instruction of type *IMMF* during state f_1. The next state will always be f_0, as indicated earlier in the state table. The $PC + 1 \rightarrow \left\{ \begin{matrix} PC \\ MA \end{matrix} \right.$ operation is executed for every *IMMF* instruction.

6.5.5   Exercises

Exercises in this section should involve simulation of processor operation. The following format is suggested.

Given: conditions before the simulation begins (i.e., the contents of relevant registers) and the value of processor inputs for the duration of the simulation.

Specify: the activity that occurs in the processor during each clock period for the duration of the simulation.

Exercises can vary in complexity depending upon the information to be specified. For example, any or all of the following may be requested:

1. The contents after each clock period of any processor or memory registers that change during that clock period (alternatively, the contents of only program-visible registers that change may be requested)

2. The word carried by each of the system buses during each clock period (alternatively, only the external buses: A, D, and RW)

3. The names of any control signals that are asserted during each clock period

4. Timing diagrams of selected control signals, registers, and buses.

Example Exercise Set

For each exercise below assume the following initial conditions, unless otherwise specified: $IX = 1234$, $SP = 5678$, $A = 24$, $B = 68$, $Q = f_0$, $CC = 00$, $M[\alpha] =$ last two digits of the hex address α (e.g., $M[1234] = 34$). Unless otherwise specified:

(a) Carry out the simulation for each exercise until Q returns to f_0.

(b) Assume that all inputs remain unasserted for the duration of the simulation.

(c) Trace changes in Q and in any program-visible registers (i.e., after each clock period of simulation, specify the contents of any such register that changes).

Eleven exercises follow, each with a different initial PC value.

1. $PC = 20AB$ 2. $PC = 2036$ 3. $PC = 20C2$
4. $PC = 20FE$ 5. $PC = 2025$ 6. $PC = 20AD$
7. $PC = 2097$

8. $PC = 2086$. $\overline{IRQ} = 0$ from the second clock period of simulation on. Continue simulation until Q returns to f_0 for the second time.

9. $PC = 208B$. Trace changes in *all* processor registers (not just program-visible registers).

10. $PC = 208E$. List all control signals that are asserted during each clock period.

11. $PC = 207A$. Sketch a timing diagram with the following lines: external buses A, D, and RW; internal buses X, Y, M, and N; control signals $ALUS$, $IDNC$, DTX, $PCTM$, $LDMAL$, and $LDDR$; registers Q, XR, YR, MA, and DR.

6.6   CONTROL UNIT VARIATIONS [26, 7, 8, 46–51]

6.6.1   State Registers and Codes
6.6.2   Microprogramming
6.6.3   Exercises

In this section we discuss two important variations of CU structure. These variations apply both to single-phase and two-phase systems (i.e., using edge-controlled or level-controlled registers).

6.6.1   State Registers and Codes

Until now we have used only the simplest possible state register, having only a parallel load operation. In this section the possible advantages of using more complex state registers are discussed. Also, state codes other than the standard base 2 code are considered.

Multioperation State Registers

In complex systems the equations for the W inputs to a simple parallel-load only state register can be very complex. A considerable savings can sometimes be achieved in state register input generation by using a multioperation state register.

For example when we are using the base 2 state code, transitions to the "next consecutive" state can be implemented by using a counter, transitions to q_0 by a clear operation, and loops to the same state by no operation. The state register of Figure 6.72 offers these possibilities. Such a register could be implemented using a 74163 circuit (Figure 5.75), or a level-controlled version of this circuit could be designed. The timing for the operations is intentionally left unspecified.

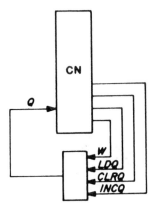

CLRQ	LDQ	INCQ	Operation	State transition
1	x	x	$0 \longrightarrow Q$	Branch to q_0
0	1	x	$W \longrightarrow Q$	q_i to q_j *
0	0	1	$Q+1 \longrightarrow Q$	q_i to q_{i+1}
0	0	0	$Q \longrightarrow Q$	q_i to q_i

$$* \; j \neq i, \; j \neq i+1$$

Figure 6.72   Multioperation state register

In addition to the parallel load input W, this register has three control inputs that must be generated by CN. The operation of the state register is defined by the table in Figure 6.72. The last column indicates the type of state transition that is represented by each operation, assuming the usual base 2 state code.

Table 6.10 is the output specification table for the DMAC of Section 6.4, using a level-controlled version of this state register (assuming the base 2 state code). The state transitions of Figure 6.50 are represented exactly by this OST.

The acronym "ACR" in the table stands for "all conditions requiring."

Notice how simple the equations for W_2, W_1, and W_0 are ($W_2 = W_1 = \bar{W}_0 = q_7 \cdot \overline{BCZ}$). This is because the value of W is a "don't care" except when the parallel load operation is used. This occurs only once in the state diagram: in state q_7 when $BC \neq 0$, the transition is to q_6, which can be achieved only by loading 110. All other state transitions are accomplished by using other state register operations.

TABLE 6.10. Output specification table

Direct output	Must be 0	Must be 1	Don't care
$CLRQ$	All others	ACR branch to q_0: q_4, $q_7 \cdot BCZ$	None
LDQ	All others	ACR branch q_i to q_j: $q_7 \cdot \overline{BCZ}$	ACR branch to q_0: q_4, $q_7 \cdot BCZ$
$INCQ$	ACR q_i to q_i transition: $q_0 \cdot \overline{SR_7}$, $q_5 \cdot \overline{BG}$, $q_1 \cdot \overline{TRQ}$, $q_2 \cdot \overline{BG}$	All others	ACR branch to q_0 or q_i to q_j: q_4, $q_7 \cdot BCZ$, $q_7 \cdot \overline{BCZ}$
W_2	ACR branch q_i to q_j, where $j = 0, 1, 2,$ or 3: none	ACR branch q_i to q_j, where $j = 4, 5, 6,$ or 7: $q_7 \cdot \overline{BCZ}$	All others
W_1	None	$q_7 \cdot \overline{BCZ}$	All others
W_0	$q_7 \cdot \overline{BCZ}$	None	All others

State Codes

The choice of a code to represent the states of a sequential machine (i.e., state assignment) is closely related to the choice of a state register, and together they can significantly affect the cost of implementation. When we are using a counter, for example, the code should be chosen to allow use of the increment operation as often as possible.

If a shift register is used, then a code that allows frequent use of the shift operation is desirable. For example, the "1-hot" code uses one state variable to represent each state. If there are four states then the words representing the four states are 0001, 0010, 0100, and 1000. This code does not require decoding to identify the state, which may be an advantage in some applications. The 1 bit circulates through the state register initiating appropriate operations in each position, much like a mechanical timer.

For a complex CU such as for the processor of Section 6.5, a compound state register, and corresponding compound state code, may be best. For example, one register may be used to represent the lowercase letter in the state name that we used, and another register could represent the subscript. The second register should have a count operation.

6.6.2   Microprogramming

Microprogramming is a technique for designing register transfer system control units. It is based upon the idea of using ROM to implement the CU combinational network. Although this idea is simple, it nevertheless leads to significant changes in CU structure.

A Hypothetical Processor

To illustrate the fundamentals of microprogramming, we will use a hypothetical 16-bit processor. The basic architecture of this processor is sketched in Figures 6.73–6.75 and Table 6.11. It has eight general-purpose registers $R0$, $R1$, ..., $R7$ that can be used for both addresses and data. Registers TS and TD are temporary registers, invisible to the programmer. Each register in Figure 6.73 is 16 bits except for CC, which is 8 bits.

System bus communication is controlled by the signals RW, AS, and ACK. A read cycle is shown in Figure 6.74. The address strobe (AS) signal from the processor indicates that an address is stable on the A bus. The acknowledge (ACK) signal from the external timing circuitry indicates that the

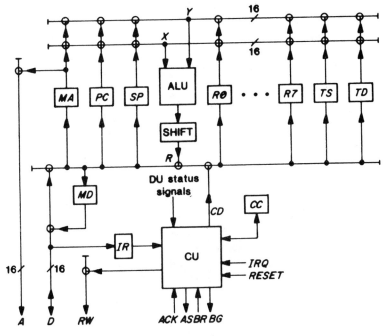

Figure 6.73   A hypothetical processor

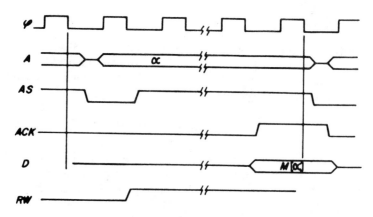

Figure 6.74   Bus read operation

address has been decoded and data is on the D bus. The processor takes the data during the next clock pulse and then clears AS. The write cycle is similar except that RW is 0 and $ACK = 1$ means that data has been taken.

The use of the "handshake" signals AS and ACK to control bus communication as described above allows the processor clock rate to be independent of the bus cycle time. This provides greater flexibility in both designing and using the processor. In processor design, for example, it is not necessary to provide separate hardware for address manipulation as in the 6800. Instead, since there are several clock periods per bus cycle, the same ALU can be used both to handle the data involved in a bus operation and to update the address in MA, PC, or SP.

The general instruction formats for the processor are outlined in Figure 6.75. Each instruction is represented by one, two, or three words. The first word specifies the operation to be performed and the address mode to be used to determine each operand. Words 2 and 3 provide immediate data or addresses for address computations.

Of the 16 possible opcodes (in the OPC field), 14 are used for two-operand instructions. The remaining 2 are used for branch and single-operand instructions. For both single- and double-operand instructions, each operand is specified by a 6-bit field, as defined in Table 6.11. The auto-increment and auto-decrement modes are useful for implementing stacks. These and most of the other address modes specified are similar to address modes used in the 68000 and 8086 microprocessors. A typical instruction is shown in Figure 6.76.

Figures 6.73–6.76 and Table 6.11 do not constitute a complete description of the architecture of this hypothetical processor. Enough information is provided, however, to allow a first-pass design of the control unit. We will discuss

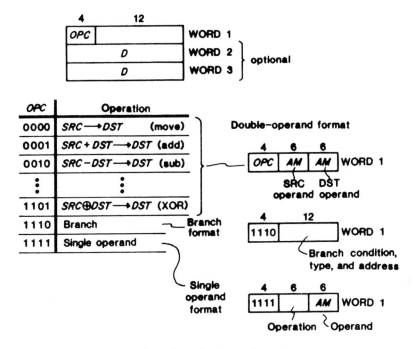

Figure 6.75   Instruction formats

briefly the design of a standard CU, and then in more detail consider the design of a microprogrammed CU.

A Standard CU

A standard CU for this processor is shown in Figure 6.77. The combinational output C consists of all the direct signals that must be generated to control the DU of Figure 6.73, and to handle processor communications. The network CSG converts the direct signals to pulse and extended signals, as necessary. Clock signals are intentionally omitted from the figure because the ideas to be discussed here apply to any form of clocking (e.g., single-phase or two-phase).

The size of the CU, either standard or microprogrammed, is determined by the number of states and the number of bits in the control word C. The length of the control word can be estimated from Figure 6.73. There are about 30 bus control inputs required (13 for X, 13 for Y, 3 for R, and 1 or 2 for A, D, and RW). This does not include any bits for selecting inputs to the CC register, which will be ignored for simplicity. There are about 23 register load con-

TABLE 6.11. Operand address modes

AM	Address mode	Operand (and address register changes)
000xxx	Register	$Ri^{①}$
001xxx	Register indirect	$M[Ri]^{①}$
010xxx	Indexed	$M[Ri + D]^{①②}$
011xxx	Auto-increment	1. $M[Ri]^{①}$ 2. $Ri + 1 \rightarrow Ri$
100xxx	Auto-decrement	1. $Ri - 1 \rightarrow Ri$ $M[Ri]^{①}$
1010xx	Short immediate	$0^{14} \circ xx$
101100	Long immediate	$D^{②}$
101101	Direct	$M[D]^{②}$
101110	Indirect	$M[M[D]]^{②}$
101111	Relative	$M[PC + D]^{②}$
11xxyy	Based-indexed	$M[Ri + Rj + D]^{②③}$

$①\, i = [xxx]_2$
$②\, D = $ word 2 or word 3
$③\, i = [xx]_2; j = [yy]_2$

ADD R5, $52C(R3)

(a)

0001 000101 010 011
0000 0101 0010 1100

(b)

$$R5 \stackrel{\wedge}{+}_2 M[R3 \stackrel{\wedge}{+}_2 052C] \longrightarrow M[R3 \stackrel{\wedge}{+}_2 052C]$$

(c)

Figure 6.76   A typical instruction: (a) symbolic representation; (b) machine code; (c) execution

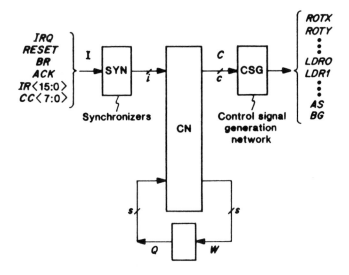

Figure 6.77   Standard CU structure

trol inputs (counting 8 for the individual bits of CC). There are about 5 control signals required to select the ALU and shift network operations. About 6 control signals are required to generate the outputs RW, AS, and BG. And finally, the output CD for injecting constants into the data unit is 16 bits. Hence, the number of bits in the control word C is approximately $c = 80$.

A sequential machine defining the operation of this processor could be constructed in the standard fashion, as described in Section 6.5. Figure 6.78 illustrates how this machine might look, using the fetch and execution of the instruction ADD R5,d(R3) as an example (Figure 6.76). No attempt is made to show how state sequences might be shared for the address computations of different instructions. Also, the interrupt response and the bus-sharing mechanism are omitted for simplicity.

The Microprogrammed CU Structure

Consider the possibility of using a ROM to implement the combinational network of Figure 6.77. The size of the ROM required would be $2^{(i+s)} \times (c + s)$. If eight state variables are needed ($s = 8$), then the ROM size is $2^{36} \times 88$. This is much too large for a practical CU.

In order to use ROM, therefore, the CU structure must be modified. The greatest reduction in ROM size can be achieved by reducing the number of ROM inputs. Each input that is eliminated halves the size of the ROM.

Figure 6.79 shows a modified CU structure that reduces ROM size by providing an input selection network, IS. This network is essentially a multiplexer with select input Q. For any state Q, it connects to the output J those bits of the input I that are "looked at" by the sequential machine during that state.

An even more dramatic reduction in ROM size is achieved by using the CU structure of Figure 6.80. This is the standard microprogrammed CU structure. The only input to the ROM is the current state Q. Hence the state is commonly referred to as the ROM address, and the state register as the ROM address register.

The address generation network AG generates the next state W (i.e., the next ROM address) as a function of the current state Q, the current input I, and an address selection word AS generated by the ROM. In a simple micro-

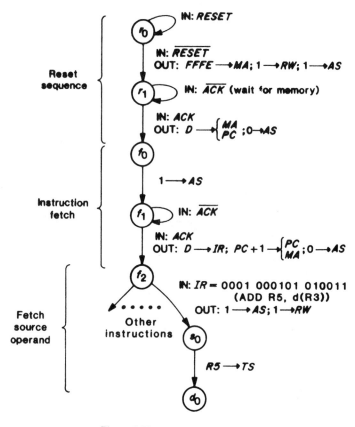

Figure 6.78   Sequential operation

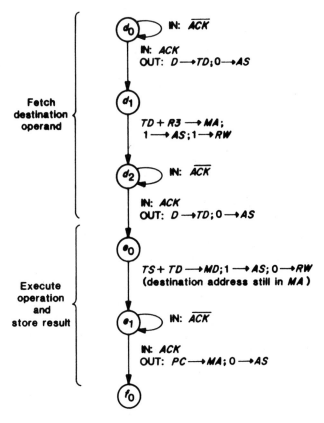

Figure 6.78 (continued)

programmed CU, AG may be a combinational network. In a more complex CU, AG may itself be a register transfer system.

A major shortcoming of this structure is that the control output C does not depend upon the input I, but only upon the state Q (i.e., this is a Moore machine rather than a Mealy machine). The output C cannot respond immediately to a change in I, but must wait until the next clock period. The structure of Figure 6.80 may be modified to alleviate this problem, if necessary, by expanding the responsibility of the AG network to include the generation of outputs that require quick response.

The Microprogram Viewpoint

When the control unit of a register transfer system is constructed as in Figure 6.80, the system begins to look like a simple computer. The ROM is the pri-

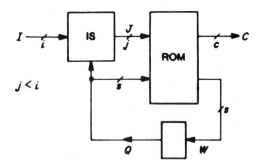

Figure 6.79   ROM-based CU with input selection network

mary memory. The words that are stored in ROM are instructions (called *microinstructions*). The sequence of words in ROM constitutes a program (the *microprogram*).

Reading a word from ROM is the instruction fetch. The instruction execution is the performance of the RT operation(s) specified by the C field of the ROM word. Execution is simpler than in a (macro)computer because every microinstruction executes in a single clock cycle. In another sense, however, execution is more complex, since each microinstruction may specify multiple RT operations and perhaps also a branch.

The microprogram viewpoint suggests a whole range of new possibilities for RT system design. For example, the idea of a subroutine may be incorporated into the control unit by providing a stack within the AG network to hold return addresses. Subroutines may be used to reduce the chip area occupied by the control unit, just as (macro)program length is reduced through the use of subroutines. Registers may be included in the AG network for use as micro-

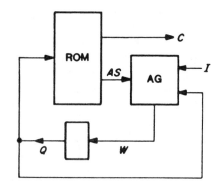

Figure 6.80   Standard microprogrammed CU structure

program index registers or loop counters, just as processor registers are used in a computer.

Further ideas come to mind if the CU ROM is replaced by RAM (called a *writable control store*). This allows microprograms that are stored off the chip to be loaded into the control memory when needed, at electronic speeds. A processor with a writable control store can be provided with a different instruction set simply by loading a different microprogram into the control memory. Hence the processor instruction set can be selected to suit the application.

Perhaps most important, the microprogram viewpoint suggests the use of software development tools for control unit design. Programs specifying the operation of the control unit may be written in an abstract language, and then assembled or compiled to produce a microprogram.

A Microprogrammed CU for Our Processor

A microprogrammed CU for our hypothetical processor is presented in Figure 6.81. The address selection field of the microinstruction word consists of three parts: a branch address field BA, an address mode field AM, and a branch condition field BC. These fields are used to control the generation of the next ROM address W as described below.

The address formation network AF is simply a wiring pattern. It forms three composite addresses $CA1$, $CA2$, and $CA3$ by combining bits of BA and IR as specified in Figure 6.81(c).

The multiplexer MUX selects one of 16 conditions to be involved in the generation of the next address. The BC field of the microinstruction controls this selection.

The RA register is used to hold ROM return addresses for microinstruction subroutine calls. Since only a single register is provided rather than a stack, subroutines cannot be nested (i.e., a subroutine cannot be called from within a subroutine).

The micro-control unit MCU has three functions:

1. It selects the next ROM address W.

2. It controls loading of the return address register RA.

3. It enables/disables the RT operations specified by the control word C.

The operation of the MCU is defined precisely in Figure 6.81(d).

The third MCU function above provides a limited capability for Mealy machine operation. The control signal ERT enables/disables the load control pulses to all DU registers. When $ERT = 0$, the RT operations specified by C are inhibited since the destination registers are not loaded.

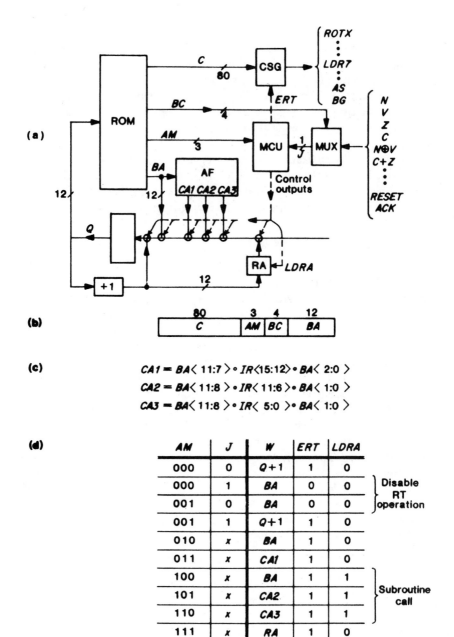

(a)

(b)

(c)

$$CA1 = BA\langle 11{:}7\rangle \circ IR\langle 15{:}12\rangle \bullet BA\langle 2{:}0\rangle$$
$$CA2 = BA\langle 11{:}8\rangle \bullet IR\langle 11{:}6\rangle \bullet BA\langle 1{:}0\rangle$$
$$CA3 = BA\langle 11{:}8\rangle \bullet IR\langle 5{:}0\rangle \bullet BA\langle 1{:}0\rangle$$

(d)

AM	J	W	ERT	LDRA	
000	0	$Q+1$	1	0	
000	1	BA	0	0	} Disable
001	0	BA	0	0	} RT operation
001	1	$Q+1$	1	0	
010	x	BA	1	0	
011	x	CA1	1	0	
100	x	BA	1	1	
101	x	CA2	1	1	} Subroutine call
110	x	CA3	1	1	
111	x	RA	1	0	

Figure 6.81   A CU for our hypothetical processor: (a) CU structure; (b) microinstruction word; (c) AF operation; (d) MCU operation

A partial microprogram for our CU is given in Table 6.12. Microinstructions to control the reset sequence and the fetch and execution of the ADD R3,d(R5) instruction are specified. Hence the partial microprogram of Table 6.12 corresponds to the partial state diagram of Figure 6.78 for the nonmicroprogrammed CU. The state names in the left column identify the microinstruction(s) corresponding to each state of Figure 6.78. Notice that some states require two microinstructions, due to the constraints imposed by the microprogrammed CU structure. By providing more MCU address modes, some of these additional microinstructions could be eliminated. Even if they are not eliminated, however, the increase in execution time will not be large since the clock rate is high.

Reducing ROM Width

The width of the microprogram memory may be reduced by encoding bits of the C field in various ways. For example, the 13 bits that control the X bus and the 13 bits that control the Y bus may each be reduced to 4 bits.

The cost of encoding the C field is speed. The encoded C word must be passed through a bank of decoders to generate the required decoded control signals.

Another way to reduce ROM width is by "field sharing." Not all bits of the ROM word are used by every microinstruction. For example, the CD bits that are used to inject constants into the DU are seldom used. The BA and BC fields are also idle frequently.

By adding an "opcode" field to the ROM word, selected bits of the microinstruction can be shared for different purposes. For example, a single-bit opcode might be used to switch one field between CD and $BC \circ BA$. That is, a single 16-bit field might serve as CD when the opcode bit is 0 and as $BC \circ BA$ when the opcode bit is 1. The opcode bit would be used outside the ROM to "steer" the shared field to the right destination. The field-sharing technique is sometimes called *bit steering* for this reason. Microprograms are sometimes longer when bit steering is used because operations that are controlled by the shared fields can no longer be done simultaneously.

The most dramatic reduction in ROM width may be achieved by complete encoding of the ROM word. A set of specific microinstructions is selected, and these are encoded in much the same way that (macro)instructions are encoded for a (macro)processor instruction set. This is sometimes called "vertical" microprogramming, as opposed to the use of a completely decoded ROM word, which is called "horizontal" microprogramming. The cost of vertical microprogramming is loss of flexibility and the necessity for extensive decoding outside the ROM.

TABLE 6.12. A partial microprogram

q	Q	C	AM	BC ($J=$)	BA
r_0	0000 0000 0000	$FFFE \rightarrow MA;\ 1 \rightarrow RW;\ 1 \rightarrow AS$	000	$RESET$	0000 0000 0000
r_1	0000 0000 0001	$D \rightarrow \begin{cases} PC \\ MA \end{cases};\ 0 \rightarrow AS$	001	ACK	0000 0000 0001
f_0	0000 0000 0010	$1 \rightarrow AS$	010	—	0000 0000 0011
f_1	0000 0000 0011	$D \rightarrow IR;\ PC+1 \rightarrow \begin{cases} PC \\ MA \end{cases};\ 0 \rightarrow AS$	001	ACK	0000 0000 0011
f_2	0000 0000 0100	$1 \rightarrow AS;\ 1 \rightarrow RW$	011	—	0001 0xxx x000
	$\cdots$				
s_0	0001 0000 1000	—	101	—	0010 xxxx xx00
d_0	0001 0000 1001	—	110	—	0011 xxxx xx00
e_0	0001 0000 1010	$TS+TD \rightarrow \begin{cases} TD \\ MD \end{cases}$	110		0100 xxxx xx00

s_0	...	...	111	—	—
d_0	0011 0100 1100	$D \rightarrow TD; 0 \rightarrow AS$	001	ACK	0011 0100 1100
d_1	0011 0100 1101	$TD + R3 \rightarrow MA; 1 \rightarrow AS; 1 \rightarrow RW$	010	—	0011 0100 1110
d_2	0011 0100 1110	$D \rightarrow TD; 0 \rightarrow AS$	001	ACK	0011 0100 1110
d_2	0011 0100 1111	—	111	—	—
	...				
e_0	0100 0100 1100	$1 \rightarrow AS; 0 \rightarrow RW$	010	—	0100 0100 1101
e_1	0100 0100 1101	$PC \rightarrow MA; 0 \rightarrow AS$	001	ACK	0100 0100 1101
e_1	0100 0100 1110	—	010	—	0000 0000 0010

6.6.3   Exercises

1. Use the state register of Figure 6.75 for the CU of the synchronous one-shot (Figure 6.10).

(a) Specify the output specification table, rows W_1, W_0, $CLRW$, LDW, and $INCW$.

(b) Write equations for these signals.

2. Repeat Exercise 1 for the OSC (Figure 6.27).

3. Use the 74198 circuit (Figure 5.78) as the state register for the synchronous one-shot (Figure 6.10). Specify the OST rows for all state register inputs and write equations.

4. Repeat Exercise 3 for the OSC (Figure 6.27).

5. Design the MCU network of Figure 6.81.

6. For the processor of Section 6.6.2, specify the machine code for each of the following instructions:

(a) ADD #$1234,$5678(R3)
(b) SUB R5,($1234)
(c) MOV (R2)+,5(R5+R6)

7. Describe the execution of each of the instructions of Exercise 6.

8. Expand the microprogram of Table 6.12 to include execution of the instructions in Exercise 6. Use existing microcode where possible.

9. Define a set of branch instructions for the processor of Section 6.6.2. Include subroutine call and return instructions. Define the machine code based upon the format specified in Figure 6.75.

10. Provide microcode to execute the branch instructions from Exercise 9.

Chapter 7

MACROCIRCUIT DESIGN

7.1   IC Interconnections
7.2   Transmission Lines
7.3   Noise

Macrocircuit design involves connecting together IC packages to form a system. There are two distinct aspects of macrocircuit design: functional and physical.

The functional aspect involves identifying the function that is performed by each IC package and providing the interconnections necessary for the packages to communicate with each other. The "function" may be a logic level function (SSI), a register transfer level function (MSI and LSI), or a PMS level function (VLSI). The functional aspects of macrocircuit design and microcircuit design are essentially the same. Most of the discussion in Chapters 3 through 6 is devoted to this aspect of digital design and applies to macrocircuit as well as microcircuit design.

The physical aspects of macrocircuit design involve the interconnections themselves. Ideally, when an output pin of one chip is connected to the input pin of another chip, the signal that is produced by the output chip appears unchanged at the input chip. In practice, this is never the case. Important considerations arise in four areas: loading, timing, transmission line effects, and noise. This chapter is devoted to these topics.

7.1   IC INTERCONNECTIONS [20, 24, 36, 42]

7.1.1   Linear Models
7.1.2   Device Specifications
7.1.3   Nonlinear Models
7.1.4   Exercises

In this section we discuss the fundamental electrical and timing considerations involved in interconnecting ICs. We restrict our attention to short interconnections, where a signal path may be represented simply as a lumped capacitance. Longer interconnecting paths are considered in the next section.

7.1.1 Linear Models

A linear model of the connection of an output terminal to an input terminal is shown in Figure 7.1(a). The complex circuitry inside each of the ICs is represented by a simple linear equivalent circuit with two regions of operation, high and low.

When the sending device attempts to establish a high output voltage (logic 1), the switch is up and the output circuit looks like an equivalent voltage source V_{OHE} in series with an equivalent output resistance R_{OH}. When the sending device attempts to output a low voltage, the switch moves down, establishing another equivalent voltage and resistance.

The equivalent circuit at the receiving end also has two operating regions, one for low input voltage and one for high input voltage. (The situation is different from that for the output circuit, however, in that the two correspond to two regions of the same v-i curve, rather than two separate v-i curves.) The two regions are represented by two values of input resistance.

The input equivalent circuit also includes a capacitance C_I that must be charged when switching to the high state and discharged when switching to the low state.

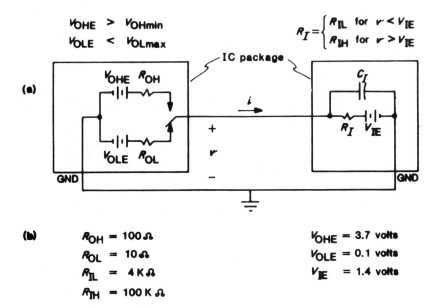

Figure 7.1   Linear interconnection model: (a) general model; (b) typical TTL values

As discussed previously, the interconnecting wire is assumed short, and may be represented simply as a lumped capacitance C_W. The value of C_W depends upon the geometry of the signal path and the dielectric constant of the insulation between the signal wire and ground. Specifically, C_W increases as the size of the signal wire increases and decreases as the distance from ground increases. Values range from about 4 pF per inch for a relatively large wire or printed circuit path that is very close to ground (e.g., 20-gauge wire separated from a ground plane by 0.25 mm of insulation) to about 0.1 pF per inch for a thin wire far from a ground wire or ground plane (e.g., a 30-gauge hookup wire 2 inches from ground).

In Figure 7.1(b) typical parameter values for TTL devices are given. These values are approximate, and may vary considerably from one manufacturer to another, or from one TTL device to another. They are not used directly in macrocircuit design calculations, and hence their precise specification is not necessary.

The important thing to notice about these parameters is their relative magnitudes. In particular, notice that the input resistances are much larger than the output resistances. Also, notice that $V_{OHE} > V_{OHmin}$ and $V_{OLE} < V_{OLmax}$. (Recall from Section 5.2 that V_{OHmin} is the minimum acceptable logic 1 output and V_{OLmax} is the maximum acceptable logic 0 output.)

nMOS interconnections may be represented by the same general model. Usually the equivalent output resistances are significantly larger than for TTL. Input resistances are also much larger. In fact, for most macrocircuit design considerations, R_{IL} and R_{IH} are both essentially infinite.

Steady-State Operation

Suppose that the output is high (i.e., the output switch is up). If $V_{OHE} > V_{IE}$ (as for TTL), then the output device will "supply" current to the input device; that is, current will flow out of the output terminal and into the input terminal, as indicated in Figure 7.2(a). Initially the current supplied will charge the capacitors. When the capacitors have reached their final value, however, there will still be a small steady-state current,

$$I_{OH} = I_{IH} = \frac{V_{OHE} - V_{IE}}{R_{OH} + R_{IH}} \cong \frac{V_{OHE} - V_{IE}}{R_{IH}} \tag{7.1}$$

The steady-state voltage will be

$$V_{OH} = V_{OHE} - I_{OH} * R_{OH} \tag{7.2}$$

The output low circuit is shown in Figure 7.2(b). If $V_{OLE} < V_{IE}$ (as for TTL), then the output device will "sink" current from the input device; that

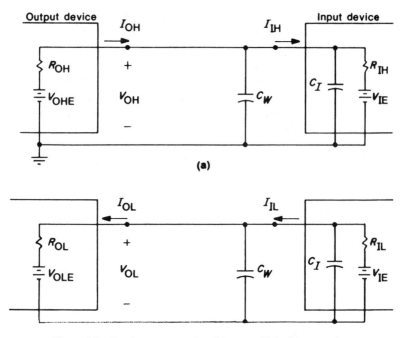

Figure 7.2   Steady-state operation: (a) output high; (b) output low

is, current will flow out of the input terminal and into the output terminal. At steady state,

$$I_{OL} = I_{IL} = \frac{V_{IE} - V_{OLE}}{R_{OL} + R_{IL}} \cong \frac{V_{IE}}{R_{IL}} \qquad (7.3)$$

and

$$V_{OL} = V_{OLE} + I_{OL} * R_{OL} \qquad (7.4)$$

For nMOS devices the input resistance is so high that the steady-state current is essentially 0 for both high and low outputs. The only current that flows is that required to charge and discharge the input and wire capacitances. The tiny "leakage current" that flows at steady state, which may be in either direction, can be ignored.

Dynamic Operation

For both TTL and nMOS devices, the input resistance is much larger than the output resistance at both high and low levels. Hence, when a switch from low to high occurs, it is the output device that supplies essentially all of the current to charge the input and wire capacitance. The circuit is essentially a first-order RC circuit.

The time constant for the low-to-high transition is $R_{OH} * C_T$, where $C_T = C_I + C_W$. The time constant for the high-to-low transition is $R_{OL} * C_T$. Since R_{OL} is less than R_{OH} for TTL, one would expect the high-to-low transition to be faster than the low-to-high transition. This is not always the case, however, because R_{OL} is quite nonlinear. It is small in the logic 0 region, but is much larger for higher voltages.

Loading

The term *loading* refers to detrimental effects on output signals that may occur as a result of device interconnections. *Static loading* refers to the ability of an output device to maintain the required logic levels at its output terminals. We will consider this type of loading first.

If an output terminal is not connected to anything, then the output current (I_{OL} or I_{OH}) is always 0. Since no voltage is dropped across the output resistance, the low output voltage will be V_{OLE} and the high output voltage will be V_{OHE}. As noted in Figure 7.1, these values are within the logic 0 and logic 1 regions, respectively.

Now suppose that the output is connected to an input terminal. Then the high output voltage will be reduced by an amount $I_{OH} * R_{OH}$, where $I_{OH} = I_{IH} \cong V_{OHE}/R_{IH}$ (equations 7.1 and 7.2). If the output is connected to a second input, then the output device must supply a steady-state current to that input as well (i.e., $I_{OH} = I_{IH1} + I_{IH2}$). Hence, I_{OH} is pulled yet lower. If too many inputs are connected to an output, then V_{OH} will drop below V_{OHmin}. The device is then overloaded.

In similar fashion, $V_{OL} = V_{OLE} < V_{OLmax}$ when an output is unloaded. When the output is connected to one input, $V_{OL} = V_{OLE} + I_{OL} * R_{OL}$, where $I_{OL} = I_{IL}$. Each additional input that is connected increases the current I_{OL} that the output must sink, until eventually $V_{OL} > V_{OLmax}$.

Dynamic loading refers to the effect of output connections on output transitions between high and low levels. Each additional input terminal that is connected to an output terminal adds the capacitance of that input plus the wiring needed to make the connection to the total capacitance that must be charged and discharged by the output. Propagation delays increase accordingly, since the time constants are proportional to the total load capacitance.

7.1.2 Device Specifications

The information that is needed by the macrocircuit designer to use an IC device is normally provided in a "data sheet" for the device. The data sheet describes the functional operation of the device and also the electrical and timing specifications, which we are concerned with in this section.

The terminology and notations used in data sheets are not standard. They vary from one manufacturer to another, and from one device to another. Every IC manufacturer publishes "data books," which contain data sheets for a family of devices together with complete explanations of the terminology and notations used in the data sheets. The reader would benefit from studying one or more nMOS or TTL data books. Typical electrical and timing specifications for these devices are described below.

Static Specifications

Static specifications have to do with steady-state operation. They are sometimes called DC (direct current) specifications because at steady state all currents are constant.

In Section 5.1 the standard TTL logic levels were specified: $V_{ILmax} = 0.8$, $V_{OLmax} = 0.4$, $V_{IHmin} = 2.0$, and $V_{OHmin} = 2.4$ volts. External nMOS logic levels are intentionally designed to be the same, so that nMOS and TTL devices can be directly interconnected.

The static specifications for a device must provide the information necessary to determine whether the required logic levels can be maintained for any proposed interconnection. This may be accomplished by specifying two numbers for each input, I_{IHmax} and I_{ILmax}, and two numbers for each output, I_{OHmax} and I_{OLmax}.

I_{IHmax} is the maximum current that will flow into an input terminal when $V_{IN} = V_{OHmin} = 2.4$. I_{ILmax} is the maximum current that will flow out of an input terminal when $V_{IN} = V_{OLmax} = 0.4$.

I_{OHmin} is the minimum current that an output is guaranteed to be able to supply while maintaining an output $V_{OUT} \geq V_{OHmin} = 2.4$. I_{OLmin} is the minimum current that an output is guaranteed to be able to sink while maintaining a legitimate low output, $V_{OUT} \leq V_{OLmax} = 0.4$.

When an output is connected to several inputs, the output current is the sum of the input currents. Correct output logic levels are guaranteed provided that

$$I_{OHmin} \geq \Sigma\, I_{IHmax} \tag{7.5}$$

and

$$I_{OLmin} \geq \Sigma\, I_{ILmax} \tag{7.6}$$

Some typical TTL static specifications are given in Table 7.1. Conditions are specified for some parameters to help establish the precise meaning of the

TABLE 7.1   Standard TTL static specifications

Parameter	Min	Typ	Max	Units	Conditions
V_{IH}	2.0			volts	
V_{IL}			0.8	volts	
V_{OH}	2.4	3.4		volts	$V_{CC} = \text{min}$ $I_{OUT} = 400\ \mu A$ [1]
V_{OL}		0.2	0.4	volts	$V_{CC} = \text{min}$ $I_{OUT} = 16\ mA$ [2]
I_{IH}			40	microamps	$V_{CC} = \text{max}$ $V_{IN} = 2.4$ volts
I_{IL}			1.6	milliamps	$V_{CC} = \text{max}$ $V_{IN} = 0.4$ volts
I_{OH}	400			microamps	$V_{OH} = 2.4$ volts $V_{CC} = \text{min}$
I_{OL}	16			milliamps	$V_{OL} = 0.4$ volts $V_{CC} = \text{min}$

[3] (braced to the last two rows, I_{OH} and I_{OL})

[1] This is I_{OHmin}
[2] This is I_{OLmin}
[3] These specifications are redundant. They duplicate the specifications V_{OH} and V_{OL} above.

specifications. Usually these are "worst-case" conditions, so that the maximum or minimum value specified is truly a worst-case specification.

Note that an output pin of a device with these specifications is capable of driving 10 inputs of devices with these same specifications. This is a direct application of the worst-case design limits expressed by equations (7.5) and 7.6).

The static specifications that we have discussed are for standard outputs driving standard inputs. There are similar specifications that apply to open-collector outputs and tristate outputs, and interconnections of these.

Power Specifications

On every TTL or nMOS device there is a ground pin (GND) and a V_{CC} or V_{DD} pin. These are connected to the power supply terminals via a low-resistance power distribution grid (e.g., Figure 2.8).

The ground terminal of the power supply is the 0-volt reference potential for all signals in the system. Ideally, the ground pin of every device is at exactly 0 volts at all times. This ideal can be approached by making the ground distribution grid sufficiently dense and massive.

The V_{CC} (or V_{DD}) terminal of the power supply is nominally at 5.0 volts. Ideally the V_{CC} pin of every device should be at exactly this level. This requires not only a good distribution grid, but also a good power supply. A good supply is one that can maintain a constant voltage at its terminals despite varying current demands.

Standard TTL and nMOS devices are designed to operate properly with $V_{CC} = 5.0 \pm 5\%$. Hence, $V_{CCmin} = 4.75$ volts and $V_{CCmax} = 5.25$ volts.

In order to choose (or design) an appropriate power supply for a system, it is necessary to know the total amount of power that must be supplied. For some devices, a maximum power dissipation specification is given for this purpose. For example, $P_{Dmax} = 1.2$ watts for the 6800 processor. The total power that must be supplied to a system (worst case) is the sum of the P_{Dmax} specifications for all devices.

Some devices do not have a maximum power dissipation specification. Instead, the maximum current flowing into the V_{CC} terminal is specified (I_{CCmax}). As illustrated in Figure 2.8, all devices in a system are connected in parallel between the V_{CC} and GND terminals of the power supply. Hence, the total current delivered by the power supply is the sum of the I_{CC} currents for the individual devices. Total power is V_{CC} times this total current.

Power dissipation is an important consideration not only for selection of a power supply, but also for temperature control. All the power that is supplied to a system is dissipated as heat. This heat must be removed from the system to keep the ambient temperature within the specified limits for the devices (usually between 0° and 70°C).

There are two types of power dissipation in digital devices: static and dynamic. For nMOS devices, power dissipation is primarily static (see Section 2.2). For high-speed TTL devices, however, dynamic power dissipation is important, and specifications may be accompanied by graphs showing dependence on clock frequency.

Timing Specifications

Timing specifications have been discussed in detail in Section 5.1. That discussion applies directly to IC devices. Numerous examples were supplied throughout Chapter 5.

The only matter related to timing specifications that was not discussed in Chapter 5 is loading. Propagation delays for IC devices are always specified for a particular load. For example, the load capacitances for the 6800 bus propagation delay specifications are 130 pF for the D bus and 90 pF for the A and RW buses. The maximum values for t_{AD} and t_{DD} in Figure 6.23 are for these loads.

Graphs are frequently provided showing propagation delay as a function of load capacitance. The graphs for 6800 bus delays are linear, with slopes of about 0.4 ns/pF.

Specifications also include a maximum capacitance for each input terminal. TTL inputs are typically around 5 pF (maximum). For the 6800 processor the maximum capacitances for input terminals range from 8.5 to 15 pF, with one notable exception. Each clock input has a maximum capacitance of 160 pF, indicating that these inputs drive many internal gates.

7.1.3 Nonlinear Models

Figure 7.1 provides a simple conceptual model, which is useful for qualitative reasoning about loading effects in macrocircuit systems. A more precise understanding of loading effects is possible if the v-i curves for inputs and outputs are used in place of the linear equivalent circuits.

Typical v-i curves for TTL devices are given in Figure 2.23. A graphical analysis of the operating point for one output driving six inputs is shown in Figure 7.3. The dashed line is the v-i characteristic for one input. The characteristic for six inputs in parallel is obtained by adding the currents of six input curves, as explained in Section 2.3. The operating points for high and low outputs are the points of intersection of the input curve with the high- and low-output curves. Note that the operating points for the six-input load are worse than for the single-input load.

The v-i curves are also helpful in visualizing dynamic operation. Suppose that the output in Figure 7.3 changes from low to high at time 0. If the switch occurs instantaneously, then the output circuit changes from the output low curve to the output high curve at time $t = 0+$. Since the voltage across the input capacitance cannot change instantaneously, the operating point changes at $t = 0+$ to the point on the high-output curve that is directly above the low operating point, as shown in Figure 7.4. The current that now flows charges the input and wire capacitance, thus increasing the voltage, and the operating point moves down the output curve until it reaches the high operating point. The rate at which it moves down the output curve depends upon the capacitance.

Actually, the output circuit does not change instantaneously. There is a continuous change in the v-i characteristics from the low curve to the high curve. The effect that this will have on the actual transition path in the v-i plane is not easy to determine precisely. In general, however, the effect will be to pull the current peak down, as shown by the dotted curve in Figure 7.4.

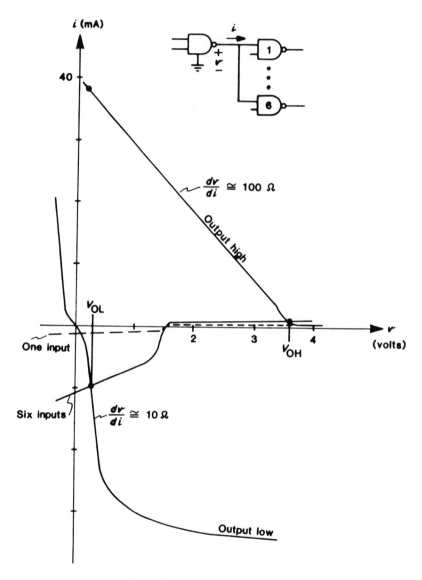

Figure 7.3   Graphical loading analysis

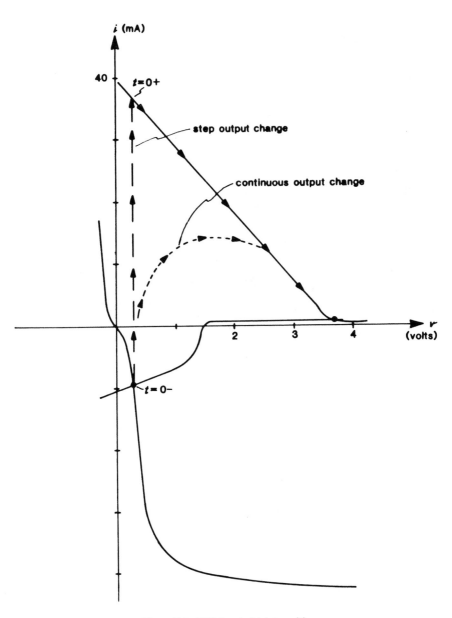

Figure 7.4   TTL low-to-high transition

7.1.4 Exercises

Suppose that the worst-case linear interconnection model (Figure 7.1) for a hypothetical logic family is as follows:

$R_{OH} = 40\ \Omega$, $R_{OL} = 20\ \Omega$, $V_{OHE} = 4.0$ volts, $V_{OLE} = 0$ volts, $V_{IE} = 1.5$ volts, $R_{IH} = 3000\ \Omega$, $R_{IL} = 2000\ \Omega$, $C_l = 10$ pF.

The following exercises deal with this model.
1. Sketch the linear v-i characteristics for the input and output circuits.

2. Specify the high and low operating points for an output driving

  (a) A single input
  (b) Two inputs

3. Assuming standard TTL logic levels, specify I_{OLmin}, I_{OHmin}, I_{ILmax}, and I_{IHmax}.

4. How many worst-case inputs can a worst-case output drive?

5. Assume that the maximum propagation delay of a particular unloaded output is 5 ns, measured from the input event that causes the output change. (This delay is due to internal capacitances.) What will be the maximum propagation delay for the same output driving a 100-pF load?

6. Repeat Exercises 1–5 for $R_{OH} = 400\ \Omega$.

7.2 TRANSMISSION LINES [20, 52–56]

  ### 7.2.1 The Digital Model
  ### 7.2.2 Computing Solutions
  ### 7.2.3 Line Termination
  ### 7.2.4 Exercises

In the preceding section we represented a signal line (wire) as a lumped capacitance. When the output device that is driving a line switches, the line voltage rises or falls exponentially with a time constant RC, where R is the output resistance of the driver and C is the line capacitance plus the input capacitance of the receiving device(s).

In this model, line voltage is a function of time, but not a function of position along the line. The voltage along the entire length of the line at any time is considered to be the same. Increasing line length simply increases capacitance, which causes the line voltage to change more slowly. But the change occurs at all points along the line simultaneously.

This predicted behavior, however, is quite different from the observed behavior of long lines. When a line driver switches, a step change is observed to occur first at the driver output. This change travels down the line at speeds ranging from about 5 to 9 in./ns, depending upon the characteristics of the line. (For comparison, the speed of light in a vacuum is $2.988 * 10^8$ m/s $=$ 10.31 in./ns. This correspondence is not surprising since both light and propagation of voltage along a signal path are forms of electromagnetic radiation.) Hence, the line voltage is a function not only of time, but also of position along the line.

When this traveling voltage wave reaches the receiving end of the line, another step change is produced (called a *reflection*) which travels back toward the sending end, where yet another reflection may occur, and so on. Eventually, the line settles down to the same steady-state voltage predicted by the short-line model.

This observed behavior is correctly predicted by a model which represents capacitance and inductance as distributed parameters along the length of a signal path (now called a transmission line). Distributed resistance may also be important, but its effects are secondary and may be discussed separately.

The distributed parameter model of a transmission line is characterized by partial differential equations, since both time and position along the line are independent variables. Although this model is not too complex for inclusion here, it is not essential and will be omitted for brevity.

We will present instead a digital transmission line model that can be derived from the distributed parameter model. The digital model directly represents the observed behavior of transmission lines described above. It is not as general as the distributed parameter model, but it is much simpler and is sufficient for our purposes.

7.2.1 The Digital Model

A transmission line consists of two conductors, as illustrated in Figure 7.5. The voltage between the two conductors at position x and time t is denoted $v(x, t)$. This line voltage is accompanied by a current $i(x, t)$. This current flows in each conductor, but in opposite directions.

Line Configurations

Many different transmission line configurations are possible, depending upon the nature of the two conductors. Four configurations commonly used

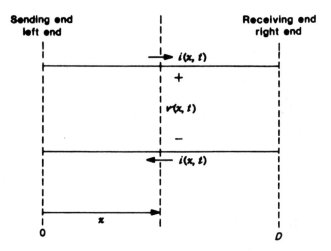

Figure 7.5   Transmission line of length D

in digital systems are shown in Figure 7.6. Other signal paths may be roughly approximated by one of these configurations.

The first configuration consists of two identical wires of radius r separated by a distance s. Flat cables consisting of many parallel wires are frequently used. Two adjacent wires in such a cable form a line of this configuration.

A *twisted pair* line is a two-wire line with the wires twisted together, about three twists per inch. Twisting the wires provides better noise immunity (Section 7.3). It does not affect the capacitance of the line, but it increases the inductance somewhat.

The next configuration is a single wire of radius r at a distance h above a ground plane. The ground plane serves as the second conductor. A nearly perfect ground plane is provided by a solid sheet of copper in the center of a multilayer printed circuit card or backplane. Alternatively, a ground plane may be approximated by a dense grid of metal strips or wires. A wire wrap connection over a ground plane of either sort is an example of this configuration.

Another example of this configuration is a flat cable with a mat of braided thin wires to serve as the ground plane. The mat serves as a common return for all signal wires in the cable.

The *stripline* configuration is similar to the single-wire above-ground configuration. The only difference is the shape of the signal line. A printed circuit path over a ground plane is of this form.

The *coaxial* line consists of a wire surrounded by a layer of insulation and then a concentric cylindrical conductor. For flexibility, the outer conductor is usually made from tightly braided fine wires and/or thin foil.

Line configuration	Capacitance (pF/m)	Inductance (μ H/m)
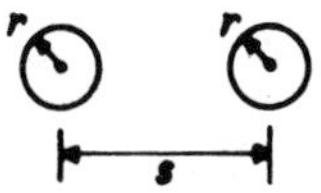 Symmetric two-wire line	$$\dfrac{12.1\epsilon_r}{\log\left[(h/r)+\sqrt{(h/r)^2-1}\,\right]}$$ where $h = s/2$	$0.92 \log(s/r)$
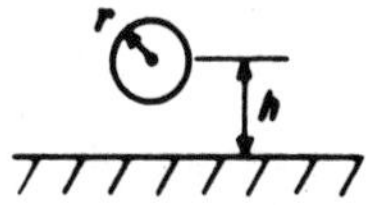 Single wire above ground	$$\dfrac{24.2\,\epsilon_r}{\log\left[(h/r)+\sqrt{(h/r)^2-1}\,\right]}$$	$0.46 \log(s/r)$ where $s = 2h$
 Coaxial line	$$\dfrac{24.2\epsilon_r}{\log(h/r)}$$	$0.46 \log(h/r)$
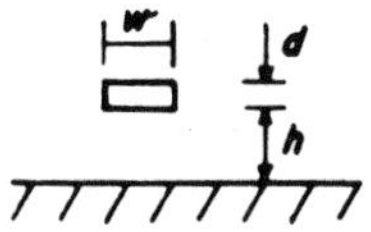 Stripline	$$\dfrac{11.5(\epsilon_r+1.41)}{\log(6h/(0.8w+d))}$$	$0.46 \log\left(\dfrac{6h}{0.8w+d}\right)$

Figure 7.6   Line configurations and parameters

Dimensions

Signal wires used in digital systems range from about 30 gauge ($r = 0.13$ mm) to 20 gauge ($r = 0.4$ mm). The minimum spacing between conductors is determined by wire insulation thickness, which ranges from about 0.15 to 0.5 mm, except for coaxial cable, where the insulation radius h varies from about 0.25 to 4 mm.

For printed circuit paths (stripline configuration), the path width w varies from about 0.25 to 3 mm, path thickness d from about 0.04 to 0.08 mm, and dielectric thickness h from about 0.4 to 2.5 mm.

Line Parameters

Every signal path has capacitance, inductance, and resistance. These parameters are not lumped at one point along the path, but are distributed along the path. Hence, they are specified "per unit length."

Capacitance and Inductance

The formulas given in Figure 7.6 may be used to compute the capacitance and inductance of various signal paths. The constant ϵ_r is the relative permittivity of the dielectric between the conductors. For air, $\epsilon_r = 1$; for common rubber and plastic insulations, ϵ_r is between 2 and 3; for epoxy fiberglass PC boards, $\epsilon_r \cong 5$.

Because of the importance of capacitance in digital systems, it is worthwhile to examine the formulas in Figure 7.6. Recall first the definition of capacitance. The capacitance between two conductors is the amount of charge that must be moved from one conductor to the other to establish 1 volt of potential difference between them. From each formula it is seen that capacitance increases as wire size increases and as the distance between conductors decreases. These qualitative relationships can be explained intuitively as follows.

The strength of the electric field between two conductors is proportional to the density of the charge distributions on the adjacent surfaces of the conductors. If conductor size increases while the total amount of charge on a conductor remains the same, then the surface charge density will decrease (density = charge per unit area). Since the density decreases the electric field intensity will decrease, thus decreasing the voltage. Hence, more charge must be moved to maintain the same voltage between the conductors. That is, capacitance (charge per unit voltage) increases as conductor size increases.

Alternatively, we might consider reducing conductor size while keeping the charge carried by the conductor constant. As conductor size shrinks, charge density and hence electric field intensity increase, causing the voltage between the conductors to increase.

Now consider holding the charge on the conductors constant and decreasing the distance between them. The surface charge density and hence the electric field intensity remain the same. Since electric field intensity is force per unit charge, the work required to move a charge from one conductor to the other decreases, because work is force times distance and distance has been decreased. But voltage is work per unit charge, hence voltage is decreased; that is, decreasing the distance between conductors while keeping the total charge fixed decreases the voltage between them. Hence, more charge must be moved to maintain a constant voltage as distance is decreased. That is,

capacitance (charge per unit voltage) increases as distance between the conductors decreases.

The formulas for inductance may be interpreted in similar fashion. When
current flows in a wire, a magnetic field is established in the space around the
wire. Conversely, a changing magnetic field around a wire will induce a current in the wire. When current in a wire increases, the magnetic field around
the wire increases. This changing magnetic field tends to oppose the increase
in current by producing a voltage in the opposite direction. The ratio of the
voltage produced to the rate of change of current is inductance: $L = v/(di/dt)$.

When the two wires of a transmission line are far apart, then the total inductance of the line is the sum of the inductances of the two wires. As the lines
are brought closer together, the magnetic fields of the two wires tend to cancel
each other, since currents are in opposite directions. Hence, the magnetic
field change is less for a given current change, so the induced voltage is less.
That is, the induced voltage for a given change in current in current per unit
time (i.e., inductance) decreases as the two conductors of a line are brought
closer together.

As an example, compute the capacitance and inductance of a two-wire line
composed of two 30-gauge wires ($r = 0.13$). Suppose that the insulation
thickness is 0.2 mm and the wires are as close together as possible; that is,
$s = 2(0.13 + 0.2) = 0.66$ mm. Suppose $\epsilon_r = 3$. Then $C = 62.6$ pF/m $= 1.59$
pF/in. and $L = 0.65$ μH/m.

Resistance

Unlike capacitance and inductance, resistance does not depend upon the geometry of a line. It is a property only of the conductors. The DC resistance of
a conductor (wire) with cross-sectional area A and length L is

$$R_{dc} = \frac{\rho L}{A} \tag{7.7}$$

where ρ is the resistivity of the material (see Section 2.3).

DC resistance is the resistance of the conductor to a steady constant current
flow. Consider, for example, a symmetric two-wire transmission line (Figure
7.6) of length D. If the receiving end is short-circuited (i.e., the two wires
connected directly together) and a voltage V is applied at the sending end,
then the steady-state current that will flow is $I = V/R_{dc}$, where $R_{dc} = \rho 2D/\pi r^2$ (since the total conductor length is $2D$ and the cross-sectional area is $A = \pi r^2$).

The resistivity of copper is $\rho = 1.72 * 10^{-8}$ Ω meters. Hence, the DC resistance of 20-gauge wire is about 0.033 Ω/m and the resistance of 30-gauge wire about 0.344 Ω/m.

As frequency increases, current tends to flow more on the outer surface of a conductor. This phenomenon, known as *skin effect*, tends to reduce the effective cross-sectional area of the conductor, thus increasing the resistance. The "skin depth" of copper as a function of frequency is

$$\delta = 66/\sqrt{f} \quad \text{mm}$$

where f is in Hertz [54]. Hence, skin effect just begins to affect 20-gauge copper wire at 26 KHz and 30-gauge wire at 270 KHz (where skin depth = radius). At 1 MHz, $R_{ac} = 0.11$ Ω/m for a 20-gauge wire. At 16 MHz, $R_{ac} = 0.8$ Ω/m for the same wire, and at 64 MHz, $R_{ac} = 1.6$ Ω/m.

Line resistance does not affect steady-state levels until lines are very long, because DC resistance is small. It can be a factor in transmitting digital signals, however, because of skin effect. Since high frequencies are attenuated more than low frequencies, pulse edges become rounded.

Characteristic Impedance and Wave Velocity

In the model that we are about to present, transmission line behavior will involve the propagation of "waves" along the line. A wave will consist of a voltage V and a current I related by a constant Z_0 called the *characteristic impedance* of the line. That is, $V = Z_0 I$. This constant is related to the capacitance and inductance of the line as follows:

$$Z_0 = \sqrt{\frac{L}{C}} \tag{7.8}$$

If C is in picofarads per meter and L is microhenries per meter, as in Figure 7.6, then Z_0 is in kilohms.

The propagation velocity of a wave along a transmission line, which we will denote c_0, is also related to L and C.

$$c_0 = 1/\sqrt{LC} \tag{7.9}$$

If C and L are in picofarads per meter and microhenries per meter, then c_0 is in meters per nanosecond.

Values of Z_0 for typical transmission lines encountered in digital systems range from 50 to 200 Ω and c_0 ranges from 6 to 8 in./ns.

Formulas for Z_0 and c_0 in terms of the parameters for various line configurations may be derived directly from Figure 7.6.

Notice that for the coaxial line and the stripline, the propagation velocity is independent of the geometric dimensions of the line; it depends only upon the dielectric constant ϵ_r. This is also approximately true for the two-wire and one-wire lines as h becomes large with respect to r.

Traveling Waves and Reflections

Consider the situation illustrated in Figure 7.7. The transmission line is driven at the left end by a digital device which can switch its output between two states. The state of the output establishes a boundary condition (i.e., a relation between v and i) at the left end of the line. The two possible boundary conditions are represented by the equations

$$f_L(v, i) = 0 \qquad (7.10)$$

and

$$g_L(v, i) = 0 \qquad (7.11)$$

For example, if this is the output device of Figure 7.1, then the boundary conditions are

$$v + iR_{OL} - V_{OLE} = 0$$

and

$$v + iR_{OH} - V_{OHE} = 0$$

Alternatively, equations (7.10) and (7.11) may represent nonlinear $v - i$ curves such as the TTL output curves of Figure 7.3.

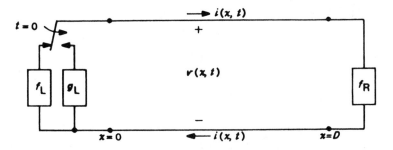

Figure 7.7   Step change in boundary conditions

At the right end of the line there is a fixed boundary condition

$$f_R(v, i) = 0$$

This may represent a gate input characteristic as in Figure 7.3 or simply a resistive load, for example.

Suppose that the switch in Figure 7.7 has been in the left position for a long time before $t = 0$ so that the transmission line is at steady state at time $t = 0$. That is, the line voltage is the same over the entire line and the line current is the same at every point as well. To be specific, let V_0 and I_0 denote the steady-state voltage and current. That is,

$$v(x, 0) = V_0 \quad \text{for all } x$$
$$i(x, 0) = I_0 \quad \text{for all } x \tag{7.12}$$

Since the boundary conditions at both ends must be satisfied, it must be that

$$f_L(V_0, I_0) = 0 \tag{7.13}$$

and

$$f_R(V_0, I_0) = 0$$

We assume that the boundary conditions are such that this pair of equations has a unique solution. Hence, the initial steady state (V_0, I_0) can be determined by solving these equations.

After $t = 0$, the voltage and current at the left end of the line must satisfy the new boundary condition $g_L(v, i) = 0$. Any voltage and current changes that occur in order to satisfy this new boundary condition will travel down the line at speed c_0, and must be related by the characteristic impedance Z_0.

Let V_{L0} and I_{L0} denote the required voltage and current changes. The subscripts denote the end at which the change occurs (left) and the time of occurrence ($t = 0$). Furthermore, let V_1 and I_1 denote the new total voltage and current at the left end. Then V_1, I_1, V_{L0}, and I_{L0} are related by the following equations

$$V_{L0} = Z_0 I_{L0}$$
$$V_1 = V_0 + V_{L0}$$
$$I_1 = I_0 + I_{L0} \tag{7.14}$$
$$g_L(V_1, I_1) = 0$$

The "wave" (V_{L0}, I_{L0}) travels down the line at speed c_0, establishing the new total voltage and current (V_1, I_1) as it goes. This wave reaches the right end at time $T = D/c_0$.

If the total voltage and current (V_1, I_1) satisfy the right boundary condition [i.e., $f_R(V_1, I_1) = 0$], then the line is at a new steady state and no further changes occur. Both boundary conditions are satisfied and the voltage and current are the same all along the line.

In general, however, the right boundary condition will not be satisfied [i.e., $f_R(V_1, I_1) \neq 0$], and a "reflected" wave (V_{R1}, I_{R1}) is generated. The subscripts denote the end at which the wave is generated (right) and the time ($t = 1$, where T is the time unit).

A positive voltage V_{R1} applied at the right end of the line will produce a current I_{R1} to the *left* in the top line of Figure 7.7 and to the right in the bottom line. Hence, V_{R1} and I_{R1} are related by $-Z_0$ rather than Z_0. If V_2 and I_2 denote the new total voltage and current at the right end, then the following equations are satisfied.

$$V_{R1} = -Z_0 I_{R1}$$
$$V_2 = V_1 + V_{R1}$$
$$I_2 = I_1 + I_{R1} \tag{7.15}$$
$$f_R(V_2, I_2) = 0$$

The wave (V_{R1}, I_{R1}) moves to the left at speed c_0, establishing a new total voltage V_2 and current I_2 as it proceeds. At time $t = 2T$ the wave reaches the left end of the line. If $g_L(V_2, I_2) = 0$, then the line is at a new steady state. If not, then another wave (V_{L2}, I_{L2}) is generated. The process continues in this fashion until the line reaches a new steady state (V_S, I_S) which satisfies both boundary conditions. That is,

$$g_L(V_S, I_S) = 0$$
$$f_R(V_S, I_S) = 0 \tag{7.16}$$

Actually, if (V_1, I_1) is not a steady state and (V_2, I_2) is not a steady state, then the final steady state (V_S, I_S) is never reached but is approached asymptotically. That is, $\lim_{n \to \infty} V_n = V_S$ and $\lim_{n \to \infty} I_n = I_S$.

This entire process is summarized in Table 7.2.

Short-Line Versus Long-Line Model

Not all interconnections in macrocircuit systems must be modeled as transmission lines. Boundary changes are actually continuous, not instantaneous. If a boundary change requires a time greater than $2T$, then the reflection from the original wave arrives at the sending end while the wave is still being produced. The original wave and the subsequent reflections are not discrete

TABLE 7.2. Response to step change in boundary conditions

Initial Conditions

$v(x, 0) = V_0$ and $i(x, 0) = I_0$ for $0 \le x \le d$

where V_0 and I_0 are such that

$f_L(V_0, I_0) = 0$

$f_R(V_0, I_0) = 0$

Traveling waves

For $j = 0, 2, 4, \ldots$ For $j = 1, 3, 5, \ldots$

$V_{Lj} = Z_0 I_{Lj}$ $V_{Rj} = -Z_0 I_{Rj}$

$g_L(V_{j+1}, I_{j+1}) = 0$ $f_R(V_{j+1}, I_{j+1}) = 0$

$V_{j+1} = V_j + V_{Lj}$ $V_{j+1} = V_j + V_{Rj}$

$I_{j+1} = I_j + I_{Lj}$ $I_{j+1} = I_j + I_{Rj}$

Steady state

$\lim_{n \to \infty} V_n = V_s$

$\lim_{n \to \infty} I_n = I_s$

$g_L(V_s, I_s) = 0$

$f_R(V_s, I_s) = 0$

---

but are merged together. In this case, the lumped model of Section 7.1 is appropriate.

The time required for a boundary change to occur is the rise time or fall time of the driver output. The general rule of thumb thus is: use the transmission line model when the rise/fall time of signals is less than $2T$, or, equivalently, $D > c_0(t_r/2)$. For high-speed ECL, the rise/fall time of signals is $t_r \cong$ 1 ns. Hence, the transmission line model should be used for interconnections as short as 3.5 in. (assuming $c_0 = 7$ in./ns). For Schottky TTL, $t_r \cong 2$ ns, hence the transmission line model is used for $D > 7$ in. For standard TTL, $t_r \cong 6$ ns, hence transmission line effects become noticeable for $D > 21$ in.

7.2.2 Computing Solutions

There is a simple graphical technique for determining the reflections that will occur on a transmission line. The technique is illustrated in Figure 7.8 for a TTL interconnection via a 100-ohm line.

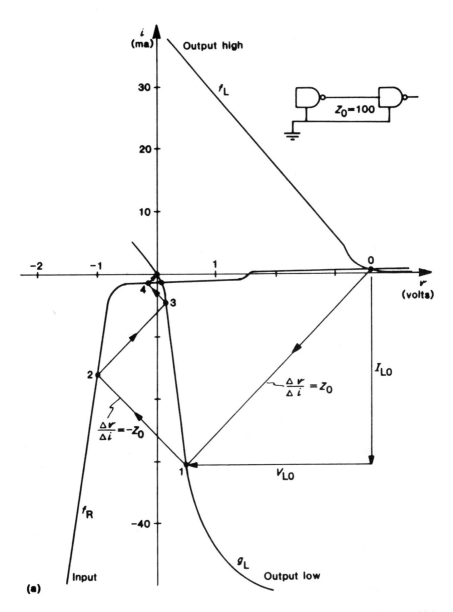

Figure 7.8   Graphical wave computations—TTL: (a) high-to-low transition; (b) low-to-high transition

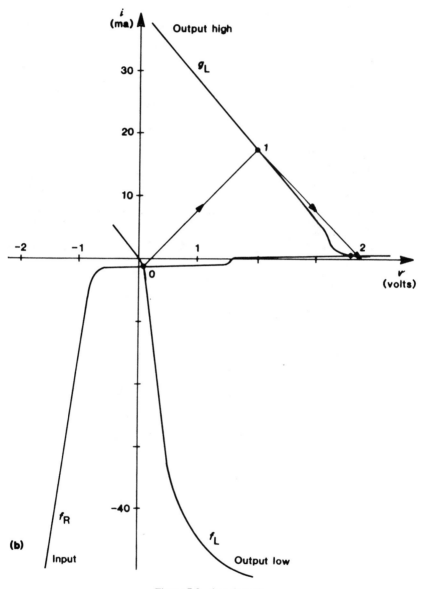

Figure 7.8   (continued)

Figure 7.8(a) shows a high-to-low transition of the output. The initial operating point is at the intersection of the f_L and f_R curves. The point is labeled 0 in the figure.

The point (V_1, I_1) is labeled 1 in the figure. As we know, $V_1 = V_0 + V_{L0}$ and $I_1 = I_0 + I_{L0}$. This point can be determined graphically as follows. We know that $V_{L0} = Z_0 I_{L0}$. But $V_{L0} = V_1 - V_0$ and $I_{L0} = I_1 - I_0$. Hence, $(V_1 - V_0)/(I_1 - I_0) = Z_0$. This can be true only if the point (V_1, I_1) is on a line of slope Z_0 through (V_0, I_0).

We also know that (V_1, I_1) must satisfy the new left boundary condition. Hence, (V_1, I_1) must also lie on the g_L curve. The point (V_1, I_1), therefore, can be determined by drawing a line of slope Z_0 through (V_0, I_0). The point where it intersects the g_L curve is (V_1, I_1).

The next point (V_2, I_2) may be determined in similar fashion. We know $V_2 = V_1 + V_{R1}$ and $I_2 = I_1 + I_{R1}$. Furthermore, $V_{R1} = -Z_0 I_{R1}$. Hence, (V_2, I_2) must lie on the line of slope $-Z_0$ through (V_1, I_1). Furthermore, (V_2, I_2) must satisfy the right boundary condition. That is, it must lie on the f_R curve. Hence, (V_2, I_2) is the intersection of the f_R curve with the line of slope $-Z_0$ through (V_1, I_1).

This process can be repeated until the operating point converges to the intersection of f_R and g_L, which is the new steady state.

In Figure 7.8(b) a low-to-high transition for the same interconnection is analyzed in the same fashion.

Timing diagrams for both transitions are shown in Figure 7.9. There are three timing diagrams for each transition: one for the left end of the line ($x = 0$); one for the middle ($x = D/2$); and one for the right end ($x = D$). Since $R_{OH} = Z_0$, the reflection (V_{R1}, I_{R1}) is absorbed when it arrives at the left end during a low-to-high transition, and no further reflections are produced.

7.2.3 Line Termination

The size and duration of the reflections that occur on a line depend upon the length and the characteristic impedance of the line, and upon the v-i characteristics of the driving and receiving devices. In some cases, reflections are not a problem; the designer simply allows enough time for the reflections to subside after each transition before requiring receiving devices to look at the line. In other cases, however, reflections cannot be tolerated, either because waiting for them to subside would introduce excessive delay, or because the reflections are of such magnitude that they may be mistaken for separate pulses. In such cases, reflections must be suppressed by *proper termination* of the line.

A line is properly terminated at either boundary if the resistance of the circuit at that boundary is the same as the characteristic impedance of the line. If this is the case then no reflection is generated at that boundary be-

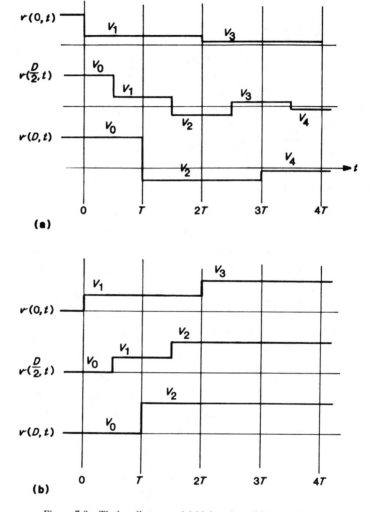

Figure 7.9   Timing diagrams: (a) high to low; (b) low to high

cause the voltage and current of an arriving wave are exactly correct for the boundary condition. If the line is properly terminated at the sending end, as in Figure 7.8(b), then one reflection is produced at the receiving end, but no further reflections occur. The line is at steady state after time $2T$. If a line is properly terminated at the receiving end, then no reflections at all are produced. Each point along the line sees a single transition, and the line reaches steady state after time T.

Since the input impedance of digital devices is usually much larger than the characteristic impedance of a transmission line, proper termination at the receiving end can be achieved by connecting a resistance Z_0 across the line. This is called *parallel termination*. The parallel combination of the high-impedance input device and the terminating resistor $R_T = Z_0$ will be essentially Z_0. The resulting *v-i* curves for a TTL interconnection are shown in Figure 7.10. It is obvious from the graphical computation technique that no reflections occur, since the line connecting the high and low operating points has exactly Z_0 slope.

There are two problems with the parallel termination of Figure 7.10, both of which result from the large steady-state current that flows when the output is high. The first is increased power dissipation. This problem is not easily avoided, and is usually accepted as the cost of suppressing reflections.

The second problem is that the high operating point may drop below V_{OHmin}. This problem may be alleviated in one or both of the following ways: (1) use line drivers rather than ordinary gates to drive terminated lines; (2) terminate lines to a voltage level other than ground.

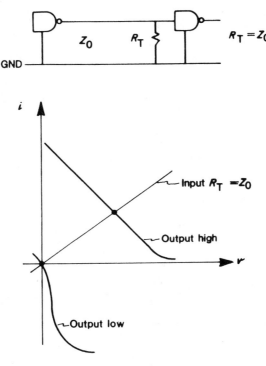

Figure 7.10   Parallel termination

A *line driver* is a gate that is capable of supplying and/or sinking larger output currents than an ordinary gate, while still maintaining the required logic levels. For example, the 96101 open-collector NAND gate can sink 48 mA while maintaining $V_{OL} \leq 0.4$ volts; the 74240 tristate buffer can source 3 mA with $V_{OH} \geq 2.4$ volts and sink 12 mA with $V_{OL} \leq 0.4$ volts.

Termination to a separate supply voltage V_T is shown in Figure 7.11(a). By making $V_T > 0$, the input *v-i* curve of Figure 7.10 is moved to the right, thus decreasing the high operating point.

Termination to a separate supply, however, is expensive. Not only is an additional power supply required, but another wire must be routed through the system (the same V_T can be used for all terminations).

An alternative is to use V_{CC} as the termination supply, as in Figure 7.11(b). This, however, may raise the low operating point above V_{OLmax}.

Another alternative is to use a split termination, as in Figure 7.11(c). The split termination is equivalent to Figure 7.11(a), with the values of V_T and R_T

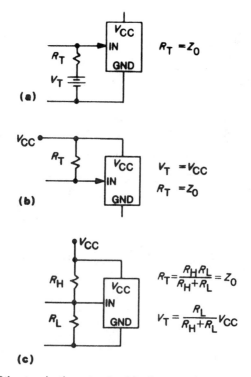

Figure 7.11   Other termination networks: (a) using a termination supply; (b) termination to V_{CC}; (c) split termination

as given in Figure 7.11(c). The values of R_L and R_H can be selected to give any Z_0 and any V_T.

Bus Terminations

A bus that has multiple inputs (drivers) and/or outputs (receivers) must be terminated at both ends to suppress reflections. Backplane buses are frequently constructed in this way, using a split termination at each end [42]. The "stubs" that connect drivers and receivers to the middle of the bus must be kept short so that they do not produce significant reflections.

Series Termination

Proper termination of a line by connecting a termination network in series with the line at the sending end is called *series termination* or *backmatching*. To be effective, this technique must be used with a gate that has the same high and low output resistance. ECL gates, for example, have $R_{OH} \cong R_{OL} \cong 7\,\Omega$. A 93-$\Omega$ resistor connected in series with an ECL output will properly terminate a 100-Ω line.

This technique cannot be used for buses, since receivers in the middle of the line will see each transition as two transitions (the original wave and the first reflection). It has the advantage over parallel termination, however, of not requiring high steady-state currents (since the high receiver input resistance is not diminished by a parallel termination).

7.2.4 Exercises

1. (a) Compute the capacitance and inductance per inch of a copper printed circuit path on a fiberglass epoxy PC card with a ground plane layer. Assume $w = 1$ mm, $d = 0.04$ mm, and $h = 0.4$ mm.

   (b) Compute the DC resistance per inch for this path.
   (c) Compute the resistance at 100 MHz.

2. Repeat Exercise 1 for a coaxial line with $r = 0.4$ mm, $h = 0.25$ mm, and $\epsilon_r = 3$. Give each parameter "per meter."

3. Write formulas for the characteristic impedance Z_0 of each of the line configurations of Figure 7.6, in terms of geometric parameters and ϵ_r. Under what circumstances is Z_0 independent of geometric parameters in each case?

4. What is Z_0 in ohms for the lines of Exercises 1 and 2? What is c_0?

5. Use the graphical technique to analyze the hypothetical interconnection of the exercises in Section 7.1.4 with $Z_0 = 100\,\Omega$. Sketch timing diagrams as in Figure 7.9.

6. Repeat Exercise 5 with each of the following termination networks:

(a) 200 Ω to ground
(b) 200 Ω to V_{CC}
(c) 200 Ω to V_{CC} and 200 Ω to ground

7. Early versions of TTL did not use the clamping diodes at the inputs, resulting in an input v-i curve that does not turn down for negative inputs; that is, $R_{IL} \cong 4000 \Omega$ for all $v < 1.4$ volts. Use the graphical technique to analyze a high-to-low transition with $Z_0 = 100$ for this gate. Compare with the modern gate (Figure 7.8).

8. (a) Analyze a TTL connection via a line with $Z_0 = 50 \Omega$. Sketch diagrams like Figures 7.8 and 7.9.

(b) Repeat for $Z_0 = 200 \Omega$.

9. Consider termination networks for a gate having the typical TTL values of Figure 7.1(b).

(a) What is the smallest resistance that may be used for termination to ground (Figure 7.10, R_T) which maintains legitimate TTL output levels?
(b) What is the smallest termination to V_{CC}? [Figure 7.11(b).]
(c) What split termination [Figure 7.11(c)] allows the smallest Z_0?

10. Repeat Exercise 9 for:

(a) The worst-case standard TTL gate specified in Table 7.1
(b) The 96101 line driver, using the specifications in Section 7.2.3
(c) The 74240 line driver, using the specifications in Section 7.2.3

11. Prove that the split termination of Figure 7.11(c) is equivalent to the termination of Figure 7.11(a).

12. For what hypothetical boundary conditions (f_L, g_L, and f_R) will reflections persist forever without subsiding?

7.3   NOISE [11, 23, 55–58]

7.3.1   Electromagnetic Radiation
7.3.2   Crosstalk
7.3.3   Common Impedance Noise

As discussed in Section 5.1.1, digital systems have a built-in noise margin that automatically eliminates the ill effects of a certain amount of noise. Relying exclusively on a large noise margin to eliminate noise problems, however, is not optimal. A large noise margin is expensive in terms of both operating costs and speed: the larger the voltage swing between low and high, the greater the power required to make the transition, and the greater the delay.

It is important to understand the common sources of noise in digital systems and to be able to limit the effects of noise so that a reasonably small noise margin will be sufficient. In this section we discuss the most significant types of noise in digital systems: electromagnetic radiation, crosstalk, and common impedance noise.

7.3.1 Electromagnetic Radiation

Electromagnetic radiation (EMR) is generated by power lines, lightning discharges, automobile ignition systems, motors, radio transmitters, and electrical systems of all sorts. It consists of oscillating electric and magnetic fields that propagate through space at the speed of light (light, in fact, is high-frequency EMR). Digital circuits may inadvertently act as receivers of EMR, resulting in noise voltages that can be mistaken for signals.

When a digital system must operate near a strong source of EMR, a shield should be used to block the EMR from entering the system. A *shield* is a layer of conducting material that surrounds the system. The electric charges in the shield move in response to the impinging EMR in such a fashion as to generate electric and magnetic fields within the shield that tend to cancel the external fields.

To be effective, a shield must completely surround a system. Signal lines that interconnect parts of the system must be enclosed within the shield. Coaxial cables can be used for this purpose: the outer conductor is part of the shield.

When a shield is placed around a system, "crosstalk" within the system may be increased due to capacitive coupling via the shield (see below). To prevent this problem, the shield must be connected to the signal ground for the system. This connection should be made at one point only, however, in order to avoid the problem of a *ground loop* (i.e., a loop in the signal ground network around which induced currents may flow) [57, 58].

A shield also prevents EMR from leaving a system. Recent U.S. government regulations require that any system built after the regulations were passed be within specified limits. Computers use EMR shields to meet these regulations.

7.3.2 Crosstalk

Within a digital system, voltage changes on one signal line can induce voltages on another line. This is known as *crosstalk*. Unless appropriate precautions are taken, these crosstalk voltages may be sufficiently large to be mistaken for intentional signals.

Crosstalk is a form of EMR. However, since the transmitter and receiver are in close proximity, circuit models are commonly used to represent crosstalk phenomena. In particular, the concepts of capacitive and inductive coupling are used to represent crosstalk.

Capacitive Coupling

The capacitance that we have been concerned with up to this point in the text is self-capacitance. The *self-capacitance* between two conductors is the charge that is moved from one conductor to the other per unit of applied voltage between the conductors. The capacitance that is involved in crosstalk is mutual capacitance. The *mutual capacitance* between two conductors is the charge that is induced on one conductor per unit voltage applied to the other conductor [58].

Noise due to capacitive coupling is illustrated in Figure 7.12. In Figure 7.12(a) the actual interconnection is represented. In Figure 7.12(b) the circuit model is shown. The output circuit of each device is represented by the linear model of Figure 7.1 with $V_{OLE} = 0$. The capacitance C_A represents the self-capacitance of input terminal A plus signal path A (with respect to ground); C_B is the self-capacitance of input B plus signal path B. C_{AB} is the mutual capacitance between paths A and B.

The timing diagrams in Figure 7.12(c) represent the noise pulse that occurs on line B when output A switches from low to high. The B output switch remains in the low position. The current i_{AB} flows briefly to charge the mutual capacitance C_{AB}. C_B charges momentarily due to i_{AB}, but eventually discharges through R_{OLB}. At steady state, $v_B = 0$ and $V_A = V_{OHA}$.

The size of the noise pulse $B\uparrow\downarrow$ is proportional to C_{AB}, and hence the noise pulse, can be eliminated entirely by surrounding path A (or path B) with a shield connected to ground, as illustrated in Figure 7.13(a). Mutual capacitance exists only when path B is in the E field due to the voltage applied between ground and path A. If A is surrounded by a grounded shield, as shown, the E field terminates on the shield, hence $C_{AB} = 0$.

It is not practical, nor is it necessary, to completely shield all lines in a digital system. It is usually sufficient to run each signal line near a ground return, and avoid putting any signal line between another signal line and its ground return.

Figure 7.13(b) shows two signal lines far from ground, with a voltage applied to path A, and path B connected to ground through a resistance as in Figure 7.12. A significant portion of the E field terminates on conductor B, hence C_{AB} is large. Figure 7.13(c) shows the same paths close to ground. Most of the E field terminates at ground rather than on B, hence C_{AB} is small.

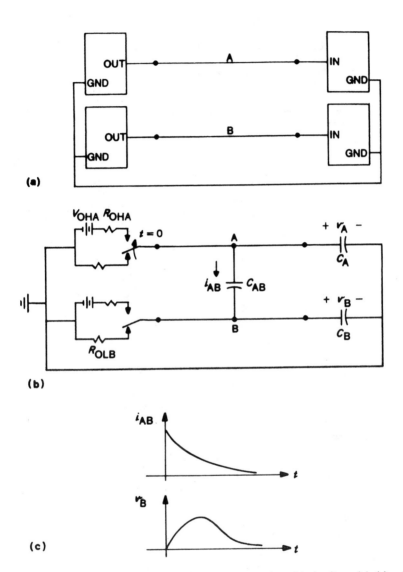

Figure 7.12 Capacitive coupling: (a) system interconnection; (b) circuit model; (c) noise pulse

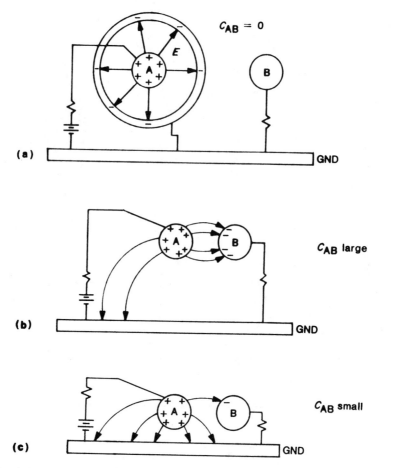

Figure 7.13   Minimizing mutual capacitance: (a) shielded line; (b) paths far from ground; (c) paths near ground

Inductive Coupling

Mutual capacitance represents the effect of the electric field created by one signal path on another signal path. *Mutual inductance* is similar, except that it is the magnetic field rather than the electric field that couples the circuits. The mutual inductance M_{AB} between signal paths A and B is the voltage induced in line A per unit current change in line B; that is, $v_B = M_{AB}(di_A/dt)$.

Mutual inductance, like mutual capacitance, can be eliminated by shielding, as in Figure 7.13(a). A current in path A will produce no magnetic field outside the shield, since the magnetic field of the return current in the shield exactly cancels the field of the signal current in the inner conductor A.

When full shielding is not practical, signal lines should be run close to ground. This reduces the mutual inductance because the field of the return current in the ground path tends to cancel the field of the signal path current everywhere except between the two paths.

Hence the guidelines for minimizing both capacitive and inductive coupling are the same: signal lines should be run close to ground; if signal lines must run alongside each other, a ground line should be run between them. For signaling between cabinets, twisted-pair lines are often used; the signal

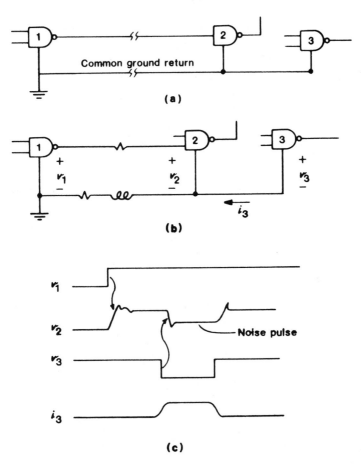

Figure 7.14   Common impedance coupling: (a) logic circuit; (b) electric circuit model; (c) timing diagram

line and its ground return are twisted together, about three twists per inch. This not only reduces crosstalk, but also reduces EMR pickup, since the induced voltages in adjacent twists tend to cancel.

7.3.3 Common Impedance Noise

When two circuits share a common conductor, varying currents in one circuit will cause voltage changes in the other circuit due to the impedance of the common conductor. This is known as *common impedance noise.*

The most important example of common impedance noise in digital systems is ground noise, that is, noise resulting from a common ground return. Ideally, ground is a perfect conductor with zero impedance, but this is never the case.

The effect of the nonzero impedance of a common ground return is illustrated in Figure 7.14. In 7.14(a), the ground symbol represents the ground side of the power supply. Gate 1 is near the power supply, and hence is connected by a very short wire to ground. Gates 2 and 3, however, are far away and are connected to ground via a common wire.

In Figure 7.14(b) the resistance and self-inductance of the common ground wire are included explicitly. Suppose that gate 1 generates a logic 1 output, say $v_1 = 2.4$ volts. Then v_2 will follow v_1 and stabilize at, say, 2.2 volts, allowing a 0.2 volt drop across the resistances of the signal wire and ground return. Later gate 3 switches from high to low. Gate 3 then must sink current through the common ground resistance and inductance. This causes a noise pulse to appear at v_2 corresponding to the voltage drop across the common ground impedance due to i_3.

Ground noise can be avoided by providing a low impedance ground network.

REFERENCES

1. Wakerly, J., *Microcomputer Architecture and Programming*, Wiley, New York, 1981.
2. Greenfield, J., and Wray, W., *Using Microprocessors and Microcomputers: The 6800 Family*, Wiley, New York, 1981.
3. Goody, R., *The Versatile Microcomputer: The Motorola Family*, Science Research Associates, Chicago, 1982.
4. Motorola, *MC6800, MC68A00, and MC68B00 Microprocessors (Data Sheet)*, Motorola Semiconductor Products Inc., Phoenix, Ariz., 1978.
5. Rafiquazzaman, M., *Microprocessors and Microcomputer Development Systems*, Harper & Row, New York, 1984.
6. Baer, J.-L., *Computer System Architecture*, Computer Science Press, Rockville, Md., 1980.
7. Hayes, J., *Computer Architecture and Organization*, McGraw-Hill, New York, 1978.
8. Tanenbaum, A., *Structured Computer Organization*, Prentice-Hall, Englewood Cliffs, N.J., 1976.
9. Marino, L., "Models", in *Encyclopedia of Computer Science*, A. Ralston, ed., Van Nostrand Reinhold, New York, 1983.
10. Gajda, W., and Biles, W., *Engineering Modelling and Computation*, Houghton Mifflin, Boston, 1978.
11. Belove, C., Schachter, H., and Schilling, D., *Digital and Analog Systems Circuits and Devices*, McGraw-Hill, New York, 1973.
12. Stone, H., *Discrete Mathematical Structures and Their Applications*, Science Research Associates, Chicago, 1973.
13. Stanat, D., and McAllister, D., *Discrete Mathematics in Computer Science*, Prentice-Hall, Englewood Cliffs, N.J., 1977.
14. Kuck, D., *The Structure of Computers and Computations*, Wiley, New York, 1978.
15. Gilbert, P., *Software Design and Development*, Science Research Associates, Chicago, 1983.
16. Bell, B., and Newell, A., *Computer Structures: Readings and Examples*, McGraw-Hill, New York, 1971.
17. Siewiorek, D., Bell, G., and Newell, A., *Computer Structures: Principles and Examples*, McGraw-Hill, New York, 1982.
18. Bell, G., Mudge, J., and McNamara, J., *Computer Engineering: A DEC View of Hardware Systems Design*, Digital Press, Bedford, Mass., 1978.
19. Millman, J., *Microelectronics: Digital and Analog Circuits and Systems*, McGraw-Hill, New York, 1979.
20. Blakslee, T., *Digital Design with Standard MSI and LSI*, 2nd ed., Wiley, New York, 1979.
21. Hayt, W., and Kemmerly, J., *Engineering Circuit Analysis*, 3rd ed., McGraw-Hill, New York, 1978.
22. Durney, C., Harris, D., and Alley, C., *Electric Circuits: Theory and Engineering Applications*, Holt, Rinehart & Winston, New York, 1982.
23. Bueche, F., *Introduction to Physics for Scientists and Engineers*, McGraw-Hill, New York, 1980.
24. D'Angelo, H., *Microcomputer Structures: An Introduction to Digital Electronics, Logic Design, and Computer Architecture*, BYTE Publications, McGraw-Hill, New York, 1981.

25. Smith, R., *Electronics: Circuits and Devices*, 2nd ed., Wiley, New York, 1980.
26. Mead, C., and Conway, L., *Introduction to VLSI Systems*, Addison-Wesley, Reading, Mass., 1980.
27. Taub, H., and Schilling, D., *Digital Integrated Electronics*, McGraw-Hill, New York, 1977.
28. Hamilton, D., and Howard, W., *Basic Integrated Circuit Engineering*, McGraw-Hill, New York, 1975.
29. Colcasser, R., *Microelectronics: Process and Device Design*, Wiley, New York, 1980.
30. Kohavi, Z., *Switching and Finite Automata Theory*, 2nd ed., McGraw-Hill, New York, 1978.
31. Roth, C., *Fundamentals of Logic Design*, 2nd ed., West Publishing Co., St. Paul, Minn., 1979.
32. Hill, F. J., and G. R. Peterson, Introduction to Switching Theory and Logical Design, 2nd edition, Wiley, New York, 1974.
33. Dietmeyer, D., *Logic Design of Digital Systems*, 2nd ed., Allyn & Bacon, Newton, Mass., 1978.
35. Unger, S., *Asynchronous Sequential Switching Circuits*, Wiley Interscience, New York, 1969.
36. Peatman, J., *The Design of Digital Systems*, McGraw-Hill, New York, 1972.
37. Waser, S., and Flynn, M., *Introduction to Arithmetic for Digital System Design*, Holt, Rinehart & Winston, New York, 1982.
38. Sterbenz, P., *Floating Point Computation*, Prentice-Hall, Englewood Cliffs, N.J., 1974.
39. Stein, M., and Munro, W., *Introduction to Machine Arithmetic*, Addison-Wesley, Reading, Mass., 1971.
40. Stevenson, D., "A Proposed Standard for Binary Floating Point Arithmetic," *Computer*, Vol. 14, pp. 51–62, March 1981.
41. Abd-alla, A., and Meltzer, A., *Principles of Digital Computer Design*, vol. 1, Prentice-Hall, Englewood Cliffs, N.J., 1976.
42. Fairchild, *TTL Data Book*, Fairchild Camera and Instrument Corp., Mountain View, CA, 1978.
43. Motorola, *Memory Data Manual*, Motorola Semiconductor Products Inc., Phoenix, Ariz., 1980.
44. Intel, *Microsystem Components Handbook*, vols. 1 and 2, Intel Corp., Santa Clara, CA, 1983.
45. Marino, L., "General Theory of Metastable Operation," *IEEE Trans. Comput.*, Vol. 30, pp. 107–115, February 1981.
46. Gschwind, H., and McCluskey, E., *Design of Digital Computers*, 2nd ed., Springer-Verlag, New York, 1975.
47. Mano, M., *Computer Systems Architecture*, 2nd ed., Prentice-Hall, Englewood Cliffs, N.J., 1982.
48. Booth, T., *Introduction to Computer Engineering: Hardware and Software Design*, 3rd ed., Wiley, New York, 1984.
49. Fletcher, W., *An Engineering Approach to Digital Design*, Prentice-Hall, Englewood Cliffs, N.J., 1980.
50. Ullman, J., *Computational Aspects of VLSI*, Computer Science Press, Rockville, Md., 1984.
51. Langdon, G., *Computer Design*, Computech Press Inc., San Jose, Calif., 1982.
52. Metzger, G., and Vabre, J., *Transmission Lines with Pulse Excitation*, Academic Press, New York, 1969.
53. Motorola, *MECL System Design Handbook*, Motorola Semiconductor Products Inc., Phoenix, Ariz., 1972.

54. Stewart, J., *Circuit Analysis of Transmission Lines*, Wiley, New York, 1958.

55. Stone, H., *Microcomputer Interfacing*, Addison-Wesley, Reading, Mass., 1982.

56. Kraus, J., and Carver, K., *Electromagnetics*, 2nd ed., Wiley, New York, 1977.

57. Ott, H., *Noise Reduction Techniques in Electronic Systems*, Wiley, New York, 1976.

58. Morrison, R., *Grounding and Shielding Techniques in Instrumentation*, 2nd ed., Wiley, New York, 1977.

INDEX

A bus (address bus), 421–425
a (ISR), address of interrupt service
    routine, 21
absolute assembler, 46
AC resistance, 546
ACCA, 15
ACCB, 15
acceptor atoms, 134
access time, 345
accumulator, 14
ACR (all conditions requiring), 513
addition, 204–219
addition instructions, 216–218
address assignment, 425
address bus, 421–425
address mode, 15
address modes, 32–36, 518
    direct, 32
    extended, 34
    immediate, 35
    indexed, 34
    inherent, 36
    relative, 35
    zero page, 34
address setup time, 345
address sharing, 425
algorithms, 75
ALU (arithmetic logic unit)   310–311
ALU IC package 74382, 311
AND operation, 147
AND-OR design 158–164
arithmetic logic unit, 310–311
ASL (arithmetic shift left), 192
ASR (arithmetic shift right), 192
assembler directives (see directives), 42
assembly language, 42–46
associative property, 149
asynchronous communication, 448
asynchronous sequential network, 156

B2 addition, 205–210
B2 addition algorithm, 207
B2 code, 4, 198
BA (bus available), 23, 424
backplanes, 85
Backus-Naur form, 44

base (of a transistor), 113
base 2 code, 4, 198
base point, 246
BC (branch condition), 23–24
BCD code, 203
BG (bus grant), 13, 21, 424, 488
binary word, 2
binary word variable, 2
bipolar gates, 116–118
bipolar transistor, 78, 112–113
bistable circuits, 331–342
bit, 2
bit slice, 311
bit synchronization, 363, 445, 449
block IO transfers, 57–62
    direct control, 57
    DMA control, 59
    interrupt control, 58
B^n, 145
Boolean formulas, 151
bottom-up design, 67
boundary conditions, 547
BR (buffer register), 438
BR (bus request), 13, 21, 424, 487
branch instruction, 16, 225–229
branch test, 31
branches, 48–53
breadboards, 85
buffer register, 56, 438
bus cycle timing, 423
bus drivers, 275–276
bus master, 10, 424
bus operations, 13, 421–425, 516
bus slave, 10, 424
bus terminations, 557
buses, 273–280, 464
    control mnemonics, 274
    drivers, 275–276
    floating, 276
    generic representation, 274
    multiplexer, 280
    open collector, 279
    open drain, 278
    precharged, 280
    simple nMOS bus, 275
    tristate, 276–277
byte, 3

BYTE1, 24
BYTE2, 24
BYTE3, 24

C (carry flag), 32
cabinets, 85
capacitance, 92-97, 140-143, 544, 560
capacitive coupling, 560
capacitor, 91
carry variables, 206
CC (condition codes) register, 19, 31-32
CCD (charge coupled device), 360
C_{gs}, 108
channel, 110, 134
character synchronization, 364, 446, 449
characteristic (floating point), 250
charge-coupled device memory, 360
checksum, 447
chip area, 454
chip enable input, 289, 301
chip layout, 136-139, 479-483, 488-490
chip select input, 289, 301
chip size and cost, 81
circuit equations, 91-92
clear input, 334
clipping diode, 105
clock skew, 410
clock track, 363
clocks, 312-317
CMOS logic, 113, 126-129
coaxial cable, 542
code ranges, 199-201, 253-254
codes, 3-4, 246-254
  2C, 4
  ASCII, 4
  base-2 (B2), 4, 198
  BCD, 203
  excess-m, 203
  fixed point, 246-249
  floating point, 249-254
  machine code, 4
  ones complement, 202
  signed-magnitude, 202
  twos complement, 199
coefficient (floating point), 250
collector, 113
combinational networks, 65, 155, 145-196,
    281-311
  ALU, 310-311
  decoders, 282-290
  model, 281-282
  multiplexers, 290-294
  PLA, 305-310
  ROM, 294-304
combining v-i curves, 106
common impedance noise, 564

commutative property, 148
compiler, 75
COMPLEMENT operation, 147
complex buses, 427
component distribution, 285
computer organization, 1-63
computer packaging and production, 76-89
concatenation, 15, 192
concurrent operation, 433-435
condition codes register, 19
contact bounce, 319
contact cut, 136
control unit, 393 (see CU)
control unit equations, 406
crosstalk, 559
CU (control unit), 393
CU combinational network, 404
CU outputs, 397, 472, 495
CU structure, 396, 470-476, 490-494, 519

D bus (data bus), 421-425
D flip-flop, 337, 340
daisy chain, 483
data bus, 421-425
data hold time, 345
data selector, 290
data setup time, 346
data sheet specifications, 272
data sheets, 533
data structures, 75
data unit, 393, 458, 489
data-base management, 75
DBE, 424
DC power supply, 97-99
debounce circuits, 321-322
decoders, 282-290
decomposition, 416
decrement operation, 222, 231, 461
delay element, 314, 322
DeMorgan's theorems, 150
dependent variables, 65
depletion mode transistor, 110
deposition process, 79
design rules, 138-143
destination operand, 6
device specifications, 533-540
diffusion, 79
digital arithmetic, 196-262
digital electronic circuits, 104-129
digital signal models, 267-272
digital signals, 263-281
diode, 105
DIR (instruction class), 499
direct addressing, 32
direct IO control, 57
direct memory access controller, 9

direct output, 397
directives, 42-44
    EQU, 42-43
    FCB, 42-43
    FDB, 42-43
    ORG, 42-43
    RMB, 42-43
discrete components, 77
distributed components, 285
distributed multiplexer bus, 280
distributed-parameter models, 70, 541
distributive property, 148
dividend, 239
division, 239-245, 257
divisor, 239
DMA controller, 9, 423-425
DMA controller design, 451-484
DMA IO control, 59
DMAC, 9, 423-425
don't care conditions, 171
donor atoms, 134
doping, 79, 134
double density recording, 365-366
double threshold, 123
drain (MOS transistor), 108
drain-source resistance, 135
DU (data unit), 393, 458, 489
dynamic loading, 533
dynamic operation, 532
dynamic power, 102
dynamic RAM, 354-358
dynamic registers, 330
dynamic systems, 65

ECL (emitter coupled logic), 113, 550
economies of scale, 87
edge connector, 83
edge signals, 269
edge-controlled load operation, 325
EL operation (extend left), 201
electric circuits, 90-104
electromagnetic radiation, 559
electronics, 70, 90-144
emitter, 113
enhancement mode transistor, 110
EQU (directive), 43
equivalent circuits, 91-93
erasable ROM (EROM), 299
error control, 4, 447
excess-m code, 203
Exclusive-OR gates, 168
exit test, 50
exponent, 250
expression, 44
EXT (instruction class), 499

extend left operation, 201
extended addressing, 34
extended logic operations, 189
extended output, 399
extended-range operations, 209
external registers, 422

FCB directive, 42
FDB directive, 43
feedback interconnection, 155
fetch-execute-interrupt operation, 20-22,
    485-488
field programmable ROM, 299
fixed-point codes, 246-249
fixed-range operations, 6, 210
flags, 19, 31-32, 226
flip-flops, 337-340
floating bus, 21, 276
floating-point base, 250
floating-point codes, 249-254
    addition, 254-255
    base, 250
    characteristic, 250
    division, 257-258
    exponent, 250
    gradual underflow, 259
    hidden bit, 252
    IEEE standard, 252
    mantissa, 250
    multiplication, 256-257
    ordering relations, 254
    overflow, 258-259
    range, 253-254
    subtraction, 256
    underflow, 258-259
    coefficient, 250
flux patterns, 361
frequency doubler, 322
full adder, 208
full duplex operation, 445
full subtractor, 229
function, 145

gate (logic), 113-123
gate (MOS transistor), 108
gate arrays, 88
gate interconnections, 123-126, 154-156
gate levels, 157
gate minimization, 158
gate networks, 152-176
gate transfer curve, 118-120
gate v-i curves, 119-120
gated D flip-flop, 340
giga- (prefix), 97
gradual underflow, 259
ground, 98

ground loop, 559
ground noise, 564

H (half carry flag), 32
H (high byte suffix), 15–16
half-adder, 218
hardware interrupt response, 20
hexadecimal, 3
hidden bit, 252
high byte, 15
HOLD, 424
hold interval, 270
hole, 134
hypothetical processor, 515

IC chip cost, 81
IC chip size, 81
IC fabrication, 78–83
IC fabrication process parameters, 138–143
idle level, 445
i_{ds}, 108
IEEE standard floating point code, 252
iff, 145
IMM (instruction class), 499
immediate access, 323
immediate access registers, 324–342
immediate addressing, 35
IMMF (instruction class), 500
IMMS (instruction class), 500
increment operation, 219, 231
IND (instruction class), 499
independent variables, 65
index range, 2
index register, 15
indexed addressing, 15, 34
inductance, 97, 545
inductive coupling, 562
inductor, 91
inertial delay, 391, 415, 419
informal circuit analysis, 100
information transfer timing, 270–271
INH (instruction class), 499
inherent addressing, 36
INHF (instruction class), 499
INHS (instruction class), 499
input capacitance, 537
input synchronization, 382–390
input transition time, 375
input-output controllers, 10
input-output devices, 9
input-output operation, 55–62
input-output processor, 72
instruction classes, 495–500
instruction register, 20
instruction set, 23–42
instruction step simulation, 51

instruction types, 23
instructions (6800 microprocessor):
    ABA, 216
    accumulator and memory group, 37
    ADCA, 217–218
    ADCB, 217–218
    ADDA, 216
    ADDB, 216
    ANDA, 190–192
    ANDB, 190–192
    ASL, 192–193
    ASLA, 192–193
    ASLB, 192–193
    ASR, 192–193
    ASRA, 192–193
    ASRB, 192–193
    BCC, 227
    BCS, 227
    BEQ, 227
    BEQ, 39
    BGE, 227
    BGT, 227
    BHI, 227
    BITA, 38, 190–192
    BITB, 38, 190–192
    BLE, 227
    BLS, 227
    BLT, 227
    BMI, 227
    BNE, 227
    BPL, 227
    BRA, 39
    branch group, 39
    BSR, 40
    BVC, 227
    BVS, 227
    CBA, 38, 227
    CC register group, 40
    CLR, 37
    CLRA, 37
    CLRB, 37
    CMPA, 38, 227
    CMPB, 38, 227
    COM, 190–192
    COMA, 190–192
    COMB, 190–192
    CPX, 39
    DAA, 217, 219
    DEC, 37
    DECA, 37
    DECB, 37
    EORA, 190–192
    EORB, 190–192
    INC, 37
    INCA, 37
    INCB, 37

instructions   (*continued*)
  IX and SP group, 38
  JMP, 40
  JSR, 40
  LDAA, 37
  LDAB, 37
  LDS, 38–39
  LDX, 38–39
  LSR, 192–193
  LSRA, 192–193
  LSRB, 192–193
  NEG, 225
  NEGA, 225
  NEGB, 225
  ORA, 190–192
  ORB, 190–192
  PSHA, 37
  PSHB, 37
  PULA, 37
  PULB, 37
  ROL, 192–193
  ROLA, 192–193
  ROLB, 192–193
  ROR, 192–193
  RORA, 192–193
  RORB, 192–193
  RTI, 40
  RTS, 40
  SBA, 225
  SBCA, 225
  SBCB, 225
  STAA, 37
  STAB, 37
  STS, 38–39
  STX, 38–39
  SUBA, 225
  SUBB, 225
  SWI, 22
  SWI, 40
  TST, 38
  TSTA, 38
  TSTB, 38
  TSX, 39
  TXS, 39
  WAI, 22
  WAI, 40
insulation, 544
insulator, 134
INT, 21, 485
integer codes, 198–204
integrated circuits, 69, 77–83
interconnections, 71–73, 529–540
  device specifications, 533–540
  dynamic operation, 532
  linear models, 530
  loading, 533

  nonlinear models, 537
  power specifications, 535
  static specifications, 534
  steady-state operation, 531
  timing specifications, 536
interrupt IO control, 58
interrupt mask, 19
interrupt request, 12
interval types, 269–272
intrinsic semiconductor, 134
INVERT operation, 147
inverter, 114
IO controllers, 10, 419–451
IO devices, 9
IOC (IO controller), 10
IOC design steps, 420
IOD (IO device), 10
IR (Instruction Register), 20
IRQ (interrupt request), 12, 21, 423, 485
isosynchronous communication, 447
IX (Index Register), 15

jump instruction, 16

K (prefix; storage capacity measure), 3
K-map, 158
Karnaugh map, 158
keyboard, 450
Kilo-, 3, 97
Kirchoff's laws, 91

L (low byte suffix), 15–16
label, 44
label definition, 48
latch circuit, 320–321, 333–336
latency time, 359
leakage current, 532
level controlled load operation, 326–328
level signals, 269
level-controlled registers, 455
levels of computer design, 68–76
  electronics, 70
  logic, 70
  physics, 69
  PMS, 71
  register transfer, 71
  software, 74
line drivers, 556
literal, 159
load operation, 2, 325–328
loading, 533
logic design, 70, 145–196
logic families, 78, 113–114
logic formulas, 148
logic gate structure, 115
logic gates, 113–123, 153

logic levels, 109, 263–266
logical adjacency, 159
loops, 49–53
low byte, 15
LSR (logical shift right), 192
lumped-parameter models, 70

M (Mega-, prefix), 3
M2[ ] notation, 15
machine code, 4, 24
machine language, 42
macrocircuit design, 529–566
macrocircuit design, functional aspects, 529
macrocircuit design, physical aspects, 529
macrocircuit implementation, 288, 301, 351
macrocircuit packaging, 83–85
macrocircuit registers, 341–343
    74163 IC, 343
    74169 IC, 345
    74198 IC, 346
    74273 IC, 342
    timing specifications, 347
magnetic bubble memory, 360
magnetic disk and tape memory, 361–366
magnetic flux, 361
main memory, 8
mantissa (floating point), 250
mask (integrated circuit), 79, 137
mask alignment error, 82
masked compare, 195
master (bus), 10
master-slave register, 341
maximum representation error, 261
Mealy machine, 371
Mega- (prefix; unit of storage capacity), 3, 97
memory, 2, 66
memory access types, 323–324
memory components, 323–367
metal, 133
metal oxide semiconductor transistor, 107
metastable operation, 384, 386
micro- (prefix), 97
microcircuit chip layout, 479–483
microcircuit control unit, 468–479
    inputs, 474
    output specification table, 477
    outputs, 472
    reset operation, 475
    state register, 471
    structure, 471, 473, 476
    timing, 478
microcircuit design rules, 138–143
microcircuit implementation, 346
microcircuit layout, 284, 299
microcircuit registers, 459–464

microcircuits, 77–83
microprogram viewpoint, 523
microprogrammed control unit, 519–526
    reducing ROM width, 525
    sequential operation, 520–521
    structure, 519
microprogramming, 515–527
milli- (prefix), 97
minimizing chip area, 454
minimum size transistor, 110
minterm, 155
mnemonic, 24
mobility, 134
models, 63–66, 530–540
    combinational networks, 281–282
    digital signals, 267–272
    linear interconnections, 530
    nonlinear interconnections, 537
    RAM, 343–346
    registers, 324–346
    sequential machine, 368–370
    transmission line, 541–550
modular design, 66–68
monostable multivibrator, 316
Moore machine, 371, 418
MOS transistors, 78, 107–111
MRE (maximum representation eror), 261
multilevel structure, 67
multioperation registers, 328–329
multioperation state registers, 512
multiphase clocks, 315
multiple output minimization, 171
multiplexers, 290–294
multiplication, 231–239
mutual capacitance, 560
mutual inductance, 562
M[ ] notation, 12

N (negative result flag), 32
n-type semiconductor, 134
NAND gate, 114
NAND-NAND design, 166–168
nano- (prefix), 97
NEG operation, 220
negative edge triggering, 325
networks, 73
next-state function, 66, 368
NMI, 12, 21, 423, 485
NMIFF, 485
nMOS, 113
nMOS external logic levels, 266–267
nMOS gates, 115–116
nMOS transistor, 107–111, 132, 134–142
    drain-source resistance, 135
    equations, 132
    fabrication, 135–138

nMOS transistor (*continued*)
  fabrication parameters, 138-143
  operation, 135
  structure, 132, 136
  threshold voltage, 135
  v-i curves, 109, 111
noise, 264-265, 558-559
  common impedance, 564
  crosstalk, 559
  electromagnetic radiation, 559
  ground, 564
  shield, 559
noise margin, 265, 558-559
non-retriggerable one-shot, 317
non-standard bus operations, 427
non-terminal symbols, 44
nonlinear resistance, 104
NOR gate, 114
NOR-NOR design, 166-168
NOT operation, 147
npn transistor, 112

object program, 42
one-shot recovery time, 317
one-shot-like devices, 319
one-shots, 316-319
ones complement code, 202
OP (opcode), 24, 31
open collector bus, 279
open drain bus, 278
operating point, 105, 106
operating system, 75
operator precedence, 148
optimal gate network design, 157-172
OR operation, 147
OR-AND design, 164-166
ordering relations, 225-229, 254
ORG (directive), 42
output function, 66, 368
output specification table (OST), 405, 435
output transients, 418
overflow, 209-210

p-type semiconductor, 134
parallel adder, 209
parallel circuit, 93
parallel input controller, 442-444
parallel output controller, 55, 436-442
parallel port IOCs, 436-444
parallel termination, 555
parasitic capacitance, 93
parity bit, 4, 447
parity bit, 447
pass transistor, 178
pass transistor propagation delay, 185-186
PC (printed circuit) cards, 83

PC (Program Counter), 16, 20
perfect conductor, 273
peripheral devices, 9
permittivity, 544
phase-locked loop, 365
photo-resist, 79
photolithography, 79
physics, 69
pico- (prefix), 97
pinchoff, 108
PLA (programmable logic array), 305-310
pMOS transistor, 107, 113
PMS (processor-memory-switch) level, 71
pnp transistor, 112
POC (parallel output controller), 55, 436-442
poly (polycrystalline silicon), 134
positive edge triggering, 326
power, 102-103, 125
power distribution, 99
power specifications, 535
power supply, 97-99
precharged bus, 280
precharging, 128, 357
primary memory, 8
printed circuit card, 83
printer interface, 55
priority encoder, 483
processor design, 484-512
processor registers, 14
processor-memory-switch level, 71
program controlled operation, 6
program counter, 16
programmability, 88
programmable logic array, 305-310
programmable one-shot, 428-436
programming (assembler language), 42-62
propagation delay, 125, 157, 185-186, 271-272
proper termination, 553
pseudo one-shots, 319, 338
pseudoinstructions, 42
pull operation (stack), 17
pull-down circuits, 115, 181
pull-up circuits, 115
pulse generators, 312-323
pulse output, 398
pulse stretcher, 323
pure delay, 314, 419
push operation, 17

quotient, 239

race problem, 455-457
RAM, 343-358
RAM organizations, 346-354

random access, 323
random access memory (RAM), 9, 343–358
range of a code, 199
RC circuit, 93–96
R_{ds}, 108, 135
read cycle, 422–423
read only memory (ROM), 294–304
read operation (dynamic RAM), 355
read operation, 2, 10, 345–348
read-write position, 358
real arithmetic, 246–262
recovery time (one-shot), 317
rectifier, 105
recursive definition, 45
refresh operation, 331, 355–356
refresh requirement, 354
register, 2
register implementation, 329–342
    bistable circuits, 331–342
    dynamic, 330
    flip-flops, 337–340
    latch circuit, 333–336
    macrocircuit registers, 341–342
    master-slave, 341
register models, 324
register transfer components, 263–291
register transfer decomposition, 416
register transfer design, 393–528
register transfer design process, 394
register transfer gate network notation, 189
register transfer level, 71
register transfer one-shot, 395–419
register transfer operations, 4–6
register transfer state diagram notation, 403
register transfer system structure, 392
register transfer timing, 409–416
REL (instruction class), 499
relative addressing, 35
relocating assembler, 46
remainder, 239
representation error, 247
RESET, 13, 21, 485
reset circuits, 321–322
reset input, 334
resistance, 134, 140–143, 545
resistivity, 134, 545
resistor, 91
resistor circuits, 91–92
resolution, 82, 138
response time, 411
retriggerable one-shot, 317
retriggerable synchronous one-shot, 390
return address, 16
ring oscillators, 313–315
ripple carry, 205
RMB directive, 43

R_{off}, 108, 116
ROL (rotate left), 192
ROM, 294–304
ROM programming, 296–299
R_{on}, 110, 115–116
ROR (rotate right), 192
R_{pd}, 116
R_{pu}, 115
RT (see register transfer)
RTL gate, 118
RW (read-write select), 353

SAM (sequential access memory), 358–366
saturation, 108
Schmitt trigger gates, 123
Schottky TTL, 550
secondary memory, 9
selectable frequency clock, 390, 418
self inductance, 97
self-capacitance, 560
semiconductor, 133
sequential access, 323
sequential access memory, 9, 358–366
sequential machine, 368–382
    coding, 372
    construction, 377–382
    ones counter, 378
    synchronization detector, 379
    synchronous one-shot, 381
sequential networks, 368–391
sequential operation, 401, 431–433, 440,
    494–511
serial adder, 209
serial port IOCs, 444–449
series circuit, 93
series termination, 557
set, 197
set input (latch circuit), 334
set membership, 197
setup interval, 270
shared data port RAM, 353
shield, 559
shift register memory, 359–360
sign bit, 200
sign extend operation (EL), 201
signal events, 269
signal ground, 104
signal path types, 273
signal paths, 273–280
signed-magnitude code, 202
single density recording, 363–364
single-port RAM, 343
single-transistor RAM cell, 357
sink current, 531
skin effect, 546
slash notation, 188

slave (bus), 10
slice, 311
small circle convention, 154, 166, 271
software, 74–75
sort, 231
source (MOS transistor), 108
source operand, 6
source program, 42
SP (Stack Pointer), 16–17
specification, 395
SR (status register), 429, 438, 452
SR flip-flop, 338–339
SSN (synchronous sequential network),
    370–377
SSN design procedure, 372
stack, 17
stack pointer, 16
standard (hardwired) CU, 517
state codes, 514
state diagram, 369
state reduction, 377
state register variations, 512–519
state table (processor), 500–510
static loading, 533
static operating specifications, 534
static operation, 531
static power, 102
static RAM, 345–354
static registers, 331–341
static systems, 65, 155
status register, 429, 438, 452
steady-state, 100
steady-state operation, 531
stick diagrams, 309
stoppable clock synchronizer, 387
storage mechanisms, 323
straight-line programs, 46–48
stray capacitance, 93
stripline, 542
structured programming, 74
stubs (transmission line), 557
subroutine return, 16
subroutines, 16, 53–54
subscript range, 2
substrate, 80, 134
subtracters, 230
subtraction, 219–225
SWIFF, 485
switch network formulas, 177
switch networks, 176–186
switches, 319–321
switching functions, 146–152
synchronization problem, 444
synchronizers, 385–390
synchronizing sequence, 364
synchronous communication, 446

synchronous pure delay, 391
synchronous sequential network, 370–377
syntax, 44–46
system bus, 7, 420–428
system bus communication, 430, 439, 454
system software, 75
system specification, 395

terminal symbols, 44
threshold voltage: diode, 105
threshold voltage: MOS transistor, 135
threshold voltage: Schmitt trigger, 123
time constant, 96
time variables, 65
timing, 373, 409, 436
timing specifications, 272, 536
top-down design, 67
transfer band, 265
transfer curves, 118–120
transistor switches, 178
transmission function, 176
transmission gate, 178
transmission lines, 540–558
    capacitance, 544
    characteristic impedance, 546
    computing solutions, 550
    configurations, 543
    digital model, 541
    dimensions, 543
    inductance, 545
    reflections, 541, 547
    resistance, 545
    steady state, 549
    terminations, 553
    travelling waves, 541, 547
    wave velocity, 546
tree networks, 178–180
tristate bus, 276–277
truth table, 146
TSC, 424
TTL (transistor-transistor logic), 113
TTL gate, 119
TTL logic levels, 266–267
TTL specifications, 535
turned-off transistor, 108
turned-on transistor, 110
twisted pair, 542
two's complement code, 199
two-dimensional ROM, 301
two-level decoder, 287
two-phase clocking, 457
two-step load operation, 336
two-terminal circuit elements, 91
two/three (2/3) level networks, 157–172
twos complement (2C) code, 4
twos complement addition, 210–216

unary subtract, 219–220
unit prefixes, 97
unsynchronized inputs, 382

V (2C overflow flag), 32
v-i curves, 105, 537–539
variables, 65
V_{CC}, 98
V_{DD}, 98
v_{ds}, 108
V_{EE}, 98
v_{gs}, 108
VMA (Valid Memory Address), 424
voltage divider, 92
voltage ranges, 109
voltage source, 91, 97
voltage-controlled oscillator, 365
V_{SS}, 98
V_{th}, 135

wafer, 80
weighted position code, 198
wire guage, 543
wire models, 273, 540–541, 549–550
wire-wrap, 85
word operations, 188–196
word variable, 2
write cycle, 422–423
write operation (dynamic RAM), 356
write operation 2, 10, 345–348
WS (write strobe signal), 348

XOR operation, 168

yield, 81

Z (ALU output), 488
Z (zero flag), 32

SPECIAL NOTATIONS

Notation	Page	Description
$x < n-1:0 >$	2	index range of binary word
$+_2, -_2, +_{2C}$ etc.	4, 204	word operations, extended range
$\hat{+}_2, \hat{-}_2, \hat{+}_{2C}$ etc.	6, 210	word operations, fixed range
$x \rightarrow y$	6	register transfer operation
$M[x]$	12	memory register x
$M2[x]$	15	double memory register
$x \circ y$	15	concatenation
$a(x)$	21	address of a memory register with name x
$x \updownarrow$	32	standard flag change
$\$$	34	hexadecimal prefix
$\#$	36	immediate addressing
V_{DD}, V_{CC}, etc.	98	double subscript power supply notation
$v_{gs}, v_{ds}, i_{ds}, C_{gs}, R_{ds}$	108–110	MOS transistor variables
R_{on}, R_{off}	108–109	transistor switch parameters
λ	138	fabrication process resolution
$\mathbf{B}^n$	145	set of n-length words
$f : x \rightarrow y$	145	function
iff	145	if and only if
$\neg$	148	complement operation
$\circ$	154	inversion circle
$\oplus$	170	Exclusive OR operation
X	189	set product (cartesian product)
$<i{:}j>$	197	set of integers
$0^n, 1^n$	198	n-tuple of 0's or 1's
$[x]_2, [x]_{2C}$, etc.	198–199	integer represented by word x under B2 code, 2C code etc.
V_{IHmin}, V_{ILmax} V_{OHmin}, V_{OLmax}	265	logic level boundaires
$x\uparrow, x\downarrow, x>, x<, x\updownarrow$	269	signal events
$[t_1, t_2]$	269	interval
t_{stp}, t_{hld}, t_{pd} t_{pdb}, t_{pde}	270–271	time intervals (setup, hold, propagation delay, etc.)
yTx	274	control signal mnemonic
$\times$	297	programmable connection
$\bullet$	297	made connection
$-$	328	don't care condition
$x(u), x(s), x(d), x(p), x(e), x(p1)$, etc.	385, 398, 473	signal type indicates in parentheses